Maritime Solidarity

Maritime Solidarity

Pacific Coast Unionism 1929-1938

Ottilie Markholt

Pacific Coast Maritime History Committee
Tacoma, Washington

Published by
Pacific Coast Maritime History Committee, Tacoma, Washington

Library of Congress Catalogue Card Number 98-068428
ISBN 0-9664397-0-8
Printed on union-made paper by
R-4 Printing, Inc., Tacoma, Washington

Front cover: Portland longshoremen picketing the *S.S. Wiliboro* at Municipal Terminal No. 1, May 9, 1934.
(*Morning Oregonian*, courtesy Oregon Historical Society, OrHi neg. 81702)

Maritime Solidarity: Pacific Coast Unionism, 1929-1938 is available at selected bookstores, or it may be ordered directly from

Pacific Coast Maritime History Committee
c/o Pierce County Central Labor Council
3049 So. 36th St., Suite 201 – Tacoma, WA 98409
Phone: (253) 473-3810

To the memory of Bob and all
working people who believed in
and fought for a better world

Contents

Acknowledgments

Many years ago, when I first set out to explore the history of Pacific Coast maritime unions as an inseparable whole, Peter B. Gill and Ralph Chaplin encouraged me to tell this story. Since then, many others have helped: Bruce LeRoy assisted in obtaining a generous grant from the Louis M. Rabinowitz Foundation that enabled me to extend research to the Atlantic Coast. At the headquarters of the International Longshoremen's Association in New York City, the officers and staff, including my union sisters, made available important Pacific Coast records. I am grateful to them.

Staffs of libraries and unions opened their archives and helped to locate documents and pictures. They include: the Chicago headquarters of the Industrial Workers of the World, the Seattle Public Library, the University of Washington Libraries, the Seattle Central Labor Council (now the King County Labor Council), the Tacoma Public Library, the Tacoma Central Labor Council (now the Pierce County Central Labor Council), the Oregon Historical Society, and the Northwest Oregon Labor Council. California libraries and unions helped greatly: the San Francisco Public Library, the Bancroft Library at the University of California, Berkeley, The Oakland Museum, the Pacific Coast Marine Firemen, Oilers, Watertenders and Wipers Association, the San Francisco Labor Council, the Los Angeles Public Library, and the Los Angeles Central Labor Council (now the Los Angeles County Federation of Labor).

Harry S. McIvaigh's support opened doors in cities beyond Tacoma. Retired union activists provided valuable documents and insights: T.A. Thronson, Edward Coester, William T. Morris, Art Will, William J. Lewis, and Charles G. Peabody. Ronald E. Magden shared Northwest union and employer documents and searched for a publisher. Stephen Schwartz and Murray Morgan also tried to interest academic presses. I appreciate the support and efforts of all these people.

Archie Green provided the final push that transformed a voluminous maritime labor history into *Maritime Solidarity*, focused on the seminal years of the 1930s. Archie critiqued the manuscript with the practiced eye of the English professor, and James Ruble gave it the final polish as copy editor. Thank you both for this valuable help.

Supporters who formed the Pacific Coast Maritime History Committee offered assistance and suggestions: Robert W. Cherny, Nellie Fox-Edwards, Greg Mowat, Lou Stewart, Bob Markholt, Ross Rieder, Allen Seager, Marcus Widenor, Shaun Maloney, Dallas DeLay, Arthur A. Almeida, Vance J. Lelli, and John C. Ehly. Thank you for your contributions.

Unions, individual members, and friends too numerous to list donated money to print the book. They include: International Longshore and Warehouse Union Local 23, International Longshore and Warehouse Union, Sailors' Union of the Pacific, International Longshore and Warehouse Union Local 4, Henry P. Anderson, The Boag Foundation, International Brotherhood of Electrical Workers Local 483, International Organization of Masters, Mates and Pilots, Office and Professional Employees International Union, Pierce County Central Labor Council, Office and Professional Employees International Local 23, United Food and Commercial Workers Local 367, Puget Sound Ports Council of the Maritime Trades Department, International Association of Fire Fighters Local 31, and Lee Markholt. Thank you all.

Labor organizations and core members of the Maritime History Committee contributed valuable resources, time, and expertise: Clyde H. Hupp; Philip M. Lelli, T.A. Thronson, and the International Longshore and Warehouse Union Local 23; Brian McWilliams, Eugene Dennis Vrana and the International Longshore and Warehouse Union; Gunnar Lundeberg and the Sailors' Union of the Pacific; John W. Thompson, Marcia Williams, and the Pierce County Central Labor Council; and Blaine Johnson. Thank you for your sustained effort.

Sympathetic organizations have provided support and resources: the Pacific Northwest Labor History Association, the Port of Tacoma, Margaret Levi and the Harry Bridges Center for Labor Studies of the University of Washington, and Caroline Gallacci and the Tacoma Historical Society. Thank you all.

I appreciate the skill and understanding of President Michael Rogers and Designer Deanna Smieja of R-4 Printing, Inc., who transformed the manuscript into this book. Thank you. Finally, I am grateful to my sons Bob and Lee and all my family for their support and encouragement.

Preface

Peter B. Gill joined the Coast Seamen's Union at Port Townsend in 1886, book no. 43. Merger with the Steamship Sailors created the Sailors' Union of the Pacific, with branches in the principal ports. By the turn of the century the young Norwegian immigrant was Seattle port agent. A rock-solid unionist, fearless and incorruptible, Pete would never drink with the employers or accept anything of value from them. When he retired in 1939 the Sailors had no provision for pensions. However, the union voted to continue his salary and commissioned him to write the history of the union as an excuse for the unprecedented retirement pay.

The 1934 strike victory swept a new generation of militant young seamen into power in the union. Although they did not always agree with him, the young activists respected the old Norwegian sitting at the roll-top desk in the corner of the hall. When the International Seamen's Union revoked the Sailors' Union charter in 1936, Pete rejected his lifelong colleagues and stuck with the union membership. He had been an international vice-president.

Bob Dombroff, my husband and one of the young firebrands in the union, suggested that I help with the union history; he knew how much I wanted to write. Pete agreed, and I accepted the assignment eagerly. So for the next three years, while our small sons played in the living room, I spent hours each day at the typewriter, first taking notes from the *Coast Seamen's Journal* and other sources; in the beginning Pete wrote a few pages summarizing union events. From there I fleshed out the story, traveling frequently to his square white house in Ballard to discuss the manuscript with him. During the three years that he lived after I finished the book in 1942, Pete tried vainly to persuade the union to publish the history. Instead, the Sailors deposited the manuscript in the Bancroft Library at Berkeley.

When Bob and I married in 1935, we both belonged to the Communist Party. Bob joined while sailing out of San Francisco after the 1934 strike, one of hundreds of young seamen who believed the Party rhetoric about fighting for a better world. We met in Seattle the fall of 1935.

I had joined earlier that year while attending the University of Washington. With fuzzy notions of reforming the world, I called myself a Socialist. I wrote a letter to the U. of W. *Daily* condemning the arrogant Sigma Nu toughs who broke up our pacifist rally the fall of 1934 and smashed our signs. Reading my indignant letter, the Party assigned a comrade to recruit me. He loaned me a copy of John Reed's *Ten Days That Shook the World* and took me around Seattle, pointing out the class struggle in every facet of city life.

My own experience confirmed the Communists' harsh view of an ugly capitalist society inviting destruction. With my dad out of work, I scrabbled among miserable jobs for the few dollars to keep myself in school. I did housework for an eminent professor, her difficult child, and her fat dog: three o'clock to eight on week days and eight to eight on Saturdays for $15.00 a month and meals. The dog lived better than my family, eating hamburger every night, whereas at home we had a pound of hamburger once a week for Sunday dinner.

I asked my Socialist friends why I should not join the Communist Party. "Communists are not nice people," they replied, offering no better arguments. In contrast to their prissy morality, I felt drawn to John Reed's masses sweeping across the Russian plains with their cry for Peace—Land—Bread. I belonged here. Knowing nothing of Marxism, Leninism, vanguards, or the ruthless doctrine of ends justifying means, I joined the Party. Soon I moved from a room in an old boardinghouse near the ship canal to an attic apartment north of the campus shared with two other comrades. That spring our campus Young Communist League organized one of the first student strikes in the country against war and European fascism.

After years of questioning, challenging, rebelling, I abandoned my critical faculties when I joined the Communist Party. I drifted away from non-Party friends. As I was right and they were wrong, we had little to say to each other. I knew beyond a doubt that communism would inevitably win because the Party said so. I nestled comfortably into the parochialism of Party life, repeating acceptable phrases and carrying out instructions. I almost went to the Soviet Union. The Party cheated on the *Voice of Action* subscription drive. Instead of awarding the prize of a trip to Russia to the real winner, a Finnish comrade in Grays Harbor, the District Bureau decided to send someone from Seattle. They picked Frances Farmer instead of me because she would generate more publicity following the trip than I could.

At the end of the spring quarter I quit college to become a full-time professional revolutionary. I had five names: my own, my Party name, the name under which I rented a room, the name under which I solicited donations for the *Voice of Action*, and a name on a post office box at Raymer's Book Store, where soldiers could write for information about communism. On summer evenings I mounted the soapbox on the Communist corner of Washington and Occidental, exhorting the skid road audience to join the Party. As I traveled around Seattle collecting money for the *Voice*, I came to realize that in embracing the ultimate revolution I had discarded everything in between. Nothing else mattered—no personal interests or goals. I had become a drudge of the revolution, plodding along submissively, "taking orders meekly with the soul of a dray horse."

The black notebook I had used at the university prompted the first crack in this glacial ice in which I had encased myself. The summer of 1935 the Party conducted a school at the Communist Finn Hall on Yesler Way for a group of promising young comrades. As I sat dutifully taking notes on the lectures of leading comrades, I realized sadly that in this classroom I would memorize facts, not challenge and evaluate ideas. Then I read J. Peters's *Manual on Party Organization.* He described how democratic centralism worked: From the bottom up Party organisms discussed an issue; then, guided by these discussions, the Central Committee decided policy. Basic Party units elected members to section committees, whose members in turn elected the district committee. But Peters's manual did not reflect Seattle's Party life. With the advent of the United Front, new policies descended on us without warning. Following the years of dual revolutionary unions and relative isolation, the United Front heralded a new strategy: Instead of attacking other workers' organizations and unions, the Party sought alliances with or attempted to capture them. Contrary to Peters, so far as I knew, no one had been elected to anything. I had been appointed to the Young Communist League Section Committee, a powerless body that did nothing. I took orders from the YCL district organizer.

Next I attended a section plenum, a general meeting of active Party members in western Washington. I listened in awe as Morris Rapport, the Communist Party district organizer, tongue-lashed comrade after comrade for his failings. He talked for hours. No victim answered back. One man wept openly. Had Rapport and other leading comrades possessed real power, in retrospect I later wondered how they would have used it. During the supper break I chattered to a young Slav miner: "The Party comes first, then the revolution, then the working class." "No, Comrade," he corrected me gravely. "First the working class, then the revolution, then the Party." I did not understand him; for me the working class remained an abstraction.

The Party welcomed my marriage to Bob in late 1935; close ties with outsiders often brought trouble. I was nineteen and Bob was twenty. He had not surrendered himself to the Party as I had. Although he understood as little about Marxism-Leninism as I did, he knew the class struggle in his blood and bones. Soon we began to discuss the disparity between the Party's fine rhetoric about fighting for the rank and file and the crude manipulation and intimidation we saw around us. Lies and deception would not build a new world. The Party line on the Sailors' Union charter revocation climaxed our misgivings: Meeting Morris Rapport on the street in early February 1936, Bob began to argue vehemently against the Communist decision to follow the charter and reorganize under the international union. "But that will destroy the Sailors' Union," Bob protested. "So what?" snapped Rapport, dismissing the shocked young Communist. "So we still have the revolution." Immediately after that confrontation we both dropped out of the Party.

Freed from the shackles of Communist orthodoxy, Bob and I began to define the new world of our hopes. We rejected the Trotskyists as just another set of commissars. While sailing out of New Orleans during the early 1930s, Bob had carried a card in the Industrial Workers of the World. After leaving the Party, he began to bring home the *Industrial Worker* and other literature regularly from the Wobbly hall at Second and Main. We pondered the idea that working people could take over the means of production and organize a society based on an economic instead of a political structure. Briefly, the summer of 1936, before the Communists and Fascists engulfed them, the Spanish anarchosyndicalists seemed to be building that new society. We read labor history. In the writings of Frank Roney, George McNeill, John Commons, and others, I learned of the great cycles of victory and defeat that marked working people's centuries of struggle in the United States.

Most important of all, I shared vicariously Bob's day-to-day struggle in the Sailor's Union and the Maritime Federation against destructive forces both inside and outside the unions. Heartbroken, I watched the maritime workers destroy their own impregnable fortress that the employers could not breach. I concluded bitterly: "We are good, blind people—obliged to lead ourselves to the New Society without advancing appreciably toward it. But we would die for what we cannot build." Our marriage failed. I tried to join the Wobblies, but they rejected a housewife.

As the Sailors' Union book took form, I realized how incomplete the history of one union must be. I would write my own history of all the maritime unions, intertwined in their great cycles of victory and defeat. I finished Pete's book, moved to Tacoma, and went to work in 1943 as office secretary for the Tacoma Metal Trades Council. I wrote for the Central Labor Council newspaper, the *Tacoma Labor Advocate*, under Ralph Chaplin's editorship and became active in my own union.

The AFL dominated Tacoma labor, a tough, militant movement embracing thousands of men and women, skilled and unskilled. Harry McIvaigh, a railroad machinist who had represented a shop crafts system federation, presided over the local movement as secretary of the Central Labor Council. He brought the concept of industrial bargaining structures for craft unions to the council. Craft unions of shipyard workers already bargained through the Metal Trades Council with the burgeoning shipbuilding industry, protected by a master agreement covering all crafts. Construction workers likewise sheltered under a Building Trades agreement for all unions, and on the job a Building Trades steward spoke for them all. When retail store employees organized, McIvaigh helped them to create a similar industrial structure: craft agreements attached to a master agreement signed by the Central Labor Council and Building Trades Council.

The major battles had been fought before I arrived in Tacoma, but their echoes reverberated throughout the movement: the 1934 maritime strike, the 1935 lumber strike, and organizing drives at the smelter and in other industries. Although we applauded CIO victories in the Midwest, the CIO in Tacoma appeared to be a Communist tactic to divide and capture. The Central Labor Council had helped the Mine, Mill and Smelter workers and the Newspaper Guild to organize. When their internationals went CIO they had to leave the council. Lumber workers suffered and employers profited from the CIO split in their union. A CIO United Construction

Workers Organizing Committee challenged the Building Trades unions without noticeable effect, and the CIO put union cards in a few scab barber shops.

I went to work for own union, Office Employees Local 23, in 1949 as office secretary. We, all of the unions, took our strength for granted. We collected dues and initiation fees because people had to join our unions to hold their jobs. A few unions tried to explain their benefits to new members. For years we failed to understand how passing time was changing our unions. Old timers who had organized them and fought battles for their survival retired and died. A new generation of compulsory union members inherited good jobs without feeling any obligation to support the unions. Eroding individual union commitment weakened the movement. Employers developed sophisticated union-busting techniques to convince people that unions should be thrown out and kept out of workplaces.

From my post at the desk in the Office Employees I watched the splendid solidarity of the 1940s crumble as employers succeeded in playing unions against each other. Sears led the open-shop drive in the retail stores, our largest bargaining unit. The employers destroyed our master agreement, enabling them to pick off weak unions. They hired many part-time employees who cared nothing about unions. From union protection and benefits in the 1950s, now, forty years later, most retail store employees have no unions, earn slightly above minimum wages, and receive few benefits.

Working in various trade union offices during those years of decline, I encountered a few strong and dedicated officers such as Harry McIlvaigh, many conscientious representatives who tried vainly to check the downward spiral, and a few self-seeking ones who exploited their unions. Like the national movement, Tacoma unions began to realize in the 1970s the urgent need to educate their members. McIlvaigh had retired, but Clyde Hupp, the new council secretary, and many delegates shared the commitment to support labor education.

I became a delegate to the Central Labor Council from my own union so I could share in the work. Some of our efforts succeeded—some failed. We tried without success to develop a labor studies program in a community college. For twelve years we put out a bimonthly bulletin, the *Labor Educator*, that I edited. We created a pictorial exhibit of some fifty poster-size photographs, "Working People and Their Unions," which has been shown in schools, union gatherings, and the Tacoma Public Library. To celebrate Labor's contribution to building Washington state, thirty-two unions wrote and published *To Live in Dignity: Pierce County Labor, 1883-1989*, an illustrated centennial history. We distributed thousands of copies to schools, libraries, and union members.

The outlines of the maritime history lay neglected for many of those years while I raised my children. A second marriage failed. In the late 1950s, at Ralph Chaplin's urging, I resumed work on the maritime history, accumulating stacks of notes from primary sources. After more years I wrote the history, thousands of pages relating in detail the story of the Pacific Coast maritime unions from their inception through the 1934 strike. In 1991 I renewed an old acquaintance with Archie Green. "What have you done with your maritime history?" he asked. "Written a tome that no one will possibly publish," I replied. With his encouragement I selected and condensed the most significant portion of the history: the cycle of building and destruction during the 1930s.

This is not the history I would have written fifty years ago. These fifty years in the union movement brought values and insights that the history reflects. I do not claim objectivity. I am passionately committed to labor. But I am so sure of the reason and justice of our cause that I quote the worst indictments of our enemies. This history is not a memoir, although lifetime judgements and reflections inevitably influence it. Nor is it interpretive history. Without intruding my opinions, I have tried to write a narrative describing a tumultuous decade on Pacific Coast waterfronts. But beneath the events here described, and more significant, is the way the participants perceived the events. What did the maritime workers see happening to their lives—their unions—their dreams? Listen to these people.

Introduction

Almost from the beginnings of maritime trade on the Pacific Coast, the men who sailed the ships and worked the cargoes combined in unions for their mutual protection. Having created viable organizations of their crafts, the workers reached out to form waterfront federations to present a common front to their employers. In 1888, the San Francisco Wharf and Wave Federation led the way.

In a massive sympathetic strike in San Francisco in 1901 the City Front Federation defeated the open-shop offensive of the Employers' Association. The victory inaugurated years of individual union strength on the waterfront. Seagoing and shoreside unions won improved wages and working conditions. Year by year the unions added to their gains with stable collective bargaining. The union network extended along the entire coast.

Each union felt that it had to preserve these gains at any cost. In time, federations became meaningless because unions could not afford to help each other with the ultimate weapon of support: the sympathetic strike. They feared to risk their individual security in a united struggle. After World War I, in the massive open-shop drive of the early 1920s, shipowners, waterfront employers, and the government broke the maritime unions one by one. Some unions disappeared entirely—others declined to a powerless handful of members. Once again the workers had no protection. As in the beginning, all groups became equal in defeat. None had gains to preserve at the expense of other unions.

Bitter years for maritime workers followed the employers' victory. During the open-shop era of the 1920s the wave of solidarity slowly built which would engulf Pacific Coast waterfronts and would propel their workers to new heights of strength and purpose. Old unionists distilled their defeats into iron resolution that fed the wave. Young workers beat their fists against the humiliations and injustices of their working lives. Their outrage and frustration powered the wave. The bitter years succeeded one another until finally the wave broke in a mighty outpouring of hope and determination, transforming the 1934 maritime strike into a stunning union victory.

This time, maritime workers institutionalized solidarity, the source of their strength, in the Maritime Federation. Their motto, "An Injury to One is an Injury to All," became holy writ. With this new power the unions wrested control of hiring from their employers and destroyed the blacklisting threat.

Employer exploitation and oppression had forced workers to combine in solidarity. As their triumph diminished employer power, it lessened the pressure that had brought them together in 1934. Other programs and promises distracted them. The Communist Party lured the discontented and embittered with the assurance that it alone held meaning and substance for the future. The CIO dazzled the nation's workers with visions of the perfect union.

Down on the docks and ships the workers struggled with the realities of their imperfect unions. Some became impatient with apparently insoluble problems. Devotion to their bright dreams replaced allegiance to the real solidarity they had created. The Maritime Federation perished.

Part One

The 1934 Strike

1

Fink Hall Years: Seamen

In a nationwide strike in 1921, shipowners and the government combined to defeat the unions of licensed and unlicensed seamen. With the triumph of the open shop, unionism survived as an act of faith. The complacent—the indifferent—the self-seeking, accretions of the years of union control, had dropped away during the struggle. Fear and humiliation dominated the harsh, rank present. Justice and dignity became frail promises for the future, to be believed by the dedicated few for whom unionism remained binding and irrevocable.

Denying the overwhelming reality of their powerlessness, men performed small acts of faith: rejected a demeaning situation, spoke out for a fellow worker, paid a month's dues. They set about patiently to rebuild their shattered unions. Ten years is a long time to deny the present and believe in the future. The decade belonged to the open-shop shipowners, but the years beyond could belong to those who persisted in trusting their promise.

Marine Service Bureau

For the shipowners, control of hiring meant control of the seamen. The Marine Employment Service operated by the Marine Service Bureau provided the means. With the shipping card and continuous discharge book, shipowners could blacklist union militants and intimidate the rest of the seamen.

To ship out of the Marine Service Bureau (fink hall), a seaman registered, received a number, and waited his turn for a job. Theoretically, the dispatcher picked the oldest registration card, but ships' officers could pick men by sending them in with notes, by telephoning for particular men, or by selecting them personally from the hall. A seaman picked for a job received an assignment card to present to the master of the vessel, who kept the card until the seaman left the ship. Then the master returned the card to the bureau, noting length of service, ability, and conduct. Registration cards expired after sixty days. In slack periods a seaman with a card less than fifty days old had little chance of shipping. If the card ran out before the man shipped, he took a new card and started again at the bottom of the list.

The Marine Service Bureau's initial success in recruiting scabs for steam schooners in 1921 encouraged offshore operators to patronize it, and soon they joined the coastwise companies in the hiring venture. Nineteen companies operating 254 vessels with total tonnage of 901,836 comprised the Pacific American Steamship Association. They operated tankers and vessels sailing to the Orient, the Pacific

Islands, and the East and Gulf coasts. Twenty-nine companies, principally steam schooner operators, owning 128 vessels totaling 132,490 tons comprised the Shipowners' Association of the Pacific Coast.

To combat the Marine Service Bureau, Andrew Furuseth, long-time secretary of the Sailors' Union of the Pacific (SUP) and president of the International Seamen's Union (ISU), urged seamen first to "get back into the union, so that you can trust each other and work together." Next, he counseled, work "The Oracle." This is what he meant: Pointing out that the shipping office would be abandoned if it caused delays in sailing, he urged seamen to jump ship when a vessel was about to leave: "The vessel is ready and the master orders the lines cast off. You cast your duds on the wharf and follow the duds. The vessel is delayed. She must find another crew. This crew may do the same thing or go up the coast and leave her there. She is again delayed. How long will the shipowners stand for that, especially in passenger vessels?"[1] The shipowners called the Oracle a "wobbly circular" which "shows the marine worker how to throw wooden shoes into the machinery of the American Merchant Marine—and incites him to do it."[2]

The unions could not resist a wage reduction in 1922, initiated by the U.S. Shipping Board, the federal agency created during World War I to administer the government-owned merchant fleet. On February 1 the Pacific American Steamship Association cut wages to $55.00 a month for able seamen, the new Shipping Board scale. The American Steamship Owners' Association paid $47.50 on intercoastal vessels. Steam schooner operators followed with a reduction from $72.50 to $65.00, and sailing vessels paid $50.00 to the Hawaiian Islands and $40.00 for other deep-water voyages. With the lumber industry picking up and lumber prices rising, seamen objected particularly to the steam schooner reduction. In spite of a 10 percent length-of-service bonus, many quit at the end of a trip. A report circulated that steam schooner operators would employ Mexican seamen to circumvent union organizers and walking delegates. In March the *Fred Baxter* cut wages from $77.50 to $60.00 after clearing the Golden Gate, which amounted to shanghaiing the crew.

Simultaneously with the wage cut, the shipowners completed control of the seamen by adopting the continuous discharge book (fink book). Besides space for discharges from each voyage, the book contained the owner's sea experience, personal description, and photograph. It stated that "no person will be employed by these associations unless he is registered at their employment office and has in his possession this certificate and discharge."[3] A seaman surrendered the book to the master when signing articles, to be returned at the end of the voyage with the discharge noting the seaman's rating, conduct, and efficiency. The bureau advised the sailor "to conduct himself so that his record will be found satisfactory for future service."[4]

Andrew Furuseth told the shipowners that the discharge book constituted "an industrial passport in which you improve upon the passport given to the negro slave prior to the war between the States, by attaching thereto the man's photo." He accused them of creating "as efficient an instrument of blacklisting as you and your advisors can together conceive."[5]

The shipowners threatened and cajoled seamen to accept the fink hall. While bureau inspectors boarded vessels at San Pedro and San Francisco to remove men not carrying fink books, San Francisco headquarters maintained a reading room and baggage room for seamen and, on occasion, provided beds and meals. A pamphlet, *A Square Deal for Marine Workers*, lectured seamen on the virtues of hard work and efficiency so "the American shipowner can afford to pay the highest wages and provide the best living conditions on his ships." The Marine Employment Service offered "a friendly refuge and the best chance of a job." The service would ship "only American citizens or men who have declared their intention of becoming citizens."[6] The Pacific District International Seamen's Union replied that the fink book and fink hall were "mere instruments of coercion which, in the long run, will create bitter resentment . . . They are badges of servitude, . . . This resentment will do more to lessen efficiency and destroy good will than any other scheme that could be devised."[7]

Albert Street Versus Shipowners' Association

The seamen turned to the courts for protection against the fink hall. Backed by the International Seamen's Union, Albert Street, a marine fireman, filed a complaint in May 1922 in the U.S. District Court, alleging that the rules imposed by the Marine Employment Service "violated the anti-trust laws and destroyed his right to freedom of contract." He stated that "he was coerced, threatened and intimidated in obeying such rules in order to make a living."[8] Refused relief in district court, Albert Street appealed to the U.S. Supreme Court, which sent the case to the Circuit Court of Appeals. In June 1924 the appeals court held that taking turns in employment was reasonable and the employment service did not violate antitrust laws.

Wages varied according to classes of vessels, types of cargoes, and shipping routes. Improved economic conditions ashore in 1923 created a shortage of skilled seamen in the lumber trade. Wages on steam schooners drifted upward until on February 1 the Shipowners' Association raised them to $75.00 for able seamen and $70.00 for firemen. The Marine Service Bureau took credit for the wage increase. The Sailors' Union turned down a proposal from the Seattle agency to strike for a raise when shipping improved in the spring. On May 14, after meeting with ISU representatives, the Shipping Board increased wages on government-owned vessels from $55.00 to $62.50, half the raise the union sought. These wages remained unchanged for the rest of the decade. On the Pacific Coast in 1924, offshore ships and coastwise general cargo and passenger carriers paid $65.00; intercoastal vessels paid the East Coast scale of $55.00.

To combat union agitators, Walter Petersen, manager of the Marine Service Bureau, explained that seamen needed the protection of the organization. He depicted the sailor as a dependent person "more or less subservient to higher authority." In the union he was "the prey of the demagogue and the radical, and he was taught that the shipowner was a rich, soulless, hard-hearted, grasping creature whose only consideration for him was the labor his sweating, toil-racked body could produce." According to Captain Petersen, by 1925 the initial "open hatred" and "profound distrust" of sailors for the bureau had changed to "trust and friendship." The Captain's title came from the Oakland police department, not the bridge of a vessel.

"Nowhere in the world," declared Petersen, "is the seafarer better paid, quartered, and fed than on the Pacific Coast of North America." He said the bureau established comfortable and sanitary crews' quarters and "food served to the crews . . . precisely the same as that which appears on the Captain's table." Ashore the bureau was "a haven of distress for those who need counsel. . . . In short, the Bureau acts IN LOCO PARENTIS, and as a guide, philosopher, and friend for the seafaring fraternity, and provides them with a greater measure of substantial, practical, and human aid than they have ever received from any of their former affiliations."[9]

Chinese Crews

During the years of union strength, shipowners looked longingly at cheap Chinese labor. A.F. Haines, first vice-president of the Pacific American Steamship Association, testified before the Senate Committee on Commerce in January 1921: "We can and do employ Chinese whenever we can get away with it with the unions. That is the only law that we have that prevents it."[10]

The government apparently held the same view. With the unions broken in 1921, the Emergency Fleet Corporation immediately began to replace whites with Asians on its vessels. In November the *Silver State* shipped 155 Chinese in the stewards' department and about 100 in the engine room. In December the *Pine Tree State* replaced the engine and stewards' departments with 132 Chinese, and the following month the *Keystone State* brought 160 Chinese for the *Bay State*. The Shipping Board and later the Dollar steamship interests used Chinese extensively on President vessels sailing out of Seattle and San Francisco. Neither the Alien Contract Labor law nor the Chinese Exclusion Act applied to Chinese shipped at Hong Kong.

Robert Dollar said he carried Chinese because they behaved better: "The worst menace to our shipping is the clause in the LaFollette bill which makes it mandatory that every member of the crew must be paid half his wages at every port of call. This causes so many desertions that many ships are using Chinese exclusively."[11] The *President Polk* paid her Chinese $11.00 a month. The following year the *President Wilson* signed on a full Chinese crew for $6.00 a month in the presence of an American consul in China and brought them back steerage. In 1928 the *S.S. Montana* replaced the entire white crew with Chinese.

Seamen complained bitterly that the government refused to enforce the safety provisions of the Seamen's Act. Federal officials gave able-bodied seaman's papers to unqualified men, handed out lifeboat tickets without adequate tests, and ignored the language clause. In December 1921 the Shipping Board arbitrarily reduced the manning scale on vessels between 7,001 and 9,000 tons from forty to thirty unlicensed seamen. The Sailors' Union protested the sweeping reductions made without considering the number required for safe navigation of individual vessels, which the Steamboat Inspection Service had heretofore determined.

Cornelius Andersen Versus the Shipowners

After losing the first court battle to close the fink hall, the Sailors' Union attacked the continuous discharge book as a monopoly restraining trade. On June 15, 1925, the Marine Service Bureau refused to register Cornelius Andersen because he had no discharge book. Three days later Andersen returned to the bureau with a note from A.J. Ryndberg, mate on the Charles Nelson Company's *Caddopeak,* requesting the bureau to ship him on the steam schooner. Again the fink hall refused to register or ship him, and the port captain refused to let the mate hire him.

Andersen sued the Shipowners' Association and Pacific American Steamship Association for $135 wages for the duration of the trip he was prevented from making because the Marine Service Bureau would not ship him and the employer would not hire him directly. Losing in district and circuit courts, Andersen appealed to the U.S. Supreme Court. On November 22, 1926, the high court ruled that in agreeing "to abide by the will of the association,"[12] the shipowners and operators had formed a combination that violated the Sherman Anti-Trust Act.

Armed with the Supreme Court decision, Cornelius Andersen sued on behalf of himself and other seamen for an injunction against the Shipowners' Association and Pacific American Steamship Association for maintaining a combination in restraint of interstate and foreign commerce. Andersen's complaint charged that the Marine Service Bureau compelled seamen seeking employment to buy and carry the continuous discharge book, register with the bureau, and ship by turn. These regulations prevented seamen from choosing their jobs and ships' officers from choosing their crews.

The shipowners declared that they did not intend to coerce or blacklist seamen and denied that they compelled the men to register at the Marine Service Bureau or carry the fink book to ship. Significantly, before the court hearing, the bureau removed from the discharge book the statement that seamen would be employed only through that agency and took down the notices posted in the hall that seamen must present the book to register for employment. Judge Frank H. Kerrigan accepted the revised instructions in the book as evidence that seamen did not need to carry it or ship through the hall. Shipowners, association representatives, and bureau agents all testified to voluntary employer patronage of the hall. In a decision at San Francisco on June 21, 1928, two years after it was introduced in the court, Judge Kerrigan denied the injunction.

Although the Marine Service Bureau convinced the court that it did not coerce seamen, the shipowners' own testimony revealed that in practice the institution controlled virtually all hiring, and seamen had to carry the fink book to ship on almost all vessels.[13] Shipowners praised the bureau's efficiency, contrasting it to the days of the union shipping office, with vessels frequently delayed and seamen often "incompetent, drunk, disloyal, and altogether unsatisfactory,"[14] according to steam schooner operator William R. Chamberlin. Length-of-service bonuses paid by some companies failed to stabilize employment. In the four years through 1925 the bureau issued 44,000 discharge books for 10,000 jobs on the Pacific Coast, a turnover of more than 100 percent a year. During 1926 and the first eleven months of 1927, the San Francisco office shipped 74 percent of those registered and the San Pedro office 76 percent.

The Shipping Board's hiring hall, the Sea Service Bureau, and the Marine Service Bureau complemented each other. In Seattle and Portland, where no branches of the latter existed, the government agency supplied seamen to private operators as well as Shipping Board vessels. The San Francisco Sea Service Bureau supplied men for nineteen Shipping Board vessels operated by Swayne & Hoyt. Slightly less than half the 15,400 men shipped annually from Seattle and Portland went through the Sea Service Bureau. In addition, at Seattle Alaska Steamship Company and the Dollar Line maintained employment offices. For the fiscal year ending July 1, 1927, the Sea Service Bureau shipped 9,627 men from Pacific Coast ports, and the Marine Service Bureau shipped almost four times as many, about 36,529 seamen.

Compulsion, Bribery, and Blacklist

Seamen flatly contradicted Walter Petersen's claim that the discharge book was not compulsory. Ferdinand Purnell carried a book in 1923 and 1924. During that time he turned down jobs from the bureau on the *Monaula* and the Standard Oil tanker *Richmond* because both vessels worked two watches and on the *Katrina Luckenbach* because of low wages. In each case the clerk told him to take out a new registration card if he wanted a different job. Three years later Purnell shipped on a Matson vessel at Honolulu. When he tried to sign on at San Francisco for another trip, the company fired him for refusing to take the book. Purnell spoke for many seamen:

> I don't like to carry them, . . . If you carry that book and go aboard a ship and the mate takes a personal dislike to you, or you don't like conditions on the ship, and either the food, or the living accommodations, and you kick about them to the mate they don't like it as a rule, and they fire you, and they will enter a bad discharge in your book; you may have twelve or fifteen other good discharges in that, and when you go to get another job on the ship they don't look at the good ones, but they look at the bad one.[15]

When the company fired George Madsen from the *Caddopeak* in 1925 for lacking a book, the port captain told him not to sail on Nelson vessels without one. After being hired by the mate, the Admiral Line refused Oscar Tybring employment on the *Admiral Seebree* because he had no book. In 1927 the fink hall inspector pulled Peter Mooi off the steam schooner *Daisy Putman* at San Pedro for not having a book.

According to I.A. Haarklau, San Pedro patrolman for the Sailors' Union, most companies insisted on hiring through the bureau. When he asked for work for union members, a master or mate usually told him, "I have got to hire men from the Marine Service Bureau."[16] Seamen affirmed that Nelson, McCormick, American-Hawaiian, Admiral Line, Grace Line, Dollar Line, Matson, Swayne & Hoyt, Standard Oil, Union Oil, and others refused to hire off the dock and sent men to the fink hall. A Union Oil tanker refused Ingolf Westvick a job because he did not go through the bureau. Martin Hoglander, with almost a quarter of a century of sea experience, had to take a book to work on a Charles Nelson vessel. He described the incident:

> The ship had been tied up for three days because they could not get a crew. It was a sailing ship; . . . I met the captain and I was with him before when he was a mate, and he said to me, "I am Captain of the 'William W. Smith' now, and I am going to make a fine trip down to Mexico, . . ." He asked me to come. I said I would go. . . . Then he turned around and said, "You must go up to the Shipowners Association and get an assignment card." I said, "What have I to do with an assignment card, I never have been around the office." I said, "You are the Master of the ship, and you hired me, what have I got to do with that card?" He said, "Well, if you want to go on that ship you will have to get a card."[17]

Seamen claimed that the fink hall and Sea Service Bureau didn't even operate honestly by their own rules. Many sailors believed that shipping clerks took bribes to ship seamen out of turn. Bureau employees took cash, and Shipping Board employees accepted gifts of Japanese kimonos, shirts, and Chinese suitcases to ship on the Oriental run.

The fink hall and fink book locked in the helpless seamen; a pervasive blacklist denied employment to those who threatened the shipowners' control of wages and conditions on the ships. Walter Petersen said of the Marine Service Bureau blacklist: "Some of the companies send us lists of men they do not want to employ; and we do not assign such men to that company but to other companies. I think Swayne & Hoyt,, the Luckenbach Steamship Company and the Matson Company have given us directions like that."[18] Edwin Nichols of the San Pedro bureau said that Standard Oil, Union Oil, and General Petroleum blacklisted a seaman named Kane. George Larsen, acting secretary of the Sailors' Union, described an incident at Richmond, where a Standard Oil tanker was taking in oil drums:

> The men were asked to work extra hours; they said, "All right, we will work, but we would like to have the same overtime as the men on the docks are paid for overtime.". . . That was refused, so, in the book was put down that these men refused to work overtime.
>
> One of these men in particular came to me and said that after he left the ship—in fact, he had been with the company some eleven months, I think, and he was almost due for a bonus, for a two weeks vacation, and he lost out on that. Furthermore, he went down to the American-Hawaiian Steamship Company and applied for a job. The mate said, "All right, have you your Shipowners Association book?" He produced the book. When the mate saw what was put in the book he questioned him about what happened on the Standard Oil tanker, and then he said: "I don't want you; furthermore, you take my advice and get off this coast, because such men as you are not wanted on this coast."[19]

The Shipping Board maintained a nationwide deferred list of undesirable seamen who would not be shipped. Mobile Port Captain M. Nicholson wrote to all masters: "It is requested that in the future if you have any trouble with your crew, or if you find any agitators among them, please submit full report to this office to enable us to place any trouble maker or undesirable on the blacklist."[20] By 1928 the deferred list contained the names of 1,125 seamen declared unfit for sea duty by Shipping Board doctors and another 1,885 seamen, "who have been placed there for various offenses such as putting emery in the bearings, assaulting officers with intent to kill, stealing ships' property, smuggling, desertion and incompetency."[21]

The Shipping Board blacklisted E.D. Cook in 1925 for persuading the crew of the Swayne & Hoyt freighter *West Nilus* to refuse to work overtime because the master would not allow overtime pay or compensatory time off. The board blacklisted another sailor for testifying in defense of a shipmate in a mutiny trial, even though the man was cleared of the charge. After a year on the blacklist, the Shipping Board refused the sailor's request to be removed.[22]

Besides the acknowledged blacklist, seamen believed that the bureau blacklisted seamen on the assignment cards. While a captain might not enter derogatory remarks in the continuous discharge book, he might well condemn a man on the assignment card returned to the bureau when the seaman left the vessel. The master's report on each seaman required by the Shipping Board served the same purpose. Blacklists of private companies and the Shipping Board circulated widely, barring seamen from sailing out of any Pacific Coast port. For many seamen, the threat of blacklist enforced submission.

Wages and Conditions at Sea

Pacific Coast shipowners created the fink hall to insure cheap, productive, docile labor at sea. The level of wages, working conditions, and living conditions measured their success.

Steam schooner wages remained at $75.00, with three watches at sea and unlimited hours of work in port loading and discharging cargo. Only the side runners on each side of the hatch, the mate's favorites assigned there to speed up the pace, received overtime. A seaman worked or quit, up to sixteen and even eighteen hours a day. Outside the Columbia River and Puget Sound, when loading and discharging cargo, the operators paid no overtime for shifting ship before 7:00 a.m. or after 5:00 p.m. After working all day loading or discharging lumber, seamen could be required to turn to and move the vessel to another dock on their own time with no extra pay. The crew worked without overtime on the day of arrival, and the master set sea watches when the vessel sailed. Officers could cut mealtime to half an hour without overtime.

On the mate's "star watch" at sea, those same favorites informed on "mess room militants," who would promptly be fired for grumbling about the trip. On some vessels the custom called for "a barrel of herring for the mate," presented by a sailor who fished part of the year. Or sailors might be required to paint the mate's or skipper's house with company paint—labor donated. With cargo worked at top speed and no penalty time, accidents increased. Many companies threatened to blacklist seamen who refused their minimal out-of-court settlements.

Steam schooners fed well for the man-killing work, but their crews endured poor living conditions. Mess rooms at best could not hold the whole crew at one sitting, and on many small steam schooners men ate on hatches and deck loads or in holds.

Seamen still slept in the forepeak, the most dangerous place in the vessel i accident. They also put up with primitive sanitary conditions. At the beginning of the trip each sailor received a bucket for washing, bathing, and washing clothes. Coos Bay Lumber Company vessels provided better quarters than on most steam schooners.

Almost equally bad conditions plagued crews on the Alaska ships sailing out of Seattle. With no steam in the fo'c'sles of some vessels, the water under the bunks froze at night on cold trips. According to one sailor, rats as big as rabbits overran the *Latouche*, and bedbugs and cockroaches abounded. The mate and purser swapped food stores for fox skins in Alaska, while the crew lived on beef stew.

Many transpacific and intercoastal vessels worked two watches. On periodic "field days" at sea, all hands worked from sunup without overtime to scrub, paint, or do other ship work. Fo'c'sles deteriorated. Many held bunks three high. Most had no heat, the crew washing midships in buckets of cold water. Some freighters skimped on fresh water to allow more cargo tonnage; then the vessel provided one bucket of water at 5:00 p.m. for the crew to wash. When provided, showers combined salt water and direct steam. In accordance with the 1915 Seamen's Act, which set minimum requirements for crews' quarters, vessels built during World War I had wash basins. Shipowners furnished no change of linen. A seaman who wanted a clean towel washed his dirty one. Intercoastal vessels had the worst quarters of all. Calmar and Luckenbach ships swarmed with rats, cockroaches, and other vermin. One sailor claimed that rats carried off his shoes. Occasionally at sailing time crews reputedly threw overboard mattresses filled with bedbugs and demanded new ones.

Offshore vessels served poor and scanty food: two eggs a week on Sunday morning. Contrary to the shipowners' claim, they all carried two pots, one for the captain's table and one for the crew's. Ships stores marked "crew's coffee, crew's eggs, crew's butter," and the like—stale or second-rate food—accounted for a greater than average incidence of stomach ailments among seamen. Some sailors took their own stores to sea. The Los Angeles Steamship Company, an exception, provided good food. The Seattle Sailors' agency noted in 1926 that the county jail allowed $1.00 a day to feed a prisoner, the federal prison 75 cents, and the shipowners 60 cents to feed a seaman.

Some seamen preferred the lighter work and higher pay on the tanker fleet, from $62.50 to $75.00, but the oil companies guarded their domain carefully against union contamination. They customarily fired a sailor for mentioning the union. In keeping with John D. Rockefeller's despotic paternalism, Standard Oil maintained a company union and welfare plan on its vessels. Seamen considered Pan American company tankers the best on the coast.

Anticipating passage of the Jones-White bill, Robert Dollar began to replace his Chinese crews with white seamen in deck and engine departments. Seamen believed that Terry LaCroix, San Francisco shipping agent, sold jobs. At Seattle, where boatswains hired deck crews for President vessels, some carried as high as 75 percent union crews, with an average of 40 percent on the entire line. A union boatswain would pick from the SUP hall. Even without an agreement, this union influence kept conditions on the President Line above those of other transpacific vessels.

Conditions aboard ships began to deteriorate about 1927. Wages varied according to I.A. Haarklau: "There is no fixed scale of wages; each company pays what they feel like, or what they can get by with, or whatever the crew is willing to accept."[23] With rising unemployment among seamen, workaways, seamen who sailed for room and board while waiting for a regular job, appeared on offshore and coastwise runs. They signed on for 25 cents a trip. Vessels sometimes "worked off" crew members, harassed them until they quit, to make room for workaways. Two vessels sailed from the Columbia River for Australia with crews of deportees furnished by the Seattle and Portland immigration offices. In 1929 the Tacoma-Oriental Steamship Company replaced white crews with Filipinos. True to the union's predictions, skilled seamen left the sea by the hundreds. Except on steam schooners, young Americans extensively replaced older foreign-born seamen during the 1920s.

Delegates of the Marine Transport Workers (MTW) of the Industrial Workers of the World (IWW) reported in 1927: *S.S. Northland*, ABs (able-bodied seamen) $75.00, food fair, fo'c'sle small, one ISU and two MTW members. *S.S. Noyo*, ABs $80.00, firemen $70.00, food bad, fo'c'sle fair, two MTW members. *S.S. Caddopeak*, ABs $75.00, firemen $70.00, two ISU and one MTW member. *S.S. Monoa*, Matson, ABs and firemen $60.00, food bad, two watches. *Industrial Solidarity* cautioned MTW delegates sending in job news: "Do not exaggerate. Conditions are bad enough without adding any unnecessary bunk."[24]

In spite of the shipowners' power, rebellion flared up now and then. A master logged a seaman sixteen times, half a day's pay for each offense, for taking coffee time in defiance of the mate's orders. When the Nelson Line *Nome City* went on two watches in 1927, the entire deck crew walked off, led by Sailors' Union members. After the captain restored three watches, the vessel sailed.

Licensed officers fared no better during the open-shop years than the crews sailing under them. Most companies compelled deck officers to join the American Shipmasters' Association of the Pacific Coast, founded years earlier as a fraternal organization and transformed into a company union after 1921. Nelson blacklisted Albert Larson for refusing to join and discharged R.B. O'Brien from two ships and refused him employment on a third for the same reason. In 1926 the president of the Shipowners' Association requested Captain V. Westerholm to hire only members of the Shipmasters' Association. When allowed to pick his officers, the owners urged him to make them join. Port captains, who hired most officers, figured prominently in the company union and collected dues.

In Seattle most deck officers shipped through the Admiral Line Officers' Club, another company union, with Grover C. Geer shipping agent for all lines. The President vessels offered the best jobs, paying $225 for first mate, $185 for second, $165 for third, and $150 for fourth mate. The company furnished uniforms and laundry.

The steam schooner scale averaged $150 for chief, $135 for second mate and $120 for third mate, with $1.00 overtime. Other vessels paid no overtime. With men bargaining individually, jobs could be good or bad depending on the skipper, but all companies drove their masters to keep costs of working cargo down. Mates on steam schooners worked on the docks when crews handled lumber, and on Alaska vessels they worked cargo, including ore, for 20 or 25 cents an hour overtime. Often they worked continuously for over twenty-four hours with no relief.

Crippled by the 1921 defeat of the other crafts, the Masters, Mates and Pilots of the Pacific, a union that had split in 1912 from the national organization, could not protect its members any better than the unlicensed seamen's unions. Many deck officers sailing out of Seattle and San Francisco kept their membership for years, but in 1929 the union was dissolved. Only Seattle Local 6 and Portland Local 17 continued to exist, composed principally of men sailing on inland waters.

Like their counterparts on deck, engineers suffered under the open shop. To work on steam schooners, the Shipowners' Association required them to resign from the Marine Engineers' Beneficial Association (MEBA) and join the American Society of Marine Engineers, the company union organized during the 1921 strike. Most offshore operators also enforced compulsory company union membership. Engineers paid $10.00 initiation fee and $1.00 monthly dues, for which they received small shipwreck and death benefits. Conditions aboard ships deteriorated and wages fell. Membership in the MEBA dropped sharply on the Pacific Coast, from 3,857 in 1922 to 1,684 in 1930, excluding locals of bay and river engineers. The MEBA left the AFL in 1923 after a three-year dispute with Pacific Coast machinists over repairs on vessels in port.

African-American Stewards' Company Union [25]

After the 1921 strike Pacific Steamship and Alaska Steamship companies continued to hire African Americans in the stewards' department on their freight and passenger vessels. They employed about 300 in winter and 500 in summer. James A. Roston, a black real estate dealer who had recruited scabs during the 1916 longshore strike and the 1921 seamen's strike, organized the Colored Marine Employees Benevolent Association of the Pacific. Formally launched on May 7, 1922, among Admiral Line employees, the organization established headquarters in Seattle, with a branch in San Francisco. Roston served as full-time paid secretary-treasurer until his death in 1924. The association appointed a "morale officer" on each ship to check up on fellow employees and report any dereliction of duty to the organization. On the recommendation of the company union, the Admiral Line punished or dismissed offenders.

The employer soon recognized the value of the association. The Admiral Line paid the rent for the offices, furnished them with discarded furniture, and contributed $50.00 a month for expenses. Membership was compulsory to work for the company. By screening applicants for employment and supervising members closely, the association forestalled agitation by militant "race men," who organized independent black unions in other parts of the country during the 1920s.

The association blunted the abrasive relations between white bosses and badly exploited African-American underlings. In spite of promises to promote blacks, the company always hired white chief and second stewards. African-American third stewards sometimes had to teach newly hired second stewards their jobs, part of which was to supervise the blacks. James Roston met each arriving ship to collect dues, hear the account of the trip, and receive an order from the chief steward for men to fill vacancies. He investigated complaints of unjust treatment or discharge against the second steward, motivated many blacks believed, by racial animosity. If he considered a grievance just, and could not settle it with the chief steward, Roston went straight to company President H.F. Alexander, avoiding the port steward and operating manager, who would uphold the second steward. Roston won enough grievances to gain the reputation among many African Americans of friend and protector.

The company paid little for black service and efficiency. While first cooks received $110.00 a month and second and third cooks $90.00, waiters, salonmen, messmen, and janitors received only $45.00 a month. The men received no pay for the eight days off in port or between trips, reducing the $45.00 to $33.00 a month. The company claimed tips brought these wages up to $90.00, but not all employees served the tipping public. They worked any sixteen hours in twenty-four with no paid overtime. Backed by the association, the Admiral Line enforced rigid discipline. The company gave thirty- to sixty-day disciplinary layoffs for "surliness to passengers," and left three or four men a month on the beach for misconduct.

Beneath the surface, an ugly racket flourished with the acquiescence of both company and association. On the Admiral Line during the 1920s gambling and drinking became almost a condition of employment for African-American stewards. The janitor ran the stewards' poker game on each trip, paying off the second steward to permit the gambling. In addition, white stewards bought whiskey in Victoria to sell to Indians and brothels in Alaska ports, as well as to the ship's crew. A steward who gambled enriched the janitor and his boss, the second steward. If he drank he enriched the steward who sold whiskey. Whites exerted pressure through janitors to keep "preachers" who neither drank nor gambled off the ships.

Many waiters sailing out of Seattle believed that a man had to gamble to work. Competent waiters charged they were fired for not contributing to the second steward's gambling cut. Admiral Line officials defended the gambling with the excuse that since African Americans had to gamble, the game should be supervised, and the janitor's cut made up for his lack of tips. Besides major extortions for gambling and whiskey, "many of the men made small gifts directly to the second stewards, to the [association] secretary, to head waiters for good stations and to the chefs for good plates of food which brought good tips."[26] These bribes averaged 50 cents to $2.00 a trip.

Revolutionary Unionists

For most seamen the new society remained an impossible dream as they faced the daily realities of the fink hall and their miserable working and living conditions on board ships. IWW Marine Transport Workers 510 addressed eloquent appeals to an increasingly indifferent audience to join the IWW and "encircle the ocean routes and the docks with ONE UNION, ONE CARD AND ONE OBJECTIVE."[27] The MTW condemned the International Seamen's Union for pouring out "money like water" to compel enforcement of the Seamen's Act, which was "dead as the dodo." The IWW charged that ISU officials avoided confrontations with shipowners, ignored seamen's complaints, conspired with employers to blacklist militants, and beat up the opposition.

Repression and harassment of the IWW continued in Pacific Coast ports after the 1923 San Pedro strike, but the raids and beatings did not silence the Wobblies. The MTW maintained halls at San Francisco, Portland, Seattle, Aberdeen, and Vancouver, B.C. A Pacific Coast MTW conference in June 1925 drew up demands for a steam schooner strike. The Wobblies voted to ask for $90.00 for sailors and firemen, $1.00 overtime, eight hours in port and at sea, clean bedding and blankets, and six paid holidays. Seamen heard no more of the strike plans.

The Communist Party (CP) infiltrated the MTW nationally and captured several minor offices by 1925, but it could not complete the takeover. Abandoning the MTW, the Communists organized the International Seamen's Club on the New York waterfront in 1927 and began attacking the IWW. The Communist *Daily Worker* advised seamen to join the ISU. A year later the Marine Workers Progressive League appeared. The several hundred members included ex-Wobblies, but the league soon barred active Wobblies from the hall.

The Communist International changed its tactics in September 1929, directing American Communists to cease their unsuccessful boring from within established unions and organize revolutionary dual unions. The Trade Union Educational League became the Trade Union Unity League, and the Marine Workers League became its maritime affiliate, the Marine Workers Industrial Union (MWIU). Wobblies and Communists squared off for a violent war of words on the waterfronts of the nation.

The Union Holds On

Membership in the Pacific District International Seamen's Union shrank as intolerable living and working conditions drove union men from the sea and employers systematically prevented union contact with nonunion seamen. In 1921 the Sailors' Union had 5,700 members, the Marine Firemen 3,300, and the Marine Cooks and Stewards 1,600, a total of 10,600 on the Pacific Coast. From a low of 1,300, probably in 1922, membership in the Sailors' Union rose to 2,500 in 1927.

To thwart the unions, shipowners barred their representatives from the docks. San Pedro patrolman I.A. Haarklau related that he could not visit most oil docks or the Los Angeles Shipyard, nor could he go aboard vessels of the Los Angeles Steamship Company, E, K. Wood, or Hammond Lumber Company. Most steam schooners compelled their mates to engage crews from the fink hall, but Weyerhaeuser boatswains selected their own crews, resulting in many union members on those vessels.

A few shipowners continued to recognize the unions. Although the owners denied it, union people believed that Oceanic Steamship Company, a Matson

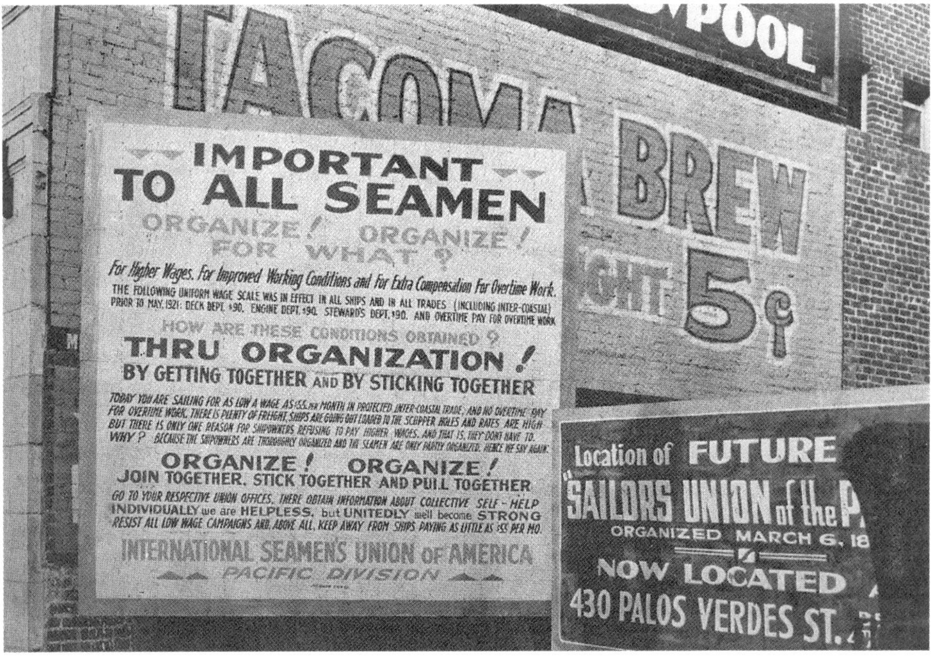

Billboard urging seamen to organize, San Pedro, 1927. (From Cornelius Andersen vs. Shipowners' Association of the Pacific Coast and Pacific American Steamship Association*)*

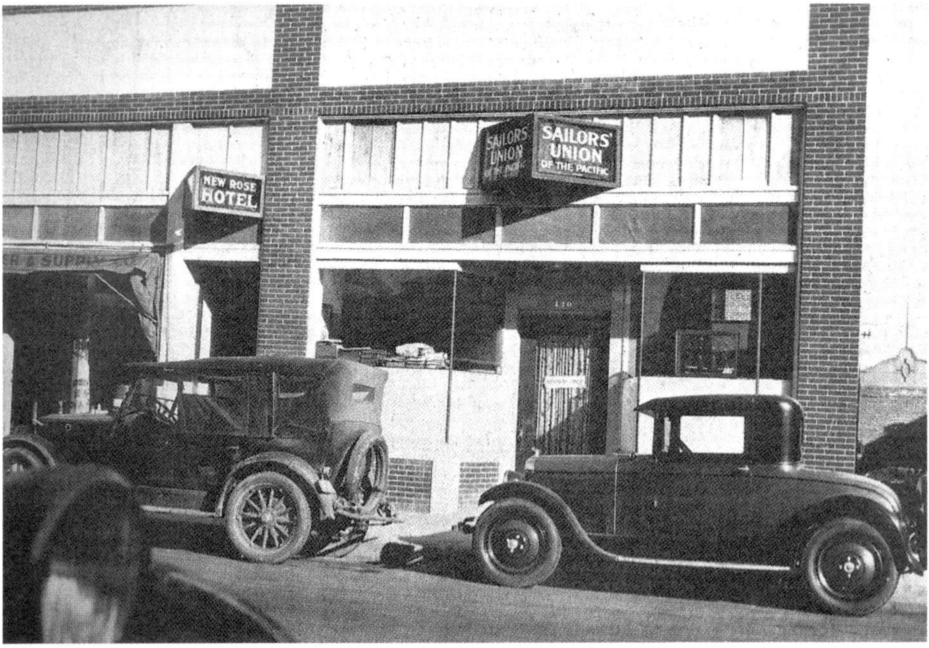

San Pedro hall, Sailors' Union of the Pacific, 1927. (From Cornelius Andersen vs. Shipowners' Association of the Pacific Coast and Pacific American Steamship Association*)*

subsidiary operating three vessels running to Australia, took union crews to avoid being tied up by the Australian Waterside Workers' Union. Honolulu sailing schooners shipped union crews because they needed experienced sailors, and some Hollywood movies used union seamen for sailing ship scenes. The Alaska Packers, operating some twenty vessels from San Francisco and Puget Sound to Alaska, took full union crews from the halls. The packers signed a three-year agreement with the Alaska Fishermen's Union the spring of 1925.

Pacific American Fisheries vessels sailing from Bellingham to Alaska observed an informal working agreement with the Seattle Sailors' agency and shipped union crews from the hall. Alaska Steamship Company vessels operating between Seattle and Alaska ports carried about half union sailors, thanks to the diligence of agent Pete Gill and patrolman Henry Nilssen. Mates shipped crews from either the union hall or the nearby Post Kellar tavern. However, the company would blacklist men who talked too much and tried to improve conditions. In spite of official disapproval, Captain Howard J. Payne, head of the Seattle Sea Service Bureau, called the union for about half his men.

By 1927 the Sailor's Union was recovering from the lost srike and Andrew Furuseth's war on the Wobblies. Although the Seattle agency expelled several men in 1923 for IWW activities, the current began to run the other way. Many former members who had joined the MTW after the strike found the revolutionary union equally powerless and returned to the Sailors' Union. On the fortieth anniversary in 1925, Andrew Furuseth exhorted members to have faith and work to rebuild the union: "The fact that for about three years from 1921 to 1924 we made progress like a crab was caused by our lack of faith. . . . The downward trend ceased more than a year ago. The upward trend since then has not been very rapid but it has been steady and we shall have more rapid progress in the future than we have had in the last year."[28]

About a year later a large sign appeared near the San Pedro waterfront urging seamen to "ORGANIZE! ORGANIZE! JOIN TOGETHER, STICK TOGETHER AND PULL TOGETHER. Go to your respective union offices. There obtain information about collective self-help. INDIVIDUALLY, we are HELPLESS, but UNITEDLY we'll become STRONG."[29]

T. Reynolds declared in a letter to the *Seamen's Journal*: "We have had five years of scab-hall control. Have we better working conditions? more money? shorter hours? better food? better sleeping accommodations? Or were we better off under union rules? If we were better off then, why not rejoin our union and bring these conditions back again. By getting together, sticking together, and fighting together for better conditions, we can get them back and hold them after we have them."[30]

Seamen endured the open-shop years of the twenties. The decade ended with the fink hall still impregnable. Fear and humiliation remained the present harsh realities. But down in San Pedro on a sun-washed street next to the New Rose Hotel, a tidy brick storefront displayed a model sailing ship in the window. Across the entrance a sign jutted over the street: "Sailors' Union of the Pacific." The few still paid their union dues.

2

Fink Hall Years: Longshoremen

> I believe that if there was any censure coming at all to the International Longshoremen's Association, it was because they didn't realize the danger of the Fink Hall system on the Pacific Coast. We didn't take the matter seriously enough. . . . I do know there was much more we could have done in San Pedro. However, it was not done and the Fink Hall system was established.[1]

Delegate W. T. "Paddy" Morris was describing to the 1927 convention of the International Longshoremen's Association (ILA) the disaster that had overwhelmed Pacific Coast longshoremen. A series of broken strikes inaugurated the decade: San Francisco in 1919, Seattle: 1920, Portland: 1922, and San Pedro: 1923. In 1919 the West Coast has been completely union—organized in the ILA in all ports except San Francisco, where the unaffiliated Riggers and Stevedores controlled the waterfront. A decade later the ILA had perhaps 1,200 members, most of them in Tacoma, the only remaining major union port.

To maintain control of the waterfront after smashing the unions, employers in Seattle, Portland, San Pedro, and smaller ports set up their own hiring halls (fink halls) and required all longshoremen to work out of those halls. The fink hall divided longshoremen: steady men against casuals competing for work. Company preferred gangs provided "a splendid opportunity for work hogs who want to work day and night," according to Morris. The fink hall also fostered an efficient blacklisting system to eliminate troublemakers and union agitators; a corrupt system that encouraged hall managers and foremen to sell jobs for liquor, money, or other favors.

Fear ruled the open-shop waterfronts. A man could lose his place in a preferred gang or be relegated to occasional undesirable jobs, or he could even be blacklisted for a complaint, a bad attitude, or union sympathy. Pacific Coast District ILA Secretary George Soule declared in 1924: "It's absolutely hopeless to carry on an organization that is going to exist as long as Fink Hall exists. Not that the men don't want to join, but they are cutting off their pay check when they come and join the I.L.A. Our only hope is to break up those Fink Halls."[2]

Seattle Fink Hall Is Established

Seattle ILA Local 38-12 struck April 30, 1920, to retain the list, a system of hiring under which the union dispatched men in rotation for jobs from the membership list, rather than allow gang bosses to pick them. African-American longshoremen considered the list system their best protection against discrimination. "The Open

Shop condition will prevail," the Waterfront Employers announced May 15, as union men returned to the docks in defeat. "Former strikers applying for work will be treated as individuals and not as members of the I.L.A."[3] The *Seattle Union Record* reported that bosses denied union longshoremen the right to register at the "fink barge," the hiring booth on the beach. The Waterfront Employers instructed their members to report "undesirables" to Captain A.A. Paysee at the barge "so these men could be eliminated from the waterfront."[4] Superintendents complained that straw bosses picked union men and left scabs without work. To avoid letting the ILA regain control of the waterfront, employers insisted that hiring must be centralized.

The same day the Waterfront Employers declared the open shop, the International Longshoremen's Association revoked the charter of Local 38-12 for striking illegally. Ten days later the international chartered ILA Local 38-16, composed of over 600 stevedores who had opposed the strike for the list system. Andy Madsen, a long-time activist in Portland and Seattle, charged that Captain Gibson and other employers had promised them recognition and the work of the port. "However, just as Local 38-16 commenced to function, they were advised they would have to hire through the Fink Hall and procure a brass check before they would be permitted to work on the waterfront."[5] Madsen referred to the numbered metal tags used on the San Francisco waterfront. On going to work, a longshoremen gave his brass check to the gang boss. At the end of the job the boss returned the check with a warrant for his pay. If the man needed money immediately, he could sell the warrant in a waterfront saloon at a heavy discount. Later the saloon would cash the warrant at face value. Sometimes gang bosses worked with certain saloons, splitting the profits on the discounted warrants. Although Seattle employers did not use brass checks, they controlled hiring by requiring registration.

In May, Pacific Steamship Company set up a company union, the Admiral Line Dock Council. In August, the Waterfront Employers replaced the fink barge with a dispatching hall. To keep the ILA off the waterfront, the employers hired Frank E. Foisie in October. In Seattle, according to Foisie, "The industry has suffered for years from recurring strikes, and striking on the job in between, much pilferage, high accident frequency, arbitrary load limits and minimum gang requirements."[6] The employers agreed to a central employment system and employee representation plan at an annual budget of $25,000.

Foisie and management representatives met with fifty hand-picked longshoremen to establish the company union. At the first mass meeting called by employers in January 1921, the longshoremen voted 319 to 209 to form a joint organization. A committee of fifteen chaired by David Madison drafted a constitution that provided for secret election of employee representatives, "the right to freedom of speech and activity and . . . no discrimination . . . against them for such," and no discrimination because of "race, creed, color, union or non-union affiliation."[7] The organization would be governed by a joint executive committee of fifteen representatives each for employers and employees, and three joint standing committees: employment, standard practices, and safety.

In a mass meeting in March 1921 about 600 longshoremen adopted by a two-thirds majority vote the constitution of the Joint Organization Through Employee Representation of Longshoremen and Truckers, and Waterfront Employers of Seattle. Unable to defeat the employer plan, Local 38-16 organized to elect its members to the joint committee, with the result that nine of the fifteen employee members of the first executive committee belonged to the union. The employees elected David Madison of Local 38-16 co-chair.

The Joint Organization cut registration in the fink hall from 1,420 to 707. First, stevedore companies formed twenty company gangs with the advice of their foremen, according to the Joint Organization minutes, "*but without* the knowledge or *influence* of the *straw bosses*."[8] Thus the employers tried to circumvent the union. Then the Employment Committee formed ten regular hall gangs selected on a point system of skills, length of service, and other considerations. Opposite James Foley's name on the stevedore list the employers noted, "Sec. [ILA] 38-16," with no points. The committee placed an additional fifty men on an extra list to serve as replacements in gangs or for peak loads. Employers encouraged the remaining longshoremen, classified as casuals, to find other work. Companies cut the trucker list to 250 by designating preferred men and evaluating them on a point system.

The gang system went into operation May 2. By then the fink hall had 435 stevedores and 272 truckers registered. Individual companies employed another 800 men. Several major employers refused to dispatch through the hall: Pacific Steamship (later Pacific Lighterage) employing 350 men, Alaska steamship with 150 men, the Port of Seattle with 50 truckers, and the railroad docks. Flour mills, grain elevators, and private warehouses also had their own hiring arrangements.

Employee representatives on the joint committee soon learned that they had no power. They lost a tie vote in April 1921 to register twelve longshoremen, most of whom had been refused registration at the fink barge. These included Arthur Curtis, organizer of Local 38-16. Again, when work picked up in September, employee representatives lost a motion to register ten more men, including six of the previously blacklisted twelve who had been refused registration. Stevedore boss W.C. Dawson put the matter bluntly: "We also found that we had made a serious mistake in allowing the employee members of the Joint Employment Committee the privilege of passing on the registration of the longshoremen. This was abused to such an extent by the men that we were obliged to take this privilege from them."[9]

Employee representatives also lost on the wage cut proposed in May 1921 after the San Francisco Blue Book company union had accepted a 10-cent reduction. Although the longshoremen objected and proposed arbitration, the employers persuaded them to agree to the cut effective August 1, reducing longshoremen from 90 cents and $1.35 overtime to 80 cents and $1.20, and truckers from 80 cents and $1.20 to 70 cents and $1.05. Employers congratulated themselves on delaying the vote from May to August: Thus they had "retained the good will of the men, which has more than made up in increased efficiency, any difference in wages that we might have gained by putting the wage reduction into effect earlier."[10]

While control of the watefront passed from the ILA to the fink hall, the union longshoremen remained hopelessly divided. In March 1921 the Seattle Central Labor Council tried without success to bring the two ILA locals together. Organization of Truckers Local 38-11 in April further complicated the situation.

The 1921 Pacific Coast District ILA convention requested the international to cancel the three Seattle charters and issue a charter for one combined local. The international revoked the charters of Locals 38-11, 38-12, and 38-16 in July. In March 1922 International President Anthony Chlopek instructed the Seattle locals to agree on a plan to amalgamate, or else in thirty days he would issue a charter to the group that wanted to remain with the international.

On April 25 the international granted the charter to Local 38-12. The action evoked a storm of protest at the Pacific Coast District convention a week later. The delegates charged that the international did not give the other locals sufficient time to comply with the edict. Chlopek rebutted that, among other reasons, he chartered Local 38-12 after receiving information that Locals 38-11 and 38-16 had endorsed a resolution from San Pedro calling on the Pacific Coast District to secede and organize a Marine Transport Workers Federation.

Paddy Morris of Tacoma criticized Chlopek for giving Local 38-12 the charter "because the other group were secessionist when 90 per cent of the members of Local 12 were members of the I.W.W."[11] Delegate Williams of Local 38-12 refuted the charge, claiming Wobblies had to drop their membership before joining the local. Union membership on the waterfront had declined. Local 38-12 claimed 165 paid-up members and Local 38-16 an average the previous three months of 187.

Dave Madison, delegate from Local 38-16, complained bitterly: "We blame the International for not giving any assistance in this controversy. Had the International carried out the wishes of the membership, this Port would not be in the shape it is today. We blame Madsen for the misrepresentation made in the [1921] International Convention, but we blame President Chlopek for the present situation."[12]

Madison said the majority of Local 38-16 members opposed the Joint Organization because they could not control it, but he conceded that the system had given the men some things the ILA could not. For example, no petty boss could fire a man, as had been the custom under the ILA. "If the union could control the plan it would not oppose it as much as they do now. . . . Whether we like the shop committee plan or not it is here, and it is here as a result of the actions of Local 12 and the International. None of us wanted the fink hall, neither did we want our charter revoked by the International without giving us a hearing."[13] Following the convention Local 38-11 merged with Local 38-16, and July 19, 1922, the merged union became a charter member of the Federation of Marine Transport Workers of the Pacific Coast, known as Local 2.

Seattle: The Union Versus the Fink Hall

The power struggle between members of the Marine Transport Workers and employers in the Joint Executive Committee of the fink hall reached a climax at the meeting August 9, 1923. Frank Foisie recorded the minutes. Employers objected to men quitting a job over a grievance. The men replied that officious foremen caused the disputes, and the organization failed to process grievances promptly. It penalized longshoremen, but not companies, for breaking rules. Committee Co-chair Dave Madison proposed a union agreement, "not to supplant the committee system, but to supplement it with an agreement." He contended:

> Under former union agreements there was less jumping the job than at present and more discipline imposed by the union on its members for violation of working rules. Again, there would be greater protection to employers to keep ships moving for even though the Marine Transport Workers Federation has enrolled a majority of the men on the waterfront, at any time some other union may organize a considerable number of them and call a strike. . . .
>
> Moreover, the men want their own organization and their own hall—they want the freedom which comes with paying for their own meeting place. The attempts at general evening meetings in the Dispatching Hall have not succeeded. The men meeting in their union could instruct their committeemen.[14]

The employers rejected the proposal and called for Madison's resignation from the committee because his full-time union job made him ineligible to participate in the Joint Organization. Lee Carls replied that the men should have the same right as the employers to be represented by paid officials, and George Kennedy noted that the employers had hired Foisie. Tom Winkler objected to Madison's registration being cancelled, as he would no doubt again work on the waterfront. Madison resigned, thus acknowledging defeat.

ILA locals and the Seattle Marine Transport Workers formed the Northwest Longshoremen's Council of Oregon, Washington and British Columbia and demanded of the Watefront Employers a restoration of the 1920 wage scale and commodity penalty rates. The employers refused to consider the demands or negotiate because they had no working relations with the ILA and Marine Transport Workers. They denied a similar request from their own employee representatives and complained that Madison was "said to have told a . . . foreman that no men would be registered except button men."[15] However, the employers did restore the 1920 scale effective January 1, 1924.

The power struggled continued. The April 1924 issue of the *Longshore Log*, published by the Joint Organization, scolded the employee representatives for trying to interfere in registering longshoremen. "The real issue," employers stated, "which ought to be frankly discussed is whether the committeemen are going to continue efforts to establish a closed shop union agreement. . . . The employers continue to say, go ahead with your union affiliation but do not make the mistake of trying to force the employers to deal with the unions or union-instructed committees."

George Kennedy replied for the longshoremen "that they do not want to take control of the business, but do want something to say as to whom they are to work with, and if the Joint Employment Committee is not to do the actual hiring of the men there is no need for such a committee."[16] The employers rejected an employee proposal to equalize wages by eliminating company gangs, which they believed did better work and provided an incentive for hall gang men to move up into company gangs.

During these years, the original ILA Local 38-12 remained small and ineffectual. Although the Port Commission and several other employers hired union longshoremen, members chronically lacked jobs. The union dispatched from the list, except when a blacklisted member's turn came for Pacific Steamship. In that case, the member went out first on the next job. The union struggled financially. In 1924 the secretary went on part time and the local moved to a cheaper hall at Western Avenue and Bell Street. With the Marine Transport Workers Federation dead, the first organizing success came in 1925. During March, April, and May, 458 men joined Local 38-12, some from Alaska Steamship and Pacific Lighterage gangs, as well as the fink hall. Frank Foisie warned that the ILA had signed up half the registered men, promising that the union would take control of jobs. But most of the new recruits soon dropped out, leaving the same small and struggling core.

The ILA had 1,300 members on the Pacific Coast in 1926, just over 7 percent of the 18,000 longshoremen. A 25-cent district organizing assessment for May, June, July, and August raised $1,060.85, and Atlantic Coast longshoremen donated $477.00. The district spent most of the money to keep an organizer in Seattle for four months, without achieving any real gains. Local 38-12 lost $917.57 in 1926. To reduce expenses the union cut the secretary's salary to $35.00 a month and allowed him to be dispatched in turn. Volunteers would keep the hall clean. The union limped along, unable to grow beyond a few hundred, but determined not to give up.

"Employers must voluntarily do more to improve conditions for the men than the unions have done and there will be nothing to fear,"[17] declared the employers' own Frank Foisie. But employers would never voluntarily grant the union's principal advantage: job control; they continued to fear and to govern arbitrarily beneath the facade of joint cooperation and harmony. Walter Freer, active in Local 38-12 until 1928, described the fink hall. Merl G. Ringenberg, scab in the 1917 Seattle streetcar strike, served as dispatcher and "dictator by tacit consent of the water front employers." Men avoided serving on the Joint Executive Committee because they feared discrimination if they spoke out and tried to represent their fellow workers honestly. Longshoremen frequently suspected committeemen "of being stool pigeons and sycophants, in order to curry favor with Ringenberg," particularly when he hand-picked them to fill vacancies between elections..

The registered men had steady jobs, while casuals, most of whom were just as efficient, made a scanty living. Freer continued: "But the casuals whether stevedores or truckers, have bait thrown to them to keep them hanging around. The bait is that they will eventually if stevedores be put on the extra board, and thence to a 'star' gang. The casual truckers or dock men may in time go on the rotating truckers list, or may be preferred by some dock."[18]

Graft and favoritism riddled the fink hall, Freer charged. Men who joined the Ballard Elks, over which Ringenberg presided as exalted ruler, reportedly received special favors. A dock foreman with an "apparent interest in a firm selling radios and radio parts . . . compelled his men to buy tickets on radios and parts" that he raffled off periodically. A chief stevedore who owned a tavern at Juanita Beach threatened men with dismissal if they didn't patronize his establishment. Allegations circulated constantly that dock foremen solicited bribes. The Joint Executive Committee minutes confirmed Freer's charge that advancement depended solely on Ringenberg and the employers. Joe Marshall protested in 1926 that the fink hall registered men who had been on the casual list only three days ahead of many old-time Seattle longshoremen on the casual board. Although the Joint Organization constitution provided for arbitration, the committee never arbitrated a deadlocked issue; the employers always had their way.

Tacoma: The Union Port

Although Tacoma employers would not renew the 1920 agreement with the ILA, they did not quite dare to set up a fink hall, concluding in July 1921 "that if an attempt were made to introduce Joint Organization at this time it would be against the wishes of organized labor, with possibly a lack of understanding by the business interests of Tacoma, and the public press."[19] The Tacoma locals had a closed shop, and gang bosses picked members for jobs from their union halls. With the Seattle waterfront open shop, the Tacoma unions could not resist the 1921 wage cut. Tacoma employers restored the 1920 scale in 1924, in line with the rest of the coast. Even without an agreement, union representatives met with employers to adjust grievances. But as long as the other ports remained unorganized, the Tacoma locals would be compelled to accept the prevailing open-shop wages and conditions.

In 1924, Tacoma Lumber Handlers Local 38-30 had about 200 members and the general cargo Local 38-3 had 500. They controlled the work of the port except the wheat docks, where 25 or 30 men worked below scale. The lumber local rejected the gang system in 1926. Two years later the Tacoma locals voted on amalgamation. The proposal carried in Local 38-3, but Local 38-30 voted no, probably because many members who had handled lumber all their lives preferred not to work general cargo or operate new machines. With half the entire membership on the coast, Tacoma became the mainstay of the Pacific Coast ILA, providing financial support and activists to hold the fragile district together.

Northwest Lumber Ports

The fink hall dominated most small ports. To break the ILA in Everett, stevedore Henry Rothschild set up a hall in 1923. After a two-week strike against the "hand-picked" system, Local 38-8 returned to work open shop. The Waterfront

ILA Local 38-3 hiring hall, Tacoma, 1920. (Courtesy Morris Thorsen)

Lumber Handlers ILA Local 38-30 hiring hall, Tacoma, 1920s. (Courtesy International Longshore and Warehouse Union Local 23)

Employers Union built a second fink hall and forced the men to register and be put in gangs. Tom Mason described the union's struggle against the blacklist: The two stevedoring companies competed for work and men. Both wanted ILA men because they knew how to handle lumber, but when the local took in a new man, "one of their stool pigeons will say that if he will take off the little blue button he will run a better chance of getting work on the Everett waterfront. . . . We all wear the dress button while we are working—the men that belong to the Local."[20] From 1924 to 1926 the local averaged 40 members out of 600 men on the front. The union charged that 120 steam schooner men belonging to the Sailors' Union refused to join the ILA. The small local could not afford a full-time secretary, and employers routinely blacklisted the part-time officer. The union no longer existed by 1926.

When the Port Blakely sawmill, sole waterfront employer, closed in 1923, the longshoremen worked out of Everett, but by 1927 the local surrendered its charter. Anacortes gave up the same year, after a four-year fight against the fink hall. Bucking the tide of defeat, Port Ludlow lumber handlers, who had worked open shop since 1918, reorganized by 1923, but their union lasted only a few years. Union longshoremen from Seattle and Tacoma migrated to Olympia when the city opened the public port in the spring of 1926, establishing a union presence on the waterfront that soon resulted in an ILA local. The employers countered with a fink hall blacklisting union members by May 1927, and the local soon disbanded.

Longshoremen in Aberdeen and Hoquiam, unorganized since World War I, responded to the 1923 surge of activity. The ILA installed a charter for Grays Harbor April 29 during a short strike. Membership reached sixty, then stopped, and the local probably disappeared by 1927.

Portland Fink Halls

The Portland waterfront was a shambles by 1923. Not one longshoreman had been dispatched from the ILA hall after October 22. Gun-toting thugs bossed the two fink halls. Local 38-4 merged with Local 38-6, and the combined local reaffiliated with the Pacific Coast District. Delegate Andy Madsen appealed to the 1923 district convention for funds: "The bulk of the membership have not made a living in the past year, and the past five months have been out completely. We have used every cent we have received for the relief of our membership. The money we need to carry on the fight against propaganda and Fink Hall we will have to depend more or less on sister locals."[21] The district could provide nothing, but Atlantic Coast longshoremen donated $100, delegates to the 1923 international convention another $160, and Tacoma longshoremen $750. The union barely survived.

Two union renegades, A.E. Barnes and Fritz Buchtmann, former ILA officers dispatching in the fink halls, proved to be the employers' most valuable servants in their program to exterminate the ILA. Most union members tried to work out of the Portland Stevedoring Company, which handled Shipping Board vessels, because the Shipping Board contract provided that every legitimate longshoreman must be allowed to work. But stool pigeons in both halls, former ILA members, fingered union men for the blacklist.

With membership down to less than twenty, the union launched a reorganization drive in December 1923. At first longshoremen responded. Old members rejoined and new ones lined up at the weekly meetings. The union scheduled forty candidates for initiation December 20. The 10-cent raise in January 1924, in accordance with the other ports, stimulated the drive. Although employers blacklisted some ILA men, more continued to join. Many recruits attended the open Sunday meetings addressed by Central Labor Council officers. By February the local had over 230 members. Then, according to Secretary Herman Larsen, the Waterfront Employers and fink hall dispatchers "set about to discriminate against any man known to carry a union card, and particularly members of Local 38-6. We found that that served as a check upon our reorganization movement. We found that the men were afraid to visit our hall; that there were members who would not even be seen around the hall of 38-6."[22]

Local 38-6 went to court to stop the discrimination. In December 1925 a court awarded Ralph Johnson, a longshoreman, damages of $4,500 against eight firms: Oregon Stevedoring Company, Pacific Steamship Company, McCormick, Luckenbach, W.J. Jones and Sons Stevedores, Brown and McCabe, Kerr, Gifford and Company, and Balfour-Guthrie and Company. The suit contended that the employers used the fink hall to prevent workers discharged from one concern being hired by another. The jury verdict substantiated the ILA's claim that waterfront employers engaged in a conspiracy to blacklist union longshoremen. Other longshoremen pressed similar claims. The successful court case did not save the local. By 1929 the union had disappeared.

Three hundred permanent men organized in twenty-five gangs worked out of the fink hall, besides 400 on the extra board and another 400 casuals. The hall claimed to rotate work for the permanent gangs, whose average weekly earnings in 1928 ranged from $29.32 to $33.91

Most small ports in Oregon fared no better. Coos Bay longshoremen managed to hold their local together and maintain good working conditions until about 1928. Then the two stevedoring companies set the longshoremen quarreling among themselves over the unequal distribution of work, and the union perished. On the Columbia River, Astoria and Rainier remained open shop after 1922, dominated by the fink hall. Bandon longshoremen, loading lumber for the one mill in town, worked open shop for two years before they reorganized in 1925 and regained control of the port. They worked eight hours for 90 cents on ships and 85 cents on the dock, with time and one-half for overtime. The tiny union remained entrenched on the mill split, the only ILA local in Oregon.

San Pedro Fink Hall

In San Pedro the ILA faced two opponents: the fink hall and the Marine Transport Workers Federation, to which Local 38-18 had defected. The 1923 district convention levied a $1.00 assessment on Pacific Coast members, expected to raise $1,000, and borrowed $500 from the international. Half the money would be used to send Otto Olson of San Diego to San Pedro to organize, and the other half to put Jack Bjorklund on as northern organizer.

Arriving in San Pedro early in April, Olson formed a small ILA nucleus before the strike engulfed the port. Loss of the strike signaled the beginning of the demise of the Transport Workers. Olson returned to San Diego after the strike. By early 1924 a group of longshoremen had reclaimed their ILA charter and reaffiliated with the district. James Reid, who had been secretary of the Transport Workers, returned to the ILA as secretary of Local 38-18.

The 1925 district convention sent Ernest Ellis of Seattle to San Pedro to organize, with his salary for two months paid by the American Federation of Labor (AFL). Tacoma Local 38-3 donated money for the drive. When Ellis came to San Pedro, Local 38-18 hired Charles Cutright, former business agent of Local 38-12, to assist him. Both men worked hard, speaking to groups of longshoremen, distributing handbills, and visiting over 300 men at their homes in the evenings. Reid reported on the drive: "The fear of the Fink Hall and the loss of their registration card is the one thing that is holding the men back from joining Local 38-18 but that feeling is now being slowly removed and the break will soon come that will put us over the top."[23]

The break did not come, and the fink hall won. By July 1927 the ILA had disappeared; the Marine Service Bureau controlled all the work of Los Angeles harbor. Of the 1,628 registered longshoremen in 1929, 603 were ship men, 604 dock men, 270 lumbermen, and 151 casuals. Average weekly earnings of the ship men for October 1929 through April 1930 ranged from $29.22 to $45.92.

Farther south in the smaller port of San Diego, employers established a fink hall during those years. From almost a closed shop in 1923, Local 38-9 declined by 1929 to a handful of men working open shop.

San Francisco: "Blue Book" Union Is Organized

The Riggers and Stevedores had dominated the port of San Francisco since 1853, an independent union not affiliated with the ILA for most of those years. The union struck September 15, 1919, for a wage increase and improved working conditions. With the docks full of scabs and the strike failing, waterfront foremen called a mass meeting December 8 to organize the Longshoremen's Association of San Francisco. The next day the Waterfront Employers' Union recognized the new organization and signed a five-year agreement. Longshoremen charged that the Harmony Club, a foremen's social club, organized the union, which claimed 1,000 charter members. They called it the "Blue Book" union, after the color of the membership books, blue, in contrast to the ILA's dark red books.

The Riggers and Stevedores called off the strike the end of December and reaffiliated with the ILA and the Pacific Coast District as Local 38-33. Members suffered discrimination because they refused to join the Blue Book union. A degrading shape-up replaced the closed shop on the waterfront: Foremen picked workers from crowds of men congregated at the pier heads competing for jobs. San Francisco employers controlled work effectively through the company union. Early in 1921 they cut longshoremen's wages to 80 cents and $1.20 overtime under a cost-of-living clause in the agreement. ILA President Chlopek found Local 38-33 in bad shape when he visited San Francisco in late 1921. Lonshoremen belonged to the Blue Book union and foremen and hatch bosses to the Harmony Club. He explained: "The said 'Harmony Club' is the key to the entire situation, as each boss selects his men and of course, he has his instructions that he cannot hire anyone who has not membership in the Waterfront Employers Union, and is in possession of 'blue book' as issued by the Waterfront Employers Union, or if his application has not been passed upon by the managers of the Waterfront Employers Union, which is in absolute control of the employees." Many former union members belonged to the Blue Book "through forced circumstances, starvation having compelled them to submit to accepting the conditions imposed by the employers."[24]

A few stubborn men kept the Riggers and Stevedores alive and attempted periodically to reorganize the port. Many of them who refused to take the Blue Book or were blacklisted, picked up work from the few companies that did not belong to the Waterfront Employers. The union shrank, moved to a small hall at 113 Steuart Street by 1921 and later moved to 92 Steuart. Following the San Pedro defeat in 1923, the international sent Otto Olson to San Francisco for two months, then laid him off for lack of funds. Longshoremen did not respond to appeals to rebuild the union, and the organizing attempt failed. The ILA cancelled Local 38-33's charter for nonpayment of per capita. San Francisco employers led the coast in the 10-cent raise back to 90 cents an hour, announced December 10, 1923.

Lee Holman, a long-time member who had been on the waterfront since 1911, spearheaded another organizing drive the following spring, for which the Blue Book blacklisted him in May. The union enrolled about 400 members. As the Riggers and Stevedores marched up Market Street in the 1924 Labor Day parade, Blue Book bosses spotted and blacklisted other members, including Harry Bridges, who had been working on the docks for two years. The union collapsed. During this time another union, the Longshore Lumbermen's Protective Association, appeared on the front.

On his way back to Seattle from San Pedro the summer of 1925, Ernest Ellis met with the Longshore Lumbermen and the ILA in San Francisco. The Riggers and Stevedores reorganized in July as Local 38-69, with Lee Holman as chairman and George McNulty secretary. Aided by donations from other ILA districts and uptown San Francisco unions, the local made good progress until funds ran out and the organizing drive stopped.

The Blue Book did nothing to try to equalize earnings for its 3,000 working members. In one company employing 354 longshoremen in 1926, 50 earned less than $15.00 a week and 51 averaged $35.00 a week or more. Sixty-five of these men worked fifteen weeks or less, and eighty-seven of them forty-eight weeks or more. In another company, average weekly wages in ten permanent gangs ranged from $27.52 to $46.65.

The Blue Book union sought legitimacy and applied for affiliation with the San

Shape-up on the Embarcadero, San Francisco, c. 1933. (Otto Hagel photo, courtesy International Longshore and Warehouse Union Library)

Francisco Labor Council. At the 1926 AFL convention Paul Scharrenberg of the Sailors' Union, Michael Casey of the San Francisco Teamsters, and John O'Connell, secretary of the Labor Council, asked ILA President Chlopek to withdraw his objections to seating the company union in the council. Chlopek consulted the ILA local and the Pacific Coast District. After agreeing reluctantly to the plan, ILA Local 38-69 reversed its stand and decided to fight the Blue Book. The ILA local joined the Labor Council in February 1927, blocking affiliation of the company union. Secretary McNulty warned the Pacific Coast District:

> We do not favor any concession being given to the "Blue Book" unless they join the I.L.A., as we are fully aware that they have no intention of joining the I.L.A. if they can get clearance from the local labor movement by simply joining the Central Labor Union and State Federation of Labor, and if they are given that concession the I.L.A. will not gain one member and can forget San Francisco for all time. You know that move would put this Local out of existence in a very short time.[25]

The ILA disregarded this warning. Blue Book officials rejected ILA affiliation, and California labor officials continued to urge acceptance of the company union. In 1927 the district, "after much deliberation consented." The Blue Book union affiliated with the State Federation of Labor in January 1928, but the Riggers and Stevedores prevented its joining the San Francisco Labor Council until March 1929, when the council unseated the Riggers and Stevedores. The Longshore Lumbermen disappeared completely, and the Riggers and Stevedores remained a name in the city directory. District Secretary Jack Bjorklund believed that with the strategy of educating instead of fighting the Blue Book union, "re-affiliation was eventually certain."[26]

African-American Longhoremen Under the Open Shop

Historically the ILA organized African-American longshoremen in separate locals with integrated bargaining councils in the South, and in integrated locals in the North. Black longshoremen had been part of the union work force in Seattle and Tacoma for years, but in the San Francisco Bay area most blacks had arrived recently to break the 1919 strike.[27] With the union powerless, African Americans on Pacific Coast waterfronts could test the employers' benevolence.

Opportunities for African Americans on Seattle docks shrank under the open shop. Following the defeat of the ILA their number declined to less than 100 by the end of 1920. All-black gangs worked on the Great Northern and Milwaukee docks and Alaska Steamship's Pier 2. About forty worked regularly out of the fink hall, and many worked in extra gangs handling penalty cargoes, such as explosives, chemicals, and goods damaged by fire or water. Samuel McCoy, an African American, testified that prior to 1929 blacks had little work out of the fink hall. Two white gangs asked him to join. He accepted provided they would also take his partner. Although the men agreed, Dispatcher Merl Ringenberg refused to allow the gang to take in the two men, fearing it would encourage more blacks to join white gangs.

Ernie Tanner, another black longshoreman, testified that in Tacoma "the color stands in their way, and they have to take the very worst jobs, the dirtiest jobs and the short jobs."[28] Tanner related a conversation with Mr. Cole, a stevedoring company official. Tanner said:

> He would expect more work from the colored gang than he got from the other gangs on the ship. I asked him why. And he said, "Well, you know you are in a minority here, and we don't have to hire you, and in return if I hire you I will expect more work from your gang." I asked him if he thought that was fair. He said, "It is not a matter of fairness with me, all the men that employ colored gangs expect more work out of them so I will expect more from you."[29]

Tanner and other African Americans from Local 38-3 presented their charges of discrimination to Seattle shipping company officials. The employers agreed to hire a specified number of blacks, but within two or three weeks the pattern of unfairness and lack of opportunity returned.

African Americans who came to California waterfronts as strikebreakers felt betrayed when the Blue Book union drove them from the San Francisco piers. By 1926 black longshoremen had work on only two docks: Panama Mail with four gangs, and Luckenbach, which employed about half African Americans. Seven years later about fifty blacks worked on the San Francisco waterfront.

Working Conditions on the Front

Without effective union pressure, wages and working conditions deteriorated under the open shop. Traditionally the West Coast had maintained a 10-cent wage differential over the East Coast, but that advantage was cut in half in 1927 when the ILA negotiated a 5-cent raise for the Atlantic ports; Pacific Coast employers chose not to follow suit. About that time the East Coast cut the work week to forty-four hours, while the West Coast continued to work forty-eight. In 1928 the North Pacific ports eliminated penalty pay for dangerous and obnoxious cargoes, although San Francisco continued to pay premium rates. Tacoma longshoremen, with union hiring and the best work rules on the coast, complained of poor working conditions and unsanitary dock facilities. They saw no improvement while the rest of the coast remained open shop.

Although the ILA nationally supported the Longshoremen and Harbor Workers Compensation Act passed in 1927, which superseded state workers' compensation laws, Pacific Coast longshoremen soon decided the act did not benefit them. Before its passage the ILA utilized legal bureaus in the major Pacific Coast ports through which injured longshoremen collected damages. Previously men could choose their doctor and hospital instead of being compelled to accept the employers' choice. In 1929 the Pacific Coast District called for amendments to the act to permit an injured longshoreman to choose his doctor, to provide compensation during the full period of total disability, and to increase minimum weekly compensation from $8.00 to $12.00. The union wanted to enable an injured longshoreman to sue a vessel with defective equipment, even if the accident involved a third party, and to base disability payments on a 330-day year.

The ILA welcomed the Northwest Waterfront Employers' proposal to institute safety measures to reduce accidents, but the union vigorously opposed the employers' attempt to require physical examinations as part of the program. Jack Bjorklund represented the ILA on the Pacific Coast Safety Code Committee that drew up coastwide safety rules in 1927. But substantive safety measures to reduce load limits and cut the appalling accident rate on the waterfront would have to wait for union muscle to enforce them.

Signs of the Awakening

By 1929 the Pacific Coast District ILA barely held on. The treasury totaled $657.15, scarcely enough to pay an organizer's salary for several months. Otto Olson wired the 1929 district convention: "May your deliberations be for the awakening of the locals of the coast."[30] While the ILA waited vainly for San Francisco to affiliate, signs of the awakening appeared in two Northwest ports.

The threat of compulsory physical examinations and an age limit of forty-five years brought Everett longshoremen back to the ILA in 1929. Old-timers who believed that they must organize to forestall the employers' plan appealed to the ILA. The district sent Paddy Morris to Everett on June 25, and a group of longshoremen soon formed a union. Local 38-76 grew to almost 250 members in July, 369 by the middle of September, and 100 percent by the end of the year. The union had its own hall and paid secretary. Conferences with employers resulted in improvements in working conditions. They agreed to adhere to regular "picking hours" and established a definite time to begin work at night. They set the noon dinner hour at twelve, instead of any time the employer chose. Small gains, but according to Arne M. Jones, the Everett members "felt that they would not be able to accomplish much for themselves until the coast is generally organized; and with this in mind they are willing to help share the burden of bringing about a thorough organization on the coast."[31]

Grays Harbor longshoremen also wanted a union. In response to their appeal, Paddy Morris went to Aberdeen the beginning of August. With district funds exhausted, the international put him on the payroll from August 5 to December 28. He found conditions on the waterfront deplorable. Aided by many local union veterans, the organizing drive went forward, and the ILA installed the charter for Grays Harbor Local 38-77 on September 17. The union grew in spite of discrimination by one of the two stevedore companies. Membership stood at about 400 by mid-October.

Then suddenly thousands of handbills attacking the ILA appeared in the harbor from the Marine Workers League: "The corrupt officialdom of the International Longshoremen's Alliance, the organization that wrecked the Longshoremen's Union of Seattle, and with the help of the A.F. of L. delivered the longshoremen body and soul to the Fink Halls, the organization that utterly neglected the longshoremen of Grays Harbor—these agents of the bosses now want to make us believe that they are going to do something to help us."[32]

"SMASH THE CORRUPT I.L.A.!" the leaflet concluded, and invited longshoremen and harbor workers to attend a mass meeting at the Finnish Hall and join the Marine Workers League. The Shingle Weavers Union started proceedings against Secretary W.H. Halloway for participating in the meeting, and the Grays Harbor Central Labor Council roundly condemned Halloway and R.H. McNeil, Marine Workers organizer, for attempting to wreck the ILA.

By December the ILA local faced trouble. Harry W. Day reported that "when it appeared that the organization was going to fall through, about eight or ten [of the members] got together and decided that they were going to pull it through."[33] The district advanced $100 to the local. A far-reaching gesture of solidarity helped: The Carpenters Union and the ILA enlisted the cooperation of the dockers union in London to refuse to handle unfair doors from McCleary. Day reported the result: The "McCleary Mill lined up 100 per cent union, and had also received word that the stevedores in London would not discharge any doors without the label and that the stevedore that loaded them must be fair."[34] Local 38-77 survived and grew, acquiring a union hall and full-time secretary.

At the end of the decade over 15,000 unorganized longshoremen on the Pacific Coast worked out of fink halls or paid the San Francisco Blue Book union for their

UNITY OF SEAMEN, LONGSHOREMEN AND HARBOR WORKERS

For an Industrial Union Based on Ship, Dock and Fleet Committees

LONGSHOREMEN AND HARBOR WORKERS OF GRAYS HARBOR!

FELLOW WORKERS:

For 20 years the longshoremen and harbor workers of Grays Harbor have been unorganized. The corrupt officialdom of International Longshoremen's Alliance, the organization that wrecked the Longshoremen's Union of Seattle, and with the help of the A. F. of L., delivered the longshoremen body and soul to the Fink Halls, the organization that utterly neglected the longshoremen of Grays Harbor—these agents of the bosses now want to make us believe that they are going to do something to help us.

We, longshoremen, know what the I. L. A. is. This Union is under the ironbound control of Ryan and his sluggers. The rank and file has no voice whatever in the affairs of the Union. Time and again Ryan has outlawed locals that were attempting to escape from his control and carry on a real struggle against the bosses.

Ryan and his sluggers of the I. L. A. can do nothing and will do nothing to help us. There is only one way in which we longshoremen and marine workers can better our conditions—through a new union—a fighting industrial union, based on ship, dock and fleet committees and embracing all marine workers from all branches of the industry irrespective of race, creed, or color.

AN INDUSTRIAL UNION BASED ON SHIP DOCK AND FLEET COMMITTEES—Such a union can only be built on an industrial basis; one industry, one union. The seamen, longshoremen and harbor workers all slave for the same bosses—the big shipping trusts—and must fight together in one union, to win the victory.

The Marine Workers League stands for a fighting Industrial Union! The Marine Workers League is organized to rally all militant seamen, longshoremen and harbor boatmen, for the purpose of building a new, fighting Marine Workers Industrial Union, based upon the class struggle. Recognizing that this union can only be built on struggle, the Marine Workers League takes an active part in the struggles of the marine workers and gives all the support within its power to the struggles of seamen all over the world.

LONGSHOREMEN AND HARBOR WORKERS:
SMASH THE CORRUPT I. L. A.!

Fight for:—

AN INDUSTRIAL UNION BASED ON SHIP, DOCK AND FLEET COMMITTEES!

UNITY OF SEAMEN, LONGSHOREMEN AND HARBOR WORKERS!

JOIN THE MARINE WORKERS LEAGUE!

MARINE WORKERS LEAGUE

Come to the Marine Workers Mass Meeting

THURSDAY NIGHT, Oct 17

At Finnish Hall, 713 East First Street

Speakers, in English and Finnish

W. H. Halloway, Sec'y International Shingle Weavers Union

R. H. McNeil, organizer Marine Workers League

Edward Turunen, well-known Finnish speaker and organizer Mother Bloor

Hear the Truth About the I. L. A. Learn More About the Marine Workers League

4

Formerly International Sea Farers Club

is to hold convention in San Francisco about November 9 & 10

Leaflet of the Marine Workers League, Grays Harbor, 1929. (Courtesy Sailors' Union of the Pacific) jobs. Company gangs and casuals pitted the favored against the unfortunate. Their submission rendered them powerless. Whatever their humiliation and resentment, they feared to oppose the fink hall and the company union.

But the fink hall was vulnerable. Longshoremen in two ports had successfully defied the blacklist to organize unions. They proved that unions could exist because employers needed their skills. They dared to demand small improvements in their working conditions and won them. No one knew how long the new ILA locals would endure, but their members saw the example of a large body of longshoremen who had defeated the fink hall years before, who worked out of their own union halls.

In Tacoma, where the business district above the waterfront merged into wholesale houses, a cluster of small hotels provided lodging for single longshoremen, and down the street the last blacksmith shop in town forged their lumber hooks. The third floor of an old brick building on the corner housed a union hall, identified by the sign over the wide stairway: "I.L.A. Local 38-3." The awakening would surely come.

3

The Vise of the Depression

"If the merchants and manufacturers had the brains that God gave geese they would realize that the only way, the certain way, the quick way, to create prosperous conditions, overcome the panic on Wall Street and to make the city hum with industrial revival, it would be to increase wages and to put more men to work."[1] With the calamity that would be known as the Great Depression a month old, editor John McGivney propounded this judgment in the *Tacoma Labor Advocate* in late November 1929. For the next three years, McGivney and much of the labor press reiterated their solution: industrial revival depended on markets—an "efficient demand" for goods. Working people, comprising three-quarters of the nation's purchasing power, needed well paid jobs to provide this demand. McGivney posed the key question in 1929: "How can masses of people with an annual purchasing power reaching the sum of $1,318, consume $8,007 worth of commodities they produce?" Obviously, they couldn't, resulting in economic breakdown.

The AFL reported 5.3 million workers unemployed by the end of 1930. For the first eleven months of 1930 accumulated wages fell $9 million, while dividends rose $405.3 billion compared to 1929. The advent of wholesale wage-slashing the fall of 1931 accelerated the downward spiral of economic chaos and misery. John McGivney declared:

> The capitalist system has broken down. For millions of our fellow creatures in the richest country in the world there is no means of existence except the scanty dole and the hard crusts that official charity may donate. Yet in this nation there is no shortage of food. There is an abundance of everything. There is dearth of no means of subsistence. There is no shortage of labor. But men are denied the opportunity of using their labor to live.[2]

The month of December 1931, 21.8 percent of union members in the United States had no work. While wages declined, unemployment rose to 10,814,000 by December 1931, 13,587,000 by December 1932, and 15,071,000 by March 1933, one-third of the workforce. Nonunion workers suffered the most severe wage cuts, confirming labor's contention that during prosperous years the unorganized could free load, but during hard times they had no protection.

Idle Ships and Destitute Seamen

The Great Depression hit the shipping industry hard. From 1929 to 1933, U.S. domestic and foreign waterborne commerce declined by nearly half. The Pacific Coast suffered less than the Atlantic, dropping 19 percent, but California commerce declined by one-third. Without the cushion of family, friends, and community, most jobless seamen suffered more than land workers, Pacific Coast fink halls swarmed with destitute seamen and other unemployed. The San Francisco hall had 80,000 registered in April 1930, one-half the number needed for the entire merchant marine, according to Victor Olander. With sailors stranded on the beach over six months waiting to ship, overcrowded seamen's missions turned away destitute seamen, and breadlines at Seamen's Institutes lengthened.

Admiral Line passengers traveling between San Francisco and Seattle dwindled to the point that the Colored Marine Employees Benevolent Association agreed to stagger work: two weeks on board ship and two weeks on the beach for a stewards' department crew, with dues suspended during layoffs. The association served coffee, sandwiches, and donuts at the San Francisco and Seattle offices.

White Angel Breadline, San Francisco, 1933. (Copyright the Dorothea Lange Collection, The Oakland Museum of California, City of Oakland. Gift of Paul S. Taylor)

Wages and Conditions at Sea

As the depression deepened seamen's wages fell, crews shrank, and working conditions deteriorated. Beginning the fall of 1931, wages on intercoastal vessels dropped from $55.00 for ABs on most lines to $33.00 on Luckenbach and as low as $25.00 on some ships. Workaways on these runs increased, as many as six on a vessel, working for 25 cents a month. They were unemployed seamen, "waiting for someone fortunate enough to be getting paid to die or quit so they can inherit his job. . . . Men who think no more of their labor than to work for rotten food and a flop on a cold steel deck!"[3] Two watches at sea came back on intercoastal and transpacific vessels. To save the cost of maintenance and repair in port, field days at sea increased, when the crew turned to to clean, paint, and repair machinery while mates took the wheel. Work often continued into the night under floodlights. Bad food grew worse. In 1933 an estimated one-third of marine hospital patients suffered from stomach ulcers.

Although the federal government continued to pay generous mail subsidies on many runs, intended in part to subsidize American seamen's pay, the entire shipping industry slashed wages. American-Hawaiian cut wages to $50.00, and the Matson luxury liners sailing out of San Francisco paid $55.00 and worked sailors twelve hours a day at sea. Tankers cut wages to $62.50, cut the food allowance, and reduced crew size. Nelson and small steam schooner operators cut wages from $75.00 and 75 cents overtime to $40.00 and 40 cents. McCormick dropped to $60.00. In the San Francisco fink hall when sailors refused to ship on a steam schooner that cut wages $5.00, the manager threatened to turn in their names to the breadlines. Alaska operators cut wages from $60.00 and 75 cents overtime to $50.00 and 60 cents. Three watches remained in effect on steam schooners and the Alaska run. With the assent of the Sailors' Union, the Pacific American Fisheries (PAF) fleet sailing out of Bellingham reduced wages from $75.00 and 75 cents to $60.00 and 60 cents.

In the black stewards' department, the Admiral Line cut first cooks from $110.00 to $90.00 and waiters from $45.00 to $36.00. Fewer passengers and meager tips further reduced waiters' earnings. When the Dollar Line began replacing Chinese in the stewards' department, in compliance with the Jones-White Act, the stewards' company union shipped African-American galley crews for four President vessels sailing out of Seattle. Alaska Steamship announced a wage cut by posting a notice on the bulletin board outside the pantry after the vessel sailed, a demonstration of the company's contempt for the crew. Waiters, messmen, and messboys received $50.00 top wages. A waiter during the tourist season could work from 6:00 a.m. to 8:00 or 9:00 p.m. with no overtime. The company sometimes paid cooks and messmen three hours' overtime for serving a midnight lunch to sailors working cargo in Alaska ports. Stewards' departments on intercoastal and offshore vessels paid lower wages. Steam schooners paid $5.00 more, as did PAF vessels, which took union crews from Seattle.

Reduced crews, speedup, and lack of proper repairs and maintenance increased hazardous conditions at sea and in port. Operators blacklisted seamen who complained. The captain of a liner testified that the company discharged him "because I made reports regarding essential repairs to lifeboat equipment."[4] In 1930 the old wooden steam schooner *Brooklyn* foundered and turned over on a trip from Eureka to San Francisco, with a loss of eighteen lives. *Industrial Solidarity* condemned the vessel as unseaworthy and badly loaded. Shipowners balked at spending a dime. Operators of the steam schooner *Daisy Putman* twice put off until "next trip" the cook's request to replace a rusty soup strainer. Finally, a wire on the strainer punctured his finger, sending him to the hospital when the wound became infected. In a court case that the owners appealed and lost, the cook collected $1,195 for damages.

Licensed officers voiced the same grievances as unlicensed seamen. Shipowners reduced base pay, eliminated overtime, and cut the subsistence allowance for masters and mates. Smaller crew size increased the work load and lengthened hours, resulting in fatigue and inefficiency. The operators cut the manning scale for marine engineers 25 percent during the 1930s, while payrolls decreased by 47.5 percent. Nationally there were 2.63 engineers for every job aboard ship. Shortage of jobs forced seamen to sail below their regular ratings. Skippers shipped as mates, mates as able seamen, able seamen as ordinary seamen, engineers as firemen, firemen as wipers, stewards as messmen, and on down the line. In fo'c'sles during those years, many AB's sea bags held captain's or mate's tickets.

Seamen's Unions

Although membership decreased with jobs, a few seamen clung tenaciously to their unions during the Great Depression. Sailors' Union membership dropped to about 800 paid up men out of 5,000 to 6,000 sailing on the coast. Seattle remained the strongest union port. Besides half the crews of Alaska vessels, steam schooners averaged 10 to 15 percent union, with another 15 percent ex-members who had dropped out after 1921. Very few union men sailed intercoastal, and not many more on transpacific runs, with the exception of the three Matson liners running to Australia.

In addition to fighting an economic battle for survival, the Marine Firemen's Union faced bankruptcy because of a corrupt official. Secretary Patrick Flynn's death in 1933 revealed the fact that he had borrowed thousands of dollars in the name of the union, which his widow inherited under the terms of his will. With 300 book members, the union changed its name to Pacific Coast Marine Firemen, Oilers, Watertenders and Wipers' Association and obtained a new charter in September 1933. In Seattle, where no branch existed, Pete Gill gave Thomas McManus, an old-time member of the Marine Firemen, desk space in the Sailors' hall. McManus received half the income from the initiation fees of the men he signed up, a commission arrangement that was not uncommon for union organizers in the 1930s.

The Marine Cooks and Stewards became the weakest of the ISU Pacific District unions, with one branch in Seattle. Union membership on Alaska Steamship vessels dwindled to about two dozen. Many men in the stewards' department who had come to the coast from Australia on Oceanic vessels during World War I liked their jobs and showed no interest in the union. Two crews had jobs the year round, and the rest drifted, working on the Alaska vessels during the March to October tourist season and sailing on Matson ships out of California ports in the winter months. Among the drifters a slightly higher percentage carried union books. On the whole coast, 5 to 8 percent of the stewards' department belonged to the union—10 percent at the most, including crews on the Oceanic vessels.

Although locals of the Masters, Mates and Pilots (MMP) on inland waters survived the depression, the organization disappeared on Pacific Coast seagoing vessels. In November 1933, the AFL loaned E.B. O'Grady to organize at San Francisco, and the national organization put on an organizer at San Pedro. The MMP chartered Local 90 for seagoing masters and mates, a coastwide union with headquarters at San Francisco.

The Marine Engineers' Beneficial Association likewise had more success keeping ferryboats and tugs organized and under agreement than seagoing vessels, where the union remained virtually ineffective. Interest in the MEBA revived in 1932 when Local 97 at San Francisco began to organize seagoing engineers. Locals existed in Seattle and Portland, and San Pedro No. 79 received a charter in November 1933.

The Revolutionary Unions

A few Wobblies could be found on many of the West Coast ships agitating for better food and quarters. Although they criticized the officials of other unions, they cooperated with the members on the ships. As the depression hung on, the IWW looked hopefully for the union upsurge among seamen. The *Industrial Worker* declared in 1931:

> The seamen have followed the events of the past two years in a mental daze, unable to picture themselves unemployed or in breadlines, or faced with wage cuts until recently. . . . Some of them still are, but the majority of them have opened their eyes to their conditions and are trying to find a way out. The International Seamen's Union's halls are gathering places for has-beens and card players. The organization has failed to enter a protest against past abuses or offer a program for future ones.[5]

Seamen themselves governed the IWW Marine Transport Workers 510, strongest in Gulf ports, where the ISU paid little attention to seamen's needs. In contrast, outsiders dominated the Marine Workers Industrial Union. The Wobblies charged that the Communist Party fraction selected the slate of officers and controlled the first MWIU national convention. The MWIU constitution, they said, followed the Russian trade union principle of "democratic centralism," with "the subordination of the lower bodies to the higher, the decisions of the higher body to be final and from which there is no appeal."[6]

With East Coast ISU officials giving seamen practically no support, the MWIU recruited young militants with some success. The MWIU attacked the other unions:

> Since 1921 [the ISU] has not made one single move to organize the seamen. It preaches class-collaboration instead of class struggle—that workers should "work in harmony" with the bosses instead of fighting them.[7]
>
> Today the M.T.W. is practically dead. The fragment that is left—comprising a few disconnected "irreconcilables" stands 100 per cent in the camp of the bosses, shows not

the slightest militancy, and is one of the bitterest enemies of the Marine Workers Industrial Union. Those former members of the M.T.W. who still retain their fighting spirit are now active in the Marine Workers Industrial Union, . . .[8]

Communist unemployed demonstration at City Hall, Tacoma, 1931. (Courtesy Tacoma Public Library)

West Coast seamen paid little attention to the MWIU. In Seattle MWIU soapboxers in front of Pier 2 and at several other locations on the waterfront during the noon hour made no impression on the seamen, according to Jack Connors of the Marine Cooks and Stewards. *Industrial Solidarity* estimated in 1930 that the MWIU had about twelve members and ten to fifteen followers in San Francisco, although the union claimed a membership of 20,000 nationally.

Better than any organizer, the depression years taught seamen how helpless they remained without a union. Although not yet ready to take a book, they began to consider a union favorably. The three rival organizations battled for their allegiance: the MWIU with militant rhetoric, rallies, and demonstrations; MTW 510 with equally militant rhetoric and the example of individual Wobblies on ships speaking out for better conditions; and, on the West Coast, conscientious ISU representatives visiting ships where they could, urging men to join, holding their unions together until the seamen should return to them.

Northwest Longshoremen

For longshoremen as well as seamen, idle ships and scarce cargoes brought hard times. In 1929, 664 registered longshoremen worked out of the Seattle fink hall, half in organized gangs earning between $170 and $190 a month, and the rest extras and casuals earning considerable less. By 1933 the employers had cut registered men to 525, and their average wages had fallen to $81.81 a month in 1932. On the Portland waterfront the average hours of work per week declined from 32.3 in 1928-29 to 16.6 in 1932. During July, August, and September 1930, an average of 154 members of the Tacoma Lumber Handlers earned about $56.23 a month.

Improved cargo-handling methods fostered speedup and increased accidents. Paddy Morris described the difference in working lumber. During World War I a twelve-man gang, four on the dock building loads and eight in the hold, did a good day's work to stow 80,000 board feet on a steam vessel in nine hours. The hold men, four on each side, could take a breathing spell while the men stowed the load sent down for the opposite side. By the 1930s, the same size gang that took in less than 130,000 to 150,000 board feet would be fired. The difference was that loads of up to 5,000 board feet, built at the mills and sent down in slings, came so fast that the hold men had no breathing spells. Winches could take the heavier loads, but the gear could not, and sometimes it snapped and broke, booms broke, and parts carried away, causing accidents. The Pacific Coast Marine Safety Code said nothing about load limits. Until the unions became strong, longshoremen would hoist loads as heavy as the gear would bear.

The depression hit the new locals in Northwest lumber ports hard when the bottom dropped out of the lumber business. In Everett the monthly longshore payroll shrank from $90,000 to $7,000. Members dropped out or fell behind in their dues, while the local fought to equalize what little work existed and prevent the employers from establishing preferred gangs. In Grays Harbor most of the mills closed, leaving thousands unemployed. Employers refused to call the ILA hall in Aberdeen for men, the only comfortable place to wait for work. The employers hall remained closed most of the time and had no toilet facilities. The Twin Harbor Stevedoring Company continued to blacklist ILA members.

By late 1930 Seattle longshoremen showed signs of abandoning the company union. On October 8, District Secretary Jack Bjorklund and Ernest Ellis, secretary of Local 38-12, met with a few key men working out of the fink hall, who believed that the depression "had shown up the true colors of the company union."[9] A month later a committee of twelve men from the fink hall met with an ILA delegation of Hugh McKennan and Tom Mason from Everett, Ellis and George Horr of Local 38-12, Paddy Morris of Tacoma Local 38-30, and Bjorklund. The fink hall committee agreed that Seattle might be organized, and the international put Morris on salary for December and January, aided by Horr, Ellis, and Robert Juarez of the Seattle local.

This time the organizing drive brought results. From November 1930 through April 1931 Local 38-12 initiated 435 new members. In May the union elected an executive committee of twenty-five to weld together the members from all over the waterfront. Each group selected its own members: seven from Local 38-12, seven

Hooverville, Seattle, 1930s. (Courtesy Museum of History and Industry, photograph #2089)

from Employers Hall stevedores, four from Employers Hall truckers, three from the Admiral Line, two from Pacific Terminal, and one each from the Port Commission and Alaska Steamship's Pier 2. The union passed a motion that "anytime the Committee from Employers Hall meet, that the members of Committee get together before the meeting to talk over things, and that no member can put anything on docket without consulting the majority of the committee."[10]

Some employers recognized that the fink hall's inability to compel employers to live up to their own rules provided a strong inducement for Seattle longshoremen to join the ILA. At the Joint Employment Committee meeting April 10, employee members complained of docks hiring men at the gate or ship's side when registered truckers from the hall should have been employed. Fishermen and relatives also cut in on the work. Speaking for the employers, William F. Varnell proposed that the committee send all employers a letter admitting the violations complained of and warning that their continuation jeopardized the Joint Organization. "The men's patience in this matter is about exhausted," he said. "It is hoped that your officers and members of the various committees will not be further embarrassed in representing you in this organization."[11] The minutes do not indicate that employers heeded the warning.

Portland Longshoremen Organize

With the Seattle organizing drive progressing, Paddy Morris and Jack Bjorklund went to Portland February 4, 1931, to visit their old friend, Con Negstad. Negstad, who had been president of an ILA local in 1916 and was active in the old union, agreed to call a meeting in his home. Thirteen trusted men came. All wanted a union, but some feared that the lack of work would deter longshoremen from organizing. Overcoming their fear of discrimination, they signed up and paid their $1.00 initiation fee. Along with most ex-ILA members, these recruits worked out of the Portland Stevedore Hall, which dispatched about 20 percent of the men for the port.

Morris stayed in Portland. The drive soon spread from the small fink hall to the big fink hall. The ILA installed a charter for Local 38-78 on March 22 at a meeting of 300 men. The employers struck back by discriminating against active members. The union put on A.J. York as full-time secretary at $125 a month and elected Con Negstad president. With over 600 members by May, the local opened a hall on Fourth Steet. The *Labor Advocate* charged that the Marine Workers Industrial Union fought the ILA drive: "They couldn't do any organizing in a union of their own brand and when another seemed to be getting along with success in sight, these disruptionists did their work."[12]

Discrimination continued. Jack O'Neil, chief dispatcher in the big hall, told some members that he "had received instructions from the employers not to hire any I.L.A. men."[13] Although Portland employers publicly denied discrimination, they

Breadline at Grandma's Kitchen, Front Street, Portland, 1930. (Courtesy Oregon Historical Society, OrHi neg. CN 010148)

acted to keep the ILA off the waterfront. A.J. York found it impossible to get work after 1931, although his former gang boss wanted to hire him. When George A. Gray asked Fritz Buchtmann, dispatcher in the small hall, why he was getting less work after he joined the ILA, "He told me that there were four companies that did not want organized men down there, either four or six companies,. . ."[14] John Beaton stated the employers discriminated against men who wore union buttons. "It was . . . blacklisting; if you belonged to an organization and wore a button in the hall you were left standing."[15] By September 1931 the union shrank. The local paid per capita to the district ILA on 174 members in October and 100 in January 1932.

Joint Northwest Bargaining

Rumors of a possible wage cut originating in New York circulated on the West Coast in September 1931. The Seattle Waterfront Employers asked employee members of the Joint Executive Committee, by now all ILA members, to consider ways of reducing operating costs without cutting wages. The employers suggested eliminating certain "unreasonable" practices, such as overtime pay for night work. The joint committee members from Local 38-12 met with committees from Locals 38-3, 38-30, and 38-76. All agreed that the employees committee would oppose any change in the Seattle wages and working rules.

Fourteen members of the employees committee sent a letter on Local 38-12 stationery to the Waterfront Employers on October 12. To reduce operating costs, they said, "We must have efficiency on the job and the cooperation of all men concerned, we your committee honestly believe that the best way to get efficiency on the job is through organization, and realizing this, an organizing drive was started about one year ago, and we have met with good results." But they stopped short of opposing the fink hall: "We your committee of employees also members of Local 38-12 I.L.A. working through this hall, are absolutely opposed to changing the system as operated through this hall, . . ."[16]

In a special meeting of the Joint Executive Committee the employers rejected the employees' letter as "a request for an International Longshoremen's Association agreement, eventually if not now," and reiterated their determination to deal with their employees as individuals. According to Merl Ringenberg's minutes, the men replied "that they believe in the system now in use; . . . and that the employers are very much mistaken in interpreting this letter either as coming from the International Longshoremen's Association or as a request for an agreement." The committee voted, one member dissenting, "that the letter be withdrawn and resubmitted without reference to the I.L.A."[17] Once again the employees retreated.

Meanwhile, the four Puget Sound locals and the Seattle employees committee agreed, according to Bjorklund, that "we would insist that the employers meet with a committee from Everett and Tacoma, and the Joint Committee to settle this wage question, knowing full well that we have the same employers in all Puget Sound ports." The employers "refused to meet us collectively on the ground that they would be according recognition to the I.L.A. "[18]

When employee members of the joint committee continued to oppose a wage cut and working rules revisions, the employers moved to regain control of their company union. Agents spread reports that the men's committee had betrayed the longshoremen and that the ILA was dictating to them. They induced "some of the weak-kneed members to circulate a petition to elect another committee and retain their relationship with the employers."[19] Jack Bjorklund persuaded the ILA members of the original committee to accept nomination, but by the time of the election most of them had withdrawn their names in fear, and the new committee had only five ILA members.

During this time the employers posted a new wage scale effective January 1, 1932: 85 cents and $1.25 overtime for longshoremen—a cut of 5 cents straight time and 10 cents overtime. The cut in straight-time pay wiped out the remaining differential between East and West Coast longshoremen. With the ILA rebellion quelled, employer Chair E.A. Quigle challenged the men: "Further, if any of you committeemen feel that you are bound to be governed by I.L.A. instructions and can not come to our meetings with open minds and participate in our deliberations with the purpose of doing the best thing that can be done under the circumstance, it is suggested that you withdraw from this committee and make room for some one who can."[20] After a few objections from the men, the committee voted unanimously to accept the employers' revisions of the working rules.

Following the Seattle employers' victory, the ILA locals decided that they had not sufficient strength to fight for a joint Puget Sound agreement, and each local should negotiate the best possible port conditions. But, Bjorklund reported, "By holding conferences of the four locals and showing the employers that we were united, we were able to get them to recede from their original demands in the way of wage reductions."[21] Tacoma longshoremen succeeded in negotiating less drastic revisions of their working rules than those imposed on Seattle.

Seattle longshoremen suffered as the depression worsened. Work and earnings reached the low point the summer of 1932. Eighteen or twenty longshoremen depended on public relief. The Joint Executive Committee voted June 3 "That limited preference for job opportunities be given according to need, that is, competent men with dependents be given a limited preference over men without dependents as far as practicable without sacrificing the employers interests too seriously."[22] Local 38-12 suffered as most of the new members dropped out. In January 1932 the union lowered the initiation fee to $1.00 and one month's dues and cut the secretary's wages to $20.00 a week. Two months later the union transferred the money in the burial fund to the general fund and sold twenty-four folding chairs for 50 cents each. In May the local cut Secretary Dewey Bennett to $10.00 a week and voted to have volunteers do the janitorial work.

Tacoma Union Dispatching

In Tacoma the depression aggravated the chronic problem of unequal distribution of earnings. With not enough work for all regular longshoremen and diminished profits for stevedores, the employers wanted to overwork the most efficient men and let the rest starve. American-Hawaiian, which had considerable work in the port, tried to induce thirty-four members to leave the ILA and form an independent union, promising them steady work. Local 38-3 discovered the plot and expelled the ringleader, ending company union attempts. Thereupon the union elected a committee to negotiate the 1932 working rules and insisted that the employers state in the new handbook, *Wage Scale, Rules and Working Conditions on the Tacoma Waterfront:* "The Tacoma Wage Scale, Rules and Working Conditions, as herein defined, were determined upon by a joint committee of employers and employees. . . . There will be no change in these rules and working conditions except on thirty days notice in writing to the chairman of the employees' or employers' committee."[23]

Traditionally the gang bosses, hatch tenders who belonged to the union, picked their gangs in the halls. By the end of 1931 the situation had become intolerable, with the most efficient men driven so hard they could stand only two or three shifts a week and the less efficient ones without work. In May 1932 Local 38-3, with the agreement of the employers, instituted the 50-50 plan. The gang bosses picked 50 percent of a gang, and the union dispatcher picked the other 50 percent, rotating the work. The plan did not equalize earnings because the same 100 men picked by the gang bosses had half the work, while the other 400 members shared the other half.

To solve the new problem, about November 1932 the local began to rotate gangs according to earnings and put the $6.00 plan in effect for the 50 percent picked by the dispatcher. (A day's work paid 85 cents times eight hours, or $6.80.) A gang boss still picked half his gang, but now the union sent out the low gang first, instead of allowing employers to request the same favorite gangs. The union placed the 50 percent picked by the dispatcher in a hiring pool, dropping a man out when he had earned $6.00. After all men had earned $6.00, the union started a new pool for all members. To appease employers, the dispatcher did not usually send out the whole list, including the least efficient members. Even so, employers objected, and the work hogs in the local complained to their bosses about sharing jobs. On March 31, 1933, the Waterfront Employers sent Local 38-3 an ultimatum that effective April 3 they would go back to the old picking system. Secretary-Dispatcher Ed Harris replied that any change would have to go through the grievance committee.

Negotiations followed, and by mutual agreement the ILA put the preferred gang system into effect May 8. The new system divided about half the longshoremen into gangs, the rest remaining in the field. As a concession, the union granted the Dollar Line, Admiral Line, and Pacific Steamship Company each two regular gangs of twenty-five men. The local dispatched the other gangs in rotation according to earnings, low gang first. About 100 warehousemen worked off a rotating list. When the earnings of a preferred gang reached $20.00 more than another gang, the company had to accept the lowest hall gang until the differential dropped below $20.00. The union set a three o'clock deadline for ordering gangs for the next day, and all gangs had to be finished and their record of the day's earnings back in the hall by that time to be eligible for dispatch. The longshoremen chose that hour to enforce a six-hour day, 8:00 a.m. to 3:00 p.m., which later became the demand for the Pacific Coast. By showing up regularly for picks, a man in the field could earn as much as a member of a preferred gang, and the $20.00 rule equalized pay between preferred and hall gangs.

The smaller Lumber Handlers Local 38-30 also acted to equalize earnings in April 1932 by adopting the rule that a member who had four hours' work, day or night, could not line up for the next pick unless fewer than necessary men showed up. In October a hatch tender was suspended for ten days for picking only four men from the eligible list for work. After Locals 38-3 and 38-30 merged April 1, 1934, the combined local integrated the lumber handlers into the dispatching system and gave Griffith and Sprague, stevedores with log cargoes, two preferred gangs.

The Tacoma unions boasted proudly that because of their work-sharing programs scarcely any longshoremen depended on relief during the depression. The locals' ability to force a dispatching system on their employers that spread work and equalized earnings during the depression revealed the ILA's strength in this single port on the otherwise open-shop Pacific Coast.

San Francisco Blue Book

By 1930 the ILA began to lose patience with the San Francisco Blue Book. When Jack Bjorklund met with company union officials and California labor officials in May, both groups asked for more time for the Blue Book to educate its members on the need for a dues increase to pay the ILA per capita tax. The ILA waited nine more months. Then President Joe Ryan requested a vote on affiliation. The officials replied that a dues increase presented a "serious obstacle to hurdle" and they doubted the success of the vote. Ryan insisted and suggested they invite Bjorklund and other labor officials to persuade the members. On April 9, without inviting any labor people to speak, the Blue Book union voted 939 to 88 against ILA affiliation. President Ryan immediately requested the AFL to expel the company union from its affiliated bodies. The state and city councils complied. The ILA was free to organize in San Francisco.

In September 1931 Jack Bjorklund went to San Francisco to evaluate the situation. First he met with a number of old ILA men compelled to belong to the Blue Book to work for certain companies. They related that "new men are constantly being hired and then taken into the union, which does not fully control the work, but is apparently content with the additional revenue derived from the initiation fees of the men who are wished on them by the employers."[24] As might be expected under these circumstances, deplorable conditions existed on the waterfront. While thousands of casuals fought for scarce jobs, shipping companies speeded up their star gangs almost beyond endurance to maximize shrinking profits.

Next Bjorklund met with the Blue Book executive board, all of whom expressed grief at being thrown out of the Labor Council. They told him they expected a less drastic wage reduction in San Francisco than they anticipated for the Atlantic Coast when the ILA agreement expired. He related:

> I told them very frankly, just what the rest of the labor movement felt about them being outlaws from the American Federation of Labor; that the longshoremen in San Francisco were well aware of the fact that Captain Peterson, manager for the Waterfront Employers, is dictating the policy of the "Blue Book Union.". . . It was all too apparent that employers had been telling them to stay out of the I.L.A. and then they would not get their wages cut as much as I.L.A. ports.[25]

Bjorklund accused the San Francisco longshoremen of freeloading on the ILA, which was responsible for every gain in longshoremen's conditions.

Finally, Bjorklund met with the remnants of the Riggers and Stevedores, who worked for independent steamship companies and docks not members of the Waterfront Employers. These men, including Lee Holman, had written to President Ryan about organizing. Although they wanted a union, according to Bjorklund, the group decided:

> With so much talk about wage cuts it would be better not to put a charter in the port of San Francisco, which would give the "Blue Book Union" officials an opportunity to say:—That if the I.L.A. officials had not butted in, we would have been able to retain our present wage scale. . . . But if shipping ever picks up, San Francisco will be organized into the I.L.A. in spite of the "Blue Book Union" officials and the assistance they are getting from some well known labor leaders in the city.[26]

The anticipated wage cut did not go according to company union predictions. Atlantic Coast longshoremen retained their straight-time rate and took a 10-cent cut in overtime in October, but in January 1932 employers cut the Pacific Coast 5 cents straight time and 10 cents overtime. The Holman group asked the 1932 district convention for an organizer and a charter. The convention recommended that a local San Francisco man be empowered to organize, with the assistance of the district and the international.

The Communists appeared on the waterfront in December 1932 with the first issue of the mimeographed *Waterfront Worker,* which sold for a penny at the shape-up near the Embarcadero. With its recitation of festering grievances, the paper found a ready response among longshoremen.

Longshoremen in Southern California ports suffered equally bad conditions. The Waterfront Employers installed a joint representation plan in the San Pedro fink hall, reputedly no better for longshoremen than the Seattle plan. Although a union nucleus remained, the men felt "that as long as San Francisco has a Blue Book Union and keep themselves apart from the I.L.A. it would be suicidal . . . to attempt to organize."[27] A small group held the ILA charter in San Diego powerless to organize until San Pedro moved.

The Vise Tightens

As the depression dragged on, most unorganized longshoremen clung fearfully to their fink hall registrations and company gangs. But resentment grew against the unequal distribution of work, the inhuman speedup, and the indignities of the fink hall and shape-up. The 1931 district convention reiterated the goal of the ILA for the past fifteen years: Longshoremen from Seattle to San Diego had the same employers, who regulated wages and working conditions coastwide through their organizations. Therefore, the longshoremen resolved, "That we pledge ourselves to work for a solid, concrete organization of longshoremen on this Coast, whose aims and objects shall be to negotiate with our employers through our District, Local 38, for a uniform agreement for the entire District."[28]

While Seattle employers repeated their pledge that wages and working conditions "shall be equal to those of the other Pacific Coast ports," some continued to cheat. Walter Freer related that in late 1932 William F. Varnell, superintendent of the Milwaukee dock, "had eighty men removed from the truckers list on the grounds of incompetency. A few weeks later it was discovered that these 'incompetent' men were working 'preferred' on his dock for 50 cents per hour, the regular rate being 75 cents."[29]

Even as the country elected a new President who promised to end the depression, another wage cut reached the waterfront. Effective October 1,1932, the North Atlantic ILA ports took a 10-cent reduction, to 75 cents and $1.10 overtime. San Francisco cut wages to 75 cents and $1.15 December 10, and Los Angeles harbor followed a week later. In Seattle the employers proposed the same cut December 15. The men objected that they could not live on less, and docks and stevedores still hired outsiders. "It is an issue of enough to eat for the men as against the hope of profit for the ship," the minutes stated. The men argued that if the Pacific Coast cut the rate practically to the New York scale, they should receive New York working conditions: "specifically, the 44-hour week, high minimum of men in a gang, two winch drivers on double winches, limited loads, etc."[30]

When the committee met a week later the men declined to accept the wage cut and asked for arbitration, as provided for in the Joint Organization constitution. The employers replied, "There is nothing to arbitrate. Our decisions are based on mutual understanding . . . when we have to go outside for someone to settle our difficulties, the end of our joint effort is in sight."[31] The wage cut went into effect January 1, 1933. Once again a committee of the defeated fink hall men asked the ILA for help. Local 38-12 would embark on another organizing drive.

Meanwhile, according to the *Labor Advocate,* the Marine Workers Industrial Union had distributed an open letter on the Seattle and Tacoma waterfronts accusing Jack Bjorklund of "preparing to play into the hands of the bosses and accept a wage cut." The ILA made no preparation to resist the cut "because Bjorklund and the shipowners are like Ryan and they are 'brothers under the skin!'"[32] The Tacoma unions had to accept the wage cut, although they continued to enforce their dispatching rules and better working conditions on the Tacoma docks.

The vise of the depression had squeezed the last illusions out of its helpless victims. They lost all belief in their employers' good intentions. Fear alone held back the rebellion against intolerable working conditions and subsistence wages. But the promise of the new President that he would end the depression and bring back prosperity began to dispel the fear. The most recent wage cut, when the shipping industry showed signs of recovery, deepened resentment. The angry murmur on the docks and in the fink halls increased.

4

The New Deal on the Waterfront

Labor's hopes for the return of good times with the New Deal focused on Section 7a of the National Industrial Recovery Act (NIRA), passed June 16, 1933. The section required that every National Recovery Administration (NRA) code guarantee to employees the right to organize and bargain collectively without interference from their employers, and also prohibited employers from forcing their employees to join a company union or refrain from joining a union of their choice. Codes in each industry would prescribe maximum hours and minimum wages which participating employers had to observe.

Skepticism tempered the general enthusiasm for some experienced unionists. Joe Clarke of the Painters Union told the Tacoma Central Labor Council that labor would get as much out of the codes as it was organized to take. John McGivney considered the act "of such immense importance that labor everywhere, organized or unorganized, should prepare to take advantage of it where they can guard against its possible abuses in unfriendly hands."[1] Passage of the NIRA coincided with the long-awaited upturn in the shipping industry. Unorganized longshoremen took hope and began to respond to ILA appeals to join the union.

San Francisco Organizes

The San Francisco waterfront began to move before the Recovery Act became law. The drive started in May 1933, according to William J. "Bill" Lewis, one of the faithful Riggers and Stevedores who periodically tried to reorganize during the 1920s. Old union members, including Lewis and Lee Holman, formed an ILA Organizing Committee. Julius G. White, member of the Proletarian Party and Albin Kullberg, reputedly a Socialist Labor Party adherent, were on the committee. Other names are missing. On ILA President Joe Ryan's recommendation the committee approached Clyde W. Deal, secretary of the Ferryboatmen's Union of the Pacific, for assistance. He gave them space in his office at No. 10 Embarcadero.

Outsiders bombarded the longshoremen with rhetoric. The *Waterfront Worker* appeared monthly denouncing the Blue Book and conditions on the docks. Soapboxers on the Embarcadero outside the piers added their appeals to organize. The MWIU had a hall on Jackson Street just off the Embarcadero north of the Ferry Building.

Disregarding these elements, the ILA Organizing Committee signed up old-timers with influence in their gangs. They charged 50 cents initiation fee and collected no dues during the organizing drive. Fred West, another Proletarian Party member from the Window Washers Union, spoke on the waterfront for the ILA. About 1,000 former members of the Riggers and Stevedores joined. A leaflet suggests the turbulence on the waterfront:

WARNING!
To All Longshoremen!

The organizing of Longshoremen on the San Francisco waterfront into the International Longshoremen's Association (I.L.A.) is meeting with the approval and support of all Longshoremen who are tired of Communistic Rot, tired of silly and senseless Soap Box Ravings and sick of Blue Book misrepresentation. Look out for desperate attempts to mislead by Communists, Fanatics or the dying Blue Book.

To be safe remember that all meetings until further notice will be held in the Labor Temple . . . and notices of such meetings will be signed by the "I.L.A. Organizing Committee."

Keep your eyes open and look out for Fakirs and Grafters.

I.L.A. Organizing Committee[2]

The leaflet probably referred to a meeting July 2 sponsored by the *Waterfront Worker* and the MWIU, attended by 100 longshoremen, the *Worker* claimed.

Success of the organizing drive alarmed the employers and their company union. AFL President William Green requested ILA President Ryan to appoint Paul Scharrenberg to deliver the Blue Book union intact to the ILA. Ryan agreed. A few days later, on June 26, the longshoremen formally organized a union and elected provisional officers, including Lee Holman president. With 2,000 members, the ILA chartered Local 38-79 on July 5, 1933. Scharrenberg wired Ryan the same day protesting his failure to consider the Blue Book. Ryan replied that Holman's group had the charter. Scharrenberg persisted:

> Regret your hasty action when everything was lined up to swing toward national affiliation 2500 men organized independently for fourteen years and working under collective bargaining and job control. Chartering of local independent association would have resulted in organizing San Pedro and San Diego under the International, but your strange maneuvering will blast these prospects. Chartering Holman's local group will cause bitter antagonism of ship owners. I therefore earnestly recommend that you revoke charter already issued and at least give local association opportunity to join like men.

Ryan shot back angrily:

> Resent tone of your telegram. San Francisco longshoremen have had opportunity to join like men for past fourteen years, but due to strange maneuvering on part of officers which you apparently condoned, they have remained outside of their International organization. . . . Cannot see why it should cause bitter antagonism of ship owners as you state in your wire, excepting ship owners favor the leaders of the men and not themselves. This is the first time I have heard a representative of the Seamen's International Union worrying about attitude of ship owners. Will appreciate your refraining from questioning or criticizing my attitude in this matter.[3]

After the 1924 failure, Harry Bridges took no part in organizing attempts. He worked in the American-Hawaiian star gang and helped to form the Albion Hall caucus while the ILA reorganized. Bridges joined Local 38-79 on July 7. MWIU members and longshoremen comprised the Albion Hall group, named for their meeting place. Besides Bridges, Henry Schmidt, former Socialist Party member, Ralph Mallen, and Roger McKenna participated. Later B.B. Jones and John Schomaker, both active Communists, joined the group. Before the meetings a Communist caucus met with Harry Jackson, MWIU organizer from New York, to plan strategy. Bridges frequently chaired the meetings of the Albion Hall group, whose program usually coincided with that of the Communist Party.

From attacking the company union and bad conditions on the docks, the *Waterfront Worker* turned its wrath on the fledgling ILA local. An anonymous letter in the July issue charged: "Monday, June 26, 1933, down comes Mr. Lee Holman selling organized labor for 50¢ apiece." The paper complained of the provisional officers:

> This slate of officials, this executive board, are not the doing of the men who signed for the I.L.A. They are self-elected. We have again and again pointed out the sell-outs put over by the high officials of the I.L.A. in other ports when the men allowed a few officials to take their union away from them and run it to suit themselves . . .[4]

The *Waterfront Worker* took credit for the agitation that led men to join the ILA. Although the paper likely influenced some of the newer men on the docks, old-timers who formed the original core group undoubtedly remembered the advantages of a union port. Local 38-79 held a mass initiation of 500 members July 27. Then the organizing drive stalled with the port scarcely more than half organized. The rest of the longshoremen hung back, intimidated by the employers' support of the Blue Book or convinced by the *Waterfront Worker* that the ILA was no good.

Organizing in the Northwest

As shipping began to improve, Northwest longshoremen looked anxiously for the union upsurge. The Portland ILA local had 10 paid-up members and Seattle 110 in April 1933, and Grays Harbor and Everett struggled to hold their charters. Two weeks after the Recovery Act became law, fifty-six delegates from Washington and Oregon ports attended a special district conference in Seattle to formulate demands for a waterfront labor code. They discussed and amended a tentative code presented by the district office, which the locals subsequently approved.

By this time Portland Local 38-78 began to revive. June receipts for applications and dues were $1,106.89, and succeeding months continued to show gains. A circular letter from the Portland Waterfront Employers did not deter men from joining the union. Portland members organized the Columbia River ports of Longview and Rainier, and the ILA chartered a local at Anacortes on Puget Sound. During July old-timers at San Pedro, Joe Simons of the Marine Transport Workers Federation and ex-Wobblies, organized the port around a nucleus of old steam schooner men and lumber handlers.

The union claimed 1,700 members by August. Late in 1933 Albin Kullberg organized a local at Stockton over stiff opposition of the boss stevedore.

The convention of the Marine Council of the Pacific in Portland July 30-31 considered the proposed longshoremen's code presented by the ILA delegates. It called for a six-hour day, thirty-four-hour week, wages of $1.00 and $1.50 overtime, union hiring halls, and preference of employment. The convention voted to work with ILA President Ryan and the Pacific Coast District to establish a national longshore code. The Portland gathering brought together for the first time in seventeen years ILA representatives from all the major Pacific Coast ports, including San Francisco and San Pedro. Lee Holman, Albin Kullberg, and Lynn Hockensmith represented local 38-79.

By late August the Northwest employers became alarmed. A special meeting of Tacoma ILA Local 38-3 on August 25, with 375 members present, gave thirty days' notice to change the agreement, asking 90 cents and $1.35 overtime. The letter to the employers threatened to "hang the hook, not only in this Port, but all Pacific Coast ports as well" if the matter was not settled satisfactorily by October 1.[5] Three days later a joint meeting of the Waterfront Employers of Seattle and Association of Washington Stevedores considered the labor outlook. W.D. Vanderbilt of Grace Line warned:

> The longshoremen are aiming to clean our house for us because of—
>
> Frequent bumping of gangs in favor of other gangs.
>
> Hiring of unregistered men by several companies independent of the central registration system (always deeply resented by the men labelled a breach of agreement because it takes away their work).
>
> Chiselling on time.
>
> Speeding up the work beyond all reason (such as 100-100 lb. sacks in a load).
>
> Glaringly unsafe methods.

The meeting concluded that a few companies violated the "explicit agreement in writing . . . consisting of the Standard Practice Handbook and the Joint Committee Minutes." The minutes continued:

> The men feeling their power, as a result of the N.I.R.A. together with organizing solidly in the I.L.A., are taking disciplinary action in their own hands against offending employers. Moreover, they indicate a fine discrimination between those members who keep their agreements and those who don't. This leads to the result that in the near future the fair employers will be compelled either to stand by their unfair competitors and oppose the men when the latter are in the right even to the extent of breaking a strike, or let the unfair employers fight the battles of their own making single-handed.

The meeting voted: "If a member wilfully and persistently breaks the agreement of the Association with the men and thereby gets into trouble with them, the consequence is that he will be left to get himself out of it."[6]

The Matson Beef

In San Francisco the Blue Book countered the ILA drive by trying to enforce the closed shop. During July and August Blue Book agents had longshoremen fired who had no books or owed back dues. In late August the ILA filed a complaint under the NRA charging that the Blue Book was a company union and that its closed-shop agreement violated Section 7a. An NRA investigating committee cleared the Blue Book of the company union charges and ruled that it held a valid closed-shop contract with the Waterfront Employers. The committee urged the Blue Book not to discriminate against members who also belonged to the ILA. Committee member John J. O'Connell, secretary of the San Francisco Labor Council, signed the report. Following the decision, the Blue Book sent a pamphlet to all members extolling their superior contract and cautioning them not to be "misled by these soap box orators who are taking advantage of the N.R.A. to try and use you for their own benefit."[7]

Local 38-79 adopted a constitution and by-laws August 15. According to Clyde Deal, the meeting adopted a democratic constitution proposed by Albin Kullberg, rather than Holman's version with power concentrated at the top. District Secretary Jack Bjorklund wired Holman "to arrange meeting as soon as possible" to nominate permanent officers. "Hold election by referendum ballot," he directed, for "several days to give all members a chance to vote."[8] The Albion Hall caucus put forward a slate opposed to Holman that included Kullberg for president, Bill Lewis, Ralph Mallen, and Lynn Hockensmith for delegates (similar to patrolmen for seamen), and twenty-five executive committee candidates. Hockensmith had been fired for wearing an ILA button.

The union held the election September 1 and 2, with Paddy Morris presiding at the meeting the 2nd. The members elected Holman president with 865 votes to 447 for Kullberg and 87 for L. Doyle, running on a "Rank and File 100%" slate. The president served full time, performing the duties of business manager. The union elected Ivan Cox as secretary and Lewis, Hockensmith, and Charles Cutright as delegates; Cutright had been business agent of Seattle Local 38-12 and later secretary of the old San Pedro local. Eighteen Albion Hall-endorsed candidates, including Harry Bridges and Henry Schmidt, won seats on the executive committee of thirty-five. Local 38-79 rented the old Riggers and Stevedores hall at 113 Steuart Street near Mission.

Longshoremen continued to rebel against the Blue Book. The *Waterfront Worker*, produced by the Albion Hall group and written by Bridges, Schmidt, Jones, and others, reported spontaneous demonstrations against showing the book on several docks. With the port still only half organized, the NRA decision seemed to reinforce the company union's power. Walter Petersen of the Waterfront Employers saw ILA strength waning. "The 'Blue Book' will survive," he said, and he was "almost positive that the Government will recognize it as the union to do business with under the N.R.A."[9] Then the employers provoked a confrontation that destroyed their company union.

The minutes of the Executive Committee of Local 38-79 indicate that the union set a trap into which the employers blundered. October 2 they noted the Blue Book

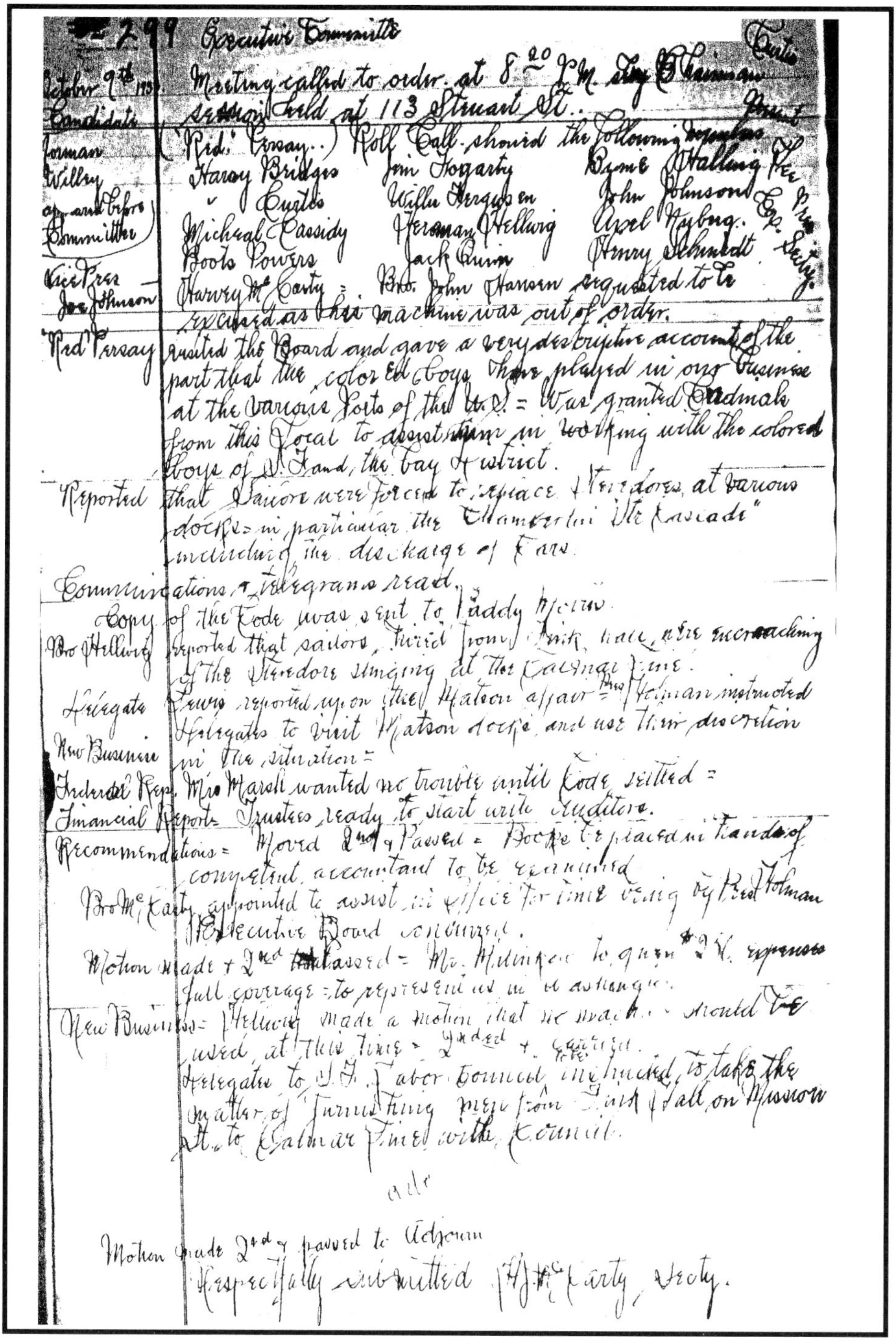

#299 Executive Committee

October 9th 1933 — Meeting called to order at 8:20 P.M. by Chairman [illegible] session held at 113 Steuart St.

Candidate Forman Willey appeared before Committee — ("Red" Prsay..) Roll Call showed the following members:

Harry Bridges, Jim Fogarty, Byrne, Hallwig Pres.
Eugles, Willie Ferguson, John Johnson
Michael Cassidy, Herman Hellwig, Axel Nyburg
Boots Powers, Jack Quinn, Henry Schmidt
Harvey McCarty = Bro. John Hansen requested to be excused as their machine was out of order.

Vice Pres Joe Johnson

"Red" Prsay visited the Board and gave a very descriptive account of the part that the colored boys have played in our business at the various Ports of the U.S. = Was granted credentials from this Local to assist him in working with the colored boys of S.F. and the bay district.

Reported that Sailors were forced to replace Stevedores at various docks = in particular the Chamberlin the Cascade including the discharge of Cars.

Communications & telegrams read.

Copy of the Code was sent to Paddy Morris.

Bro Hellwig reported that sailors, hired from Fink hall, were encroaching of the Stevedores [illegible] at the Calmar Line.

Delegate Lewis reported upon the Matson affair = Pres Holman instructed Delegates to visit Matson docks and use their discretion in the situation =

New Business

Federal Rep. Mrs Marsh wanted no trouble until Code settled =

Financial Report = Trustees ready to start with auditors.

Recommendations = Moved 2nd & Passed = Books be placed in hands of competent accountant to be examined

Bro McCarty appointed to assist in office for time being by Pres Holman. Executive Board concurred.

Motion made & 2nd & passed = Mr. [illegible] to given $25 expenses full coverage = to represent us in [illegible]

New Business = Hellwig made a motion that no machine should be used at this time = 2nded & carried.

Delegates to S.F. Labor Council instructed to take the matter of furnishing men from Fink Hall on Mission St. to Calmar Lines with Council.

Motion made 2nd & passed to Adjourn

Respectfully submitted H.J. McCarty, Secty.

Meeting of the San Francisco ILA Local 38-79 Executive Committee October 9, 1933, plans the Matson confrontation. (Courtesy International Longshore and Warehouse Union Library)

drive to "increase membership as heavy as possible by November 1, 1993" to win recognition under the code. The next item relates, "Matson Foremen say only 2 men on job who are not members of I.L.A." When the Executive Committee met a week later, "Delegate Lewis reported upon the Matson affair. Pres. Holman instructed delegates to visit Matson docks and use their discretion in the situation. Federal Rep. [Ernie] Marsh wanted no trouble until code settled."[10] Thus the union seems to have planned the events that followed.

The next morning, on October 10, Matson fired four ILA members for inefficiency, although one was a fourteen-year employee. Delegate Lynn Hockensmith charged the company fired them for refusing to show their fink books on going to work and demanded their immediate reinstatement. When Matson rejected the demand, 400 longshoremen struck the company at one o'clock. The walkout stopped loading of the *Yale* and unloading of the *Moana*, *Monterey* and *Manulani*. The company recruited unemployed, the crew, and clerks who went down to the dock after office hours to finish loading the *Yale*, which sailed two hours late. Lee Holman warned that unless the strike was settled by noon the next day, all bay shipping would be tied up.

Federal Mediator Marsh proposed that all strikers return to their jobs without discrimination and the men's discharge be arbitrated. The Albion Hall group had another agenda. People distributed handbills on the front calling on longshoremen to extend the strike. By then the *Maunalei* had docked. International President Ryan threatened to tie up all Matson vessels if the strike continued. Twenty-eight non-union longshoremen sent from the port of Crockett departed "after looking the situation over."

The ILA meeting October 12 voted to accept arbitration, defeating a resolution, likely from the Albion Hall group, to strike the entire port, and requested strike sanction from the international as a last resort. Jack Bjorklund notified Tacoma employers that longshoremen would work no Matson ships in Puget Sound unless the company agreed to arbitrate. A conference between Matson operations manager Hugh Gallagher, Lynn Hockensmith, and Bill Lewis ended in a deadlock. Strikers massed at the Matson piers booed and jeered the scabs, and a rock thrown through the window of a car full of scabs injured one. After first refusing, the company agreed to arbitrate.

Following a two-hour meeting between George Creel, regional NRA administrator, and an ILA committee of Charles Cutright, Hockensmith, Henry Smith [Schmidt?], Albin Kullberg, and Roger McKenna, the longshoremen agreed to return to work after the employer dismissed the scabs. The morning of the 14th Matson paid off the scabs and police escorted them to their homes. The strikers returned to work, and Creel appointed the arbitration board. Instead of holding the arbitration, on October 18 Creel's office issued a statement: "The executive committee of the Water Front Employers' Association has consented to an immediate adjustment of all differences that led to a recent strike of longshoremen. This amicable settlement representing the desire of the employers and employees to meet the request of the government obviates the necessity of any decision of the arbitration board, . . ."[11]

Matson reinstated the fired men, and Bill Lewis informed Hugh Gallagher that longshoremen would no longer show their fink books when going to work. The union made a bonfire of the hated books in a vacant lot across the Embarcadero from Pier 32.[12] The Matson victory proved ILA strength and set off the final union surge. Soon longshoremen on all the docks deserted the Blue Book for the ILA. Local 38-79 issued credentials to "Red" Persay, an African-American stevedore to help sign up black longshoremen. Once again San Francisco longshoremen carried union books.

The tempo of organizing increased on the rest of the coast as well. The ILA chartered locals at Astoria and St. Helens on the Columbia River in August, while Paddy Morris organized the small lumber towns of Port Gamble and Port Ludlow on Puget Sound and Port Angeles on the coast. He ranged as far south as San Diego, where the fink hall still controlled the waterfront. In San Pedro thieves broke into the ILA office and stole the membership list. "However," the *Labor Advocate* commented, "the secretary had a copy of the list and the 1,700 men will lose none of their standing because of the employers' pilfering."[13] Longshoremen at Olympia on Puget Sound, Raymond on Willapa Harbor, and the San Francisco ship clerks organized in September and October. The *Advocate* reported September 22 that the ILA had taken in 10,000 new members in the last two months.

Seattle: The Joint Organization Collapses

Seattle longshoremen finally rebelled against the fink hall. The union initiated sixty-two men in September. In a meeting of the fink hall joint committee September 13, employee representatives, including ILA members Bill Craft, Ed Ridley, and F.E. Whelpley, asked a wage increase, an ILA agreement, and control of dispatching. The employers refused, explaining that the increase must come from New York, and they reiterated their determination not to deal with the ILA.

The Communists jumped on the employers' subsequent public statement that men were free to join the ILA. The *Voice of Action*, official organ of the Seattle Unemployed Citizens League that the Party had recently captured, headlined, "I.LA. BETRAYER OF STEVEDORES." The paper charged: "The Seattle I.L.A. is the safest possible pacifier. It has the pretences of a real organization of workers, yet is almost as safe as the company union system, as far as the bosses are concerned. Right under our very nose, in the 'closed shop' of Tacoma, the men have been betrayed by Bjorklund and Paddy Morris."[14]

The MWIU declared: "This plan to officially sponsor the I.L.A. is deliberately planned to behead the growing support to militant industrial unionism."[15] The Communists were wrong. Rather than embracing the ILA, the employers tried to save face and appease their rebellious longshoremen.

The ILA North Atlantic agreement concluded November 4 provided for a 10-cent increase in straight and overtime. With the Blue Book asking for more, San Francisco employers urged Seattle to put the New York increase in effect immediately. When the Joint Executive Committee met November 15, the employers offered the men 85 cents and $1.25, the same as San Francisco offered the company union. The employees rejected the offer, stating they first wanted ILA recognition and believed they would eventually settle for 90 cents and $1.35. The joint committee minutes related:

> The men's committeemen then began resigning as individuals; until a spokesman for the group resigned for the committee as a whole advising this was decided upon under instructions from the local I.L.A. of which all the committeemen were members.
>
> They announced that a new committee of five had been officially appointed by the I.L.A. in whose favor the present committee resigned and requested that the employers recognize them as representing the rank and file.

The employers refused to recognize an ILA committee and condemned the union's coastwide "force program." The minutes continued:

> The men's representatives claim that they want to take over the Dispatching Hall. This claim is based on the desire to compel men to join the union, . . .
>
> The relative indifference of the men's representatives to a wage increase and their desire to do nothing until the I.L.A. demand recognition is still further evidence of the policy of force.
>
> This is further borne out by the decision of the men to force an I.L.A. committee on the employers by disbanding the present one.[16]

Privately the employers feared trouble. They agreed that "all ports on the Pacific Coast would soon be faced with a demand for a single I.L.A. agreement up and down the Coast, and that the employers in every port should be doing something."[17] This time the Seattle employers could not manipulate their employees to recreate the Joint Organization.

The Portland Waterfront Employers announced that they had negotiated an agreement with their longshoremen effective November 14 for 85 cents and $1.25 overtime. The Portland ILA, with about 700 members, vehemently denied the agreement represented genuine collective bargaining. Portland stevedores enforced working rules below those on Puget Sound and paid penalty rates on fewer cargoes covering fewer gang members. The one hour for meals could be changed by mutual consent.

The IWW still believed that the ILA was a tool of the bosses. A Wobbly correspondent wrote from Port Angeles:

> It looks to me as though the employers in the marine industry have dug up from the grave their old stand-by, boss-controlled pet the ILA, to try and stem the tide of the rising revolt in the marine industry. If they can hoodwink the west coast marine industry slaves into agreement again, they figure everything will be rosy for years to come.[18]

Not all longshoremen who had once belonged to the IWW now agreed with this assessment of the ILA. The fink hall years may have convinced many that the Wobblies would never abolish capitalism by the general strike and take over the means of production. Perhaps they decided to settle for the immediate goals of a trade union and signed agreement, which the IWW forbid. Whatever their reasoning, many ex-Wobblies helped to build the ILA during the early 1930s, bringing with them the conviction that militant economic action was the surest way to gain union demands.

Walter Freer, Seattle trucker and Wobbly during World War I, served as president of Local 38-12 by 1923 and held various offices in the union before he moved to Tacoma. Soon he became active in Local 38-3, along with Robert Hardin, another ex-Wobbly. Steve Reay, secretary of Local 38-30, had been a Wobbly before the war. "Big Ed" Harris, secretary-dispatcher of Local 38-3, and others—about fifteen active members—had carried Wobbly cards.

NRA Code Hearings

Although every NRA code guaranteed working people the right to organize unions and bargain collectively without employer interference, nothing in the law compelled employers to sign a code in the first place. The shipping industry, already permitted under the Shipping Act of 1916 to organize and negotiate conference agreements regulating competition, had little to gain from those privileges accorded other industries under NRA codes. Employers and employees did not negotiate labor provisions as equals. Unions might submit proposed labor codes and government representatives might even recommend their adoption, but employers did not have to sign any code that did not please them.

In this inferior position, the Pacific Coast District ILA sent a delegation to the shipping code hearings in Washington, D.C. Paddy Morris, Matt Meehan, secretary of the Portland local, and A.H. Petersen, secretary of the San Pedro local, represented the district. Seattle Local 38-12 sent Bill Craft, and the San Francisco longshoremen paid Henry P. Melnikow of the Pacific Coast Labor Bureau, who represented the Masters, Mates and Pilots and Marine Engineers, an extra $50.00 to speak for them. Hearings were delayed until the ILA settled the North Atlantic agreement. When sessions began November 4, the shipowners proposed a forty-eight-hour week averaged over four weeks and wages of 30 to 40 cents an hour.

The Atlantic and Gulf ILA asked for the new North Atlantic scale of 85 cents and $1.20 overtime on a forty-four-hour week. The Pacific Coast asked $1.00, $1.50 overtime, and a thirty-four-hour week: six hours Monday through Friday and four on Saturday. The $1.00 an hour for six hours totaled $6.00, the same daily wage for which they worked eight hours at 75 cents. In effect, to create more jobs the Pacific District proposed to cut two hours off the workday without decreasing wages. Dr. Boris Stern of the Department of Labor supported the longshoremen's demand for higher wages. He estimated that half of the men earned only a subsistence wage. Raising pay from 85 cents to a $1.00 an hour would increase the cost of freight-handling less than 3 percent, he argued, an amount stevedores could easily pass along. Dr. Stern also proposed government hiring halls.

Following the hearings, the Pacific Coast District held a special convention in Portland November 22-25 to plan strategy. The longshoremen condemned the Stern plan, believing that "the government supervision would leave the fink hall intact in all but name, and it is known that this plan was foisted upon the code hearings by fink hall managers . . . They hope to be continued as fink supervisors of government hiring halls, and against this the longshoremen are adamant."[19] They reiterated their demand "that the hiring of longshoremen in all ports of the Pacific Coast shall be done through the I.L.A. and that I.L.A. men be hired whenever available."[20] The delegates instructed the district secretary to invite the employers in the five major ports to meet and bargain collectively with the district. If they refused to negotiate as a coastwide unit by December 10, the district would send out a referendum ballot on whether or not to strike.

Seattle employers replied that an election would be necessary to determine their employees' representatives. They posted the new scale of 85 cents and $1.25 effective December 11. San Pedro and Portland ignored the ILA letter, and San Francisco employers replied that they negotiated with the Blue Book. After stalling for two months, the company union signed a one-year agreement for 85 cents and $1.25 effective December 10. Tacoma employers put the scale into effect and agreed to meet with the ILA to discuss local issues. Everett employers posted the new rates in the fink hall, where the ILA forced adoption of a virtual list system. The union omitted about forty longshoremen termed incompetent by the employers from the list.

As instructed by the convention, the ILA district office prepared the strike ballots. Instead of sending them out, President Ryan requested the district to take a referendum on what organization the longshoremen wished to have represent them. The district complied. The vote of more than 8,000 for the ILA, over 90 percent of the ballots cast, should have proved conclusively that the ILA represented Pacific Coast longshoremen.

Shipowners Stall Codes

Organized seamen found the NRA equally frustrating. The International Seamen's Union gathered signatures of 12,000 organized and unorganized seamen designating the union to represent them and pledging to join as soon as they were financially able. The union presented these pledges to the NRA. The Pacific District ISU drafted a seamen's code providing $75.00 a month and 75 cents overtime for able seamen and firemen, thirty-four hours a week in port and fifty-six at sea, an improved manning scale, preferential hiring, and all seamen shipped through shipping commissioners. Without waiting for a code, on August 31 the Pacific District unions of the ISU, the Sailors' Union, Marine Firemen, and Marine Cooks and Stewards, presented demands to Pacific Coast shipowners similar to their code proposals. They received no response.

The shipowners' recommended code presented at the November hearings said nothing about wages or hiring. Later they proposed $40.00 a month minimum for able seamen and firemen. The ISU asked $75.00 and the Marine Workers Industrial Union $65.00. The Pacific District ISU appealed to the National Labor Board January 11, 1934, to compel the employers to recognize the union. The board replied that it had no jurisdiction over the shipping industry until the code was signed.

Pacific Coast longshoremen fretted as the union delayed the strike vote pending settlement of the code. The *Labor Advocate* reported that "locals up and down the entire coast are clamoring for prompt action without further delay in taking the vote."[21] Morale was excellent. The longshoremen were united "almost to a man" on union recognition and abolition of the fink hall. The Seattle local, with over 600 members, comprised an amalgam of separate groups. An investigating committee for new applicants named January 18 included Pete Erickson and Robert Collins for the old ILA; Shelvy Daffron, stevedore, and F. Whelpley, trucker, for the employers hall; Louis F. Taggart for the Port Commission; Frank Miller for Alaska Steamship; and E. Johnson for Pacific Steamship Company.

Northwest employers watched unhappily as the ILA grew. They still could not compel their own members to abide by their dispatching rules. A special meeting of dock operators December 21 discussed how to give hall truckers more work to prevent their turning to the ILA. Of the 122 registered truckers, 62 worked for single companies and 60 worked from the casual board. These earned an average of less than $10.00 a week because the companies continued to hire men not registered. Frank Foisie reported in January that in many Sound ports the situation "is passing to the I.L.A." The union completely controlled Port Angeles, "and even where there has been sole employer control in Bellingham," the employers feared the future. The ILA claimed Olympia 100 percent, and Tacoma labor relations were "very unsatisfactory," with a "great deal of propaganda" for union demands. Harvey Wells "did not like the feeling that exists over there among the men." Everett was "growing very critical," according to Joseph Weber, and "employers should very quickly check the authority which the men are taking upon themselves." With the list system in effect, "under which no production can be had," the ILA secretary had become "in effect the dispatcher."[22]

George Creel at San Francisco understood the longshoremen's mood. On January 4, 1934, he wired William H. Davis, shipping code administrator, stressing the need for haste in completing the code, ending the message, "Strike pending." Again January 16 he pleaded with Davis: "Advise me date of creation and method of selection of employee representation stop, Urge utmost care in this respect as attitude of large employers has aroused deep distrust of unions stop. . . . Situation very serious and postponement dangerous stop."[23]

The second shipping code hearings were held January 31 to February 2. The proposed longshore labor provision gave nothing to the Pacific Coast ILA except the promise of recognition and minimum wages below union demands. The employers found new reasons to delay signing the code. The Shipping Board, representing their interests, stepped in to claim the right to regulate the industry, and the American Steamship Owners' Association objected that foreign-flag vessels, carrying 85 percent of foreign trade, could not be brought under the code.

Whatever the shipowners' excuses, West Coast longshoremen would wait no longer. The San Francisco longshoremen requested the district secretary "to submit to all locals of the district the following propositions:"

> First, that the date of our annual convention be advanced from May 7, 1934 to February 25, 1934; that this be held in San Francisco on the ground that San Francisco is being made the center of attack; that when the locals select a delegate they draw up a plan of

> action to enforce our demand; to instruct them how long we will wait before the code is signed before giving an ultimatum; to instruct them as to whether or not they are in favor of taking a strike vote to enforce our demands regarding hours, wages and working conditions.[24]

Some members, including Paddy Morris, considered the convention premature, but they recognized that the locals demanded action and would not be put off. The referendum passed overwhelmingly. To meet the objection that the small Northwest locals could not afford to send delegates to San Francisco, Local 38-79 offered to pay their transportation. Later the convention authorized a 25-cent assessment to pay part of that expense. The *Voice of Action* termed the meeting a "rank and file" convention and stated that "no paid officials are invited to the conference."[25] In fact, the convention was no more or less rank and file than any other, and paid local officers, as well as working longshoremen, served as delegates. All, including the district officers, had both a voice and a vote.

Communist policy changed during these months of ferment among West Coast longshoremen. The official Party program was still to build Trade Union Unity League unions under its hegemony, the MWIU on the waterfront, but as the Party attracted a few followers in the ILA, the line began to change. Whereas the *Waterfront Worker* in San Francisco originally brought forward the MWIU, by September 1933 when Harry Bridges became editor, the paper claimed to speak for the ILA rank and file. Party officials criticized the *Worker* for concentrating on capturing the ILA, rather than recruiting for the MWIU. A dissenting Party member replied that most longshoremen thought the MWIU was primarily for seamen.

In Seattle the *Voice of Action* veered around from a sweeping condemnation of the ILA in early October to asserting two months later that "the rank and file longshoremen [in the ILA] recognize the strong tactics and the fighting program of the Marine Workers Industrial Union." The MWIU stated: "With such a group working within the I.L.A., broadening the rank and file struggle as they broaden organizationally, it will be only a question of time before the Ryans, Paddy Morrises and other gangster elements today in control of the I.L.A. will find it very unhealthy on the Seattle waterfront."[26]

According to Tacoma longshoreman T.A. "Tiny" Thronson, Communists worked skillfully within the ILA or any union. They came to a meeting with a set agenda and positioned their members strategically in the hall. If outnumbered, they prolonged the meeting until late in the evening, waiting for rank and filers to go home. With these tactics a minority controlled meetings.

The San Francisco Convention

Fifty-four delegates from seventeen ports assembled Sunday, February 25, 1934, for the district ILA convention in San Francisco, and six small locals, five in the Northwest, sent proxy votes. To allow the new locals full representation, the convention based voting strength on average per capita tax paid August through

January, rather than since the last convention in May. A local had one vote for every 100 members or fraction thereof, and the district officers one-half vote each. The eighty-three votes probably represented 7,500 paid up members. After the first day District President Dewey Bennett relinquished the chair because of a bad cold. Paddy Morris defeated Harry Bridges for temporary chair, and the convention reelected him daily.

The delegates were determined to force their employers to bargain. They elected a committee by area caucuses to meet with the Waterfront Employers March 5: A.H. Petersen, San Pedro; Bill Lewis, San Francisco; Jack Ahern of Portland, Columbia River; Ed Krumholz of Aberdeen, Willapa and Grays Harbor; and George Miller of Tacoma, Puget Sound, plus District President Dewey Bennett and Secretary Jack Bjorklund. They wired President Roosevelt, NRA Administrator Hugh Johnson, Shipping Code Administrator John Weaver, Senator Robert Wagner, chairman of the National Labor Board, and ILA President Ryan:

> Administrator Weaver's non-insistence upon adequate protection for the longshore industry has forced the Pacific Coast District longshoremen . . . to take steps to protect their own welfare and force collective bargaining to obtain our original demands stop. The action of the government in not providing a code proves that it is either impotent or negligent stop. We have today passed resolutions giving the shipowners and operators until March 7, 1934, to meet with us for this purpose stop.[27]

The question of whether to stay in session Sunday and then adjourn, or recess Sunday and wait to hear the negotiating committee's report of the meeting Monday provoked a roll call vote. San Pedro proposed the early adjournment to save delegates the expense of an extra day. Paddy Morris left the chair to urge the delegates not to adjourn before hearing the report of the meeting with the employers. He warned that if the convention adjourned without a definite answer from the employers and a concrete plan of action, "outside forces" would work on local unions "and inside of a week you will have a dozen individual locals out in a dozen individual strikes."[28] This, he feared, would destroy the locals. Morris probably referred to the Communists, whose current strategy encouraged quickie strikes by ships' crews and longshoremen. The roll call to recess Sunday and thus prolong the convention carried 49.49 to 32.51. The half of the San Francisco delegation that voted consistently with the Communist bloc and several delegates who wanted to go home early joined San Pedro in the minority vote.

On the Embarcadero a *Waterfront Worker* extra headlined, "FAKERS MOVE FOR BETRAYAL!" accusing Morris, Bjorklund, and Pedro Pete (A.H. Petersen) of supporting the Ryan Plan for government fink halls. It urged longshoremen to "clean house of these fakers" and "elect rank & file officials." A cartoon showed King Morris ruling delegates out of order and Bjorklund altering the minutes on Morris's orders.[29]

In reply to Joe Ryan's telegram cautioning the convention against radicals in certain ports who were "dissatisfied with the Ryan and Bjorklund conservative type of leader-

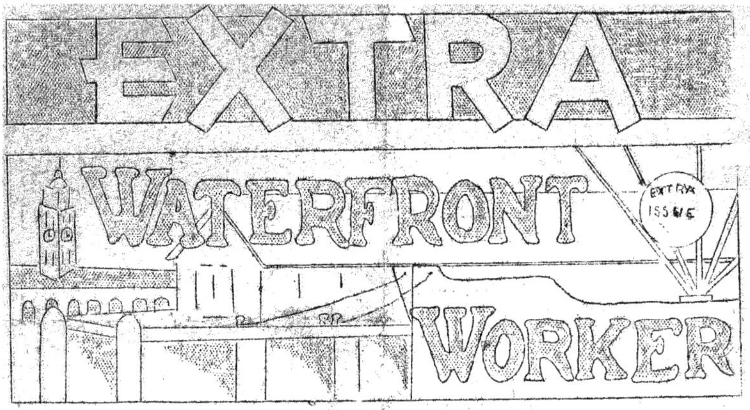

FAKERS MOVE FOR BETRAYAL!

The West Coast Dist. Convention of the ILA, has overwhelmingly voted
down the Ryan Plan: the system of Gov't Fink Halls, designed to remove
50,000 men from the industry--with compusory arbitration thru a "Nat'a
Ind. Relations Board". This plan, which Morris, Bjorklund, and Pedro Pet
have been attempting to railroad thru--one piece at a time, has been exposed in the Waterfront Worker time after time. Locals such as Portlan
& Tacoma, who in the past, endorsed the phoney Portland Convention, ar
now aware of the true nature of the Ryan Plan.

The W.F.W. now warns the men that they must BEWARE OF INTRODUCTION O
ANY PART OF THIS PHONEY SKUNK PLAN BY THE BACK DOOR, WHICH THE FAKERS AR
NOW TRYING TO DO. THAT IS, BEWARE OF MEDIATION--REGIONAL OR OTHERWISE! IT
THREATENS THE UNITY OF THE COAST! INSIST ON DIRECT NEGOTIATIONS WITH THE
SHIPOWNERS-ALL AGREEMENTS SUBMITTED TO BE VOTED BY THE MEMBERSHIP BEFORE
FINAL ACCEPTANCE.

Also, the Convention will not have completed it's work if it has not
laid a solid basis for united action with teamsters and seamen. Already,
we are informed, an ILA local in Norfolk, Va., (Coal Trimmers) is winning
back jobs because seamen, organized in the Marine Workers Ind. Union,
have struck, demanding that they no longer be forced to trim coal.

We must clean house of these fakers! Elect Rank & File officials who
will honestly work for the best interests of the members--not themselves

FOR THE RANK AND FILE CODE! FOR COAST-WISE RECOGNITION!

FOR UNITY OF ALL MARINE WORKERS!!

Waterfront Worker *attacking the incumbent majority in the Pacific Coast District ILA convention, San Francisco, February 1934. (Author's Collection)*

ship,"[30] the delegates wired back "that each and every and all locals on the Pacific Coast are 100 percent loyal to the International Longshoremen's Association."[31] Having disposed of the rumor of a split in the union, the delegates passed the major strategy resolution signed by seventeen members of Local 38-79, including Harry Bridges and Bill Lewis, leaders of the opposing factions in the San Francisco local. The resolution as amended provided:

1. That we negotiate and deal with the shipowners only as a district.
2. Recognition of the ILA, embodying our original demands.
3. That we will not arbitrate these demands on the grounds we have nothing to arbitrate.
4. If favorable consideration is not given these demands by March 7, negotiations shall be broken off and a date shall be set not later than ten days after the convention, to take a strike vote by the Pacific Coast District.[32]

During the debate on the strike vote Paddy Morris urged the delegates: "You want to be sure that you do this one thing and that is that you get every damned member in the local to vote if you think the time has come to strike, try and educate your fellow member to that effect also. FOR IF WE DO TAKE A STRIKE VOTE, FOR GOD'S SAKE MAKE IT A BIG REPRESENTATIVE VOTE. DO THE JOB WELL AND NOT HALF-HEARTEDLY."[33]

Thus armed with a plan of action, the ILA committee met with the Waterfront Employers. As the longshoremen anticipated, the session accomplished nothing. Thomas G. Plant of American-Hawaiian, president of the Waterfront Employers, headed the shipowners' committee. He repeated that they could only represent San Francisco, that the employers could not form a coastwide bargaining organization because different operators belonged to the waterfront employers in each port. The longshoremen argued that in fact the employers cooperated as a coastwide unit on such issues as wages.

Then, according to Jack Bjorklund, Plant asked what the longshoremen wanted. "So I explained . . . that we wanted recognition of our organization. He said that was closed shop. I said, absolutely! He said that was absolutely out of the question,"[34] claiming the closed shop was illegal under the NRA. A.H. Petersen pointed out that East Coast shipowners had signed a closed-shop agreement with the ILA. The employers replied "that the shipowners on the East Coast take one view of the Recovery Act and the shipowners on the West Coast were taking an entirely different view of it."[35]

Bjorklund warned that "when you say that you cannot deal for these other ports and then these other ports pass the buck on and state that they cannot do anything unless they do it in San Francisco, that will not go," because "the men have exhausted all the patience within them to tolerate"[36] conditions in some ports. He read the employers a statement: "We were instructed from the convention to notify the shipowners that in the event they did not meet with us by March 7th, the deadline was set and we would then proceed to take a strike vote."[37] When the employers objected to "radicalism" in the ILA, Bjorklund replied that they created Communists by exploiting workers.

The ILA committee reported back to the convention that the employers refused to grant recognition or the closed shop. Jack Ahern declared that "you couldn't have convinced those fellows with anything, for no matter what you said they had an answer for it. As soon as we walked in we might just as well have walked out, for it was useless to bring up anything; . . ."[38] Harry Bridges made a long speech criticizing the committee's report and advocating strike action. He commented on the shipowners' objections to radicals:

> I notice today that we are all radicals, because the conservative policy was voted down. . . . Also they all say this fighting and arguing and bickering will not get us anything, and so forth, and that is the question where the radical element comes up. That is why they class me under the radical element. I have never denied it. . . .
>
> That is their pet scheme and idea to point out a few men whom they say are disrupting their organization; they simply point that out because these few men with the best interests of their organization at heart want to strike; and it is my idea that we should pursue such a course in our organization to get what we should have, and not what they want to give us. If they won't consent, we must force it. That is my idea and I think the rest of the delegates think along the same lines, and I don't think that they are "Reds" either.[39]

Bridges urged the delegates not to "take any notice of what the shipowners think or say about us" and elect district officers "who are not favorable to the shipowners." Stung by the tone of the speech, Petersen fired back:

> Brother Bridges talked about the strike under the radical element. Has nobody else ever been on strike? Remember, Mr. Bridges, the radical element never ended a strike, nor can they claim the strike as their foster-child. Many of us who have advocated trying to go along conservative lines are just as much in favor of going out on strike if the necessity arises as any radical.[40]

Bjorklund jumped in: "As for the radical element, you claim that you are a radical. I don't know how radical you are. I believe with Brother Petersen that it is not the radicals who do the fighting for organization on the Pacific Coast and get results. I have been on more strikes than most of the men around here, and I have been called a radical and now I am called a conservative."[41]

Paddy Morris reminded the delegates that "we have a very much more serious proposition before us" than fighting about radicals or conservatives. He continued:

> I want to say this, however, on the question of radicals and conservatives, that while the radicals were prating about strikes in theory, the conservatives were out practicing it, while the radicals preached and prated about it. I am also a radical. But I do know this that the employers can use the term radical and conservative and they will do so if they think they can split us. . . .
>
> As I told you once before, it doesn't make any difference to the boss whether you are a radical or a conservative. The main consideration and thing is, are you trying to put your hand in his pocket and take some of his money out. . . . Now, boys don't think that

> the business man is worrying about the radical or the conservative element, for he is not. But when he sees a group of men getting together, he immediately thinks they want to take some of his dough away from him. That is why we are here, to get some of his dough; slip our hands into his pocket and get some dough out, and if we cannot do it peaceably we will try to get it in some other way, the best possible means of doing so.[42]

ILA District Constitution

While they waited for the meeting with the Waterfront Employers, the delegates took care of other business in this first regular convention of the reorganized Pacific Coast District. In the nine months since the last convention, the California ports had organized and membership had increased almost tenfold. Most importantly, the delegates needed to write a new district constitution. Debate centered around the method of election and recall of officers. The convention provided for a nine-member executive board, three from each state, including a president and secretary, no two from the same local. Communist bloc delegates opposed geographical representation, contending that the best men should be elected, no matter how many came from the same local or state. The constitution provided for a referendum to recall officers "upon written demand of 20 percent of the membership."[43]

Communist front organizations received a cold reception. The convention denied admittance to delegations from the Marine Workers Industrial Union and the International Labor Defense. The body passed a motion by Titus Humphrey, an African-American delegate from Local 38-79, calling on members to oppose racial discrimination and give equal consideration to blacks and whites. The delegates concurred in a resolution from Local 38-3 to work for a blanket ILA agreement with a common expiration date for all districts, and one from Local 38-79 to establish gang committees on each dock to handle grievances and enforce union rules.

A resolution from Local 38-12 instructed the incoming executive board to work for formation of a waterfront federation, and one by members of Local 38-79 instructed the board "to have ILA locals in each Pacific Coast Port, to call port conferences of all Marine Unions and Marine Workers, whether organized or unorganized. These conferences to be called for the purpose to organize united support behind our demands."[44] Based on information from Joe Ryan that the code would likely be signed on March 22, the convention adopted a resolution from Tacoma delegates to strike March 23 "if our strike demands are not met by our employers on March 22nd."[45]

The international would pay salaries of $60.00 a week, the amount international organizers received, to the district president and secretary, provided the Pacific Coast District located one office in the north and the other in the center or south. Election of officers at the close of the convention followed factional lines. Communist bloc candidate Henry Schmidt of San Francisco Local 38-79 received 15-3/4 votes for president, from half of the Local 38-79 delegates, Pilcher and Isaksen of Everett with their Anacortes proxy, Houly of Raymond, and Adams of Portland. Elmer Bruce of San Pedro Local 38-82, supported by the ex-Wobblies, received 23-2/5 votes, from the San Pedro delegates and their San Diego proxy, Krumholz of Aberdeen, and one Seattle delegate. Bill Lewis of San Francisco Local 38-79 received 43-17/20 votes, a clear majority from the rest of the convention. The body reelected Jack Bjorklund secretary-treasurer by acclamation. Delegates caucused by states to nominate executive board members.

Over the years the Pacific Coast District had survived internal fights. Radicals and conservatives had dominated conventions and district offices. Within the ILA, Socialist Labor Party adherent Paddy Morris worked with Democratic Party regular Jack Bjorklund. Regardless of political differences, they trusted each other.

During these years, for the first time, a few members followed the instructions of an outside group in matters traditionally considered internal union business. The directives that governed these members came from the Communist International, which decreed that in all mass organizations, "even if there are only two Party members in such organizations and bodies, Communist factions must be formed for the purpose of strengthening the Party's influence and for carrying out its policies in these organizations and bodies."[46] The Executive Committee of the Communist International directed that the factions "must be subordinate to corresponding Party organs— . . . Such Party organs must issue the necessary instructions to the communist factions . . . in accordance with the directives received from the higher Party organs. . . . In all questions on which decisions were made by corresponding Party organizations the factions must strictly abide by these decisions."[47]

The Central Committee of the Communist Party U.S.A. instructed new members in 1932: "From now on, the decisions of the Party and the decisions of the Communist International are your highest commands."[48] Anti-Communists in the ILA and other unions objected not so much to Communist "radicalism," which many refused to acknowledge as authentic, but to people carrying out the Party line rather than acting on their own convictions. On many issues their policies might coincide, as they did in the district convention, but in a showdown the Party would come first and the ILA second. Union members could not trust people thus committed. For this reason anti-Communists of all descriptions would unite to keep Communists from capturing their organizations.

Strike Vote

The delegates returned to their home ports to prepare for the strike that seemed inevitable. After a final meeting March 7, at which the Waterfront Employers again refused to bargain coastwide or consider a closed-shop agreement, the district ILA put out the strike ballot. The vote to strike was 6,616 to 599 (92 percent), with Anacortes the only local voting no.

After almost a year of futile talking the longshoremen would use their strongest weapon: economic action. They shared no part of the recovery in the shipping industry. The rising cost of living threatened their average wage of $40.00 a month, which yielded a bare subsistence. The 10-cent raise the beginning of the year did not compensate for the climb in retail prices since then. Mechanization decreased jobs, as much as 30 percent on some docks, and larger loads and speedup increased accidents and injuries. February became the worst month for accidents since the passage of the Longshoremen and Harbor Workers Act. Only elimination of the open shop and fink hall could change these wretched conditions.

Neither the Communists nor the Wobblies believed the ILA would fight. The *Voice of Action* declared: "Nothing would please some of the I.L.A. officials and the shipowners, who have been working close together, than to smash the strike in the beginning and hogtie the membership to compulsory arbitration, decasualization plan, etc., which has been in the back of their minds from the beginning."[49] The *Industrial Worker* warned that ILA officials would sign a meaningless agreement and thus prevent a strike.

Contrary to the predictions of their critics, union longshoremen geared up for war. They called on labor to boycott firms using struck ships to carry their freight. The Tacoma ILA warned members not to buy major items on monthly installments and advised them to establish credit at a grocery store and butcher shop. After years of resistance, the Tacoma Lumber Handlers voted to amalgamate with the general cargo local. The employers had tried to play the unions off against each other, but the increase in mixed cargoes finally persuaded the lumber local to merge. The new Local 38-97 received a charter on April 1, 1934.

The Sailors' Union had been watching intently as the strike threat developed, speculating on the longshoremen's chances of success and wondering how seamen would respond to picket lines. Bill Lewis talked with Pete Gill, Seattle agent, whom he knew from his days as a steam schooner sailor before coming ashore to work on the San Francisco docks. Of the SUP officials, Lewis believed Gill would be most sympathetic to the longshoremen. At the San Francisco headquarters meeting March 19 the union advised members under agreement to continue to work, but "that our members in all other vessels, especially in the steam schooners, be advised to leave such vessels in case a strike is called by the longshoremen and that in doing so they are not merely doing so out of sympathy with the strikers but also because of the low wages and rotten conditions prevailing."[50]

The San Francisco Waterfront Employers also prepared for the strike. In full-page ads in Bay area newspapers March 19 and 21 they warned longshoremen "that if you strike, it is your own act . . . It is your own job and your livelihood that you give up. The ships will be kept working."[51] Up and down the coast employers planned to recruit scabs from among the unemployed. Although publicly employers deplored the strike, George Creel related in a letter to the National Labor Board, "The shippers are confident of victory and gave me to understand confidentially that even if they lost two or three million, it would be worth that to destroy the union."[52] The *Pacific Shipper* called the closed-shop demand un-American—the issue was "whether the I.L.A. shall dictate to the employers." Collective bargaining was "merely the pretext of labor leaders mad for power."[53]

On the eve of the strike the *Labor Advocate* condemned the outrageous position of the shipping companies: "rather than yield one iota of their autocratic and despotic position, the companies would force upon the coast a strike." The paper cited the government's generosity to the industry in mail subsidies, loans, and sales of ships, concluding: "It is the same organization of shipping concerns which now presents an iron front against any such concessions as recognition of the union and are preparing with the dollars given them by the American people to crush labor organizations on this coast."[54] March 21 the ILA District Executive Board refused requests from Senator Wagner and ILA President Ryan to take no drastic action. Bill Lewis wired Ryan: "The sentiment of the men is so strong that a strike cannot be averted unless the President intervenes."[55]

April 3 Agreement

March 22: With the longshoremen ready to strike the next morning, President Roosevelt wired District President Lewis urging him to call off the strike until an impartial board could be appointed to conduct hearings and make recommendations for settlement of the controversy. With the deadline only hours away, Lewis polled district executive board members up and down the coast. Reluctantly they agreed to accede to the President's request. Lewis wired Roosevelt:

> Strike order by virtually unanimous vote of longshoremen of the Pacific Coast represent the deepest conviction of 12,000 workers that justice could not be had except by showing our economic strength.
>
> In compliance with your request, however, we are postponing strike action at this time under your pledge to appoint an impartial commission to conduct hearings and make recommendations, believing that the evidence of the justice of our cause is bound to change present unbearable conditions.[56]

Some locals criticized Lewis for delaying the strike. The Communists tried to exploit the situation: "LONGSHORE STRIKE BETRAYED!" the *Voice of Action* proclaimed in a banner head. After a heated debate the San Francisco longshoremen concurred in the postponement because, Local 38-79 stated:

> We realized that Lewis had been placed in a pretty tough spot at the very last minute almost by the President's request when Roosevelt should have sent his request for cooperation to the shipowners who have stalled both the code and our demands for many months . . . Consequently the Frisco I.L.A. resolved that the strike committee of the San Francisco bay district concurred in the action of the Pacific Coast board, including President Lewis in postponing the strike at the request of the President of the United States.[57]

President Roosevelt appointed a Mediation Board composed of the chairmen of Regional Labor boards: Judge Charles A. Reynolds of Seattle, Dean Henry F. Grady of San Francisco, and Dr. J.L. Leonard of Los Angeles. The board held hearings in San Francisco March 28-31, attended by the ILA District Executive Board and representatives of the waterfront employers of San Francisco, Seattle, and Portland. Los Angeles employers refused to attend. The board recommended that the Regional

Labor boards hold representation elections, that joint hiring halls be operated in each port, and that an arbitration board determine wages and hours for the entire coast.

The San Francisco employers rejected the board's recommendations on April 3, reiterating their position that each port must be treated separately. They agreed to recognize and bargain with the ILA for San Francisco only and proposed to establish a joint hiring hall. The ILA District Executive Board accepted the "gentlemen's agreement with reluctance but in the spirit of peace." The Regional Labor boards would hold elections in other ports. Three days of meetings between employers and the ILA produced no results. The Mediation Board on April 7 rejected the longshoremen's demand for a coastwide settlement as contrary to the April 3 agreement. In a stormy meeting April 9, in which a strong minority led by Harry Bridges opposed acceptance, Local 38-79 approved the April 3 agreement. The district officers turned over negotiations to the San Francisco local and returned to their home ports.

Local 38-79 suspended President Lee Holman from office for exceeding his authority and refused President Ryan's request to reinstate him. Holman had told the Mediation Board he opposed coastwide bargaining and the coastwide strike vote. As expected, Regional Labor Board elections in other ports yielded overwhelming majorities for the ILA. After a lively discussion a meeting of 550 members in Portland April 8 defeated a proposal to strike immediately and voted to go along with the district. Down south the employers formed the Longshoremen's Mutual Protective Association of Los Angeles and Long Beach Harbors, a company union claiming 300 members.

The San Francisco talks, which began April 16, yielded minimal progress. With wages and hours issues deadlocked, the longshoremen invoked mediation. On April 30 Local 38-79 notified the Waterfront Employers "that unless something definite shall have been arrived at," by Monday evening, May 7, negotiations would be discontinued.[58] Mediation sessions May 2-5 produced nothing. May 6 the ILA refused the employers' proposal for national mediation. May 7 Tom Plant dispatched a letter to Bill Lewis, hand-carried, proposing that the employers issue a statement on the progress of negotiations. After reading the letter Lewis told the messenger there would be no answer.

Senator Wagner appealed to the district not to strike, seconded by wires to all locals from President Ryan directing compliance with the National Labor Board chairman's request. The district refused to postpone the strike. President Bill Lewis instructed Secretary Jack Bjorklund to wire all locals to vote immediately on whether to strike Wednesday, May 9, at 8:00 a.m. The meeting May 7 of 1,500 members of Local 38-79 broke off negotiations and voted to strike.

May 8

All along the coast stevedore bosses worked their gangs extra hours to finish loading and clear vessels before the strike. In a full-page newspaper ad addressed to the longshoremen of the San Francisco Bay area, the Waterfront Employers again warned against the strike. Speaking for the district, Bill Lewis told the press: "No one, not even President Roosevelt, can stop this strike now except an agreement on the part of our employers to conform to our demands."[59] Dean Grady wired from Washington, D.C., to delay strike action, and Dr. Leonard flew to San Francisco to persuade Lewis to postpone the walkout. The district president could not be found, and no one in the ILA hall knew where he was.

But behind the defiant words of Lewis, the union worried about how solid the men actually were in key ports. By the morning of the 8th the ILA district secretary had strike votes back from every local except Seattle and San Pedro, major ports that must strike. Jack Bjorklund persuaded San Pedro to call a stop-work meeting for that night and wire the results to him. Many Tacoma longshoremen considered Seattle the weakest link on the coast, in spite of the March strike vote of 995 to 92. Bjorklund suggested to Pete Erickson, president of Local 38-12 and a strong union man, that the Seattle union call a mass meeting of all longshoremen that evening and take a strike vote.

About 1,500 men attended the meeting, including many nonmembers. Delegations from Everett and Tacoma urged the Seattle longshoremen to strike. By eight o'clock people began to drift away, not wanting to be counted. "Bolt the door!" President Erickson shouted, and the meeting continued. Sentiment wavered. Some wanted to wait for strike authorization from President Ryan, who had urged postponement. A wire from Senator Homer T. Bone, former labor attorney, also pleaded for delay.

The first vote showed 60 percent against striking, but the local president kept the meeting in session while waiting for news from San Pedro. Near midnight Jack Bjorklund arrived with a wire that a meeting of 1,000 men in San Pedro voted to strike. The crowd cheered the news. Then someone asked if the telegram was a true copy. Bjorklund replied that they would have to take his word. After more discussion, at one o'clock in the morning, by voice vote the meeting reconsidered the previous action and voted to strike. On the docks nearby, gangs worked all night to finish loading vessels.

With this shaky support in the largest Northwest port, the strike was on. In a few hours the battle would begin: the struggle that would determine the future of unions on the Pacific Coast.

5

Strike!

On Wednesday, May 9, at 8:00 a.m., 12,000 longshoremen struck Pacific Coast ports from Bellingham, fifty miles below the Canadian border, to San Diego, twenty miles above the Mexican border—almost 1,700 miles of coastline. In Seattle 2,000 struck (including nonunion men)—700 in Tacoma—1,100 in Portland—3,000 in San Francisco—and 1,800 in San Pedro. The small ports struck solidly, 250 in Grays Harbor and Everett, 150 in Olympia, and so on. Unorganized longshoremen in Eureka joined the strike. The *Labor Advocate* summed up:

> They listened to the promises of the NRA; they harkened to the pleading of Senator Wagner; they obeyed the request as a command of President Roosevelt and they got in return—nothing. . . .
>
> The end had been reached at last. The patience they had so enduringly shown, the control they had so determinedly manifested had reached the end. The strike became not merely a necessity. It had become the only step that manhood could take against oppression, repression and industrial serfdom.[1]

The waterfronts remained relatively quiet the first day. In Seattle the union put out a token force of 300 pickets. Encouraged by the reluctant vote, the Waterfront Employers believed the longshoremen would change their minds about striking. In Tacoma and Portland the ILA told off members into squads and shifts and prepared to picket in force. At San Francisco, District President Lewis met with Teamsters Union officers. He reported later:

> Having been through several previous strikes in San Francisco, I realized the necessity of having the teamsters help. If the teamsters are on strike in San Francisco, it is virtually a general strike. The teamsters were contacted and their aid was asked, . . . They were distinctly told that we expected more than just a refusal to go on the dock proper; for the 1919 strike was broken through this means. They agreed to cooperate to the best of their ability.[2]

On the Embarcadero police, many on motorcycles, charged a crowd of strikers trying to stop scabs being delivered in an armored van to the floating scab hotel *Diana Dollar* at Pier 22. Police arrested several pickets. They dispersed 500 strikers gathered at the Luckenbach docks, where a gang of black longshoremen worked. The other remaining nonunion black gang struck with the ILA. In San Pedro the Marine Service Bureau claimed 300 scabs were working or standing by—the union said 40 scabs.

Portland longshoremen picketing the S.S. Wiliboro *at Municipal Terminal No. 1, May 9, 1934. (* Morning Oregonian, *courtesy Oregon Historical Society, OrHi neg. 81702)*

The relative quiet lasted one day. On May 10 the war began as employers in the four largest ports prepared to work cargo with scabs and strikers mobilized their resources to keep the ports closed. Bill Lewis declared for the ILA: "The men will remain out until our demands are met by the employers. The strike will be carried on to the finish."[3]

Portland

"STRIKERS IN CONTROL!" the *Portland News-Telegram* headlined. "Crews Employed to Work Ships Trapped in Employers' Hall – Police Chief Threatens Strikers With Action – Lunches for Besieged Group Go to Union Forces."[4] The ILA won the first round. The Waterfront Employers notified all registered longshoremen to report to the fink hall May 10 or be dropped from the rolls, and advertised for 500 scabs. Instead of scores of penitent strikers, about 150 young scabs showed up. Soon 600 strikers surrounded the fink hall. Shortly after 9:30 a.m. a bus drove up to take gangs to work. "Tip her over," the crowd shouted, and as the men began to rock the bus the driver jumped. Strikers climbed in and promptly filled the seats. Police persuaded them to leave the bus peacefully, "but by the time the bus was again ready for the strikebreakers, there was no air in the tires." The disabled bus was towed away, and a second bus drove up. A nineteen-year-old scab emerging from the building met a fist in his face. Police attempting to escort scabs to the bus gave up when strikers pushed them back, and the bus drove away to prevent damage.

Then Police Chief B.L. Lawson arrived with a tear gas squad of thirty men. Strikers met with silence his threat of police action if they prevented scabs from leaving and proceeding to the docks. He left shortly after, promising to return at the "first hint of violence." The strikers blockaded the fink hall all day, "good-natured but menacing, using their fists whenever arguments failed, but letting the other side make the first move," the *News-Telegram* reported. The strikers bought out a caterer who arrived with box lunches for the men inside. The crowd in the hall dwindled as the scabs, mostly youth seventeen to nineteen years old, came out and surrendered their work cards. After keeping them imprisoned for ten hours, the picket allowed the rest to leave with the admonition not to scab.

With twenty-four vessels tied up, the sixteen-mile waterfront became a "seething threat of mass action." The strikers released all perishables on the docks and 2,400 sacks of sugar for canneries processing farmers' berries. Union members and unorganized seamen left their vessels. After the Central Labor Council declared the steamship companies unfair, the Teamsters pledged not to haul to or from the docks.

Defeated the first day, the waterfront employers and Portland police prepared for a showdown. The city hired 125 extra waterfront police. Of those who applied for the

Police protect scabs leaving fink hall from angry strikers, Portland, May 11, 1934. (Morning Oregonian*, courtesy Oregon Historical Society, OrHi neg. 81704)*

jobs, the department rejected eight because of criminal records. Employers reportedly paid scab herders $2.00 a head for recruits. This time, instead of a defenseless bus, the employers brought a truck surrounded by prowl cars to the fink hall. While police held strikers at bay, scabs dashed from the hall to the truck, and the convoy proceeded to the McCormick terminal. A fight started in front of the dock when pickets stopped the truck and began pulling out scabs. Reinforcements rushed from the ILA hall. About 1,000 strikers fought hand to hand with police, disarming 16 special deputies and chasing away a squad of 20 or more before they reached the dock gates.

At the Luckenbach dock strikers sifted through police lines and persuaded a gang of scabs not to work. After a convoy of police and deputy sheriffs delivered a crew of scabs to Pier B of Municipal Terminal 1, strikers rushed the gate and drove off the strikebreakers in a free-for-all fight. At the McCormick terminal 400 unarmed strikers swept past 26 specials armed with guns and clubs, battered through two barricades, and stoned and boarded the *Admiral Evans*, which had arrived from Astoria to house scabs. Finding no scabs, they beat several police officers and threw one overboard to swim to shore. The strikers allowed the gang of twenty-five scabs to leave the dock after handing over their work cards, and they permitted another forty to leave the fink hall toward evening.

Police arrested four strikers, reputed to be a "strong arm squad." Chief Lawson threatened to use "tear gas—then bullets." For the third day scabs worked no vessels. The *News-Telegram* commented: "There was rough stuff in the wake of the strike, and prospects of more bitter fighting as the grim workers of the waterfront made their stand, knowing that if they fail there will be 1100 permanent vacancies where they once worked."[5]

The City Council appealed to President Roosevelt to settle the strike, and Mayor Joseph Carson, Jr., and Sheriff Martin Pratt of Multnomah County requested Governor Julius L. Meier to call out the National Guard. The Central Labor Council replied to the militia threat with a resolution May 14 "that we favor and will advocate a general strike of all workers if and when the guard is called out to police the waterfront."[6] Labor people expected seventy-five uptown unions to strike if the governor summoned troops.

The last eleven longshoremen who had remained at work, winch drivers and gang bosses, quit May 14 and joined the strikers. As penalty for holding out, the union sentenced them to carry picket banners in front of the fink hall. In accordance with instructions from the Waterfront Employers' Union in San Francisco, fifty-one steamship companies announced they would quit calling at Portland if the port did not provide adequate protection by noon May 15. The next day the employers closed the fink hall and suspended operations.

Seattle

In contrast to the fierce resistance Portland employers encountered, Seattle shipowners met little opposition as they recruited scabs to work the fourteen vessels in port. On May 10, 150 scabs worked on three piers. The employers towed laid-up vessels to docks for "floating boarding houses," the *Admiral Rogers* to Pier 41, the *Queen* to Pacific Steamship terminal, and the *Redondo* to Pier 2. On Senator Wagner's plea for arbitration, the Teamsters Union reversed its earlier promise of support. The next day 200 scabs worked six vessels. Sheriff Claude Bannick deputized 100 guards, claiming that radicals had threatened to fire the docks. Teamsters hauled goods to and from the piers.

Bert Farmer, assigned by the Everett strike committee to stiffen up the Seattle strike, blamed Local 38-12's weakness on "the fact there was five factions of men united into one hall and were not familiar with who was who and all hanging around the hall waiting for the next man to do something and had no men on the picket line consequently the docks were full of strikebreakers."[7]

The employers recruited about 100 students from University of Washington fraternity houses to scab at 5 cents over the regular scale. The student body demanded they be suspended from school, and the U. of W. *Daily* said editorially: "Judas sold his soul for thirty pieces of silver, according to the Bible, and the university students today are offered the chance to sell their self-respect and the good-will of the university for ninety cents an hour."[8] President Hugo Winkenwerder warned that students cutting classes to work would get no credit for courses, but when anonymous leaflets appeared on the campus inviting students to participate in a waterfront demonstration, Winkenwerder declared: "I am even more opposed to the efforts to enlist students to take part in demonstrations."[9] Scabs might be bad, but Communists were worse. The ivory tower must remain intact.

Everett longshoremen came out solidly. At Grays Harbor employers tried to load three vessels, and one gang worked at Port Angeles. Anacortes longshoremen, who had returned their ILA charter, refused to cross picket lines of strikers from Bellingham. The strike wave spilled over into Canada May 12 when the Vancouver and District Waterfront Workers' Association voted 602 to 223 to strike if negotiations with the British Columbia Shipping Federation did not yield a satisfactory agreement, and Vancouver and Victoria longshoremen voted to refuse to "handle trans-shipments from Seattle or to Seattle from struck ships,"[10] plugging a loophole in the strike across the border.

In Tacoma the Waterfront Employers made no move to recruit scabs to work the five idle vessels. Nor did they request extra police. The union held daily meetings and maintained four-hour picket watches around the clock. When the steam schooner *Lake Francis* docked at the Defiance Mill May 10, the seven crew members struck, leaving master and mates to move the vessel to Seattle.

Although Tacoma strikers controlled their port, ominous news came from the rest of the coast: disaster threatened the strike. The union called a special meeting for 5:00 a.m. Saturday, May 12. Members recalled bitter memories of the 1916 defeat. If they could close up Seattle the strike had a chance of success. Six hundred Tacoma members piled into trucks and headed for Seattle, where 150 Everett longshoremen joined them. Paddy Morris, who chaired the Tacoma strike committee, likely planned the joint venture with his old friend in Everett, Tom Mason. They did not approach

Seattle longshoremen. After the spectacle of the strike vote meeting and their desultory picketing, Tacoma had little faith in them. The *Seattle Post-Intelligencer* headlined the action: "2,000 Longshore Strikers Raid 12 Ships; Stop Work; 'No Troops Now,'—[Governor] Martin."[11]

The raid began about 8:30 at the McCormick Piers 6 and 7, where the strikers, led by George Soule of the Tacoma Flying Squad, wrecked the wooden barriers and rushed to where the steamers *Lake Francis* and *Silverado* were loading. The men boarded the vessels and hauled off the scabs. They smashed several heads in the fight and threw the foreman of Pier 7 into the water when he resisted. The raiders then split into two groups, one under Soule and the other led by Big Ed Harris, Tacoma ILA secretary. Strikers from Local 38-12, striking seamen, sympathetic teamsters, loggers, and other workers swelled their ranks as the strikers moved south along the waterfront, leap-frogging from dock to dock. The *P-I* related:

> The raiding mob struck at twelve ships in the harbor during the day and halted work on all but one of them. In most cases the mob was orderly, giving the workers a chance to leave their jobs voluntarily. A committee of strikers would board a ship and request the strike-breakers to leave. When they agreed the strikers would form two lines and the workers would have to walk a gauntlet while the mob jeered and shouted imprecations. . . .
>
> There was no police interference at any dock while the raids progressed, the officers on duty mingling with the mob and marching with the members from dock to dock. The mob was too large for the officers to check.[12]

From the McCormick docks the raiders went to the *Cadretta* of the Nelson Line and the *Kirkpatrick* of Northwestern Company. After a long argument on the *Dorothy Luckenbach* and *Moldanger*, the scabs left voluntarily. At the Pacific Steamship terminal, sixteen armed guards fell back when they saw the size of the crowd and allowed the strikers to take twenty-five scabs off the *Ruth Alexander*, which sailed for California partially loaded. Scabs on the *Kansan* at the American-Hawaiian dock left readily, and the Isthmian steamer *Steel Maker* discharged her scabs before the raiders arrived. The captain of the *Steel Mariner* threatened to kill the first man who set foot on his ship. The ship had no scabs on board. Scabs working the *Europa* in the East Waterway quit without resistance.

At Alaska Steamship's Pier 2, where the *Yukon* had finished loading that afternoon, the raiders demanded that the eighty-five scabs housed on the *Redondo* come ashore, threatening to break down the gates to get them. After the company finally agreed to discharge the scabs, the strikers sent them through the crowd with a warning not to return to the waterfront. Finally, the raiders headed for the Grace Line *Santa Rosa*, loading at the Bell Street terminal. As the strikers arrived, the big steel door began to roll down. Boosted up by his fellows, a Tacoma longshoreman held the door on his shoulders while the raiders scrambled under and into the covered dock area. A handful of police tried unsuccessfully to stop them as they battered down two doors with heavy timbers and fought their way to the ship's side. The scabs fled through the port opening into the liner. Hearing the uproar, the mates appeared with drawn

2,000 Longshore Strikers Raid 12 Ships; Stop Work; 'No Troops Now,'—Martin

Mob Smashes Barriers and Compels Emergency Crews to Halt Vessel Loading

Dore Denies State Guardsmen Are Needed; 100 Extra Police Sworn in by City

Sweeping along the waterfront from the Bell St. terminal to the East Waterway, a mob of striking longshoremen paralyzed Seattle shipping yesterday afternoon.

The mob, augmented by sympathizers and Communist agitators and including 600 strikers from Tacoma and 150 from Everett, numbered more than 2,000.

Unrestrained by the police, they swarmed aboard twelve ships, hauling strike breakers from their work—in some cases in the face of the ships' officers' drawn revolvers.

While the raids were in progress, a special meeting of the Waterfront Employers' Association was hurriedly called, and it was decided to suspend all waterfront operations until adequate protection is provided for the strike breakers.

TROOPS SOUGHT

A committee, headed by Watson Barr, Seattle, manager of the Interocean Steamship Corporation, called at once on Mayor John F. Dore and asked him to appeal to Gov. Clarence D. Martin to call out the national guard.

The committee got scant satisfaction from the mayor.

Although he said he would not give them a definite answer until noon today, he indicated strongly that he would not ask for state troops.

"I see no reason why the police can't handle the situation," Dore observed. "And if the police can handle it, we certainly don't want any troops—we don't want to have anybody killed."

MARTIN READY

Governor Martin declared last night that he will not hesitate to call out the guard if [illegible]

Employers' Association, announced that his organization will take no action until it receives Dore's final word today.

The raiding mob struck at twelve ships in the harbor during the day and halted work on all but one of them. In most cases the mob was orderly, giving the workers a chance to leave their jobs voluntarily. A committee of strikers would board the ship and request the strike breakers to leave. When they agreed, the strikers would form in two lines and the workers would have to walk a gantlet while the mob jeered and shouted imprecations.

2 MEN ARRESTED

There was no police interference at any dock while the raids progressed, the officers on duty mingling with the mob and marching with the members from dock to dock. The mob was too large for the officers to check.

Two arrests were made during the day and one man was taken to the hospital as a result of the raids. Fred Erber, twenty-six, a seaman, was jailed for interfering with a newspaper photographer and threatening to break his camera. He was later released on his personal recognizance. J. S. Lockett, forty-seven, was arrested for creating a disturbance at 1st Ave. S. and Atlantic St. and was required to post $25 bail.

THROWN INTO WATER

Phil R. Greuger, 3120 37th Place, dock foreman at Pier No. 7, was seized by the mob and thrown into the water when he resisted them. He managed to swim ashore and was taken to the City hospital suffering from exposure.

Strikers raid Seattle docks, May 12, 1934. (Seattle Post-Intelligencer) guns and threatened to shoot anyone who attempted to follow the scabs. The strikers retreated without their quarry. Cases of citrus fruit broke and scattered in the melee, and police arrested two men during the raid.

The Waterfront Employers, meeting in emergency session during the raid, decided to suspend work until their scabs could be protected. They requested Mayor John F. Dore to ask Governor Clarence D. Martin to call out the National Guard. Instead, the mayor declared a state of emergency and ordered 100 extra police sworn in for waterfront duty. Tom Plant advised San Francisco employers that Northwest waterfronts were "entirely under the control of an organized mob. . . . Reports indicate that in the absence of adequate protection it will be impossible to load and unload cargo at Columbia River and Puget Sound without risk of damage to cargo and ships."[13] They demanded troops, threatening an embargo. A special meeting of the San Francisco Waterfront Employers Sunday morning May 13, instructed Northwest agents of all shipping companies to "serve notice upon your Mayor and Governor that unless satisfactory assurance of full and adequate protection is furnished by Noon Tuesday, May 15, it will be necessary for us . . . to discontinue our service to and from your port and such service cannot be resumed until the required protection is furnished."[14]

In Seattle May 15 Mayor Dore attempted to restore the law and order he promised employers. He dispatched sixty-five police officers to Pier 2, where the *Victoria* would load for Alaska. Strikers had released the cargo of fresh salmon on her arrival. About 2,000 strikers let army and mail trucks pass, but persuaded union teamsters delivering cargo to turn back. Police made no attempt to interfere. After strikers had turned back half a dozen trucks, the company gave up, and Dave Beck, secretary of the Joint Council of Teamsters, announced that teamsters would not pick up or deliver merchandise at the docks until the strike ended.

Mayor Dore wired Interior Secretary Harold L. Ickes for federal troops to assure shipments to Alaska and asked Governor Martin for state militia intervention. Business interests deluged Martin with demands to call out the National Guard, and Mayor Frank H. Richmond of Walla Walla offered to send scabs from eastern Washington to move wheat. Pacific Steamship Company suspended all freight and passenger service to coastal ports between Seattle and San Diego until Portland and Seattle provided adequate protection for scabs, and Luckenbach threatened to stop calling at Seattle.

Governor Martin met with representatives of employers and labor on May 15. The union delegation included President James Taylor of the Washington State Federation of Labor, Dave Beck of the Seattle Teamsters, Harry McIlvaigh, secretary of the Tacoma Central Labor Council, Paddy Morris and George Smith of the Tacoma longshoremen, and two representatives each from the Olympia and Grays Harbor ILA locals. All stressed that employers must grant union recognition before peace could be restored to the waterfront. Intent on breaking the strike, the employers concentrated on demands for state militia. The unions argued against sending troops, as no serious violence had occurred. Labor won a victory when Governor Martin decided not to intervene until efforts to reach a peaceful settlement had been exhausted.

The following night at the Tacoma Central Labor Council meeting it was "Moved and seconded that if troops are used to break Longshoremen's strike, Council call general strike, and that letter be addressed to Chamber of Commerce notifying that if they are successful in their efforts to have troops called out to try to break strike, Labor Movement will retaliate with general strike. Motion carried unanimously."[15] Dave Beck's majority in the Seattle Central Labor Council defeated a similar resolution for a general strike. Beck commented: "A central labor council has no power to call a general strike, and it is foolish to talk about it."[16]

With water transport the only link to most of Alaska, the longshoremen recognized the danger of being accused of letting Alaskans starve. The strikers had to find a way to feed Alaska on their terms without capitulating to the operators. The morning after the governor's conference, a special meeting of the Seattle longshoremen voted to load the *Victoria* with a cargo of food. They would work a six-hour day for the rate of pay agreed on at the end of the strike. What could Alaska Steamship Company say to that? Refuse and let Alaska starve? The union had proved that the vessel could not be loaded with scabs. The company admitted its helplessness and accepted the offer. Watching the mercy ship load, Bert Farmer declared: "We saw 7 ton steel girders, a ten ton ore screen, and a hundred dredge buckets . . . They were loading bricks, cement, coal, drilling mach., steel rails, hay, chain, wood pipe, cable, lumber, and many other things that would be hard to digest."[17]

The *Victoria* sailed May 18. Mayor Dore declared furiously that Seattle was "ruled by a Soviet of longshoremen."[18] He invited the mayors of forty Washington cities to confer on united action to break the strike. The mayors of Wenatchee, Ellensburg, Colfax, and Mount Vernon attended and duly resolved to urge the governor to call out the National Guard. The dismal response to Dore's invitation constituted another victory for the strikers. Most public officials would not panic yet.

San Francisco

Scabs unloaded seven of the thirty-five vessels tied up at San Francisco May 10. By the next morning the employers claimed 533 scabs had been recruited out of 1,200 needed. On May 12, 500 strikers broke through police lines and stormed the fink hall at 256 Mission, hurling a barrage of rocks and clubs that broke windows and injured six police officers. The employers then moved their recruiting office to Pier 14, as scabs were afraid to report to the Mission Street hall and police declared they could not protect scabs being transported to the docks.

The San Franciso waterfront seemed almost a natural fortress. Huge concrete piers jutted out into the bay along a three-and-one-half mile stretch of the Embarcadero, the thoroughfare encircling San Francisco from Fisherman's Wharf to the China Basin. Spurs of the state-owned Belt Line Railway along the Embarcadero ran onto the piers, and heavy steel rolling doors protected truck access to the terminals. The employers withdrew behind these fortifications. The Waterfront Employers issued a bulletin to all members May 13: "PROTECTION AGAINST ATTACK FROM THE

Scabs leaving a San Francisco pier, May 10, 1934. (Courtesy San Francisco Public Library)

Same scabs being loaded into an armored van to transport them safely to their quarters. (Courtesy San Francisco Public Library)

OPEN BULKHEADS BETWEEN PIERS."[19] The bulletin instructed members to construct fences of corrugated iron topped with barbed wire from the pier sheds to the bulkheads between the piers.

Behind the impregnable barrier of concrete, steel, and iron, scabs unloaded vessels, transported to the docks by water from their quarters on the *Diana Dollar*. While scabs worked the ships, 1,000 longshoremen paraded daily with strike placards along the Embarcadero behind an American flag and the ILA banner. An ILA speedboat warned off scabs being brought from the East Bay. In the first of a series of actions to dramatize their cause, strikers and sympathizers, 4,000 strong, marched up Market Street, Sunday, May 13, and held a mass meeting at the Civic Center. The MWIU-sponsored United Front Seamen's Committee marched with their own banners, but the ILA barred political slogans to prevent the MWIU from exploiting the event.

Scab herders roamed the Berkeley campus. Although President Robert Gordon Sproul announced that the University of California was not furnishing strikebreakers, the longshoremen charged that fraternity houses recruited scabs, and at San Pedro the ILA listed two University of Southern California football stars among scabs. The Communist front National Students League at Berkeley distributed leaflets in East Bay urging students not to scab. After strikers complained that San Francisco officials told people on relief to go to work on the waterfront, the Board of Supervisors instructed the Emergency Relief Administration not to advise or suggest "to relief clients that they take employment where strike conditions prevail," and "not to permit solicitation of persons housed or fed" at relief facilities to scab.[20]

The longshoremen desperately needed support from the teamsters. The Teamsters Union reneged on its initial pledge not to haul into or out of struck docks, citing a contract clause discouraging sympathetic strikes, but rank-and-file sentiment and mass picket lines soon restored teamster support. In response to an appeal from the ILA, a special meeting of 3,000 San Francisco teamsters May 13 voted overwhelmingly to boycott the waterfront entirely. They quoted a contract provision allowing them to refuse to work under unsafe conditions, such as a crowd of angry strikers surrounding the cab of a truck. Following the vote, many members headed for the docks to join the picket line.

The embargo helped greatly in San Francisco. Scabs could unload cargo behind waterfront fortifications—employers reported 900 scabs working twenty-four vessels on May 15—but they could not move merchandise from the piers; nor could they deliver outbound cargo for empty holds. The day after the Teamsters' vote, Bay Area Boilermakers and Machinists declared an embargo on all scab vessels. With the teamsters' sympathetic action, the Belt Line road remained the only means to transport merchandise out of and into the besieged docks. In spite of strong sympathy of many members, the railroad brotherhoods refused to boycott the scab freight. Strikers parked cars on the tracks, lay down on the tracks, and stood massed in front of approaching trains until the Board of State Harbor Commissioners threatened to call for the National Guard to protect the free movement of the railroad.

Pickets could not stop the Belt Line Railroad on the Embarcadero, San Francisco, 1934. (Courtesy San Francisco Public Library)

Anticipating employer efforts to recruit scabs, the strikers asked the African-American community for support. The weekly newspaper, *The Spokesman*, greeted ILA overtures skeptically. "LONGSHOREMEN APPEAL TO NEGRO FOR STRIKE SUPPORT; IS ALL-WHITE POLICY OF UNION TOTTERING?" the paper headlined May 10. Local 38-79 presented a letter for publication asking Bay Area blacks not to scab. Eugene "Dutch" Dietrich stated the union had over sixty black members and promised an open policy and recognition of the black gang that had struck. A week later thirty black scabs from Oakland arrived at San Francisco docks. Thereupon, 500 strikers poured into Oakland to halt recruiting. Several strikers received injuries in a battle with fifty scabs. *The Spokesman* editorialized: "Black Scabs on the Waterfront—an Ultimatum to Labor Unions."

> After all, the kind of labor represented by the striking longshoremen—union labor—never seems to need the loyalty of Aframerican workers until it calls a strike. As long as the unions are getting what they want, any person darker than a sunburned Swede is black-balled the moment he sticks his head in the meeting room. But when the union boys want to wrest a few extra hours or dollars from the "bosses," the atmosphere becomes thick with mellow friendship, warm invitations, and loud hurrahs for "our black brothers."

Nor did the bosses prove any better friends of the black worker. "The employers use him for a cat's paw, discarding him no sooner than he has done the dirty work of breaking the strike." The paper welcomed "the small sign of change" in the ILA's recent recruitment of African Americans, but it warned: "Union officials, take heed: the present dock strike contains an ultimatum from long-suffering Negro workers! Open the membership of your union, or risk the success of your strike! Negros must be strikers or strike-breakers. If they are not permitted to help you, they will hinder you."[21]

Declaring that "Negroes have been the bludgeons of capital since the first slaves were landed on American soil," a month later the paper urged class solidarity: "Union labor's greatest enemy is not the strike-breaker, but the employer who uses the strike-breaker to defeat it. The strike-breaker's greatest enemy is not union labor, but the employer who uses him as a tool against his class."[22] Local 38-79 issued an appeal "TO ALL NEGRO PEOPLE" May 16, denying employer charges that "the I.L.A. will not accept Negroes." In fact, African Americans participated actively in the union, and five "colored brothers" served on the strike committee.[23]

Instead of a compact circle of piers that could be easily fortified, the waterfront across the bay at Oakland meandered along the Inner Harbor opposite the Alameda docks. Blacks scabs soon went to work in Oakland. On May 17 a crowd of 400 strikers broke through police lines at the Oakland municipal pier and attacked 72 scabs loading the Japanese freighter *Oregon Maru* with scrap iron. They injured six—one seriously. Some of the injured lay on the dock for hours without medical aid because private ambulances refused to go the pier, claiming they had received anonymous death threats. The ILA deplored threats against doctors and ambulance drivers and pledged that no such interference would be tolerated and the union would render all possible aid to the injured men. After the fight, the scabs demanded to be armed and deputized.

On the 19th, 250 strikers swept past 30 police officers at the Sunset Lumber Company docks in Oakland and swarmed over the steam schooner *Noyo*. The fourteen scabs retreated to the engine room and barricaded themselves against the crowd, remaining there for several hours. Some scabs thereafter refused to work on the Oakland docks. Both E.K. Wood and Sunset Lumber companies closed because of the inability to transport their products. They could not find scab sailors with experience handling lumber.

North of Oakland at Crockett, longshoremen completed organization during the first days of the strike. They tied up the port and sent representatives to the San Francisco strike committee.

San Pedro

Down south, striking longshoremen could not stop work on the sprawling docks at San Pedro, Wilmington, and Long Beach, covering over forty miles of waterfront that comprised Los Angeles harbor. Although the ILA struck solidly, the employers managed to keep the port open, backed by the resources of the open-shop Merchants' and Manufacturers' Association of Los Angeles. On May 10 the employers claimed 507 scabs were at work, 266 from Los Angeles and the rest company union men. The union counted only half that number, not more than fifty of them longshoremen. Cooks and stewards on two vessels refused to feed scabs. With Los Angeles teamsters only partially organized, their boycott did not shut off trucking to and from the docks.

In the principal scab encampment, scabs slept on two old sailing ships, the *Indiana* and *William H. Harriman*, moored at Berth 40 at Wilmington. A stockade surrounded large tents for the cook house and mess hall. The employers denied a report that carpenters and plumbers hired to fit the old ships quit in support of the strikers. A cook reportedly left for the same reason after wrecking the galley range. The employers quartered more scabs at the nearby Grace Line terminal Berth 146 and at Terminal Island in a circus tent in the Crescent Wharf Company's pipe yard. They transported other scabs to the docks in guarded autos and water taxis. The ILA patrolled the waterfront in 200-man details on three-hour shifts and hired three fishing boats from which to yell their appeals to scabs. Some quit and joined the strikers. The black Los Angeles Longshoremen's Association refused to scab. President Hayes Self and Treasurer Kennedy, retired longshoremen and ex-ILA members, related to the union that both employers and the company union tried unsuccessfully to persuade their members to go to work.

Beneath the peaceful picketing, the strikers' anger and frustration mounted. May 14 the employers claimed 1,300 men worked nineteen ships, and forty-eight vessels had sailed since the strike began. The union said 600 men worked. Late that afternoon a group of strikers held an informal meeting at White Point. Peaceful picketing would not win the strike, many argued. Strikers had closed the northern ports with forthright action. Scabs hurled unanswered insults at them. They beat and threw out a striker who sneaked into the stockade to count scabs. About 10:30 the police learned that the stockade would be attacked that night. Armed with tear gas bombs they hastened to the encampment. The *San Pedro News-Pilot* reported the tragedy:

"ONE SLAIN, SCORE INJURED IN STRIKE RIOT AT WEST BASIN – Tear Gas, Bullets Employed to Quell Longshoremen's Mob – Strikebreakers' Stockade Fired and Men Beaten at Grace Line Terminal."[24] Blinding searchlights and a barrage of tear gas from police and bullets from guards met the raiders as they approached the stockade. Some carried ball bats, clubs, and saps. A guard's bullet killed Richard J. Parker, twenty, unarmed, as he stumbled forward with his arms in front of his face, blinded by tear gas. He had joined the ILA the previous day. A bullet in his chest fatally wounded John Knudsen, fifty-one, ILA member. The raiders' objectives were the 400 scabs on the sailing ships. They tore down part of the stockade and burned the mess tent before being repulsed. When police exhausted the tear gas, they used clubs on the strikers. After being turned back at the stockade, the raiders forced their way into the Grace Line terminal and beat scabs quartered there before police drove them away. Police arrested six strikers. The ILA denied knowledge of the raid.

Besides Parker and Kundsen, guards shot six strikers, and twenty scabs and strikers were otherwise injured. Eyewitnesses reported that no raiders had guns. Walter Hannefield, Los Angeles detective agency guard whose bullet killed Parker, claimed he fired in the air. Police released him after a few days' detention and he never stood trial for the murder. The Los Angeles police force had previously dismissed the killer for stealing, in the wake of charges of attempted extortion and consorting with underworld characters connected with commercial vice and narcotics traffic.

The day after the attack the employers repaired the stockade and surrounded it with a wire barricade. San Pedro became an occupied town, as 320 police guarded the waterfront. The Los Angeles Central Labor Council protested against "the alleged promiscuous arming of strike breakers and 'scab herders' at San Pedro," and demanded "that such practice be stopped, and if there is to be a general arming, Unionists be given the same favors as those hired by employers to shoot down strikers."[25] The council charged that ex-convicts and at least six men "cashiered dishonerably out of the navy" worked as armed guards.

The union buried Richard Parker on May 22. Five thousand strikers and sympathizers, led by an ILA color guard bearing the American flag and union banner, marched in the funeral procession, and 10,000 lined the streets as the two-mile-long cortege passed. Many stepped from the curb to join the ranks of the marchers. Portland strikers held a memorial service for Parker on the waterfront. John Knudsen died in the hospital of his bullet wound on June 5. Parker and Knudsen became the first martyrs. More bullets—more funeral processions would punctuate the bitter struggle.

Seamen Strike

The seamen's strike during the second week of the conflict greatly strengthened the longshoremen's position. Many union and nonunion seamen quit their ships even before the strike began, particularly in the Northwest. Others stayed with their vessels, some furnishing steam for scabs or working cargo. Alaska Steamship threatened to blacklist seamen who struck. The attitude of the Sailors' Union in each port likely influenced crews. In San Francisco Secretary George Larsen counseled members to remain on board pending official action. In Seattle crews stayed with their ships awaiting a strike vote, and in Portland Carl Carter advised seamen to quit as individuals. Larsen and Pete Gill, veterans with memories of union strength before the 1921 defeat, doubted whether sailors would respond to a strike call—they failed to recognize the latent rebellion among young unorganized seamen that would trigger their immediate support and send them flocking to union halls. Carter predicted that most sailors would strike. Seamen at Portland joined ILA picket lines immediately.

The Sailors' Union meeting May 14 at San Francisco voted to work ships under union agreement and strike the rest for $75.00 and 75 cents overtime, three watches, and other union conditions. The meeting voted to ballot coastwide on the strike call the following day and elected Larsen and Paul Scharrenberg to meet with ILA Local 38-79 "to bring about an agreement whereby neither sailors nor longshoremen on strike shall return to work until the demands of both have been satisfied."[26] Seattle sailors and firemen struck the same night. The union invited all ships' crews to the meeting, members vouching for nonmembers. Sailors and firemen voted by secret ballot over 100 in favor and 2 against to strike all noncontract ships. The SUP coastwide ballot was 131 to 15 to strike. San Francisco voted 55 to 14 for the walkout, Seattle 54 to 0, Portland 14 to 0, and San Pedro 8 to 1.

The Marine Firemen and Marine Cooks and Stewards also took strike votes, with the result that on May 16, one week after the longshoremen, 4,000 sailors and firemen struck all noncontract ships, and a day later 700 cooks and stewards walked out. The union did not tie up the Pacific American Fisheries fleet out of Bellingham or the steam schooner *Lumberman*. The strike amounted to an act of faith and desperation

STRIKE-SEAMEN-STRIKE

International Seamen's Union of America

PACIFIC DISTRICT

The Sailors' Union of the Pacific, the Pacific Coast Marine Firemen, Oilers, Watertenders and Wipers' Association, and the Marine Cooks and Stewards' Association of the Pacific Coast are on strike for enforcement of the wages and working conditions submitted at the Shipping Code hearing held at Washington, D. C., November 10, 1933.

These demands provide for $75.00 per month for Sailors and Firemen, and 75 cents per hour overtime, abolition of the scab shipping offices, for union recognition and full union conditions.

Now is the time to fight for better conditions and remedy long standing grievances.

ALL SEAMEN UNITE! PULL TOGETHER!

Seamen's strike call, May 16, 1934. (Courtesy Sailors' Union of the Pacific) for the partially organized seamen. Sound trade union practice dictated that a union organize an overwhelming majority, as the ILA had done, before challenging such a formidable opponent as the shipping industry. Success in the seamen's strike depended not on the loyal union minority, but on the unknown majority who had abandoned the unions or never joined.

The shipowners' policy of segregating black and white crews in the stewards' department on separate vessels and fostering the Admiral Line company union among African Americans resulted in a virtually all-white union on the Pacific Coast, contrary to ISU practice in other districts. The Marine Cooks and Stewards' Association of the Atlantic and Gulf had a large black membership. At the beginning of the strike the Pacific Coast Marine Cooks and Stewards proposed to the company union that they join the walkout, promising equal shipping rights and a minimum of two official positions if the union won. The company union split. James Roston, son of the black scab herder in Seattle who had organized the association, urged loyalty to the employers and recruited scabs in San Francisco during the strike. Members' decisions reflected the divisions in the African-American community. Those who struck likely shared the integrationist views of unions and civil rights organizations. As in other departments, some walked off because they feared the strikers' wrath. The strike destroyed the company union. By the end of the conflict about 300 black stewards had joined the Marine Cooks and Stewards. With Pacific Steamship vessels tied up the first week of the strike, employers recruited some association members to scab on other ships, and many left the waterfront.

Democratic procedures such as meetings and membership votes did not delay the Marine Workers Industrial Union. In a leaflet May 9 the San Francisco MWIU called on all crews to elect delegates to a "final strike conference" May 10. The conference set up a United Front Seamen's Central Strike Committee and called the strike for May 12: "ALL CREWS TO REMAIN ON SHIPS—BUT NO WORK AFTER SATURDAY 8 A.M."[27] The committee claimed to represent 350 employed and 800 unemployed seamen. Similar MWIU-sponsored committees appeared in Seattle, Portland, and San Pedro. Thereafter, the MWIU would assert that it had forced reluctant ISU officials to call the strike. The *Voice of Action* headlined May 15: "Seamen Out under Militant MWIU Leadership in 4 Northwest Ports," and the San Francisco MWIU claimed credit for crews of thirteen vessels walking off at the beginning of the strike.

The MWIU claims are suspect. First, considering its minimal influence during the strike, the United Front Committee could not have had 1,150 adherents on May 12. Second, far from being stampeded by the Communists, the SUP had decided back in March to strike for seamen's demands if the ILA struck. The instruction to remain on ships while striking contradicted all past practice among maritime workers, and no further reference to it appeared in the press or MWIU leaflets. Either the group abandoned the tactic immediately or seamen paid no attention to it.

Most seamen responded to the ISU strike call. At Seattle on May 16, 200 strikers persuaded 50 sailors and firemen to strike the *President Grant*, leaving the Chinese stewards' department and a cargo of silk aboard, and the 25-man crew of the Associated Oil tanker *H.M. Whittier* quit. The *Steel Maker* and *Steel Mariner* sailed for San Francisco after the crews refused to strike, and the American-Hawaiian *Columbian* moved into the stream when the crew chose to stay aboard. The next day seamen and engineers struck the *Alaska*, the Sunset Pacific tanker *Brandywine*, and Grace liner *Charcas*. A crowd of striking seamen rushed the Todd Dry Dock gates when a truck entered, swarmed over three *Luckenbach* vessels, the *Edward, Florence*, and *Jacob*, and persuaded the crews to quit. Seamen struck the *Northland* on arrival from Alaska. At Tacoma, crews of the tanker *Topila* and *S.S. Golden Cloud* struck.

The marine unions put out pickets and pulled crews off ships at Portland and San Francisco. San Pedro immediately felt the seamen's strike. Of the eight ships tied up May 19, four could find no crews, and the fink hall lacked forty-seven scabs for replacements. The *Lurline* prepared to sail with a new scab crew of forty-five, and the Matson-Oceanic liner *Monterey* arrived from Australia with a union crew that would strike.

Back in Washington, D.C., Andrew Furuseth read press reports that Communists controlled the burgeoning strike and asked San Francisco for information. George Larsen replied:

> Shipowners have sown the wind and are reaping the whirlwind stop. They defeated the maritime unions in 1921 with aid of Harding Administration stop. They stripped maritime personnel of wages and conditions until wage reductions reached 65 percent stop. Married seamen of all trades unable to support their families sought work as longshoremen, teamsters and other shore work suffering the hardships of newcomers stop. The shipowners after the defeat of seamen imposed harder and harder conditions on longshoremen stop.... Present flareup of trades wherever possible is not directed by labor union officials for they are swept along by this deep-seated resentment against the shipowners stop. The communists are loudmouthed but not in control stop. I am doing all I can to unite our side with the common cause stop. This is our only salvation stop. . . .[28]

The licensed officers formed the last link in the chain of maritime solidarity forged in the great strike. Masters, Mates and Pilots Local 90 had only 350 members, 18 percent of the officers on affected vessels, and the Marine Engineers scarcely had better numbers. Many officers shared the union convictions of unlicensed seamen. Others realized that if they did not support the strike and sailed with scabs, they would face the deadly hostility of union crews after the strike. Both motives induced them to walk out. On May 19 Masters, Mates and Pilots Local 90 and Marine Engineers No. 97 of San Francisco voted to strike for recognition and improved wages and working conditions. Two days later they called their members off all vessels, pledging to remain out until all striking organizations reached satisfactory settlements. A San Francisco member described the engineers' meeting:

> The longshoremen and other dock workers were on strike and engineers were placed in the position of strike-breakers if they stayed with their jobs and furnished steam for strike-breaking longshoremen to work cargo. This is a position in which no true union

man wishes to place himself, and I am proud to say the majority of engineers were of the same mind and came to the meeting demanding something be done.[29]

The Seattle unions of licensed officers equivocated. After hearing a committee from the Sailors' Union, Masters, Mates and Pilots Local 6 voted May 18 to refuse to work with scabs. The union voted two days later to ask the Alaska operators for a wage increase and union recognition and discuss strike action if the employers refused their demands.

The Seattle Marine Engineers No. 38 refused to strike. Business Agent William Peel explained May 21: "We do not want our action construed as casting any reflection on the action of the engineers in San Francisco. Conditions are different there, but in Seattle we are receiving good treatment from the steamship lines and do not feel a strike is justified."[30] Regardless of the association's stand, engineers sailing out of Seattle left their vessels along with unlicensed seamen.

The shipowners dismissed the licensed officers' strike as of small consequence as not many officers heeded the strike call. But those who struck, highly skilled personnel, proved to be most difficult to replace. Old-timers tell one story of 1934 with knowing smiles. The engineers on a Swayne & Hoyt freighter struck when she arrived in San Francisco. When she was ready to proceed to sea with a crew of scabs, they discovered that the engines would not run. Instead of trying to make repairs during the strike, the wise port engineer laid the vessel up for the duration. After the strike he rehired the engineers who had struck, and they promptly put the ship in working order. True or not, from the earliest days of collective action, skilled mechanics had found ways to protect their jobs and make strikebreaking costly for employers. The IWW talked much about sabotage, but the skilled trades practiced it quietly, with the firm conviction that the tools with which they produced profits for their employers belonged equally to them.

The Battle for Public Opinion

Before the strike was a week old, the employers blamed the longshoremen for closure of lumber and flour mills and other firms in the Northwest. The press reported over 1,000 idled by the strike in Tacoma, and the South Bend and Raymond Chamber of Commerce claimed that the strike of 110 longshoremen affected the jobs of 1,500 other workers. Weyerhaeuser closed two mills in Everett and planned to shut down operations at Longview affecting between 2,500 and 3,000 workers. Two mills at Coos Bay closed, as did two at Portland employing 600 men. Three Aberdeen mills closed, throwing nearly 1,000 out of work. Five mills and one logging camp at Olympia shut down, adding 525 men to the jobless army. The Associated Press estimated May 17 over 5,800 idled in Washington and Oregon as an indirect result of the strike.

The strikers denied responsibility for many of the closures. Some plants shut down because of filled production quotas, others for lack of orders. The supposed strike casualties included a lumber mill that shipped almost exclusively by rail. The two Tacoma flour mills had shut down for the annual cleaning, required by insurance companies to prevent dust explosions. Some people defended the strikers. In answer to a radio speech by Seattle Chamber of Commerce President Alfred Lundin, Mrs. W.A. Carlson, president of the Tacoma League of Women Voters, wrote: "The sooner chambers of commerce and others realize that industrial peace can come only by recognizing the right of workers to form their *own voluntary organizations* and permit them to deal collectively with organized industry, the sooner we will have industrial peace, greater purchasing power and better business."[31]

By the end of the first week employers began to realize how hard the strike would be to break. Gloom replaced confidence. The *Pacific Shipper* lamented: "The efforts to keep traffic moving through the employment of non-union workers, which had seemed so promising the previous week, were set practically at naught by the resurgence of violence and intimidation and by the spreading of the strike to draymen, dock clerks, bargemen, and on American flag vessels to deck and engine crews."[32] The strike "virtually embargoed" Northwest ports, and California ports fared scarcely better. Inbound freight not moved and outbound freight not loaded piled up on congested piers. The tie-up diverted coastwise and transcontinental traffic to railroads. The seamen's strike "hit coastal ships the worst, and was partly responsible for the complete paralysis of this trade."

The paper reported "dire threats" to dynamite piers and punish families of steamship officials and scabs. It blamed Reds for everything: "Professional agitators appeared to have the conduct of the strike entirely in their hands, even as they are believed to have inspired it." Employers held out to save the country from revolution. With many shippers believing the demands "merely cloak an attempt on the part of labor captains of a radical complexion to seize prestige and power, if not to undermine the social order, the operators gave little if any consideration to an acquiescence to the strikers' demands, despite the straits to which the industry was reduced."[33]

Soup Kitchens and Strike Support

The shipowners had money, political influence, and the power to award or withhold jobs. The strikers had numbers, skills that transformed ships and cargoes into profits, and a vast reservoir of support that took form in each community. To strike is a bold affirmation of human dignity, but it is also a rejection of the employer's paycheck. People must eat. Strikers and their families must be fed. Soup kitchens and commissaries are as important as picket lines.

The maritime unions had no strike funds built up. Most ILA locals were less than a year old, their treasuries pinched by the conferences and conventions that preceded the strike. The seagoing unions, with their few dues-paying members, had lived from hand to mouth for years to keep their halls open. The Sailors' Union voted at the outset to pay no strike benefits. Most uptown unions could offer only limited help. The depression had depleted their membership and drained their resources also. But more important than numerical or financial strength, all union people shared the hope and courage that swept maritime workers into their great struggle. The waterfront strike belonged to them. "No man is an Island, . . ." The great wave of solidarity built.

Although negotiations depended on the district officials, the strikers fought their battle day by day in every port, large and small. ILA locals organized strike committees immediately to handle picketing, relief, publicity, and other matters, and seamen formed committees when they struck. In Seattle delegates from the Sailors' Union, Marine Firemen, and Marine Cooks and Stewards constituted the ISU strike committee. Henry Whiting of the Sailors chaired the committee at first, succeeded by Harry Lundeberg.

Seattle picket lines stiffened after the May 12 raid. Seamen and longshoremen both picketed at every dock. Forty black ILA members took an active part in the strike. By May 21 the SUP had over 200 pickets, both members and pledges, standing eight-hour picket watches or performing comparable strike duty. Two picket launches patrolled Elliott Bay. After two weeks of meal tickets in restaurants, the Seattle ILA opened a soup kitchen in the hall to feed single strikers and a commissary for groceries for those with families. Black cooks and stewards from the Admiral Line helped in the soup kitchen. The Central Labor Council mobilized relief and support. Although the Teamsters unions continued to block use of the ultimate weapon, a general strike, they donated $1,000 a month to the striking longshoremen, and other unions contributed generously.

Strike relief for seamen centered around the Sailors' Union building at the foot of Seneca. The union installed a range and gas stoves on the vacant third floor and set up a soup kitchen that fed 400 to 500 strikers. Cooks and stewards solicited contributions and prepared the food, which sailors transported to the picket lines. Fish donated by the Alaska Fishermen's Union became a mainstay. Some strikers ate at relief stations for the unemployed. Longshoremen slept in their own beds at night, but most seamen, single transients, lived between trips in waterfront hotels. They must have a place to sleep, as well as food. The fortunate ones kept their rooms on credit. Almost 100 slept in the union building on the third floor on paper or sacks, and another 50 downstairs in the main hall on benches or four chairs pulled together. A few had blankets or cots, and some slept in autos.

Fifty-two squads of longshoremen picketed the Portland docks, with little to do after the port shut down. When rain began to fall, they lit bonfires and built shacks of scraps of lumber, corrugated iron, and composition roofing. At the Admiral dock they put in a stove and brewed coffee. A picture of Captain Kidd boarding the *Admiral Evans* decorated the interior. A wooden six-shooter and daggers hung in front, whittled and carved as the pickets whiled away the time on the quiet waterfront. In another picket shack on the Oceanic dock they made coffee on an improvised stove. Striking seamen elected an ISU strike committee, which met jointly with the ILA committee. By May 21 the SUP had 150 pickets out.

Portland unions rallied immediately to provide relief for their waterfront strikers. An afternoon meeting of local union officers donated $400, and the Central Labor Council meeting that night elected a committee to raise funds to feed strikers and their families. The council opened a commissary for family relief in the basement of the Labor Temple and a soup kitchen near the waterfront to feed single men. A restaurant

Milk for pickets from a sympathetic waterfront cafe, Portland, May 1934. Note the union button on the waitress's uniform. (Morning Oregonian, *courtesy Oregon Historical Society, OrHi neg. 81691)*

ILA picket shack, Admiral Dock, Portland, 1934. (Courtesy Pacific Northwest Labor History Association)

in the same building as the ILA hall announced that no longshoreman would be refused a meal for lack of money, and restaurants donated sandwiches and buttermilk for the picket lines. A delegation from the United Farmers' League offered the strikers "everything that can be produced on a farm."[34] Women's unions and auxiliaries organized strike aid. The Faloma Fishermen's Union donated one fish from each drift's catch to the strikers in appreciation for their help in a strike the previous year. Striking seamen ate in the ILA soup kitchen.

The San Francisco ILA strike committee, chaired by Harry Bridges, set up committees for relief, defense, publicity, picketing, and other matters. Bridges, John Schomaker, Henry Schmidt, all of the Albion Hall group, Charles Cutright, and John McClellan constituted the executive committee, and Ralph Mallen chaired the publicity committee. The defense committee arranged bail and legal services for arrested strikers. Sympathizers donated money and food. In contrast to other ports, the San Francisco strike committee accepted help from Communists and their front organizations provided they adhered to strike policy. For awhile the Communist weekly *Western Worker* issued Local 38-79's official bulletin. Sam Telford of the MWIU, representing the United Front Seamen's Strike Committee, met with the ILA strike committee May 12 to arrange for joint committees.

Three hundred attended the regular SUP meeting at headquarters May 21 and elected a strike committee of W.W. Caves, chair, Carl Lynch, J. McLaughlin, Fred A. Nunce, and Nils Jensen. The SUP appointed a negotiating committee of Caves, Edward Schieler, and Herman Bach. The union issued strike cards and buttons to nonmembers provided they would perform strike duties. Strike card men had "all the privileges of the Union, except that they could not vote on any financial matters, in-as-much as it was the full book members who were paying the bills. The strike card men, however, had a full voice and vote in any matters concerned with the strike."[35] The Marine Firemen and Marine Cooks and Stewards adopted the same policy. The SUP hall at the foot of Clay Street stayed open around the clock. Seamen slept where they could, none in the hall. By May 24, 640 members and pledges picketed on three watches, four on and eight off. Between 3,000 and 4,000 strikers of all crafts picketed.

At first the ILA issued meal tickets for waterfront restaurants, but soon the unions set up a joint relief kitchen for all strikers at 84 Embarcadero, the address of the Blue Book hall in the early 1920s. The kitchen fed over 1,000 strikers three hot meals a day and sent coffee and sandwiches twice to pickets on night duty. Uptown unions donated money, and members volunteered their help in support work and the soup kitchen. Two doctors offered their services to treat strikers and their families. Women relatives of ILA members organized an auxiliary June 5 to contribute their strength.

In San Pedro most seamen remained on their vessels until the strike call May 16. About one-third of those who struck belonged to the ISU, according to one sailor, and on steam schooners 90 percent had been ISU members. The MWIU had forty or fifty on strike. About 75 to 100 licensed officers, including radio operators, participated

Members of Marine Cooks and Stewards Union serve strikers. (Courtesy San Francisco Public Library)

Soup kitchen at 84 Embarcadero, San Francisco, 1934. (Courtesy San Francisco Public Library)

actively in the strike and picketed with the seamen. Initially the seamen formed three separate strike committees, ISU, MWIU, and unorganized seamen, but later they merged into the ISU strike committee, that met jointly with the ILA committee.

The seamen pulled crews off ships and policed the town, challenging sailors on the street for strike clearances and sending them to the SUP hall to register for picket duty. Soon it wasn't safe around town without a picket card. Sailors, firemen, and cooks and stewards participated equally in strike activities. At first waterfront hotels and restaurants took the walkout lightly, waiting to pick a winner, but as the strikers proved their strength proprietors began to cooperate and notify pickets when scabs were around. A striker working at the Don Hotel in Wilmington, which fed extra police from Los Angeles, regularly picked up information and passed it on to the unions, enabling the strikers to anticipate movements of ships, scabs, and police.

Three relief groups operated in San Pedro. The ILA had a soup kitchen and commissary; the Seamen's Institute fed strikers three times a day; and the MWIU set up the Workers' International Relief. About seventy or eighty men slept at the Seamen's Institute, a few in hotels and rooming houses, and others at the Sailors' hall on Palos Verdes, in shacks on the beach, and in boxcars. Women relatives formed an ILA auxiliary on May 15 to solicit provisions and money from merchants and work with the union relief committee. The San Pedro Eagles Lodge gave a dinner and entertainment for 700 longshoremen. Some restaurants in the harbor "posted signs that reserved the right to refuse patronage, which meant they would not feed 'scabs.' They also announced they would feed any of the Union men who might be without funds."[36] The Los Angeles Central Labor Council appealed for donations of food and money. The council urged unemployed union people to go daily to employment offices that recruited scabs to persuade prospective recruits not to scab. As in other ports, uptown unions donated to relief funds, and sympathetic Hollywood stars contributed generously.

Red Herring

While shipowners and strikers battled for ascendancy on the waterfront, politicians scurried around frantically to get the strikers back to work. The strike presented a painful dilemma for elected officials who wanted to please everyone. The Roosevelt Administration had to make good on vague promises or lose needed labor support. Unwilling to exert any real pressure on the shipping industry to bargain with its employees, the federal government resumed the mediation shuffle. On May 11 the President's Board wired the National Labor Board to request ILA President Joseph P. Ryan to come to San Francisco immediately.

Acting on instructions from San Francisco, shipowners' Northwest representatives delivered their ultimatum to mayors and governors that their firms would discontinue service to Seattle and Portland unless they received adequate protection. May 15 the governors of Washington, Oregon, and California appealed to President Roosevelt to intervene in the strike. On that date, "for the first time in history not a freighter left a Pacific Coast port," according to the *San Francisco Examiner*. The governors' plea brought Assistant Secretary of Labor Edward F. McGrady, former AFL legislative representative, to San Francisco to settle the strike.

McGrady met separately with employers and longshoremen. President Bill Lewis, Vice-President Cliff Thurston of Portland, Secretary Jack Bjorklund, Paddy Morris of Tacoma, John Finnegan of the San Francisco Ship Clerks, and A.H. Petersen of San Pedro represented the district ILA. Frank Foisie from Seattle and representatives from Los Angeles joined the employers' team. When Local 38-79 voted May 19 to require ILA negotiators to refer all proposals back to the locals for approval and pledged to remain out until the demands of all striking unions were met, McGrady declared angrily: "Communists are throwing a monkey wrench into the situation. . . . There is an element among the longshoremen that lives on strike and does not want a settlement."[37]

McGrady was half right. The Communists hoped to use the strike to recruit members and gain control of the maritime unions. To that end their shrill propaganda saturated the waterfront, supporting the strikers but attacking all elected officials and activists who did not submit to their direction. But, contrary to his observation, Communists did not control the ILA. The union needed no vote to limit the authority of negotiators. Established district policy required that the entire membership decide such an important issue as the strike settlement, and sentiment for solidarity grew among all strikers. J.W. Mailliard, Jr., president of the San Francisco Chamber of Commerce, escalated the attack, calling for removal of "Communistic agitators . . . as the official spokesmen of labor . . ."[38]

The longshoremen defended ILA officers and members as "a true cross-section of Americanism. The strike is in effect to procure work enough to support their families as Americans."[39] Ben Osborne, secretary of the Oregon State Federation of Labor, charged: "Waterfront employers are endeavoring to draw across the trail the red herring of communism in order to divert public attention from their own sins. . . . The reds in this controversy are the employers whose policies are breeders of communism and whose acts would have precipitated violence had not the strikers been men of coolness."[40]

The *Labor Advocate* dismissed the Communist tag, reminding readers that "organization work in San Francisco by the I.L.A., as in every other port . . . was carried out successfully only in the teeth of the bitter opposition of the communists. They tried to pack meetings; they opposed organization tooth and nail and one of these disrupters stated frankly he preferred the open shop and a business dispatcher appointed by the boss."[41]

Starving Alaskans

Pressure on the strikers to release Alaska vessels increased. A dispatch from Anchorage May 22 warned that the supply of butter and eggs would be exhausted in ten days, little flour remained, and all of Alaska would be without supplies in a month. The question of releasing Alaska vessels led to the formation of the Joint Northwest Strike Committee. The ILA district negotiating committee warned that employers threatened to withdraw from mediation if the strikers did not release the PAF cannery fleet. The Tacoma ILA sent out a call to all Washington and Columbia River locals to meet May 24 on the Alaska situation.

Sixty-two delegates from eight Washington locals met in the Tacoma Labor Temple. After hours of discussion, the meeting wired Bill Lewis and Jack Bjorklund for information on whether the San Francisco local had released any cannery vessels. Not receiving a definite answer from them, the meeting adjourned at 4:30 a.m. with no decision. The delegates wired Joe Ryan, by then in San Francisco, "demand that you pull [strike] EAST GULF COAST and GREAT LAKES at once."[42]

When the Joint Northwest Strike Committee convened May 26, Con Negstad represented Portland and carried proxies from Astoria, Vancouver, and St. Helens. The committee elected Walter Freer and Ed Harris, both of Tacoma, permanent chair and recording secretary respectively. With Alaska Governor Troy in San Francisco demanding release of vessels, Ryan and District Secretary Bjorklund urged the committee to comply. Federal mediators Ernie Marsh and Charles Hope added to their pleas. After much heated debate the meeting voted 28 to 10 on a roll call to release one vessel for Southwestern Alaska. Everett and Raymond, Communist dominated; Grays Harbor, probably a mixture of ex-Wobblies and Communists; and five of the twenty-two Seattle delegates voted against releasing the ship. The rest of the ports voted in favor. Another identical roll call decided that the ship would be a Northland Transportation Company vessel because that company had been fair to the unions, and "that the cargo must be of a needy nature—such as—medicine, foodstuffs, clothing and any necessary government supplies. . . . Also the loading must be 100 percent union men and that the crew or any other party connected in any way with the loading or movement of said ship must also be 100 percent O.K."[43] The *North Wind* sailed May 29 with the union crew from the previous trip dispatched by the Sailors' Union. Word from San Francisco that Local 38-79 was not working cannery vessels ended debate on releasing PAF ships.

Formation of the Joint Northwest Strike Committee set the pattern for the remainder of the strike. The northern locals, large and small, continued to act together, joined later by the striking seamen, and the strikers in other ports met the employers' increasing efforts to break the strike with similar joint committees.

6

Negotiations

While the northern locals wrestled with the Alaska problem, the ILA district negotiators presented proposals to the employers May 24: that employers bargain with the ILA according to Section 7a of the NIRA; that the ILA control hiring halls; that wages and hours be arbitrated with retroactive pay; and that the seamen's strike be settled satisfactorily before longshoremen returned to work. They demanded an answer by noon May 26. If employers rejected the proposals, the longshoremen would press for a hot cargo boycott and seek support for congressional legislation opposing ship subsidies and mail contracts.

At this point International President Joseph P. Ryan arrived in San Francisco. "At no time," Bill Lewis stated, "was his aid asked by the District officials."[1] Mediators, employers, and the press treated Ryan as an authority whose opinions amounted to policy decisions. President Ryan may have understood the needs of East and Gulf Coast longshoremen, but his press statements showed his ignorance of West Coast demands. He said May 26: "We don't give a hoot for the closed shop. All we are interested in is recognition with preference."[2] He dismissed the mutual support pact with the marine unions. The same morning 800 members of Local 38-79 voted to remain on strike until employers met their demands for a closed shop, union hiring halls, and a satisfactory settlement for the seamen. The Associated Press speculated on the local's "virtual repudiation of Joseph P. Ryan."[3]

The ILA district negotiators did not air their disagreements with Ryan in the press, but Harry Bridges followed the Communist style of public attacks, stating: "Settlement for mere recognition may mean a lot to national heads of the International Longshoremen's Association who get fat salaries, but the workers are going to hold out for nothing less than a closed shop."[4] In a wire to Ed Harris May 25, Paddy Morris foresaw the inevitable struggle more clearly than Ryan:

> Met employers this forenoon—again this afternoon with a subcommittee—Committee deadlocked on question of hiring halls—looks like a finish fight—In the event negotiations are broken off we are preparing ground for a Pacific Coast Waterfront Federation—We believe this is the opportune time to start it, and such a Federation would firmly cement our forces together.[5]

The *Pacific Shipper* admitted the strike's effectiveness. Strikers "virtually blockaded" Northwest ports, with twenty-five ships waiting in Puget Sound and twenty-four tied up in the Columbia River. Fifty vessels waited to unload in San Francisco Bay, and in

Los Angeles harbor, with thirty vessels tied up, "steamship operators were hampered by striking crews and other obstacles."[6] From the idle docks the employers turned to the negotiating table.

President J.W. Mailliard, Jr., of the San Francisco Chamber of Commerce said May 24: "We do not wish to make a statement pending the outcome of negotiations . . ., following which the merchants will open the port of San Francisco to commerce."[7] The Waterfront Employers' Union statement the next day called the Blue Book a "bona fide union of longshoremen" (present tense) and contended that the Seattle, Portland, and San Pedro fink halls "assured a satisfactory hiring and dispatching system, and an equitable distribution of work." The statement asserted that the "sole purpose" of the longshoremen's demands for the closed shop and union hiring halls "is to deny the worker any freedom of choice, but to force him to belong to one union whether he wishes to or not."[8]

The May 28 Offer

In this chilling atmosphere the talks proceeded. While the negotiators met May 28, police on foot and horseback attacked the ILA parade on the Embarcadero as it crossed over to the sidewalk in front of the docks at Pier 18. Strikers condemned the unprovoked assault. Police said the men broke ranks for a rush on Pier 20. The *San Francisco Chronicle* described the confrontation:

> In a terrific surge of violence climaxing the twentieth day of the longshoremen's strike, nearly 1000 striking stevedores staged a bloody pitched battle with police yesterday afternoon on the San Francisco water front. Casualties were many as officers and strikers battled savagely at close range. . . .
>
> Under command of Lieutenant Joseph Mignola, a squad of police armed with sawed-off shotguns fired into the ranks of a group of strikers who were attempting to cover their advance on Pier 18 under a barrage of bricks and cobblestones. . . .
>
> Splotches of blood appeared on scores of faces. Police suffered heavily from the barrage of bricks and stones. Their own clubs wreaked equal damage.
>
> Across from Pier 18 one group of strikers found a pile of bricks and began hurling them with devastating accuracy into the approaching ranks of patrolmen.
>
> It was then that Lieutenant Mignola gave his men the order to fire. The officers drew pistols and fired over the heads of the strikers.
>
> When the barrage continued they leveled their sawed-off shotguns and fired directly into the line.[9]

Police shot one man in the back; four police officers, three strikers, and a newspaper reporter were hospitalized for their injuries, and scores were hurt less severely. Police arrested six strikers. Chief Quinn decreed that henceforth all pickets must remain on the town side of the Embarcadero.

The ILA fared no better in the Matson Building a few blocks away, where Joe Ryan agreed to recommend an employers' offer that granted neither union hiring halls nor preference of employment and ignored the seamen's demands. Paddy

Morris, Cliff Thurston, and Jack Bjorklund walked out an hour before the session ended, expressing dissatisfaction with the proceedings. Although no one signed the document, Ryan, Ed McGrady, and the press hailed the May 28 proposal as a strike settlement.

The Waterfront Employers of Seattle, Portland, San Francisco, and Los Angeles agreed to recognize the ILA for collective bargaining. A joint committee in each port would administer a joint hiring hall. There would be no discrimination against union or nonunion men; employers would be free to select men and men free to select their jobs; "and within those principles the employers will cooperate in spreading the work." Employers would pay expenses of the halls and salaries of their employees and "be responsible for the registration and dispatching records." The ILA would maintain and pay the salaries of "representatives in each hall, to see that there is no discrimination,"[10] and ILA representatives would have the right to inspect registration and dispatching records. The employers agreed to arbitrate wages and hours. They included Los Angeles in the proposal, the only concession over their previous position.

Ryan praised the offer: "This gives us exactly what the longshoremen have fought for and is all we want. It gives recognition to the I.L.A. in all disputes and provides for collective bargaining."[11] San Francisco longshoremen disagreed and roundly condemned the proposal for failing to meet their demands.

Northwest Locals Reject Offer

The Northwest negotiators, Morris, Thurston, and Bjorklund returned to Tacoma for the May 29 Joint Northwest Strike Committee meeting to consider the proposal. After they reported on the negotiations, the meeting voted unanimously to reject the offer and concur in the action of the Tacoma local, which had gone on record "as being absolutely opposed to any proposition being even entertained by District #38, I.L.A., which first does not recognize our original demand, which was absolutely 'closed' or 'Union Shop,' . . . and FURTHERMORE—that this Conference go on record as standing 100 per cent behind our original demands."[12]

Joe Ryan followed the negotiators to Tacoma to try to sell the employers' proposal. Instead, according to Ed Harris, after a long discussion and exchange of views, the delegates convinced Ryan of the importance of union hiring halls. After thirteen hours the meeting adjourned. At the Portland meeting the next night Ryan recommended rejection of the offer, and 1,000 members voted it down with "a roaring cheer." He also spoke against the proposal in Seattle, Everett, Olympia, and Grays Harbor. The San Francisco strikers confirmed their initial rejection with a secret ballot vote of 2,404 to 78. Only the small North Bend, Oregon, local voted for the offer. Down the coast A.H. Petersen recommended acceptance because it included the Los Angeles Waterfront Employers, but San Pedro rejected the proposal in a standing vote of 1,000 members. Ryan wired Luckenbach headquarters in New York to accept union hiring halls, warning that "trouble will undoubtedly follow on east coast" unless the company agreed.[13] Jack Bjorklund commented:

Joint Northwest Strike Committee outside the Seattle Labor Temple, 1934. (Courtesy Pacific Northwest Labor History Association)

> I have never seen the longshoremen's members so completely in accord upon any single issue as they are on this one. There is no possibility any settlement of the strike can be reached unless the employers agree to let the longshoremen have their own hiring halls and do their own dispatching of men.[14]

The Communists saw in the May 28 offer a plot by the district negotiators and Ryan to betray the rank and file. The Portland MWIU *Waterfront Striker* charged June 1 that Ryan and the district officials attempted to sell out the strike, and the San Francisco *Waterfront Worker* of June 12 attacked Ryan and Paddy Morris for trying to put over fink halls.

Probably the district negotiators expected the May 28 offer would be rejected. Tiny Thronson, a member of the Tacoma strike committee, believes the union sent the proposal to a vote to silence those who criticized the ILA for not taking a secret ballot strike vote May 8, and to demonstrate the strikers' solidarity. Ed McGrady flew back to Washington, D.C., declaring: "Both sides have adopted the law of the jungle. . . . The law of the jungle is force. It will mean more destruction, pitched battles—even murder."[15]

San Francisco Police Violence

Police violence against strikers, which San Francisco employers fully condoned, placed them in an awkward position. In a bulletin to members May 29 the Waterfront Employers complained:

> The local riots of yesterday (Monday) have been played up in the New York papers this morning to such an extent that dangerously large amounts of cargo shipments intercoastal from New York to San Francisco are being cancelled. In the interests of California business, and the accuracy of news transmission of California conditions, it is requested that you use the following material . . . for direct transmission to New York and other Eastern papers.

The suggested press release expressed "optimism on the waterfront situation" and stated that intercoastal and transpacific cargo loadings were "running approximately on schedule." The release quoted Mayor Angelo J. Rossi that "with the exception of the minor localized disturbances of yesterday, this has been the most peaceful strike in my knowledge in San Francisco."[16]

A provocative demonstration by the Young Communist League on May 30 to celebrate National Youth Day garnered headlines and martyrs. After being denied a parade permit, about 250 young men and women assembled at Third and Howard and marched toward the Embarcadero. When the parade stopped in front of the ILA hall at Steuart and Mission, 100 waiting police charged into the crowd with nightsticks, cracking heads at random. They injured twenty-five, one critically, including bystanders and strikers who rushed to the young people's defense. The Communist Party exploited the incident fully, with a mass meeting the next night sponsored by the International Labor Defense. While youth with bandaged heads sat on the platform, speakers from striking unions, community organizations, and the Communist Party addressed an overflow crowd. On Sunday, June 3, 5,000 strikers, their families, and sympathizers marched up Market Street to the Civic Center, where speakers denounced police brutality.

At this point, with press fanfare and employers' support, Lee Holman announced formation of a new union. Local 38-79 dismissed the "union" as press propaganda. While waiting for the shipowners' next move, the unions tightened up the strike in San Francisco. Employers circumvented the Teamster boycott of San Francisco docks by sending cargo unloaded by scabs in Belt Line boxcars to distant industrial sidings, where union teamsters picked it up. Strikers began following the hot cargo and picketing the cars, as far away as Los Angeles. As a result of the pickets and an appeal, the Teamsters Union voted June 7 to boycott all scab cargo at any location.

On June 8 Marine Engineers, completely organized on San Francisco Bay tugs, voted to refuse to move scab vessels, thereby immobilizing them at their location for the rest of the strike and obliging arriving ships to drop anchor in the bay. Masters, Mates and Pilots Local 90 challenged the Waterfront Employers' public statements of benevolent labor policies:

> Can anyone conceive of a more complete and definite repudiation of the methods used by the members of the W.F.E.U. than the present revolt among all those employed by them against the conditions these employers have so ruthlessly imposed for years? . . .
>
> . . . They forgot to inform the public that all the marine unions are on strike against their unfair practices as well as the low wages and long hours they imposed. They fail to mention their company unions that they have fostered and endowed for years, and that under these company unions the wages have been continually reduced, the working conditions getting steadily worse, and that to be known as a union man meant being fired and no known union men hired.[17]

Besides the British Columbia longshoremen's boycott, international support came from the Australian and New Zealand dockers' unions, the Central Union of Transport Workers in Amsterdam and Rotterdam, and dock workers at Gothenburg, Sweden, all pledging to embargo unfair vessels. On June 7 1,000 New York longshoremen handling freight from West Coast ports struck the *Lena Luckenbach* and *President Cleveland* in sympathy with the Pacific Coast. ILA officials sent them back to work the next day.

While employers publicized their "peaceful strike" for eastern consumption, they made plans to open the port by force, an action sure to provoke the bloodshed of which McGrady warned. San Francisco business interests decided June 5 to turn over strike strategy to the Industrial Association, the open-shop organization that had broken previous strikes. For the present the Waterfront Employers and Industrial Association kept their alliance secret, although reports circulated that the employers prepared to open the port. Still trying to break the deadlock, McGrady proposed a joint hiring hall, with expenses shared equally and employers and the union each paying the salary of its committee. A government representative would manage the hall. Disregarding Ryan's endorsement, the ILA district negotiators rejected the plan, offering instead to sign an agreement with any port or steamship company that would accept the union hiring hall. "We shall insist on complete control of hiring halls," declared Bill Lewis.[18] The employers refused.

Guerrilla Warfare at San Pedro

The San Pedro strikers fought hard to obstruct the work of the port. Police arrested seamen for beating scabs and held an IWW member for several days for inciting violence and spotting scabs. Two strikers drew thirty days for beating a detective in a Wilmington cafe. On May 23 between 150 and 200 pickets stopped a Pacific Electric train loaded with 150 scabs from Los Angeles, blocking the tracks for half an hour or more while they harangued the scabs. They persuaded all but seventeen to go back to Los Angeles and paid their return fare. The Marine Service Bureau put the original number at seventy-five and forty reported for work. Faced with such encounters, the employers soon abandoned attempts to transport scabs directly from Los Angeles by bus or train. After that agents hired scabs in a Los Angeles hotel room, took them by bus to Ventura, and loaded them into speed boats for San Pedro.

Police harassed the Communists, and the unions rebuffed them in their bid for prominence. May 19 police raided the MWIU hall, where fifteen people listened to an exhortation for more militant picketing. They seized literature, including a bulletin, "We must arm ourselves," and arrested fourteen, eleven of them charged under the old criminal syndicalism law. ISU and ILA officials repudiated Red interference, but the MWIU attracted a few fiery young militants.

African Americans continued to refuse to scab. The 750 members of the Los Angeles Longshoremen's Association rejected the employers' offer of a ten-year agreement at going wages or higher if they would go to work. The ILA denied a reported promise that if association members did not scab and if the union won, the association could have four full gangs on the docks.

The strike broadened and intensified. Between 600 and 700 Los Angeles County truck drivers refused to deliver freight to the waterfront. Ship Scalers, Cleaners and Painters, organized in an ILA local before the walkout, struck in sympathy, and several hundred licensed officers defined their status. Meetings of Masters, Mates and Pilots Local 90 and Marine Engineers No. 79 on May 25 and 26 voted to recommend that their members resign their positions on ships with scab crews or scab longshoremen working cargo. The strikers sought public support with periodic mass meetings to explain the issues, and 1,500 people attended an ILA benefit dance May 31.

Police activity increased in proportion to strike activity. The end of May employers erected five fences with gates across streets near the terminals. Police checked entering cars to prevent strikers from congregating at the docks. They limited pickets to the hours of 6:00 a.m. to 6:00 p.m., although they did not strictly enforce the severe antipicketing ordinance. Nearly 2,000 seamen and longshoremen swelled picket lines. To prevent harassment by strikers, employers began convoying trucks to the docks in caravans guarded by police. As in San Francisco, Belt Line railroad employees handled scab cargo. The night of June 1 police waiting with clubs routed a "mob" of 200 "communists" marching on the Terminal Island scab camp, and the next morning 150 strikers demonstrated at the Matson terminal when 150 scabs for the *Lurline* arrived from Los Angeles with police escort. Police arrested five strikers for assault. By June 7, 600 extra police patrolled the harbor on twelve-hour shifts, forbidden to fraternize with strikers. Police found saps and baseball bats in strikers' cars.

Crews continued to strike as vessels arrived. The ISU reported June 1 that 2,500 seamen had quit work in San Pedro. Coinciding with similar publicity in Portland and San Francisco, the Longshoremen's Protective Association announced June 7 that it had signed up 1,000 members, 650 of them experienced longshoremen registered with the fink hall including 350 from the ILA. Union Secretary Petersen laughed at the claims, declaring that no members had deserted. With 1,665 men working twenty-five ships, the employers stopped recruiting strikebreakers for the docks. A few scabs rebelled. Employers denied reports that seven gangs of them on the Luckenbach docks and others on the *Diamond Head* had struck because of poor food. In response to court orders, the shipowners fitted out the *Covena* for a cook ship, berthed between the sailing vessels at Wilmington, and evacuated the scab stockade.

Strikers stoned autos June 6; police jailed twenty-four for disorders, and a group of fifty strikers stopped trucks and persuaded drivers to return to Los Angeles. The next day pickets stoned eight officers of the United Fruit liner *Chiriqui*, and that night someone dropped homemade bombs on the Terminal Island scab camp, injuring a guard. Pickets stoned scabs working on the *West Palmas* June 8 at the Swayne & Hoyt docks on Terminal Island. When scabs rushed at their tormentors, the strikers drove them back onto the dock, where pickets and scabs fought with fists, clubs, and pitchforks while a crowd of 200 watched. Police arrested several strikers for assault.

A major skirmish took place June 11 at the Panama Pacific terminal when 200 strikers with two trucks rushed into the pier after a false alarm of a demonstration at Wilmington had drawn off some of the police. The strikers attacked scabs loading the *California* with pick handles and clubs, and police responded with clubs and billies in the fifteen-minute battle. Reportedly the raiders sought a scab veteran hatch tender. Police arrested seven strikers. After the battle the *California* laid fire hoses on deck to repulse another attack.

Hunger threatened strikers' families in spite of generous contributions from Los Angeles unions and small business and professional people in the harbor. The Los Angeles County Welfare Bureau agreed to provide food until federal funds became available. About 1,800 strikers' families received boxes with a four-day supply of food. Most of the day June 6 a line a block long and four deep filed through the relief station. The *Los Angeles Times* condemned the federal ruling that classified strikers as "unemployed" and therefore entitled to public relief: "This strike, thus paid for from the public purse, has run the gamut of anti-social activity. It has included riot, arson, murder, unprovoked assault, wilful destruction, sniping, defiance of public authority, the spread of Communism, interference with the normal course of business, damage to wholly innocent persons and business unconcerned in the issue and general menace to the public welfare."[19]

The *Times* accused the government of "taking sides in the strike" and called the strike itself "plain extortion and racketeering." The editorial charged: "Largely to blame is the government policy of encouraging strikes through the National Labor Board, the attempt to force the American Federation of Labor down industry's throat by law, the payment of doles to strikers in the guise of 'relief' and other forms of subsidy and encouragement." The paper urged the government to "stop coddling labor leaders for political purposes and step in to preserve order and keep traffic moving, by force if necessary."[20]

Defending the open shop proved expensive. The Los Angeles Steamship Association June 7 considered a 50 percent increase in carloading charges to shippers. "Use of unskilled longshoremen, their housing and feeding, employment of guards, and other expenses incident to the strike have made the increase necessary, it was stated."[21] The ILA asserted: "The financial loss to the shipowners is greater here than in any other port on the Pacific. From reliable sources we have gleaned the information that the average cost per ton is now $3.60 which is four times what it should be without taking into consideration the police overhead, cost of transporting strike breakers and recruiting them."[22] The *Los Angeles Citizen* charged that the Merchants' and Manufacturers' Association dictated the extreme open-shop stance of the Waterfront Employers because it financed the battle to break the ILA.

Employers asserted that Communists controlled the strike. The latter encountered rough treatment, reminiscent of the IWW free speech fight a decade earlier. In a demonstration sponsored by the United Front Seamen's Central Strike Committee June 11, 300 Reds stormed the San Pedro police station, according to wire service reports, to protest police brutality and seizure of pamphlets during a raid on the committee's hall. The demonstrators, including some women, assembled in a vacant lot four blocks away and moved toward the city hall, "like Russian revolution scenes in the movies," the *News-Pilot* said. Striking longshoremen ignored pleas to join the march. The demonstration lasted about half an hour when police arrived and dispersed the protestors with riot sticks arresting several. Red raids the next night failed to catch any victims.

The employers claimed June 11 to have 500 men registered before the strike at work, including strikers from northern ports. The ILA replied that their ranks remained unbroken. A letter to all locals declared: "The situation here appears better every day. . . . The turnover of scabs is over 50 percent weekly. It costs the shipowners $3.60 per scab delivered to their corrals. We have successfully forced them through legal action to quit housing and feeding any scabs on any city-owned property."[23]

Secretary A.H. Petersen urged all locals to disregard press reports of defeat from San Pedro, "for they are false and misleading and are only designed to attempt to break down the morale of the I.L.A. in other ports and to save the face of the Merchants' and Manufacturers' Association of Los Angeles who promised the shipowners that the strike would be broken within a period of two weeks. We are now entering the fifth week of the strike and our ranks remain one hundred percent solid."[24]

Northwest Picket Lines Hold

The Portland waterfront remained quiet in spite of the Chamber of Commerce's demand that Mayor Carson take the "necessary steps" to restore law and order. Shortly after midnight on May 24, ISU pickets boarded the tanker *Kewanee* at Linnton and persuaded seventeen of the crew to leave. The ILA charged that dynamite found in an auto near the waterfront might be a plant to discredit the strikers. Members of Marine Engineers No. 41 resolved May 20 to remain on ships and keep up steam for lights and protection of cargo, provided they received full pay, but they would not furnish steam to scabs or sail with scab crews.

Police and strikers massed at the Admiral Line dock where a steamer prepared to unload fruit, and pickets turned back two trucks at the gate. Mayor Carson and Police Chief Lawson arrived with machine gun and tear gas squads, but picket lines held against the sixty-five officers. Four days later police and pickets again converged at the Admiral Line dock, and the department put officers on twelve-hour shifts. The Central Labor Council condemned the long shifts and attempts to move cargo from the docks, and declared unfair all goods unloaded by scabs at San Francisco and trucked to Portland.

While Lee Holman made news in San Francisco, Portland employers tried to organize a "conservative union." The ILA said no strikers deserted to this group, and Joe Ryan declared firmly, referring to both ports, "There will be only one longshoremen's union, and that will be the I.L.A."[25]

Contrary to their claims, the Communists attracted few followers on the Portland waterfront. The *News-Telegram* reported May 14 that the MWIU asked for police protection after a raid on their hall, allegedly by longshoremen. The MWIU related in the *Voice of Action* that rank-and-file seamen repudiated SUP agent Carl Carter and followed the MWIU to the united front picket line. Instead, according to the press, about May 17 the ILA prevented an MWIU parade that would have resulted in a pitched battle with ISU pickets. The battle occurred a week later when ISU pickets beat MWIU pickets and destroyed their banners. An MWIU committee visited the SUP agent and "demanded the right to be allowed to be on the front and do some picketing."[26] Carter and the ILA strike committee agreed to permit the MWIU to picket, provided they did not soapbox or distribute literature. The MWIU had about 5 pickets on the front, as against 350 ISU pickets. The ILA would "keep order," presumably prevent hostile seamen from beating up MWIU members. Pickets greeted an MWIU parade May 25, permitted by the ILA and ISU, with "stoney stares," according to the press.

The crew of the States Line steamer *Illinois* walked off when she docked June 7. ISU pickets boarded the tanker *Kekoshee* and took off the crew of twenty-four. The pickets escorted the crew to the bus depot and ordered them to buy tickets out of town, then to the union hall, where the strikers gave the crew a meal and held them until time for the bus to leave. Mayor Carson threatened twelve police officers with dismissal for failing to protect the crew, but the captain of the *Kekoshee* testified at their hearing that strikers used no force to take the crew off, no police were around, and none were called. Many patrolmen sympathized with the strikers. Several on waterfront duty suggested donating a day's pay, and one charged that "the fellows who are trying to break this strike by using police and guns are the ones who cut our pay."[27]

Following rejection of the May 28 offer, Seattle employers pressed the new Mayor Charles Smith to settle the strike or provide protection to open the port, and King County Sheriff Claude Bannick deputized 50 waterfront guards. Twenty strikers raided a cabinet shop June 2 and seized 209 riot clubs worth $103, after overpowering a deputy sheriff who was supervising their manufacture. Sweeping past three guards, 100 longshoremen boarded several of the seven vessels lying at Pier 41 on June 9 in search of scabs. Police evicted them peaceably.

Strikers in Washington ports appreciated the portion of the *North Wind* payroll set aside for emergency relief. Seattle, Tacoma, Everett, Bellingham, and Olympia each received $250; Raymond and Grays Harbor $150; and Port Ludlow, Port Gamble, Port Angeles, and Port Townsend $50.00.

Newly organized Flour and Cereal Workers came to the Joint Northwest Strike Committee for help to gain union recognition and complete organization at the Fisher Flouring Mills. After being turned down decisively in an interview with company officials, the strike committee decided reluctantly "that the present time was not quite the right time to be involving ourselves into more trouble, so the matter was laid over indefinitely."[28] The incident foretold future patterns. As the union resurgence rolled on during the next few years, workers in many industries would look to the maritime unions for support.

The strike already delayed the fishing season in Bristol Bay. The Alaska Fishermen's Union joined the Alaska Packers to urge release of vessels so the season would not be altogether lost. On June 4 the Seattle longshoremen released five Alaska vessels to be worked under union conditions, including the *Mary D* of the Pacific American Fisheries out of Bellingham, the *Mazuma* of the Everett Packing Company, and the Northland Transportation's *North Haven* and *North King*, loaded at Portland, to ship essential supplies.

Captain John Fox, secretary of the Masters, Mates and Pilots Local 6, earned the nickname "Finky Fox" among militant seamen for allowing union mates on tugs to haul scabs and scab cargo. In line with the policy of Marine Engineers in other ports, members of No. 38 in Seattle stayed aboard struck ships but refused to sail with scabs or furnish steam for scab longshoremen. On June 7 the captain of the General Petroleum tanker *Brandywine*, lying in Elliott Bay without a crew, told the union engineers on board that they would move to another anchorage. Instead, off West Point, the tug *Adolph J* came alongside and put thirty scabs aboard the tanker, indicating that she planned to put to sea. When the engineers refused to work, the captain sent the scabs ashore in the ship's lifeboats. The *Brandywine* put back to Seattle, where the assistant engineers quit. When she returned to the dock, pickets beat the three-man crew of the *Adolph J* and attempted to sink the tug. Pete Gill filed a protest with customs agents over the *Brandywine* putting to sea without a crew. Two days later the tanker sailed with a full scab crew.

Whether coincidental or related to the *Brandywine* incident, the Joint Northwest Strike Committee summoned Fox and Joe Ruddy, also of the Masters, Mates and Pilots, to appear the next day "regarding their men still being aboard several ships which were considered unfair."[29] After lengthy discussions the strike committee dropped the matter, but seamen later related that Fox's members hauled scabs to vessels, hooked onto scab vessels, and towed barges with scab cargo out to vessels. One striker told of a committee from the Sailors' Union finding Fox hiding under his desk when they visited him to persuade him to cooperate with the strikers.

The Party Line

Communists pursued a two-part strike strategy on the coast. For longshoremen, demand rank-and-file decision-making instead of entrusting elected officers with responsibility. Praise those officials who followed the Party line and condemn those who opposed it. A *Voice of Action* article in May singled out Everett and San Francisco as the only locals with good leadership.

For seamen the Party built the MWIU, still the official seamen's union, and at the same time developed a fraction in the ISU. Using the MWIU front, the Party created United Front Seamen's Strike committees in each port to woo unattached seamen and embarrass ISU activists at a time when all good union people supported the concept of solidarity. One MWIU leaflet declared: "All along the Coast the M.W.I.U. has worked for unity and is gradually achieving it. In spite of Pete Gill, the Seattle local of the I.S.U. voted to recognize the M.W.I.U. as a striking Marine Union and to co-operate as much as possible with their pickets."[30]

The Communists attacked ISU officials for ignoring the United Front. A bulletin to all ISU members issued by the MWIU and United Front Committee at San Francisco called upon the ISU to cooperate: "SO FAR WHAT STEPS HAVE BEEN TAKEN BY THE I.S.U. OFFICIALS TO SEE THAT THE STRIKE IS CARRIED ON IN SUCH A MANNER THAT IT CAN BE WON? JUST ASK ANY RANK AND FILE I.S.U. MEMBER—NOTHING HAS BEEN DONE." Another MWIU leaflet accused Paul Scharrenberg, Selim Silver, and George Larsen of "kissing the boots of the shipowners and kicking at the militant MWIU. . . . Why should Scharrenberg, Silver and Larsen want to attack the MWIU? BECAUSE EVERY ATTEMPT THESE FAKERS HAVE MADE TO SELL-OUT HAS BEEN EXPOSED BY THE MWIU."[31]

In most ports the striking unions could easily dismiss the MWIU demand for parity, but in San Francisco the group had a powerful ally in longshore activists who followed the Party line. Early in the strike an MWIU leaflet urged San Francisco longshoremen to "DEMAND THAT THE MWIU REPRESENTATIVES BE CALLED IN ON THE CENTRAL STRIKE COMMITTEE OF THE I.L.A. IN ORDER THAT THE CLOSEST COORDINATION OF STRIKING SEAMEN AND LONGSHOREMEN MAY BE OBTAINED."[32] On May 30 the longshoremen demanded that the Sailors' Union call a mass meeting of all rank-and-file seamen, including the MWIU, to formulate demands, or the longshoremen would call one themselves. Rejecting the ultimatum, the Sailors strike committee instead held an ISU mass meeting June 1, attended by 1,800 seamen. The meeting reiterated the seamen's demands and their pledge to remain out until employers met longshoremen's demands. The next day the longshoremen agreed to support the majority union as determined by an election. No one doubted that this would be the ISU.

The Alaska Agreement

The federal government's threat to charter and operate vessels for Alaska brought the Alaska operators and the ILA to the bargaining table. The Joint Northwest Strike Committee reconvened June 5. Negotiations began that afternoon with a conference in Mayor Charles Smith's office, attended by the entire strike committee, Jack Bjorklund, Joe Ryan, Dave Beck, and representatives of the shipowners. Two days of negotiations produced a compromise agreement giving the unions closed shop and dispatching, but protecting Alaska Steamship's eight-five finks who refused to join the union. Delegates to the strike committee from all ports except Seattle and Everett had full power to act without referring the agreement back to their members. In a stormy meeting Local 38-12 finally gave its delegates that authority, and Everett followed.

The longshoremen signed the Alaska agreement June 8, in spite of objections from the San Francisco local. Joe Ryan and Jack Bjorkland signed for the ILA and representatives of Alaska Steamship, Northland Transportation, Santa Anna Steamship, Wills Navigation, and Arctic Transportation companies for the employers. Mayor Charles Smith signed as a witness. The agreement ran to September 30, 1934, the expiration date of the North Atlantic ILA agreement.

The agreement granted the ILA a closed shop and provided that all men would be dispatched from ILA halls. It set wages at the Tacoma prestrike scale, with any increase resulting from the strike settlement retroactive, and hours according to the ILA shipping code demands: a six-hour day, thirty-four-hour week. The agreement applied only to "vessels and cargo to and from Alaska direct, or to local products from British Columbia." The operators agreed not to "charter or operate any vessel or vessels belonging to an unfair company," and longshoremen would not be required to handle any unfair cargo or any cargo transshipped from any unfair vessel or dock. The pact protected marine groups with a provision "that all crews and all ships under this Agreement shall be hired under terms that are satisfactory to their respective organizations affiliated with the A.F. of L. or recognized as having jurisdiction over the work."[33] The district ILA sent the agreement to the locals, explaining the "terrific pressure" to turn public opinion against the longshoremen. "We are also convinced that the Waterfront Employers Union was bitterly opposed to the release of these ships," the letter stated.[34]

The Joint Northwest Strike Committee agreed that Local 38-12 would handle dispatching. For every eleven gangs furnished, Seattle would provide five, Tacoma three, Everett two, and Olympia one. Other Northwest ports would supply gangs as needed. The men would receive 50 percent of their earnings, the local to which they belonged 25 percent, and the strike committee the remaining 25 percent, to be distributed for emergency relief to locals not participating in the work.

The marine groups asked a wage increase from Alaska operators before they would sign agreements. Sailors' Union pickets kept the ships tied up until June 9, when the last union reached a settlement. Sailors; Firemen; Cooks and Stewards; Masters, Mates and Pilots; and Marine Engineers signed agreements. The sailors and firemen gained wage increases of $5.00 a month and 10 cents overtime, to $60.00 a month and 60 cents overtime. The longshoremen noted that the agreements contained no reference to union longshoremen and set the expiration date at September 30, 1935, instead of 1934. The agreement covered about 1,200 of the 25,000 strikers on the coast: 500 longshoremen, 600 unlicensed seamen, and 125 licensed officers.

Many strikers regretted the Alaska agreement because it breached their demand for a coastwide settlement; others approved it. San Pedro longshoremen advised the rest of the coast that "the sentiment of the men is that it is perfectly satisfactory . . . if the rest of the shipowners would concur in the same type of agreement, the strike could be settled."[35] In San Francisco the Sailors Union approved the agreement after lengthy discussion, but the San Pedro ISU voted 671 to 14 to refuse to sail the motor ship *Sierra* of the Arctic Transportation Company up the coast under the agreement.

Speaking for the Communists, the *Voice of Action* headlined: "RYAN PUTS OVER STRIKE-SPLITTING PROGRAM," and called the agreement "the greatest step yet made to smash the coastwide longshoremen's strike."[36] The District Committee of the Communist Party told Seattle longshoremen in a leaflet:

> Ryan, Lewis, Morton, Morris and the rest of the misleaders have succeeded to split the mighty unified front of the longshoremen and seamen, . . . Their action has already proven that they intend to "settle" the strike by signing separate agreements with each company, by calling on Mayor Smith of Seattle to intimidate the men, and finally by accepting the old wage scale, and leaving the final settlement to an arbitration board set up by Roosevelt's strikebreaking NRA machine.[37]

But who really won? Perhaps the operators regretted the agreement even more. Ralph Lomen of the Arctic Transportation Company declared: "It is certainly a victory for the longshoremen. I congratulate them. They got just about what they wanted."[38] Alfred Lundin of the Chamber of Commerce told Paul Eliel of the San Francisco Industrial Association that the "agreement was signed because of fear that the Federal Government would take over and operate the vessels on the Alaska run."[39] Lundin denounced the agreement:

> It is the "closed shop," and that means destruction of the commerce of the Port of Seattle. It is my opinion that coastal, intercoastal and overseas shipowners cannot and will not consent to sign any agreement that places the unions, not in partnership, but in absolute control on the waterfront—control of the job, with dictatorship to say what freight they class as "fair" and what "unfair."
>
> This is not the American plan permitting collective bargaining, but would mean ruin for the Port of Seattle in competition with free ports to the north and south, and would mean the enforced unionization of every concern that does business over Seattle's docks. . . . Seattle is not ready for any such abject surrender to union domination.[40]

Northwest Negotiations

At the invitation of the ILA locals, delegates from the Sailors, Marine Firemen, and Marine Cooks and Stewards joined the Joint Northwest Strike Committee June 12. Not content with the Alaska agreement, Mayor Smith demanded a strike settlement, or he would open the port by force. Alfred Lundin concurred: "This port must be opened—and it must be free."[41] In response to the Mayor's request, a committee of Seattle longshoremen met with employers "with instructions to settle the strike upon some plan similar to the Alaska Agreement, providing it was on a Coastwide basis."[42] The committee reported no progress and dissolved. A new committee of Cliff Thurston, Harry Pilcher, Paddy Morris, Jack Bjorklund, and Bill Craft met with

Seattle employers the next day and accomplished nothing. The strike committee rejected an open-shop employers' proposal June 14.

The labor community pressured Portland longshoremen to settle. According to Joe Ryan, representatives of the Portland Central Labor Council and Oregon State Federation of Labor "told our strike committee and some of our membership in my presence that the strike had gone on so long that they could no longer support them; that it began to look as if there would be a break and asked our men to consider some sort of arbitration or a compromise and return to work, . . . The Governor of Oregon was going to call out the troops until the Central body and the State Federation of Labor changed his mind."[43]

As a result of the meeting, the longshoremen agreed to cooperate with a mediation board composed of Governor Julius L. Meier, Franklin T. Griffin, president of the Portland Electric Power Company, and H.V. Alward, manager of the Bank of California. The Portland plan, endorsed by the employers, recognized the ILA as collective bargaining agent and provided for joint control of the hiring hall and arbitration of wages and conditions. The Portland ILA Executive Board endorsed the plan only if it became the basis for settlement in other ports. A meeting of representatives of about fifty Portland unions endorsed the plan. After lengthy discussion, the Joint Northwest Strike Committee dismissed the proposal. Most delegates considered it "nothing but an open shop agreement" that "would unquestionably soon break our ranks if we ever adopted same upon a Coastwide plan."[44] When the rest of the coast except San Pedro rejected the plan, the Portland ILA had no obligation to agree to a local settlement.

While Governor Meier mediated, Mayor Carson beat the war drum. In a radio speech June 9 he called for the use of force to break the strike and condemned people who contributed to strike relief. The strikers acquired their share of city weapons when a party raided a planing mill and took a quantity of nightsticks intended for the police. The tanker *Tejon* sailed June 13, the first vessel to get out since the beginning of the strike. The company brought the crew in speed boats and trucks, men jumped aboard, and someone chopped the hawser in two, all before pickets had time to mass. She swung into the channel full speed ahead, narrowly missing the loaded tanker *Kekoshee* anchored nearby. The Portland Waterfront Employers polled 600 registered longshoremen on the strike. Of the eighty-two ballots returned, about three-fourths opposed the strike and approved the employers' position. The ILA said scabs returned the ballots.

In Seattle Mayor Smith prepared to open the port. The *P-I* June 11 reported a concerted move to break the strike. The operators mobilized a large force of private guards, and the police department procured 500 new riot clubs. The tanker *LaBrea* sailed June 13 after twenty-five scabs armed with clubs fought their way through the picket line. Someone fired four shots at the strikers. Mayor Smith assumed personal command of the police force June 14, and Sheriff Bannick had 500 deputies ready, 90 percent with police or military experience. The mayor used his new weapons the next day at the Todd drydock , where 50 police stood off 400 strikers trying to take mates and engineers from the *Edward Luckenbach* and *Florence Luckenbach*. The *P-I* described police tactics: "Tanks of gas are connected with the manifolds of two police cars, at the Todd plant entrance, backed toward the street, with motors running. The cars are capable of discharging 800,000 cubic feet of gas, sufficient to quell any rush, according to Patrolman L.M. Norris, . . ."[45] Patrolmen with riot guns backed up the gas, with more in a harbor boat, and special squads of 100 stood ready for trouble.

The department put police on twelve-hour shifts and added twenty new horses to the force. It issued special revolver shells loaded with tear gas to officers on waterfront duty. Chief Howard ordered sporting goods stores and pawn shops to lock up all firearms and ball bats. Police confiscated over 100 bats, rubber hose lengths, and clubs in raids, and tore down the picket shacks at Todds. They took forty-eight hickory bats from a car in front of the Sailors' Union hall at 5:30 a.m. with two men asleep in it. Pickets patrolled roads leading to Todds, looking for food trucks attempting to stock the yards preparatory to bringing in scabs. The Seattle longshoremen declared that Smith's use of force would cancel the Alaska agreement, as they understood it to require that no strikebreakers worked other cargo in the port.

Tacoma employers organized their own Citizens' Emergency Committee to open the port, chaired by John Prins of the Metropolitan Life Insurance Company. He declared: "For Tacoma to allow its docks to remain closed to shipping after the movement of freight through Seattle has possibly been restored is unthinkable."[46] Paddy Morris replied for the ILA: "They're not going to be able to get any workers around here to do the work. And if they did, they would be incompetent and would hurt the dock and ship operators worse than they would hurt us. It's absolutely absurd."[47] The Tacoma Central Labor Council condemned use of armed guards and called upon all affiliated organizations "to use their economic and political power against any person, firm or organization"[48] involved in bringing armed guards to Washington waterfronts.

The Industrial Association Takes Charge

San Francisco employers resolved to end the strike, either by imposing their terms on the unions or opening the port by force. They made public the secret alliance of Waterfront Employers' Union, Chamber of Commerce, and Industrial Association in an exchange of letters. In a communication June 12, Chamber of Commerce President J.W. Mailliard, Jr., recited the damage caused by the strike and requested the Industrial Association to "immediately assume the responsibility of determining a method of ending this intolerable situation." He charged that the strike had cost San Francisco millions of dollars: "Approximately $40,000,000 worth of merchandise lies on docks, in warehouses and in the holds of 96 ships, stalled here by the strike. Freight entering the port for the first month of the strike was less by 600,000 tons, worth another $40,000,000 than in the month preceding the calling of the strike. Meantime, shipping that belongs to San Francisco is being diverted to Los Angeles where the port has been kept open."[49]

President John F. Forbes replied the next day for the Industrial Association accepting the responsibility "of determining a method of ending the intolerable conditions which are now existing in San Francisco as a result of the waterfront strike."[50] The ILA district negotiators refused to bargain with the Industrial Association, demanding the right to meet the employers for whom their members actually worked.

The day before the Chamber of Commerce initiated the drive to open the port, the San Francisco longshoremen appealed to all Bay Area unions for a general strike. In contrast to the Portland and Tacoma labor movements, where the ILA held a prominent place in the Central Labor Council, the San Francisco ILA had little influence in that body. In Portland and Tacoma the general strike resolutions of the central councils made specific threats to keep the National Guard off the waterfronts. In San Francisco the general strike call appealed for a demonstration of labor solidarity. The fact that the Communist Party regarded the general strike as a prime tool to radicalize the masses did not lessen its attraction for the embattled maritime workers and their friends. While the employers' attack escalated, sentiment for the general strike grew.

Mayors, who controlled the police, became necessary allies to break the strike. The mayors of Seattle and Portland would readily furnish protection for scabs at the operators' behest, but in San Francisco Mayor Rossi hesitated to alienate the labor community, with which he had strong ties. His refusal to guarantee protection for scab teamsters kept the port closed. Therefore, the employers concentrated their pressure on the mayor.

After Michael Casey of the Teamsters met with Rossi June 12, he telephoned Joe Ryan in Seattle to come to San Francisco immediately. Dave Beck also hastened south. Bill Lewis met Ryan at the airport, reminding him of the district's autonomy and the fact that any agreement would have to be ratified by the membership to be binding. Ryan described the meeting June 13 with the mayor and Lewis: "Mayor Rossi informed us he had gone as far as he could. He said, 'I'm tired of taking abuse from the rest of the citizens, saying I am yellow and am not able to cope with the Communists.'"[51]

The Waterfront Employers rejected a proposal by Ryan similar to the North Atlantic agreement. Tom Plant called preferential hiring "the closed shop," which was "contrary to the National Recovery Act."[52] Ryan replied that Plant's American-Hawaiian Steamship Company had signed the North Atlantic agreement, which the New York Shipping Association evidently found compatible with the NRA.

Mayor Rossi Capitulates

With Ryan's proposal out of the way, the employers carried out their plan for an amicable settlement on their terms. The morning of June 14 Joe Ryan and Michael Casey, J.P. McLaughlin, and Dave Beck of the Teamsters met with the officers and staff of the Industrial Association. The session excluded ILA district officials. According to Paul Eliel, member of the association's special advisory strike committee, Ryan assured the group that the rank-and-file longshoremen would accept an agreement satisfactory to him and the Teamsters. Likewise, Casey and Beck said union teamsters would haul freight if Ryan approved the agreement. After receiving these pledges from the union officials, Tom Plant and Albert E. Boynton, managing director of the Industrial Association, met with Mayor Rossi. Later that afternoon Rossi convened a conference in his office attended by Ryan, the Teamster officials, John O'Connell of the Labor Council, Plant, and representatives of the Industrial Association. Ryan described the mayor's capitulation:

> He said, "Plant, you and Ryan, if you don't get together and settle this question by tomorrow, then I will declare that the police shall protect the non-union teamster who wants to go in and carry freight into that waterfront."
>
> He was holding out against the powerful Industrial Association of San Francisco. . . . he held the fort for weeks and would not let them organize a draymen's organization to go in and take the place of the International Brotherhood of Teamsters. Mike Casey and McLaughlin and O'Connell were his labor advisers, just the same as George Meany, Jimmy Quinn and I are labor advisors to Mayor LaGuardia of the City of New York.
>
> . . . I went back to my room and figured the magnificent strike I had seen carried on in Portland, Grays Harbor, Olympia, Aberdeen, Tacoma, Seattle and the rest of the ports that I visited in the Northwest. The Waitresses' Union gave their time gratis to the men in Portland in the commissary, and every organization donated, even to the farmer bringing in potatoes and everything of that sort to help their men in this strike. On the other hand, the Mayor of Portland, Oregon, when the Police Department would not beat our men up on the waterfront, swore in two hundred deputy sheriffs, but the longshoremen got clubs and chased the two hundred deputy sheriffs out of there.[53]
>
> . . . when [Beck, Casey, and O'Connell] urged me in the presence of the Mayor of San Francisco that I not disrupt their organization; and told me that they couldn't hold it any longer; that it would not be fair to their membership to sacrifice their agreements, I felt that something must be done and done quickly.
>
> The Industrial Association, . . . is out to crush organized labor and they were organizing draymen and told Mr. Casey, Mr. O'Connell and Mr. McLaughlin, . . . that if they didn't carry out their agreement they had available all the men they wanted to work on the waterfront.[54]

Ryan saw no alternative but to reach a settlement, no matter how bad the terms. He agreed to negotiate privately with Tom Plant. At this point Lee Holman, the discredited president of Local 38-79, made another bid for legitimacy. He announced that Ryan had promised him an ILA charter if the San Francisco local refused to abide by the international constitution. Ryan denied the promise.

The Industrial Association tried without success to persuade federal and state officials to pressure Ryan to put into effect immediately the April 3 understanding or the May 28 offer as a settlement. In a long telegram to President Roosevelt June 15 the association warned that unless the strike ended "within the next few days" the ports would be opened "and it appears inevitable that an industrial conflict of character too serious to contemplate will be the outcome."[55] The association predicted a sympathetic strike if nonunion teamsters began hauling cargo. The association also sent wires to the Labor Department and Edward F. McGrady urging them to intercede personally with the President, as well as to the California congressional delegation and Governor Frank F. Merriam. Neither Roosevelt nor the Labor Department replied.

The June 16 Agreement

Joe Ryan and Tom Plant retired to the shipping executive's home June 15 to negotiate. By the end of the day they had drafted an agreement; early the next morning the Waterfront Employers met and accepted the draft, subject to approval by the Industrial Association. The association complied promptly. Meanwhile, Ryan summoned the ILA district board, officers of the San Francisco local, and officers of the marine unions, E.B. O'Grady, Masters, Mates and Pilots, Randolph Meriwether, Marine Engineers, Paul Scharrenberg, Sailors' Union, John McGovern, Marine Firemen, and Eugene Burke, Marine Cooks and Stewards, to a meeting in his room at the Whitcomb Hotel the same morning. Harry Bridges charged that Ryan hand-picked representatives of Local 38-79 to acquiesce. Ryan described the meeting: "These men went over the agreement; the Seamen's representatives asked me questions, and they all agreed that in face of the determined effort by the Industrial Association to keep the strike going and break up our organization, through putting on non-union teamsters in the teamsters' places, the right thing to do was to go along."[56] Bill Lewis related that the marine unions demanded that the ILA pull the East Coast longshoremen off the job. During the meeting Ryan approached their officers one by one and asked if they would also pull their crafts. Each one declared no—the strike must be confined to the West Coast.

Employers and labor representatives met in Mayor Rossi's office that afternoon. Lewis described the meeting:

> Only one copy of the proposed settlement was present and after a great deal of discussion lasting until well after 5:30 P.M. representatives of the various groups affixed their signatures to the document. Peterson and myself refused to sign it stating we did not have the power to sign anything and any agreement reached there would have to be ratified by the members of the District. It was not until after 7 o'clock that copies of the agreement were available to us.[57]

T.G. Plant signed the agreement for the Waterfront Employers' unions of San Francisco, Seattle, Portland, and Los Angeles; Joseph P. Ryan for the International Longshoremen's Association, and J.E. Finnegan for the Pacific Coast District ILA. Michael Casey and John P. McLaughlin of San Francisco and Dave Beck of Seattle signed for the Teamsters' Union to "guarantee the observance of this agreement" by the longshoremen. Charles A. Reynolds and J. L. Leonard of the President's Mediation Board and Mayor Rossi also signed as guarantors for the longshoremen, and John F. Forbes of the Industrial Association signed as guarantor for the Waterfront Employers. According to Lewis, Finnegan signed with the understanding from Casey that his union ship clerks would get a hearing before the Mediation Board. No one explained how the guarantors would enforce the agreement.

The agreement recognized the ILA as collective bargaining agent and established joint committees in each port to register longshoremen and manage the hiring halls, expenses to be borne equally. The agreement protected the open shop by a section prohibiting discrimination because of union membership or nonmembership, but nonmembers were required to pay their pro rata share of the longshoremen's expenses for the hiring hall. Employers would be free to select their men from among those registered, perpetuating company gangs and unequal earnings. Wages and hours would be arbitrated, the settlement retroactive to June 18, when the longshoremen would return to work. A sentence similar to the New York longshore agreement barred sympathetic strikes. The agreement ran to September 30, 1934, with an automatic renewal provision. The pact did not mention settlement of the marine workers' demands.

According to prearrangement, the San Francisco papers June 16 carried editorials that the strike MUST end, but the real news hit the streets later: "SAN FRANCISCO STRIKE ENDS: PORT OPENS MONDAY," the *Chronicle* headlined. Joe Ryan was optimistic:

> Under any circumstances the longshoremen will go back to work Monday. There is no question but that they will approve and ratify it. . . . Under the settlement we retain the right to discipline our members, which means that we can kick out any member who doesn't abide by the majority's rule.
>
> The man who doesn't belong to the union, . . . must pay the same pro rata share for the upkeep of the hiring hall as the man who does belong to the union, so there is no reason for keeping out of the union. This will mean that in four months at the most we will have a closed shop.[58]

Michael Casey asserted for the Teamsters: "Our men will return to work Monday [June 18] regardless of what action is taken by the longshoremen . . . No ratification by our membership is necessary,"[59] and Dave Beck announced the strike settlement and flew back to Seattle. Bill Lewis declared: "While it is not everything we wanted, we plan to make every effort to sell the plan to the membership and get them to approve it."[60] But Dewey Bennett of the Seattle ILA doubted acceptance without the union hiring hall: "I can't see that it differs so much from the agreement we turned down."[61]

Strikers Reject Agreement

The agreement took strikers, seamen and longshoremen alike, by surprise. With their ranks solid and morale high, they had no idea that the strike threatened to collapse and they must salvage what they could from the ruins. They saw the employers' warlike preparations to open the ports as a renewed challenge to their resources and determination, not inevitable defeat. They simply could not understand why Ryan agreed to the June 16 terms. The seamen cried foul. Selim Silver of the Sailors' Union said: "We agreed verbally not to return to work until the demands of all unions had been met. We expect the longshoremen to keep their end of the bargain."[62] In Seattle Dave Beck declared that the seamen were covered by an "understanding" that all strikers would immediately be reemployed without discrimination and their demands submitted to arbitration. Pete Gill replied for the Sailors: "You can thank Mr. Beck for his cooperation but we don't appreciate it. We were left out in the cold."[63]

Randolph Meriwether of the Marine Engineers asserted: "Regardless of recent reports of an agreement signed by Mr. Ryan, . . . we are standing united for a settlement satisfactory to all the striking unions," and the executive committee of the Masters, Mates and Pilots declared: "We wish to state no settlement has been made. We are all standing united for a settlement satisfactory to all unions on strike."[64] In a wire to the national president of the Masters, Mates and Pilots, E.B. O'Grady charged the agreement "completely deserts the other organizations." He requested the president to inform President Ryan that it "destroys the greatest and most uniform position ever existing."[65]

The district ILA called special meetings in all ports Sunday, June 17, to vote on the agreement. Joe Ryan charged that "radicals" packed the San Francisco meeting to insure rejection of the agreement. Strikers jammed the Eagles Auditorium to overflowing before the meeting started, according to Judge Reynolds's eyewitness account to Paul Eliel. By the time Ryan arrived, almost half an hour late, speakers from the floor had "whipped the meeting into a frenzy of anti-agreement sentiment." When he defended the agreement, "about fifteen longshoremen marched up on the platform and literally threatened Ryan with physical violence unless he withdrew his active support of the proposal."[66] The *Chronicle* reported that Ryan called for joint negotiations:

> I would not leave this hall until I had named a joint strike committee from all unions affected. Get your proposals together and present them jointly in a body. I was not aware the strike was so widespread or I would not have agreed to the peace plan, which I must say wasn't bad. . . . If you stick together I firmly believe you will be in a position to ask a general strike. [It is] no longer a fight of the maritime unions, but an open shop fight between organized labor and the open shop.[67]

E.B. O'Grady of the Masters, Mates and Pilots, W.W. Caves, chair of the Sailors' Union strike committee, and representatives of other unions also spoke. The meeting voted unanimously by acclamation to reject the agreement because it left out the marine crafts. Then the meeting endorsed participation in the Joint Marine Strike Committee already being organized. After the meeting Joe Ryan told the press: "It is no longer a longshoremen's strike. It has become a waterfront strike. I am going to take a back seat and let someone else take a hand at settling it." Asked if charters would be pulled, he replied, "If the men feel that loyalty to other unions makes it necessary to refuse the agreement there will be no reprisals."[68]

Michael Casey qualified his previous promise that the teamsters would go back to work: "We will make no move until the situation clarifies. . . . sending teamsters to the waterfront today would only result in confusion and possibly worse. After today it might be another story." Bill Lewis added: "I don't believe the teamsters will haul scab cargo no matter who orders them to. But if they try to do it anyway a mighty serious situation will result."[69]

Tacoma, Seattle, San Diego, and other ports rejected the agreement unanimously, and Portland by 97 percent. San Pedro accepted the agreement 638 to 584, but the local voted to remain on strike. Secretary Petersen explained the vote expressed the strikers' sentiment on the terms of the agreement alone, and it was not their intention to ignore the seamen. The day they voted the *Mariposa* arrived in port with a crerw of 300, almost all of whom struck.

The June 16 agreement represented the employers' last attempt to defeat the strikers by negotiations. Its reception proved that the longshoremen would not accept an open-shop agreement and that they would not desert that seamen. The employers would not offer an acceptable agreement, and they would not recognize the seamen's unions. Municipal authorities prepared to use police to open the major ports. The strikers prepared to resist scabs and police with all their strength. The greatest economic struggle ever undertaken by organized working people on the Pacific Coast approached its climax.

7

Open the Ports!

Between five and six thousand pickets massed on the San Francisco waterfront Monday morning, June 18. In observance of the agreement, no scabs worked and no union teamsters showed up to haul cargo. ILA district officers and the signatories to the agreement met in Mayor Rossi's office "to discuss the stand of the teamsters on the rejected agreement," according to District President Bill Lewis. "President Casey of the Teamsters was asked what his union would do to enforce the agreement but he stated that the teamsters' signatures were only affixed as observers to the agreement."[1] Rossi pleaded for more negotiations, offering to act as mediator.

By Monday afternoon the employers put the scabs back to work, and Tom Plant wrote an indignant letter to the Industrial Association charging Joe Ryan and Teamsters officials with breaking faith. He reiterated that the "Waterfront Employers' Union has no power or jurisdiction to discuss or negotiate demands of sailors or other marine workers," concluding: "This immediate repudiation of an agreement made in good faith is convincing evidence that the control of the Longshoremen's Association is dominated by the radical element and Communists . . . Further evidence of this is afforded by the fact that a majority of the committee of five selected at the longshoremen's meeting on Sunday have been active in the affairs of the Communist organization."[2] Presumably he referred to Harry Bridges, Henry Schmidt, and John Schomaker, identified with the Albion Hall caucus.

The employers' outrage was for public consumption. Privately, they apparently doubted that the agreement would end the strike. While Plant and Ryan negotiated, the Industrial Association prepared to open the port. It rented warehouses, bought trucks and other equipment, and organized the Atlas Trucking Company. Monday afternoon the association unveiled the new firm. Meanwhile, in the Fishermen's Hall near the Embarcadero, the Joint Marine Strike Committee created a single organization of all crafts to negotiate with the Waterfront Employers.

All along the coast June 18 the strike remained equally firm. No longshoremen returned to work, and no union teamsters went near the docks. In Seattle the Joint Northwest Strike Committee planned a strategy to meet the expected offensive. Down in San Pedro the ILA called on the marine crafts to form a joint committee.

Uptown in all the port cities newspaper headlines screamed for law and order to end the strike while citizens' committees recruited scabs and armed deputies. On the other side of town, union people's support grew for the strikers' cause which they increasingly identified as a fight for their own survival. Warning against the employers' attack on the closed shop, the *Labor Clarion* hailed this growing solidarity:

> Alarmed at the possibility that this position might be assumed generally by employers, workers in other groups have been impelled to stand behind the marine and waterfront workers under the general belief that they represented the "shock troops" in the general defense of the trade union position against the assault upon the union shop and for the installation of the "open shop" even in industries which had recognized union contracts for generations.[3]

Joint Marine Strike Committee

The unions formed the Joint Marine Strike Committee several days before the June 16 agreement, probably on the initiative of the ISU. W.W. Caves reported to the ISU strike committee June 12 on his recent trip to Seattle to investigate release of Alaska vessels. There he found all the striking unions cooperating in the Joint Northwest Strike Committee. Perhaps he suggested that San Francisco form a similar organization, for the ISU strike committee voted to meet jointly with the ILA committee.

In the absence of minutes, it appears that delegates from striking maritime and shipyard unions held a conference the next day at the Fishermen's Hall on Clay Street, H. Woods of the Sailors' Union presiding. Evidently, when the group seated delegates from the Marine Workers Industrial Union, the ISU representatives withdrew, crippling the committee. The meeting June 14 hastened to repair the damage: The delegates voted to ask the MWIU to withdraw, to ask the Marine Engineers to withdraw their resignation, and to have H. Woods resume the chair. The meeting the next day voted to return the credentials of the MWIU. Harry Bridges, John Schomaker, Charles Cutright, John McClellan, and Henry Schmidt, the executive committee of the strike committee, served as Local 38-79 delegates.

The Joint Marine Strike Committee, which became the hub of strike strategy, comprised seven maritime unions striking for their own demands: Longshoremen; Ship Clerks; Masters, Mates and Pilots; Marine Engineers; Sailors; Marine Firemen; and Marine Cooks and Stewards, and three shipyard unions striking in sympathy: Machinists Local 68 and Boilermakers Local 6 of San Francisco, and Machinists Local 234 of Oakland. In a five to four vote by organizations the committee elected Harry Bridges over E.B. O'Grady of the Masters, Mates and Pilots as permanent chair. The Marine Workers Industrial Union did not give up easily. The committee voted down 16 to 13 a motion June 18 to seat delegates as observers, and the next day tabled a letter repeating the request. The member unions exchanged signed pledges of mutual support:

> We, the undersigned organizations, individually and severally, hereby agree to refuse to return to work until such time as a satisfactory agreement is arrived at between employers of labor in the marine industries and the organizations signatory to this agreement. We also direct that a joint committee from each of the organizations signatory to this

agreement shall become the negotiation committee, who shall institute and complete negotiations between employers of labor in the marine industry and the organizations signatory to this agreement, subject to ratification of all crafts and strikers involved.[4]

"Hear Why the Ryan Agreement was Rejected," read the leaflet announcing the public meeting June 19 sponsored by the Joint Marine Strike Committee. A striker penciled "News Items" on the back:

1. A fink by the name of James Roston is shipping scabs. He lives in Room U-7 of the Panama Hotel. He ships from Annabelle's joint, next door.
2. The shipowners expected to fool the teamsters back to carrying freight away from the stagnated docks, thru lying reports in the newspapers they control. But yesterday morning, the time set for the "return to work," the teamsters failed to show up, thus strengthening the solidarity of the workers. . . .
3. The Wisconsin of the States Line, which was on the hook since Wednesday, came off 100% yesterday, including 2 mates and an engineer. They came off in a launch.[5]

Over 10,000 strikers and sympathizers crowded the Civic Auditorium June 19. Hisses and boos punctuated Mayor Rossi's speech, but mention by another speaker of a general strike brought vociferous approval. The meeting adopted two resolutions, one addressed to President Roosevelt and Congress "asking that heavily subsidized ship companies be required to cooperate with the policies of the Administration in granting living wages and decent conditions,"[6] and the other calling on Atlantic Coast seamen and longshoremen to strike in sympathy. For the first time in over forty-five years no vessel entered San Francisco Bay that day.

Almost the entire Joint Marine Strike Committee met with Mayor Rossi June 19 and presented official demands: "1. Absolute assurance that protection against discrimination of any character whatsoever, or blacklisting because of union or strike activities. 2. Joint settlements for all unions involved."[7] Rossi asked for specific proposals to transmit to the Waterfront Employers. In reply to the Joint Marine Strike Committee's request to negotiate, Tom Plant reiterated the Waterfront Employers' refusal to bargain with the seafaring unions. The meeting the next day arranged by the mayor accomplished nothing. The Joint Committee submitted the longshoremen's demands. Plant came with a prepared statement again refusing to negotiate with the committee and then withdrew.

The press reported the strike cost San Francisco $700,000 a day, $1.00 for each inhabitant. The *Pacific Shipper* asserted that the effect of rejection of the June 16 agreement "was to crystallize civic and industrial sentiment in the belief that the strike could be broken only by meeting force with force." The paper declared that the shipowners regarded the longshoremen's determination to stand by the marine crafts "as a mere subterfuge by which the Communist element could extend their reign of thuggery indefinitely."[8] The ILA strike committee concluded that "the employers of labor in the marine industry have no desire to settle the strike peacefully and amicably."[9]

The employers still tried to enlist President Roosevelt's intervention. In a long telegram June 19 the Industrial Association recited the repudiation of the June 16 agreement at a "rump meeting" and warned of "crisis threatening destruction of property and serious loss of life in various ports . . . unless you act to compel performance on the part of Longshoremen's Unions of the agreement signed by their International President."[10] Instead of trying to coerce the ILA, Secretary of Labor Perkins requested employers and longshoremen to arbitrate the hiring hall as the sole remaining point at issue. Both refused. According to Paul Eliel, the Industrial Association followed up Plant's refusal with a request to Michael Casey to call AFL President William Green, explain the strike situation to him, and ask him to transmit the information to Secretary Perkins. Casey complied.

In spite of the Waterfront Employers' repeated refusal to recognize any union but the ILA, the rest of the striking unions submitted their demands to Mayor Rossi. The International Seamen's Union asked recognition, "absolute assurance against discrimination of any character whatsoever, or blacklisting because of union or strike activities," and "abolition of any shipowners employment bureau in any form." The Masters, Mates and Pilots asked preference of employment, no discrimination for strike activities, the right of union representatives to visit ships and be present when seamen signed articles, reemployment of all strikers, and a satisfactory settlement for all striking unions. The Marine Engineers made similar demands. The ILA Ship Clerks, called checkers in Northwest ports, asked recognition and no discrimination for union or strike activities. They wanted "a preferential agreement covering hours, wages and working conditions similar to the one now in effect at the Port of New York between our organization and the New York Shipping Association."[11]

On June 20 the Joint Marine Strike Committee adopted a system of proportionate representation of one vote for each 500 strikers or fraction thereof. This probably gave six votes to ILA Local 38-79, three each to the Sailors and Marine Firemen, two to the Marine Cooks and Stewards, and one each to the Masters, Mates and Pilots, Marine Engineers, Ship Clerks, Machinists, and Boilermakers. The Teamsters' meeting the next night rejected the invitation of E.B. O'Grady and Harry Bridges to send delegates to the Joint Marine Strike Committee. The waterfront boycott would continue, but the Teamsters would remain free of mutual pledges of support.

By mid-June strike relief became an acute problem in the war between shipowners' pocketbooks and strikers' stomachs. The San Francisco Labor Council estimated almost 7,000 AFL strikers to take care of: 3,000 longshoremen, 3,000 unlicensed seamen and more as ships arrived, 450 masters, mates and pilots, between 94 and 125 machinists, between 97 and 110 boilermakers, and 300 ship clerks, besides 500 unaffiliated marine engineers. Teamsters and Ferryboatmen supported their own strikers. The joint relief kitchen at 84 Embarcadero served 3,300 meals a day. Uptown unions donated thousands of dollars, two Teamster locals each $1,000. Receipts for the week reported June 22 totaled $2,245. A strikers' committee told the Citizens' Emergency Relief Committee June 20 that probably from 1,500 to 2,000 strikers would soon need relief. Family and shelter feeding cost $70,000 a month, according to the relief director. The ILA Women's Auxiliary opened a headquarters on Market Street and enlisted strikers' wives to picket stores receiving unfair freight.

The Communist Issue

Anti-Communist militants among the strikers emphatically rejected employers' charges of Communist influence. Within the Sailors' Union a controversy developed over the united-front demand by the Marine Workers Industrial Union. On June 12 the ISU strike committee voted to exclude the MWIU from all future meetings, and two days later passed a resolution denying that the strike was Communist controlled and repudiating "any and all Communist organizations including the so-called Marine Workers Industrial Union."[12] The next evening Harry Bridges denounced the anti-Communist resolution at a seamen's mass meeting as "dangerous to the complete unity of strikers."[13] At the ILA meeting June 17 W.W. Caves repudiated the anti-Communist resolution of the ISU strike committee and called a seamen's mass meeting that evening, at which he defended the MWIU.

The following day the Hearst *Call-Bulletin* published statements by Caves attacking the Sailors' Union officials and demanding support for the united front. When Secretary George Larsen suspended Caves from the strike committee for the public attack, angry union members invaded Larsen's office to protest the action. The regular meeting that night reinstated Caves to the strike committee and elected him to the Joint Marine Strike Committee, along with Jack O'Brien, Justus Swanson, Herbert Mills, and Herman Bach. A stormy meeting of the SUP strike committee June 20 ended with Caves's removal as chair and a warning to make no more public statements for the committee. Mills became chair, and the committee voted to oppose seating the MWIU in the Joint Marine Strike Committee. The SUP suspended Caves from the strike committee June 24 "because he has not been around for three days, and because his attitude and general disposition seems to inject a spirit of dissention in the Committee."[14]

Besides agitating for a seamen's united front, the MWIU organized striking ship scalers. The Joint Marine Strike Committee rejected Harry Jackson's plea to seat delegates from over 300 scalers organized in the MWIU. The ILA strike bulletin in the *Western Worker* criticized the ISU for obstructing "complete unity": "Haven't we learnt yet that our strength lies in unity in our ranks? We longshoremen know that the Marine Workers Industrial Union was the first to call out the seamen to support us. They called the strike May 11. We know that it is this splendid cooperation which made the strike 100% from the beginning. They have been on the picket line with us and in all fights."[15]

The San Francisco Labor Council also repudiated Communist involvement in a resolution passed June 22 by a vote of 129 to 22, with over 250 delegates present and a "large communistic claque in attendance as visitors," the *Labor Clarion* reported. The resolution, introduced by Paul Scharrenberg, denounced Communist attacks on AFL unions and their officers and resolved, "That we repudiate all Communist organizations, especially the so-called Marine Industrial Union, and denounce their efforts to inject themselves into an industrial conflict for the sole purpose of making converts to communism; . . ."[16] Both E.B. O'Grady and Harry Bridges opposed the resolution. Anticipating a motion for a general strike, the maritime unions turned out in force, but the "prolonged and at times acrimonious debate" on the resolution sidetracked the general strike call. The meeting voted down 66 to 29 a motion by Mike Casey to investigate each delegate for Communist affiliation.

Regular meetings of the ILA and Sailors' Union also adopted the anti-Communist resolution. True to form, the Communist Party replied with a leaflet condemning AFL and Labor Council officials as "only bosses agents":

> They do not want the longshoremen to win! They know that a victory for the longshoremen will encourage the membership of all unions to follow the example of the longshoremen—take rank and file control, and follow a fighting policy.
>
> Scharrenberg and Larsen of the seamen have been doing everything in their power . . . to still the voice of the rank and file. Since the last seamen's meeting, when over 1000 repudiated their splitting policy, they have decided not to call any more mass meetings. Scharrenberg wants the fink hall to stay.[17]

The Communist issue divided picket lines as well as union meetings. The ILA strike bulletin June 25 reminded pickets that "the only weapon we have is SOLIDARITY: No matter what union or faction one may belong to – if a man is a striker – he's a friend – and let the employer see that the WORKERS ARE ALL FOR ONE AND ONE FOR ALL . . ."[18]

San Pedro

After the ILA rejected the June 16 agreement, the San Pedro unions formed a joint strike committee on the initiative of the ILA. With the port open, the striking ILA Ship Scalers, nearly 1,000 strong, composed almost entirely of Chicano workers, was "instrumental in retarding the movement of ships,"[19] according to Local 38-82 President W.R. Patterson. Although Communists had a limited following among seamen, the ILA shunned them. The union appointed a committee to try any member "who expressed radical sentiments," according to the *News-Pilot.* If found guilty, presumably of being a Communist, the member would be expelled. Sporadic violence continued. The press reported beatings and arrests almost daily, and June 19 someone found a tin box containing eight homemade bombs near the Texaco oil reservoir. On June 23 about 300 pickets, believed to be led by the United Front Seamen's Committee, stormed the pier at Berth 90, armed with rocks, clubs, and pieces of pipe. Both sides suffered injuries.

The steam schooner operators' attempt to reopen the coastwise lumber trade, tied up since mid-May, provoked more violence. Police arrested eleven seamen June 24 at the McCormick lumber yard, where they intended to work over some scabs. Four days later police with clubs dispersed 200 strikers attempting to raid the E.K. Wood lumber yard, where fifteen scabs from a labor camp discharged a cargo of Northwest lumber from the *Cascade*, tied up since May 28. Police attacked pickets with gas bombs the night of June 27, and the next day arrested thirty-two strikers in a picket boat for shouting insults at scabs. They released the pickets a day later without charges, to resume their marine patrol. The *Lena Luckenbach* could not discharge cargo June 30 because her engineers refused to furnish steam for scabs. They offered to take the vessel to sea provided the crew included no scabs, an impossibility because no union seamen would sign on. While it lasted, their action amounted to a sit-in, immobilizing the vessel.

The employers announced a new peak of activity June 27, with 1,748 men working twenty-one ships. Nine freighters and one tanker sailed, but the work proved costly. A letter from T.G. Plant of the San Francisco Waterfront Employers' Union June 21 to Eugene Mills, president of the San Pedro Marine Service Bureau, complaining of expenses, confirmed the strikers' charges that San Francisco shipowners really controlled the southern port. Plant objected to the average expense of approximately $7,000 a day. Instead of guards costing $100,000 for wages and board, city police should protect scabs. Individual employers should pay the daily expense to house and feed the scabs they used.

Seattle: Smith Cove

The Joint Northwest Strike Committee reconvened June 18 at Seattle amid Mayor Smith's warlike preparations to open the port. The committee rejected a proposal of the salmon terminal operators to sign an agreement similar to the Alaska agreement, but the delegates released canned salmon consigned to relief agencies, some destined to feed the San Pedro strikers. The committee stipulated that freight car numbers must be furnished and the salmon traced to its actual destination. When Alaska Steamship Company paid for Saturday work $300 short at the old rate, the committee secured payment of the correct amount.

To answer employer charges that the unions did not want to settle the strike, the Joint Northwest Strike Committee drafted a counterproposal to the June 16 agreement. It provided for union recognition, registration of longshoremen employed prior to January 1, 1934, a joint policy committee to determine the method of dispatching and act as a grievance committee, dispatching from ILA halls, and arbitration of wages and hours. Crews of all ships would be hired under terms satisfactory to their unions. The employers rejected the proposal.

The delegates requested Joe Ryan June 18 "to embargo all strike-affected ships and cargoes originating in or coming into any Atlantic or Gulf port."[20] He refused, stating that he would not "sacrifice the efforts of nineteen years of constructive negotiations between ourselves and our employers for a group of maritime organizations who are not in a position to reciprocate until such time as they demonstrate the strength of their own international organizations."[21]

Then the strike committee appealed directly to Atlantic and Gulf ILA locals to "place an embargo on all ships and cargoes loaded by scabs on the Pacific Coast. We need not urge you to do this on behalf of labor solidarity, but we do ask you as members of our ILA not to aid the enemy by handling cargo which is unfair to your Brother members and fellow workers. We are fighting the battle of the union as against the open shop. It is as much your fight as ours, and because it is, we do not hesitate to call on you for this cooperation."[22]

"POLICE WILL OPEN PORT TODAY!" the *Post-Intelligencer* headlined June 20. The city and county assembled an army of 560: 300 city police, 200 deputies, and 60 state troopers. With eighteen ships waiting to unload, the employers planned to begin work at Piers 40 and 41 at Smith Cove. Police Chief George F. Howard told the entire force massed at headquarters: "We are not looking for trouble, but we are prepared for it. . . . See that your guns are in good shape. But use them only in the last extremity for the protection of life and property. . . . A strike council was appointed in this city weeks ago. The man at the head of it is one of the most prominent communists on the Pacific Coast. That's all."[23]

Taking pickets by surprise, about 8:00 a.m. a long caravan of cabs, trucks, and buses appeared at Pier 40 with 400 police and armed guards. The employers brought forty-eight scabs from West Seattle in a launch guarded by two coast guard cutters, and a fire engine company stood by with hoses ready. They shifted the *Admiral Rogers* from Pier 40 to 41 to serve as mess hall and lodging for scabs. Toward noon 100 pickets gathered. They turned back trucks loaded with food and supplies for police and scabs and persuaded a City Light line crew not to install a flood light for the police. Pickets beat a teamster. At noon the Sailors' Union sent stew, buns, and coffee to the pickets.

Pickets attempt to block a train at Smith Cove, Seattle, June 20, 1934. (Courtesy Museum of History and Industry, Seattle Post-Intelligencer *Collection, photograph #23998)*

Up the tracks leading to the piers another 100 pickets sat down in front of a Great Northern switch engine headed onto the pier to shift freight cars so scabs could unload the cargo of silk aboard the *President Grant*, tied up since May 16. After talking with the strikers the engineer returned to the yards. Two hundred police protected the land end of Pier 40, and fifty deputies guarded the scabs at the end of the dock two blocks away. The employers expressed satisfaction with the day's work.

While the employers fortified Pier 40, the Joint Northwest Strike Committee adopted a motion, "That we notify Mayor Smith of Seattle that unless he removes police from Seattle docks, we shall cease all work on the Alaska ships,"[24] and sent a committee of Jack Bjorklund, Bill Craft, Ed Harris, all ILA, Henry Whiting, Sailor's Union, and George Laws, Marine Firemen, to meet with the mayor. The delegation made no progress. That night the Seattle Central Labor Council voted to request Mayor Smith and the City Council to withdraw police from the waterfront and request Sheriff Bannick to withdraw special deputies. The Labor Council adjourned without acting on a motion for a general strike "if police and armed guards were not withdrawn in 24 hours."[25]

After another meeting the next morning with Mayor Smith produced no results, the Joint Northwest Strike Committee requested the Seattle Central Labor Council Advisory Board to intercede with the mayor. Pickets at Smith Cove, reinforced by Tacoma longshoremen, turned back a train before 8:00 a.m. and another around 11:00. Then Mayor Smith and Chief Howard visited the scene. The next time pickets sat down on the tracks, sixteen mounted officers rode into the strikers swinging clubs; they injured three strikers. Cars with supplies for police went into the dock. Someone mixed salt with sugar delivered to police, spoiling their coffee. Pickets beat up a group of magazine salesmen that refused to stop before the sales crew convinced them they were not scabs. A coast guard cutter and harbor patrol boat kept two picket launches away from the docks.

Word reached the Joint Northwest Strike Committee early in the afternoon of an impending raid at Pier 40 incited by outsiders. The entire committee went down to Smith Cove to prevent it. The press reported the committee's intervention: "'We're not going to send you men through the barricade against machine guns and gas when you have only your bare hands,' one of the speakers told the crowd. 'We've given the police until 7 o'clock to withdraw from the pier. If they don't comply with our demand we'll pull every man off the Alaska ships—and that will mean that every ship in the harbor will be tied up.'"[26]

The committee averted the raid. Sheriff Bannick told a strikers' committee that he could not disarm the special deputies because their guns belonged to the Citizens' Committee, and the district attorney told another committee that the law permitted armed guards aboard vessels within the three-mile limit. Late that afternoon scabs began unloading the British *M.S. Modavia* at Pier 40.

At 8:30 the committee of Bjorklund, Craft, Morris, Laws, Whiting, and Harris returned to the strike committee from their final meeting with Mayor Smith and the Labor Council Advisory Board. The minutes reported: "Stated they had a very hot session with the Mayor, but that he would absolutely not remove his police from the docks." The Joint Northwest Strike Committee voted to "pull men from Alaska ships at once" and wired Portland, San Francisco, San Pedro, and Joe Ryan: "Mayor Smith breaks faith and spirit of Alaska agreement by placing police on docks when no lives or property were at stake there being no scabs or pickets on said docks—N.West Strike Committee has ordered work ceased on all Alaska ships at once this includes all Marine Groups—Employers making no progress—Morale good."[27]

Work stopped on the Alaska vessels at 9:30 that night. All crafts walked off except marine engineers left aboard to assure the safety of the vessels. The employers and Alaska Governor Troy condemned the strikers for tying up the ships, and Alaska Steamship Company threatened to sue them for loss or delay caused by the stoppage. Dave Beck joined the chorus condemning the strikers for breaking the agreement and pledged to "handle cargoes from any spot where it is safe for us to do so."[28]

Tacoma: The Milwaukee Dock

Tacoma employers planned to open the port simultaneously with Seattle. The Citizens' Emergency Committee declared in a newspaper ad June 18: "THE PORT OF TACOMA WILL BE OPEN! . . . 600 TACOME LONGSHOREMEN HAVE NO RIGHT – NOR WILL THEY BE PERMITTED TO DICTATE – THE FUTURE OF 106,000 PEOPLE."[29]

Tacoma longshoremen prepared to resist. The evening of June 19 unknown persons seized a truck loaded with cots and mattresses for scabs to be housed on the Milwaukee Dock. They deflated the truck tires and threw the contents on the ground. That night they took the scab foreman from his home and beat him severely. A friendly police officer tipped off the longshoremen that a bus load of special deputies would arrive from Seattle the morning of the 20th. When the Grayhound pulled into the depot at 4:30 a.m., a dozen strikers watched thirty-one specials get off.

Police escorted the deputies, together with local recruits and trucks loaded with bedding, food, and other supplies, to the Milwaukee Dock, where over 100 pickets had already gathered. There, representatives of the Citizens' Committee found the gates locked. Meanwhile, the specials climbed out of the cars into the waiting crowd of strikers. At the request of the longshoremen, police searched and disarmed the deputies, seizing an assortment of guns, clubs, hand grenades, and tear gas bombs. Then, after a "brief but firm parley with Tacoma longshoremen," the specials decided to give up and return to Seattle. Police escorted them back to the bus depot. No scabs showed up at the docks. Three young men hired as watchmen observed the confrontation. After seeing the deputies' arsenal and hearing the strikers' description of their duties, they quit and departed with the strikers. J.C. Osborne, head of the Associated Industries, had deputized the watchmen illegally. The labor legal bureau collected a full day's pay for them after the Citizens' Committee offered half. The *Tacoma News Tribune* headline read: "EFFORTS TO OPEN PORT HERE FAIL."[30]

That night the Tacoma Central Labor Council adopted a strong statement endorsing the proposed agreement of the Joint Northwest Strike Committee and condemning the Citizens' Emergency Committee. The council called for a boycott of "individuals, firms and organizations guilty of aiding in any way the efforts of the Tacoma Citizens' Emergency Committee to carry out their strikebreaking policy."[31]

The Citizens' Committee still insisted that "the port must open." ILA representatives met with the Tacoma Port Commission June 23, with the result that the next morning the ILA pulled pickets from the Port docks and teamsters hauled cooperage supplies and wheat from the piers. Monday morning, the 25th, the ILA and Port officials met again. After an hour's session the Port officials invited the Citizens' Committee to send a representative. The committee refused. The next day the Port Commission rejected the committee's demand to resume work with police protection, and June 29 the committee announced it was abandoning plans to begin operations because the Port Commission refused to cooperate.

Failing to open the port by force, the Waterfront Employers tried to soften up the strikers with a folksy personal letter from President Sam Stocking July 3. He recited alarming facts of diverted cargoes, trade permanently lost, and the resulting damage to the strikers as longshoremen and taxpayers, ending with the appeal: "Let's get back to work, Men, and keep Tacoma on the map. It's your city and mine."[32]

Outrage in Longview-Kelso over employers' attempts to open the ports threatened to boil over in a general strike. About 600 loggers, sawmill workers, warehousemen, and pulp mill workers walked out at noon June 20. People expected the Electrical Workers, Retail Clerks, and Teamsters to take strike votes later that day. The Central Labor Council wired the Tacoma and Seattle councils: "Longview-Kelso Central Labor Council representing 3500 workers, condemns use of armed guards for forceful opening of Pacific Coast ports. We are prepared to use whatever means are necessary to protect members of the I.L.A."[33] After a few days, when the general strike failed to materialize, the loggers and mill workers returned to work.

General Strike Call

Work limped along at Smith Cove in Seattle. June 22 forty more scabs arrived by launch to work the Tacoma-Oriental steamer *Everett.* After many failures two food trucks got through the picket lines. The *Modavia* sailed June 23 with 5,800 cases of salmon. Pickets permitted a switch engine to enter Pier 40 to remove empty cars. The next day the employers ran the first trainload of cargo into the pier at 4:00 a.m. under mounted police escort. The night of June 24 pickets greased tracks leading to Smith Cove with crude oil, repeating the operation the next night with axle grease. After that police patrolled the tracks. Strikers beat four scabs coming out of the Alaska Building June 25. The press June 26 reported 400 Tacoma longshoremen massed in Seattle. June 28 eighty pickets persuaded the crew of a fourteen-car train not to enter Pier 40. Then the twenty mounted police and their horses moved from a dock warehouse to tents near the tracks for quicker response. Someone bombed the Northern Pacific yard manager's home, tearing a hole in the lawn. The employers claimed 165 scabs at work, guarded by 200 specials. International President Ryan refused another request to embargo hot ships on the Atlantic and Gulf.

ILA members sought an injunction to prevent the Port of Seattle from housing guards on public property. After the City Council refused by a five to four vote to confirm the appointment of special police, Mayor Smith reappointed 102 of them, wages to be paid and provisions furnished by the Citizens' Committee. The longshoremen again went to court to enjoin the mayor and Chief Howard from soliciting money and supplies for special police, contending the use of private contributions for the police violated the city charter. They charged that the mayor conspired with the Waterfront Employers and Citizens' Committee to break the strike.

In British Columbia June 22 members of the Vancouver and New Westminster Waterfront Workers refused to unload the *Kingsley* carrying a shipment of fruit from California, nor would they handle 250 boxes of silver arrived from China for reshipment to San Francisco and New York. Four days later 500 Vancouver longshoremen took forty scabs off the *Kingsley*, using a tank car for a battering ram to crash the barricade. The Vancouver union and Joint Northwest Strike Committee exchanged fraternal delegates to meetings.

Many deck officers sailing out of Seattle had belonged to Masters, Mates and Pilots Local 6 before the coastwide Local 90 was organized. For over a month while the port lay idle, Local 6 delayed the strike call, left to the discretion of Secretary John Fox, and members stayed with their vessels. The local finally struck June 26, calling out masters and mates on the *Everett* and *Admiral Chase*, being worked by scabs. Ten days later Seattle Marine Engineers' Beneficial Association No. 38 officially struck, seven weeks after the rest of the coast.

The night of June 27, ILA pickets spotted a dozen black scab cooks and stewards boarding a Bainbridge Island ferry. Following the boat across the sound in a launch, the strikers beat the ferry to Port Blakely and hid in bushes near the dock. A tug would pick up the scabs there and take them back to the *Admiral Chase* at Pier 40, a long way around to avoid pickets. When the scabs left the ferry, the strikers jumped out, beat them, and chased them into the woods. The next morning two came out of the woods and begged a ride back to Seattle, where one went to the Marine Hospital. Blacks among the pickets "later laughed over the incident, agreeing that they did not 'beat the stewards good, but just scared them.'"[34]

In a letter June 26 to the 106 Seattle unions, the ILA called for a general strike if police remained on the docks, and the strikers demanded action in the Central Labor Council meeting the next night:

> Communication from Marine Cooks & Stewards & Firemen Requesting general strike of all locals, also from Longshoremen Resolution requesting all affiliated locals to take immediate steps to vote the institution of a general strike. Moved letter be filed, amended council go on record favoring general strike. Ruled out of order by the chairman, as it was in direct conflict with laws of the A.F. of L. A telegram from President Green was read advising against sympathetic strike. After considerable discussion, motion carried.[35]

The *Voice of Action* gave William Green's wire front-page coverage to prove the treachery of AFL officials: "The Central Labor Council of Seattle must not either countenance or favor a sympathetic strike on the part of workers not involved in the longshoremen's controversy," he said. A sympathetic strike violated AFL laws, broke contracts, and antagonized the public. He urged the council "to become actively aggressive in opposing sympathetic strike."[36]

The Communists tried to take advantage of the strikers' anger and frustration over the employers' opening the port. The Communist Party staged a demonstration June 26 across from the ILA hall, addressed by Roy Hudson, national secretary of the MWIU. Speakers called for a general strike, and the meeting endorsed a demonstration June 29 at Pier 40 against police and armed guards. The Joint Northwest Strike Committee passed a motion opposing "any and all demonstrations unless approved by our organization."[37] The press reported 750 demonstrated at Pier 40.

The *Labor Advocate* labeled the attempt to open Seattle a failure. The scabs, mostly University of Washington students related to shipping interests, grumbled because they paid $1.00 a day for poor food and exhorbitant prices for cigarettes. The paper reported:

> [Eighty scabs quit work] upon being assured of not being molested by the pickets and they said to the longshoremen that more would quit if they thought they could get away without being attacked by union men.
>
> Pier 40 . . . is made over into a regular fort, with an amazing array of arms and ammunition ready to repel any attack of the pickets. It takes about 600 armed men to protect 120 at work and costs to the city and county are enormous. The strikers have made no attempt to molest anyone and content themselves with jeering at the scabs trying to do work they don't understand. Half the number of regular union longshoremen would handle all the work the scabs are doing in much less than one-twentieth of the time.[38]

Alaska Agreement Renewed

Tired of the Waterfront Employers' intransigence, foreign shippers approached the Joint Northwest Strike Committee for a separate settlement. Representatives of the Tacoma Port Commission proposed that they load foreign ships at their docks, paying union scale and doing their own stevedoring. The strike committee rejected these overtures. With freight congested at Pier 40, the employers began work at Pier 41 June 30, provoking anew the strikers' rage and frustration. That afternoon several thousand men massed at the pier, threatening to raid the dock.

Hours later, at dusk on the Standard Oil docks at Point Wells north of Seattle, W.C. Douglas, a company guard, shot Shelvy Daffron in the back. Daffron died the next day. According to the *Labor Advocate*, a party of twenty or twenty-five men, mostly seamen, went to Point Wells to try to induce the crews of two tankers to quit. The daily press reported a striker heard a guard mutter, "Give it to 'em," before the guards opened fire, and guards clubbed the retreating pickets. Company officials claimed that sixty strikers rushed the dock and fought with thirty guards. The longshoremen denied that the strikers returned gunfire. Charged with manslaughter, Douglas never stood trial. The ILA buried Shelvy Daffron, a member of Local 38-12, on July 6 in a funeral attended by 15,000. Six thousand strikers and sympathizers marched the three miles to the cemetery in silence.

Pressure built rapidly to resume Alaska shipping. With Mayor Smith absolutely refusing to withdraw police from the Seattle waterfront, July 5 the Joint Northwest Strike Committee considered working Alaska ships in neutral ports: "After two hours discussion the following motion was made—MOTION—That if armed guards are removed, we will work said ships in any Port, and will continue to work them until armed guards are used. If armed guards are used, we will then cease work and order our members back on the picket lines, and this will be our position, regardless of who may be working the ships.—(AYE)"[39]

Later that day Colonel Ohlson of the Department of the Interior and Judge Reynolds met with the committee. According to the minutes, they told the delegates that working ships in a neutral port "was a smart move on our parts, and possibly would be quite a set back to several parties . . . to their own line of battle. However, these ships must be loaded they stated and if not in neutral ports by us, then they surely would be loaded by the Government with the aid of Troops."[40] Word of negotiations between the Joint Northwest Strike Committee and the Alaska operators to work vessels in Tacoma evoked a chorus of open-shop objections. The Tacoma Chamber of Commerce, Waterfront Employers, Citizens' Emergency Committee, and Alaska shippers of Tacoma resolved "that we hereby petition the dock owners and operators of the city, including the Port Commission, to decline the offer of the Alaska steamship operators and the International Longshoremen's Association to temporarily use the Tacoma docks during the strike emergency."[41]

Disregarding these objections, the operators agreed to the unions' terms, and the strikers resumed work under the Alaska agreement July 6 at Tacoma. Teamsters hauled freight piled up on Seattle docks to Tacoma, except for twenty-four knocked down coal cars for the Alaska Railroad, which the strikers released to load in Seattle. The Joint Northwest Strike Committee explained to the San Francisco Joint Marine Strike Committee that resumption of work at Tacoma "put the Mayor of Seattle in a very bad light because a great many citizens blamed the Mayor's stubbornness for the loss of Alaska shipping."[42] The committee ordered work suspended at Seattle, Tacoma, and Everett during the funeral of Shelvy Daffron.

Portland: The Strikebound Port

"As far as we are concerned the strike ended Monday," E.C. Davis of the Waterfront Employers declared June 18 after Portland longshoremen along with other unions up and down the coast rejected the Ryan agreement. He charged that "the citizens of Oregon face an organized band of unruly men led by radicals who are not strikers but who are intent on enforcing their selfish wills on our citizens by force of violence."[43] The Chamber of Commerce pledged to "utilize its entire resources in cooperation with the constituted authorities and the other groups of citizens and business interests to open the port."[44] The fink hall reopened, steam was up on several vessels, and walking bosses appeared on the docks. Strikers massed at dock gates to resist, turning back engineers at the McCormick dock, but they released 400 cases of lemons to be unloaded by union longshoremen, and seamen put a union crew aboard the tanker

Kekoshee to unload 2 million gallons of gasoline declared a fire hazard. The City Council authorized hiring 200 specials instead of the 500 requested by Mayor Carson and tied two to two on a vote to censure him for offering to deputize eastern Oregon farmers to help open the port. Commissioner J.E. Bennett told Carson:

> The small minority in this thing is the half dozen boat owners and bankers. Yet we make no effort to bring any pressure to bear on them. The chances are if the banking crowd had kept out of this strike it would have been settled a long time ago. I don't think there is anything in the charter that gives you the right to deputize any farmers from eastern Oregon.
>
> All the way through the strike the striking longshoremen have been pictured as the villains in this plot. They are not the villains. They are the victims. The bankers and the boat owners are the villains.[45]

Mayor Carson deployed his troops like a general. He armed and deputized all guards, watchmen, and dock employees to augment the 200 special police paid by private funds. As the law prohibited use of state troopers to break strikes, they took over the functions of the regular police force, mobilized for waterfront duty with riot equipment. The Citizens' Emergency Committee hired another 100 private guards at $5.00 a day. At Portland's northwest city limits downstream from the main part of town, Municipal Terminal 4 at St. Johns and the Linnton oil docks across the river became the battle zone. The mayor prepared facilities to house and feed 200 police at the terminal.

Special police who guarded scabs at "Fort Carson" (Terminal No. 4) marching from the restaurant to their quarters, Portland, June 28, 1934. (Courtesy Oregon Historical Society, OrHi neg. 81703)

"POLICE WIN DOCK VICTORY!" the *News-Telegram* headlined June 20 after the tanker *Lio* docked and unloaded at Linnton. Before they left the station, armed with shotguns and tear gas, Chief Lawson exhorted the police to "fight till the last man." High fences topped with barbed wire and double-locked gates protected the oil docks, heavily guarded by police where railroad tracks entered the docks. A police boat kept the ILA launch from approaching the tanker. The pickets, reinforced by loggers, mill workers, fishermen, and longshoremen from Longview and Astoria, milled helplessly around outside the locked gates of the General Petroleum dock. Linnton was "a fortress complete with barbed wire entanglements and a small army of police,"[46] the reporter commented.

Union teamsters refused to haul oil from Linnton, and massed pickets, mostly seamen, kept scab teamsters out of the dock. Pickets blocking tracks prevented train crews from moving all but six tank cars. The tanker *Kewanee* sailed June 22 with a scab crew, followed the next day by the *Alladin* and *Lio*, which departed six men short when they quit at sailing time. The seamen released gas for hospitals, dairies, airmail planes, and institutions for old people, babies, and orphans, provided union teamsters hauled it.

The public took sides. Commissioner Bennett demanded the names of those contributing to the fund for special police. Wheat farmers of Wasco County and other regions called on Mayor Carson to open the port. A veterans' group requested the City Council to bond each special policeman for $10,000, charging they were young thugs hired to attack longshoremen, 80 percent of whom were World War veterans. The Independent Merchants' Association passed a resolution "favoring the demands of the International Longshoremen's Association and appealing to the employers to recognize this organization and to fairly and honestly consider its demands as to conduct of hiring halls, hours and wages."[47] The strikers sent speakers to community organizations to refute the hostile press. They charged that to force longshoremen back to work authorities evicted those living in government housing for failure to pay the $15.00-a-month rent.

Preparations to open the port moved forward. The night of June 25-26, the employers brought 225 specials to Terminal 4 and moved the *Admiral Evans* from the McCormick dock to accommodate them. The ILA protested against housing men on Terminal 4 as illegal use of public property. The other four commissioners tabled Mayor Carson's request for an appropriation of $20,000 to hire 500 special police for ten days. Five tankers proceeded up the Columbia to Portland.

In a letter June 26 the ILA pleaded with Mayor Carson to abandon his war preparations, charging that under the guise of preserving law and order he provoked a violent confrontation: "We know that your machine gun nests have been planted and that your bombs are ready. And, we say to you, that any loss of life, or any murder that occurs, or any women and children who shall be left husbandless and fatherless by your actions, the BLOOD will be on your hands."[48] The mayor ignored the plea.

The press charged that beat-up gangs roamed the city. Police arrested three strikers June 27 for beating two specials from The Dalles in a hotel lobby. The ILA notified Northwest locals of three organizers from the Columbia River Longshoremen's Association in the area, and the press reported the company union as active in five Washington ports. Strikers kidnapped a company union member with thirty-three years on the Portland waterfront, questioned him, and finally beat him when he refused to join them. The ILA estimated the company union had forty scabs lined up.

The ILA doubled picket lines and held reserves in the hall. Nearly 500 armed regular and special police and sixteen scabs camped at Terminal 4. Three hundred fifty strikers surrounded the terminal, about 100 at the gates and the rest lying in ambush in the brush armed with clubs, ready to rush the docks if the gates opened. The night of the 28th police drove pickets away with threats of guns and tear gas. After a British steamer, half loaded when the strike began, moved to Terminal 4 the next day, the crew threatened to beat any scab that set foot on her. Police held the largest picket boat for approaching too near the British ship. They confiscated clubs and arrested nineteen strikers. When word of the boat seizure reached strike headquarters, hundreds of angry pickets gathered at the terminal. Police drove them back half a mile up the road, allowing eighty to remain at the gate. Then the strikers obtained permission from sympathetic families to camp on their property adjacent to the terminal. "Cossack Orders," the *News-Telegram* termed a police order June 29 barring reporters from Terminal 4.

The uptown unions actively supported the strikers. Besides maintaining the commissary and soup kitchen, costing about $300 a day, officials of the State Federation of Labor, Central Labor Council, and other unions met daily in an advisory committee of about forty-five. The Union County sheriff turned down a request to provide special police after consulting with the LaGrande Central Labor Council. By a vote of three to two the Portland City Council rejected the longshoremen's offer to load wheat ships under union conditions. City health officers inspected the twenty-five picket shacks on the front and found them sanitary.

According to an ISU estimate, the MWIU had about twenty-five members in Portland. Unable to influence strike policy, it alternately criticized the ILA and demanded a united front. In a bulletin July 3 the MWIU attacked "Negstad, Carter, Craycraft and Company" for opposing "militant action and mass picketing," not permitting the "unemployed and 'reds'" on picket lines, and releasing certain cargoes. After the striking unions rejected a united-front proposal, the MWIU pleaded: "STRIKERS, RANK AND FILE CONTROL, A REAL UNITED FRONT, AND IMMEDIATE MILITANT ACTION WILL TIE UP TERMINAL FOUR AND WIN OUR STRIKE!"[49]

By July 3 five tankers discharged oil at Linnton. The next day police arrested fifty-four pickets, mostly seamen, for defying an order limiting pickets within the fire emergency zone. Released on $10.00 bail, they returned to the picket line. Thereafter police did not enforce the limitation. National Guard officers surveyed the ground around Terminal 4 for machine gun positions. Eighty-four scabs, twenty of them

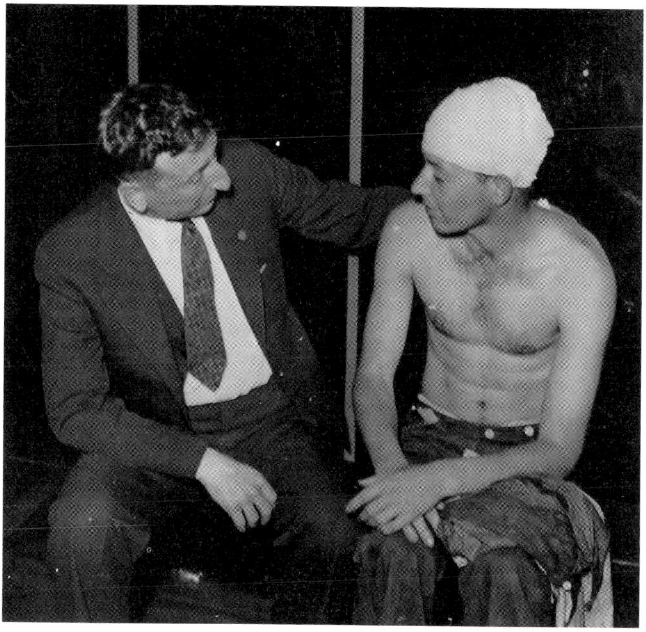

Union attorney consulting in jail with a striking seamen arrested in a confrontation with police at the Linnton oil docks near Portland, July 6, 1934. (Courtesy Oregon Historical Society, OrHi neg. 81697)

from the company union, worked at the terminal July 5, guarded by 333 specials. The ILA claimed it cost the employers $3.42 for every sack of flour loaded. The strikers watched from the top of the hill with binoculars, making no effort to rush the docks. At Linnton pickets persuaded a train crew not to move tank cars onto the docks. Later that day, when the train approached with a new crew, 500 pickets rushed from the brush and hills along the docks, hurling rocks through the windows of the engineer's cab and attempting to pull the crew from the engine. In a pitched battle police drove them back with tear gas and night sticks, but the train crew decided not to move the cars.

The Battle of Terminal 4

A major confrontation at Terminal 4 began July 6 when a heavily guarded train with fifteen freight cars approached through the gulch. With the train about a mile from the gates, a crowd of pickets climbed down through the fields, put a log on the tracks, and lay down across them, stopping the train. While the engineer and police officers retired to the terminal to discuss the situation, pickets brought soap, lard, and axle grease from their camp, greased the rails, and again lay down on the tracks, armed with fence rails. Soon an army of seventy-five officers, headed by Chief Lawson, came down the tracks. With men lying in his path, the engineer refused to go forward. As the train backed away hundreds of pickets rushed through the fields. Police fired a heavy barrage of tear gas down the gulch and up the hill toward the advancing pickets, gassing police, reporters, photographers, and pickets. Lawson ordered the officers "to storm up the hill after the . . . pickets gathered at the crest." They had gone a short ways over a field of corn and potatoes when an angry young farmer ordered them off, "shouting that they had killed his pig with their gas." The strikers had permission to use his property, but not the police. The officers retreated, with "strikers banked on top of the hill against the sky snarling and yowling their candid and unflattering opinion of the gas barrage."[50]

The next morning police squads blocked roads leading to the terminal, stopping carload after carload of strikers until they stretched back to St. Johns over a mile away. They held back all but forty pickets over two miles from the tracks as another train proceeded toward the terminal. Just 500 yards from the gates it halted, and a "man reported to be from the grievance committee of the American Railway brotherhood conferred shortly with the engineer, who then announced he would go no further," and backed out, reportedly at the delegate's request. The *News-Telegram* continued: "In a towering rage over failure of his strategy, Lawson ordered all his men—regulars, specials, dock guards—back into the terminal. The jubilant pickets gave a rousing cheer for the train crew, then swarmed after the police, finally camping closer to the gates then they had ever been before."[51]

Amid rumors that the National Guard might be called out, the uptown unions prepared for action. "GENERAL STRIKE PLANS PUSHED," the *News-Telegram* headlined July 10, as the Central Labor Council asked all unions to ballot on the general strike before the end of the week and the Strategy Committee met to work out details for emergency distribution of milk and hospital supplies. The press reported July 11 that 80 of the 105 Portland unions had returned ballots, all in favor of striking. The committee emphasized that the "movement is, and will remain, under the direction of recognized and legitimate labor organizations."[52] In a gesture of support, twenty women belonging to a textile union relieved pickets at the McCormick dock, away from the battle zone.

After his failure to get trains into Terminal 4, Chief Lawson withdrew all but fifty regular police from the terminal, touching off a wave of resignations among the specials. To stop the supposed influx of "reds" from San Francisco planning to rush Terminal 4, as the MWIU urged, police rounded up 100 transients who arrived by boxcar. The strikers released gasoline to fill 300 empty city storage tanks, sending along a picket to monitor the operation. A seaman from a tanker swam ashore, contacted the ISU hall, and when he reported the tanker was unfair, all but three of the crew quit.

Chief Lawson's final attempt to open Terminal 4 on July 11 ended in bloodshed. Again police turned back all but the forty regular pickets, but many left their cars and drifted down toward the tracks, hiding in the brush. Armed specials stood six feet apart in a long semicircle over the seven acres of brush surrounding the terminal. The train approached at ten o'clock, forty cars drawn by two locomotives pushing ahead a flatcar with a picked shotgun squad of fifty police on it. More armed officers walked beside the train. As it slowed, pickets laid heavy rails across the tracks and uncoupled the airbrake hoses on several cars. The jolt threw James E. Bateman, a brakeman, from the side of a car. A throng of strikers on either side of the tracks hurled rocks at the flatcar. Then, according to the strikers, Chief Lawson, in the cupola of the caboose behind the engines, ordered the police to "shoot to kill" and fired the first shot. A burst of gunfire from the flatcar wounded four pickets, two critically. Strikers denied that they fired first, as none were armed, and they asserted that police shot to kill, as all injuries were above the waist. Police bullets riddled trees in Pier Park woods, several yards from where small girls played.

Police refused to allow the train to be cut in two so a badly injured longshoreman could be put into an auto. Instead, pickets "with police pistols leveled at them carried him over the bumpers between the cars."[53] The train backed away from the terminal, followed by enraged pickets and a few of their wives. Some pickets tried to pry up railroad tracks after the train had passed, "working in a furious frenzy, some of them near hysteria." All day "restless, bitter longshoremen milled around Terminal No. 4."[54]

In a stormy session of the City Council that afternoon, the Central Labor Council Strategy Committee demanded immediate removal of Chief Lawson, "discontinuance of attempts at shipping activity at the public docks," and removal of all special police from the docks. Ben Osborne, secretary of the Oregon State Federation of Labor, accused Mayor Carson of "trying to provoke labor riots in Portland by causing helpless men to be shot down in an effort to force" Governor Meier to call out the National Guard. Matt Meehan opened a package and unrolled a bloody, bullet-riddled shirt on the press table. "You're responsible for this," he shouted at Carson. "'I accept the responsibility,' Carson retorted with a stubborn toss of his head."[55]

The council voted three to one to ask the mayor to remove Chief Lawson and to request the shipowners to discontinue attempts to work ships, but the commissioners would not withdraw police from the waterfront. Carson refused to remove Lawson. Police doubled the guard at Terminal 4 and sent in more ammunition. Thirty specials decided not to quit when shown that the terminal provided their safest refuge. Pickets turned back county and city trucks at Linnton and provision trucks for the police camp at Terminal 4.

The waterfront remained quiet the next day. "Flowers, scarlet and white, marked the place on the road near Pier park where four pickets fell under police bullets in Wednesday's grim battle."[56] Strikers roped off the blood-stained area and posted a guard there to prevent passersby from walking on it. Police and railroad officials announced there would be no further attempts to bring a train into Terminal 4. James Bateman died of his injuries July 13. At the terminal, police placed specials in shallow trenches barricaded with sandbags to protect them from pickets on the hill pelting them with buckshot from a slingshot. Employers installed floodlights so guards could see the pickets and their camp on the wooded hill.

Support for the strikers came from many sources. The National Association for the Advancement of Colored People pledged that it would do its utmost to persuade African Americans not to scab, declaring: "We realize as a race that if your program is a success you will have accomplished much for all working people."[57] The cooperative Farmers' National Grain Corporation refused an appeal of the Portland Chamber of Commerce for a $1,000 donation with the tart reply: "The Farmers' National will try to bear up under the displeasure of the grain trade, but we will not contribute money to break down organized effort by laboring men to improve conditions."[58] With ballots returned from 85 of the 105 Portland unions, all in favor of striking, the maritime workers demanded that the general strike begin at once. The Strategy Committee waited for word from San Francisco. People expected that a general strike there would trigger the Portland strike.

Coastwide Bargaining Committee

Following rejection of the June 16 agreement, San Pedro and Northwest strikers simultaneously proposed a coastwide marine federation. The San Pedro ILA suggested June 19 that a committee of two each from Puget Sound, Columbia River, San Francisco, and San Pedro, plus representatives of each participating district organization, should start functioning in San Francisco immediately. Two days later the Joint Northwest Strike Committee recommended a coastwide negotiating committee of twelve, composed of a longshoreman, a representative of the marine unions, and a teamster each from Washington, Oregon, Northern California, and Southern California. The committee elected Ed Krumholz of Grays Harbor to represent Washington longshoremen and appropriated $100 each from the Alaska emergency fund for expenses for Krumholz and Cliff Thurston, elected by Portland to represent Oregon longshoremen.

The San Francisco Joint Marine Strike Committee tabled a proposal for a federation June 23. The *Waterfront Worker* attacked the proposed federation June 25, charging that "the fakers Paddy Morris, Bjorklund, Lewis & Co. are attempting to build Marine Federations, so built that only the top officials will be delegates. All this is done to closely control the labor movement and prevent rank and file control."[59] The Joint Marine Strike Committee seated representatives from the rest of the coast as they arrived in San Francisco: Cliff Thurston from the Columbia River, A.H. Petersen from San Pedro, Ed Krumholz from Grays Harbor, J.R. Snee from the Portland Marine Engineers, George Nutting of Portland and Henry L. Whiting of Seattle, both from the Sailors' Union, representing the ISU, and W.H. Weale from the San Pedro Marine Engineers. No teamsters participated.

While the union delegates converged on San Francisco, the Industrial Association proceeded with plans to open the port. Representatives of the Industrial Association, Chamber of Commerce, State Harbor Commission, and Police Department met for two and a half hours in Chief Quinn's office June 23 to work out detailed plans. Still pleading for delay, Mayor Rossi declared that "the police are not going to be used to 'open up' anything. Their business is to preserve law and order." But Governor Merriam announced that he would "take steps to force the issue and open up state property to the resumption of commerce."[60] Chief Quinn promised the employers every available police officer in San Francisco if necessary to protect the waterfront, and the *Examiner* reported that twelve "big men" had arrived from Los Angeles to drive scab trucks. The employers claimed 1,600 scabs were working. The San Francisco Bay Carloading Conference put a 100 percent surcharge on carloading rates, blaming the scabs' inexperience and extra expense of bringing them from out of town and feeding them.

Pickets harassed scabs wherever they could. The press reported that in Oakland strikers released the brakes on a gondola car, sending it crashing through a dock barricade. Then they boarded the *William McKinley*, beat the watchman, and smashed portholes. In San Francisco strikers threw bottles of creosote through the windows of scabs' homes and painted their houses yellow.

Edward McGrady returned to San Francisco June 24 to try to prevent the bloody confrontation that threatened the city. The Joint Marine Strike Committee branded claims of strikers in other ports ready and willing to return to work "incorrect and untrue," asserting that reports of delegates from other ports "prove absolutely that the solidarity of the marine groups on strike is unimpaired."[61]

President Roosevelt appointed the National Longshoremen's Board June 26 under provisions of the recently passed Labor Disputes Act. The board, composed of Archbishop Edward J. Hanna of the Catholic Diocese of San Francisco, chair; O.K. Cushing, a San Francisco attorney; and Edward McGrady, would investigate the strike, take testimony, and endeavor to bring about a settlement. While the press, which clamored for the government to force the strikers back to work, hailed the appointment, the unions greeted the development with silence or suspicion. Keith J. Middleton, in San Francisco representing the Seattle Waterfront Employers, told his group privately:

> Bishop Hanna is a very estimable gentleman but is an old man and he doubted if he would be able to make a very valuable contribution to the Board. Mr. Cushing is an attorney in San Francisco, in high standing with his profession and a man of high intellectual integrity. He and Bishop Hanna would no doubt work closely together. Mr. McGrady is and has been ready to accept any expedience.[62]

Middleton guessed wrong. Cushing, defending the employers' view, not McGrady, would be the odd one on the board. On Mayor Rossi's appeal, the Industrial Association agreed June 27 to postpone the port opening twenty-four hours. In a final attempt to reach agreement with their employers, an ILA negotiating team of District President Bill Lewis, A.H. Petersen of San Pedro, Cliff Thurston of Portland, Ed Krumholz of Grays Harbor, Charles Cutright of San Francisco, and International President Joe Ryan drafted a proposal similar to the June 16 agreement, except that it provided that all men would be dispatched from ILA halls by an ILA dispatcher. The offer depended on a satisfactory settlement for the seamen and acceptance by an ILA referendum vote. Bridges opposed the proposal, and the San Francisco ILA strike committee announced that the rank and file would repudiate it.

Ryan retorted angrily that "the action of the local strike committee has given the employers a lack of confidence in the leaders of the strike in San Francisco." He blamed Bridges for refusing to abide by a majority decision and declared that Bridges "does not want the strike settled and it is my firm belief that he is acting for the communists."[63] The employers rejected the offer, branding it "the closed shop worded a little differently."[64] Joe Ryan left San Francisco that night, announcing, "I can't see any use sticking around here arguing with a bunch of obstinate employers who could end this thing in a minute by coming half way."[65]

At Archbishop Hanna's request the Industrial Association again postponed the port opening to July 2. The longshoremen refused the board's request to arbitrate all issues, and the shipowners objected to the board's proposal to hold representation elections for the marine groups, claiming they were too widely scattered and the vote would take too long.

"Tighten Up Those Picket Lines!"

The unions braced themselves for the port opening. The Pacific District ISU began issuing a strike bulletin June 25. The first one reminded strike card members of the Sailors, Marine Firemen, and Marine Cooks and Stewards that they would "have a vote on any final settlement of the strike, and that there will be no DISCRIMINATION against any man, who has done his duty with us in this fight when it comes to shipping when the strike is over."[66] The second bulletin instructed pickets: "When you meet a scab or a suspected scab, take care of him where you find him. DO NOT BRING HIM UP TO THE HALL! DO NOT CART HIM AROUND IN SQUAD CARS!" The bulletin urged the 1,700 SUP pickets:

> TIGHTEN UP THOSE PICKET LINES! When your number is called, be in the Hall. Most of you are slacking up on the night watches. . . . Portland and Seattle are standing twelve hour watches, AND NINETY PERCENT OF THE MEN CALLED IN THOSE PORTS *STAND THEIR WATCHES.* This is not a game! It is our last stand. Our backs are against the wall. If we lose this fight, we might as well all quit the sea. . . . The men on the picket line are our best and only weapon. *That means YOU.*[67]

The ILA strike bulletin June 29 urged all pickets to "hold themselves prepared to mobilize in front of docks on short notice. This move is necessary as an attempt may be made to open the docks momentarily."[68] The same morning picket captains of the ten striking unions of the Joint Marine Strike Committee met to reorganize the picket system. All would picket jointly on six-hour watches, and all pickets would receive three meals a day instead of two. They put sailors living in the relief shelter on a special day watch. The unions named four wharf captains, "two on each side of the Ferry Building to keep a constant check on the men. Pickets will be checked every hour, and there will be no more hiding behind box-cars. . . . This is the time when we NEED the pickets. You who do your duty, pass the word along to the slackers."[69]

During these days of impending crisis, the Marine Workers Industrial Union kept up the attack on the ISU in the *Fo'c'sle Head.* It claimed to represent rank-and-file seamen and accused the ISU of rejecting united-front demands from fear of its officers. The ISU replied that it already supported joint settlement for all marine workers before any striking groups returned to work, no discrimination against any striker regardless of affiliation, and complete abolition of all fink halls. On the demand for seamen's hiring halls in all ports, "to be controlled by democratically elected committees of seamen on the beach," the ISU replied that it would "never recognize A HIRING HALL RUN BY FARMERS AND COAL MINERS!"[70] Refuting claims that the MWIU represented the rank and file, the Sailors' Union pointed out that the MWIU fed about 350 men daily in the relief kitchen, most of them registered as scalers, while the SUP fed 1,970 seamen.

The *Joint Marine Journal* replaced the ISU strike bulletin July 2, issued jointly by the ISU, Masters, Mates and Pilots, Marine Engineers, and Ferryboatmen's Union. The lead article proclaimed:

> The purpose of this publication, is to foster the rapidly growing idea of UNITED ACTION among all striking unions. This sheet is as representative of licensed officers as it is of members of the unlicensed personnel of ships. . . . Masters Mates and Sailors — Engineers and Firemen — are at last United with the Longshoremen, in a mutual endeavor to gain the recognition, and the respect that is our heritage. Men! We are fighting for the right to make a decent living, and to conduct our own affairs. WE MUST WIN! And when victory is ours, this Federation of Waterfront Trades must REMAIN to protect the rights we have gained! . . . This is the first time in Maritime history, that we have all worked together, and the shipowners can't believe it yet. . . . and with a common aim, and a common purpose; all working TOGETHER for the good of all — we will go over the top, AND NONE SHALL GO BACK TO WORK UNTIL ALL GO BACK, AND UNTIL ALL GO BACK WITH VICTORY!

The Masters, Mates and Pilots declared: "With every ship adding to our ranks as they arrive, there can be no question as to the results of our efforts, . . . *WE ARE ON STRIKE!* . . . BECAUSE WE WANT BETTER LIVING CONDITIONS – BETTER WAGES AND SHORTER HOURS! Get out on the Picket Lines men and – DO YOUR DUTY!"

The Marine Engineers hailed the new "spirit of unity and solidarity" among all crafts:

> The many years of blacklisting and oppression, cuts in wages and personnel, long working hours and rationalization schemes, the seed sown by the shipowners has borne fruit. . . .
>
> . . . All squabbles and differences between engineers about organization or no organization were forgotten. . . . The American Society [company union] came over to the M.E.B.A. in groups and many are now among its most active members on the picket lines and other strike duties. It is clear that the Marine Engineers are tired of playing the role of Simon Legree over their subordinates aboard ship, and that they will no longer act as policemen, strikebreakers and scab herders for the shipowners.[71]

The National Longshoremen's Board appealed to all parties July 2 to submit all issues to arbitration, after all strikers returned to their former jobs without discrimination. Immediately following the longshoremen's arbitration, the board would "take up the grievances and demands of the maritime unions." The board promised to exercise its power to order representation elections for marine employees and to "use its good offices to bring about an arrangement making it unnecessary for seamen meanwhile to apply for work to the Marine Service Bureau."[72] Attorney General Cummings ruled that employers need not organize a single association to negotiate with marine employees—leaving the obligation to bargain up to individual companies.

Promises of arbitration and elections did not satisfy the strikers. The *Joint Marine Journal* rejected the appeal: "To Seamen this will mean that you will go back to work under EXACTLY THE SAME CONDITIONS YOU LEFT, and then you will be allowed to vote, as an individual employee of the steamship company, . . . You answer NO — Today! . . . Don't allow yourselves to be misled, and ABOVE ALL — DON'T WEAKEN NOW!"[73] Seamen rejected the proposition decisively. Andrew Furuseth, eighty-year-old secretary of the Sailors' Union and president of the ISU, who had arrived in San Francisco June 27, went down to San Pedro to urge acceptance of the proposal. Seamen heckled him at meetings July 3 and voted the next day 727 to 181 against returning to work pending aribitration.

Eight thousand strikers and sympathizers congregated on the waterfront July 2 waiting for the employers to try to move cargo. Just before the scheduled time, at Mayor Rossi's repeated pleas, the Industrial Association agreed to a last postponement to July 3 at one o'clock. The ILA credited the massed pickets for the decision: "WE HAVE SHOWN MR. SHIPOWNER AND THE S.F. INDUSTRIAL ASSOCIATION THAT WE CAN BE ON THE JOB WHEN WE ARE NEEDED . . . KEEP YOURSELVES IN READINESS TO BE CALLED TO THE FRONT AT ANY MOMENT. HOLD TOGETHER, BOYS! WE HAVE DEMONSTRATED OUR STRENGHT THIS AFTERNOON."[74]

The day brought one more crisis. That evening the Industrial Association moved five trucks into Pier 38, the McCormick dock, where one vessel lay alongside. Describing the confrontation between police and 1,500 strikers shortly after six o'clock, the *Chronicle* reported:

> Within the brief moments while the big steel door was rising, word was passed down the water front, and pickets ran to a point opposite the pier.
>
> They yelled and cursed as five old trucks rattled across the Embarcadero and into the pier. The door slammed shut and the crash of its closing drove the strikers across the way into a near frenzy.
>
> "Might as well get them now," yelled one of the pickets.
>
> "Let's go!" shouted the others.
>
> Mounted patrolmen wheeled their horses into a straight line in readiness to charge into the advancing pickets. The officers on foot drew their revolvers, and others armed with gas guns gave their weapons a last-minute inspection. Second by second, the danger of a bloody clash increased.
>
> Then came the idea that averted, at least for a matter of hours, what appeared to be the certainty of bloodshed. Two members of the strike committee were permitted to go inside the pier and reassure themselves that no effort was being made to load the trucks. The strikers brought the word to their comrades, and the majority of the crowd began drifting away slowly and uneasily.
>
> Hundreds remained through the night maintaining their vigil beside a bonfire that shed a ruddy glare on the gray walls of the piers across the Embarcadero.[75]

The next day the employers would open the port.

8

Bloody Thursday

Prelude July 3

The battle to open the port of San Francisco began July 3 at Pier 38 on the south end of the Embarcadero. Chief Quinn had almost 700 police ready, and the Joint Marine Strike Committee appealed to all unions to send their unemployed members down to the waterfront. Early in the morning strikers and sympathizers began to gather, swelling to a crowd of over 5,000, many carrying rocks and railroad spikes. Toward noon police moved them back to clear the area between the dock and the Atlas warehouse two blocks away on King Street. A train crew spotted a string of empty boxcars on a siding across the Embarcadero south of the pier, and police cars blocked the thoroughfare on the north. The *Chronicle* described the confrontation:

"At 1:15 the big steel door of the pier slowly went up, and two trucks, closely followed by a third, rumbled out," headed for the warehouse. Strikers broke through police lines to a vacant lot across the street from the rear entrance of the warehouse, where thousands of stacked bricks from a demolished building provided ammunition, and opened a barrage on the first truck. Mounted police wielding nightsticks rode into the crowd, followed by foot police, who fired several shots in the air and drove the mob back with tear gas and riot clubs. Rocks shattered the windshields of several police cars, including Chief Quinn's. The reporter continued:

> Determined to clear all strikers from the area around which the deadline had been drawn, the police began chasing them up Second street. Bricks and rocks were hurled at the officers, finding their mark in many cases, as the police moved forward under a barrage of gas bombs.
>
> Some of the bombs were thrown by hand, and the strikers picked up some of these before they were discharged and tossed them back into the police lines.[1]

Fighting between small detachments continued as police forced pickets back from the waterfront; waves of tear gas engulfed the entire district, and bricks and stones littered the streets. Thousands watched the four-hour battle from Rincon Hill. The fighting stopped streetcars, and police escorted commuters bound for the Southern Pacific station at Third and Townsend through the melee. A police bullet hit Eugene Dunbar in the ankle, then ricocheted through a bank window and wounded a teller. Pickets stopped several trucks not connected with the Industrial Association, hauled out and beat their nonunion drivers, and overturned the trucks. The battle ended at

5:00 p.m. when the Atlas trucks stopped hauling from Pier 38. The employers claimed the five trucks had made eighteen round trips. Reports of injuries listed thirteen police officers, sixteen strikers, several scabs, and the bank teller; in addition, countless strikers did not report their injuries. Police clubbed and arrested Frank Webb, Sailors' Union picket captain. At the foot of Clay on the Embarcadero, well away from the battle zone, pickets beat up a group of scabs who had ventured off the docks for a few drinks. After the skirmish police picked up Argonne Reinhardt, a scab from Los Angeles, from the gutter and threw him in the drunk tank. He died that night from a fractured skull.

In a paid ad the Industrial Association claimed the port was open, thanks to "the full protection of the authorities in this peaceful undertaking. The men employed to move our trucks are unarmed. They ride the trucks alone."[2] The ILA strike bulletin charged the attempt to move cargo was "ONLY INTENDED TO FRIGHTEN SOME OF THE STRIKERS INTO RETURNING TO WORK PENDING ARBITRATION." In fact, the Industrial Association had "moved a half dozen old trucks with unlicensed drivers and gunmen. The freight they claim to be moving is empty boxes."[3]

The night of July 3 Matson ordered fourteen refrigerator cars spotted on Pier 30. They contained perishable fruit and vegetables for the freighter *Manukai*, scheduled to sail the next day. The train crew walked off when pickets surrounded the engine, and a second crew likewise refused to defy the pickets. The railroad brotherhoods would not sanction loan of crews from other railroads, so the Belt Line finally recruited a scab crew to move the cars. As the crew backed a string of empties from the pier, strikers threw a switch, derailing several cars.

After the Joint Marine Strike Committee rejected Governor Frank Merriam's plea to leave the Belt Line alone, the governor announced he would call out the National Guard July 5 to protect the state-owned railroad. Adjunct General Seth E. Howard promised 1,000 men within thirty minutes of the governor's order, equipped with gas masks and vomiting gas that incapacitated a person for two days. The police sent a rush call to the federal government for more tear gas bombs from Alcatraz to replenish the depleted supply. The *Joint Marine Journal* appealed for pickets:

> Get on the line, Brothers, and keep the port closed – until the MARITIME UNIONS, and the I.L.A., working together with common ideals – go over the top with VICTORY!
>
> Striking seamen: The newspapers tell us that the Industrial Association will try again tomorrow, Thursday. The battle isn't over—it is just beginning. We suggest that each and every one of you be on the "Front" tomorrow to protect YOUR job and to voice your protest. IT IS UP TO *YOU!*[4]

Battle of Rincon Hill

Thursday morning, July 5, thousands responded to the appeal for pickets, only now, contrary to orders of the Joint Marine Strike Committee, perhaps a few carried guns instead of rocks in their pockets. With only a scattering of pickets around, the

Industrial Association sent five more Atlas trucks into Pier 38 before 6:00 a.m. Nearly 800 police stood ready to protect life and property. The strikers recognized the Atlas operation as a symbolic action to break their morale and bring troops to the waterfront, but cargo moving across other docks presented a more ominous threat to the strike. The major battles of Bloody Thursday centered around strikers' attempts to prevent the Belt Line from shifting cars.

"Fighting reminiscent of world war battles," wrote an AP correspondent, "raged on the San Francisco waterfront today as striking pickets fought hand to hand with police against the roaring blasts of pistols and riot guns and the blinding fumes from tear gas bombs."[5] The battle of Rincon Hill started about eight when a crew shunted two refrigerator cars into the Matson docks, amid shouts of 2,000 pickets massed nearby. A *News* reporter described the battle:

> Police decided to clear the Embarcadero. The crowd fought back, hurling rocks. In the midst of the fight, smoke began curling up from the two box cars, standing on a sidetrack about a block away. The cars were surrounded by milling, fighting strikers.
>
> Fire engines arrived. According to police, strikers hurled rocks at the apparatus. The call went out for tear gas.
>
> A tear gas squad . . . swung into action. Flanking them were police with riot guns. Gas pistols popped and grenades flew through the air.
>
> Men were felled by police clubs. Others ran, cursing and clawing at their eyes, out of the clouds of stinging gas.
>
> Radio cars sped to the scene. The crowd gave back. Soon it was on the run, radio cars in pursuit. The strikers ran north to Harrison street. Police continued to herd them along.
>
> The crowd was driven back to Bryant street from Beale to Main streets, but here it grew menacing again. Rioters hid behind materials intended for the bay bridge and hurled rocks.
>
> The main battle had veered onto Rincon Hill. It started when a gang of 500 men rushed down the Harrison street bridge toward the melee below. They were cursing, hurling rocks. Police said at least one man was firing a revolver.
>
> The fight raged up the bridge and into the streets. The situation had grown so serious that police were abandoning any attempt to herd the rioters along. The long nightsticks were rising and falling like pistons. When a man went down he stayed there until radio cars had a chance to pick him up. . . .
>
> The police cars took a terrific beating from stones hurled by rioters. Hardly a machine in the war zone did not have a broken top, smashed window or dented fender.
>
> Bullets from police revolvers spattered against houses on Rincon Hill, imperilling women and children inside. Police claimed the strikers returned their fire, blamed the wounding of at least one man to the rioters' guns. . . .

Stray police bullets whizzing past shut down the Bay Bridge construction job at 9:30. At intervals along Harrison the strikers threw up barricades of planks and ladders that stopped autos but not mounted police with their nightsticks and trampling hooves. The reporter continued:

Police gas strikers near the Embarcadero, San Francisco, July 5, 1934. (Courtesy Sailors' Union of the Pacific)

Plainclothes police subdue a striker, Bloody Thursday. (Courtesy San Francisco Public Library)

> So much tear gas was used that the officers had to send for a fresh supply. New, long riot sticks, with which police had been equipped, battered heads and left a wake of still forms on the streets. As the riot neared its end, a machine load of rifles and riot guns was taken to the scene, distributed among plainclothesmen.
>
> When the riot was over, police set a deadline which cut off most of the south end of the waterfront. Officers with shotguns and tear gas were posted to see that no striker advanced beyond the lines, which began at First and Harrison, led to the Embarcadero, thence to the foot of Berry street, up to Third and Brannan, down Brannan to Second, and back across Harrison.[6]

The battle was ended by 10:30. Injuries put six strikers in the hospital, at least three hit by police bullets, and they took care of many more injuries among themselves. Police searched Rincon Hill and building tops for snipers and kept pickets moving away from the front. "A big truck passed one group which was being shepherded by officers. Out of the cab leaned a grinning driver, a union teamster's button shining on his cap. 'We'll be with you tomorrow,' he shouted."[7]

The Joint Marine Strike Committee met during this time. Shortly before eleven, according to the minutes,

> A report of the strike situation was made . . . by Brother Schmidt, of the I.L.A. which is received by him through a telephonic communication; and on receipt of the information thus conveyed, it was moved, seconded and carried that the Committee adjourn immediately, and that the full Joint Marine Strike Committee call on Mayor Rossi and the Board of Supervisors at once, and demand that the inhuman persecution and terrorizing of men on strike by the San Francisco Police Department be stopped.[8]

The Killings

Hostilities ceased at noon when the scabs knocked off for lunch. Pickets routed from the south end of the Embarcadero made their way back to the waterfront north of the deadline. The battle began again shortly after one when a Belt Line locomotive hauled a boxcar into Pier 18 and emerged with a long string of cars. Police guarding the train claimed a shot came from a crowd of strikers across the Embarcadero between Howard and Folsom. Newspapers said someone threw a rock, but other witnesses saw nothing thrown. Foot police hurled tear gas and mounted police charged into the pickets. Eyewitness Donald Mackenzie Brown reported: "The pickets retreated in a surging mass, stopping as they went to hurl back the tear-gas bombs, to throw rocks, bricks, spikes, anything they could lay hands on. But against the gas and guns of the officers these missiles were but a feeble protest. I saw no officer seriously injured thereby."[9]

Strikers carried away many of their comrades who fell under police clubs. Tear gas and gunfire dislodged a picket in a parking lot hurling rocks from an innertube slingshot. Police estimated the crowd at 5,000. Munition salesmen accompanied the police and demonstrated their gas guns. At the foot of Howard, police fired bombs and bullets into the lobby of the Seaboard Hotel, frequented by striking seamen. Choking, cursing men stumbled out. The attack critically injured James Engle,

Striker hit by a gas projectile in front of the Seaboard Hotel, Bloody Thursday. (Courtesy San Francisco Public Library)

twenty-six, shot in the body and his skull fractured by a blow, and a bullet wounded another man. An exploding grenade hit a man standing in front of the hotel, severely burning him on the chest. The enraged pickets tore cobblestones from the street and hurled them at the police. The AP correspondent reported: "The police replied savagely—this time lowering their pistols and shotguns to get effective results from their fire. One by one the strikers fell and their ranks drew back, but they fought fiercely as they retreated and police cars bearing three machine guns rushed to the scene . . . Gradually the strikers gave way and the machine guns were not brought into action."[10]

Brown watched as police forced pickets up Howard and across Steuart:

> Suddenly bedlam broke over Steuart Street. Struggling knots of longshoremen, closely pressed by officers mounted and on foot, swarmed everywhere. The air was filled with blinding gas. The howl of sirens. The low boom of gas guns. The crack of pistol-fire. The whine of bullets. The shouts and curses of sweating men. Everywhere was a rhythmical waving of arms—like trees in the wind—swinging clubs, swinging fists, hurling rocks, hurling bombs. As the police moved from one group to the next, men lay bloody, unconscious, or in convulsions—in gutters, on the sidewalks, in the streets. Around on [Mission] Street, a plainclothes-man dismounted from a radio car, waved his shotgun nervously at the shouting pickets who scattered. I saw nothing thrown at him. Suddenly he fired up and down the street and two men fell in a pool of gore—one evidently dead, the other, half attempting to rise, but weakening fast. A gas bomb struck another standing on the curb—struck the side of his head, leaving him in blinded agony.[11]

The two men who fell on Mission around the corner from the ILA hall were longshoremen Howard S. Sperry, shot in the back, and Charles S. Olson, critically wounded in the arm, face, and chest. Sperry, returning from his picket shift in the relief kitchen to have his strike card punched at the hall, died soon after in the emergency hospital. Eyewitness accounts of the shooting varied. One man said that a piece of brick hit the officer in the leg before he fired—another that no one threw bricks before the shots, but pickets shouted, "Let's tip his car over!" The official police report, mistakenly listing Olson as dead, stated:

> A general riot of about six thousand men broke out at Steuart and Mission Streets in the middle of the afternoon. At this time all radio patrol cars were ordered to this area. Two inspectors of police, while responding to this call found themselves surrounded by these rioters before the arrival of the other officers. The rioters blocked the car and shouted "Kill them," and attempted to overturn the police car. During this time the inspectors were being struck by showers of bricks and rocks. Feeling that their lives were in danger, the officers fired two shots from a shotgun and several shots from their revolvers at the men who were attempting to overturn the car. The two men who were struck with the bullets from the inspectors' guns later died.[12]

A block away on Spear near Mission a man was found shot in the back and taken to an emergency hospital. As doctors worked over the dying man, he refused to give his name. "I'm an intelligence officer for the International Labor Defense, and that's all I'll tell you,"[13] he declared. Police identified the man from fingerprints taken after his death as George Counderakis, Communist activist from New York. Later union people identified the unclaimed body in the morgue as that of Nickolas Bordoise, Greek immigrant, San Francisco resident for twelve years, and member of the Cooks and Waiters Union. No one recognized the other name.

About twenty minutes after the killings, police bombed the ILA hall. The longshoremen described the attack:

> While two of our members were lying in their own blood on the sidewalk – shot in the *back* – and our union headquarters was filled with injured and gassed members – the police deliberately fired gas bombs into our headquarters . . .
>
> . . . doctors were taking care of the wounded—and men were lying in agony on the floors—the police, . . . shot tear gas bombs into the hall, and stationed officers with drawn guns at the entrance to see no one was allowed to get out and escape from the gas ordeal.
>
> While this attack was in full swing, four anonymous telephone calls were received at ILA headquarters. In each instance—after each attack—a voice would ask "Now are you willing to arbitrate?"[14]

The AP correspondent reported: "Ralph Mallen of the longshoremen's publicity committee, emerged from the building carrying a man stripped to the waist and blood smeared. The man had been shot through the shoulder. Mallen said two other men with bullet wounds were lying in the building but the tear gas had prevented him from reaching them."[15]

Charles S. Olson (next to building) and Howard S. Sperry, shot by police at Steuart and Mission streets, Bloody Thursday. (Courtesy San Francisco Public Library)

Strikers' memorial to Sperry and Olson, Bloody Thursday. (Courtesy San Francisco Public Library)

Donald Brown described the brutal attack in the street:

> The night sticks were the worst. The long hardwood clubs lay onto skulls with sickening force, again and again till a face was hardly recognizable.
>
> But an insane courage drove on the strikers. In the face of bullets, gas, clubs, horses' hooves, death; against fast patrol cars and the radio, they fought back with rocks and bolts till the street was a mess of debris. One policeman was thrown from a horse, cracking his head on the pavement. Another suffered a cut face when he failed to dodge a heavy rock. . . .
>
> About two o'clock the fighting subsided, the sirens stopped blowing, and the strikers melted away.[16]

During the fighting Atlas trucks made ten trips from Pier 38 to the warehouse. In a long and acrimonious session with Mayor Rossi, the Joint Marine Strike Committee demanded that the mayor withdraw all police from the waterfront. He refused, repeating his pledge to protect life and property and make the streets safe for all citizens without interference from strikers. Eyewitnesses reported acts of senseless police brutality. A seaman and a reporter saw two officers hitting a young striker on the shins with their nightsticks in front of the Harbor Emergency Hospital. "As he fell to the sidewalk, other officers came up. All of them beat him on the head with their nightsticks."[17] An ISU observer stationed at the hospital to see that wounded strikers received proper treatment related: "An injured seaman, Joseph Silver of 80 Corn Street, was brought in by Police Officer 1178 to be treated for wounds. While the doctor was dressing his wounds he asked the patient how he came to be hurt. Silver replied that Officer 1178 had struck him. Whereupon said officer called him a 'damned liar' and assaulted the patient while still under the doctor's care. He was forcibly withheld by hospital attendants."[18]

Defeat

Shortly before three o'clock word spread among the strikers that Governor Merriam had ordered out the National Guard, renewing their fury and triggering the final battle of the day. Pickets surged down Mission in a desperate effort to regain the waterfront. Police used nausea gas to repulse them. Brown described the scene:

> They came from everywhere with fresh loads of iron and stone. They swarmed onto the Embarcadero, outnumbering the police by enormous odds. The police answer to this was gas, and still more gas. These bombs appeared to have longer range than those used in the morning, and exploded on impact. Volley after volley of these crashed into the closely packed mob, searing flesh, blinding, and choking. Where the ranks broke, mounted officers drove in with clubs, trampling those who could not get out of the way. Again the sirens screamed, and carload after carload of officers and plainclothes-men armed with more tear gas and shotguns swung into action. Many were especially equipped with gas masks.
>
> The congestion at the foot of Market Street was becoming fantastic. The spectators were standing so thickly on the bridge over the under-pass that the structure was in

danger of collapse. Automobiles were packed in the subway below, stopping all traffic. . . . And all the while, ferry-loads of commuters were being emptied into the Ferry Building, and ferryloads of automobiles from Oakland and Alameda were being dumped at the auto entrance, a little to the south and in the midst of the heavy fighting.

At the height of this confusion, the battle reached white heat. More and more gun-fire came into play. Bullets crashed into office windows, scattering the curious employees, sending showers of glass onto the crowded sidewalks below. . . . Police vainly tried to drive the masses of spectators back from the combat zone, but they were thrust into it by the discharging auto ferries and street-cars. Some, trying to escape from the stalled trolleys, fell before the hail of slugs. Two men were shot. A bystander at the auto ferry fell screaming.

The superior technical equipment of the uniformed forces was too much for any human flesh, regardless of numerical superiority. The Embarcadero was cleared of strikers. There remained the broken windows, scattered glass, rocks, spikes, empty shotgun shells, and drying blood. . . .

As the amazed spectators began to disperse after four o'clock, . . . I went up Market and turned into Steuart Street, where the police were mopping up the remaining combatants. Near the ILA headquarters two men were helping a staggering picket away from the fray. He was stripped to the waist showing a gaping bullet hole in his back. Tear gas fumes were drifting out of the open door of the ILA hall, where wounded were being given first aid.[19]

By five o'clock the strikers gave up—driven off the waterfront. Police permitted fifteen men at a time to go through their lines for the evening meal at the relief kitchen. Official casualty figures reported 2 dead and 109 injured, 32 by police bullets, and the rest gassed, clubbed, or hit by missiles. A few police officers and bystanders were injured, and strikers clubbed the *News* photographer. Strikers accounted for most of the 109 casualties and included only those treated at hospitals. Many injured strikers sought private treatment to avoid possible arrest at hospitals. About fifty seamen sustained injuries. At the Marine Firemen's Union meeting that night the secretary reported:

The Police Department are living up to their Cossack tactics by starting to use riot guns, revolvers and tear-gas. They sent over a hundred to the Hospital suffering from club beatings and gunshot wounds. Then they capped a glorious day of blood spilling by going in front of the I.L.A. hall and killing two defenseless longshoremen by shooting them in the back. They killed one more, bringing the total to three. To the disgrace of San Francisco, our Police Department has the backing of a spineless mayor in the blood-spilling orgy. A delegation appealed to him to stop the bloodshed before the two longshoremen were killed. He told the strikers that we must have law and order. His interpretation of law and order is to shoot defenseless men in the back to death. Women and children also. But what can the workers expect of boot-licking politicians?[20]

Early in the evening the National Guard began to occupy the waterfront. With rifles and bayonets protruding from trucks, the first hundred soldiers moved out of the Armory at Fourteenth and Mission. More arrived from Oakland. The scattering of pickets on the town side of the Embarcadero, some huddled around small fires in

California National Guard occupies the San Francisco waterfront, Bloody Thursday. (Courtesy International Longshore and Warehouse Union Library)

vacant lots, made no demonstration. By morning 2,000 troops camped on the Embarcadero. Col. R.E. Middlestadt ordered the troops to "avoid shooting if possible, but if it becomes necessary to discharge your rifles, shoot for effect."[21] Capt. Bedford W. Boyes elaborated: "We want strikers to realize that we are soldiers and not policemen. We do not intend to engage in hand-to-hand combat. We are not going to hit anyone on the head with clubs because we are not equipped with them."[22]

Police Chief Quinn deplored the Guard's arrival. The press reported: "'We have the situation in hand and I'm afraid the National Guard coming will result in much bloodshed and many deaths,' said Chief Quinn. 'In a situation like this the National Guard sets a deadline and then shoots anyone who crosses it. The strikers don't understand these kinds of orders and are quite likely to barge across deadlines. And rifles are being put in the hands of inexperienced men.'"[23]

The strikers chalked a memorial on the sidewalk where Sperry and Olson fell: "POLICE MURDER – 2 ILA MEN KILLED – SHOT IN THE BACK." Flowers bordered the square and covered the bloodstains where the bodies had lain. Strikers propped a small American flag and an ILA banner against the building beside an extra edition with an account of the killing. A police patrol came by and "destroyed the flowers and the American flag, throwing the remnants into the patrol wagon."[24] The next morning the strikers protested the desecration to Mayor Rossi and replaced the memorial. The ILA posted a guard, and police did not again violate the spot. Hundreds of passersby stopped to look, and strike sympathizers came down to pray or ponder the message of the bloodstains.

Labor Is Outraged

The San Francisco waterfront remained quiet July 6, "bristling with the steely threat of army machine guns, bayonets, rifles and nausea gas bombs."[25] "A STRANGE OPENING," the *Joint Marine Journal* commented: "The National Guard stands with fixed bayonets, in front of every pier . . . with machine guns on bridges, roofs, and other points of vantage. Pickets are restricted by a ring of steel . . . a half dozen trucks make furtive trips from one pier to a warehouse three blocks away . . ."[26] A Communist Party leaflet appealed to guardsmen to "REFUSE TO BE THUGS AND MURDERERS. . . . JOIN IN A GENERAL STRIKE! REFUSE ORDERS TO SHOOT DOWN STRIKERS, PICKETS AND LABOR UNIONISTS!!!"[27]

"Bloody Thursday," as July 5 would be known among maritime workers, evoked a nationwide protest from union people. AFL President William Green wired Mayor Rossi condemning his use of police to aid "unreasonable employers to compel striking workers to accept their terms." He wired Governor Merriam: "Bayonets, soldiers and machine guns are not the instrumentalities which should be used in the settlement of differences which arise between employers and employees,"[28] and urged him to demand that the employers negotiate a settlement immediately. Rossi protested his impartiality and claimed that the police were never the aggressors, and Merriam emphasized the National Guards's sole function to protect life and property. ILA President Joe Ryan warned: "We cannot be expected to keep our men at work on the Atlantic Coast for employers who are calling out troops to shoot down men who simply want a decent system of hiring."[29]

The *Labor Clarion* declared: "The Industrial Association deliberately precipitated the crisis by an insincere gesture to remove goods from the docks to a warehouse a few blocks away, knowing in advance that the move would be contested by strikers and sympathizers and that bloodshed was inevitable. It savored of premeditation and planned provocation of strife."[30]

From New York July 6 the Central Committee of the Communist Party directed: "Organize protest meetings, and strong solidarity actions! Pass resolutions in your organizations for the right to organize, strike and picket! For a general strike of Pacific Coast workers! For the spreading of the strike to the entire maritime industry of the country."[31]

Not only Communists called for a Pacific Coast general strike. Outraged by the Bloody Thursday events, Ben T. Osborne, secretary of the Oregon State Federation of Labor, proposed that the state federations of labor of Washington, Oregon, and California call a general strike of all Pacific Coast workers, to begin July 12, if employers did not meet the demands of the maritime workers by that date. The executive committee of the Oregon State Federation withdrew the letter, explaining that Osborne had acted without proper authorization.

Copy

JOINT LETTER

7-7-34

Paul Scharrenberg, Secretary
California State Federation of Labor
San Francisco, California.
and
James Taylor, President
Washington State Federation of Labor
Seattle, Washington.

Dear Sirs and Brothers:

The waterfront strike has now reached a stage where it is now longer a controversey between the workers engaged in that industry and their employers. The establishing of vigilante committees; the setting up by ship owners and chambers of commerce, through their industrial associations, their own police departments, and in some instances that includes the taking over of the control of county and city police departments; and the instituting of military rule with utterances of the commanding officers to "Shoot to kill", constitutes a situation which demands emphatic actions by all workers of the three states, Washington, California, and Oregon, acting together as one.

The demands of the strikers are for the recognition of cardinal principles to which the labor movement is committed. The growing demand for general and concerted action to place the power of all organized workers behind the marine craft organization is well recognized by all. The States Federations are properly the bodies to coordinate these forces and to lead the workers in an orderly and efficient manner.

If the officers of the State Federations of California and Washington agree with this plan of action, it is my suggestion that the Secretary of the California State Federation of Labor presentx to the waterfront employers and the ship owners' organizations, through the President's Board in San Francisco, on behalf of the three State Federations of Labor the following demands:

1st: All employers who employ workers engaged in marine work shall recognize the chosen representatives of the union as the representative of all workers in their respective crafts for the purpose of collective bargaining.

2nd: That all workers shall be employed through the union.

3rd: That employers will immediately after the men return to work enter into negotiations with the organizations to execute an agreement governing terms and conditions of employment, rates of pay, hours of work, etc. (wages and hours subject to arbitration).

It is further my suggestion that the President's Board be notified that unless the ship owners and employers agree ta the principles herin enunciated, that a general strike will be called of all organized workers in the three Pacific Coast States on Thursday, the 12th day of July, 1934, at the hour of twelve o'clock noon.

Sincerely and fraternally yours,
BEN T. OSBORNE
Executive Secretary of the Oregon
State Federation of Labor.

BTO:NC

Ben T. Osborne letter July 7, 1934, calling for a coastwide general strike. (Author's Collection)

The Funeral

The strikers buried their dead with a mass funeral. The ILA strike bulletin July 7 announced: "On Monday the workers of San Francisco will give their answer to the blood-baths of the S.F. Industrial Association and the Shipowners through their paid murder agents, by turning out EN MASSE – to conduct the bodies of those slain martyrs to their final resting place."[32] The seamen's bulletin said:

> Each organization will form its own unit in the demonstration and are requested to have their own flag, as well as the National Flag. NO PLACARDS OF ANY DESCRIPTION WILL BE ALLOWED.
>
> Seamen! Make it your business to be there. It is your duty! We cannot honor these men too highly. All other Unions in the city of San Francisco will be there, to honor our dead, and we must be there also.[33]

The bodies of Sperry and Bordoise lay in state at ILA headquarters all day Sunday, attended by an honor guard of ILA war veterans. Flowers filled the small hall over Harry's Lunch. Only the wreath sent by the Police Department was missing—returned by the strikers. Thousands filed silently past the caskets. "OUR BROTHERS," the memorial leaflet read;

Funeral of Howard S. Sperry and Nickolas Bordoise begins at Steuart and Mission streets, July 9, 1934. (Courtesy Sailors' Union of the Pacific)

HOWARD S. SPERRY – a longshoreman – a World War Veteran . . . STRIKING FOR THE RIGHT TO EARN A DECENT LIVING – under decent conditions . . .

HOWARD SPERRY'S STRIKE CARD NEEDS PUNCHING NO MORE!

HIS DUTY IS DONE – HIS STRIKE CARD IS FILED AWAY.

. . . . A MARTYR TO THE CAUSE OF LABOR.

. . . WE MUST – AND SHALL – WIN FOR THE WORKERS OF THE WATER-FRONT THE THINGS FOR WHICH HOWARD S. SPERRY STRUCK – AND DIED! A DECENT ILA CONTROLLED HIRING HALL – AND AN END TO THE ROTTEN COMPANY UNION SYSTEM WHICH HAS HELD US IN PEONAGE FOR FOURTEEN YEARS.

NICKOLAS BORDOISE – a resident of San Francisco for twelve years. A member of Cooks & Waiters Union #44 for ten years. Also a member of the International Labor Defense. Not a striker himself – but merely a visitor to the water front – looking to the welfare of his fellow-workers on strike!

HAIL AND FAREWELL! OUR BROTHERS! WE SHALL NOT FORGET![34]

On July 9, a hundred people gathered in the ILA hall for the brief service at 12:30, as thousands packed the street below to share the service over a public address system. The *Chronicle* reporter wrote:

> No minister of the cloth was present—only a few of the "comrades" and a group of their women—wives, mothers, sweethearts, and even little children. . . .
>
> Here and there in the group a child whimpered, restless in the close atmosphere with the cloying scent of many flowers. Veterans in their old army uniforms, already gray with the years since the war in which they served, stood guard over the caskets—vastly different than those youthful National Guardsmen on the Embarcadero a block away.

A.F. Walker, a former longshoreman, spoke a few words over the caskets: "We are here to pay respects to you, in the hope that your sacrifice will not have been in vain. . . ." Two men sang. Then pallbearers carried the caskets down the narrow stairway and placed them on two flatbed trucks surrounded by flowers. Longshoremen piled the rest of the flowers on two more trucks. The cortege proceeded across Steuart, turned left, and moved up Market.

A group of men, eight abreast, led the procession wearing arm badges with the legend, "I.L.A. War Vet." "They marched, enough of them to have formed a goodly company of soldiers, with an American Flag and the banner of the International Longshoremen's Association in the van." The *Chronicle* reporter described the procession:

> In life they wouldn't have commanded a second glance on the streets of San Francisco, but in death they were borne the length of Market street in a stupendous and reverent procession that astounded the city. More than 15,000 men and women marched in that procession.
>
> Howard S. Sperry, war veteran and striking longshoreman, and Nickolas Bordoise, an unemployed fry cook, were transformed in death into heroic symbols of labor.
>
> While the entire city gasped in amazement yesterday, these two men who were killed in the bloody riots of last Thursday on the water front were given the most amazing mass funeral San Francisco has ever seen.

Funeral cortege moves up Market Street. (Courtesy The Bancroft Library, Charles M. Kurtz Collection, photograph #1959.003:112-pic)

A solemn procession that had the strange aspect of a silent parade moved at a snail's pace up Market street . . . until its entire length stretched from the Ferry to Seventh street—was the funeral cortege of the war veteran and the fry cook.

It was a silent, grim-faced precession that moved slowly, deliberately through the city.

And for the hour it took to pass along down town life came to a full stop and stared.

Many more thousands of people from all walks of life formed deep banks on both sides of Market street. While the noon-day crowds formed a large part of the spectators, there were many who waited long especially for the procession.

With bared heads they stood silently and respectfully as the longshoremen and maritime workers carried their dead.

Overhead fluttered the pennons and banners of the Knights Templar, colorful symbols which added to the incongruity of this silent procession, watched by silent crowds.

There was a band just like any band that might march in a parade—blue uniforms, sun glinting from trombones and trumpets—but no stirring march tune, no lilting air was heard. Just the dull roll of muffled drums and the steady dirge of the funeral march.

The funeral procession of labor had its touch of color, however. There in the center of the strange cavalcade were uniforms, the uniforms of the United States Army and Navy—and an American Flag.

But the flag was draped over the coffin of Howard S. Sperry, the war veteran, and the uniforms were worn by men who had seen service in the World war—men who had worked cargo on the docks of San Francisco before their bitter clash with their employers.

The uniformed men marched with lagging pace in a guard of honor around the flower-decked truck which carried the casket of Sperry. Behind them came the second truck, also banked with flowers, but accompanied only by the funeral director. On this was borne the casket of Bordoise, the fry cook and union man, who also lost his life because of his devotion to the cause of labor.

Four cars with the relatives of the dead followed the caskets. Next came the union contingents led by William J. Lewis, president of the Pacific Coast District ILA and Harry Bridges, chairman of the Joint Marine Strike Committee, followed by the fifty members of the committee. The reporter continued:

Then came the mighty show of strength that amazed the citizens who packed the sidewalks and pressed out into the street.

Eight abreast, line on line they came, their bared heads in view as far as the eye could see down the broad length of Market street—longshoremen, sailors, marine engineers, masters, mates and pilots, firemen, water tenders, machinists, welders. Here they came as far as you could see in a silent orderly line of march, a mass demonstration of protest which transcended anything of the like San Francisco had seen. . . .

And any who doubted the solid sympathy of the labor movement with the striking unions were shamed by that demonstration.

Unique was that monster procession, for the thousands of spectators were not held back by any police ropes, nor were there any police to regulate traffic, aside from the few officers who customarily stand at the intersections.

And the police stood aside, melted into the crowd for the most part. This was not their parade. The marine workers had given due notice they would handle the demonstration and pledged their solemn word a funeral it would be, not more, not less.

No placards would be a shown, they said, and none were. No communist agitators would be tolerated, they promised. And none were. Only one communist dared show his color before that reverent procession. His attempts to distribute copies of The Western Worker at Stockton and Market streets met with summary action from the "traffic car" of striking longshoremen which preceded the procession. His papers were taken from him and he was sent spinning through the crowd. . . .

Market street traffic halted and then vanished from the street as the procession approached. Street cars were rerouted on Mission street and the longshoremen had the street to themselves and their dead. . . .

And San Francisco bared its head, irrespective of opinion or affiliation, to let the maritime workers bury their dead in peace.[35]

The procession ended at Duggan's funeral parlors on Seventeenth near Valencia. That night the Veterans of Foreign Wars post to which Howard Sperry had belonged held a service there for him, and the next day he was buried in the Presidio National Cemetery. The Communist Party conducted a Red funeral for Nickolas Bordoise at Cypress Lawn Cemetery.

Pickets resumed their regular duties after Bloody Thursday, instructed "not to Boo the National Guard, not to engage them in any manner and to keep all men away from the picket lines who have been indulging in intoxicating liquors."[36] The Joint Marine Strike Committee appealed without result to Santa Fe and Southern Pacific crews to refuse "to shunt cars in to the strike area," urging that the "strike must be won if all the railroad men will stop the movement of cars carrying scab cargo."[37] Twenty-two seamen remained in the Marine Hospital July 12, "some with severe and minor lacerations about the head and body, and others with gunshot wounds."[38] James Engle and Charles Olson, critically injured July 5, showed improvement. Dissention flared up again in the ISU after the bloody port opening. Rumors circulated that some seamen would agree to arbitrate all demands—that the Marine Cooks had sold out. The *Joint Marine Journal* warned July 7:

Our adversaries tried to split the I.L.A. by attacking certain of their leaders through the medium of newspapers. They failed. So they started on the I.S.U., . . .

ARE YOU GOING TO FALL FOR IT? ARE YOU GOING TO GIVE UP NOW AFTER THIS LONG SPLENDID FIGHT? ARE YOU GOING TO PLOT AGAINST YOUR OWN UNION? ARE YOU CRAZY? . . .

Now is the time that we need to show our solidarity . . . our UNITY. HOW CAN WE EXPECT OTHER WELL KNIT UNIONS UP TOWN TO BACK US UP – IF WE ARE GOING TO ALLOW THE ENEMY TO SPLIT US?[39]

The Sailors' Union meeting July 7 reorganized the strike committee with "Fighting Boz" Evans as chair and added three strike card men, nonmembers actively participating in the strike. The meeting also elected a new negotiating committee chaired by Herbert Mills with four more SUP members and one strike card member

National Guard on the Embarcadero, San Francisco, 1934. (Courtesy Sailors' Union of the Pacific)

to be added as an observer. Beginning July 11 all ISU unions reregistered their strikers and issued new strike cards. The Sailors' Union demanded loyalty from strikers. Before a man could reregister, the union required a pledge to "work with and for this Union during the strike" and "support the duly elected officers and committees." The striker had to "disavow Communism in all its forms" and swear he was "not a member of any dual organization,"[40] meaning the MWIU.

At the onset of the Industrial Association's offensive, uptown unions stepped up their support. On June 29 the Chauffeurs' Union pledged $1,000 a week for fifteen weeks, and the Web Pressmen levied a 50-cent assessment. The California State Federation of Labor issued a statewide appeal June 12 to all affiliates for strike relief contributions. The American Radio Telegraphists' Association struck July 15, although many radio operators had already left their ships and joined the picket lines. They demanded union recognition, an eight-hour day, and wages of $125 to $105 a month depending on the vessel. The union claimed 1,500 members nationally, 600 on the West Coast.

The mass funeral and testimony of prestrike conditions on the waterfront swung public opinion toward the strikers. To counter these influences, the Waterfront Employers ran full-page newspaper ads defending their position. They also appealed directly to the strikers. In a series of individual letters to "the real longshoremen," the

Waterfront Employers' Union praised the June 16 agreement and offered to answer questions "in strictest confidence." They attacked the ILA demand for control of the hiring hall as a scheme to provide work for union members not regular longshoremen.

While the Waterfront Employers tried to soften up their employees, the Industrial Association appealed to business people for more funds to smash the unions. A letter July 12 asked recipients for a pledge to be paid in installments on call of the association at any time within five years. Signers of the appeal included Republican National Committeeman William H. Crocker, president of the Crocker First National Bank; Kenneth R. Kingsbury, president of Standard Oil Company of California; F.B. Anderson, president of the Bank of California; and Wallace M. Alexander, Hawaiian sugar factor and one of the controlling figures of the Matson Navigation Company.

National Longshoremen's Board Hearings

With the threat of a general strike hanging over San Francisco, the National Longshoremen's Board held public hearings July 9-11. Paul Scharrenberg presented the ISU proposals adopted by coastwide vote July 2. The union asked recognition for the purpose of collective bargaining or, if the shipowners refused, a representation election before the seamen went back to work. "The men must not be required to return to work through the shipowners' employment bureaus, and shall be returned to their positions without discrimination for union activity or strike activity."[41] Negotiations would begin immediately after the seamen's return to the ships, and matters still in dispute after thirty days would be arbitrated, wages to be retroactive to the date of return to work.

E.B. O'Grady and Capt. Oscar E. Rolstad presented the demands of the Masters, Mates and Pilots. The union asked for recognition for collective bargaining and no discrimination for strike activity. Negotiations should begin promptly, and unresolved issues should be arbitrated. They stipulated that satisfactory arrangements must be made with the other striking unions. Sam Kagel presented similar demands for the Marine Engineers' Beneficial Association.

District President Lewis stated the ILA position July 4 in a reply to the Board's plea for arbitration:

> Before submitting to arbitration, or requesting our members to take a referendum vote thereon, two important qualifications must be considered.
>
> 1. There must be a basis of settlement established for the Maritime Groups, and all other groups affected which will be acceptable to them, covering recognition of their organizations, and arbitration, if necessary of their proposals.
>
> 2. In your letter no mention is made concerning the hiring of Longshoremen while arbitration is proceeding. The longshoremen under any circumstances would not return to the existing halls, for such action might be construed as a tacit consent to their perpetuation. The question of hiring halls must be settled before the men return to work.[42]

In oral testimony Harry Bridges declared: "Unless the I.L.A. can control those hiring halls the right of longshoremen to organize is just a farce." Citing the open-shop guarantee and the employers' right to select employees, he charged that "the joint hiring hall, as proposed by the employers, is not a joint hiring hall at all, but a shipowners hiring hall, with an impotent I.L.A. observer."[43]

Speaking for the employers, Tom Plant reiterated their willingness to abide by the June 16 agreement for longshoremen and their inability to recognize or deal with the marine unions. He cited official police reports of violence: 4 dead, 266 injured, 63 percent strikebreakers and 10 percent police, and 40 cases of sabotage. Plant charged that teamsters had been driven from the waterfront by threats and intimidation.

In a final effort to avert the impending general strike, July 10 the Longshoremen's Board asked employers and unions to submit to unconditional arbitration. The spectacle of over 15,000 grim union people marching up Market Street the day before may have induced the shipowners to make a concession. The Waterfront Employers of San Francisco, Seattle, Portland, and Los Angeles agreed to unconditional arbitration with the ILA, and forty-two steamship companies agreed "to meet with representatives of their seafaring employees for the purpose of collective bargaining, such representatives to be selected in elections held in such manner as your board shall determine."[44] The Seattle Waterfront Employers accepted with the stipulation that "non-union operations along the coast to remain status quo" until the arbitration decision was rendered and accepted, and that Tacoma would be included on the same basis as other ports.[45]

ILA District President Lewis agreed to conduct a coastwide referendum on whether the union would arbitrate, provided the hiring hall issue was settled and the marine unions reached an understanding. On July 12 a circular letter to all locals went out over Lewis's mimeographed signature urging acceptance of arbitration. Lewis repudiated the letter, put out "without my knowledge and it does not in any way express my opinion. A.H. Petersen sent the letter to the district locals as purely his own convictions, . . ."[46] Lewis reiterated the ILA insistence that the closed shop and hiring halls could not be arbitrated.

In another letter to the board July 15, Lewis, Bridges, Cliff Thurston of Portland, and John Finnegan of the district executive board, stated that the ILA "cannot agree to take a referendum vote on the question of submitting everything in dispute to arbitration"[47] until the hiring hall question was settled and the maritime unions arrived at a satisfactory understanding with the shipowners.

The unlicensed seamen agreed to vote coastwide on arbitration. The ISU pointed out, however, that the shipowners had not agreed to arbitrate with the marine unions, that collective bargaining might go on indefinitely without an agreement being reached. The *Joint Marine Journal* urged seamen to refuse to arbitrate control of hiring:

> The main fight of the seamen is for the abolition of the infamous Fink Hall. Are we going to ARBITRATE that question? The Fink Hall must go, and all shipowners employment bureaus must go with it. That includes these little shipping offices on the docks, where the college boys (who are scabbing now) used to come with their letters . . . and get jobs . . . and go to sea . . . while we stood around all day and every day . . . waiting . . . waiting . . . chased away by police, if too big a crowd of hungry *seamen*

gathered there . . . cursed at and run around . . . until we lost all hopes and didn't care if we went to work or not . . .

STRIKERS!!! THE QUESTION OF HIRING HALLS CANNOT BE ARBITRATED!!! . . .

THINK BEFORE YOU VOTE!!! DON'T SELL YOURSELF OUT!!![48]

The coastwide ISU vote rejected arbitration 1,980 to 1,558. The San Francisco Sailors voted 607 to 258 against arbitration and the San Pedro ISU 540 to 452. The Seattle Sailors voted 256 to 23 for arbitration and the Portland Sailors and Marine Firemen 182 to 5 in favor. Besides union hiring halls, the strikers wanted better living and working conditions. A seaman wrote to the *Joint Marine Journal*:

> There is no better time than now for the President's Board to select a committee of anybody versed in sanitation to go on board some of those steam schooners and vessels at anchor and see for themselves the crews quarters and how we have to live.
>
> They could also get the ships logs from some of those coast wise vessels and see where the crew had to make three or more shifts during the night and then turn to at eight in the morning and work until five.[49]

Soldiers harassed pickets on the Embarcadero and strikers working in the relief kitchen, in some cases cutting off their buttons "with accompanying opprobrious remarks." Local 38-79 Secretary Ivan Cox interviewed the Adjutant General, "who stated that no National Guardsman has any right – nor any orders – to use their bayonets to flip union buttons off the coats of any man."[50] The ILA strike bulletin counseled patience in the face of the difficulties in maintaining the relief kitchen. City health officials inspected the premises three times a day.

General Strike Call

General strike sentiment had been building before Bloody Thursday. In a letter July 3 the Joint Marine Strike Committee urged "all A.F. of L. unions to elect delegates to a conference to be held . . . Saturday, July 7th – to discuss and prepare for a general strike of the workers in the Bay region."[51] While police clubbed strikers July 5, a Joint Marine Strike Committee leaflet called upon union people to instruct their Labor Council delegates to vote for a general strike:

> The San Francisco Industrial Association and the San Francisco police have started a reign of terror on the waterfront by shooting, gassing and bombing the workers, . . .
>
> . . . For your own future protection and to help your fellow union men ACTION and DECISIVE ACTION must be taken immediately by all organized workers. The only effective weapon that will . . . force the shipowners to grant the strikers their just demands is the GENERAL STRIKE.[52]

An ILA leaflet the next day urged all trade unionists to plan for a general strike: "FOR EIGHT LONG WEEKS WE HAVE BEEN FIGHTING YOUR FIGHT ALSO! ARE YOU GOING TO PERMIT THE SCABBY – UNION-BUSTING

OPEN SHOP POLICY OF THE SAN FRANCISCO INDUSTRIAL ASSOCIATION AND THE SHIPOWNERS TO WIN? – AND SET THE ORGANIZED LABOR MOVEMENT BACK TWENTY YEARS?"[53]

At this point the San Francisco Labor Council stepped in to take charge of the burgeoning general strike movement. July 6, by a vote of 165 to 8 the delegates created a Strike Strategy Committee "to consult and advise with" the maritime unions. Council President Edward F. Vandeleur of the Street Railway Carmen's Union appointed a committee of seven: Daniel P. Haggerty of the Machinists, past president of the California State Federation of Labor and San Francisco Labor Council; M.S. Maxwell, president of the California State Federation of Butchers; Frank Brown, secretary of the Molders Union; John O'Connell of the Teamsters, secretary of the Labor Council; George Kidwell, secretary-treasurer of the Bakery Wagon Drivers; Charles A. Derry of the Typographical Union, editor of the *Labor Clarion*, and himself as chair. The meeting adopted unanimously a resolution by the Joint Marine Strike Committee upholding the longshoremen's refusal to arbitrate the question of hiring halls and condemned Governor Merriam for calling out the National Guard in "the unwarranted display of force and compulsion in the settlement of an industrial dispute."[54]

Ralph Mallen, delegate to the Labor Council, reported in the ILA strike bulletin: "The S.F. Labor Council has not blocked a General Strike. The Council has set up a committee to make plans for a strike that will stop every industry in the city."[55] John O'Connell stated: "This strategy committee is a sane move now. It will lead to organized movement in case of a general strike later and would mean that brains and not brawn would direct us."[56] Saturday, July 7, the Joint Marine Strike Committee voted to cooperate with the Labor Council's strategy committee. Fourteen unions had already voted for a general strike. The Strike Strategy Committee declared July 8: "We mean to give the shipowners and the National Longshoremen's Board every chance to settle this crisis peacefully and we want to act reasonably and not violently. But we do not intend to yield one inch of the ground to which these men are justly entitled, and if their rights are overlooked we are ready to unleash the full strength of organized labor in San Francisco."[57]

At the Teamsters' Union special meeting that day Michael Casey tried without success to persuade the members against a strike. He warned that a sympathetic strike violated their agreement and international rules, and they would not receive the $10.00-a-week strike benefit. "In all my years of leading these men," he declared later, "I have never seen them so worked up, so determined to walk out."[58] The strike ballot read: "Do you wish to continue working after Wednesday under present conditions?"[59] By a vote of 1,220 to 271 the members said NO. Another meeting Wednesday night would make the final decision. General strike sentiment also grew in East Bay communities. Oakland teamsters voted the same day 369 to 54 to strike July 12.

Impatient teamsters demanded action at the meeting in San Francisco the 11th. Boos and catcalls greeted the strategy committee's urgent plea from the Longshoremen's Board to delay the strike until the maritime unions could vote on arbitration. The demonstration drove the Labor Council representatives from the dais. Members called insistently for Bridges, who was waiting outside with several hundred strikers. The teamsters greeted him with an ovation, and after his speech the meeting voted by acclamation to strike at seven o'clock the next morning. The vote brought out 3,700 teamsters. The Strike Strategy Committee admitted that a general strike had become inevitable: "The offer of the employers to arbitrate appears to have come too late. . . . The action of the Teamsters' Union . . . is an indication of the feeling of union labor throughout the city, and indeed along the entire Coast."[60]

According to the AFL constitution, no central labor council could call a strike. The power rested solely with affiliated local unions. But a council could request them to ballot on the question of a sympathetic strike, and could convene a meeting of delegates from unions voting in the affirmative to form a general strike committee, a body separate from and independent of the council. This procedure preserved both the cohesiveness of the labor movement in the community and the autonomy of local unions in strike actions.

On recommendation of the Strike Strategy Committee, the Labor Council called a meeting Saturday morning, July 14, to act on the general strike demand. Already 32,000 members of thirteen unions were on strike. Delegates from 115 unions representing 65,000 of San Francisco's 75,000 organized workers attended. The group ejected representatives of the Marine Workers Industrial Union. After E.B. O'Grady declined the nomination, the delegates elected Edward Vandeleur to chair the General Strike Committee. Clyde W. Deal of the Ferryboatmen defeated Harry Bridges for vice-chair 262 to 203, and George Kidwell of the Bakery Wagon Drivers was unopposed for secretary. By a vote of 315 to 15, with 245 not authorized to vote, the committee ordered "all Unions that have taken strike action to call out their members, Monday, July 16th, at 8 a.m., and that all other Unions that have not acted be asked to take action at once."[61]

From the beginning a clear division appeared, as in the contest for vice-chair. The maritime unions and other militants wanted to shut down everything. They wanted to go for broke, to throw labor's entire resources into a struggle equal in intensity and devotion to that of the maritime strikers. They believed that such a struggle could force the shipowners to grant the maritime workers' demands. Conservative union people who controlled the Labor Council wanted to confine the strike and exempt essential consumer services to avoid antagonizing the public. They feared that employers would use the strike as an excuse to break unions and that organized labor would be weakened by the drastic act. They wanted a small, disciplined strike, a reasonable gesture of support for the maritime strikers that would not jeopardize the labor movement. ILA District President Bill Lewis later reported that "when these unions went on strike, they immediately took over the direction of the strike to the almost total exclusion of the longshoremen who had very little to say concerning the policies of the strike."[62]

Joe Ryan suggested that Labor Council officials sanctioned the general strike to destroy Communist influence on the waterfront. The Communist Party agreed:

And if these leaders later "sanctioned" the General Strike, it was with the express purpose not only to escape the isolation, which they already suffered among the marine workers, among the rest of the workers, but also as Ryan stated not merely to break the general strike, but also to oust the Left-wing leadership in the San Francisco marine strike as a prelude to breaking the strike of the marine workers. *The efforts to break the general strike did not develop with these leaders in the course of the general strike.* It was planned before the strike, which they could not stop, began.[63]

The General Strike

City and state officials prepared to crush the strike. Calling the strike the "worst calamity since the disaster of 1906," Mayor Rossi assumed emergency powers and threatened the city with martial law. Police Chief Quinn swore in 500 extra deputies, and Governor Merriam sent in 3,000 more National Guardsmen. Chief Quinn ordered stores and pawnshops to remove firearms from their windows, and hospital emergency wards prepared to receive casualties. Mayor Rossi organized a Citizens' Committee of Five Hundred composed of business and professional people. Replying to the mayor's fears of riot and insurrection, the General Strike Committee emphatically denied any revolutionary motives and charged that "certain leaders of the attack upon us which has forced this strike action have sought for their selfish ends to prey upon the patriotism of the people, to prejudice the city and the nation against organized labor by false declarations that the present situation is due to 'red' or revolutionary impulses."[64]

The *Labor Clarion* charged: "Newspapers interested only in catering to the wishes of influential advertisers and in swelling circulation figures have taken advantage of the troublous times to class as a communist every person who expresses advanced ideas, no matter how patriotic they may be nor what unselfish motives may actuate them." It condemned Governor Merriam for precipitating the general strike by ordering troops to the waterfront and then advising citizens to arm themselves against unarmed strikers. The paper demanded:

> For what purpose did he order the troops to San Francisco if not to protect the citizens? Are the governor's intemperate utterances to be interpreted as an acknowledgement that the military force was brought here merely at the demand of the waterfront employers to break the strike by intimidating the strikers? . . .
>
> No matter what incendiary statements may be issued by Governor Merriam, he cannot evade the responsibility for the military occupation of San Francisco and the spirit of unrest thereby created.[65]

The *Joint Marine Journal* counseled moderation:

> Our adversaries are the Shipowners, and the San Francisco Industrial Association. We are NOT FIGHTING AGAINST INNOCENT WOMEN AND LITTLE CHILDREN! . . .
>
> A General Strike is a desperate remedy, and can easily lead to unforeseen terror, misery and starvation. It is intended as a gigantic mass protest of all labor, against unjust

grievance. Let us take care that we are not carried away by our enthusiasm or our bitterness, to the extent of harming the innocent. A General Strike is aimed at the capitalistic interests . . . . and NOT at our Brothers of the working classes.[66]

The Teamsters' strike July 12 shut off gasoline supplies, and mass picketing of highways at the south city limits, the only land access to the peninsula, stopped all commercial trucks except those bearing exempted food, produce, or essential supplies. Practically all San Francisco unions struck July 16. The strike committee instructed those producing and delivering milk, bread, and ice to remain at work, as well as those engaged in essential public safety and health services. The printers refused to strike the newspapers, and the Electrical Workers remained at work at Pacific Gas and Electric utility. The Ferryboatmen, headed by Clyde W. Deal, struck the Golden Gate and Key System ferries to East Bay, but they left the ferries owned by railroads in operation. Streetcar operators and taxi drivers struck, halting public transportation. The Chinese Laundry Workers Union, Si Fook Tong, with 600 members, joined the strike. Oakland struck July 17, followed by other East Bay communities. Over 100,000 people were on strike in the Bay area, and another 470,000 unorganized workers were indirectly involved.

The daily press ran stories of immanent food shortages and editorials that Communists plotted the strike. The *Chronicle* declared July 16:

> Organized labor and communism have nothing in common. There are no unions in Russia, where these radicals get their orders.
>
> Are the sane, sober workingmen of San Francisco to permit these communists to use them for their purpose of wreckage, a wreckage bound to carry the unions down with it?[67]

The Hearst press thundered:

> There are many thousands of honest, upright, god-fearing, hard-working union men now part of the so-called general strike.
>
> The total of these against the handful of Communistic radicals, who have gotten them into this mess, is so overwhelming as to make us wonder how they have permitted themselves to be led from wise leadership into this revolt against their very selves. . . .
>
> Communists—an amazingly small number of them—but an amazingly skillful number of them—are in the saddle today.[68]

Declaring that "It is war now," the *Los Angeles Times* called for federal troops and vigilantes to break the strike:

> On the one side are the forces of law and order; on the other a group of Red-directed insurrectionists who, in their bloody defiance of authority, disgrace the name of honest and patriotic American labor. That they have been able to force thousands of workers unwillingly to lend support to this assault upon their own city is one of the most vicious phases of the closed-shop system, which makes the livelihood of union members dependent upon the blind obedience to their officials' orders.[69]

From the beginning the General Strike Committee exempted restaurants, increasing the number and adding other retail services each day. Employers and public officials condemned the permit system for exempt establishments and vehicles as a usurpation of their authority. To protect their civil service standing, streetcar operators on the municipal White Front line returned to work July 17 on the committee's recommendation.

The Communist Party took credit for the general strike. Earl Browder, general secretary, claimed in the New York *Daily Worker* that 1,200 Communists "are directing the workers of San Francisco in the logical path to a better life."[70] The *Western Worker* declared:

> All workers of the West Coast should FOLLOW 'FRISCO AND STRIKE IN UNITED RANKS. A GENERAL STRIKE of the entire West Coast will once and for all establish the rights of the workingmen. . . .
>
> You can strengthen this strike and win through strengthening the ranks of the militant workers, especially by JOINING THE COMMUNIST PARTY. . . .
>
> It is the Communist Party which: INITIATED THE GENERAL STRIKE—FIGHTS ALL SELL-OUT MANEUVERS—IS THE MOST ACTIVE MILITANT FORCE—CALLS FOR GENERAL MARINE STRIKE IN U.S.—WON SEAMEN TO COME OUT WITH LONGSHOREMEN![71]

The paper referred to the MWIU strike call.

Newspaper owners organized the Newspaper Publishers' Council the first day of the strike to convince the public that the strike heralded a Communist revolution. John Francis Nylan, general counsel for the Hearst papers, headed the group. Besides printing daily horror stories, the publishers used General Hugh Johnson, head of the National Recovery Administration, for their purpose, according to an article by Earl Burke in *Editor and Publisher*. The general arrived in San Francisco July 16 to accept an honorary Phi Beta Kappa key from the University of California. In a session lasting until 3:00 a.m., the publishers persuaded Johnson to abandon his position that the longshoremen's demands for union hiring halls should be granted before arbitration. Nylan told him that they might "even have to ask him to leave San Francisco"[72] if he refused to cooperate. The next day at Berkeley, after affirming labor's right to organize and bargain collectively and calling the shipping industry's position "extreme and unreasonable," General Johnson denounced the general strike as "a menace to the government. It is civil war. . . . When the means of food supply—milk to children—necessities of life to the whole people are threatened that is bloody insurrection."[73]

The National Longshoremen's Board deplored the general strike and again urged unconditional arbitration. The General Strike Committee meeting July 17 agreed, repudiating its previous support of the maritime strikers' position. The resolution introduced by George Kidwell called on the governors of the Pacific Coast states and mayors of all affected port cities to appeal to President Roosevelt to request all waterfront employers and unions to agree to unconditional arbitration. After a heated debate lasting many hours the delegates adopted the resolution on a standing vote 207 to 180.

Harry Bridges charged that unaccredited delegates packed the meeting and the chair denied a roll call vote. The employers hailed the action as a break in labor's united front. The chair ruled out of order a resolution introduced by Bridges reaffirming the Labor Council's resolution of support for union hiring halls. The *Western Worker* called the vote for arbitration "THE MOST SHAMEFUL BETRAYAL OF WORKERS IN AMERICAN LABOR HISTORY!" It charged that Vandeleur, Kidwell, and Casey were "collaborating with the thugs and gunmen of the Industrial Association."[74]

The morning of the fourth day, July 19, Kidwell introduced another resolution in the General Strike Committee meeting:

> That this General Strike Committee . . . now proposes that upon acceptance by the shipowners, employers of the striking maritime workers, of the terms of the President's Longshoremen's Board for settlement of this strike, that this General Strike Committee will accept such a basis for the immediate termination of the strike.

Charles Derry of the Typographical Union introduced an amendment:

> That this General Strike Committee hereby advises all those unions that are now out on strike out of sympathy with the maritime workers and longshoremen to immediately resume work, and that we pledge every resource, moral and financial, for the continued prosecution and the successful termination of the maritime workers and longshoremen's strike.[75]

The debate narrowed to the demand that the employers arbitrate with the seamen as a basis for ending the general strike, or ending it immediately without any conditions attached. After an hour's debate, the delegates adopted the Derry amendment by a standing vote of 191 to 174. Then they passed the resolution as amended. The meeting adjourned at 1:15.

The general strike ended. Workers began returning to their jobs as word spread through the city. The Teamsters Union meeting that night voted to take a secret ballot the following day: "The General Strike Committee has ordered all men on sympathy strike with the longshoremen to return to work. Are you in favor of returning to work?"[76] The vote to return carried 1,138 to 283. The next morning union teamsters began hauling to and from the waterfront.

9

Strike Settlement

The maritime strikers fought alone, without teamster support and instructed by the rest of the union movement to accept arbitration. Whatever their private feelings of betrayal and bitterness, publicly they refused to acknowledge defeat. The Joint Marine Strike Committee thanked "the entire labor movement for its tremendous show of unity."[1] The *Joint Marine Journal* summed up:

> The collapse of the so-called General Strike, does not mean that we can be forced to return to work against our will and dictates of our conscience. . . . We will finish what we started, and the only finish we will consider is a victorious finish.
>
> The shipowners seem very happy this morning. We note that they have radioed their ships, to come home to San Francisco because the public has shown them that "San Francisco Knows How." Well, Mr. Shipowner, we know how, too, and we will show the crews of your ships "how" when they arrive.
>
> Strikers, remember that your status is not changed, and our strike will not be over until YOU VOTE to return to work and end it.[2]

General Strike Aftermath

Assessments of the significance of the general strike varied. AFL President William Green lectured San Francisco workers on their "grave mistake" in striking:

> When a sympathetic strike occurs, the issues primarily responsible for the strike become subordinated and a new conflict arises between those engaged in the strike and government authorities.
>
> The sympathetic strike is immediately accepted as a challenge to government and because the government must be supreme, it is compelled to bring all its resources into action. That means that the workers on strike are no longer fighting against the employers who were responsible for creating the original issue which caused the strike, but instead the fight is between the City, State and Federal Governments on the one side and the strikers on the other.
>
> Everyone must know and understand that in such a conflict the government must win; it cannot surrender. It must establish its supremacy, and usually the result of such a conflict is that the government wins and strikers lose, and the employers against whom the original strike was directed become the beneficiaries.[3]

The *Los Angeles Times* gloated editorially over "The Strike That Failed." Banker William H. Crocker predicted victory for the open-shoppers:

> This strike is the best thing that ever happened to San Francisco. It's costing us money, certainly. We've lost millions on the waterfront in the last few months. But it's a good investment—a marvelous investment. It's solving the labor problem for years to come, perhaps forever.
>
> Mark my words. When this nonsense is out of the way and the men have been driven back to their jobs we won't have to worry about them any more. They'll have learned their lesson. Not only do I believe we'll never have another general strike, but I don't think we'll have a strike of any kind in San Francisco during this generation. Labor is licked.[4]

A new York columnist disagreed:

> New York feeling is that nothing has been settled and that the battle against "union domination" will be stiffer than ever from now on.
>
> Financial insiders get word that conservative labor leaders pulled some Machiavelli stuff that strengthened their grip considerably. They could have fought the general strike harder than they did—perhaps even headed it off.
>
> To do so would have stirred lasting bitterness not only among out-and-out radicals but also among the rank and file of union members. This in turn might have soon cost the conservative heads their jobs and handed the unions over entirely to radical control. . . .
>
> By swimming with the tide instead of trying to buck it, the conservatives kept command. This enabled them to minimize friction with the public and thus prevented serious damage to union prestige. The rank and file has now discovered for itself that the general strike was futile and that its experienced leaders knew their potatoes.
>
> This isn't to say that radicalism within the unions is abolished—but radicals won't find it so easy to gain recruits for awhile.[5]

The Red raids began July 17 with a vigilante attack on the Marine Workers Industrial Union hall, followed by the arrest of ninety "vagrants" who were trapped by National Guardsmen blocking both ends of Jackson Street near the hall. For two days vigilantes armed with baseball bats, hatchets, and axes rampaged through San Francisco, wrecking offices and halls of Communists and front organizations and beating the occupants. Police followed up to arrest the victims. Vigilantes raided the *Western Worker*, Workers School, Mission Workers Neighborhood House, Workers Ex-Servicemen's League, International Labor Defense, Communist offices and book-store, and other places. The terror spread to East Bay communities and along the coast. The raiders wrecked IWW halls and a Finnish Workers Center in Berkeley having no Communist connection. Police arrested over 450 in San Francisco, including 150 at a meeting in a vacant lot on Howard in the Skid Road area.

Public officials helped create the vigilante atmosphere, beginning with Mayor Rossi's Citizens' Committee in late June, a joint venture with the American Legion to rid San Francisco of Communists. In his radio speech July 16, Governor Merriam urged workers to undertake a "more active and intensive drive to rid this state and nation of alien radical agitators . . . if they are to enjoy the confidence of the people."[6]

According to the *New York Times*, the raids were premeditated: "The first indication of the concerted drive against radicals came from Charles Wheeler, vice-president of the McCormick Steamship Line, who said in a talk at the Rotary Club here today [July 17] that the raids would start soon. He intimated government consent had been obtained for the raids."[7]

A *New York Post* editorial charged: "General Johnson's irresponsible talk about 'subversive elements' to be driven out 'like rats' from the ranks of labor is encouraging the 'vigilantes' (thugs hired by the industrialists?) and the police in a brutal, illegal and unconstitutional attack on radical elements unmatched outside of Fascist Germany."[8]

The *Labor Clarion* condemned police complicity in the terror:

> While the city of San Francisco was occupied by some five thousand state troops and the city police force has been augmented by the addition of several hundred patrolmen, a series of outrages against property and individual liberty were perpetrated, accompanied by brutal beatings of alleged "reds," which has no equal for savagery in all the history of labor troubles in California. That the police were aware of the identity of the "vigilantes" is common report.
>
> The activities of the peace guardians seems to have been confined to "mopping up" after the various raids and arresting every person found on the premises and booking them on various charges, including vagrancy, disturbing the peace, distributing communistic literature, and so on.
>
> No intimation that any members of the raiding parties have been arrested or even interrupted in their depredations has been noticed in the reports of police activities.
>
> The situation grows out of a hysterical campaign inaugurated by the newspapers, which have insisted that the waterfront strike and subsequent sympathetic strike were engineered by communists. That it was part of the plan to terrorize strikers there can be no doubt.[9]

Municipal Court Judge Sylvain J. Lazarus, who heard the cases of those arrested, declared July 23: "I am disgusted to think that this good old town should have acted like a pack of mad wolves. I don't know who is responsible, but it should be traced back to its source. Boys never before arrested were thrown in jail for a week, and aging men were also subject to that humiliation. My heart bleeds for them."[10]

The American Civil Liberties Union, International Labor Defense, IWW General Defense Committee, League for Industrial Democracy, National Committee for the Defense of Political Prisoners, and Non-Partisan Labor Defense formed a Committee for Workers Rights. Subsequently the American Civil Liberties Union won suits against the cities of Richmond, Berkeley, and San Francisco, based on responsibility of police and public authorities for some of the raids. Authorities did not try or punish any vigilantes.

San Pedro

The sounds of Bloody Thursday reverberated in San Pedro. The ILA lengthened picket shifts from four to six hours, resulting in 600 men on a shift and a total of

1,200 from all crafts. The strikers could not persuade the 300 union employees of the Harbor Belt Line Railroad to quit. The railroad fired a crew of six for refusing to defy pickets. Although thirty police armed with clubs and revolvers rode the locomotives, strikers derailed an engine and a car at Wilmington.

In San Pedro calls for a general strike increased as the San Francisco strike date approached. The 1,200 members of the Fishermen's and Cannery Workers' Industrial Union stood ready to walk out in sympathy. A Communist delegation clamored for admission to the Los Angeles Central Labor Council meeting July 13 and distributed leaflets calling on all "A.F. of L., T.U.U.L., and Independent Unions to act at once and force the calling of a general strike and join the coastwise strike."[11] The council left the general strike question to local unions, instead proposing a buyers' boycott of all firms belonging to the Merchants' and Manufacturers' Association. The council appealed to all union members for a voluntary assessment of 25 cents a week for relief for the 1,300 families of strikers who needed food.

Three hundred strikers and scabs battled at Wilmington July 13 when a picket car tried to force a car of scabs off the road. A scab stabbed a striker, and police arrested ten, including a scab who threatened strikers with a gun. The ILA demanded the right to arm strikers after scabs carrying guns without permits shot several pickets. Police searched scabs' cars and seized six guns. They arrested several men reported to be scabs for giving fictitious names and addresses tobuy guns.

San Pedro police duplicated the Red raids of the Bay area. July 16 they broke up a Communist meeting of 400 and arrested two for advocating violence: the "San Francisco spirit," according to the *News-Pilot.* Two days later police raided the MWIU hall, seized membership lists and literature, and arrested the occupants for vagrancy. When officers returned the next morning looking for more "vagrants," fifteen MWIU members met them at the door with baseball bats. Police arrested ten in the ensuing battle. A "For Rent" sign appeared on the MWIU hall July 20.

South of San Pedro, the port of San Diego remained open, with the steamer *Humboldt* tied up at Pier 1 for a scab dormitory. Strikers beat scabs and stoned their cars, and police arrested pickets as they harassed shipping.

Seattle: Battle of Pier 41

While police battled strikers in San Francisco, the Seattle waterfront simmered on the verge of a violent eruption. Police moved picket lines back of the railroad tracks at Smith Cove July 3, permitting only three pickets from each organization near the gates and keeping the tracks clear with a police cordon. The department dismissed two officers for failure to aid the son-in-law of a steamship official being beaten by strikers, and suspended two more for failure to arrest pickets beating a scab. Scabs worked and trains moved freely at Piers 40 and 41. July 9 pickets stopped the car of Steve S. Watson, a guard from Smith Cove who ventured uptown, overturned the car, hauled him out and beat him. A shot rang out, fatally wounding the guard. After headlines blamed "Reds" for the death, a coroner's jury found that the bullet came from Watson's gun as he tried to pull it during the scuffle. Sheriff Bannick ordered all guards to stay on the docks. The first scab ship sailed from Bellingham, loaded by loggers employed by the mill company. They worked behind a sixteen-foot fence protected by special deputies. At Ketchikan, Alaska, police intercepted taxis of union seamen and firemen from the *Yukon,* armed with belaying pins, on their way to talk to the scab crew of a tanker at the Standard Oil docks.

The Washington State Federation of Labor convention passed strong resolutions demanding removal of armed guards from the docks and commending Governor Martin for his fairness in the strike. A meeting in Tacoma sponsored by the Central Labor Council to protest attempts to drive away the Alaska trade drew a crowd of 5,000, and a strike support meeting at the Seattle Civic Auditorium brought out 3,000. The Marine Workers Industrial Union called a demonstration, "On to Pier 40!" for Saturday, July 14, repudiated by the Joint Northwest Strike Committee. That evening when the *President Jackson* arrived at the Atlantic Street dock from Pier 41, police dispersed a crowd of angry pickets threatening to cut the mooring lines.

With scabs working vessels at Smith Cove, the Seattle Waterfront Employers attempted to coax their longshoremen back to work. They polled 895 longshoremen on whether they wanted a secret ballot vote on the June 16 agreement. The longshoremen returned 260 ballots, less than a third, with 13 "no" votes. The employers reported July 16 that they had collected $41,500 in strike assessments from their members, out of which they had spent $36,000; daily expenses amounted to about $600. The Associated Industries appealed to all employers to "deal with those who believe in and support the open shop and who are meeting every closed shop attack by this business co-operation. . . . See that the money you and your family spend does not go into channels that pay those who are damaging not only your business but that of all Seattle."[12]

After police forced them back from the tracks at Smith Cove, the strikers tried to persuade the four railroad unions to honor their picket lines. The brotherhoods hesitated: contracts would be violated and members might be fired. When they finally and definitely refused, the strikers took the offensive to regain their positions at the piers. Strikers from Tacoma, Everett, and other Sound ports joined Seattle men the morning of July 18 in a charge of 1,500 on Pier 41, where scabs worked the *President Grant* and a tanker. Police drove them back with clubs and nausea gas; pickets fought with stones and clubs. Fifty strikers slipped past police lines to the dock near the *President Grant*, later joined by the bulk of the pickets. A dozen strikers had broken heads, and six gas victims received medical attention at the ILA hall nearby. A skirmish broke out at the foot of Madison Street when fifty pickets attacked eight deputy sheriffs returning from escorting special deputies to a boat headed for Smith Cove.

That night the longshoremen reported to the Central Labor Council meeting that at Smith Cove "they had regained ground that was lost and everything was peaceable now. The reason for this move was to stop freight cars moving." The Flour, Feed and Cereal Workers from Fisher's Mill reported that "Members refused to load boats for Smiths Cove,"[13] A few uptown unions had voted for sympathetic action, but the council tabled a motion for a general strike requested by maritime delegates.

Five hundred pickets camped at the entrance to the piers all night, vowing to prevent trains from moving. Three hundred police guarded the docks armed with submachine guns, shotguns, gas guns and grenades, revolvers, and riot clubs. Police Chief Howard resigned after Mayor Smith went over his head to take personal command of the forces at Pier 41. The pickets held their positions unchallenged for a day. In the first action the morning of July 20, police dispersed with gas 700 strikers who were trying to erect a barricade to stop a train at Railroad Avenue and Madison. Strikers accused railroads of picking the crew for long years of service to guarantee obedience to orders. The train proceeded to Smith Cove, where police waited. The *Post-Inteligencer* described the battle:

> Police gas bomb squads were established at regular intervals all along the Garfield Street Bridge, while at particular vantage points snipers were planted with long-range gas guns capable of hurling 37 millimeter gas shells at a distance of 450 feet or more. Behind the bridge the mounted police squad was mobilized to keep the mob out of the railroad yards, while platoons of foot police with riot guns were assembled on the docks at places where they would be least likely to get the effects of their comrades' gas bombs.
>
> When everything was in readiness Captains Comstock and Olmstead, accompanied by Sergeant John H. Harrington, began circulating quietly among the mob on the docks.
>
> "Better start moving," the officers advised the men. "If you don't we'll have to move you."
>
> One strike leader, who identified himself as a marine fireman, heeded their warning.
>
> "I think the best thing to do is to leave peaceably," he exhorted his followers. "We can't do anything against the police."
>
> Possibly a hundred strikers heeded his advice and followed him out. But the remaining 600, emboldened by their success two days before, elected to stand their ground. Not knowing that the police had only a small supply of gas equipment on hand at the time of the first battle, they had the impression that they had nothing worse to expect—and they boasted they "could take it."
>
> "We're ready for your perfume!" one of the strikers jeered, and there was an echo of catcalls.
>
> "All right," one of the officers replied, grim-lipped. "Let 'em have it."
>
> As he spoke the squad stationed farther west on the Garfield Street Bridge went into action, tossing a barrage of gas grenades into the crowd below.
>
> At first the bombs had no effect. In some instances, when the policemen had not held the grenades long enough before dropping them, the rioters picked them up and hurled them back at the officers on the bridge. But as the nauseating, blinding fumes spread the fight went out of the mob and they broke and ran.
>
> Some of the men made for the railroad yards north of the terminals, as had been

> anticipated, but they were met by the mounted squad and more gas bombs, and they headed for Elliott Avenue and safety. . . .
>
> When the mob tried to make a stand at the east end of the dock the long distance gas bombs went into play. End over end the projectiles hurled, most of them exploding directly over the heads of the strikers and showering them with gas. . . .
>
> The rioters were bewildered by the long-range bombs. They couldn't understand where they were coming from and some of them, in terror of the unknown, plunged headlong into the water, to be fished out a few minutes later by their comrades or policemen.[14]

The battle lasted twenty minutes, leaving the entire dock clear, gates open, and trains moving by eight o'clock. Police gassed hundreds, including some of the attackers. Six pickets and three officers were hospitalized. A gas bomb hit Olaf Helland, member of the Sailors' Union, in the temple; he died on August 6. Police with submachine guns stood guard at barricades of bales of wool from the terminal, anticipating another attack that did not come. During these days police raided the

Police with submachine guns guarding Pier 41, Seattle, July 20, 1934. (Courtesy Museum of History and Industry, Seattle Post-Intelligencer *Collection, photograph #24007)*

Marine Workers Industrial Union hall, *Voice of Action,* Co-op Bookstore, and other Communist locations, seizing records and literature. They arrested sixty, most of whom were soon released.

Shipowners could find few scab seamen. Saul Haas, collector of customs, refused to clear the *President Grant* for the Orient July 21 because she lacked eleven of the nineteen able seamen required by law. She listed to starboard because scabs stowed the cargo improperly. A Seattle ISU dispatch reported:

> She was supposed to sail on Saturday noon but she got away on Sunday at noon. The Collector of Customs talked over the radio and said that the reason that the ship could not sail was because her crew consisted of "high school kids and bindle stiffs, and of the eight alleged certificated AB's, only three knew the Port side from the Starboard side, and that the ship was in the hands of a decidedly incompetent crew."
>
> . . . The Coast Guards and the Steamboat Inspectors were all under fire. There were big headlines in the papers here Saturday saying that the liner could not sail because of inexperienced seamen. It made the public realize that the seaman is supposed to be an experienced man and not just anybody the shipowners pick up here and there from schools and skidroads.[15]

On instructions from the Secretary of Commerce, Haas released the vessel with a $500 fine for the crew shortage. The *West Cactus* also sailed late for lack of seamen, and the *President Jefferson* made no attempt to recruit scabs.

Sympathetic unions accounted for the overwhelming share of strike donations, although small business people and friends also contributed. The Northwest Joint Council of Teamsters donated $1,000 a month to the Tacoma longshoremen. The Tacoma ILA July 21 listed donations to the strike fund of $3,259.59. They included $350 from the Central Labor Council, $250 from the Carpenters, $228.75 from the Building Laborers, $150 from the Smeltermen, and $100 each from the Meat Cutters, Typographical Union, Teamsters Local 313, Bricklayers, Civil Service League, and Street Car Men, besides $25.00 in car tokens. Miners unions at Black Diamond and Carbonado contributed $73.33, Spokane unions $57.00, and Yakima unions $165.65. Another undated list of donations totaled $456.75 received from small businesses and individuals. British Columbia longshoremen also contributed.

Portland: Poised for a General Strike

"PORTLAND STRIKE DUE TOMORROW!" the *Post-Intelligencer* headlined Tuesday, July 17. Instead, the Strategy Committee delayed the strike call because of Senator Wagner's arrival that night. The committee promised twenty-four hours' notice of the strike, while housewives laid in supplies of canned goods, vegetables and milk. The oil companies refused to unload 300,000 gallons of gasoline for harvest machines released by the strikers, apparently preferring to incite farmers against the unions. As in other ports, police and vigilantes staged Red raids, wrecking the MWIU hall July 16 and taking records, literature, a revolver, and several clubs.

Senator Wagner came to Portland in response to Governor Meier's request to President Roosevelt to intervene. He spent Wednesday meeting first with the unions and then the employers. As the senator's party and a group of local labor men left Terminal 4 that evening, armed guards showered their two cars with ten bullets, wounding Charles W. Hope, secretary of the Northwest Regional Labor Board, in the leg. Police arrested five specials, and the employers apologized profusely, but no guards were prosecuted. Provided the governor did not summon state troops, the Strategy Committee agreed to postpone the general strike call until Senator Wagner could present his findings on the Portland situation to the Longshoremen's Board in San Francisco.

Less than three hours after the unions promised to delay the strike, Governor Meier ordered the National Guard mobilized in response to Mayor Carson's declaration that a "state of actual insurrection" existed. The governor stated he had received over 500 telegrams begging him to open the port, citing ruined crops and cargoes diverted to other ports. He ordered the mobilization "to prevent loss of life and bloodshed" upon being notified by steamship companies and dock operators that work would be resumed the next day. "Every man who desires to work," he declared, "and has an opportunity to do so is entitled to the protection of organized society in his lawful enterprises."[16]

Senator Wagner fumed: "I regret that the governor felt it necessary to call out the militia at this time, particularly since the labor strategy committee has assured today that there would be no general strike pending efforts at an adjustment of the longshoremen's dispute at San Francisco."[17] Labor charged "that the employers are determined to prevent a settlement, fearing that the government board will award to the strikers their just demands, and that they are now proceeding to precipitate a condition which will preclude a settlement. We are astonished that the governor is allowing himself to be used in this manner by the employers."[18]

Eleven hundred guardsmen camped at Clackamas, ten miles from Portland, armed with bayonets, machine guns, light howitzers, and gas, ready to move in if strikers interfered with the port opening. Hostile crowds of strikers watched a small contingent arrive at the Portland armory Thursday night. Released from its promise by the mobilization, the Strategy Committee threatened the general strike if guardsmen set foot on the waterfront.

Protected by ninety police and sheriff's deputies armed with guns and tear gas, the steamer *San Julian* began loading ties for the Orient at the foot of Everett Street, where a dynamite explosion earlier that day had torn a hole in the fence around the dock. A crowd of 150 pickets cursing and throwing rocks fell back under police threats. Fifteen gasoline trucks, each with an armed guard and accompanied by a police convoy, delivered gas from Linnton to service stations, easing the acute gas shortage. The next day another vessel began to load grain. Pickets remained peaceful but vigilant. Police ordered seven heavily armed specials heading up town for some fun back to the docks under escort, followed by wisecracking strikers. ILA President

Oregon National Guard erects a barricade at the Multnomah County Armory, Portland, July 1934. (Oregon Journal*, Courtesy Oregon Historical Society, OrHi neg. CN 005984)*

Con Negstad commented on the port opening: "At the rate they are loading now, they can probably send out one ship a month. They have fewer men working now than they had in the first days of the strike."[19] Citizens circulated two petitions to recall Mayor Carson, neither sponsored by labor. The ILA Women's Auxiliary, organized during the strike, picketed Meier and Frank department store, in which the governor was part owner. Their signs read, "Bullets Don't Make Money." At first store guards shoved them around, but after strikers appeared on the picket line and shoved back, the guards let the women alone. Week after week, donations poured into the Longshoremen's Relief Fund from unions and well-wishers. In all, the Central Labor Council collected about $12,000 to feed the strikers.

Labor speeded up general strike plans, fueled by anger over the guard mobilization. Previously uncommitted unions endorsed the strike. It was expected that key unions, the Street Carmen, Electrical Workers in the utilities, and Teamsters, would go out first. The Joint Northwest Strike Committee endorsed the strike, "but only along the lines of a general strike in a spasmotic plan for better results."[20] Kelso-Longview unions stood ready to strike with Portland. A resolution by the Citizens' Co-operative Association of Oregon City placed responsibility for the threatened strike on Governor Meier, and Ben Osborne of the State Federation of Labor declared that if called, the strike would be "a revolt against industrial autocracy,"

Confrontation between strikers and harbor police as S.S. San Julian sails, Portland, July 20, 1934. (Courtesy Pacific Northwest Labor History Association)

rather than an "insurrection." The situation was "balanced on a pin," the *Joint Marine Journal* reported.

George A. White, commander of the National Guard, finally persuaded Governor Meier not to order the troops to the waterfront, according to Charles Peabody of the Portland ILA. In a meeting between the commander, the governor, and ILA officers, White pointed out that the state militia had not been called out in thirty years in an Oregon labor dispute. Their recent use in other parts of the country, White urged, had brought discredit to the institution.

Shipowners Agree to Arbitrate

With the end of the San Francisco general strike, efforts once more focused on settling the waterfront conflict. July 20 the Joint Northwest Strike Committee voted seventeen to ten to send five delegates to San Francisco. Six of the ten "no" votes came from the Communist-dominated ports of Bellingham, Everett, and Raymond, and the other four from Grays Harbor, the Wobbly stronghold. Perhaps they did not want to augment anti-Communist forces in San Francisco. The committee elected

William Veaux and William Craft of Seattle, Paddy Morris of Tacoma, Joe Sumption of Olympia, and Ed Krumholz of Grays Harbor to go to San Francisco. Cliff Thurston remained there representing Portland.

Although ILA President Joe Ryan disagreed with strike policy, he continued to refuse Lee Holman's application for a San Francisco charter. In a final effort to persuade the longshoremen to settle separately, Ryan wrote the Pacific Coast District July 19, repeating his charge that the marine unions rode on the ILA's shoulders. The Joint Northwest Strike Committee replied July 24, pointing out that seamen comprised the majority of strikers:

> It is the unalterable conviction of the longshoremen of the Northwest that without the aid of the marine crafts, the strike would have been broken within the first two weeks. . . . The employers can get all the scabs they want for longshore work, but they cannot get sufficient licensed officers and seamen to do them much good unless the organized marine crafts break ranks. They will not break ranks as long as they have the support of the longshoremen. The longshoremen having solicited the help of the marine crafts, do not feel that they are riding on our shoulders, as you say, and we are in duty bound to support the marine crafts until a settlement for all can be made. . . .
>
> While your statement that the marine crafts have not helped the longshoremen in the past is undoubtedly true; it is also true that the longshoremen have not helped them either. We live and learn and hope to profit by our mistakes. We hope and expect that all the striking crafts will return to work at the same time as organized bodies with agreements satisfactory to them, and not as demoralized hungry individuals.
>
> We hope the above statements will convince you that while the help of the teamsters is valuable, it is by no means decisive, and that the organization of the Pacific Coast Marine Federation is a vital necessity to the workers in the entire industry. With such a federation, we believe strikes would seldom be resorted to, but when strikes are unavoidable, they would be 100% effective.[21]

In spite of bayonets protecting scabs in San Francisco and union teamsters ready to cross their picket lines, the Marine Engineers expressed optimism July 20:

> One thing we do know, is that we are gaining ground all the time. General Johnson is working for us, and working fast. Senator Wagner, Labor's best friend, is on his way down from Portland and will arrive here sometime today.
>
> Postmaster General James A. Farley is on his way here to join General Johnson and Senator Wagner to aid the Longshoremen's Board in arriving at a settlement of this dispute. It looks like some of these Steamship Lines are going to lose some of their fat mail contracts unless they wake up real pronto.[22]

The Engineers' optimism seemed justified. After an all-day conference July 20 between representatives of the Waterfront Employers' Union, Industrial Association, newspaper publishers, and several steamship companies, the group issued a statement:

> In view of the stand of the Teamsters' Union in returning to work and other developments to bring about industrial peace and harmony, the members of this conference

believe that in the event the Longshoremen's Union should vote to submit all differences to arbitration by the President's Board, the steamship owners should agree to add to their offer already made and should agree to arbitrate hours, wages and working conditions with the maritime unions.

Following the conference steamship representatives consulted the numerous companies involved and have obtained their adherence to a plan of arbitration, if the Longshoremen's Union will make such course possible.[23]

The Industrial Association account of the strike does not mention mail subsidies, but Drew Pearson and Robert S. Allen noted in the "Washington Merry-Go-Round" that on July 17 President Roosevelt empowered Postmaster General Farley to investigate ocean mail contracts and cancel or modify those considered unwarranted. Two days later Farley announced he was going to San Francisco as an "arbitrator." Reckoned on the basis of pounds of mail carried, the annual subsidies of $26 million would be reduced to $3 million. All six of the big shipping companies involved in the strike received heavy subsidies. Pearson and Allen pointed out: "Secretary Perkins, General Johnson and Assistant Secretary McGrady, chairman of the federal long-shoremen's board, consider these companies basically responsible for the failure of the peace agreement. . . . The government has legal power to crack down on these juicy contracts. The conclusion is obvious."[24]

Finally, the spectacle of employers defying New Deal promises to labor forced the federal government to force the shipping industry to offer the same terms to the marine crafts that it offered to the longshoremen. The terms satisfied neither group: unconditional arbitration, but they were equal. The longshore locals agreed to a coastwide ballot conducted by the National Longshoremen's Board: "Will the I.L.A. agree to submit to arbitration by the President's Board the issues in dispute in the Longshoremen's strike, and be bound by the decision of the Board?"[25]

Voting in the ILA halls began July 22, conducted by government representatives. Proof of union membership, not port registration, determined eligibility. In San Francisco the National Guard permitted ILA representatives to patrol the waterfront to pick up members to take to the hall to vote. In San Pedro thirteen members voted in jail, and in Portland pickets left their posts in squads, marched to the hall to vote, and back to the docks. District President Lewis visited Portland, Seattle, and Tacoma locals advising them to accept arbitration "mainly because the employers had agreed to abide by the arbitration decision of the board in regard to the maritime unions . . ."[26] The press reported that in a special meeting of Local 38-79, Harry Bridges urged members not to return to work until both seamen and longshoremen gained union hiring halls. In a wire to Edward McGrady the Tacoma strike committee objected strongly to arbitrating the union dispatching system in effect in that port. The board would make no promises. Fear of losing the hiring hall may account for most of the eighty-seven votes against arbitration in Tacoma. In Portland, the *Labor Advocate* reported:

> The longshoremen were asked to provide a body guard for J.S. Meyers who watched the voting in the I.L.A. hall for the longshoremen's labor board, when he returned to his hotel and later to the airport with the ballots. Information had been received by the officials that some inveterate open shoppers intended to steal the ballots to prevent an amicable settlement. The guard kept them at a distance.[27]

The longshoremen's decision to vote on unconditional arbitration left the marine crafts in a critical position. Andrew Furuseth appealed to an open meeting of sailors in San Francisco July 21 to "stand steady" and not lose hope:

> Two things cannot be arbitrated. One is Union Recognition, and the other is the abolition of the shipowners employment bureaus. . . . The shipowners have spent more, trying to break this strike, THAN THE INCREASE IN WAGES WOULD HAVE COST THEM FOR YEARS TO COME. There is no question of their ability to pay. Wages don't worry them. What they have fought is the building up of a strong union, . . .
>
> [Some men, particularly younger ones.] are beginning to figure that the strike is almost over, and that they can beat the gun, by a little hand-shaking with shipping agents now. This morning, at least twenty men were seen entering the piers; and the other night a big party was held in the infamous Fink Hall. Sandwiches, beer and coffee were served according to our reports, and after refreshments were over, THE MEN PRESENT SIGNED UP TO GO OUT ON CERTAIN SHIPS. All these men are known, and also many more are known, who are trying to beat the gun. Many of them figure that they can get a Quartermasters berth, or a water tenders berth today, where they would have to go as a wiper or ordinary seaman next week. STRIKERS these men ARE WORSE THAN SCABS. If we start going back individually now, it will break the strike.
>
> STAND STEADY! DON'T FALTER! DON'T WEAKEN! We don't see any longshoremen sneaking down to the piers, to slap the boss on the back. ARE THE SEAMEN GOING TO BE KNOWN AS WEAK SISTERS???[28]

Licensed officers likewise stood firm. The Marine Engineers declared July 23: "We do not contemplate any separate settlements. . . . We will not be frightened back to the ships, and we will not be KIDDED into going back to work ahead of our fellow strikers, by the shipowners agents." The Masters, Mates and Pilots stated: "We are still on strike, and we will stay on strike until we have a fair basis of settlement that can be accepted by fair men. We do not intend to desert the Longshoremen or any other striking Unions, and all reports to the contrary are deliberate LIES. Shipowners propaganda."[29]

The Joint Marine Strike Committee called for a solid front, resolving July 23 "that after taking the ballot on arbitration the question of time of return to work must be settled, together with all striking groups in conference, and . . . that under no circumstances shall any one of the striking groups be left alone, but return to work shall be by all simultaneously at an agreed time and condition."[30]

Longshoremen Accept Arbitration

San Francisco longshoremen maintained picket lines around the clock, instructing members to "only picket as near their respective docks as permitted by the militia –

and avoid further conflicts with soldiers if possible." The strike bulletin warned against "the rumors and poisonous lies of the daily press" intended to confuse them. The bulletin reported July 23: "The Shipowners expected a great many 'stevies' to rush the docks this morning ready to go to work – and it must have been a great surprise to Mr. Shipowner to see a solid picket line – instead of a line of men wanting to work."[31] July 25 the Masters, Mates and Pilots protested release by the ISU of the steam schooner *Lumberman,* leaving the licensed officers in a "tough spot." Seamen's delegates promised to rescind the action.

Major questions faced the strikers: If the longshoremen's vote carried, would they return to work before the seamen? Who were strikebreakers, all those who worked during the strike, or only new employees hired after the strike began? How would seamen and longshoremen be hired during arbitration proceedings? When a seamen's delegation appeared before the ILA strike committee July 23 to ask the first question, the San Francisco longshoremen suspended balloting for a short time. The ILA bulletin reported:

> The seamen are insisting that they will not return to work through the FINK HALLS. The NATIONAL LONGSHOREMEN'S BOARD says that this is a matter for Arbitration. . . .
>
> The Strike Committee at once sent a delegation of ten members, to interview the NATIONAL LONGSHOREMEN'S BOARD, and try and find out what they could do in this case.
>
> The NATIONAL LONGSHOREMEN'S BOARD, advised the delegation that the voting continue, and also said that if the vote for Arbitration carried, they would ask the I.L.A. to return to work as soon as possible, also the Seamen, but they would not make any bargain about the shipping of Seamen through the FINK HALL.
>
> . . . We don't want to be placed in a position where we would be going to work and scabbing on the Sailors. They would look at us in the same light as we regard the Teamsters.[32]

The employers insisted that only new employees hired to replace strikers be dismissed to fulfill their pledge to discharge strikebreakers. The strikers classified anyone who worked during the strike as a scab who must go before they returned to work. The Longshoremen's Board upheld the employers, citing previous National Labor Board rulings. This meant working with the Alaska Steamship finks in Seattle and about 100 scabs in San Pedro. It meant sailing with former shipmates who refused to strike.

Over 2,000 ISU strikers gathered July 26 "in an enthusiastic meeting that will long be remembered by all those that were present." The *Joint Marine Journal* reported:

> All doubts about the solidarity of the waterfront workers were completely removed. We KNOW now that seamen and longshoremen are SOLIDLY together in one fighting unit that will not be broken. Brothers Paddy Morris, Craft, Bill Veaux, Krumholz and Joe Sumption from the northwest carried this message to the seamen. Then Brother Harry Bridges confirmed the position of the San Francisco Longshoremen

and the meeting adjourned with three rousing cheers for the Longshoremen! Old timers, who never thought they would live to see the day left the meeting with tears in their eyes . . . and a song in their hearts![33]

In response to a request from the Longshoremen's Board, the forty-two steamship companies confirmed their press release in an official agreement to arbitrate wages, hours, and working conditions. They made no mention of hiring halls. On July 27 the companies advised the board that as a basis for the seamen to return to work they were willing:

a—To discharge any man who was employed after the strike was called (May 16) who prior to that date was not following the sea regularly as an occupation. Such vacancies as made will be available to men not now employed.

b—To agree not to discriminate in any way in employment against any man because of union affiliation or strike activity.

c—That where there are employment halls your board may appoint a representative to supervise the operation to see that there is no unfairness or discrimination.

d—That any question of unfairness or discrimination shall be at once referred to a representative of your board for decision.[34]

With incomplete returns indicating an overwhelming majority of longshoremen in favor of arbitration, the Waterfront Employers notified the board the same day that they were willing:

a—To discharge all men performing longshore work who were employed after the strike was called, who were not regularly employed as longshoremen at the respective ports prior to the calling of the strike, the men to be discharged on the return of the longshoremen to work. This will . . . provide employment for the men now on strike as it then existed.

b—No discrimination of any kind will be made against any man because of membership in the union or because of strike activities.

c—Any adjustment of wages shall be retroactive to the date of return of the men to work.

d—San Francisco has no hiring hall but other ports have such halls. Where such halls exist, your board shall appoint representatives to supervise their operations, and the local I.L.A. shall have the right to appoint observers to see that the halls are run fairly without discrimination. Pending arbitration there shall be no change in the method of hiring or dispatching men and all other previous conditions of hiring and employment shall apply.

e—Any question of unfairness or discrimination is to be at once submitted to your board for decision, the parties to be bound thereby.[35]

The ILA District Executive Board protested the terms to the Longshoremen's Board:

The attitude of the employers in stating that the longshoremen must return through the existing halls certainly does not sustain their contention that they are willing to do everything in their power to promote harmony.

The longshoremen were willing to have the hiring done from neutral ground without using the employers or the union hall. Despite their protestations of collaboration in every manner, they still insist upon being treated as the victor retaining the spoils.[36]

The board did not sustain their objections. The ILA strike bulletin described the situation July 27: "The shipowners are playing checkers with us now. They make a phony move – and then wait for us to make the next move. They have placed an ad in the papers which says 'Longshoremen and winchdrivers wanted.' After promising to fire all scabs before we return to work, they now advertise for more scabs. This, of course, is being done in an attempt to demoralize us."[37]

The longshoremen voted 6,504 to 1,525 to arbitrate, 81 percent. A tabulation by ports gave Portland 96 percent for arbitration, San Pedro 89 percent, Seattle 88 percent, and Tacoma 84 percent. Everett, with strong Communist influence, voted 110 to 109 against arbitration, and Raymond 61 to 37 against. Grays Harbor voted 53 percent for arbitration. In the San Francisco hall of Local 38-79, 2,014 voted for and 722 against arbitration, 74 percent, and in the Oakland hall 302 for and 37 against, 89 percent.

Although everyone expected the strike to end in a few days, confrontations continued on the waterfronts. At Seattle scabs worked ten ships at Smith Cove. Strikers beat scabs, and police arrested three strikers. Pickets stoned two tugs. July 28 thirty strikers attacked fifteen scabs loading the *Emma Alexander* at the Pacific Steamship terminal. At Tacoma the Grace liner *Cuzco*, anchored in the stream for over a week, pulled alongside the smelter. When a scab jumped on the dock to make the lines fast, striking seamen beat him severely. ILA pickets rescued the man and put him back aboard the vessel, which moved out into the stream again. At San Francisco scabs knifed three strikers in a battle, and at Oakland police arrested eleven pickets July 28. At San Pedro, while strikers stoned scabs' cars and police arrested pickets, the ILA began to form members into gangs. By July 23, the union had organized fifty-six gangs comprising about 1,000 men.

At Portland July 23 police dispersed seamen pickets at Linnton trying to block oil deliveries. Pending instructions from the district, the ILA picketed state hiring halls opened July 26 by Governor Meier. Strikers shoved a freight car across the entrance of the Luckenbach docks, vowing to stop all freight moving from terminals. An engineer refused to take a train into the Oceanic terminal after pickets warned him to halt. Police arrested 236 pickets July 29 for defying Mayor Carson's order limiting them to three at a dock. Governor Meier threatened to use the National Guard if the port was not open by Monday, July 30.

The National Longshoremen's Board conducted the promised representation election for seamen. The ballot read: "By what person, persons, or organizations do you wish to be represented for purposes of collective bargaining with your employer?"[38] A discharge from a voyage made after May 8, 1933, entitled a seaman to vote. Balloting began July 28 in San Francisco and the next day in other ports. The steamship companies protested to the board against the single polling booth: "Conditions

Strike log from the Joint Marine Journal, *San Francisco, August 1934. (T. Cameron, artist, courtesy International Longshore and Warehouse Union Library)*

TUT TUT TUT!
DON'T WE LOOK SNAZY THOUGH?
CAMERON
ONE MORE SPOT WILL DO IT!
SCAB HOTEL
D—x ☆!!
BLUB!
?
STRIKE BREAKERS ATTEMPTING TO SWIM THE BAY WHEN STRIKE IS OVER
SEAMEN VOTE HERE

in San Francisco . . . make it practically impossible for sailors now upon the ships to go to the polling place to vote. . . . [It] is so heavily picketed and surrounded by representatives of the Unions which called the strike, that it would be worth the life of a man on a ship to go to the booth to vote."[39] The board kept polling places in each port open until October 22 to enable crews of ships at sea to vote.

The *Joint Marine Journal* appealed to unlicensed seamen to vote for the ISU: "From 1921 till 1934 this Union has of course not been recognized and the reason . . . is that YOU AND YOU AND YOU . . . seamen, refused to join it for one reason or the other. You did not support your union, and so your union could not support you. Since the 16th of May, however, you, over 10,000 strong on this coast have showed that you learned the value of organization."[40] The *Journal* warned licensed men:

> Above all, don't vote for the Company Union. A Company Union is the Employers method of controlling labor. When you join a Company Union, you sacrifice ALL of your rights as a free man. If you get fed up with abuses, you can only quit your job. You have no redress through a strike. You can't call any other unions out to help you. You are alone – an individual. If, on the other hand you belong to a national or International Union . . . you have an ORGANIZATION back of you . . . you will be able to make an effective protest through your ORGANIZATION.[41]

Without waiting for the election, the Shipowners' Association of the Pacific Coast, principally steam schooner operators employing about 1,200 seamen, agreed July 28 to recognize the ISU. The association included twenty of the forty-two companies. Except for the fink hall years of 1921-1934, this association had bargained with the unlicensed seamen almost since the turn of the century.

End of the Strike

During these days the strikers faced a threat more serious than police clubs. The Longshoremen's Board wanted to get them back to work, overlooking pledges of solidarity. The ILA vote constituted a big victory for the board, revealing that the longshoremen threatened to break, regardless of the marine unions. If the unions could maintain solidarity and mutual trust, although the long battle ended with nothing more than recognition and arbitration, they could still hope to achieve their goals. If they destroyed the solidarity and returned to work fragmented, they would surrender the momentum and sense of power developed during the strike. The strikers understood this, although their needs diverged. The longshoremen wanted to return to work, but the seamen still hoped to win better terms. None could afford to destroy the solidarity, and they knew it.

With the board pressing them to set the date, the longshoremen stalled for time and worked frantically to persuade the seamen to go back to work. July 28 ILA delegates to the Joint Marine Strike Committee called on all unions to end the strike, and the ILA District Executive Board voted to accept the employers' conditions for returning to work. A special ILA strike bulletin that day reported:

Our District officials, in conjunction with the Joint Marine Strike Committee have been meeting day and night for the last three days to iron out the problem of getting rid of the strikebreakers and returning to work as we came out. We feel now, if the employers live up to the *promises they have made through the Press*, in regards to getting rid of strikebreakers, that the longshoremen and all maritime workers will be back at work the first of the week, possibly Monday morning.[42]

The bulletin moved too fast. The licensed officers wanted more specific guarantees against discrimination, and the unlicensed seamen refused to ship through the fink halls. The seafaring unions held mass meetings Sunday forenoon, July 29. Stephen Schwartz described an ILA delegation's visit to the Sailors' Union:

Paddy Morris, I.L.A. official from Tacoma, argued that the general strike had failed, that the dockworkers had been forced to vote for arbitration, and that even removal of the fink halls would be made dependent on arbitration. Although the government had promised to do away with the fink halls pending the arbitrators' decision, the federal authorities had then reversed themselves and declared that the halls could continue to function under the stewardship of a federal representative. "The labor unions are tired of the fight," said Morris. "The return of the teamsters has weakened our position. . . . We don't feel the fight is over—it has just begun. This is merely a truce. The shipowners have lined up all capital on their side, and it is a battle between Labor and Capital."[43]

Bill Craft and others from Seattle and Portland argued that all strikers should now return together and build the Marine Federation. Harry Bridges told the seamen: "I think the longshoreman is ready to break tomorrow. I don't think that they will last. They have had enough of it. They have their families to support. They are discouraged by the teamsters going back to work. They didn't get enough support from the council . . . I disagree with our officials in lots of things they have done. I agree on this point. I think they are right . . ."[44]

After the longshoremen left, the meeting considered the shipowners' letter of July 27 proposing that the seamen go back to work through the fink halls with a union observer present. Although the longshoremen seemed about to break, the seamen simply could not end their strike with the fink hall intact. Then Andrew Furuseth suggested the dramatic act that would destroy the hated institution: the strikers would burn their fink books, key to the system of intimidation and blacklisting that had enslaved them. Schwartz related his appeal:

"What do you think my proposition is? It is horrible and yet it is the most beautiful you can ever think of. We will build a fire in this lot nearby if we can get the police's permission to do it. We are going to build a fire. Alongside of that fire we will have a can of petroleum and each man who has got a fink hall book will come along there and he will dip it into the petroleum and throw it on the fire. . . .

"The only thing I ask of you is first that you will endorse the answer to the letter . . . If you believe as I do and are willing to do as I suggest to you, bring your fink books and let us burn them—burn them—burn all of that." He asked dramatically, "Will you do that?" The men answered by virtually unanimous cheers.

"The burning will begin tomorrow at 12 o'clock," the "old man" shouted.[45]

The meeting voted to endorse unconditional arbitration and the shipowners' terms for return to work. The membership meeting the next day would make the vote official.

In Seattle July 29 the Joint Northwest Strike Committee approved the ILA District Executive Board's recommendation to return to work under the employers' conditions, and that evening a special meeting of San Francisco Local 38-79 concurred in the board's recommendation to return to work Tuesday morning, July 31. The date allowed for the official vote of the ISU Monday, practically certain after the seamen's mass meeting endorsed the terms for return. Representatives of the Masters, Mates and Pilots pleaded vainly to delay the return to work. The ILA meeting instructed all longshoremen to go to work in their regular gangs, and those not working in steady gangs to report to the union hall for assignment. No gang could work more than fifteen hours, including meal breaks, without a rest period, and no gang could work more than forty-eight hours in a week. The union negotiated the rules just before the strike. The meeting voted to fine any member $5.00 "who is caught soliciting work in front of the docks." The ILA strike bulletin summed up July 30:

> Nowhere in the entire world has the marine industry ever been tied up as it was on this Coast. Labor has demonstrated its mighty power and can do it again in the future if necessary. By maintaining unity and solidarity with the other marine crafts, we will gain the respect of all organized labor – and the employers. We did not lose the strike! The marine unions are a permanent force that must be recognized and reckoned with. The employers figured they would beat us in a couple of weeks, but they made a bad mistake and a very costly mistake. . . .
>
> Today will probably be spent filing the hooks to be ready for 8 AM tomorrow. All who worked in steady gangs get your dope today. Extra gangs and extra men get dope in the morning at I.L.A. headquarters.[46]

The licensed officers could not hold out alone. By noon July 30 San Francisco had the results of meetings in other ports along the coast, a majority vote to return to work. The Masters, Mates and Pilots and Marine Engineers notified the Longshoremen's Board in a joint statement:

> As other striking unions have declared their intention of returning to work, and in a sincere desire to continue the unity which has been established during this strike between all the unions,
>
> We are pleased to notify you at this time that all licensed personnel of the West Coast have been directed to return to their respective positions on Tuesday, July 31, at 6 a.m., and that the strike now in force will terminate as of that date and time.[47]

The ISU voted 4,305 to 509 to return to work. Over a thousand seamen gathered July 30 in the vacant lot at the foot of Clay and Embarcadero. There they built a huge bonfire. As Andrew Furuseth watched and the crowd cheered, the seamen burned the hated gray continuous discharge books. They dumped boxes in the fire containing

Seamen burn fink books, San Francisco, July 30, 1934. (Courtesy San Francisco Public Library)

thousands of books, collected before and during the strike when men joined the union. The strikers erected a wooden cross marked "Fink Hall Grave" over the ashes. Seamen at Portland burned their fink books the same day in a large bonfire on a lot near the McCormick terminal.

In San Pedro between 1,500 and 2,000 seamen remained on strike against all but steam schooners when the rest of the coast returned to work the next day. They had voted to go back believing they would not have to ship through the fink hall. Now they refused. At 10:00 a.m. on August 1, about 1,000 seamen burned their fink books in a mock funeral ceremony. Then the ISU agreed that crews for offshore vessels would be shipped through the fink hall with a union observer. The fink book burnings not only destroyed the shipowners' network of blacklisting and intimidation, but more significantly, announced the seamen's determination to take control of their own lives.

As the strike ended, the Communist Party line did not waiver: the Party assigned all credit to its followers—all blame to its critics. The *Voice of Action* headlined: "Maritime Strikers Betrayed, Undefeated – Government and A.F.L. Leadership Succeed in Betrayal of Workers."[48] Sam Darcy, district organizer, boasted that "there

San Pedro seamen burn fink books. (Voice of the Federation)

would have been no maritime or general strike except for the work of our Party."[49] William F. Dunne stated: "The strike reached its highest point in San Francisco because the influence of the Communist Party in the waterfront unions was strong enough to defeat the reactionary leadership." He charged that "treachery" of AFL and ILA officials nationally and in the Bay Area, Seattle, and Portland labor councils "made it impossible for the working class to bring all its force to bear against the unprecedented mobilization of the forces of the employers and the government."[50] He summed up: "The influence of the M.W.I.U. in the strike movement was far greater than its membership figures would indicate. It was the initiator of the united front program which solidified the ranks of the marine workers and it had a great part in the general strike in the Bay Counties."[51]

Most maritime workers would not agree that the Communist Party played a decisive part in their struggle. Instead, they would accept the view expressed by Harry Lundeberg a year after the strike in the first issue of the *Voice of the Federation*, weekly paper of the newly formed federation:

> The keel of the Maritime Federation of the Pacific was laid in the 1934 strike of the maritime workers on the Pacific Coast who stood solidly against the shipowners and allowed nothing to break their solidarity.
>
> The fact that the maritime unions withstood for [eighty-three] days the concentrated onslaught of the shipowners and the industrialists of the Pacific Coast was due mainly to the fact that old methods, such as one maritime craft staying on the job while another craft would be on strike, were discarded, and in the 1934 strike all crafts walked out practically together and thus were able to put up a united front against the shipowners.[52]

In retrospect maritime workers would recognize the 1934 strike as the great watershed between the fink hall years and the years of union strength. But what had they to show for the eighty-three-day strike as they prepared to return to work Tuesday morning? They had embarrassed the New Deal to the point of forcing their employers to recognize and arbitrate with their unions. Beyond that, on paper, they had nothing—no hiring halls, no improved wages, working or living conditions. On paper they gained no victory to celebrate—just a grim standoff that moved the struggle from picket lines to hearing rooms. But union strength is determined more by each member's concept of unionism than it is by written documents. The maritime workers knew that together they were strong. They remained as determined as the day they struck to use that united strength to achieve their union hiring halls and improved wages, working and living conditions.

Part Two

The Maritime Federation Years

10

Confirming the Victory

Strikers claimed without question the jobs on the ships and docks. They refused to accept the employers' limited definition of strikebreakers and disregarded the ruling of the National Longshoremen's Board upholding the employers. They would not work with scabs. Moreover, they would support the right of anyone else to refuse to work with scabs. Employers could either accept these conditions or face picket lines and work stoppages.

The Associated Press reported that on Tuesday morning, July 31, 10,000 longshoremen and 8,000 unlicensed seamen returned to work in Pacific Coast ports. Seamen shipped off the docks, except at San Pedro, where the fink hall dispatched them to offshore vessels. There the last longshore scabs left the stockades and ships where they had been housed, and the last of the 500 metropolitan police on duty during the strike left the harbor. In Seattle, Portland, San Pedro, and smaller ports, the fink hall dispatched longshoremen, monitored by ILA and government observers. In San Francisco extras shaped up at pier heads as before.

Cleaning Up the Waterfronts

Tie-ups began immediately over scabs. Seattle longshoremen refused to work American Mail and Tacoma-Oriental vessels with scabs still aboard. Tacoma longshoremen would not work the Grace liner at the smelter and a Panama Pacific ship with scab crews. Portland longshoremen refused to work with scabs. All along the coast the unions protested the failure of some companies to take back strikers, and the employers filed objections to the unions' refusal to work vessels with scab crews. The Longshoremen's Board condemned the work stoppages and told the unions to use the grievance procedure.

The rush of work after the strike brought new men to San Francisco docks in violation of the settlement. In a bulletin August 10, Local 38-79 proposed "to immediately appoint a gang steward for every gang whose business it will be to check every man in his gang in order to insure that extra men be hired from the hall and not in front of the docks." It advocated direct action: "We may receive some betterment of conditions through arbitration, but it may be in the far future, so it behooves us to take an aggressive attitude and establish and improve the working conditions on our own initiative."[1] The Waterfront Employers charged that the bulletin caused work stoppages on two passenger vessels and proved the union's irresponsibility. The ILA replied that a special committee, not the union itself, put out the bulletin.

Local 38-79 kept its promise to the African-American community. Immediately after the strike ended, seventy-nine gangs of seventeen men each went to work. Thirty-five of these gangs included four or five African Americans. The black weekly *Spokesman* praised the union for pledging the "open door" policy to African Americans. From about 50 before the strike, black membership rose to over 200 by September. The union sent mixed gangs out in rotation. By contrast, according to the *Spokesman*, the San Pedro local did not put members of the Colored Longshoremen's Association to work as promised. With ninety gangs working in Los Angeles harbor, the association claimed the right to at least ten gangs. The paper charged that "the union has sought to tie up the work for themselves, forgetting the sacrifice made by the colored men who refused to scab for a principle."[2]

Portland waterfront employers deliberately provoked violence to discredit the ILA. After the strike both union men and scabs worked out of the fink hall with their own dispatchers. As instructed, on Friday morning, August 3, the longshoremen reported to the hall instead of to the ships for work. With the hall full of union men, a group of finks marched up in a body. In spite of the ILA dispatcher's efforts to keep order, about 200 men started fighting outside the hall. He sent home the ILA men for the day, and closed the hall. The union saw the incident as an employers' trap. After that the employers hired the finks from the Columbia River Longshoremen's Association hall, opened contrary to the strike settlement. The employers also recruited additional scabs to make up five gangs, in violation of the agreement. Twenty-five union gangs worked out of the fink hall at North Ninth and Everett.

On Monday, August 20, Luckenbach asked for one ILA gang to work with four gangs of finks. No men would work with the scabs. Dispatcher Matt Meehan protested that this was a lockout. After consulting with other ILA officials he climbed up on a table and told the longshoremen: "They are going to use Columbia River men today on the Luckenbach boat, so the Luckenbach gangs won't have any work today, so they can go over to the Luckenbach dock and picket, and any other men who are not employed today can go over there and do the same. Get your banners and go."[3]

About 125 longshoremen picketed Luckenbach. Other angry men went over to the company union hall, where the finks, anticipating possible trouble, waited inside for an escort to the dock. A fight broke out among the scabs in the hall, many of whom were armed. Shots rang out, one of them killing James Conner, a college student scab. Police immediately began arresting union men. During the next two weeks they arrested twenty-eight ILA members, charged with first degree murder and held without bail.

Meanwhile, a few days after the shooting, some of the finks began talking. One of them confessed he fired shots inside the hall, and another identified the killer as Carl Grammer, a scab gang boss. Police arrested him. It became evident that no one outside the hall had fired any shots. Nevertheless, the district attorney announced the ILA men would be prosecuted. Oregon law provided that when a death occurred as a result of a riot, all who participated in it were guilty of second degree murder. The longshoremen cried "Frame-up!" charging that employers deliberately provoked the riot to upset the arbitration proceedings, a repetition of the August 3 disturbance when they sent finks to the dispatching hall to make trouble.

The entire union movement rallied to defend the accused. Portland Local 38-78 provided relief for the families of the jailed members: money for food, fuel, rent, and other necessities. Oregon labor formed a defense committee of three ILA members and Gust Anderson, secretary of the Portland Central Labor Council, Ben Osborne of the State Federation, and I.A. Snyder of the railroad brotherhoods. The committee collected and disbursed funds for family relief and legal defense and publicized the case nationwide. Pacific Coast District ILA locals contributed most of the money, \$30,290, and outside sources added \$2,998. Seattle Local 38-12 donated \$1,000 and assessed members \$1.00 a month for three months; San Francisco Local 38-79 donated \$4,683; and San Pedro Local 38-82 \$1,800.

A grand jury indicted thirty-three union men and one scab in December on four counts each of assault and rioting. The jury returned no indictments against those inside the hall, although "proof was offered at the preliminary hearing that not less than six or seven carried and used pistols."[4] The prosecution dropped the murder charges against the ILA men. The defense committee put up bail of \$1,000 each, and they returned to work. The men demanded separate trials. In the first trial in May 1935 a jury found Art Shearer not guilty of felonious assault. Evidence showed that men inside the hall threw the first rock and fired the first shot. The rest of the defendants were released.

Longshore Arbitration Award

The Longshoremen's Board began arbitration hearings in San Francisco August 8. From the Northwest William Vaux and William Craft represented Seattle; Paddy Morris and Ed Harris, Tacoma; Ed Krumholz, Grays Harbor; and Cliff Thurston, Portland. Harry Bridges spoke for San Francisco, A.H. Petersen for San Pedro, and Bill Lewis for the district ILA. Labor consultant Henry P. Melnikow assisted the union. Frank P. Foisie and attorney Herman Phleger represented the Waterfront Employers.

Neither side would budge from its position before the strike. The longshoremen demanded preference of employment; union hiring halls; the six-hour day and thirty-hour week; wages of \$1.00 an hour and \$1.50 overtime, with premium pay for penalty cargoes; load limits; and a broad definition of longshoremen to include dock workers, grain handlers, and warehousemen. The employers demanded prestrike wages and working conditions and perpetuation of their open-shop fink halls. They argued that to grant the union hiring hall "would constitute almost a death blow to the shipping industry upon this coast."[5] They contended that "to compel a non-union man to seek employment through a union hall in San Francisco would be to write his death warrant," that "I.L.A. dispatching means a closed union shop."[6] The employers wanted a narrow definition of longshoremen, the right to determine load limits, gang size, and other working conditions, and maintenance of prestrike conditions except as specifically altered by the award.

Amid a steady barrage of complaints from both sides, the Longshoremen's Board held hearings in San Francisco, San Pedro, Portland, and Seattle. The employers complained of twenty-nine strikes and work stoppages between August 1 and October 12, most of them caused by failure to discharge scabs or reinstate strikers. During that time seamen and longshoremen lodged 448 complaints of discrimination and denial of jobs.

Frank Foisie hailed the new employer solidarity: "One outstanding benefit has accrued to shipping as a result of the strike; shipping leaders are together on this coast for the first time in its history in a truly significant fashion." He urged them to stick together against the union:

> No member has the right to waive any of the pre-strike conditions under I.L.A. pressure since this in effect constitutes a breach of contract with fellow members, and it is imperative that there be no letting down even to the point of permitting a ship to be tied up by the I.L.A. with all hands then standing by in support of the member against whom the tie-up is directed.
>
> It is the unanimous opinion of all person contacted in other ports that there is no hope that we can secure a cooperative agreement with the I.L.A. under present leadership and with the present temper of the men.[7]

The longshoremen's arbitration award, handed down October 12, provided for the open shop, a joint hiring hall with an ILA dispatcher in each port, and a joint labor relations committee of three each from the ILA and the employers to administer the hall and settle disputes. The award raised wages for longshoremen, narrowly defined, from 85 to 95 cents straight time and $1.25 to $1.40 overtime on a six-hour day, thirty-hour week, retroactive to July 31. Premium pay for penalty cargoes remained at the same differential above the base rate. In separate awards the board gave grain handlers 80 cents and $1.20 and dock workers, including warehousemen, 70 cents and $1.05, with the same hours.

One sentence would become the longshoremen's legal defense of hot-cargo boycotts: "The employers shall be free to select their men within those eligible under the policies jointly determined, and the men likewise shall be free to select their jobs." The board rejected the union demand for load limits, ruling instead: "The employer shall be free, without interference or restraint from the International Longshoremen's Association, to introduce labor saving devices and to institute such methods of discharging and loading cargo as he considers best suited to the conduct of his business, provided such methods of discharging and loading are not inimical to the safety or health of the employees."[8] Archbishop Hanna and Edward F. McGrady signed the award. Attorney O.K. Cushing concurred, except in the wage provisions.

Bill Lewis, Paddy Morris, and A.H. Petersen, speaking for the ILA, expressed satisfaction with the award, pointing out proudly that the longshoremen became the first substantial group on the Pacific Coast to achieve the AFL goal of the thirty-hour week. The *Waterfront Worker* declared the joint hiring hall was "exactly the same as Ryan's sellout June 16th agreement."[9] Harry Jackson asserted for the MWIU, "While they have gained in wages, the manner in which the decision was made is a smooth attempt to break the union."[10] The Seattle Waterfront Employers refused to recognize the six-hour-day provision as retroactive and resolved to oppose interference with their right to set load limits.

The board held separate elections for checkers, resulting in ILA representation for 450 men employed by forty-one companies. The board set wages at 90 cents and \$1.25 overtime on an eight-hour day.

Job Actions

The award brought no peace to West Coast waterfronts. Within seventy-two hours of the decision, separate strikes tied up four vessels in San Francisco. With work stopped completely at two terminals October 15, the employers blamed the continual strikes on "radical and irresponsible leadership, more concerned with prolonging than terminating the difficulties."[11] The *Waterfront Worker* declared October 22: "Struggle along the docks has succeeded very largely in keeping off scabs and cutting down on the speedup, and the way in which this award works out depends largely on the militancy of the longshoremen in keeping up the struggle. . . ." The paper urged:

> By working slower and making smaller loads, we will get more wages, which according to the shipowners economics will increase our purchasing power. Then we can buy some of the stuff we shove around on the docks now. The gang and dock steward system which we have inaugurated is most satisfactory in keeping job control, and must become a permanent thing. . . . Full JOB CONTROL is our final objective . . . the right to say where and how we shall work.[12]

In Seattle longshoremen tied up vessels, refusing to hoist more than forty cases of salmon or fresh fruit to a load. The Waterfront Employers resolved October 22 to stand firm on their right to determine load limits. They complained that government representatives continued to be "indecisive and ineffective." Other problems plagued Washington employers. The Tacoma local demanded overtime for working the long hatch through the meal hour, even with a different crew, and Everett demanded a fixed noon meal hour. Everett employers embargoed the port November 13 to force longshoremen to go through the fink hall instead of hiring off the docks. The ILA tied up Bellingham demanding Pacific American Fisheries warehouse work. At Grays Harbor the union controlled dispatching and virtually dictated working conditions.

In a dispute at San Pedro employers ordered longshoremen to discharge loads of 3,150 pounds of potash and 2,850 pounds of cement. The fourth day the men refused to work unless employers cut loads to about 2,100 pounds. The employers complied under protest. Arbitrator Dodd condemned the employers for speedup and lack of concern for safety and the longshoremen for the work stoppage. Employers up and down the coast attempted to evade the six-hour day and overtime after 3:00 p.m. by working two gangs four hours each. The arbitrator ruled that "six hours a day means that every employee dispatched to a job has a right to expect six hours of employment, provided sufficient work is available to warrant a work day of that duration."[13]

The turmoil continued at San Francisco. Eighteen strikes occurred during the first month after the award. The Waterfront Employers wired Secretary of Labor Frances Perkins October 31 and again November 14 protesting the "repeated daily violations" of the award and "repeated acts of violence" by union members. They charged the local with "the deliberate intention . . . to disregard its obligations under the award." The wire claimed that the employers had just received "an ultimatum from the union officials that the employers agree before Monday to all their demands not granted in the award."[14]

On the Dollar docks before the strike, longshoremen had been discharging fifteen cases of coconuts to the sling load. Shortly after the strike they cut the number to twelve. On October 29 the union complained that the employer again ordered the men to load fifteen cases. When the *President Wilson* arrived November 16, Dollar fired four gangs of longshoremen in succession for refusing to put on the extra three cases, and the vessel sailed without unloading the coconuts. Five days later, when the *President Coolidge* arrived from Manilla with more coconuts, the same thing happened, and again the ship sailed with the coconuts in her hold.

The employers appealed to the arbitrator, contending that the men violated the award by striking and demanding that the award be amended to provide for disciplinary action. The union replied that the men were free to select their jobs. The *Waterfront Worker* charged that strikes "were deliberately provoked by the employers, . . . They are doing this in order to worsen conditions, and if we fight back they pretend that we only want to make trouble."[15] A longshoreman on the Matson docks commented in the *Waterfront Worker:* "If the shipowners want big loads, why can't we give it to them?—but we can take our time. They are out to break the union, . . . and it would be wrong policy at this time to strike, so stay on the job, boys, and slow down —take it easy. We can force the shipowners to be good dogs in damn short order."[16]

Judge M.C. Sloss, the arbitrator, ruled January 4, 1935, that the men should work as directed by the employer and upheld the fifteen cases of coconuts. While recognizing the right of individuals to refuse jobs, he noted in a subsequent award the "plain distinction between individual cessation and an organized or collective stoppage of work. Such collective or combined stoppage is not consistent with the observance of the award." Although the union itself did not violate the award, it was "the duty of the I.L.A. officials, . . . promptly to induce the men to resume work or to furnish another gang so that work may continue without interruption."[17] While job action continued to reduce load limits generally, the San Francisco Waterfront Employers drew up a schedule in April 1935 with an average limit of 2,100 pounds. Local 38-79 pressed for a limit of 1,800 pounds.

Communist Bloc Line

San Francisco longshoremen elected Harry Bridges president of Local 38-79 in September 1934 by a vote of 1,283 to 432. The waterfront seethed with invective. The *Waterfront Worker* continued to vilify the ILA district officers. In November the paper attacked "Fink Ryan" and his "loyal henchmen" on the Pacific Coast. "The

District officials, Lewis, Morris, Pedro Pete and the rest of those 'officials' did nothing to organize and help win the strike. On the contrary, they worked overtime to betray us. Now, they are working to split us up."[18] A week later the paper called Morris "a dangerous faker, a Ryan man, and a shipowner's representative in the ranks of the workers."[19] The paper also attacked rank-and-file members of Local 38-79. Steve A. Door, Book No. 3879, protested in a letter to the *Waterfront Worker* December 17:

> You claim to be a worker's paper. If you are for the workers half as much as you claim why do you hide behind anonymity? . . . Anyone who exercises the privilege of a member and objects to what he thinks is wrong, even though the clique favors it. This poor sucker is held up for ridicule. Of course some people don't mind being ridiculed and continue to make bursts at the meeting.
>
> But you are stopping many honest members from being more active for fear of the Worker. . . . Stop some of your scandal mongering and print two-sided constructive arguments and you will be doing something.[20]

In March 1935 a group of self-styled conservative members of Local 38-79 began putting out *The New Waterfront Worker*, a mimeographed sheet with format similar to the original publication. The paper charged that during the 1934 strike Harry Bridges "spent most of his time fighting the membership in an effort to put over the program of the CENTRAL COMMITTEE of the Communist Party." "It is common knowledge along the Front," the paper asserted, "that anyone daring to disobey the demands of the Misleader [Bridges] will find himself a subject for invective in the journal of the Communist Party put out on the Waterfront, the Waterfront Worker."[21] To defeat this "clique control" the paper urged members to attend meetings, become active in the union, and work to improve it. The old *Waterfront Worker* called the new paper a shipowners' sheet. Local 38-79 reelected Harry Bridges president in September 1935 by a vote of 2,318 to 286, but many of the Albion Hall candidates lost out. Ivan Cox defeated Albion Hall leader Henry Schmidt for secretary 1,104 to 932.

In Seattle the *Voice of Action* continued to echo the Party line. In August 1934 it called on the rank and file of Local 38-12 to throw out Pete Erickson, Dewey Bennett, Louis Taggart, and Ed Morton, charging they sold out the strike and "sabotaged mass picketing at Pier 40."[22] Another *Waterfront Worker* appeared in October in Seattle, the expression of "militant ILA members'" in the Northwest. Like the *Voice*, its policy coincided with the Communist Party line.

Hiring Halls

The provisions of the award that labor relations committees should register longshoremen and set up joint hiring halls touched off more battles. In each port the employers tried to get their small groups of finks registered and give them work. They appealed the union's contention that longshoremen had to be physically present at the hall to be dispatched, arguing that nonunion men would be intimidated. Seattle employers demanded that the Labor Relations Committee register their forty-eight Alaska Steamship finks, who had been prevented from working since October 22.

Judge Sloss ruled in January 1935 that longshoremen need not appear at the hiring hall, and April 10 Arbitrator Harry Hazel ordered the Seattle Labor Relations Committee to register forty-two of the Alaska finks. The committee complied, and the dispatcher assured the employers that if the men came to the hall they would be sent out in regular order; he had heard no threats against them. Local 38-12 voted April 18 to take in all eligible registered men. Those who had done less that fifty pickets during the 1934 strike would be assessed 50 cents a picket not done, and those doing no pickets would be assessed $100 and barred from ever holding office.

Meanwhile, Local 38-12 took control of the dispatching. The union instructed all men to come to the new ILA hall at 68 Pike Street to be dispatched on Monday, January 21. The employers refused to recognize the hall. While 1,300 longshoremen remained idle, Merl Ringenberg tried vainly to dispatch from the employers' hall. Most men he sent to work did not report, and those who did quit on arrival. Thus they crippled the employers' hall. The union picketed the fink hall. Late that night the employers caved in and admitted that the hiring hall was "in fact an I.L.A. hall with the dispatching of men in the hands of the I.L.A."[23] Work resumed the next morning.

The San Pedro Labor Relations Committee also registered the finks. During January Local 38-82 resolved not to work with them. F.S. Gregory of the San Francisco Waterfront Employers charged in a wire to Secretary of Labor Perkins that the longshoremen had "attempted to prevent qualified nonunion men from working through physical violence" and struck companies attempting to employ them. Although the union refused to admit them, it was "formally demanding of the employers that they permanently cease to employ any nonunion men."[24] Arbitrator Watkins ruled March 11 that men need not appear at the hall, and refusal to work with nonunion men violated the award. The hiring hall in San Francisco finally opened on March 4, 1935, at 33 Clay Street. As in other ports, the three elected dispatchers belonged to the ILA. A month later Local 38-79 moved to new quarters next door.

Longshoremen did not like the old working rules, which the award had left untouched. Delegates from Washington ILA locals formulated uniform working rules in February 1935, which the locals adopted and tried to put into effect. After some Seattle and Tacoma employers gave in and accepted the union rules, the Waterfront Employers and the ILA negotiated uniform working rules for Puget Sound and Grays and Willapa harbors in May. The employers gained their demand to vary the meal time within two hours and gave in on other points. The longshoremen gained improvements in penalty pay and working rules, but they waived the demand for uniform load limits.

Cleaning Up the Ships

Seamen cleaned up their ships after the strike. The shipowners offered to discharge all scabs who had not gone to sea before the strike. The Longshoremen's Board contended that all strikers should be returned to their former positions without discrimination. The seamen's unions, licensed and unlicensed, aimed at nothing less than completely union crews, shipped from their union halls, on all vessels calling at West Coast ports. While they waited for formal recognition, the seamen worked constantly toward that end.

Some steamship companies flatly refused to return seamen who had struck to their former positions. The National Longshoremen's Board reported that one company rehired only twenty-three of forty-five complainants, twelve licensed officers and eleven unlicensed seamen. "Complainants seeking reinstatement were constantly informed that their places were filled by capable seamen whom the company would not transfer or discharge," the board reported. The vice-president and general manager of the company "referred to the Board as 'pinks'" and "charged that the activities of communists, sluggers and agitators were encouraged and condoned by the Board's general attitude and inactivity." Another company declared that the three complainants "were deserters and not strikers entitled to reinstatement."[25] The Masters, Mates and Pilots reported to the Seattle Central Labor Council August 1 that the American Mail Line discriminated against union men.

During August at San Francisco the Sailors' Union handled about 300 discrimination cases, only 30 of which they settled satisfactorily. The Dollar Line and tankers were the worst offenders. Seamen frequently took direct action to rid their vessels of scabs. At San Francisco on September 20, 200 seamen struck the *President Taft*, *President Wilson*, and *Admiral Nulton*, demanding discharge of 17 scabs on the *Taft*. The 400 longshoremen stopped work, teamsters respected the picket line, and union taxi drivers refused to take passengers to the pier. At four o'clock the company fired the scabs. The *Pacific Seaman* hailed the victory "as conclusive proof that the unity and solidarity which flowered in the recent strike has not disappeared from San Francisco's waterfront."[26] But the victory was flawed: scab engineers remained on the *President Taft*.

Crews battled on other "half and half" President vessels. Scabs and union men on the *President Grant* "staged a big row" in Hong Kong, and crews of the *Hoover, Hayes, Adams, Coolidge*, and *General Lee* fought in Manila. Trouble continued on the *President Grant*. In Hong Kong on February 3, 1935, Alvin Chown, scab carpenter, knifed Bruce Lindberg, nineteen-year-old member of the Marine Firemen. The murderer was never punished.

The tankers remained as determined as ever to keep the unions out. Soon after the strike ended, the collector of customs at Seattle found three tankers unseaworthy because they lacked sufficient able seamen. Writing from San Pedro, R.J. Evans protested September 11 to the Longshoremen's Board that Sailors' Union members had to go to other ports to get work because of "the arrogant attitude that the oil companies have taken in regards to taking back the men who left their employ."[27] At the end of the strike the tankers formed the Pacific American Tankship Association and notified the Longshoremen's Board that "No one has any authority to commit the members of this Association in any matter since [July 30] except the officers of our Association."[28] In November Carl Carter, Portland SUP agent, notified the officers of the General Petroleum tanker *Tejon* that unless the company discharged five scabs hired after May 18 who had never sailed, he would pull the unioin men off. The company appealed to the board, contending that the Tankship Association letter absolved it from the terms of the July 27 agreement. Not so, the board replied, and the company paid off the five scabs.

Unlicensed seamen flocked to their unions after the strike. By August 11 the Sailors' Union had taken in 130 new members and reinstated 36 old ones; the Marine Firemen took in 254 members, and the Marine Cooks and Stewards 60. Scabs tried to join, "and they have more different stories to tell, trying to get clearance cards than a dog has fleas . . . but they aren't getting them," the *ISU Journal* declared.[29] Some scabs went to the East Coast, took ISU books, and returned to San Francisco. There the unions took up their books and expelled them. The union dealt thus with five men in October. By the end of the year the Marine Firemen had over 4,000 members and pledges.

The Marine Workers Industrial Union still claimed equal status with the International Seamen's Union. When Frank Webb, SUP patrolman, told the MWIU crew of the *Oakmar* at San Francisco in October that they would have to join the ISU or quit, the *Waterfront Worker* accused him of "trying to create a dues paying racket, and further splitting the seamen."[30] An expelled member of the ISU charged that ISU delegates "go aboard ship and report M.W.I.U. men to fink mates and have them knocked off."[31]

The Sailors' Union and Marine Firemen demanded 1934 strike clearances, but the Marine Cooks and Stewards had a different situation. Although the Colored Marine Employees Benevolent Association had disbanded, the majority of the stewards' department on large vessels did not strike, and the union could not replace them. To prevent their being formed into another company union, the Marine Cooks and Stewards voted in September to take in 1934 scabs under special conditions. True to its promise to the association at the beginning of the strike, the union put Revels Cayton on as assistant in San Francisco and Fred Sexias, a chef on Alaska vessels, in Seattle.

The unions of licensed officers fought stubbornly against shipowners' attempts to form new company unions. The Licensed Officers Association pressured masters and mates to join. The Masters, Mates and Pilots declared: "There is no place for company unions among intelligent free men,"[32] adding a month later: "The day has definitely passed when the licensed officer can hope by taking a position of isolation to be able to benefit himself, or to obtain better wages and conditions. . . . Regardless of title, you are selling your labor; you require all the assistance organized labor can give you, and you cannot expect to be always receiving without cooperation."[33]

Seamen's Awards and Agreements

With 12,293 votes cast by seamen, the National Longshoremen's Board closed the polls in major ports on October 22, 1934. At the end of the strike the steam schooner operators, organized in the Shipowners' Association of the Pacific Coast, had recognized the International Seamen's Union. As the ballot count proceeded, offshore operators also recognized the union: Grace Lines and Panama Mail on November 6,

McCormick, Dollar, Matson and subsidiaries, Pacific Steamship, States Line, and Swayne & Hoyt in December, American Mail January 30, 1935, and Nelson February 6. Only American-Hawaiian with its three subsidiaries and the tankers refused to recognize the ISU until the board certified it as bargaining agent. On the tankers the ISU received 709 votes, the Standard Oil company union 221, the Marine Workers Industrial Union 24, and other unions 23.

When the unlicensed seamen began negotiations with the steam schooner operators, the unions demanded $75.00 and 75 cents overtime for able seamen and firemen. The operators offered $62.50, 60 cents overtime on cargo work, and 30 cents on ship work. The Marine Firemen rejected the offer 122 to 22, and the Sailors' Union turned it down by a ratio of 15 to 1. The Sailors insisted on union preference, union-controlled shipping, an equal overtime rate for all work, and abolition of day men. When negotiations bogged down in November, the unions and the Shipowners' Association agreed to arbitrate.

The steam schooner award February 2, 1935, gave members of the Sailors' Union, Marine Firemen, and Marine Cooks and Stewards "preference of employment in their respective capabilities when available." It provided that "no seafaring employee shall be required as a condition of receiving employment to register with any private hiring hall or similar employment institution. All employment shall be direct from the offices of the unions or from the docks. The rotation or tag system of employment shall not be used."[34] So much for the fink hall. Next the seamen would get rid of shipping off the docks. The award set wages for sailors and firemen at $70.00 and overtime 70 cents on an eight-hour day, fifty-six hour week.

After the strike, wages on offshore vessels drifted up to a top of $50.00 for able seamen, but conditions remained deplorable. Many Dollar vessels still had "four men jammed into a little two-by-four room, that [was] certified to accommodate three seamen,"[35] and Matson still worked two watches. Even after certification American-Hawaiian and its subsidiaries refused to recognize the International Seamen's Union until crews of the *Nevadan* and *Oregonian* struck for recognition in Portland and won. After the Pacific American Steamship Association granted preference of employment, the ISU agreed to arbitrate other issues.

Besides union preference, the offshore award handed down April 15, 1935, abolished the fink hall, providing hiring on the docks or through union offices at the employer's option. But, the award said, preference of employment "shall not be construed to require the discharge of any employee who may not desire to join the union, or to apply to prompt reshipment; or to absence due to illness or accident." Moreover, it provided that the union "shall not discriminate against the steamship companies by refusing to sail under licensed officers, including chief stewards, irrespective of their office or non-affiliation with any particular organization or association."[36] Thus the operators tried to protect their scabs. The award raised wages for able seamen and firemen from $50.00 to $62.50 and for messmen and waiters from $40.00 to $50.00. It limited work at sea Saturday afternoons, Sundays, and holidays, but companies paid overtime in time back instead of cash. The unions considered the award generally disappointing.

Rather than include the Alaska operators in the offshore arbitration, the seamen negotiated directly with them. On March 6 the Sailors' Union, Marine Firemen, and Marine Cooks and Stewards signed agreements with Alaska Steamship, Northland Transportation, Wills Navigation, and Santa Anna Steamship companies providing for union preference of employment and hiring through the union halls or off the docks. The pact raised wages for able seamen and firemen from $60.00 and 60 cents overtime to $70.00 and 70 cents; it raised pay $10.00 a month for cooks and waiters. The raises, retroactive to June 9, 1934, covered 1,500 men on 25 ships. The owners estimated the back pay would cost $50,000.

The unions moved to take control of shipping. The constitutions of the unlicensed seamen's unions established San Francisco as the coastwide headquarters and vested meetings in that port with authority to initiate policy and overrule branch actions. SUP headquarters' meetings led the battle for union shipping. According to Carl Tillman, right after the strike few jobs came into the San Francisco Sailors' hall. In October the union voted down the first motion to ship through the hall 79 to 17. During the following week some crews demanded replacements through the hall, and a few more jobs came in. The chair ruled another motion for union shipping out of order because it would antagonize the steam schooner owners. The next week more jobs came through the hall, but the motion failed again 67 to 38. Tillman described the final victory: "During the fourth week the McCormick Steamship Co. and many other smaller companies fell into line. Monday night, with 200 men at the meeting, everyone demanded that shipping be done through the hall." The motion passed unanimously. "About six weeks later the holdouts of the Matson Navigation and Dollar Steamship companies had to give in."[37] Thereafter, from 350 to 500 men a week shipped through the hall at San Francisco. The union suspended the shipping cards for thirty to sixty days for chiselers who violated the rules. Although the awards permitted shipping off the docks, seamen insisted on shipping through their unions.

The branches also demanded hiring through the union. At San Pedro in October 1934 seamen refused to ship through the fink hall. The SUP instructed all members on ships "not to allow any man on board the vessel who does not come from the Union Hall."[38] In Seattle and Portland, likewise, most jobs went through the halls. Seattle put a ninety-day limit on shipping cards in July 1935 "to eliminate 'stump ranchers' from coming in with a six- or seven-month-old card."[39] Meanwhile, up and down the coast the unions continued to tie up vessels to get rid of scabs.

Taking in former members of the Colored Marine Employees did not necessarily result in complete integration and checkerboard crews in the Marine Cooks and Stewards Union. San Francisco headquarters voted in July to ship through the hall, with preference for the oldest man ashore. The Seattle branch maintained a separate hall for African Americans until the union caught the black patrolman approaching steamship companies to replace white crews with black. With the support of African

Americans as well as whites, the union affirmed the principle of equal shipping rights regardless of color and closed the black hall in Seattle.

During these months after the strike, union crews improved their living conditions at sea. Vincent J. Malone of the Marine Firemen described the unions' gains aboard ship:

> Port captains, port engineers, ship captains, and chief engineers who had long run ships as if they were in the slave trade, now had to deal with resurgent militant union men, who . . . now wanted, above all things, decent conditions on the ships. . . . ship after ship was tied up because recalcitrant port captains refused to do anything about vessels that were loaded with bedbugs; again and again ships remained immovable at the dock because some grafting port steward had failed to realize a new day had dawned and that decent first grade stores, meat, vegetables and milk had to be provided; fresh milk, chicken and ice cream appeared on the mess tables of freighters . . . the thin straw and excelsior mattresses—the Donkey Breakfasts—went overboard; through the portholes went the miserable cracked enamel mugs and plates . . . and in their place appeared regular crockery ware; ships coffee dreg grade disappeared and the crews got regular first grade coffee; . . . quarters were rebuilt and cleaned out; clean white linen was provided regularly instead of blue sheets intermittently.
>
> And as they came in, the poor deluded shipowners' Ishmaels on the few ships that did manage to sail, the scabs who evermore were to carry in their sorry souls the knowledge they had betrayed their brother working stiffs for a miserable forty dollars a month, these miserable vermin were turned out in the streets and back to the farms, accompanied by the hoots, the jeers, the derision, the contempt of the longshoremen, the firemen and the sailors, and here and there, plenty of good solid kicks and blows.[40]

Licensed Officers' Negotiation

Pacific Coast shipowners had negotiated with licensed officers for many years before the 1921 disaster inaugurated the open shop on their vessels. Union victories in the seamen's elections brought them to the bargaining table again, however unwillingly. In spite of shipowners' pressure, their carefully nurtured company unions lost out on most steamship lines. The Masters, Mates and Pilots won certification in all companies except Donovan Lumber and Redwood Steamship among the steam schooner operators; and Dollar, American-Hawaiian, and Panama Mail among the offshore operators, where no organization received a majority. Mates and engineers on Swayne & Hoyt vessels chose a company union.

On steam schooners the Marine Engineers won elections in all except Donovan Lumber, National Steamship, and Redwood Steamship, where no union won, and Hobbs Wall, where the company union won. The union won in all offshore companies except Swayne & Hoyt. On the tanker fleet the licensed officers' unions won elections 100 percent on Associated Oil, Hillcone, Richfield Oil, Union Oil, and General Petroleum. No union won on Texas Oil, and on the Standard Oil fleet the company union won in all departments.

A coastwide conference of Marine Engineers the end of October 1934 formulated uniform demands. The Marine Engineers and Masters, Mates and Pilots signed agreements with the steam schooner operators in April 1935, and later that month the MEBA and nineteen offshore operators agreed to arbitrate their remaining unsettled issues. The award for engineers in August granted wage increases averaging 14.7 percent retroactive to March 1. The pact provided for a fifty-six-hour week for watch engineers and forty-four hours in port. The arbitrator denied demands for preferential hiring and a night engineer in port.

In the balloting, of 149 engineers employed by American-Hawaiian and its subsidiary, Oceanic and Oriental Navigation, 38 voted, 37 of them for the MEBA. The remaining 111 who did not vote were either indifferent or scabs afraid to go near the polling booth. The union signed an agreement with the company in June providing for wage increases, three watches, overtime Saturday afternoons and Sundays in port, and two weeks' vacation with pay. Addition of a fourth engineer created thirty-six more jobs. Membership in San Francisco increased 40 percent during 1935, to 1,400, and in San Pedro 50 percent to 350, in spite of the loss of the tankers.

Shipowners demanded the undivided allegiance of captains and mates of their vessels. The certification votes proved that they frequently did not get it. Licensed officers, as well as unlicensed seamen, cleaned up their ships. In Seattle March 14, 1935, the crew of the American Mail liner *President Jefferson* struck. The Sailors' Union demanded replacement of a scab carpenter, and the Masters, Mates and Pilots demanded union junior mates. Longshoremen respected the mates' picket line, and the pickets turned back trucks at Pier 41. The company fired the scab carpenter but refused to hire union mates. A.F. Haines, vice-president of American Mail, accused the union of trying to dictate management policies. After two days' delay the company agreed to demote one mate, and the vessel sailed.

The steamship companies refused to concede or arbitrate the union's demand for preferential hiring. Twelve major lines announced March 26 that they were willing to arbitrate wages, hours, and working conditions, but they flatly refused to cede their "entire freedom of selection of masters and licensed deck officers for our vessels." They said their "duty to the public" prevented their surrendering the "right and duty to select competent master and officers."[41] The Masters, Mates and Pilots reached an agreement in May with the majority of the offshore operators without arbitration, and Luckenbach agreed the end of the month to sign an agreement with the union.

The American Radio Telegraphists' Association, the last shipboard union to be formed, completed organization following the strike and negotiated agreements with the steamship companies. After a threatened coastwide strike in February 1935, McCormick granted wage increases of from \$75 to \$100 a month on coastwise vessels and \$85 to \$110 on intercoastal vessels, an eight-hour day, first-class accommodations, and union hiring. From 200 members on the Pacific Coast in July 1934, the union grew to 700 a year later.

East Coast Seamen

Victory on the West Coast galvanized East Coast seamen into action. The majority wanted to join a union and fight to improve conditions. With thousands of pledges, the Atlantic divisions of the International Seamen's Union demanded recognition and collective bargaining agreements from their employers. The shipowners stalled until the unions set an October 8 strike date. At the last minute the ISU called off the strike when thirty-six companies agreed to recognize the union and negotiate. In New York the United Front Committee, formed by the Marine Workers Industrial Union, went ahead with the strike, which collapsed after a week.

Without waiting for an agreement, most intercoastal companies calling at Pacific Coast ports voluntarily raised wages. Not so Luckenbach, which paid $35.00 a month for able seamen. While negotiations for an agreement dragged on, twenty sailors and firemen struck the *Robert Luckenbach* when she docked at Seattle December 3. The crew of the *Dorothy Luckenbach* also walked off when she arrived, and the *Florence Luckenbach* and *Paul Luckenbach* anchored in the stream to prevent their crews from joining the strike. The crew tied up the *Jacob Luckenbach* in Tacoma. Longshoremen and teamsters respected their picket lines. The seamen went back aboard their vessels December 13 with pay raised to $50.00 for able seamen, $60.00 for firemen, and proportionate increases in other classifications.

The intercoastal Shepard Line paid $40.00 a month for a twelve-hour day on deck, and provided "lousy and crummy" quarters, with tin mess gear and no linen. The vessels had carried nonunion Filipino crews since they began operating in 1929. In January 1935 the Seattle Sailors picketed the *Wind Rush* and *Harpoon*, demanding union crews. The company paid off the scabs, shipped SUP crews, raised wages, and agreed to improve working and living conditions. The Atlantic agreement, effective January 1, 1935, covered almost all steamship lines and provided for preference of employment and wages of $57.50 for able seamen. Direct action brought additional companies into line. In March the Calmar, Shepard, and Isthmian intercoastal lines agreed to recognize the Eastern and Gulf Sailors and sign the Atlantic agreement after seamen tied up their vessels in Pacific ports. These actions succeeded because longshoremen respected seamen's picket lines.

By 1935 the Communist Party's long zig to the left with revolutionary unions dual to the AFL ended. It embarked on another zag to the right: boring from within established unions and the united front. The Party directed Trade Union Unity League unions to liquidate or merge with AFL unions and their members to form "rank and file" caucuses. The Marine Workers Industrial Union proposed a merger to the International Seamen's Union in January 1935. Most ISU divisions ignored the proposal. Pacific Coast unions already accepted MWIU members individually rather than pull them off ships.

When the Seattle Sailors rejected the merger, the *Voice of Action* chastised Harry Lundeberg, "apparently an honest, sincere union member," for supporting "the stand of Buckmaster, Morton and Taggart in condemning the Marine Workers Industrial Union's criticism of the reactionary officials, Scharrenberg and Olander."[42] The *Waterfront Worker* deplored the ISU's attitude and urged all longshoremen to "talk to the seamen they meet up with as this unity move among the seamen sure affects us."[43]

A new paper appeared on the San Francisco waterfront, *The Seamen's Lookout*, dubbed *The Seamen's Sellout* by anti-Communists. It criticized the Atlantic agreement and Sailors' Union officials for dominating meetings and railroading actions. It called for amendments to the SUP constitution to abolish the six-month probationary membership and cut eligibility for office from three years to one, changes that would benefit former MWIU members.

The Tanker Strike

The tanker operators remained the most adamant union opponents. Pacific District ISU officials represented the unlicensed seamen in negotiations with all companies except Standard Oil that began January 25. The operators refused preferential hiring, conceded by other companies on both East and West coasts, and began hiring Filipino workaways who could replace their crews in a strike. Without a vote of the unions, on March 9 Paul Scharrenberg called a strike on the tankers for preference of employment.

Taken by surprise, the members struck the ships as they arrived in port. By March 12 five tankers lay idle in San Francisco Bay, three at Portland, one at Seattle, and others at San Diego and Long Beach. At San Pedro striking crews of eight tankers occupied a federal relief transient camp. Five major tanker operators withdrew their offer of an open-shop agreement on March 19 and announced a "fight to the finish" against the unions.[44] Members of the Masters, Mates and Pilots, Marine Engineers, and American Radio Telegraphists, who had walked off in support at the beginning of the strike, struck March 21 over "refusal in writing from tanker operators to discuss or arbitrate all working conditions."[45]

With thirty-six tankers tied up on the coast, at San Francisco on March 25 the unions formed the Council of Marine Crafts, in which members of the Joint Tanker Strike Committee participated. The *Waterfront Worker* reported April 1 that all striking unions met together "with the exception of two; namely, the Sailors' Union and the Firemen's Union. Due to the maneuvering of the officials of these two unions, the members withdrew their delegates from the Marine Council."[46]

A new paper, the *Seamen's Voice*, "published by a Real Rank and File Group of I.S.U. Seamen," had a different version. It charged that when the strike began "the Reds (by Reds we mean Bridges, [E.B.] O'Grady and [Roy] Pyle) started to muscle into our business, although they were not asked. Why? Because they want another General Strike, so we would have to go Red with them all the way." The paper asserted that the joint strike committee and Marine Council "kicked out" the Sailors' Union delegates for refusing "to sign a phoney agreement *without* the consent of the Union, but *they would not sign any paper until there had been a vote of the Sailors' Union Rank and File.*" The paper recommended that anyone "should be dumped" who "distributed Bridges literature."[47] The Marine Council announced March 25 that there would be no general strike to support the tanker strike.

While tanker operators recruited scabs, Secretary of Labor Perkins appointed a mediation board composed of Albert A. Rosenshine of San Francisco, Senator Daniel

C. Murphy of California, and Thomas C. Ridgeway of Los Angeles. On April 5 the oil companies offered wage increases, reemployment of strikers as vacancies occurred, and the right of union patrolmen to visit ships. The unions rejected the offer because it did not grant preference of employment and agreed that none would return to work until all gained union preference. The uptown unions supported the striking seamen. Charging that Standard Oil spearheaded the open-shop stance, state federations of labor and central labor councils put the company on the unfair list.

In San Francisco Lee Holman recruited scabs until police arrested him for operating an employment bureau without a license. Japanese seamen, with a strong union and a history of cooperation with the AFL, refused to scab. When the tanker *Gertrude Kellogg* reached Seattle with a scab crew, according to the *West Coast Sailors*, "Finky Fox towboats put Tanker Schmitt and 20 gunmen on board" to prevent about forty sailors and firemen from attempting to take off the finks, "and live steamhoses were stretched along the deck of the *Gertrude Kellogg* to give the striking seamen and firemen 'the works.'"[48]

Besides tanker seamen, other workers on the coast walked off their jobs. In California, warehousemen at the C & H sugar refinery at Crockett struck for recognition, and longshoremen picketed Seattle flour mill docks. Workers uptown also organized. Every day an old gray bus, spattered with egg and the windows covered with chicken wire, hauled scabs to the Olympic Garment factory, where employees, mostly women, struck for a closed shop.

The Seattle Chamber of Commerce organized the Committee of Five Hundred to combat the union drive. Chamber President Alfred Lundin wired Secretary of Labor Perkins and Assistant Secretary McGrady April 16 protesting the government's "temporizing" and failure to compel the maritime unions to live up to the awards. He charged that those unions "are now reliably reported as being out of control."[49] The same day the Committee of Five Hundred ran a display ad in the *Seattle Star* quoting a member of the Masters, Mates and Pilots who had been first mate on a tanker. "WE ARE VICTIMS OF A HANDFUL OF RADICALS," he charged. "Let it be known that we are not in sympathy with the radical racketeers, and we are inviting a clubbing, and our families may be marked for cowardly attack." He congratulated the Committee of Five Hundred: "You are not fighting unionism, but the stifling union domination of a few radical musketeers that care nothing for our homes, families, our very lives."[50]

The oil companies announced April 16 that fifteen of their thirty-two tankers operated on the Pacific Coast with scabs. They delivered an ultimatum a few days later that if the unions did not accept the April 5 proposals by April 26, they would withdraw the offer and close the tankers to union seamen. The Joint Tanker Strike Committee reaffirmed its rejection of the open-shop offer. The founding convention of the Maritime Federation resolved April 24 that if all other means to settle the strike failed, the federation would take a strike vote of its 35,000 members. Two weeks later the Pacific Coast District ILA convention voted that if the seamen's unions decided to strike all vessels the longshoremen would then ballot on a coastwide support strike.

The tanker operators refused to meet with the federation executive board. The strike threat prompted Secretary of Labor Perkins to appoint a new arbitration board May 16 composed of O.K. Cushing, Selah Chamberlain, and Paul Sinsheimer. The arbitrators proposed that the unions approve the board's wage and hour proposals and terminate the strike and boycott, strikers to be reemployed as needed before hiring new employees. The unions rejected the proposals, and the membership voted 1,232 to 66 to terminate the strike June 17. The unions continued to boycott Standard Oil service stations. Loss of the strike set back organization on tankers for years, particularly among licensed deck officers. Some members of the Masters, Mates and Pilots struck and lost their jobs—others scabbed. Thereafter, many tanker officers shunned the union.

The Modesto Frame-up

Standard Oil did more than spearhead opposition to unions. On the night of April 20, Stanislaus County peace officers and Standard Oil special agents stopped two cars near the country town of Patterson, searched the cars, and arrested ten of the eleven men in them. They claimed to find dynamite, lengths of fuse, detonating caps, and two blackjacks in one car, and similar items in a nearby ditch. Hal Marchant, the eleventh man, who represented Portland on the Joint Tanker Strike Committee, turned out to be a private detective employed by Standard Oil. A grand jury charged all but James Scrudder, a stool pigeon for the San Francisco Police Department, with conspiracy to dynamite the Del Puerto Hotel in Patterson and assault scabs housed there, and also with illegal possession of the dynamite and weapons.

The Modesto victims: striking tanker seamen framed by the Standard Oil Company, April 1935. Back row, left to right, John Rodgers, John Burrows, Henry Silva, Victor Johnson, Robert Fitzgerald, John Sousa. Seated, Patsy Ciambrelli, Reuel Stanfield. (Voice of the Federation)

The indicted men included two members of the Joint Tanker Strike Committee, Victor Johnson and Reuel Stanfield; the rest were rank and filers recruited at the last minute. Four belonged to the Marine Firemen. The unions charged Standard Oil framed the men. The trial began July 9 at Modesto. Witnesses for the prosecution asserted the men intended to blow up the hotel and Standard Oil stations with the dynamite and fuses. The defense claimed they made the trip to verify a report of scabs housed at the Del Puerto and possibly put a picket line on the hotel. They charged that Standard Oil detectives planted the explosives and blackjacks. Early in August the jury found eight of the defendants guilty of reckless and malicious possession of dynamite on the public highway. They received sentences of from six months to five years in San Quentin and Folsom prisons. The prosecution dropped the charges against the ninth defendant, who was critically ill. The unions asserted that Standard Oil pressure produced the guilty verdict, upheld on appeal.

Another stool pigeon surfaced in Portland. William Moore of the Marine Firemen and Maxie Weisbarth of the Sailors' Union drew sentences on May 16 of nine months in jail for assault and battery and inciting to riot. Moore then accused three other strikers of dynamiting a Standard Oil station in Portland April 15. During the trial of Joseph G. O'Brien, Moore admitted that he turned state's evidence to collect a $1,000 reward from Standard Oil. After a jury acquitted O'Brien, the prosecution dropped charges against the other two defendants.

Harry Lundeberg declared that "the failure of [the tanker] strike can be laid at the door of Paul Scharrenberg, who called this strike prematurely, without consulting the membership and notwithstanding that no preparations for carrying on this strike had been made."[51] Scharrenberg was a long-time member of the Sailors' Union, secretary of the California State Federation of Labor, editor of the *Seamen's Journal*, and a vice-president of the International Seamen's Union. Now the Sailors' Union investigated his past record. Besides calling the tanker strike without authority, the special committee found that:

1. He urged the ISU in 1933 to help Walter Petersen of the San Francisco fink hall lobby to defeat a bill raising citizenship requirements of American vessels from 50 to 66-2/3 percent. This would have enabled the Dollar Line to retain Chinese crews, when half the American seamen had no work.
2. While harbor commissioner he deputized Petersen's fink hall runners with guns so they could go aboard all vessels and force seamen to carry fink books.
3. When the SUP sent him to Washington, D.C., to work for a seamen's code under the NRA, he worked instead to establish a shipping board composed of equal representation of the government, shipowners, and seamen.
4. As editor of the *Seamen's Journal* he supported a compensation law that would deprive seamen of the right to libel a vessel and sue for damages.
5. He openly sided with the Blue Book union against the ILA in San Francisco in 1933.

Scharrenberg refused to attend the trial, asserting in the *Seamen's Journal* that the charges "were framed by the henchmen of an alien Communist, the notorious Harry Bridges" and that the trial "was personally conducted by Harry Lundenberg, . . . who came from Seattle especially to manage the affair."[52] By a coastwide vote of 322 to 54 the Sailors' Union expelled Scharrenberg June 3.

The State Federation of Labor, the International Seaman's Union, Hugh Gallagher of Matson, the Hearst press, and others raised a great public outcry against the expulsion. After some controversy Office Employees Union Local 13188 accepted Scharrenberg's application for membership by a vote of 4 to 2. At the San Francisco headquarters meeting on July 15, 450 members reaffirmed the expulsion. The SUP denounced him as a "renegade," "an enemy of the labor movement who rode on the backs of the seamen . . . and did nothing for them but only for himself and shipowners.'" The union declared that the tanker strike call "was nothing more than a deliberate attempt to wreck the Maritime Unions on the Pacific Coast, and would have succeeded in throwing the coast into turmoil had not the Maritime Federation of the Pacific stepped in and ended the strike."[53]

Except for the tanker fiasco, the maritime workers had utilized well the months since their return to work to push toward the objectives for which they had struck. Elections under the new labor laws compelled their employers to recognize and bargain with their unions. Negotiations and arbitrations brought wage increases and improved working conditions, and direct actions established de facto control of their hiring halls. Each new gain increased their strength and confidence and added momentum to the union advance.

11

Hot Cargo

More than any other single event, the maritime workers' victory in 1934 propelled the union upsurge forward among working people on the entire Pacific Coast. In Washington and Oregon the organizing drive among loggers and lumber mill workers gathered momentum. Farther north, British Columbia longshoremen, who had suffered the same exploitation during the open-shop years as their southern brothers, began to organize. In the San Francisco Bay area the union fever infected men who worked next to the triumphant longshoremen for much lower wages. Packers, warehouse workers, and bargemen organized and demanded better pay and working conditions. In the spring of 1935 this organizing ferment would erupt in confrontations and strikes.

During the months following the 1934 strike the maritime workers had been occupied with arbitrations, negotiations, and cleaning up the ships and docks. By the end of 1934 they had achieved a working relationship that included union hiring with all their employers except the tanker operators. Next they would define and formalize their relations with each other.

Maritime Federation Is Planned

In the Northwest, talk of a federation resumed in November. The Seattle longshoremen voted December 6 that "the local go ahead with the Marine Federation, to get as many of the Local Unions into the Federation as possible and to ask the co-operation of the District."[1] Seattle Local 38-12, the Sailors' Union, and others organized the Puget Sound Federation the middle of January 1935. The *Voice of Action* condemned the proposed constitution, drawn up by Paddy Morris, because it excluded dual unions, thus barring the MWIU. The paper suggested organizing an opposition rank-and-file federation. In San Francisco the Masters, Mates and Pilots; Marine Engineers; Marine Cooks and Stewards; ILA Checkers; and Machinists formed the Council of Marine Crafts. The Sailors' Union and Local 38-79 did not participate. According to John Kucin, when he asked Harry Bridges why the longshoremen had not joined, Bridges replied, "I don't like that set-up, when I get ready to go for a Federation I will form it."[2]

Paddy Morris succeeded Jack Bjorklund as Pacific Coast District ILA secretary in January after Bjorklund became Pierce County sheriff. In response to Morris's suggestion, the district ILA invited representatives of the five other organizations "directly employed in the marine transportation industry" to meet in San Francisco on February 18 to plan a coastwide marine federation. Reciting the need to organize "to maintain the conditions established by the recent strike settlement, and to further advance those conditions," the letter cautioned that "special attention should be given to the question of representation so that the interests of all organizations, large and small, shall be safeguarded."[3] The ILA invited the Brotherhood of Teamsters; International Seamen's Union; Masters, Mates and Pilots; Marine Engineers; and American Radio Telegraphists to the conference.

The Communists had been predicting for months that the district ILA would sell out the federation concept. The *Waterfront Worker* headlined January 14: "FAKERS MOVE TO CONTROL FEDERATION," charging: "Paddy Morris, the old faker, made it quite clear at our last membership meeting that they, (the fakers) had already taken steps to control the Maritime Federation when it is set up. . . . Lewis backed Morris up in his statements that we had to deal with the elected officials of the various organizations, . . ."[4]

The next meeting of San Francisco Local 38-79 adopted the "Declaration of Principles for Formation of Marine Federation," calling for "democratic control of the Federation through elections, whereby each member votes as an individual member of the Federation and not as a member of a union. This form of organization keeps the control in the hands of the Rank and File." The *Waterfront Worker* urged the union to promote the program: "We have no time to lose. The employers are moving fast—they have already begun organizing their Pacific Coast Federation. With the many tricks these scoundrels have up their sleeves we cannot afford to take chances."[5] The paper attacked the ILA conference call for leaving out Machinists, Boilermakers, and other shoreside unions, and labeled the proposal "a Federation to castrate the mighty power of the workers and to better serve the interests of the shipowners."[6] Harry Bridges toured the coast before the conference to explain Local 38-79's position.

Delegates from eight coastwide organizations met in San Francisco February 18 to found the Maritime Federation: Longshoremen; Masters, Mates and Pilots; Marine Engineers; Sailors' Union; Marine Firemen; Marine Cooks and Stewards; Ferryboatmen's Union; and Radio Telegraphists. The Teamsters did not accept the invitation. Five delegates chosen by the subdistricts represented the ILA: Art Will for Puget Sound, Ed Krumholz for Grays and Willapa harbors, M.D. Rodgers for the Columbia River, Harry Bridges for Northern California, and a member from San Pedro for Southern California. E.B. O'Grady of the San Francisco Masters, Mates and Pilots chaired the conference, and Roy Pyle of the Radio Telegraphists was secretary. The organizations represented 35,000 workers.

For ten days the delegates wrestled with a constitution to submit to the unions that would participate in the actual founding convention. After all their bombast about one-member-one-vote, the Communists, who apparently controlled a working majority in the conference, settled for a compromise permitting small organizations proportionately more votes. The conference sent the draft constitution to the parent organizations with a call for the founding convention in Seattle April 15. The *Voice of Action* applauded the constitution "drafted under the militant chairmanship of

Frisco ILA president Harry Bridges." According to that paper, the Seattle Marine Federation expelled John "Finky" Fox as delegate March 15, "notorious for his attempts to set up a waterfront federation affiliated to the Chamber of Commerce and his recent strike breaking actions of towing the Robert Luckenbach from the dock during the recent (M.W.I.U.) strike."[7]

Maritime Federation Founding Convention

When the delegates assembled in Seattle April 15, 1935, for the founding convention of the Maritime Federation, it appeared that the Communists had lost their majority. E.B. O'Grady defeated Karl Isaksen of the Everett longshoremen for chair 38 to 30. The convention seated delegates from the Alaska Fishermen, affiliated with the ISU, but "tabled indefinitely" the question of seating the Ferryboatmen's Union after the unlicensed seamen objected that the "organization cannot live up to the principles of the Federation."[8] The founding organizations pledged to pay per capita tax on 33,663 members, on which convention voting strength was based: ILA, 12,000; Sailors' Union, 6,800; Marine Firemen, 5,000; Marine Cooks and Stewards, 4,000; Alaska Fishermen, 1,500; Marine Engineers, 2,146; Masters, Mates and Pilots, 1,617; and Radio Telegraphists, 600. Prior to the convention most organizations had ratified the draft constitution with reservations and amendments, and a few at both ends of the ideological spectrum had adopted it as written. The convention hammered out the final document.

The delegates adopted a pro rata voting schedule: 1 to 250 members, 3 votes; 251-500, 6 votes; 501-750, 8 votes; 751-1,000, 10 votes; one additional vote for each 250 members to 10,000; and one for each 350 above that. Where the draft constitution stated that the federation would be composed of bona fide labor unions whose members were "employed in connection with the shipping and marine transportation industry," the convention specified labor unions "who work in conjunction with and who are in conformity with the principles of the American Federation of Labor" and "whose members are directly engaged in connection with shipping and marine transportation."[9] Throughout the life of the federation the controversy about seating peripheral organizations would continue. The Alaska Fishermen's Union, voting with the Communist bloc, became the first example. Most non-Communists tried to limit the federation to basic crafts directly engaged in the industry, while the Communist bloc attempted to include other organizations whose votes they controlled.

The provision for a federation vote to end a serious dispute or strike occasioned the first roll call vote. The draft constitution proposed that the vote should "not be recorded as a vote by organization, but as a majority vote of the affiliated memberships of the Federation voting as a whole." By a vote of 78.23 to 72.94 the convention provided that the vote should be recorded by organizations "with each union allowed a number of votes equal to the per capita tax paid averaged over 12 months." While a majority vote of the combined membership would decide all issues, the vote of each organization would "be increased in proportion to the total number of votes cast until each organization attained its full vote."[10] Thus the delegates gave seafaring unions, many of whose members would have no opportunity to vote, an equal voice with shoreside unions.

The convention divided on this and other votes along ideological lines. Delegates from the Alaska Fishermen, Radio Telegraphists, and ILA Local 38-79 of San Francisco composed the solid Communist bloc. Harry Pilcher and Karl Isaksen of Everett Local 38-76, J.R. Jones of Grays Harbor Local 38-77, Hugh Adams of Portland Local 38-78, C. Wisner of Raymond Local 38-92, Herbert Mills of the Sailors, and Earl King of the Marine Firemen also voted with the bloc. The Masters, Mates and Pilots, Marine Engineers, the rest of the Marine Firemen, ILA delegates from Seattle 38-12, San Pedro 38-82, Tacoma 38-97, the rest of Portland 38-78, and most of the small locals voted solidly against the bloc.

A roll call vote of 94.95 to 58.73 defeated endorsement of political action and a labor party, and another roll call rejected May Day as the workers' holiday 107.34 to 47.63. The convention authorized one or two district councils in each state or province composed of locals of affiliated unions. Additional organizations could join the federation upon approval by a majority of district councils. The delegates provided for two full-time officers, president and secretary-treasurer, and voted to pay a per capita tax of 5 cents a month to the federation, 2 cents of it for the district councils.

The licensed officers made their stand on voting strength for executive committee members. The draft constitution proposed an executive board composed of four members of each affiliated organization with prorated votes. Speaking for the Marine Engineers, Fred M. Kelley of San Francisco warned that their delegates would recommend rejection of the constitution if the convention adopted the proposal. The substitute, adopted 81.04 to 73.96, provided that in each district council each affiliated organization should select one member for the district council executive committee, and those combined executive committees would comprise the federation executive committee. Thus the delegates rejected sheer numbers in favor of recognition that the interests of key small crafts, such as licensed officers, must be protected. Over Communist opposition the delegates added a paragraph prohibiting the executive committee from assuming "the power to negotiate agreements or settle disputes without first being instructed by the membership of the union concerned in such agreements or disputes."[11]

For president of the federation Paddy Morris nominated Art Will of the Seattle longshoremen, and Herbert Mills nominated Harry Lundeberg, patrolman of the Seattle Sailors, supported by the Communist bloc. Two Sailors' Union delegates who had been voting with the anti-Communists voted for Lundeberg, giving their union brother the victory 78.31 to 76.69. For vice-president Fred W. Friedl of the San Pedro Marine Firemen defeated Communist candidate Karl Isaksen of the Everett longshoremen 80.80 to 74.20. After San Pedro police shot Friedl by mistake in June, Lundeberg appointed William Fischer, ex-Wobbly logger and dispatcher for Portland ILA Local 38-78 to succeed him.

For secretary-treasurer John Kucin of the San Pedro Masters, Mates and Pilots nominated Fred Kelley of the Marine Engineers, and the Communists supported Roy Pyle of the Radio Telegraphists. Two Sailors' Union delegates refused to follow instructions to vote for Pyle. Shortly before the vote Carl Carter, Portland branch agent, left the hall, giving his vote to William Buckmaster of Seattle. With Buckmaster not voting, Kelley won the election 75.78 to 72.40. For failure to obey instructions the union reprimanded Buckmaster. The Pacific Coast District ILA spent $1,242.42 of the $1,500.00 set aside by the Joint Northwest Strike Committee to found the federation.

The Communists hailed the election of "Harry Lundeberg, fighting progressive . . . to the presidency,"[12] but the *Voice of Action* called upon the federation to "cast from its leadership Paddy Morris, Art Will, Whitney, Thurston, Carter and all those who supported the treacherous constitutional amendments."[13] The *Waterfront Worker* deplored the "inadequate representation accorded to the I.L.A. on the Executive Board," pointing at Morris, Thurston, and other ILA delegates "who led the fight and voted, along with convention reactionaries, for this clause."[14] Actually, twenty-two of the thirty-one ILA delegates voted for the clause limiting ILA representation.

The Seattle federation became District Council No. 1, with 8,754 members, and the San Francisco federation District Council No. 2 with 15,456 members. Harry Bridges defeated E.B. O'Grady for president 98 to 40, and the council elected Mervyn R. Rathborne of the ARTA secretary. Besides the coastwide organizations, delegates from the local Boilermakers, Machinists, and Caulkers were seated in the council. The Communists would always control the Bay Area District Council. Columbia River unions organized District Council No. 3 with 4,252 members, and San Pedro organized District Council No. 4 with 5,436 members. The hoped-for British Columbia council did not materialize.

Fittingly, the new federation dedicated to solidarity adopted the motto of the Industrial Workers of the World, "An injury to one is an injury to all." It harked back to the nineteenth century Knights of Labor declaration that "An injury to one is the concern of all." The federation launched the *Voice of the Federation* in June, a weekly newspaper published in San Francisco. Although ideological lines hardened, the paper, like the federation itself, aimed to contain the warring factions within its pages. It would report news impartially, publish official statements of member unions, and print rank-and-file letters. Maritime unionists assumed that the federation and its voice were so important that they could encompass all differences. Beginning as a four-page tabloid without regular financial backing, the paper had grown by November to six full pages, practically self-supporting, with a circulation of 13,000 a week. Locals in each port subscribed for bundle orders, and the paper carried ads for union establishments catering to the needs of maritime workers.

Pacific Coast District ILA Convention

On the eve of the Northwest lumber strike, Pacific Coast longshoremen assembled in convention in Portland May 5. The district numbered 12,000 members in forty-eight locals, seventeen of them chartered since the strike. In Alaska, Juneau and Cordova longshoremen organized locals, as well as walking bosses on Puget Sound. San Francisco Local 38-79 had over 3,700 members, almost a third of the entire district. The delegates prepared for the inevitable continuing struggle. Over the opposition of San Francisco they authorized the district executive board to negotiate an agreement to replace the award expiring September 30, and to include checkers and clerks, under separate awards, in the longshoremen's agreement. They resolved to support the Timber Workers' strike and refuse to touch unfair lumber. The convention levied a 25-cent assessment to send five delegates to the coming international convention. The delegates voted to work toward standard load limits of 1,800 pounds where jitneys operated and 1,400 pounds where loads were hoisted without mechanical devices, and to recommend a system of dock and gang stewards for all locals.

To facilitate communication the convention established a weekly paper to be mailed to each member, financed by a referendum vote to raise per capita to the district from 5 to 10 cents a month. Locals would receive space for reports in proportion to their size, and the district secretary would edit the paper; the *Pacific Coast Longshoreman* began publication August 12, 1935. The convention endorsed the Maritime Federation action declaring July 5 a holiday in memory of those strikers killed in 1934, and the delegates levied a 25-cent assessment to establish a fund for the widow and children of Ray Morency, striking ILA warehouseman shot by a scab at Stockton April 26, 1935. The delegates instructed the incoming executive board to plan financial assistance for locals affected by the lumber strike. While commending their good works, the convention turned down pleas from ladies' auxiliaries in Seattle and San Pedro for official status and the right to use the emblem for recognition.

The most heated controversy centered on the method of electing officers. The Communist bloc introduced a resolution to elect all district officers by referendum, amended to elect only the president and secretary by referendum. The rest of the board members would be elected as before by state caucuses at the convention. On a roll call the amendment passed 72-3/5 to 43-1/20, and the subsequent coastwide referendum approved the constitutional amendment.

Bill Lewis of San Francisco Local 38-79 defeated Harry Bridges of the same local for district president 69-4/5 to 50-1/5, and Paddy Morris of Tacoma defeated Hugh Adams of Portland for secretary 79-1/5 to 39-4/5. Delegates reelected Cliff Thurston of Portland vice-president. In the California caucus for executive board members, the San Francisco votes elected Joe Simons, the only Communist bloc delegate from San Pedro, to the executive board.

The Pacific Coast District sent five delegates to the ILA international convention in New York City in July: Robert Hardin of Tacoma from Puget Sound, J.R. Jones of Aberdeen from Grays and Willapa harbors, M.D. Rodgers of Longview from the Columbia River, Harry Bridges from Northern California, and Joe Simons from Southern California. The convention rejected a resolution by Bridges to remove A.H. Petersen as international organizer because "his activities have been more in the interests of the employer than they have the membership."[15] Bridges and President Joe Ryan engaged in an acrimonious debate on their activities during and after the 1934 strike. Bridges was "tied up with the Communist Party," Ryan asserted. "I believe he has a lot of real sincerity in his endeavor to do something for his brother members . . . and he has a natural hatred for the employers because he worked under intolerable conditions for eleven years. This is the Communists' opportunity. They see he is active, and have grabbed him up and are pushing him on."[16]

The convention rejected Pacific Coast resolutions for the six-hour day, to build regional maritime federations, and other proposals. The delegation itself was split. Jones and Simons supported Bridges, and Hardin and Rodgers opposed him, although they had no use for Ryan. The delegates elected Hardin and Rodgers vice-presidents and left another spot open on the executive board for the Pacific Coast; the ILA subsequently named Bill Lewis. The west Coast delegation opposed Ryan's reelection as international president, opposed approval of his signing the June 16 agreement, and opposed raising the salaries of paid officers. The *A.F. of L. Rank and File Federationist* charged that Ryan had assumed complete power in the union with a resolution providing that "any union or unit of the I.L.A. that breaches the terms of any contract —shall be automatically suspended from the I.L.A."[17] Ryan denied press rumors during the convention that he would revoke the San Francisco charter. The *Labor Advocate* carried Robert Hardin's report of the convention:

> A few young men of ability who might have been groomed into possible opposition candidates to Ryan were so invincibly opposed to the communist activities that they would have resented any support from such sources. The halo built around Harry Bridges by the Daily Worker in New York, the Western Worker in San Francisco and the Voice of Action in Seattle and communist leaflets that have been scattered around the water front of New York City and the cities on the Great Lakes telling how the conditions enjoyed by the Pacific Coast District were obtained under the leadership of Bridges and the guidance of the communist party only, confused the issue to uniting all in a solid front for Ryan, Hardin said.
>
> "One conclusion," said Hardin, "that can be drawn from this convention is that as long as there is an element inside the I.L.A. that there can be any question raised as to their activities being formed and directed from outside the A.F.of L., no definite progress can be made. Whatever changes or reforms that will come about inside the I.L. A., the issues will be confused when they are sponsored by a group whose activities outside can be thus questioned."[18]

Employers Organize Coastwide

During the months following the strike, the employers watched with increasing alarm as union longshoremen nibbled away at control of their waterfronts. The end of 1934 Thomas G. Plant, president of the San Francisco Waterfront Employers, met with Frank Foisie in Seattle. They discussed the need for a concerted labor plan and concluded that they must unite coastwide in an organization comparable to the ILA. Waterfront employers in other ports concurred, and in January they hired Harold

Ebey of the Hamburg-American Line as coast coordinator. The employers protested to Secretary of Labor Perkins the longshoremen's continued violations of the arbitration award. Frank Foisie described their dilemma in February:

> The truth, however unpalatable, is that the I.L.A. is with us now and it or its equivalent will, no doubt, be with us indefinitely in the future. It is irresponsible in both leadership and membership. . . . shipping management must provide labor leadership to the longshoremen, while aiding by every bit of resource in us to foster the growth of responsible leadership from within the ranks of the longshoremen. . . . The object would seem to be to influence the direction of I.L.A. purpose rather than to thwart it; this in spite of daily evidence of bad faith.[19]

The middle of March the Seattle Waterfront Employers considered a lockout as "the one means of forcing public attention on the marine strike evil. It may be necessary to break over the back of the administration through newspapers, the government's failure to enforce the Award which it sponsored."[20] An organizing drive in April among warehouse workers at the California Packing Corporation in Alameda provided the opportunity to try the lockout weapon. ILA Warehousemen Local 38-44 struck after the company fired a number of employees, presumably for union activity. On April 17, 1935, members of San Francisco Local 38-79 refused to unload freight cars from the struck plant at the Encinal terminals. Cal-Pak proposed to the Waterfront Employers to distribute its products on many docks in the San Francisco Bay area, with the understanding that steamship and stevedore companies would discharge all longshoremen who refused to handle the products. The employers agreed, resolving:

> That the Steamship Companies will do all in their power to try and unload any California Packing Corporation products presented for shipment at San Francisco in freight cars or trucks, and in the event men will not handle such cargo they will be fired and new gangs ordered from the Hiring Hall, and that the men discharged will not be worked elsewhere on the ship or dock the same day.[21]

Cal-Pack's strategy worked. Rather than face a port lockout, Local 38-79 backed down and worked the scab cargo. Frank Foisie, who replaced Harold Ebey as coast coordinator during this time, commented in a letter June 8, "The Cal-Pack stand against the I.L.A. warehousemen's union has resulted in a complete stemming of the tide for the most, at least against the I.L.A. warehouse encroachment on industrial docks down here."[22]

A major section of the Waterfront Employers resolved May 31 to try to change Local 38-79's officers. Foisie reported June 5: "The Waterfront Employers of San Francisco are working with Ryan and the district officials toward securing responsible leadership on the part of the I.L.A. on advice that an agreement can no longer exist." They hoped to persuade the international president to revoke the San Francisco local's charter "because of flagrant violations and acknowledged communist control."[23]

Then Foisie probed for another opening. Maritime workers had pledged to refuse to touch scab lumber. When Puget Sound mills opened with scabs June 21, bringing the National Guard to Tacoma two days later, he demanded that longshoremen load the hot lumber. On Saturday, the 22nd, Paddy Morris took George Smith of Tacoma, Dewey Bennett and Art Whitehead of Seattle, and Arne M. Jones and Joe Sumption of the district executive board to meet with the employer representative. Foisie delivered an ultimatum that longshoremen must work the lumber Monday, or the employers would break with the union coastwide. Morris replied:

> You are placing before us two very unpleasant alternatives. We don't want to break with the employers; we don't want to refuse aid to our fellow unionists. . . . It will be the lesser evil to break with the employers than to order our men to go thru picket lines of state police and militia with tear gas and saps. So we will not go thru the picket line to handle any lumber.[24]

The employers did not carry out their threat to lock out the longshoremen.

Point Clear *Hot Cargo*

More hot cargo reached Pacific Coast docks. In British Columbia longshoremen reorganized after their open-shop years. Fraternal delegates from the Vancouver and District Waterfront Workers' Association had attended the Maritime Federation and ILA conventions, and union people on both sides of the border looked forward to formal affiliation of Canadian maritime workers. The British Columbia Shipping Federation locked out the Vancouver longshoremen on June 4, 1935, for refusing to handle paper loaded by scabs at Powell River. The employers' preparations before the lockout indicated that they planned to destroy the union. Refusing to go back to work in an open shop, the longshoremen struck. Canadian seamen joined them. Police charged strikers June 18, sending nine to the hospital.

When the Swayne & Hoyt steamer *Point Clear* docked at Powell River to load, union engineers refused steam to scabs. A scab engineer furnished the steam, and the vessel proceeded to San Francisco. When she arrived June 22 the union engineers walked off, demanding that the scab be fired, and the union picketed the vessel. After longshoremen refused to cross the picket line, the company paid off the crew under protest. The Sailors' Union voted June 24 to refuse "to handle or transport cargo from British Columbia ports, or any other ports where strike conditions prevail."[25] The next night District Council No. 2 of the Maritime Federation declared the *Point Clear* cargo hot. Many maritime workers believed that the security of their Pacific Coast unions depended on defeating the British Columbia Shipping Federation.

The San Francisco Waterfront Employers became inpatient. President T.G. Plant, dubbed "Tear Gas" Plant by union people, reported June 25: "We have worked all angles—the Department of Labor, J.P. Ryan, Lewis, Petersen, and other conservative I.L.A. leaders on this Coast. Our only apparent hope of progress lay in trying to persuade the conservative leaders that if they wanted to preserve anything for the I.L.A. they would have to set their house in order."[26] Two days later he wired District President Lewis and ILA President Ryan protesting the longshoremen's refusal to cross the *Point Clear* picket line. He castigated their action as "constituting such a

Police route strikers with tear gas on Ballantyne Pier, Vancouver, B.C., June 18, 1935. (A/P Wide World Photos)

deliberate and outrageous violation of the agreement . . . and culminating as it does a long series of deliberate and outrageous violations serves again to prove that the officials of the San Francisco local are proceeding on a wilful policy of abrogation of the award and are doing everything in their power to provoke and prolong strife."[27] Plant again called upon them to remove Local 38-79's "radical leadership" and threatened to terminate the agreement if the longshoremen did not work the *Point Clear*.

The ILA District Executive Board protested that the Marine Engineers should have invoked the machinery of the Maritime Federation before picketing the *Point Clear*. The Engineers replied that they had. The board sent two questions to a coastwide referendum: Shall the ILA declare July 5 a holiday, and shall the longshoremen refuse to handle British Columbia cargo? On June 29 the Waterfront Employers began blacklisting gangs that refused to work the *Point Clear*. Frank C. Gregory explained to the employers "that if a split could be caused between the local I.L.A. and the International and district officials, it would be much better and cheaper a way to bring about a climax to the matter."[28]

While the *Point Clear* remained tied up at Pier 54, the maritime unions honored their martyrs on July 5, the anniversary of Bloody Thursday: Olaf Helland and Shelvy Daffron, killed in Seattle during the 1934 strike; Howard Sperry and Nickolas Bordoise in San Francisco; Richard Parker and John Knudsen in San Pedro; and Bruce Lindberg in Hong Kong. Up and down the coast waterfronts shut down. At Seattle, longshoremen worked no ships. Shelvy Daffron's widow and Bruce Lindberg's mother led the parade of 5,000 maritime workers. Seventeen vessels lay idle at Portland, where unlicensed seamen and longshoremen formed picket lines at seven in the morning. While seamen on two ships performed some work, crews of three English vessels refused to furnish steam and joined in the observance. San Pedro men did little work as the unions marked the day.

After being explicitly denied the holiday, San Francisco Local 38-79 voted to open the hiring hall and dispatch as usual, but until one o'clock no men could be found to send out. After that, according to employers, only a few men showed up—according to the union, plenty of men showed up. The unions put out a ceremonial picket line at the docks in the morning. At Steuart and Mission, where two longshoremen fell on July 5, they posted an honor guard from sunrise to sunset, and flowers banked the spot. In a spectacle reminiscent of the funeral, during the forenoon 25,000 workers marched up Market Street in a parade two miles long. In several ports huge mass meetings in the evening climaxed the day's events.

McCormick Steamship Company discharged Captain Salo, master of the *Charles L. Wheeler* for marching in the San Francisco July 5 parade. The crew struck in protest, joining members of the Masters, Mates and Pilots on the picket line. Four days later, with four more McCormick vessels tied up, the company denied firing the captain and offered to transfer him to the *Silverado*. Salo accepted, and the company paid the crew for the four days they picketed.

After thirty gangs had been blacklisted for refusing to work *Point Clear* cargo, the employers lifted the blacklist, and pickets remained on the vessel. Gregory reported that "it was originally planned to isolate San Francisco, but conditions have now changed and if we go ahead and precipitate trouble the whole coast would show a united front."[29] By then the ILA had declared British Columbia cargo unfair in the coastwide referendum, and all Maritime Federation district councils had voted to refuse the cargo. U.S. and foreign seamen supported the Vancouver longshoremen with various actions as the strike dragged on, and other Pacific Coast maritime workers aided the strikers with donations and assessments voted by their members.

Washington Conference

While the longshoremen boycotted British Columbia scab cargo and Northwest hot lumber, the September 30, 1935, expiration date of the award approached. The Waterfront Employers of Seattle, Portland, San Francisco, and Los Angeles notified the district ILA the end of July that they would renew the award for a year provided the ILA would guarantee that strikes, work stoppages, and violations would cease. The employers' continued clamor finally induced Assistant Secretary of Labor McGrady to summon maritime union representatives to Washington, D.C. to confer on the tie-ups. "Flour is rotting in the holds of the ships," he declared; "perishable goods are destroyed, newspaper publishing being curtailed account of the paper being held."

He had received 175 protests from businessmen and publishers on the Pacific Coast. The stoppages were "an intolerable situation and one which cannot be allowed to continue."[30]

The ILA district sent Paddy Morris from Washington, Cliff Thurston from Oregon, and Harry Bridges from California, uninstructed, to the August 5 conference. The Sailors' Union sent Harry Lundeberg, Carl Tillman, and Lee Barlow, and the Masters, Mates and Pilots sent Captains O.E. Rolstad and V. Westerholm. Lundeberg reported that the conference proved to be the severest test yet for the Maritime Federation. The shipowners hoped to split the organization by insisting on separate craft conferences and craft votes on British Columbia cargo. The federation stood out clearly as their main target, Lundeberg said: "Although the shipowners and their allies termed the Maritime Federation a 'superimposed outlaw' organization and 'not recognized,' the fact that they recognized the *POWER* of the Federation was evident in every conference held in Washington."[31] Forsaking their Pacific Coast unions, Victor Olander and Andrew Furuseth of the ISU joined the shipowners and Edward McGrady in demanding release of all vessels tied up on the Pacific Coast. Besides the *Point Clear*, they included the *Point Arena, West Mahwah, Point Ancha, Golden State*, and others, some idled because the unions could find no seamen willing to sign on for a voyage to British Columbia. McGrady pleaded with the delegates for over six hours to release the vessels, and the shipowners made renewal of the agreements contingent on their release. The delegates finally agreed to recommend a coastwide referendum on British Columbia cargo.

Frank Foisie reported to the Seattle Waterfront Employers that the Washington conference accomplished "very little," and he called for more protests to the federal government and chambers of commerce. The San Francisco Waterfront Employers said that the "radical element in all the marine unions seems to be very jubilant over the developments in Washington" because they had given McGrady the "run-around."[32] Twelve vessels lay idle on the coast.

San Francisco Local 38-79 complained periodically of outside pressure to remove its officers. In an open letter to Pacific Coast members August 2, the union expressed alarm at newspaper reports that the employers' offer to renew the agreement included "THE PROVISO THAT THE SAN FRANCISCO LOCAL LEADERSHIP BE REMOVED."[33] The letter urged all locals to support San Francisco's right to elect its own officers. After receiving several protest letters, Secretary Paddy Morris assured all locals August 21 that the district was "unanimously upholding" the right of a local union "to elect and retain the officers that its membership elects" and that "the right of local autonomy in such a matter has never been questioned." Reports to the contrary in the capitalist and anonymous press, he said, "are based upon ulterior motives to create suspicion and engender disruption in the solidarity of the organization." He chided the "sensation-mongers" in San Francisco: "This office does not believe that the building up of a straw man and then tumbling him over for the notoriety and effect such useless action may bring will result in any good to our organization."[34]

Both the ILA and Maritime Federation put out hot cargo ballots. The ILA turned down Federation President Lundeberg's plea to vote with the rest of the unions. ILA District President Bill Lewis threatened to prefer charges against any local voting the federation ballot: the ILA must act as a district, not as individual independent locals. He directed the threat against Local 38-79, which opposed the district officers at every opportunity. At this point the regular Powell River longshoremen, who belonged to the Vancouver and District Waterfront Workers' Association, informed the ILA that the casuals who worked only during peak periods, not they, had struck. An investigating committee from Northwest District Council No. 1 recommended terminating the boycott, as the strike could not be won.

The district ILA put two questions on the ballot: to remove the British Columbia hot cargo ban and to renew the agreement for a year. The district board recommended calling off the boycott because vessels worked by the Pacific Coast ILA handled only 2 percent of British Columbia commerce, too small an amount to help the strikers. The ban would be symbolic, not worth the risk of a strike. The members voted 8,468 to 1,329, 86.4 percent to renew the agreement. They sustained the hot cargo ban by a vote of 5,243 to 4,784, 52.3 percent. San Francisco voted 89.4 percent for the ban and Portland 63.9 percent. San Pedro voted against the ban 78.2 percent, Seattle 85.2 percent, and Tacoma 84.3 percent. In the Maritime Federation ballot the rest of the unions voted 18,448 to 961, 95 percent, to continue the Vancouver boycott.

The Washington, D.C., conference demonstrated that the federal government could not compel union members to handle hot cargo. Seeking other means to coerce their workers to obey, the shipowners turned to their uptown allies. Over 200 representatives of chambers of commerce and industrial associations from principal Pacific Coast port cities met in early September. Maritime workers interpreted the secret conclave, sponsored by the San Francisco Waterfront Employers, as a strategy session to smash their unions. The *Voice of the Federation* reported ominous speeches. Roger Lapham of the American-Hawaiian company feared that "we will be maneuvered into a position where you other business men will demand that we arbitrate. . . . The forces of union labor are increasing in power. This is particularly true along the Pacific waterfronts. Public opinion is essential if this tendency is to be checked."

Herman Phleger, counsel for the San Francisco Waterfront Employers, emphasized "our duty to try to build responsible unions. We have endeavored in the last year to encourage responsible union leadership . . . but our efforts in that direction are fruitless." Alfred Lundin, president of the Seattle Chamber of Commerce, warned: "Further progress of the maritime worker unions under their present leaders bodes disaster. The shipowners and commercial interests cannot win their fight without public support."[35] Following the conference the chambers of commerce of Seattle, Tacoma, Portland, Oakland, San Francisco, Los Angeles, and San Diego, and the Washington Industrial Council placed full-page ads in the daily press calling for strict observance of the awards. "Without it," the ad stated, "our Pacific Coast commerce will be destroyed and the extensive commercial and industrial interests we represent seriously damaged." The ad charged maritime workers with violating the awards in refusing to handle cargo and conniving with other unions to "dominate many lines of business and industry not directly concerned in maritime controversies, but whose products move by water." The employers' organizations pledged "THEMSELVES TO STAND TOGETHER IN SUPPORT OF THE PUBLIC INTEREST."[36]

Sloss Hot Cargo Decision

Two labor disputes in the San Francisco Bay area provided the shipowners with the means they sought to force the ILA to handle hot cargo. Dissatisfied with their representation, deckhands on barges and boats plying the Sacramento and San Joaquin rivers left the Ferryboatmen's Union and organized ILA Bargemen's locals at San Francisco and Stockton. About 800 men struck seventeen companies on July 2, 1935, for union recognition and improved wages and conditions. The Bargemen claimed that Clyde Deal, secretary of the Ferryboatmen, recruited scabs. River Lines, paying 27 cents an hour, operated the *M.S. Fort Sutter*, protected by armed guards. By mid-September all but three companies had settled with the Bargmen.

In the other dispute the Santa Cruz Packing Company in Oakland locked out fifty warehousemen on August 8 for joining ILA Local 38-44 and demanding union recognition. They made 30 cents an hour. Work continued with scabs guarded by armed detectives. Western Pacific train crews refused to cross the Warehousemen's picket line to shunt cars onto the company's siding, but Southern Pacific crews disregarded the strike. Members of San Francisco Local 38-79 refused to touch River Lines or Santa Cruz cargo.

Employers coastwide pledged support as the San Francisco Waterfront Employers prepared for a showdown with their longshoremen. In a special meeting of the Labor Relations Committee September 11 the employers demanded that longshoremen work Santa Cruz and River Lines cargo. Harry Bridges and other officials denied that the union boycotted the cargo: "the I.L.A. officials had tried to get the longshoremen to work them, but . . . the union was powerless to compel its members to work against their will."[37]

By prearrangement with the employers, on September 21 the River Lines' *Sutter* dumped cargo on twelve San Francisco docks, and Southern Pacific crews spotted cars of Santa Cruz freight on San Francisco piers and at three Oakland terminals. The longshoremen would not touch any of it. Tom Plant warned: "The men who refused to handle cargo of these companies have suspended themselves from further employment by us. We shall demand the registration of such additional men as may be necessary to insure normal movement of all cargo. . . . We will countenance no further violations."[38] The employers demanded Local 38-79 arbitrate the hot cargo tie-up. Hitherto the ILA had always refused to arbitrate the issue. Without consulting the district ILA, Bridges agreed. Prior to the hearing the Local 38-79 Labor Relations Committee met with District President Bill Lewis and labor consultant Henry P. Melnikow. Lewis later related:

> Inasmuch as the District Council No. 2 of the Maritime Federation had previously gone on record in favor of the Bargemen arbitrating their dispute, and the case of the

Santa Cruz Packing Co. was in the hands of the national labor board, I advised Brother Bridges not to arbitrate these issues but to go to the interested unions and have them release the cargo; and further advised him to go to Judge Sloss and refuse to arbitrate. But this advice was refused even though I told them that their action would undoubtedly involve the entire Pacific Coast.[39]

Judge Sloss heard the case September 23. Employers' counsel Herman Phleger tried to trap Lewis into admitting that a strike was in effect:

Phleger: Do you take the position that the membership of the I.L.A. on this coast will handle British Columbia cargo?
Lewis: We never instructed them otherwise.
Phleger: In other words the embargo resulting from the referendum vote is withdrawn, is it?
Lewis: The vote was not taken to place any embargo on Vancouver cargo. It was just to find out how the membership stood on that particular issue.[40]

During the hearing the longshoremen demanded that the employers abide by the May 6, 1935, decision of Judge Sloss awarding overtime pay for work performed between 3:00 and 5:00 p.m. The employers replied that the longshoremen could have their money when they filed individual claims for it. Back pay for the 12,000 longshoremen on the coast amounted to about $500,000. The employers announced that hereafter they would insist on the six-hour day instead of paying overtime for the two extra hours. This would mean registering an additional 1,100 longshoremen and reducing average earnings by 25 percent. The union objected both to the employers' demand for individual claims and their plan to limit gangs to six hours. While the port waited for the referee's ruling, the Waterfront Employers blacklisted 1,300 longshoremen for refusing to handle hot cargo. They removed the list of registered men from the joint hall to their office in the Matson Building so they could pick and choose whom to blacklist.

Judge Sloss ruled September 27 that the refusal of members of Local 38-79 to handle British Columbia cargo amounted to a sympathetic strike and a violation of the award. He stated that the longshoremen's concerted refusal "goes far beyond the exercise by individuals of their personal right to accept or refuse jobs," and violated the award. He dismissed the longshoremen's argument that picket lines and armed guards constituted unsafe working conditions: "I am satisfied that the real ground and basis for the refusal to work was the unwillingness to handle 'hot cargo,' and not the presence of the picket lines."[41] The referee declined to rule on whether a longshoreman violating the award forfeited his right to be employed, but he agreed that the employer could require registration of additional men if ILA members refused to handle hot cargo.

The employers were jubilant. Harry Bridges had promised officially that his union would abide by the decision. Therefore, he must compel his members to handle the hot cargo. Stalling for time, the district ILA demanded a rehearing. Judge Sloss refused. The employers offered to reinstate the 1,400 blacklisted longshoremen if they would work ALL cargo as directed. Seventeen ships lay idle, with others unable to unload and a few ready to sail partially loaded. The *Chronicle* predicted that longshoremen would continue to boycott scab cargo.

Effects of the Sloss Award

The *Waterfront Worker* roundly condemned the Sloss decision. "He would send us back to the Blue Book and the Fink Hall! HE WOULD MAKE SCABS OF US ALL! . . . DON'T HANDLE HOT CARGO! PREPARE TO MEET THE SHIPOWNERS' ATTACK IN A MILITANT MANNER!"[42] However, instead of meeting the shipowners' attack "in a militant manner" and being provoked into a strike, the unions made haste to get rid of the hot cargo by having it declared fair.

By September 28, the employers had tied up twenty-nine ships and blacklisted 1,640 longshoremen. That afternoon the executive committee of Federation District Council No. 2 recommended that the Bargemen and Warehousemen lift their boycotts while they negotiated settlements. Federal mediators handled the River Lines dispute, and the regional labor board investigated the Santa Cruz lockout. The unions agreed, thus releasing all vessels except the *Point Clear.* The district ILA held that only a membership referendum could lift the boycott.

The employers refused to end their blacklist until longshoremen agreed to work the *Point Clear*. By October 4, thirty-four of the forty-nine ships in port where tied up. With pickets gone, union firemen went aboard the *Point Clear*, but no longshoremen appeared. In retaliation against the blacklist, the union enforced the 120-hours-a-month work limit. To alleviate the shortage of longshoremen the employers threatened to register additional men regardless of union affiliation. Bridges warned that this action might precipitate a strike. The executive committee of District Council No. 2 voted October 5 to "request the ILA District Board to take a vote on Vancouver cargo and that pending the ballot we work the BC cargo if it becomes necessary to avert a strike."[43]

In an "extra" the next day the *Voice of the Federation* accused the shipowners of deliberately trying to provoke the maritime unions into a strike to smash them and of lying to the public that the unions had caused the port lockout and bankrupted Pacific Steamship Company. Harry Lundeberg declared that the maritime workers did not want trouble, but they did not intend to "be forced back into the slavery conditions under which they worked prior to the 1934 strike, which is the evident objective of the shipowners."[44]

In accordance with Judge Sloss's ruling October 6 that they violated the award, the employers lifted the blacklist. The next day the British Columbia strikers released their hot cargo, and October 8 San Francisco longshoremen resumed work on all vessels without regard for the 120-hour limit. As the waterfront returned to normal, the employers could claim a victory in forcing the longshoremen to abandon their support of the British Columbia strikers. Acknowledging defeat, the Canadians called off their strike December 9 and went back to work open shop.

The Sloss decision outraged the district ILA. In a front-page article in the *Pacific Coast Longshoreman*, Paddy Morris declared that the ruling was "loaded with dynamite for our organization." Citing the possibility that the decision could force union members to act as strikebreakers against sister locals, he asserted: "We like to live in peace and satisfaction with employers. But there is a point where peace is more deadly than struggle." The district could not be expected to jettison its principles of solidarity and cooperation with "a great federation of workers" to preserve agreements. "The employers cannot expect it. Our membership would not intend it. And our organization cannot countenance it. . . . But whether employers are agreeable or not, labor's first duty is to labor, and when that duty is challenged, that challenge should not be ignored." In an editorial on "Hot Cargo" the paper declared:

> There are some matters which strictly are not arbitrable, and in our estimation, succor and support for sister locals in the association . . . is, in reality, one of them.
>
> The very unity of the Pacific coast district organization depends upon that and no local should assume responsibility for arbitrating any question of the sort. . . .
>
> There are some things of more importance than awards or agreements and that is the defense of our organization and its co-operation with the rest of the labor movement.[45]

Ole Oleson of the Sailors' Union asserted that the Sloss decision "was no more than we had a right to expect . . . from a man who holds his office by the grace of big business." He declared: "It was a mistake in the first place to go to their boards with proposals of any kind. We should never have put ourselves in the equivocal position of discussing the issue at all. We should have simply said, as becomes good union men, 'We will not under any circumstances consider working hot cargo of any kind or from any where.'"[46] Harry Lundeberg warned that release of the British Columbia cargo settled nothing: "If union men are to be forced by the employers into working 'hot cargo' it will only be a matter of time before the Maritime Unions on the Pacific Coast will be beaten into subjection and broken."[47]

San Francisco employers' success with the port lockout encouraged the Seattle Waterfront Employers to embark on a similar program against Local 38-12. After O.D. Fisher refused to negotiate an agreement, ILA Warehousemen's Local 38-117 and Federal Local 19169 covering the inside workers voted 5 to 1 to strike his flour mill. The 300 employees struck October 3, 1935, when the mill signed an agreement with a company union. The Seattle Central Labor Council put Fisher products on the unfair list, and union supporters persuaded grocers to cover up their Fisher flour. Union employees in bakeries and restaurants also rejected the flour. For eight months longshoremen had been refusing to load ships at the Fisher dock, where warehousemen received only 55 cents; now they boycotted the flour completely. Seattle Waterfront Employers prepared to force their longshoremen to handle the hot flour or face a port blacklist. O.D. Fisher agreed to cooperate, and Frank Foisie and the San Francisco policy committee approved the plan.

By the end of October the employers had spotted fourteen freight cars of scab flour on as many commercial docks. They had flour shipments booked on American-Hawaiian, Luckenbach, Calmar, McCormick, Gulf Pacific, Nelson, Pacific Steamship,

Alaska Steamship, Northland, and Matson vessels. All dock workers, once ordered, would be assigned to work hot flour and then discharged; none could be released and later employed on another job. The program started November 1. The first day the employers discharged ninety-two dock workers. The Seattle Port Commission declined to lock out workers on its docks, and Pacific Steamship Company did not comply with the blacklist. The longshoremen charged a port conspiracy to reduce dock wages to 55 cents. Over the ILA's protests that they had not been given a fair hearing, Arbitrator Harry Hazel ruled November 12 that refusal to handle hot cargo violated the award.

The program did not work as it had in San Francisco. Although 818 men had been discharged by the end of November, the Seattle longshoremen showed no signs of abandoning the Fisher strikers. Union dispatchers, who still controlled the hiring hall, would not send men to docks just to be discharged for refusing to touch Fisher flour. Contrary to employers' orders, the dispatchers sent out blacklisted men. At the Luckenbach dock on Sunday morning, December 8, the employer refused to accept three discharged men. Thereupon, all five gangs quit. The Waterfront Employers met the next day. "It was emphasized that either the attempt to force the handling of 'hot cargo' must be abandoned or all lines must stand together and be prepared not to call I.L.A. men for work as long as one company is unable to get men from the hall without employing men already discharged." The meeting recommended to the San Francisco policy committee "that unless all lines having Fisher flour agree to tie up their ships if, or as long as, one line is unable to get men, the 'hot cargo' program be called off on Wednesday morning."[48]

The employers abandoned the blacklist and returned the cars of stale flour to the mill. In late January the two unions won recognition and later union agreements with Fisher Flouring Mills. Of the 300 employees who struck, only four returned to work during the sixteen-week strike. Moreover, the Seattle longshoremen had ignored the arbitrator's decision and upheld the principle that the question of working hot cargo could not be arbitrated or in any way compromised.

12

Testing the Federation

Adhering to the principle that "An injury to one is an injury to all," Pacific Coast maritime workers, and particularly unlicensed seamen, greatly improved their working and living conditions with job actions during 1935. The principle required mutual cooperation and sacrifice to succeed. The craft that tied up a vessel expected and received support from other crafts. The workers usually gained their point because employers chose to yield on a specific issue to keep their ships sailing and cargo moving.

The hot cargo ban depended similarly on cooperation to support other union people. Declaring the *Point Clear* and British Columbia cargo fair did not mean repudiating the principle of refusing to touch scab cargo. After Judge Sloss's harsh decision instructing longshoremen to work hot cargo, both the district ILA and members of the Sailors' Union proclaimed defiantly that regardless of agreements and arbitrations union people would not scab on each other. The debate over the right of one craft to decide unilaterally on policies of job action and hot cargo without consulting other crafts would bring together delegates from affiliated unions in an emergency convention of the Maritime Federation.

Sailors' Union Job Action

All the awards and agreements expired on the same date, September 30, 1935, in the midst of the hot cargo confrontation. The Longshoremen renewed the award, which became an agreement, for a year without changes, but the marine unions wanted to negotiate improvements in their wages and working conditions. The unlicensed seamen asked a six-hour day in port and shipping through the union hall for all departments, a guarantee that no member of a crew would be required to go through or work behind a picket line, and ten holidays, including Bloody Thursday. Instead of time back they demanded cash overtime and pay equal to that of longshoremen when working cargo. On board each vessel they wanted a radio operator and adequate sanitary facilities. The Radio Telegraphists asked for a wage increase and a picket line clause, and the licensed officers wanted to negotiate improvements in their agreements. Neither the offshore companies nor the steam schooner operators would concede anything.

"SAILORS DENIED COLLECTIVE BARGAINING," The *Voice of the Federation* proclaimed in a banner head October 17. "Embittered toward all forms of negotiating . . . by the deliberate stalling on the part of the shipowners . . . the seamen have turned their back on 'negotiations' in favor of 'job action,'"[1] the paper reported.

The Sailors' Union would demand $1.00 an hour for working cargo after 5:00 p.m., Sundays and holidays, and when shifting ship in port during those hours. Shipowners paid 70 cents overtime. Maritime Federation President Harry Lundeberg declared that the labor relations board had done nothing for the seamen, and the Sailors' Union would continue to refuse arbitration "until such time as the shipowners see fit to deal with us collectively." He cited the gains through job action:

> The living and eating quarters of the seamen are as a rule in terrible condition, poor heating and ventilation systems, rotten sleeping quarters, messrooms so small that men must wait in turn for another to eat. This condition and many others exist on most of the ships. The only way these conditions were remedied was by the action of the men themselves refusing to live and work under such conditions.[2]

Reflecting Communist policy, the *Voice of the Federation* editorially condemned "indiscriminate, unorganized or unjustifiable job action,"[3] and the *Waterfront Worker* asserted that the Sailors patrolmen played into the shipowners' hands by initiating job actions. In a special meeting, "primed," according to Lundeberg, the Sailors' Union voted to refer job action to an emergency convention of the Maritime Federation called for mid-November. The editorial and postponement touched off a storm of protest among seamen. In rank-and-file letters they defended their "right to take *job action* when they see fit." Harry Lundeberg declared that those who advocated committees and conferences "are people who are trying their damndest to kill the seamen's strongest weapon. . . . THE MEN ON THE SHIPS ARE CAPABLE OF PICKING THE RIGHT TIME AND PLACE. . . . Those who want to supervise are loyal to the principle of defeatism."[4] Similar protests came from Seattle and Portland.

The *Waterfront Worker* recommended "that these 'direct actionists,' who are inspiring STRIKE actions under the guise of JOB action, that they wake up and recognize the UNANIMOUS sentiment of the Rank and File, who are AGAINST such PREMATURE STRIKE ACTION, BUT WHO ARE, AS ARE WE, HEARTILY IN FAVOR OF WELL-PLANNED, CLEVER JOB ACTION." In a cartoon labeled "Direct Actionists," a worker rummaged in an overturned garbage can, while a Wobbly rushed up, exclaiming, "Let me at it."[5]

About the time that members of San Francisco Local 38-79 hoisted scab cargo from the hold of the *Point Clear*, the *Katrina Luckenbach*, loaded by scab longshoremen, steamed out of New Orleans headed for the Pacific Coast. East Gulf ILA ports struck October 1 for a wage increase, joined by the West Gulf in sympathy October 11. Paddy Morris wired the strikers that Pacific Coast longshoremen "will refuse to handle any cargo loaded by scabs on the Gulf Coast regardless of the award."[6] The Sailors' Union instructed members to support the strike and refuse to work or sail behind picket lines. Crews that quit in Gulf ports in support of the ILA strikers formed a West Coast Seamen's Committee, and the Sailors' Union donated $20.00 a week to the strikers.

The Pacific Coast District on November 1 instructed all locals to refuse to handle scab cargo from Gulf ports. Accordingly, when the *Katrina Luckenbach* arrived in San

Pedro the next day, Local 38-82 tied her up. Tom Plant termed the action "open defiance" of the recent Sloss award. The *Matthew Luckenbach* soon joined the *Katrina.* San Pedro longshoremen steadfastly refused to work hot vessels from the Gulf. With a growing fleet tied up there, the San Francisco Waterfront Employers appealed to Secretary of Labor Perkins to make the unions live up to their agreements.

The *Daily Commercial News* called the labor secretary's reply that the federal government had no power to enforce agreements "a frank admission of the futility of government arbitration as a means of settling industrial disputes. . . . [It] is a sad commentary on the attitude of the administration, and it must remove any hope anyone may have held that the government, which forced arbitration on the maritime industry last year, through the government-appointed board, will be of any assistance in clearing up the intolerable situation that now exists."[7]

Disregarding an international convention mandate, President Joe Ryan refused to order East Coast longshoremen to boycott Gulf hot cargo. Without support from Atlantic Coast ports, the East Gulf strike failed. In late November, with a federal mediation board undertaking to settle the East Gulf strike, the Pacific District ILA released the Luckenbach vessels at Ryan's request. Unbeknownst to the Pacific Coast District, Ryan did not consult the Gulf strikers. The San Pedro local worked the *Katrina* November 28; the Sailors' Union shipped a new crew, and the vessel proceeded to San Francisco. After the East Gulf strikers protested the release of any Gulf vessels, the district renewed the ban December 3. With East Gulf ports working while mediation proceeded, the district ILA and East Gulf Strike Committee released all vessels tied up on the Pacific Coast on December 9, and the West Gulf strike ended December 12. California longshoremen had made good Paddy Morris's defiant words that the ILA would not touch hot cargo regardless of awards.

Maritime Federation Emergency Convention

Communist jitters over Gulf hot cargo headed for the Pacific Coast and the Sailors' job action prompted Federation District Council No. 2's resolution October 7 to call an emergency convention. Citing the coastwide employers' "carefully planned attempt to disrupt and destroy the various Maritime Unions . . . also the Federation itself," and the "individual opinions and actions that have . . . served in part to disorganize [the federation's] unity of purpose," the council called for the convention in San Francisco.[8] For reasons that are not recorded, Seattle, Tacoma, and most other Washington and Columbia River ILA locals did not send delegates, and the *Pacific Coast Longshoreman* ignored the convention. Perhaps they did not want to debate the unofficial hot cargo boycott in Seattle against Fisher flour, or perhaps they chose not to become involved in the confrontation between the Communists and the Sailors' Union over job action. For whatever reason, the anti-Communist ILA bloc stayed away.

Meanwhile an angry bloc of seamen formed, led by the Sailors' Union, who did not want the Communist Party telling them what to do on their steam schooners. Aside from idealogical groupings, the fundamental question lay rooted in the very nature of the Maritime Federation: "Who decides the extent that a union must jeopardize its members to support another union?" Debate during the twelve-day convention that opened November 12 centered on this question of mutual support as related to Gulf hot cargo and steam schooner job action.

Local 38-79 introduced a resolution supporting the ILA in refusing to handle Gulf hot cargo, calling for a federation referendum on the ban, and pledging that the federation "will stand ready to take further action in support of the Gulf strike." The resolution as passed, amended by Sailors' Union delegates, provided "That in the event a serious situation develops in any Port . . . due to the refusal of any component organization . . . to handle or transport any cargo TO AND/OR FROM any Gulf Ports," the federation would immediately take a vote to determine whether the federation would strike in support of the locked-out union.[9]

Late in the convention Harry Bridges introduced a resolution defining job action as action attempting to gain new concessions or enforce an award or agreement, but excluding "action taken for demands such as increases in wages, shorter hours, etc., where such things are distinctly covered by the wording of an agreement or an award." The exclusion hit directly at the Sailors' Union steam schooner action. The resolution called for consultation with other affected unions, a majority decision "as to what extent the job action be prosecuted or continued," and immediate discontinuance when the action threatened to "provoke a strike or lockout."[10] In other words, the union initiating the action would be powerless to make decisions.

The Sailors' Union replied the next day with a minority resolution, "That when job action is considered necessary, and is taken in an organized manner, after proper consultation with other workers on the job who would be affected that we go on record as recognizing the rights of Maritime workers of any organization to use job action when it is deemed necessary and is done in an organized manner."[11] After a hot debate the convention voted down the minority resolution 81.14 to 69.79. The unlicensed seamen, except Earl King, who abstained, and another marine fireman, the Masters, Mates and Pilots, and part of the Marine Engineers voted for the resolution. The ILA delegates in a bloc, the San Francisco Machinists, the Radio Telegraphists, one fireman, and the majority of Marine Engineers voted against the resolution. The Alaska Fishermen abstained, probably because they felt too much pressure from the unlicensed seamen to vote against them. Aside from the Marine Engineers, who simply didn't like sailors tying up ships, the delegates voted on ideological lines. The convention adopted a compromise resolution that eliminated the exclusion of demands covered by an award, but retained committee consultation and majority decision-making.

On paper the Communist bloc won a victory in circumscribing job action, but two months later the steam schooner sailors resumed their campaign. Perhaps the most lasting result of the convention would be the emergence of a bloc of young, militant anti-Communist seamen, some of them Wobblies or ex-Wobblies. Communist attacks on Harry Lundeberg and the San Francisco patrolmen solidified the group. An editorial in the *Western Worker* during the convention proclaimed, "We need Maritime Unity—Not Beef Squads," and charged that in a union meeting Lundeberg threatened "open violence against those who do not agree with his rather individualistic policy." Lundeberg replied that he conducted the meeting in question properly and asserted: "It is this handful of so-called sailors who are the ones that are trying to thwart the wishes of the rank and file of the men on the ships, and ram down their throats by hook or by crook their own ideas relative to arbitration."[12]

Ideological War

Usually the *Pacific Coast Longshoreman* ignored the *Waterfront Worker's* attacks and innuendoes, but when the paper called union activist Fred West a "labor faker" and questioned his role in helping to organize San Francisco in 1933, Paddy Morris blasted the paper. The article implied that West wanted "easy work so he would be called a Stevedore" and that Lee Holman finally "paid him off" for a rumored $50.00. Answering the attack in the San Francisco Labor Council's *Labor Clarion*, West stated that at the request of some active stevedores he spoke on the waterfront for about fifteen days during the organizing campaign, always making clear that he was not a longshoreman. Some days he received $1.50 for meals—nothing more. Paddy Morris printed the *Waterfront Worker* attack and West's answer in the *Pacific Coast Longshoreman* December 2 with the headline: "Scurrilous Sheet Protects Its Writers by Anonymity While Doing Stool Pigeon's Work – Rats Try To Undermine Solidarity By Baseless Attacks On Fellow Workers." He accused the "anonymous vermin who are trying to create disruption and strife within the ranks of organized labor by the publication of the Waterfront Worker, week after week," of "doing the bosses' dirty work whether paid for it or not."[13]

The *Waterfront Worker* replied that Morris made "a desperate effort to clear himself of the proven charges made against him . . . in our past issues." The article answered charges of "mud-slinging" and a suggestion that it consolidate with the *Voice of the Federation*. The *Voice*, "being the OFFICIAL organ of the Maritime Federation . . . cannot say many of the things which the WATERFRONT WORKER can say—and which *must* be said." In other words, the *Voice* could not print the anonymous accusations and innuendoes that appeared in the *Worker*. The paper defended "our so-called 'mud slinging'—we are mighty proud to have been able to expose before the eyes of the West Coast maritime workers the activities of such labor-fakers and misleaders as Joe Ryan, Burglar Lewis, Pedro Pete, and—yes—even Paddy Morris." The paper used the derogatory name for Bill Lewis after discovering a youthful brush with the law. The *Waterfront Worker* defended anonymity as necessary to protect its writers and correspondents from being "victimized by the shipowners just as attempts are always made to 'get rid' of militants."[14]

Another acrimonious exchange occurred in the *Pacific Coast Longshoreman* after Paddy Morris ridiculed District Council No. 2's demand for a congressional investigation of the shipowners' plot to destroy the maritime unions. He warned that "such appeals" could result in "a greater government control of employment. . . . And we want less, not more, government interference with our hiring halls."[15] In reply Henry Schmidt, San Francisco Local 38-79 Publicity Committee, chided the ILA paper for joining "the shipowners in making derogatory remarks about our Local officials."[16] Walter Freer of Tacoma Local 38-97 pursued the debate in the *Pacific Coast Longshoreman* with the assertion that Harry Bridges proposed the congressional investigation for "propaganda to boost [his] badly depreciated stock." Freer wrote:

> Bridges is hungry for the district presidency. His attempts to build a reputation for himself have been flat and dismal failures. He arbitrated hot cargo in utter defiance of the district; . . . If Bridges had consulted the district thru its officers as he should have done, he would have been flatly forbidden to arbitrate. To scab or not to scab cannot be arbitrated by union men. Furthermore, anyone with brains enough to last him over night, would know what the award inevitably would be. If he claims he had authority from his local union, the answer is, no local has any such power. The immediate consequence up here was that Examiner Hazel handed down an order based on the Sloss award, without the formality of arbitration that we had to work Fisher's flour. We ignored the order and won the strike; but the order would not have been served on us had Bridges not set himself up as bigger than the district and been hit over the head with an order to work hot cargo.
>
> Bridges nearly broke his neck getting the embargo lifted on British Columbia cargo . . . The northwest was involved ten times as much as Frisco in the British Columbia strike; yet we did not squawk, though we knew the strike was lost in July. . . . We sent ship after ship back across the Pacific with British Columbia cargo untouched during the six months of the strike. We refused to handle cargo at Fisher's mill for ten months and refused to handle it anywhere during the duration of the Fisher strike. We kept lumber tied up during the three months lumber strike . . .[17]

Harry Bridges himself answered Morris and Freer, charging the district officials created a "smoke screen" to "conceal their own questionable actions and shortcomings" as the district convention and election approached. He accused them of protecting Joe Ryan's reputation during the Gulf strike and hinted that the district's opposition to an investigation might be explained by fear of exposing the officials' nefarious, under-handed schemes. Bridges stated: "The entire membership of the Frisco local still has the minutes with the resolution where Paddy Morris tried to send us back to work with the scab sailors during the 1934 strike." Morris called this statement "a lie out of whole cloth, and known as such to Bridges and his friends, . . . unless some of these authors have since added forgery to their accomplishments as panic stricken liars."[18] Thus the Communist bloc and the anti-Communist veterans sparred to present the record.

Employers' Suspension Program

Although the employers had forced the San Francisco longshoremen to retreat on British Columbia hot cargo, they still contended with a belligerent work force not in the least cowed or obedient. Gregory Harrison, attorney for the San Francisco Waterfront Employers, told the Pacific Traffic Association in November that "unless shippers resist the Maritime Federation, the maritime unions will have a strangle hold on the transportation facilities of the country."[19] The Board of Directors of the

Waterfront Employers meeting December 9 adopted a suspension program that, according to President Thomas G. Plant, called for "suspension of agreements with the I.L.A. for violations of the Award; employers would continue to operate under the provisions of the Award and pay the same wages and grant the same conditions but would hire the men at the docks and relations with the I.L.A. would not be resumed until the violations were corrected or removed."[20]

The employers anticipated that the program would precipitate a longshoremen's strike, and for their success in this battle they needed the support of shippers and business interests in all the Pacific Coast ports. The minutes described Plant's reasoning:

> The time has arrived when it was necessary to have a show-down with the Maritime Unions . . . that there could be no hope of a strike by the I.L.A. as that was not its strategy; that they would continue the quickie strikes, job action and guerilla warfare until the employers had no resistance left . . . that the Maritime Federation has now extended their influence to the Gulf and Atlantic, and that . . . if Mr. Bridges gets a foothold in the East it would be disastrous to the shipping industry.[21]

Elisha Hansen, chief attorney for the shipowners in Washington, D.C., demanded that the federal government prosecute the Maritime Federation as an illegal conspiracy. Louis Stark, *New York Times* labor editor, reported December 31 that "if the government refuses to declare the maritime unions on the Pacific Coast an illegal conspiracy, that there is organized a strong vigilante organization, strong enough and ready to protect the interests of the shipping companies."[22]

Early in January John F. Forbes, president of the San Francisco Industrial Association, called another coastwide meeting of representatives of chambers of commerce, employers' associations, and shipping interests, to gain support for the suspension program. He told the participants: "During the last couple of years we on the Pacific Coast have just taken one hell of a beating. We have got it good and hard up and down the coast everywhere. We have seen these people take one unit after another, and we have sat back and haven't done very much about it."

With job action resumed on the steam schooners, Forbes declared that the power of the Maritime Federation "is so evident that right at the moment nobody can ship any lumber up and down the Pacific Coast; and it seems unless the condition is corrected, that the lumber mills will have to close down." The meeting approved the suspension program "in principle," and business people in other ports subsequently consented "to a surcharge being put on freight to carry the cost of the fight."[23]

The suspension program would cover all shipping lines, including three intercoastal companies that dealt with the East Coast ILA. The Waterfront Employers secured their approval, provided the East Coast ILA received a preferential agreement and the suspension applied only to San Francisco. The "Atlantic and Pacific Lines were now in agreement on the suspension program and that the shipping interests were prepared to move ahead when the opportunity presents itself."[24] Thus the employers set the trap to destroy San Francisco Local 38-79.

District Council No. 2 warned January 22 that the "shipowners and their allies" would soon make a "broad attack" on the federation and its affiliated unions. The program included a press attack and organization of vigilantes "to help the employers carry through their program." Claiming constant violations, the employers would be "forced to suspend awards and agreements until 'responsible' authority is established in the unions and the 'irresponsible' and 'Communistic' elements are removed."[25] The Pacific Coast District prepared to defend Local 38-79. About a week later Joe Ryan notified District President Bill Lewis that he wanted to revoke the San Francisco charter. Lewis replied "that any attempt to take the charter away from the Pacific Coast would be fought to the bitter end. It was a shipowners' policy, and we would fight it to the last ditch. I also told him as far as the Pacific Coast District was concerned that they were able to handle themselves."[26]

Sailors Union Charter Revoked

By mid-1935 the officers of the International Seamen's Union made plans to discipline their defiant Pacific District unions, which belonged to an unauthorized organization, the Maritime Federation. These district unions tried to eliminate the international from their collective bargaining arrangements. The Sailors' Union led the rebellion: it refused to reinstate Paul Scharrenberg's membership and persisted in giving books to former members of the Marine Workers Industrial Union. Pacific Coast shipowners saw here a possible opportunity to split the seamen, similar to their efforts with the longshoremen. Frank Foisie testified before the Senate LaFollette committee that as early as July 1935 the employers wrote to ISU officials as "part of a working understanding leading toward the revocation of the Communist controlled marine union; a program similar to that of the International Longshoremen's Association."[27]

Rumors of the threat to revoke the Sailors' Union charter circulated on the San Francisco waterfront. The end of December the ISU announced the opening of an office in San Francisco "to safeguard the interests of the international union." Harry Lundeberg warned that the action was "probably a move to be ready to LIFT THE CHARTER of the Sailors' Union of the Pacific."[28] Meanwhile, in a resolution signed by 300 men and passed December 16, 1935, the steam schooner sailors demanded a six-hour day in port. Instead of negotiating, the shipowners tied up their vessels when crews refused to work over six hours. Lundeberg described events in a letter to SUP activist Bob Dombroff January 22, 1936: "The shipowners tied the steam-schooners up for lack of business, they said they didn't lock the men out, the Sailors didn't strike. . . . The steamschooner situation is ready to break anytime now . . . The only thing that holds it back right now is the shipowners are waiting for the I.S.U. Convention to yank the West Coast charter."[29] A few operators agreed to six hours; by February 3, sixty-seven vessels lay idle, officially for lack of business.

The first ISU convention since 1930 opened in Washington, D.C. on January 13, 1936. The Pacific Coast Marine Firemen sent six delegates, the Marine Cooks and Stewards three, and the Sailors' Union sent Ed Coester of Portland and Al Quittenton of San Pedro. The Alaska Fishermen had a delegate, and Clyde W. Deal represented the Ferryboatmen's Union. The rest of the districts around the nation outvoted the Pacific Coast almost two to one. The delegates concurred in Secretary Victor Olander's condemnation of the Maritime Federation because it violated the rules of the international and the AFL by providing a method to initiate and end strikes. Therefore, the convention directed the Pacific District unions "to immediately sever their connection" with the federation.[30] The next day pickets appeared at the ISU office in San Francisco. In place of the outlawed federation the convention proposed a National Maritime Labor Council composed of chief executives of the Masters, Mates and Pilots, Marine Engineers' Beneficial Association, and International Seamen's Union. The delegates tabled most of the West Coast resolutions, including one protesting the proposed continuous service book in the antilabor Copeland bill and upholding the union hiring hall.

As anticipated, the convention expelled the Sailors' Union on January 27 for taking in members of a dual organization, violating awards and agreements, and refusing to reinstate Paul Scharrenberg. The ISU also charged that headquarters elected a chair from the floor and the union loaned $5,000 to the Modesto Defense Committee. The delegates voted 292 to 186, the entire West Coast, to expel the Sailors and "organize the loyal members into a District Union."[31] On this issue alone Clyde Deal, subsequently elected sixth vice-president, supported the Sailors' Union; otherwise he voted with the international officers. The next day the ISU obtained a restraining order in federal court tying up all Sailors' Union funds. The union denied violating awards and agreements and charged the shipowners with refusing to bargain. As for taking in members of a dual organization, the Sailors' Union required MWIU members to renounce their allegiance to that union and its principles and destroy their books before accepting them.

Expulsion of the Sailors' Union enabled the ISU officers to achieve their principal objective: the authority to rule the union without democratic constraints or challenges by their members. Without the 57 votes of the expelled union, the ISU officers had the two-thirds majority necessary to amend the international constitution. The amendments, which gave the international executive board and secretary-treasurer unlimited power over the district unions and their members, became effective without approval of the membership.

In the midst of this crisis the Pacific District unions elected new officers, with mixed results. For secretary-treasurer of the Sailors' Union Harry Lundeberg defeated Herbert Mills, the Communist bloc candidate, by a vote of 1,496 to 466, 76 percent, but Albert Quittenton, Communist choice, defeated Robert Stowell for assistant secretary 1,217 to 573. Lundeberg took office February 3. The Marine Firemen elected Communist bloc candidate Earl King secretary-treasurer by a two to one vote, and the Marine Cooks and Stewards reelected veteran Eugene Burke secretary-treasurer. Burke accommodated himself to the Communists as they gained influence in the union.

Seamen rallied immediately to support the outlawed Sailors' Union. With 1,000 present at the regular headquarters meeting January 27, the day they lost their charter, the members voted to operate as the "American Seamen's Union" to keep their hall open. The Seattle branch protested that the new name established a dual union. Three days later in special meetings along the coast the union voted to print cards pledging members "to fight to keep the charter of the S.U.P. and to uphold its present constitution in the A.F. of L. and to resist any and all attempts by certain officials of the I.S.U. or others to reorganize our union or take away our fundamental democratic rights as union men."[32] This action ended the new name. Within a week 3,400 members signed the pledge cards. A mass meeting of unlicensed seamen at San Francisco resolved to create emergency committees of the three crafts in each port, and the Marine Firemen and Marine Cooks and Stewards resolved to mobilize support for the Sailors' Union throughout the labor movement.

The National Organization of Masters, Mates and Pilots also interfered in the internal affairs of Local 90. District Council No. 2 adopted an ambiguous statement January 28 by Harry Bridges calling for "cool thinking and cool action." He charged that internationals plotted to split the Maritime Federation:

> The basic reason for withdrawal of the Sailors' Charter and attack on the Masters, Mates and Pilots, is to split these unions with the hope that the other unions will take sides, . . . and with the fervent wish that the other unions will take the side of the expelled unions, and therefore open the way for the lifting of more charters and splitting of all maritime unions.
>
> It should be clear that our course should be opposite. . . . The Maritime Federation cannot support any union or group that advocates, First, setting up an independent dual group outside of a national or international organization. Second, it cannot support any group that is now in and advocates withdrawal from the American Federation of Labor. . . . The fight must be to remain in the international and the American Federation of Labor through abiding by the International Constitution and carrying on the fight by contesting the constitutionality and legality of any expulsion through legal methods.[33]

The *Waterfront Worker* spoke more plainly. Sketching a scenario of a reorganized union of loyal members with job control, the *Worker* urged sailors to join the new union instead of boycotting it: "If a new 'legal' S.U. of P. is set up and is boycotted, this would be turning the whole apparatus over to FINKS! But if 6,800 militant, determined Rank and File members are prepared to go along with the Charter, then the International will think twice before it serves the Sailors' with the formal notification of revocation."[34] The Sailors' Union disregarded this gratuitous advice. Some members believed the Communist Party advocated following the charter with the hope of capturing the union. They reasoned that the ISU officials and shipowners would expel and blacklist Harry Lundeberg and other militant activists. With these adamant anti-Communists out of the way, the Party would have a better chance to capture the union.

The Sailors' Union requested all labor bodies, the Maritime Federation and its affiliates to "take a position against employment of seamen from any other source than the union hall of the SUP."[35] Northwest District Council No. 1 and William

Fischer, who succeeded Harry Lundeberg as federation president, immediately concurred, and President Bill Lewis stated that "the ILA District would recognize no other union than the men who fought with them in 1934 on the picket lines."[36] Bay Area District Council No. 2 tabled the request. In obedience to ISU orders, the Marine Firemen, Marine Cooks and Stewards, and Alaska Fishermen withdrew from the Maritime Federation. The *Pacific Coast Longshoreman* asserted that solidarity did not depend on formal organization and urged maritime workers to remain united in purpose even if some of them had to leave the federation.

Recognizing that it could not fight on all fronts at once, the Sailors' Union voted February 3 to return to work on the steam schooners with an eight-hour day. The operators refused to call the hall for men, claiming they dealt with the ISU. International Secretary Victor Olander urged that "the ships be put into operation," continuing:

> I am firmly convinced that the men who actually go to sea have not been responsible for the chaotic condition which has prevailed on the Pacific coast in recent months. They have been misled and misinformed and their affairs have been miserably mishandled by incompetent officials and committees who have acted as puppets under the manipulation of political extremists unknown to the membership of the union.[37]

The operators stated they would ship men only from the docks—the sailors remained in the union hall. After two days the shipowners called the hall for men and the union furnished crews. The Sailors claimed victory in the organized return to work, "and there is no doubt that had it not been for the action of the International in linking hands openly with the shipowners we would have won out in our fight."[38]

The federal court dissolved the temporary restraining order against the Sailors Union February 5 and denied a further injunction sought by the ISU. Then the international tied up SUP funds in four banks, leaving the union "without a penny to operate on" or pay the phone bill for the dispatching office. Nor could the union use dues money collected on the old union books. To provide funds for current operations, the members set up the Sailors' Union Emergency Committee and issued new union books. Subsequently the Sailors' Union defeated another ISU attempt in the state courts to seize SUP property.

In late February ISU Vice-President Ivan F. Hunter headed for the Pacific Coast to organize a new union. SUP agent Pete Gill, who had been first vice-president, met him in Seattle when he changed trains. "Go back," Gill told him. "The men don't want you."[39] But Hunter ignored the advice. The Sailors' Union resolved "that we condemn any and all who advocate following the policy of Olander and Scharrenberg to reorganize and follow the CHARTER at any price." The union warned members and all organized labor:

> THIS FINK UNION WILL BE DUAL TO THE SAILORS' UNION OF THE PACIFIC, E.C., AND ANY SEAMEN SHIPPING THROUGH THIS SO-CALLED UNION WILL BE CONSIDERED SCABS! . . .

. . . IF YOU WANT TO KEEP THESE CONDITIONS WHICH WERE WON BY THE SAILORS' UNION OF THE PACIFIC THRU AND AFTER THE 1934 STRIKE STAY THE HELL AWAY FROM 64 PINE STREET OR ANY OTHER FINK HALL THEY MIGHT ATTEMPT TO OPEN.[40]

Tom Plant reported to the Board of Directors of the Waterfront Employers February 26, 1936: "A program of reorganization of a new union was now under way that some of the members of the Pacific American Steamship Association had discussed the purposes fully with Mr. Hunter, . . . and had promised him that they would take sailors from the new union when the newly-organized union was prepared to furnish them, which would probably be within a week or ten days."[41]

The Pacific American Steamship Association, the organization of offshore operators, notified the Sailors' Union the next day that its members would no longer deal with the "disfranchised body." The association pointed out that in 1934 its employees had designated the International Seamen's Union to represent them, and the agreement and award specified the ISU. Employer representatives on the Labor Relations Committee refused to meet with the union to discuss grievances. Paddy Morris commented in the *Pacific Coast Longshoreman*: "Apparently the only folks on the waterfront who rejoice in the present strangulation of the [Sailors' Union] appear to be the shipowners who hope to benefit by the disintegration of the union forces."[42] In District Council No. 2 the Sailors' hiring hall resolution lay on the table for several weeks until SUP delegate Carl Tillman succeeded in having it adopted. Then Local 38-79 concurred, opposing "the employment of seamen from any other source than the hall of the SUP."[43]

With over 5,200 pledge cards signed, the Sailors' Union filed a court action March 2 declaring the charter revocation invalid and seeking to restrain the international from setting up a new district union. The union contended that the ISU convention was illegal because officials appointed all delegates except those from the West Coast, instead of their being elected according to the provisions of the constitution. The court granted the temporary injunction April 15. Charging restraint of trade, the Shipowners' Association filed suit against the Sailors' Union, Marine Firemen, and Marine Cooks and Stewards April 2 to prevent operation of their hiring halls. The Sailors resolved to strike the coast if the courts outlawed union hiring halls. Federal Judge Louderback dismissed the suit nine months later. Harry Lundeberg declared that the ISU officials' "final act of revoking our charter has exposed these fakirs in their true role, as real unadulterated agents of the shipowners, TAKING THEIR ORDERS FROM THE SHIPOWNERS."[44] In a letter to Bob Dombroff April 2 he commented on the Communist Party line:

We have certainly had little or no support in the SUP during this crisis from the "comrades"; in the last few months they have criticized us time and again and tried all kinds of petty schemes to disrupt. You can rest assured if we had followed the policy which Telford openly advocated on the floor of our meeting "FOLLOW THE CHARTER AT ANY PRICE" – "REORGANIZE WITH SCHARRENBERG IF

NECESSARY", the SUP would not be in existence today. It seems funny to me that party policy coincides or jibs with that of the reactionaries, whether intentional or not. For instance, when Bridges stated openly in the District Council #2 here that if the ISU shipped a crew on board of any vessel he would HAVE TO TELL HIS MEN TO RECOGNIZE THEM – because THEY BELONGED TO THE A.F. of L. and when he was asked point blank what he would do if the Sailors threw a picket line around the dock he said he would have to order his men to go through. Well, I think this is "finky" – a bunch of weak-kneed bastards. They can see NOW what a lousy mistake they made, but of course they will never admit it. He said this some six weeks ago, before they knew how strong we were – and they are now coming around and talking about "backing us up", etc.[45]

Newspaper attacks, "shipowners' lying propaganda," reached a peak April 13 in a *San Francisco Chronicle* editorial:

> Under the radical leadership which has assumed control—. . . the Sailors' Union . . . has been inciting its members to insubordination and mutiny for the deliberate purpose of destroying the American merchant marine. . . .
>
> Because the tactics of the radical leadership of the suspended Sailors' Union involves mutiny at sea, peril to passengers and ships and the destruction of the American merchant marine, not only responsible union men of all crafts ashore but all the people should resist all efforts to force radical unionism on American shipping.[46]

The Sailors' Union replied with 50,000 leaflets refuting the accusations and a libel suit for $100,000 against the newspaper.

The ISU executive board summoned the officers of the Sailors' Union to attend a meeting in Chicago May 25, 1936, to consider the charter revocation. In a scathing reply endorsed by SUP meetings, Harry Lundeberg refused. He denied that the international, which claimed the Sailors' Union no longer existed, had any right to order that union to do anything. "Before the Sailors' Union . . . is obligated to pay any attention whatsoever to any notice from the International Seamen's Union, you are required, by common sense as well as by law, to withdraw each and every legal action . . . [and] to take your hands off the funds of the Sailors' Union." Lundeberg maintained that the convention, the charter revocation, the new constitution, and the new officers were all illegal and in violation of the old constitution. He charged that the shipowners alone could profit by the international's war on the Sailors' Union and warned that the union would fight "without reservation and without cessation for the rights of the sailors on this Coast." He concluded:

> Above all, we refuse to let you say with one breath that you have already thrown us out of the International Seamen's Union and that the Sailors' Union of the Pacific has no legal existence—and then, with your next vain breath, call us to Chicago to discipline us in what you have prepared as a cut and dried performance whereby you can again try to do what you did so illegally and so foolishly at the February convention.[47]

The Sailors' Union petitioned the National Labor Relations Board May 11 for a coastwide representation election between the union and the international. In spite of the hostility of the offshore and coastwise shipowners' associations, by the middle of May the Sailors' Union had signed direct agreements with about fifteen companies on the Pacific Coast.

The Santa Rosa *Lockout*

While the Sailors' Union fought for its charter, East Coast seamen began their own rebellion against ISU officials, encouraged by the Communist Party. The end of 1935 the ISU demanded a $5.00 wage increase to bring the Atlantic agreement up to the West Coast offshore scale of $62.50 for AB. In San Francisco early in January 1936, 350 unlicensed seamen, crew of the Panama Pacific luxury liner *Pennsylvania*, struck for West Coast articles. The owners rounded up a scab crew to sail the vessel back to New York without taking passengers or calling at San Pedro. The Sailors' Union provided the strikers with food and lodging, and ILA Local 38-79 resolved January 7:

> That we, . . . go on record as refusing to work any ship from the East Coast that is manned by men who have replaced crews taking action . . . to gain the equivalent of the wages and conditions on the Pacific Coast, [and refusing] to work any ship from the East . . . loaded by Eastern longshoremen who have replaced longshore gangs which have refused to work in support of Eastern seamen taking action in East Coast ports.[48]

Federation District Council No. 2 concurred in the resolution, although the federation constitution provided for a coastwide referendum in a dispute that might involve more than one craft.

About two months later another Panama Pacific liner, the *California*, arrived at San Pedro. This time the crew refused to sail the vessel until they received the $5.00 raise. They stayed on board and served meals to the 441 passengers. Secretary of Labor Perkins called their action a strike, but Secretary of Commerce Daniel Roper labeled it mutiny and demanded punishment. After three days the *California* sailed for New York. On her arrival, the master logged sixty crew members and fired the leaders. Thereupon the crew struck, touching off a rank-and-file strike over the vigorous opposition of ISU officials. Joe Curran, *California* ship's delegate, chaired the ISU Provisional Strike Committee. Disregarding the unsanctioned strike, the international renewed the Atlantic agreement effective March 15 with the $5.00 wage increase. Members had no part in negotiating or ratifying the contract covering thirty-eight steamship companies.

A banner head in the *Voice of the Federation* March 26 proclaimed: "STRIKE IS SPREADING ON EASTERN COAST." Two weeks later the *Voice* reported eighteen vessels tied up and 2,400 striking ISU members registered for picket duty. The Sailors' Union on March 30 declared the Grace Line *Santa Rosa*, bound from New York to San Pedro, hot, and voted to donate $100 a week to the East Coast strikers. The next night District Council No. 2 concurred in the *Santa Rosa* ban.

In spite of glowing accounts in the *Voice*, apparently Harry Bridges and ARTA official Mervyn Rathborne, secretary of District Council No. 2, felt uneasy about the East Coast. Bridges received a vague letter April 1 from strike leader Joe Curran, which he answered the same day, requesting concrete information, "the true details of any ships that are coming out here . . . how [crews] are procured and what they constitute, etc."[49] The same day Rathborne wired Roy Pyle of the Radio Telegraphists in New York:

> Urgent important that you forward following information soon as possible stop. First official communication that can be read to District Council Number Two giving details regarding number of ships on strike stop. Numbers of seamen out stop. Ports affected stop. . . . Second confidential report giving back ground and your personal opinions of entire situation stop. Important you keep us informed stop. No reliable information here.[50]

There is no evidence that Bridges and Rathborne shared their doubts with the district council delegates. April 7 the council made plans to picket the vessel. At this meeting Council President Harry Bridges "reported a conversation which he had had with President Ford of Grace Lines to the delegates. HE TOLD THEM THE SANTA ROSA WOULD BE PICKETED UPON ITS ARRIVAL AND WOULD NOT BE WORKED BY THE LONGSHOREMEN. He further told Ford that the only method upon which work could be effected would be to effect a settlement of the difficulty in New York between Grace and Co. and the strike committee headed by Joseph Curran."[51]

District Council No. 3 concurred in the San Francisco ban, and District Council No. 1 voted to respect a picket line. Although the *Santa Rosa* would dock first at San Pedro, District Council No. 4 had not received a single letter or wire from the East Coast strikers. With some misgivings over the lack of information, the council voted to work mail and baggage only. Unknown to the unions, this coincided with the plan the Waterfront Employers adopted on April 11, to bring the *Santa Rosa* to San Francisco to unload all her cargo and thus implement their suspension program to lock out the port. Several hundred seamen pickets greeted the vessel when she docked at San Pedro the morning of April 13. After longshoremen removed mail and baggage, other gangs refused to go through the picket line to unload the 1,500 tons of cargo for that port. The ship departed for San Francisco less than an hour after her arrival.

With the hot ship steaming north, the situation began to look different for Local 38-79. At the request of Harry Bridges, District Council No. 2 met that afternoon to determine a policy on the *Santa Rosa*. Delegates from the licensed officers stated that they would not pull their West Coast members because their unions never declared the vessel unfair. Wires for information to Joe Curran and Roy Pyle brought the chilling reply that the strike had little impact, with only two vessels tied up. Pyle advised the unions to "by all means avoid a showdown on this issue."[52] That night Local 38-79 voted to work the *Santa Rosa* and instructed federation council delegates to have her declared fair.

With 1,000 pickets waiting for the *Santa Rosa* at Pier 35, District Council No. 2 met again at nine the next morning. After hearing 38-79's plea to declare her fair, the

Maritime Federation pickets waiting for the S.S. Santa Rosa *on the Embarcadero, San Francisco, April 14, 1936. (Courtesy San Francisco Public Library)*

delegates voted instead to send down a committee to check the crew's books. According to Harry Lundeberg, the Communist bloc "tried to say it was a bum beef and the Sailors' Union . . . was to blame for it."[53] The vessel docked at eleven. After unloading mail and baggage, longshoremen refused to go through the picket line to work cargo. The council reconvened at two, with three members of the *Santa Rosa*'s crew present. They related that 75 percent of the crew had been on the ship the previous trip, that they had ISU cards, and when she sailed two pickets stood on the dock with signs, one reading: "This ship is unfair," and the other, "This ship is fair."[54] At 3:30, while the delegates debated a motion to declare the vessel fair, a messenger handed Harry Bridges a letter from the Waterfront Employers, which stated:

> You are advised that all relations with your union have been suspended and will not be resumed unless and until your union gives satisfactory assurance . . . that all causes of the violations have been removed and will not recur.
>
> In the meantime the employers will maintain the provisions of the award governing wages, hours and working conditions of longshoremen, and all members of your union . . . may receive employment under arrangements that will be made by the employers.[55]

The trap set by the Waterfront Employers snapped shut.

On hearing the ultimatum the council declared the *Santa Rosa* fair, and Bridges notified the employers that Local 38-79 was "at all times prepared to live up to the award" and work the *Santa Rosa*. According to Paddy Morris, he "pleaded with" Fred

Doelker, Grace Line Pacific Coast manager, to "let him send men to work the Santa Rosa."[56] The employers replied to the pleas of Bridges by enclosing a copy of their letter of April 15 to District President Lewis:

> As you were advised yesterday, Waterfront Employers Association of San Francisco have suspended all relations with the International Longshoremen's Association, Local 38-79. This action was forced upon the employers by wilful and persistent violations of the fundamental provisions of the Award of the Government Arbitration Board, and decisions of the Federal Arbitrator, culminating in refusal of Local 38-79 to work the S.S. SANTA ROSA.
>
> Suspension of relations with Local 38-79 was directed solely against the radical and subversive leadership of the Local which has fallen under the domination of Communist agitators. Employers have no desire or intention to abrogate the Award or break off dealings with the International Longshoremen's Association, District 38.
>
> They are prepared to meet with you at any time.[57]

Local 38-79 answered the employers April 16, "May we suggest that if and when the members of our Association be allowed some say in the choosing of the officers of your Association, we will stand ready to extend a like prerogative to you. . . . The officers of the Local as presently constituted will be in office until September 1936 and as such, on local questions dealing with Local 38-79, I.L.A., you will deal with them and no others.[58]

Bill Lewis assured the employers April 15 that "the district is willing and anxious to resume relationship on an equitable basis as soon as possible. . . . You have already been advised by Local 38-79 concerning their willingness to resume an amicable relationship."[59] Longshoremen ignored the employers' bulletins posted along the front urging them to hire at the docks, and employers refused to take men from the hiring hall. Although the *San Francisco Chronicle* ignored the whole story, the Associated Press carried a full report. "SHIP OPERATORS BLACKLIST UNIONS," the *Oregonian* headlined April 15, and the next day the subhead proclaimed. "Organized Employers Seek to Crush Longshore Radical Leaders." By April 16 operators had diverted five vessels from San Francisco to other ports, threatening to involve additional locals. Paddy Morris hastened to San Francisco.

The employers advised the ILA district April 16 that they would meet "when you furnish us with authorization from the members of the San Francisco local for you to act in their behalf." Lewis countered that the district officers were "not in position to conduct any negotiations with the employers" in behalf of the local; "compliance with the requirements of the award for local conditions must be approved by the rank and file longshoremen of the local involved." In the next letter the employers denied press reports that they wanted to abolish the hiring hall or change the award. They would reestablish all conditions under the award "as soon as it is possible to resume relationships with the San Francisco local."[60] Lewis and Morris arranged a meeting with the Waterfront Employers and the Labor Relations Committee of Local 38-79.

Meanwhile, labor rallied to support the locked-out longshoremen. The perceived plot to destroy hiring halls touched a raw nerve. The San Francisco Labor Council and Joint Council of Teamsters voted their support, and the Seattle Central Labor Council wired "its fullest support to longshoremen in their struggle against the shipowners." All the maritime unions pledged support, and members of the Sailors' Union stood ready to strike in their defense.

Bill Lewis and Paddy Morris represented the district ILA in the meeting April 18 in the Matson Building; William Marlowe, Charles Connors, R. Goulet, and J.E. Hogan the Labor Relations Committee for Local 38-79; T.G. Plant, Joseph A. Lunny, Hugh Gallagher, E.T. Ford, and J.J. Walsh the Waterfront Employers. Lewis later described the meeting: With newspaper headlines reporting cargo diverted "to every point on the Pacific Coast," and the employers refusing to take the men back pending an agreement, Lewis accused the employers of "looking to spread this all over the Pacific Coast. . . . So I says, 'You are not going to get by with that stuff. Morris is going to Seattle and I will stay at San Francisco, and we will have a good strike! They caucused, and then they said, 'We will agree that the men won't be required to work the other California ports until this question is disposed of.'"[61]

The all-day meeting hammered out a memorandum of agreement. First, the Waterfront Employers agreed "that none of the Locals of the Pacific Coast District will be required to work cargo diverted from San Francisco pending the acceptance of the agreement." The agreement reaffirmed the award and stated that local questions, disputes, and grievances would be handled by the local Labor Relations Committee and coastwide questions by the district. It pledged that all parties would perform all provisions of the award and decisions of the Labor Relations Committee and arbitrator. The parties agreed that Judge Sloss "shall underwrite this agreement."[62] The Waterfront Employers would resume relations with Local 38-79 and order longshoremen from the hiring hall when the organizations approved and signed the agreement. The memorandum, signed by those attending the meeting, allowed until April 21 at 8:00 a.m. for ratification.

That same evening, after consulting with Local 38-79's Publicity Committee (Henry Schmidt), the members of the Labor Relations Committee officially repudiated the memorandum. They said they had "overstepped their authority" in signing it, and they found "on further analysis that by having the tentative memorandum underwritten by the District Officials we automatically relinquish the autonomy of the local."[63] The next morning Sunday, April 19, Harry Bridges flew to Portland for a mass meeting. The *Oregonian* headlined the event, "BRIDGES BERATES 'RYAN HENCHMEN.'" He denounced the memorandum and condemned Lewis and Morris as henchmen of ILA President Joe Ryan, "a shipowners' tool."

At another meeting in San Francisco that same Sunday, Judge Sloss explained to the signers of the memorandum the basis on which he would be willing to act as arbitrator. At the request of the 38-79 Labor Relations Committee he put those conditions in writing. He agreed to serve on condition that all awards "shall be promptly obeyed and complied with, in letter and spirit." He asserted in paragraph 4 that the

ILA and its members "have consistently and repeatedly disregarded the awards of the arbitrator on two important questions":

> (1) The ruling that the Union, or its members acting collectively, have not the right to refuse to do work, or to stop work, because of any dispute regarding conditions, but that it is their duty to continue to do the work, as directed, pending the settlement of the controversy . . . This presents the issue of "job action," a procedure which is inconsistent with the carrying out of the Award.
>
> (2) The refusal to handle "hot cargo," i.e., cargo affected by some controversy involving labor disputes outside the scope of the Award . . . The rulings of the arbitrator on this question have not been accepted and the union and its members have maintained their position that they will not handle such cargo so long as it remains under the ban imposed by other labor organizations.[64]

That night the *Santa Rosa* sailed for San Pedro, still carrying the 6,000 tons of cargo for the two California ports. When a special committee of the San Francisco Labor Council met Monday morning with officials of San Francisco Local 38-79 and the district ILA, Bridges still objected to the agreement. Finally Lewis told him "that there was only one thing lousy with that agreement, 'Harry, you have got the men out in the street, Bill Lewis is getting them back, and you couldn't do it.'"[65]

Bridges arrived late at the longshoremen's meeting that night because he appeared first before the Teamsters meeting to get a resolution of support. He walked rapidly to the stage and announced: "While the fakers were drawing up a phony agreement I was getting you the support of the Labor Movement."[66] The Teamsters' resolution provided "that this organization endorse the stand taken by the membership and officials of I.L.A. 38-79 and express their full confidence in same."[67] Bridges continued, "There are two ways of settling a thing like this, you can go up to the shipowners and talk it over with them as to whether you return under their conditions, or you can go out and get some support so you can return under your own conditions."[68] Then the members heard the April 18 memorandum and Judge Sloss's letter read and adopted a long resolution by Bridges to ratify the agreement.

The following day Judge Sloss called the parties together to execute the final agreement. At the shipowners' request it included paragraph 4 from the Sloss letter condemning job action and hot cargo work stoppages. The next morning the longshoremen went back to work. Harry Lundeberg observed that now the longshoremen would have to work hot cargo, adding: "Bridges also stated in the district council meeting [April 21] that if any picket lines were established over *phoney beefs* as he called it that they would be removed by the longshoremen."[69] He aimed the threat at the Sailors' Union.

Paddy Morris deplored the conduct of Harry Bridges in the "*Santa Rosa* imbroglio" and criticized the Maritime Federation's disregard of its own constitution. He contended that the District Council No. 2 resolution January 7 declaring East Coast vessels hot amounted to a strike call without the required coastwide referendum authorizing it. Morris said that initially the *Santa Rosa* concerned either San Pedro, the first port of call, or the district ILA, not the San Francisco local, and that Bridges had no business talking to Grace Line President Ford and informing him of the union ban. He pointed out that as soon as Bridges learned that San Pedro longshoremen had not been required to work the *Santa Rosa*, that she was headed for San Francisco, the boycott became a "lousy beef." By voting April 13 to work the *Santa Rosa* at Bridges's urging, the San Francisco longshoremen agreed to scab on their fellow workers in San Pedro. After repudiating and denouncing the April 18 agreement, Bridges signed it, with the addition of the odious paragraph 4, included as a result of his objections to the original draft. Morris called Bridges a "noisy flannel-mouthed fraud" and his conduct cowardly, contemptible, and "utterly unprincipled."[70]

Publicity Committee Chair Henry Schmidt replied that the April 18 draft agreement "was cunningly worded and ambiguous" and "contained a hidden threat of not only stringent enforcement of the award, . . . but the definite possibility of some modification of the award or additional power to the arbitrator and the Pacific Coast District." Without explaining how, Schmidt asserted that Local 38-79's resolution accepting the agreement protected the union from this threat. He criticized the district for "being in such a hurry to rush in to negotiate a settlement with the employers on the employers' terms" and warned that the district officials would try "to confuse the issue before the eyes of the rank and file." Schmidt implied a plot between shipowners, district officers, and Judge Sloss to discredit and control the officers of Local 38-79 and suggested that "Jos. P. Ryan has not yet given up his fond hope of bringing the west coast locals under the same control that he has on the east coast."[71]

Without any documentary evidence, Bridges and Schmidt used the *Santa Rosa* crisis and the way the district settled it to repeat again the charges that Lewis and Morris were "Ryan henchmen" and therefore shipowners' agents. On the contrary, the correspondence between the Waterfront Employers and the district ILA shows that Lewis and Morris refused to be used. The shipowners' suspension plan failed and Local 38-79's integrity was preserved, not because of Bridge's cleverly worded resolution, but because Bill Lewis insisted from the beginning of the crisis that the shipowners must respect that integrity before the district ILA would meet with them. Once they understood that the district would defend the San Francisco local, the employers had two options left: they could either force a coastwide strike or back down and resume relations with Local 38-79. They chose the latter.

1936 Pacific Coast District ILA Convention

The 1936 Pacific Coast District ILA convention, which opened in San Pedro May 4, became as much a contest for power as a conference to decide coastwide issues. The Communist bloc aimed to establish by reports, resolutions, and censure, that the district officials, principally Bill Lewis, Paddy Morris, and A.H. Petersen, international representative appointed by Joe Ryan, had not represented the members honestly or capably. Those officers firmly intended to prove instead, that they had served well and that Harry Bridges and his followers had made the mistakes.

Delegates to the convention of the Pacific Coast District, International Longshoremen's Association, San Pedro, May 1936. (Voice of the Federation)

The first confrontation occurred on May 7 when Bridges corrected the minutes and Morris accused the San Francisco delegation of quibbling. "Because there are certain issues that are coming on the floor . . . and they don't want those issues to come on the floor, and they figure that if they kill the time for a couple of weeks you would not have the chance to bring them up, . . ."[72] Bridges, in turn, accused Morris of altering the minutes of the first Portland conference and the 1934 district convention. More discussion followed that the delegates ordered expunged from the record. The next confrontation came over seating International Representative A.H. Petersen with voice. Local 38-79 delegates argued that he should be denied a seat because Joe Ryan appointed him. When the anti-Communists demanded a roll call, the Bridges faction backed off, and Petersen received all but a few votes.

President Lewis brought an "ILA Convention News" bulletin from Local 38-79 dated May 11 to the floor of the convention on May 12. The bulletin stated:

> In line with Paddy Morris' policy of protecting Ryan and blasting the rank and file, the speech of fraternal delegate Stein, vice-president of the New Orleans local, was deliberately distorted in the minutes of the May 5 session . . . Morris tried to confuse the issue by raising the phony charge that the San Francisco delegation was deliberately attempting to prolong the convention. . . .

> Directly answering Morris' attack, Bridges stated that his speech was the speech of a clever politician. Morris was relying on the fact that many of the delegates were new delegates, and could, so Morris believed, be impressed by clever speeches. The fact remains, however, Bridges said, that the past Minutes have been juggled and confused for the sole purpose of confusing the membership, . . .[73]

Morris exploded. He moved to prefer charges against the local "for conduct unbecoming union men in taking part in the character assassination of the District Secretary without any foundation or fact to back it up." In response to a question as to whether the minutes distorted his speech, Charles Stein replied, "I don't make that assertion."[74] Local 38-79 delegates repudiated the unsigned article, although they admitted the union put out the bulletin.

After a long discussion the convention voted 64 to 75.5, with 20.5 not voting, not to permit Morris to file the charges. The vote revealed a consistent Communist bloc of seventy odd votes, as against sixty-four for the incumbent officials. The argument resumed after the vote. Morris asserted that the material in the San Francisco bulletin had been expunged from the minutes. "The San Francisco delegates deny that they said or that they gave that information to Local 38-79, but they haven't informed this delegation how it was transferred from the waste paper basket of the Carpenters Hall in San Pedro to the Union Hall of Local 38-79 in San Francisco."[75]

In the afternoon session the Committee on Officers Reports, chaired by Eugene Dietrich of Local 38-79, brought in a recommendation to nonconcur in Secretary-Treasurer Morris's report because of certain actions. On instructions from his local, Dietrich censured Morris for the policies and articles in the *Pacific Coast Longshoreman*, "specifically the last three issues," which "contained a lot of political propaganda." The committee also recommended nonconcurrence in President Lewis's report, stating by way of "constructive criticism" that the officers had not complied "with resolutions that directly effected the solidarity of our organization." Dietrich also presented charges by Local 38-79, which were later withdrawn. Heide of the San Francisco Warehousemen moved to concur in the report. "PRESIDENT LEWIS: No, no, we are not going to concur in anything at all. I am going to make a report."

Vice-President Thurston took the chair while Lewis answered the charges. On his failure to get a uniform coastwide agreement for the checkers, Lewis related that the San Francisco employers' intransigence had resulted in separate agreements for San Pedro and Portland before a San Francisco agreement could be negotiated. Lewis described the British Columbia hot cargo arbitration, which he opposed and Harry Bridges agreed to. He recalled that when Henry Schrimpf asked Bridges in a Local 38-79 meeting, "What right have you or anybody else to arbitrate hot cargo?" Bridges replied, "There were two courses for me to pursue, one was to arbitrate the question, and the other was to strike, and I knew you wouldn't strike."[76]

In the Gulf hot cargo situation, Lewis faulted New Orleans longshoremen for communicating with Bridges rather than with the district officers. He repeated the criticism on the *Santa Rosa*, that Bridges "didn't only usurp the function of the

Federation or the I.L.A., he usurped everything, and did individual dealing with the shipowner."[77] He reminded Dietrich, by way of "constructive criticism," that "you have got to function as a district, otherwise they can take San Francisco Local and San Pedro Local and separate us, and they can break you up just like you do a cracker. One local can't function without the assistance of the other. If you are going to have District officials, you have to back them up 100 per cent."[78]

A.H. Petersen and Paddy Morris elaborated on the *Santa Rosa* negotiations and settlement. The Communist bloc delegates had enough of the recital, but Vice-President Thurston would not permit them to shut up the accused men. Morris defended his controversial articles in the *Pacific Coast Longshoreman* because certain individuals who "were brazenly usurping the functions of the District"[79] had to be called to task. He charged that after the Washington, D.C., conference Bridges opposed informing the members of the Waterfront Employers' threat to break relations if the ILA did not lift the British Columbia hot cargo ban, stating, "If the price we have to pay for the award is the dumping of our brothers in Vancouver, it is too big a price; to hell with the award."[80] But when the pinch came he asked the strikers to lift the ban.

Morris asserted that Gulf officials did not keep the district properly informed during the strike: "Individuals not representing the District were getting information from Darcy and Spencer. Darcy and Spencer knew perfectly well who I am. Why didn't they correspond with me—a nicely prearranged plan to put the District officials in the hot grease."[81]

Then Harry Bridges took the floor to answer Lewis and Morris. He criticized the district officers for being hard to find and uncooperative—"they duck out of town, or duck the issue when things come up."[82] Lewis replied that "many a time" he had gone to Bridges's office "and couldn't get in."[83] Bridges reiterated that the hot cargo arbitration was a district matter. He did not remember the details of his contact with the British Columbia strikers, but he maintained that he had described the San Francisco lockout and left the decision up to them. Robert Collins of Seattle Local 38-12 asked Bridges if he had said "That you were going to work the cargo anyhow." Bridges replied that he had not "made a specific demand on them to lift the cargo." But Art Whitehead, also of the Seattle local, said that W. Mitchell, secretary of the Vancouver and District Waterfront Workers' Association and strike committee told them "that if they didn't lift the ban you were going to dump them."[84]

On the *Santa Rosa*, Bridges said that Ford of Grace Line called him and said the ship carried no scabs, that the seamen received $5.00 a month more than West Coast scale, and that "practically all of the original crew from . . . San Francisco" remained on the vessel. Bridges blamed the Sailors' Union for declaring the *Santa Rosa* hot and said that he tried vainly to "get the dope to answer these arguments in the Council and couldn't do it." But Lewis observed that "the first time you were concerned about getting any official information was when the ship was on her way to San Francisco."[85]

The next morning William Craft of Local 38-12 moved to expunge "all of this politics or whatever you may call it, investigations, and get down to resolutions."

Morris objected, demanding the right to defend himself. Lewis refused to accept the motion to expunge: "I want every man on the Pacific Coast to know what transpired. I want it to appear in cold facts, and so far as I'm concerned there will be nothing expunged from that record."[86] After more discussion the convention referred the officers reports back to committee. Then Bridges moved "that the discussion of the past two or three days on the past issues be expunged from the record."[87] Lewis objected vehemently. Henry Schrimpf of Local 38-79 offered an amendment that when correcting the minutes any delegate "shall be able to delete anything from those minutes." The amendment, said Lewis, "is that we delete not the irrelevant matter but whatever the Delegates wish to omit. Under those circumstances any man can make a statement on this floor and then he goes to work and finds out that it probably does not sound so good to him, and he can delete it."[88] No one seconded the amendment. The motion to expunge lost 33 to 35.

Debate on the past record finally ended with Bridges protesting that he did not have enough time to say half of what he wanted to. The delegates proceeded to consider the resolutions. They chose May 30 over July 5 to commemorate Maritime Memorial Day. They voted down a Farmer-Labor party and endorsed Franklin D. Roosevelt for reelection. The convention endorsed the Committee for Industrial Organization, still a part of the AFL. In response to the ILA's increasingly industrial character, the delegates provided for coastwide conferences for checkers and other distinct crafts. Similarly, they voted that only locals directly involved could vote on agreements, strikes, lockouts, and hot cargo bans. They recognized ladies' auxiliaries, organized during the 1934 strike, as beneficial and worthy of encouragement.

The convention supported Hawaiian longshoremen's request for ILA charters and approved charters for Vancouver and New Westminster in British Columbia. In a postscript on the hot cargo ban, the convention passed a resolution introduced by delegates from Portland Local 38-78 to "use every effort to assist the longshoremen in British Columbia, who after a protracted and bloody strike, were left on the street" and to "condemn any person or persons who assisted in getting [them] in this position."[89] The convention requested the international to restore the charters of the two New Orleans locals revoked during the Gulf strike.

The delegates adopted referendum voting for constitutional amendments, but rejected a Communist bloc resolution for referendum for primary nominations for district offices by a roll call vote of 71.56 to 85.44. After defeating a proposal for visiting cards between locals, the delegates approved a transfer system. With San Francisco locals 38-79 and 38-44 opposing it, the delegates voted 101 to 53 to create a convention fund. The convention concurred in the officers reports without further discussion.

Action on the agreement expiring September 30 generated major concern. The delegates formulated a detailed referendum ballot to determine whether to open the agreement and what to ask for. They also requested the Maritime Federation to adopt a policy "for the simultaneous renewal, amending, or termination of agreements in order that all Maritime Unions may work in cooperation."[90]

Neither Bill Lewis nor Paddy Morris would accept nomination for office again. The anti-Communists nominated Cliff Thurston of Portland for president and Elmer Bruce of San Pedro for secretary. The Communist bloc nominated Harry Bridges for president and Matt Meehan of Portland for secretary. For district organizer the delegates nominated Eugene Dietrich of San Francisco, Paul Heide of the San Francisco Warehousemen, Joe Simons of San Pedro, and William Craft of Seattle. The delegates elected the executive board in the subdistrict caucuses: Art Whitehead of Seattle and Andy Larsen of Tacoma for Puget Sound; Ed Krumholz of Aberdeen and C.W. Wisner of Raymond for Grays Harbor; Conrad Negstad of Portland, vice- president, and Joseph J. Thomas of Astoria and M.D. Rodgers of Longview for the Columbia River; Henry Schmidt of Local 38-79 and Walter Mahaffey of the Stockton Bargemen for Northern California; and F.E. Ward of the San Pedro Checkers, Lee Gholson of the San Pedro Longshoremen, and D.C. Mays of San Diego for Southern California.

Originally the ILA expected the convention to last no more than eleven days so the Maritime Federation convention could begin May 15 in the same city. Many delegates represented their locals in both gatherings. Then the federation postponed its opening to May 18, but the ILA convention did not adjourn until May 19.

Predictably, with almost 4,000 members, Locals 38-79 controlled the referendum vote for officers. Harry Bridges defeated Cliff Thurston for president 8,381 to 2,740, and Matt Meehan defeated Elmer Bruce for secretary 6,523 to 3,189. As Eugene Dietrich received the highest vote, Joe Ryan appointed him international organizer. After years of critical opposition, unchallenged control of the ILA District would give the Communists the opportunity to demonstrate their superior strategy in the approaching coastwide confrontation with their employers.

1936 Maritime Federation Convention

With the ILA convention still in session, President Bill Fischer called the Maritime Federation convention to order May 15, appointed credentials and rules committees, and then recessed the body until the longshoremen finished their deliberations. Five days later the convention opened with 118 delegates representing nine unions. Three distinct groups brought their programs to the convention: the Communist bloc, led by delegates from Local 38-79 and the Radio Telegraphists, who aimed to control the federation and capture the offices; a group of longshoremen and licensed officers, committed to the federation and opposed to Communist control; and the Sailors' Union, anti-Communist but also fighting its own battle with shipowners and the international. Pondering the year's struggles, the hot cargo crises and controversial jobs actions, the delegates again wrestled with the problem of how much power to entrust to the federation and how much to reserve for the affiliated unions.

The convention decided external issues with relatively little controversy. The delegates supported the CIO, concurred in the district ILA boycott of war cargoes, endorsed a National Maritime Federation, supported ILA charters and a federation district council in Hawaii, and voted to issue a 25-cent "Free Mooney and Billings" stamp to raise money for the imprisoned class war veterans. The delegates recommended that the district councils sponsor educational programs, monthly mass meetings, and recreation centers. The convention rejected a Farmer-Labor party by a roll call vote of 67.138 to 81.175 and endorsed President Roosevelt for reelection. The delegates sent to referendum a proposal for a one-hour coastwide work stoppage to support the Modesto Boys and a 5-cent monthly assessment for the Maritime Federation of the Gulf, both approved by the members. In another referendum on a Maritime Memorial Day and date, members voted to observe July 5.

To maximize union strength in the anticipated negotiations with their employers when the awards and agreements expired September 30, the delegates resolved that all organizations should cooperate in presenting their demands. They recommended that the unions include clauses granting preference of employment, prohibiting discrimination for union activity, protecting the right to refuse to cross a picket line, and other items, and that they agree on a uniform beginning and termination date.

After an audit the convention dismissed an accusation made in District Council No. 2 that the *Voice of the Federation* books were "very shady," but the delegates created an editorial board of the elected federation officers, president, vice-president, secretary-treasurer, and three trustees, to supervise the paper's policies. The board would also select the editor, subject to approval of a majority of the district councils. In general, the Communist bloc supported and the anti-Communists opposed centralization and paid officials within the federation. The delegates defeated proposals to pay district council coordinators or secretaries and rejected a plan for mandatory executive subcommittee meetings. The convention proposed a constitutional amendment, adopted by a 93 percent referendum vote: "The Federation recognizes the fullest autonomy of each affiliated organization in the government of its internal affairs, and nothing in this constitution shall be construed as being in conflict with the constitution of the American Federation of Labor or the constitution of any organization affiliated with the Maritime Federation of the Pacific."[91]

The delegates backed off from direct federation involvement in strikes. The old constitution provided that if the federation executive committee could not settle a dispute with employers referred to it by a component organization, the committee would take a strike vote by referendum of the whole membership. Likewise, the federation could end a strike by referendum. The proposed change, adopted by a 90 percent referendum vote, provided: "The Executive Committee, if unable to adjust any dispute, may refer the dispute, by majority vote of the executive committee, to component organizations for a membership vote." Thus, each union, not the federation, would take the strike vote. The convention added a sentence that the federation "believes in the policy and adheres to the principle of a referendum vote, by the entire membership . . . on all major issues,"[92] and left unchanged the method of counting votes.

Controversy swirled around the beleaguered Sailors' Union. The delegates tabled a resolution by the union to take a federation referendum immediately on calling a coastwide strike if the employers destroyed the hiring hall of any union. Resolution 42, introduced by the Communist bloc, provoked a bitter fight over the last resolve, which provided:

> That the Convention go on record as condemning such attacks by the employers and their employer-controlled press, and anti-labor associations; and that we also condemn any efforts on the part of any individual or groups that deliberately propose the establishing of the Maritime Federation as a non-A.F. of L. or independent organization or who propose the secession of any affiliated union from the A.F. of L. and its Central Bodies, and International.

A minority report condemned the last resolve:

> [It] is an attack upon the Sailors' Union for not giving up their democratic rights and reorganizing under the bureaucratic ISU Executive Board. The Sailors' Union in order to survive has been unwillingly forced into the position that is condemned in the resolution, that of being denied membership in the A.F. of L., the International, and two Central Labor Bodies. . . . The course that is advocated in this resolution is to abandon the Sailors' Union of the Pacific, . . . and reorganize under the International, . . .

The report proposed to substitute for the end of the resolve, "and that we also condemn the various International officials who with their union-smashing tactics are trying to break up the A.F. of L. and its principles by attempting to take away the democratic rights of the membership."[93] After lengthy debate a roll call to table lost 78.178 to 81.025. Two days later the delegates resumed a debate on the resolution in a committee of the whole. Back in convention, they tabled it by a vote of 109.327 to 48.131.

The final attack on the Sailors' Union proscribed job action. Although the delegates had voted June 1 to table a resolution condemning job action, Harry Bridges persisted with the subject. The last day of the convention he introduced a motion, "That any action taken by an organization involving members of other organizations to the extent of forcing them off the job, must be in strict conformity with the provisions of the Maritime Federation constitution before such action is recognized by the Federation."[94] After lengthy debate the delegates approved it, amended to read, "any major action," and referred it to a referendum vote, with Harry Lundeberg, Ed Coester, and Charles Cates of the Sailors, and Charles May, John Kucin, and B.H. Greenwood of the Masters, Mates and Pilots recorded as voting no. The referendum carried by 83 percent. However, the Sailors' Union had the last word. In the night session, the final business before election of officers, the convention adopted unanimously a resolution supporting the union. After reciting the international's attacks that "may cause the S.U.P. to take strike action," the resolution pledged "our wholehearted moral, economic support to the S.U.P." and recognized "the S.U.P. and the men who went on strike in 1934 with all other marine groups."[95]

As the convention moved through twenty stormy days, differences between the anti-Communist bloc and the Sailors' Union diminished. The bloc supported the Sailors against the Communist attempt to condemn their charter position. Henry Schrimpf surprised many delegates by defecting from the Communist bloc. A working longshoreman and union activist, Shrimpf had represented Local 38-79 at the 1935 ILA and Maritime Federation conventions, along with Harry Bridges and

Henry Schmidt, voting solidly with them in the Communist bloc. He voted with the Communists in the recent ILA convention and during most of this meeting. But on June 7, in the second discussion and roll call vote on Resolution 42 condemning the Sailors' Union, he defended the Sailors on the floor and voted with them.

The delegates reelected the incumbents to office, rejecting the Communist bloc challengers. For president William Fischer of the Portland Longshoremen defeated James Engstrom of the Seattle Marine Firemen 84.333 to 71.802; for vice-president Harry Christoffersen of the San Pedro Sailors defeated C.D. Bentley of the San Francisco Marine Engineers 86.060 to 73.928; and for secretary-treasurer Fred M. Kelley of the San Francisco Marine Engineers defeated Max Watson of the San Francisco Marine Cooks and Stewards 86.531 to 71.123. Schrimpf did not vote for president, and he voted against the Communist bloc for vice-president and secretary-treasurer. The Communist press noted the new alignment: "It is reported that Lundeberg and the Sailors delegation, as well as Schrimpf of the ILA 38-79 supported the Fischer-Kelley slate, which caused a great deal of surprise among rank and filers, especially with regard to supporting Kelley, who also received the support of the Paddy Morris-Lewis-Bruce clique."[96]

With seats on the newly created editorial board of the *Voice of the Federation*, the trustees became key officers. The anti-Communists supported Henry Schrimpf of Local 38-79, nominated by Harry Lundeberg, Roy M. Farrell of the San Francisco Marine Firemen, and Bob Dombroff of the Seattle Sailors. The Communist bloc supported Mervyn Rathborne of the San Francisco Radio Telegraphists, C.D. Bentley of the San Francisco Marine Engineers, and John Brost of the Portland ILA. The delegates elected Schrimpf with 84.645 votes, Bentley with 84.578, and Dombroff with 73.801, squeezing out Rathborne by 2.664 votes.

As the convention wound down a *Voice* editorial reminded members that "the purpose and aim of the Federation has not yet been consummated. . . . the road to this objective requires not only the best judgment, but courage, loyalty and devotion to the principles forming the base of the existence of our united movement, which was born and developed in struggle." Accepting dissention as inevitable, the editorial warned:

> Nevertheless, no one can possibly be useful or even remotely constructive, if his interest does not serve the Maritime Federation of the Pacific. *There can be no split affection between it and other organizations. It must come first.* Issues of a principled character must not only be posed openly before the membership, but those sponsoring them are obliged to do so. . . . At no time in the experience of our organization has there been a more crying need for solidarity. No one can possibly serve the Federation unless this unity is paramount.[97]

Many members agreed that the federation represented the finest flowering of waterfront unionism—their ultimate strength, to be preserved and defended against all harm.

13

The 1936-1937 Strike

Ever since the end of the 1934 strike maritime workers had been pushing constantly to extend control over their working lives, and their employers had been shoving back with all their might to stop the advance. With mutual support of job actions and the employers' inability to find any but union people to move their cargoes, the workers had made substantial gains during those two years of pushing and shoving. Both sides prepared for a showdown. The employers firmly resolved to take back their lost power over the workers on their ships and docks. The unions resolved with equal determination to surrender nothing and improve their wages and working conditions.

Union people waited restlessly for negotiations to begin. By fall they would either have confirmed their strength in new agreements or be on strike fighting for the existence of their organizations. When the Seattle Newspaper Guild struck the Hearst *Post-Intelligencer* in mid-August, seamen and longshoremen swarmed to the Guild picket line, as if rehearsing for their own struggle. Meanwhile, Congress intervened to aid the employers.

Copeland Fink Book

As shipowners watched control of seamen on both coasts slip from their grasp following the 1934 strike, they turned to the federal government for legislation to bring their unruly servants to time. Senator Royal S. Copeland and Congressman Schuyler O. Bland introduced legislation in 1935 to reform the system of mail subsidies and control and discipline merchant seamen. The bills would compel a seaman to carry a continuous discharge book containing the seaman's photograph and fingerprints, similar to the fink book on the Pacific Coast. After each voyage the master would note in the book the seaman's character, conduct, and ability. A rumor also circulated that the Shipping Board would reopen Sea Service bureaus on the Pacific Coast.

Seamen protested vigorously against the book as a device to gag and blacklist militants. As the final bill neared passage, Joseph B. Weaver, director of the Bureau of Marine Inspection and Navigation, confirmed their fears in an interview in the *Boston Globe* June 21, 1936. Questioned about radicalism among merchant seamen, he stated:

> The new legislation to deal with this menace is the most far-reaching of its kind ever put through and consists principally of the adoption of a continuous discharge book, which will be virtually a service record of every seaman and is patterned somewhat after a passport.

> . . . [The book] will contain a full account of the man's work as well as notations that mark the owner as a breeder of dissatisfaction or a trouble maker.
>
> . . . when a seaman leaves one vessel his chances of signing on some other ship will depend entirely on this record. Under this system undesirables will be kept ashore and many cases of outbreaks among crews of American ships that have occurred recently will be avoided in the future.[1]

An overwhelming majority of Pacific Coast unlicensed seamen signed protest cards declaring that they would "never accept the book as a condition of employment."[2] The Sailors' Union passed a motion June 22 forbidding any member to carry the book under penalty of being classed as a scab, and wired President Roosevelt that "we will not accept nor recognize any book but our own union book."[3] Over the seamen's protests Congress passed the Merchant Marine Act of 1936 on June 25. The Sailors' Union resolved that compelling seamen to carry the book "is one of the most vicious abridgements of the constitutional rights of citizens, carrying with it all the implications of slavery, finger-printing, blacklisting, fink halls, and nullifying each and every democratic right which the Seamen fought so valiently for in 1934."[4]

When the law became effective in six months, unlicensed seamen on offshore vessels would be required to carry the despised government fink book and obtain a certificate of service. The provision for the certificate required men to surrender their able seaman and lifeboat tickets and submit to a reexamination. The Sailors' Union protested that the examination might be so strict that an older seaman who had passed the tests in his youth would be unable to qualify, "regardless of how capable a man may be. In other words, . . . it is left in the hands of a few whether thousands of good old seaman will be thrown aside and will be faced with the prospect of living on charity as paupers, after spending their youth and manhood making profits for the shipowners."[5]

Moreover, the certificate could be suspended or revoked for misbehavior, negligence, or unskillfulness. The seamen declared that the clause "sets up the most vicious blacklisting system ever heard of." It could be used to discriminate against seamen who struck ships while under articles, technically desertion. "So under this law," the Sailors' Union concluded, "one part of the Government could easily become a strike breaking agency, which no doubt some gentlemen intend it should be."[6] The act replaced the Shipping Board and Emergency Fleet Corporation with the Maritime Commission to enforce the provisions relating to ship subsidies and construction, as well as those relating to seamen.

Sailors' Union vs. International

The Sailors' Union emerged victorious from the court battles in which the International Seamen's Union tried to seize the funds and property of its expelled district union. Judge Michael D. Roche ruled June 9 in the U.S. District Court for Northern California that "there was no cause for action in any of the courts"[7] and dismissed the temporary restraining order against the Sailors. Thereupon the international gave up and withdrew the remaining six suits in federal and state courts against the expelled union, thus releasing SUP funds and property. The action did not affect the charter nor the Sailors' Union petition for an injunction to restrain the ISU from establishing another West Coast union.

Failing to destroy the Sailors' Union, the ISU opened negotiations to restore the charter on the international's terms. The ISU proposed to allow the union to negotiate directly with its employers and to allow the Pacific District unions to belong to the Maritime Federation provided that body did not conflict with the AFL. The Sailors' Union offered to reconsider its expulsion of Paul Scharrenberg the previous year; to rescind the "Crooks Resolution," which authorized admission of former members of the Communist Marine Workers Industrial Union, provided "no present member of the Sailors' Union shall lose his membership on that account;"[8] and to comply with other requirements of the international. However, the union flatly refused to be bound by the new amendments to the international constitution, insisting that the ISU submit them to a referendum of the entire membership before they became binding.

The Pacific Coast District ILA, controlled by Harry Bridges and his confederates, inquired about the negotiations. ISU Secretary-Treasurer Ivan Hunter replied July 14 that he would not suspend the amendments nor order a referendum on their validity. According to Bridges, the ILA District Executive Board decided that Hunter's letter "definitely laid a favorable basis regarding the restoration of the charter of the Sailors' Union, . . ."[9] In the National Labor Relations Board hearing in July, the international could not show that it represented a single sailor, as against 6,200 pledge cards for the SUP. Reflecting Communist bloc strategy, the Marine Firemen supported the international's contention that the Pacific District unions should bargain as a unit.

Ivan Hunter addressed "An Open Appeal" to the SUP July 24 to accept his proposal "to bring harmony between the Sailors' Union of the Pacific and the International Seamen's Union." San Francisco Local 38-79 voted "that we request the Sailors' Union to accept the return of their charter under the terms offered by the International Seamen's Union of America," with the understanding that "if the I.S.U. attempts to enforce the constitution to the DETRIMENT" of the Sailors, the ILA would support them.[10] The Sailors replied to Hunter's appeal with "An Open Letter from the Rank and File of the Sailors' Union of the Pacific" signed by eighteen San Francisco activists. Rather than bring harmony, they declared, the proposal would force the union to accept the illegal amendments, under which the ISU Executive Board could take over the funds, property, and entire union. Moreover, the international favored government fink halls and fink books, which it would attempt to force on the union.

The ideological complexion of seamen's unions in each port depended on the dominant voices in the weekly meetings. Besides port agents and patrolmen, who routinely attended meetings, articulate seamen from ships that happened to be in port could influence a meeting. As in other controversies, support for the Sailors' Union divided along factional lines. The Seattle and San Pedro federation district councils backed them, as did the Seattle, Portland, and San Pedro Marine Firemen, the

Portland and San Pedro Marine Cooks and Stewards, San Francisco Marine Engineers, and San Pedro Masters, Mates and Pilots. The Radio Telegraphists helped to distribute Hunter's appeal. SUP member S. Sorenson commented on a statement in the Communist *Maritime Worker* that "a small minority" blocked "efforts to force the sailors to accept the charter back on the conditions laid down by the International."

"Why don't the Communist party mind their own business?" he concluded. "What do they mean by a small minority group, when the whole coast is opposed? Only the C.P. and its stooges go for Hunter and Co.—and they are certainly very strange bedfellows!"[11] Local 38-79 finally voted August 17 to support the Sailors' Union, "in-as-much as they have stated that they want to be a part of the American Federation of Labor."[12] Clamor to accept the international terms subsided as the maritime unions prepared to negotiate with their employers.

King-Ramsey-Conner Case

During the summer of waiting, while the employers assured the public of their desire for waterfront peace, they concocted another frame-up to portray maritime unionists as thugs and murderers. Someone stabbed to death George W. Alberts, chief engineer on the Swayne & Hoyt freighter *Point Lobos*, in his cabin on March 22, 1936. For months police could not solve the murder. Then without warning on August 27, they arrested Earl King, secretary of the Marine Firemen, and Ernest Ramsey, patrolman, in San Francisco and George Wallace, a member of the union, in Brownsville, Texas. King was a lifelong union activist and a prominent Communist bloc adherent. Police picked up Frank Conner in Seattle a few days later. He had been the Marine Firemen's delegate on the *Point Lobos* at the time of the killing.

The grand jury indicted these four men and another fireman, Ben Zakovitz, for the murder of Alberts. The Marine Firemen immediately set up a defense committee supported by other maritime and uptown unions. Wallace refused the union's offer of funds for an attorney, choosing instead to be represented by a public defender, who worked closely with the prosecution. Alameda County District Attorney Earl Warren conducted the trial, which began November 12. The prosecutor disqualified all prospective jurors having union connections. Depending on testimony of Wallace and Albert Murphy, assistant secretary of the Marine Firemen, the prosecution tried to prove that King had ordered Murphy to give Ramsey money to hire Wallace and others to beat up the chief engineer. Wallace fingered Zakovitz, who could not be found, as the murderer, and named Conner and himself as accomplices. Union documents and testimony of officers on board the vessel at the time of the murder contradicted the story.

During the trial a bizarre plot unfolded: the district attorney's office had bugged a hotel room in which Murphy and his friend Frank Guidera tried to entrap and incriminate King. Swayne & Hoyt promised Roscoe Slade, who had been first assistant engineer on the *Point Lobos*, a ten-year job in South America for coloring his testimony, and the company paid two mates scheduled to testify for the prosecution each $175 a month, although by this time the strike had begun. After the trial a tape turned up linking the San Francisco police and representatives of an employers association to the frame-up.

At the close of the trial, Judge Frank M. Ogden, a colleague of Warren's, commented on the evidence. He accepted Wallace's story and rejected contradictory testimony. Guided by the judge's remarks, the jury convicted King, Ramsey, Conner, and Wallace of second degree murder on January 5, 1937. The Marine Firemen tried and expelled Albert Murphy for his police stool pigeon activities, and the Marine Cooks and Stewards took like action against Frank Guidera. After they had served years in San Quentin, Governor Culbert Olson pardoned King, Ramsey, and Conner.

Negotiations Begin

The longshoremen voted 6,357 to 2,083 to open the agreement; also over 90 percent voted for union preference, the six-hour day, coastwide uniform working conditions and penalty rates, and a wage increase to $1.00 straight time and $1.50 overtime. During August and September they assessed themselves $2.50 each month for a strike fund. The employers prepared for war when the current agreements expired. In a coastwide conference June 15-16, representatives of the Waterfront Employers of Seattle, Portland, San Francisco, and Los Angeles, the Pacific American Steamship Association, the Shipowners' Association of the Pacific Coast, and the Alaska operators formed the Coast Committee for the Shipowners, chaired by Tom Plant. The employers, said Plant, "must get together on a plan similar to that of the Maritime Federation to the policy of 'one for all and all for one.'"[13] Before the longshoremen could even present their demands, the employers took the offensive. The Coast Committee notified the ILA July 29 that they wished to modify the award and asked the union to agree to arbitrate all issues not settled by September 1, 1936. The longshoremen refused.

A month later the Coast Committee proposed changes that would strip longshoremen of their gains since 1934. They demanded a narrow definition of longshore work to evade the provisions of the award for many dock workers and changes in language to enable them to work one eight-hour or two six-hour shifts at straight time. In place of the fixed hourly rate they proposed an "efficiency wage" that would result in speedup and piece work. They wanted to reduce penalty pay and eliminate most travel pay. The employers proposed that the port labor relations committee, not the union, select the dispatcher, and that the committee be given power to impose severe penalties—loss of working time and blacklist—on longshoremen for violating the agreement. They would forbid sympathetic strikes. The employers warned the ILA: "If you permit the Award to terminate on September 30, we will then be obliged to advise you of the conditions under which we would be willing to continue the relationship, and that we would not be willing to continue the present conditions of the Award after that date."[14]

The ILA declared that the demands would "bring back the speed-up system, blacklisting, favoritism and starvation standards of living." "Your proposals," the union concluded, "are of such a nature that we . . . are in doubt at this time whether you are honestly and in good faith trying to arrive at an agreement."[15] The members voted 9,409 to 310 to reject the owners' proposals. To gain favor with the public, employer publicity emphasized their willingness to arbitrate as the means to assure waterfront peace—the union's refusal invited turmoil. Tom Plant asked International President Joe Ryan to "procure acceptance by the I.L.A. of the principle of arbitration." In reply Ryan urged that the differences be settled by direct negotiations. As for the demand for two straight-time six-hour shifts, he "would never submit that question to arbitration and any company that attempts to enforce the same will be immediately declared unfair in every port where we have jurisdiction."[16]

The Coast Committee tried to provoke federal intervention. John J. Walsh, representing the foreign lines, noted his conversation with Assistant Secretary of Labor Edward F. McGrady September 19:

> Walsh said employers had determined their program and were going to stay with it. McGrady said: "Won't you go along on the present agreement for a while?" Walsh said Sept. 30th is the deadline and if I.L.A. has agreed to arbitrate by that date, employers are going to push new wages and conditions under which they would employ men. McGrady said it will raise hell, and Walsh said maybe so, but everyone had his mind made up and would die a quick death [rather] than by slow strangulation. McGrady said can I tell the President you are going through with it on Sept. 30th. Walsh said absolutely.[17]

The employers attempted to commit the Maritime Commission to insist on arbitration by October 15 as a condition for extending the agreement beyond September 30. Tom Plant reported to the Waterfront Employers October 1 "that the Maritime Commission was a new agency that had been brought into the picture and might offer definite help to the shipowners in working out their problems with maritime labor."[18]

The seafaring groups encountered equal difficulties with their employers. Although the NLRB delayed a decision, both the steam schooner operators and the offshore companies agreed to recognize the Sailors' Union Emergency Committee as bargaining agent, and the international did not interfere in the direct negotiations of the Marine Firemen and Marine Cooks and Stewards. The unlicensed seamen wanted more money, cash overtime instead of time back, and their hiring halls confirmed in writing in the agreement. The Sailors wanted the six-hour day for cargo work on steam schooners, and the Marine Cooks and Stewards wanted an eight-hour day at sea.

The Sailors' Union levied a $5.00 strike assessment and voted 1,928 to 295 to terminate the agreements and awards. The union cautioned that with negotiations in progress the shipowners were "only waiting for something to holler about."[19] Crews should wait until they reached San Francisco to settle minor disputes. However, the union would not be intimidated by employer threats. The Sailors backed Charles Brenner, delegate, when the master of the Dollar Line *President Hoover* refused to sign him on for another trip. Brenner and others had charged Captain Yardley with violating rules of safety at sea. When the union refused to ship a replacement, the offshore operators threatened to break off negotiations and advertised for scabs. Harry Lundeberg declared: "If the Dollar Line or any other line is allowed to discriminate or blackball any man or spokesman for the union, it will mean that we will be back to the old blackball system that we had before the '34 strike. Fear of discrimination will face every man, . . ."[20] The *President Hoover* sailed with her original crew, including Brenner, and Dollar sued the Sailors' Union for $80,000 damages for delaying the vessel.

When the offshore operators finally met with the Sailors' Union on September 17 they offered harsh and unacceptable terms. They proposed that each side should post a $20,000 surety bond for performance of the agreement; that the shipowners would be free to hire nonunion men if the union could not supply satisfactory help, and union men would not refuse to work with or discriminate against them; and that union members would comply with "statutes of the United States relating to merchant seamen."[21] This statement would force seamen to accept the Copeland fink book and certificate of efficiency. The employers agreed to preference of employment but not union hiring halls and reserved the right to fire or refuse to hire a seaman for any cause. They demanded cuts in wages and working conditions and provision for a labor relations board to settle disputes. The licensed officers and radio operators had no more success with their demands for preference of employment and wage increases. As with the other crafts, the shipowners demanded that the unions arbitrate all issues not resolved by September 30.

At the invitation of the Maritime Federation, the coastwide negotiating committees of the separate crafts began meeting jointly August 22. The unions would exchange information and agree on uniform policies. Thus the meetings would ensure united action while preserving each union's autonomy. Over the objections of the Sailors' Union, each craft had one vote regardless of size.

Shipowners Stall

From the outset the unions questioned the employers' sincerity. On September 1 the Coast Committee for the Shipowners released to all shippers the correspondence with the unions, charging them "'with one or two exceptions'—with daily violations of contracts merely for the purpose of creating trouble and delay."[22] To gain public sympathy the employers lamented loudly the unions' repeated refusal to arbitrate. The *Voice of the Federation* charged September 24: "As far as the shipowners are concerned, the negotiations have thus far been a sounding board for their bales of propaganda. They came there merely to play a part which they had already decided upon."

As September 30 approached with little progress, the unions considered extending the negotiations. The licensed groups had only begun to meet with their employers, and the Marine Cooks and Stewards had rejected the offshore operators proposal 724 to 27 and refused to arbitrate as well. The Joint Negotiation Committee voted September 25 to request a fifteen-day extension. With a presidential election less than two months away, the federal government intervened to avert a strike. The newly appointed Maritime Commission, with undefined power over labor relations, requested a sixty-day truce. The ILA and Radio Telegraphists favored thirty, and the unlicensed seamen insisted on fifteen. The Joint Negotiation Committee voted September 29 to accept the thirty-day truce. The employers refused, seemingly determined to force arbitration or a strike or a lockout. Local 38-79 reported: "Just how well their plans have been laid can be seen from the fact that 30 hours before the deadline the docks are practically free of cargo. The Admiral Line and McCormick Steamship Company have refused freight as early as last Tuesday and the last ships of both lines have cleared port. No ships are scheduled to sail from here after Saturday of this week."[23] At the last minute, September 30, the shipowners agreed to the fifteen-day extension.

Assistant Secretary of Labor Edward F. McGrady later confirmed the fact that the employers had been planning a prolonged lockout to break the unions. From Seattle, the Marine Firemen reported that "a large tent . . . has been put up in back of the dock at Pier 41, and numerous carloads of sleeping cots, kitchen utensils and equipment, and loads of canned food have been put aboard the President Madison (a ship lying along side the dock for several years.)"[24] The September 30 issue of the University of California student paper at Berkeley headlined: "Attempts at Arbitration Appear Hopeless; Shipowners Expect Violence From Longshoremen," and military training students at the university received a hypothetical problem to solve: They had to make a plan to defend the campus against gangs armed with clubs, pistols, and stolen rifles during a waterfront and general strike.

To counter such slander and the hostile daily press, the unions took their case to the public. In San Pedro the federation district council sponsored a weekly radio program, and the unions bombarded newspapers with their story. In Seattle the Longshoremen appropriated $1,000 for publicity. Several radio broadcasts featured the union cause, and the union sponsored two mass meetings, one addressed by Mayor John F. Dore with 5,000 present. The *Guild Daily*, published by striking *P-I* unionists, printed 20,000 copies of a special insert, "Presenting the Union's Side."

The days passed with little accomplished. Ed Coester noted bitterly that the offshore operators had conceded one point, "that all dishes shall be crockery ware" – a condition already in effect. But "that the shipowners concede this might be mutually AGREED UPON denotes progress."[25] The "SUP Notes" commented on the seamen's impatience with the shipowners' stalling:

> On many ships the crews sent telegrams after telegrams demanding strike action be taken. On many ships the crews got tired of the delays and took action themselves. Before the official Strike Orders were issued, ships up and down the Coast were tied up, and several ships on the East Coast and Gulf. . . . When the Shipowners mentioned Arbitration on all issues involved, the Seamen pulled their belt in a notch and stood ready to use their Economic Action on the Picket Line.[26]

By October 13 Edward McGrady and the federal mediators returned to the Joint Negotiation Committee to urge another extension until the Maritime Commission, the new federal agency created by the Merchant Marine Act of 1936, could hold a hearing. With the Sailors' Union and Marine Cooks and Stewards opposed, the committee voted to extend negotiations to October 26, when the Maritime

Commission would become effective. The employers assented to an indefinite extension. The unions polled their members to strike at midnight October 28 unless the employers met the two fundamental demands of each union, which were: Marine Engineers, preferences of employment and uniform manning; Masters, Mates and Pilots, preference of employment and cash overtime; Radio Telegraphists and Marine Cooks and Stewards, hiring halls and an eight-hour day; Marine Firemen and Sailors' Union, hiring halls and cash overtime; and Longshoremen, hiring halls and the six-hour day.

The Maritime Commission objected to the unions' time limit. "It must insist," the wire read, "on compliance with its demands until the investigations are completed and the findings are announced." The Joint Negotiation Committee replied to this "veiled threat":

> [The unions] have attempted to cooperate to the fullest extent with the Maritime Commission to avoid a tie up. The present fifteen day extension granted at the request of the commission has resulted in great unrest on the part of our membership due to the employers' attitude in refusing bona-fide negotiations. This situation has been aggrevated by the commission's latest assumption of authority not yet in effect, when the public and unions were looking to them to take a neutral and pacifying attitude.[27]

In a statement to all members in the *Voice* October 22 the ILA District Executive Board accused the Sailors' Union and Marine Cooks and Stewards of repudiating the joint committee decision to take a strike vote, thereby threatening to split the federation. Had the committee agreed to the request of the two unions, the ILA charged, "it would have meant just dodging the question and finally being forced into an unconditional extension such as the employers had requested, for perhaps another year."[28]

The Sailors' Union and Marine Cooks and Stewards replied that the accusation was false—based on selective quotations from committee minutes that did not present an accurate account of the disagreement over policy. "The statement makes an effort to place upon the Sailors' Union of the Pacific and the Marine Cooks and Stewards' the responsibility for anything that may happen which might be detrimental to the Maritime Federation." They warned of the "grave danger" of "the campaign which has been started to discredit any position which may not agree with that of those responsible for the I.L.A. statement. The greatest enemy to unity is any attitude which seeks to choke criticism, take advantage of differences of opinion for factional purposes and try to raise a lynch spirit against a minority opinion."[29]

Rear Admiral Harry G. Hamlet arrived in San Francisco on October 18 representing the Maritime Commission. He proposed that the industry continue to work under present awards and contracts for a year. The employers agreed; the unions continued to try to negotiate. Modifying their initial outrageous proposals, the Waterfront Employers offered to renew the ILA agreement for longshoremen and checkers. The Longshoremen rejected an offer by twenty-six eastern and foreign steamship lines of an agreement granting the desired wage increase because it did not include the seafaring unions. The ILA also negotiated with the steam schooner operators. The unions voted over 90 percent to authorize a strike October 28. Harry Lundeberg reported to the Sailors' Union branches October 25:

> Joint Negotiating Committee met on Saturday [the 24th] with Hamlet in order to impress upon him the seriousness of the situation and see whether he could find ways and means of forcing the shipowners to concede the minimum demands and gave him a written statement that if these demands were not met by Wednesday the unions would be out.
>
> The Admiral said he was powerless to make the shipowners come through with these demands. The only solution he could offer on Saturday was a further extension.

The Sailors strike vote carried 1,861 to 136. "Only a miracle" now could prevent a strike, he concluded. "The branches, therefore, should make the necessary arrangements."[30]

The four major West Coast steamship lines, Dollar, Matson, Swayne & Hoyt, and American-Hawaiian, formed the core of employer opposition. All day the 28th the seafaring unions met one by one with Tom Plant for the Coast Committee of the Shipowners. None gained their fundamental demands. All refused to sign separate agreements without settlements for the other unions. Plant declared further negotiations would be useless. The Joint Negotiation Committee voted that night to delay the strike in the hope of reaching agreements with the steam schooner operators. The Sailors and Firemen had reached agreements, although other crafts had not come to terms.

When the committee met the morning of the 29th, the Radio Telegraphists and Marine Engineers moved for a twenty-four-hour postponement, supported by the Communist bloc. During the stormy meeting that followed, Harry Bridges announced that regardless of other unions the ILA intended to wire all locals that the strike would take effect at midnight the 29th if "no satisfactory arrangement" had been reached. The delegates had no choice but to go along with the ILA. Negotiations during the day produced no settlement. When the delegates reconvened at nine they tabled Marine Firemen Roy Farrell's motion to strike at midnight. The Marine Cooks and Stewards reported that their members "were going to strike tonight for the 8-hour day."[31] Shortly before eleven the weary delegates broke for a belated supper. When they returned they voted unanimously to strike. Immediately they notified their union halls filled with waiting members. Five hundred Marine Firemen thundered their approval and began registering to picket. Other unions activated their strike committees at once and sent pickets down to the waterfront. Hugh O'Neill, chair of the Marine Firemen's Negotiations Committee, spoke for many members:

> The negotiations of the past few months were nothing but a farce. The shipowners never at any time intended to negotiate anything with us. They went through the motion in order to save their faces with the public, and while fooling the public into believing that they were trying to avert a tie-up of shipping, they were not only preparing for a tie-up but doing everything they could to cause one.[32]

Strike!

Down on the Embarcadero longshoremen ceased work, and crews of the *President Hoover*, the banana boats, and other vessels, packed and ready, shouldered their sea bags and came ashore. Word sped by wire up and down the coast to federation district council meetings waiting for the expected strike call. Along the entire Pacific Coast work stopped on the docks and crews walked off their ships. Strike committees met first thing in the morning, and clusters of pickets took up their stations at each dock. All except a few licensed officers responded to the strike call, tying up 136 vessels in the major ports: 27 at Seattle, 30 at Portland, 57 at San Francisco and Oakland, and 22 at San Pedro. Additional crews struck as more ships arrived daily. The picket line stretched the length of the Pacific Coast for 1,700 miles. Only the unorganized tankers continued to sail.

Both the unions and the employers declared they had made every effort to avoid the strike. Edward McGrady termed the walkout "sheer madness," a "challenge to the welfare of the nation."[33] Joseph B. Weaver, director of the Bureau of Marine Inspection and Navigation, called for immediate appropriation of funds to open government hiring halls for seagoing personnel. Tom Plant called the strike "outright defiance of Federal interest and authority."[34] Although Plant asserted that the

Seamen pickets around an oil drum, Seattle, November 2, 1936. (Seattle Star)

shipowners "have no plans to continue operations at present," Mayor Angelo Rossi proclaimed a state of emergency in San Francisco, and Chief of Police Quinn sent 108 extra police officers to the waterfront. Seven patrol cars cruised the area, their occupants armed with shotguns and tear gas bombs. Los Angeles Chief James E. Davis put police on twelve-hour shifts and dispatched 400 to the harbor area. Mayor Joseph Carson warned that "law and order will prevail in Portland,"[35] and in Seattle paid newspaper ads invited citizens to "Clip, Sign and Mail" coupons enrolling them in the Law and Order League, with membership "strictly confidential." The ad asked if they would "respond to a call by public officials for emergency service."[36]

The shipowners demanded that either the unions or the government place skeleton crews on struck vessels for protection against fire, theft, or destruction of merchandise, and that perishable cargo and ship stores be removed. The Joint Policy Committee, formerly the Joint Negotiation Committee, voted October 31 not to permit masters and chief engineers to remain aboard vessels, but it authorized removal of perishable ship stores. The shipowners then hired watchmen for each vessel. The Maritime Commission investigation opened in San Francisco on November 2 with a statement by employers' attorney Gregory Harrison. After listening for fifteen minutes, attorneys for the unions walked out in protest against the commission's apparent intention to function as an arbitration board. At noon Admiral Hamlet adjourned the hearings indefinitely.

Strike or not, longshoremen would work in an emergency if they received proper treatment. At San Pedro November 1 Panama Pacific executives, bare-handed and sweating, grabbed the lines of the approaching *S.S. California*, warped her to the dock, and tied her up, amid the cheers of passengers and longshoremen standing by. When the Matson line *Mariposa* arrived a short time later, longshoremen handled the lines for their asking wage of $1.00 an hour. They also furnished men to help crew and firemen fight a fire in the hold of the *Edward Luckenbach* when she arrived from New York. At Seattle when 250 tons of fishmeal aboard the *Latouche* reached a dangerously high temperature, the strike committee dispatched seamen and longshoremen to remove the cargo, half their wages to go to the joint kitchen fund.

The hostile press recalled the violence of the 1934 strike and deplored the loss of jobs and hardships the strike imposed on workers in other industries. The West Coast Lumbermen's Association said November 2 that by the end of the week production of lumber mills would be down to 25 percent and 20,000 loggers and mill workers would be either without jobs or working part time.

Countering the animosity of the business community, the union movement responded to the strike with immediate moral and financial support. The Lumber and Sawmill Workers assessed its 70,000 members $1.00 each for the Northwest strikers. Thus the union acknowledged the maritime workers' contribution to victory in the 1935 lumber strike when they refused to touch hot lumber and kept forty-two vessels tied up on the coast. Other unions donated generously, and the San Francisco Laborers Local 261 pledged up to $10,000 for strike relief if needed. The Boat Owners Cooperative Association of San Pedro and San Francisco donated $3,488.60.

Hot Bananas

The unions released all fair cargo on the docks when the strike began and perishable ship stores that would spoil for lack of refrigeration. But the question of releasing perishable cargo, also bound to spoil without refrigeration, generated a major difference in strike policy. Again the unions split along ideological lines. Arguing that the strikers must not antagonize the public, the Communist bloc and some conservatives, principally among the licensed officers, wanted to release all perishable cargo. Their opponents, militants and ex-Wobblies, replied that the shippers knew the danger of a strike and had insurance to cover their losses—that the unions must make the strike as effective as possible.

The Joint Policy Committee voted November 3 to request the local strike committees "to provide men to remove perishable cargoes on struck ships."[37] San Francisco agreed, Seattle and San Pedro refused, and Portland delayed action. The committee wired Seattle: "Joint Policy Committee very strongly urges you to conform to yesterday's action on perishable cargo stop. Very great pressure from US Labor Dept. local press and public stop. We feel unified coast policy on this issue extremely important."[38]

The perishable cargo controversy focused on the ripening bananas in the holds of vessels at San Pedro. The importer to whom the 4,216 stems of bananas on the *California* were consigned went to court November 7 to secure a libel on the cargo. Federal Judge Paul J. McCormick granted the request, instructing U.S. Marshal Robert Clark to employ people "at not less than the union scale" to unload the bananas, provided the consignee posted a $7,500 bond against damage to the ship. According to a United Press dispatch, Harry Bridges wired the strike committee "to place union longshoremen aboard the California to work the cargo."[39] The strikers did not budge. Meanwhile, the United Fruit liner *Talamanca* approached San Pedro November 2 with her refrigerated holds full of bananas. Rather than dock and lose both crew and refrigeration, she cruised in the roadstead.

In spite of Joint Policy Committee pressure, the coast remained deadlocked. The San Pedro Strike Committee sent Elmer Bruce of the ILA, John Kucin of the Masters, Mates and Pilots, Britt Webster of the Sailors, and A.C. Correa of the Marine Engineers to San Francisco to present their views. On November 8 the Joint Policy Committee denied them the floor until after voting to begin handling perishable cargo the next morning. Then the committee permitted them to speak, when their opinions no longer mattered. The Marine Firemen's meeting refused to hear them, persuaded by Communist bloc adherent Walter Stack's opposition. *The West Coast Sailors* apologized to the San Pedro delegation for San Francisco's shabby treatment.

The Sailors' Union voted coastwide 1,166 to 58 on November 7 not to work perishables. The Columbia River Joint Strike Committee voted not to work, and Seattle voted November 8 to work. Attorney General Homer Cummings delayed execution of the San Pedro court order. The Joint Policy Committee recommended November 11 that "no consideration be given to removal of perishable cargo or action thereon until shippers withdraw court orders instructing U.S. marshal to remove perishables."[40] The $10,000 worth of bananas on the *California* lay buried under

Picketing hot bananas on the S.S. California, *San Pedro, November 1936. (*The ISU Pilot, *New York)*

2,500 cubic feet of nonperishables.

The San Pedro strikers charged that the employers practiced "a deliberate fraud" on the judge in their request for libel—that their "real purpose was to put the U.S. government in such a position that it would have to act as a giant strike breaking agency."[41] Asked what he would do if the marshal ordered him to work, one longshoreman replied that there was "nothing to stop them from unloading them bananas one by one." What really worried him was "getting up steam on the vessels."[42]

Marshal Clark reported that an attempt to unload the bananas would invite violence, and he would be forced to demand a $10 million federal bond from the shipowners before carrying out the order. He testified that union officials warned him of trouble if he attempted to unload the bananas. The *Voice of the Federation* related: "'Have you had telephone calls offering help in unloading the cargo?' [U.S. District Attorney] Hall asked. 'Yes, from gunmen and detective agencies,' the marshal smiled quietly. 'But I need banana men.'" Hall contended that "no actual controversy existed between the libelant and the respondent shipowner," and moved "to dismiss the suit on the ground that it is a sham and collusive."[43] The following week the court dismissed the petition. A fleet of garbage trucks hauled 1,600 stems of bananas, poured ashore on the Matson docks and smelling horribly, to the city dump. In January San Pedro longshoremen unloaded cocoa beans for medicine, turning over their pay to the strike committee, but they refused to touch 2,000 tons of Argentine corn for poultry feed, declaring, "We are on strike—and when we strike we don't work cargo."[44]

Secretary of Labor Perkins urged the unions and employers to negotiate. The unions agreed, but Tom Plant declared that the strike was "the culmination of two years of planned violation by the unions of all awards and agreements."[45] He elaborated: "Union leaders insist that they shall be the ones to determine in whose hands owners must entrust their ships. They have called a strike in an attempt to seize this and other means of completely controlling the maritime industry. To resume negotiations under current circumstances would be useless."[46]

Although most of the unions had reached tentative agreements with the steam schooner operators before the strike, the coastwise employers refused to negotiate. Turning to the offshore owners, the assistant secretary of labor persuaded Tom Plant to meet with the Sailors and Firemen. The encounter November 17 accomplished nothing. Plant reiterated the employers' objections to union hiring halls. "He stated," Harry Lundeberg reported, "that the shipowners wanted full and entire selection of crews without any stipulations . . . that this was the shipowners' right; that they were the ones *WHO OWNED THE SHIPS*, and should have the power to say whether a man worked or not."[47] Negotiations ended.

Joint Policy Committee Takes Over

Shipowners and the press might try to scare the public with stories about "Communist radicals" leading the strike and plotting to take over the American Merchant Marine. Actually, measured in terms of aggressive class struggle against the shipowners, the Communist bloc became the conservatives. At the beginning of the strike, without authorization from their unions, the delegates comprising the Joint Negotiation Committee voted to continue its existence as the Joint Policy Committee. The same coalition of conservative licensed officers and Communist bloc followers that had urged caution and delay before the strike continued to control the committee. They favored working perishable cargo to appease public opinion and generally stressed the importance of courting the public to win the strike. Their opposition, centered around the Sailors' Union and the San Pedro longshoremen, advocated policies that would exert the greatest economic pressure on the shipowners to grant the unions' demands.

Originally created to exchange information about the status of negotiations, the committee assumed the right to set coastwide policy. The committee voted November 6 to restrict sources of strike news for the *Voice of the Federation* because the editor printed a report that the Atlantic Coast ILA worked hot West Coast ships. Ed Krumholz of the Grays Harbor longshoremen objected to "gagging the press." Four days later editor Barney Mayes and several of the editorial board appeared before the committee to protest the gag order. Henry Schrimpf declared that "Any official strike news received by the Editorial Staff shall be published in the 'Voice,'" and Mayes defended the policy of printing both sides of controversial labor issues. Harry Bridges, seconded by Walter Stack, replied that "WE have to decide policy of strike" and objected to "injecting independent industrial unionism" in the paper.[48]

Five ILA executive board members voted against Bridges's position: Ed Krumholz, C.J. Miller, Andy Larsen, Lee Gholson, and Con Negstad. Harry Lundeberg commented in a letter to Bob Dombroff: "It seems as if these five members are impressed with the sentiment of the rank and file and that of the District Councils in Seattle and San Pedro against this so-called Joint Policy Committee and seem to feel that there must be a control established immediately before this policy committee becomes a cheap addition of the C.P."[49]

Strikers in other ports protested against the self-appointed committee. Asserting that it was "acting without proper authority from the rank and file membership of the maritime unions," the Seattle Sailors demanded November 9 that the Joint Policy Committee be disbanded and that the Maritime Federation Executive Board, enlarged by one member from each craft from each port, assume its duties, voting to be on a per capita basis.[50] The Northwest Joint Strike Committee nonconcurred, killing the proposal.

The Portland longshoremen demanded information: "What constitutes the Joint Policy Committee? How many organizations vote on it? What are its powers?"[51] In the committee itself November 10 Ed Krumholz moved to "dissolve this Policy Committee until we resume negotiations." Charlie Cates, Sailors, seconded the motion "because we have DICTATED POLICIES instead of recommending them to the Strike Committees."[52] The motion lost. To facilitate communication between the major ports, the Maritime Federation installed teletype equipment in the San Francisco and district council offices in November.

The strikers unanimously condemned shipowners' attempts to paint their unions red, but they objected strenuously when Communists tried to exploit this sentiment to discredit their critics. An article appeared in the *N.W. Joint Strike Committee Bulletin* January 21 describing "stoolies," which were "found in many unions where they do their masters bidding and carry on his dirty work from the inside." They were "either super-conservative or super-militant," explained the writer:

> For example, if they customarily comb their hair, wear a necktie and carry themselves with a slight degree of dignity they become conservatives; whereas on the other hand if they never had a necktie on in their life they become super-militants. . . . they find a way to work very closely together on nearly all issues and to unite in an attack on sincere union men who oppose them. One of their favorite methods of attack is to follow out the example of their masters the shipowners and Willie Hearst by raising the redscare and shouting "communist" and "Moscow agents" at honest union men.[53]

In other words, anti-Communists in the unions were shipowners' agents. The Seattle Sailors labeled the article "a new and subtle form of 'militant-baiting' . . . just keep track of all guys whose policy is to the left of the Communist Party and if he doesn't wear a necktie, why nail him quick because he is a 'stoolie.'" The correspondent concluded:

> We are sorry to have to say this but someone must take the lead to prevent our strike bulletin from being used for any cheap red-baiting. We hope that the infantile mind responsible for such trash will stick to the job of printing strike news in our North-West Joint Strike Bulletin. We praise the fine work being done by the publicity committee and hope that it accepts this criticism with the friendly spirit in which it is given.[54]

East Coast Seamen

Encouraged by West Coast support, the East Coast seamen's rebellion against their corrupt and autocratic officials swept forward irresistibly. As the struggle escalated, the international's increasingly repressive and violent tactics drove more and more seamen into the Seamen's Defense Committee, chaired by Joseph Curran. By the end of October 1936 the committee's weekly paper, *The I.S.U. Pilot* had grown to an eight-page tabloid. The paper's editorial policy indicated that the Communist bloc controlled the movement.

The Seamen's Defense Committee called on Atlantic and Gulf seamen to sit down in sympathy with the Pacific Coast strike. Beginning in New York, the sit-down spread to Boston, Philadelphia, Baltimore, Houston, New Orleans, and other ports, affecting 14,919 seamen and 214 ships by November 5, according to Curran. East Coast seamen struck November 6 for West Coast wages and conditions. In reply to their plea for West Coast support, the Joint Policy Committee wired Curran that it would "recommend to membership here that if effective strike takes place on East and Gulf coasts West Coast will support insofar intercoastal ships are concerned."[55]

ISU officials branded the strike illegal and prepared to smash it. David Grange called on "loyal members to stand by their ships and take them to sea in fulfillment of the agreement," which ran until December 31, 1937. He labeled Curran "a dummy on the knee of the communists."[56] Joe Ryan said that by the middle of December the Communist Party had advanced $3,700 to the Strike Strategy Committee and would give an additional $3,000 that Curran said he needed. The *Pilot* ran ten pages with many pictures and claimed a circulation of over 30,000.

Earlier in the year the Sailors' Union had been the East Coast seamen's staunchest supporter, feeding and housing stranded members and donating to their strike. The Seamen's Defense Committee opened halls in San Francisco and San Pedro, over the protests of the Sailors' Union that the halls "can only create confusion at this time and aid the labor fakers of the ISU in their assertions that the East Coast members cannot receive proper treatment on this Coast . . ."[57] The East Coast men, represented by Peter Innes, refused to accept strike relief from the West Coast unions. Instead, in late November Innes submitted a bill to New York for feeding East Coast strikers in

San Pedro. With over 1,500 West Coast men being fed and housed by the Seamen's Defense Committee in Atlantic and Gulf ports, the Sailors' Union deplored this seemingly forced separation. The East Coast men in San Pedro rejected the union's request to close their hall and accept West Coast strike cards.

Union longshoremen internationally supported the seamen. Members of the Confederation of Mexican Workers refused to discharge the Grace liner *Santa Elena* in Ensenada, and French dockers at Havre would not unload cargo from two vessels with scab East Coast crews.

Two days into the strike the press bewailed Alaska's serious plight, with a supply of perishables to last less than a fortnight. The strikers negotiated with Col. O.F. Ohlson for the Interior Department to operate vessels chartered from the Alaska Packers. Under the agreement signed November 27 the unions won their entire demands, including eight hours for cooks and stewards.

In 1934 the unions had negotiated a similar agreement with the Alaska operators. This time, however, the *West Coast Sailors* noted, the Alaska operators joined the Coast Committee for the Shipowners. "If they had stayed in Seattle and attended to their business, . . . instead of listening to the siren's song of T.G. Plant & Co. it is very likely that they could have been supplying Alaska now instead of watching the good old Alaska Packers dipping up the gravy with nothing to lose."[58] The Bureau of Indian Affairs steamer *Boxer* sailed from Seattle December 5 with relief supplies, followed by the Alaska Packers *Arctic* the next day and the *General W.C. Gorgas* the middle of December. This time no one attacked the agreement as a sell-out.

Strikers questioned the plight of starving Alaskans. (SUP striker Robert L. Scanlon in N.W. Joint Strike Committee Bulletin*)*

At the outset the unions instructed crews to return to their home ports. Then, on November 2 the Joint Policy Committee ordered seamen to strike at once in any American port. The new order stemmed from the employers' refusal "to negotiate the two fundamental issues of each organization," said Federation Secretary Kelley. "It was not our intention to tie up the whole world, but it is our intention to get the demands for which we struck."[59] Crews of three Alaska vessels struck at Vancouver, B.C., and ILA locals at Juneau, Cordova, Ketchikan, and Seward joined the strike, causing the Alaska Railroad to suspend operations. Six ships in Alaska waters returned home without unloading. Juneau longshoremen discharged medical supplies and drugs only.

Six vessels lay idle in Hawaii with 900 seamen on strike, joined by union longshoremen at Honolulu and Hilo. Governor Joseph B. Poindexter appealed to Edward McGrady to secure release of the *Lurline* and *President Pierce*, homeward bound, to bring 600 stranded passengers back to the mainland. The Joint Policy Committee ordered the Honolulu strikers to release the ships. The local strike committee agreed, provided union longshoremen worked them and the employers included the Hawaiian locals in future negotiations. The employers refused, and the ships remained tied up. Subsequently the homeward bound Matson liner *Monterey* picked up 447 people, boarding them from pineapple barges in Honolulu harbor to prevent the crew from striking.

The strikers agreed to clear relief ships for Hawaii under the same conditions as the Alaska agreement, but Col. Ohlson could find no return cargoes to make the trip pay its way. Foreign vessels and an army transport supplied the Islands with canned milk and medical supplies. In late November 1,600 seamen and longshoremen picketed in Honolulu. An efficient soup kitchen had served 15,000 meals since opening, but the problem of lodgings remained acute. Men slept on Japanese mats on the floor of the union hall. Supporters later donated bedding, and some merchants aided the strikers. The maritime workers stood firm in this far Pacific outpost, a microcosm of the struggle on the mainland.

14

On the Picket Lines

Beneath the clamor over whether to release hot bananas or let them rot, the strike held strong—plenty strong enough to surmount differences over working perishable cargo and other policies, because the many thousand strikers knew they must stand solid or be destroyed. Surrounded by the pressures of an indifferent or hostile society, they must support and nurture this voluntary organization, this federation of unions that they transformed into an army to fight a war with the shipowners.

Up and down the coast strikers mobilized for the day-to-day challenge of keeping the ships tied up. In most major ports the Maritime Federation district councils became joint strike committees to coordinate activities and set policies. Relief committees provided for the most urgent needs: food for strikers and their families and lodging for seamen. The strikers set picket watches to patrol the waterfront around the clock and named publicity committees to tell their story to the community.

Northwest Strike Committee

With 3,000 on strike in Seattle by October 31, 1936, pickets dispatched from the ILA and Sailors' Union halls stood six-hour watches, later changed to eight on and forty off. The Sailors bought a truck for $275 and fixed it up to haul pickets, "dry and in comfort," to their stations. Not anticipating that scabs would invade the deserted piers, the pickets camped beside the railroad tracks across Alaskan Way from the docks. They erected small shanties and built fires in oil drums to protect themselves from the November cold and rain. The Northwest Joint Strike Committee urged pickets not to leave a mess at their stations and to "KEEP YOUR FIRES DOWN." The Seattle Fire Department soon required covers and two lengths of stovepipe for the drums. The *Strike Bulletin* reported November 6:

> All is quiet on the waterfront. . . . The silence is only broken now and then when the patrol captains and the coffee car goes the rounds. When their mission is fulfilled silence returns and the only thing audible is the voices of the men on duty talking about past achievements and the noise of a burning wood fire. The nights are pretty chilly and a little fire goes a long way to drive away that desire for two overcoats instead of one.[1]

Until the soup kitchen opened the unions issued restaurant meal tickets to their members, and the relief committee sent coffee and sandwiches to the picket lines from temporary kitchens. The joint soup kitchen, run by the Marine Cooks and Stewards, opened at 1400 Western Avenue on November 13, with a seating capacity of 240. Each union paid for the meals for its members. By December the kitchen served 1,500 men three meals a day at a cost of 10 cents a meal. The committee opened a commissary to distribute groceries to strikers with families. Union foraging committees solicited donations for the soup kitchen and commissary from wholesalers and produce dealers, and the strike committee purchased the rest of the food. Members of the ILA and Maritime Federation women's auxiliaries helped in the commissary. After the strike committee released seven refrigerator cars of eggs from a cold storage warehouse, the Washington Co-Op donated two cases to the relief kitchen.

By mid-November the Sailors had secured beds for 35 pickets, and early in December the Joint Strike Committee opened a dormitory over the soup kitchen, dubbed the "Glacier Palace" by the strikers, to accommodate 150 single men. Both the Sailors and Firemen operated volunteer barber shops in their halls. "Nothing like tonsorial perfection on the picket line," the *Strike Bulletin* quipped. Fuel companies donated wood and coal to the strikers, and the Commonwealth Co-Op Shoe Shop offered to repair their shoes free. Dr. Weiss, member of Seattle Warehousemen's ILA Local 38-117, and himself on strike against Blumaur-Frank Drug Company, donated his services to the strikers. The relief committee appealed for donations of coats, pants, sweaters, and shoes for strikers and magazines for sick members. Sympathizers also contributed women's and children's clothing. The committee urged strikers falling behind in installment payments to get help from their unions if they could not negotiate extensions.

Beginning November 10 the Northwest Joint Strike Committee added more members and met daily to deal with the multitude of problems arising from the strike. It acted on an endless stream of requests to release cargo or grant access to dock facilities. While most fair cargo remained on the docks until November 11, the strikers released a few items for their friends: newsprint for the *Guild Daily* and linens from the McCormick dock for the women's sewing project of the Works Progress Administration. They released ten tons of perishable ship stores—meat, butter, and eggs—from the *Eldorado* to be donated to the Salvation Army. At the health department's request they authorized unloading of the 200 frozen reindeer carcasses aboard the *Victoria*. In January they released the 1936 salmon pack for car loading, and they acceded to the Alaska Trollers Co-Op request to move a quantity of frozen fish in the territory, provided they used union boats and labor.

Local union strike committees handled their own problems, such as picket assignments, eligibility for relief, discipline, and the like. The Sailors' Union committee preferred charges against the crew of the *Donna Lane* for permitting the vessel to discharge cargo at Prince Rupert after the strike began. The Joint Strike Committee recommended that unions assess working members 50 percent of their wages, half for the committee and half for their own unions. The *Strike Bulletin* complained that when longshoremen loaded the Alaska relief ship *Arctic* a few job hogs managed to get in two shifts instead of sharing the work fairly.

On the fourth day of the strike Austin E. Griffiths, who had been endorsed by labor, introduced an ordinance in the Seattle City Council to ban picketing within fifty feet of an establishment and outlaw mass picketing (more than two people) entirely. Widespread opposition killed the measure. The strikers arranged radio programs, wrote press releases, and held mass meetings to counteract the shipowners' propaganda in the daily press, and members of the Maritime Federation Women's Auxiliary explained the strike to community groups. The strikers distributed 20,000 copies of the *Guild Daily* insert, "Presenting the Unions' Side," and sent speakers to Spokane and Grand Coulee in eastern Washington. To educate their own members, the strike committee sponsored classes in labor history and cultural events.

In addition to participating in the Northwest Joint Strike Committee, the unions in Washington lumber ports conducted their own strike. In Grays Harbor, where several ships lay idle, the unions formed a joint strike committee to coordinate picketing and other activities. In Everett the ILA Ladies Auxiliary managed the soup kitchen. The women put on a dance in early November that netted $200 for relief. At Christmas the auxiliary and the local gave a party for 200 children of strikers, complete with music, a clown, and Santa Claus. The auxiliary provided fruit, nuts, candy, and toys, and the Carpenters Union gave each child a fifty-cent piece.

Defeat of the British Columbia longshoremen in 1935 left the Vancouver waterfront dominated by the Shipping Federation and two company unions. During 1936 the ILA chartered small locals of longshoremen at Victoria, New Westminster, and some who worked coastwise vessels in Vancouver, but none controlled the work of the ports. Kingsley Navigation, with vessels running from Vancouver to U.S. Ports, employed ILA members, and the Seafarers' Industrial Union, an independent Canadian seamen's union, had partially organized Kingsley vessels. On the eve of the confrontation down south, the company joined the Shipping Federation and notified Vancouver ILA Local 38-126 that it would no longer employ union longshoremen.

As the strike shut down U.S. ports from Alaska to San Diego, Washington and Oregon fruit growers sent their crops by rail to Vancouver, and foreign steamers changed their course to avoid the strikebound ports. The *Seattle Star* headlined November 2: "Shippers Indicate Vancouver Will Benefit Much From Coast Strike." True to their prediction, the port hummed with activity. The Pacific Coast District ILA called out Vancouver and Victoria locals, promising that they would be included in the agreement.

Local 38-126 picketed the Vancouver waterfront and appealed in vain to company union men to stop scabbing and join the ILA, repeating the promise: "The I.L.A. can and does guarantee that any agreement signed by the District Negotiating Committee will apply to the whole Pacific Coast, *including all B.C. locals*."[2] The scabs did not respond, and cargo moved unimpeded across Vancouver docks while shipping increased threefold. Merchants sent goods diverted from U.S. ports and offloaded at Vancouver south by rail to Seattle, Portland, and California. Washington strikers traced the hot cargo across the border, published boxcar numbers, and picketed the cars on sidings, preventing them from being unloaded. For example, they identified hot pulp and paper in Great Northern, Chicago Northwestern, Reading, and New York Central boxcars. They reported January 12: "So far, we have been 100 per cent effective in blockading this leak of hot cargo."[3] But train crews in the Southern Pacific and Western Pacific yards in the Bay Area reportedly handled B.C. hot cargo. Union teamsters refused to touch cargo from picketed boxcars, including four of them on an Oakland siding filled with hot bananas from the Gulf, and a crew in San Pedro refused to move a car of hot bananas.

Announcing that they had "no quarrel with the public," Portland longshoremen authorized removal from the docks of fair cargo discharged before the strike. The union also permitted individual farmers driving their own trucks or employing union teamsters to haul their fruit to waterfront cold storage facilities. In Portland about 1,500 longshoremen and 700 seamen struck, with more seamen joining the picket lines as their ships docked. Approximately 20 strikers picketed every dock and terminal. Local 38-78 put out 105 squads of twelve men each, picketing eight hours on and thirty-two off. The union took in twenty-five walking bosses, many of whom had not belonged since the 1934 strike. The unlicensed seamen's unions bought an old school bus for $75.00 to haul pickets to their stations. As elsewhere, the Marine Cooks and Stewards operated the joint soup kitchen. Steamboat inspectors harassed mates and engineers on the lines, demanding to see their papers and threatening to revoke their licenses. An estimated thousand pickets patrolled the Columbia River ports.

The Ladies Auxiliary of Portland ILA Local 38-78 gave a Christmas party for strikers' children. (Voice of the Federation)

The unions met daily in the Columbia River Joint Strike Committee, distinct from Maritime Federation District Council No. 3. Charles Peabody described the Portland situation November 7:

> We are not accepting the top strike committee plans as promulgated by Krolek [Radio Telegraphists] and some of that gang. . . . All groups meet together and mutually discuss their problems; each group handles their own personal business and joint policies are brought before all groups.
>
> Repeated attempts have been made to bring us under some plan which would turn all finances, relief, defense, etc. over to a central Committee. The SUP, MM&P, MEBA, MFOW&W, are going along with the ILA idea and everything is working smoothly. The only objections are those that arise from Krolek.[4]

In the Joint Policy Committee Con Negstad objected "to certain remarks and insinuations repeatedly cast on this floor by certain individuals re Portland Longshoremen not cooperating with rest of striking groups; farther ILA 38-78 has a fund, which a certain minority other than members from 38-78 are attempting to divert into a general fund for all strike groups."[5]

San Francisco On Strike

Thousands of seamen thronged their union halls in San Francisco the first day to take out strike cards, prepared to keep the ships tied up until employers granted their demands. The 350 pickets the unions put out "were alternately rainsoaked and dried as they stood around in a torrent or found what little shelter they could under awnings or in the recesses of doorways."[6] Later they erected shacks across the Embarcadero from the piers for shelter and built bonfires to keep warm. The ILA appealed for bedding to protect Marin County pickets against the chilly nights.

An estimated 10,000 federation members struck in the Bay Area, with the number increasing as ships reached port. District Council No. 2 became the San Francisco Port Strike Committee, responsible for collecting funds, feeding and housing strikers, legal defense, and publicity. The individual unions assigned pickets, coordinated by the joint committee. They picketed six hours on and twenty-four off. The Port Strike Committee kept a central defense office open twenty-four fours and operated a first aid station.

The *Chronicle* estimated the number of pickets in December at 17,000, which may include several thousand involved in other strikes. The Masters, Mates and Pilots patrolled the bay in a picket launch. The unions warned pickets against interfering with the Belt Line railroad, which had provided the excuse in 1934 for calling out the National Guard. Cars of vigilantes reportedly cruised uptown, beating up men with union buttons, and a rumor circulated that the employers were bringing 1934 scabs to San Francisco.

Until the joint soup kitchen opened, pickets received half-price restaurant meal tickets. The kitchen in the old location at 84 Embarcadero began serving November 9, fitted up with a first-class stove, crockery, and linoleum on the floor. Staffed by

Picket shack, San Francisco, 1936-1937 strike. (Courtesy International Longshore and Warehouse Union Library)

Inside a picket shack on the quiet waterfront, San Francisco. (Courtesy San Francisco Public Library)

East Bay picket shack, 1936-1937 strike. (Lou Rabb photo, courtesy International Longshore and Warehouse Union Library)

members of the Marine Cooks and Stewards, the facility served 7,000 meals a day and put up 3,000 lunches for pickets on night duty. Each union paid for the meals for its members with color-coded tickets punched for each meal. The kitchen fed people at an estimated cost of 12-1/2 cents a day. The Marine Cooks and Stewards bulletin December 15 reported income for the kitchen of $22,928.14. Assessments from federation unions raised $9,583.99, donations from other unions $7,134.92, and donations from outside of labor $6,209.23. Benefit dances and public meetings also helped to raise money.

Unions outside the Maritime Federation gave over $36,000 to the San Francisco strikers. Donations included $1,100 from Book Binders and Bindery Women Local 31-125, $1,155 from Chauffeurs Local 265, $2,600 from Laborers Local 261, $2,471.40 from the Deep Sea and Purse Seine Fishermen, $4,750 from Fish Reduction Workers Local 20249, $3,800 from the Inland Boatmen (formerly Ferryboatmen), and $1,000 from Musicians Local 6. Unions in Denver, Newark, Salt Lake City, and Cheyenne sent contributions.

The unions published their own separate bulletins: ILA 38-79 *Strike Bulletin*, *West Coast Sailors*, Marine Cooks and Stewards *Strike Bulletin*, and so on. In addition to union publications, the anonymous *Maritime Mirror* appeared October 1, an attractive tabloid replete with many illustrations, columns, features, and sports, but with no acknowledged sponsor or means of support. Editorially it professed to be by

Strikers lined up at the soup kitchen, 84 Embarcadero, San Francisco, 1936-1937 strike. (Courtesy International Longshore and Warehouse Union Library)

Striking marine cooks and stewards staffed the San Francisco soup kitchen. (Courtesy International Longshore and Warehouse Union Library)

and for union labor, lauding Harry Lundeberg and the militants and violently attacking Communists in the unions. The entire labor movement, anti-Communists as well as Communists, condemned the sheet as disruptive and provocative. The other anonymous piece, a mimeographed leaflet "issued by a group of rank and file members" of the Marine Cooks and Stewards, appeared regularly with the slogan, "Destroy Communism before it destroys our unions." It criticized union policies and opposed the strike. Bulletin No. 161 condemned the strike as a costly mistake engineered by the Communist Party.

Lee Holman, renegade expelled from the ILA, appeared in December with a new union, the Maritime and Transportation Servicemen's Union, many of the members men from out of town with police records. A brawl erupted when strikers tried to stop Holman's men from distributing the *American Citizen*, an antilabor newspaper. In a raid on Holman's hall on Howard Street police confiscated pick handles, lengths of pipe, and two dirks. Strikers suspected that the group had staged the three nighttime attacks on the *Voice of the Federation* office, when vandals threw rocks through the plate glass windows. Union people speculated that employer money financed Holman's activities, possibly to influence public opinion in favor of an antipicketing ordinance on the ballot March 9. In the final provocative demonstration after the strike, Holman sent a crowd of 300 men to the ILA hiring hall seeking work.

The strikers assessed stiff penalties for drunkenness. The Sailor's Union at San Francisco fined members $5.00 for conduct "unbecoming union men," and in Portland the union lifted strikers' union buttons for the offense. The Seattle Sailors required a member to apologize to a meeting for being drunk in the hall. The 1,500 member Maritime Patrol kept order in San Francisco with two squad cars that cruised the waterfront, picking up drunks and taking them to their quarters. In Everett the ILA Purity Squad did the same. The San Pedro ILA voted the same penalties for pickets showing up drunk or with liquor as for men reporting for work drunk: $10.00 fine for the first offense, ten-day suspension from work for the second, and thirty days for the third.

Picketing Los Angeles Harbor

The San Pedro Joint Central Strike Committee (Southern California District Council No. 4) put out 1,400 pickets, later reduced to 900, on the forty-seven miles of waterfront that comprised Los Angeles harbor. When the Long Beach police dug up an ancient antipicketing ordinance to arrest two ILA pickets, the strike committee informed the police "that they were dispatching 2,000 pickets at once! And if they arrested 2 they'd have to arrest 2,000."[7] That ended the arrests. Following East Coast orders, crews on the *California, President Wilson*, and several freighters sat down instead of walking off. After four days aboard the vessels they joined the strikers ashore. By November 10, fifty-four vessels lay idle, including five from East and Gulf ports, and another ten or eleven cruised outside the breakwater; 5,300 Maritime Federation members and 800 East Coast seamen were on strike.

Initially the unions fed strikers in the Belmont Cafe and the Mariner before the relief kitchen in the Trocadero Club opened, fitted up with $1,000 worth of

Staff of the Maritime Federation Central Kitchen, San Pedro, 1936-1937 strike. (Courtesy International Longshore and Warehouse Union Library)

equipment. The facility, run by the Marine Cooks and Stewards, seated 600. By late November the kitchen served 3,600 meals a day costing $3,000 to $4,000 a week. The strikers also operated smaller kitchens at Long Beach and Wilmington. Many waterfront cafes gave pickets coffee and doughnuts, and several served free breakfasts, including the Harbor Union Cafe in Long Beach, where waitresses donated two hours of labor daily to feed the pickets. The ILA Ladies Auxiliary took care of family relief, providing for about 1,500 families by mid-November.

Union people and sympathizers donated generously for strike relief. The Los Angeles Central Labor Council asked its 50,000 members for an assessment of 25 cents a week. Farmers donated vegetables in return for a few hours of work by crews of strikers, and merchants donated meat, ice, gas, and oil. A coffee company gave ten pounds every other day. Friends loaned gas pumps and restaurant equipment. A barber let a striking seaman cut hair in his shop, and a Wilmington barber gave strikers free haircuts. A picket card admitted people to the Crystal Ballroom at Long Beach. As the holidays approached with no settlement, a jewelry store extended credit for Christmas presents. The strikers raised money with dances and entertainments. A benefit boxing show netted over $1,750 for the relief fund. Cash donations from all sources totaled $60,662.06: $8,348.41 from outside unions, $14, 796.89 collected by the Los Angeles Central Labor Council, $3,169.19 by the Long Beach Central Labor Council, $1,664.32 by the San Pedro Central Labor Council, and $32,683.25 donated directly by community supporters.

At first, the 4,100 seamen on strike lacked lodgings. The Catholic Church provided a building accommodating 500, and the strikers rented two hotels, the Mason and Del Mar, housing another 500. After the Red Cross, Community Chest, and YMCA refused to help, the strike committee equipped the hotels with new cots, bedding, and linen. For the period November 23 to December 2, the relief committee housed 2,637 men at a cost of $1,437.49, providing them with face and bath towels and clean linen weekly. Besides these lodgings, some waterfront hotels extended credit to strikers.

Initially a striking longshoreman's wife administered first aid from her home. Then the strikers set up a first aid hospital in a building donated rent-free, staffed by two doctors, a dentist, an orderly, and nurses. The hospital had treated 800 cases by the end of November.

To circumvent San Pedro's antipicketing ordinance, which forbade sandwich signs, pickets from uptown unions would stand in front of an unfair establishment selling labor papers to signal a boycott. Owl drug stores provided the current target. Striking seamen from out of town occasionally blundered into the stores. One clerk, noticing the maritime strike buttons, asked the customer, "What are you doing in here? Don't you see the pickets outside?"[8]

The Joint Central Strike Committee adopted a single strike card for all crafts and handed out the *Maritime Strike News* daily to strikers and the public on the streets. After incurring lively censure for a pro-Bridges report of a meeting, the publicity committee decided that printing controversial information "caused more harm than good" and confined the bulletin to local strike news. In addition to sponsoring public mass meetings, the strikers took their case to the community over the radio. Elmer Bruce, chair of the Central Strike Committee, Roy Donnelly, president of San Pedro ILA Local 38-82, and others spoke on the air, and Bruce debated the question, "Is the Present Maritime Strike Justified?" with employer representative Frank Foisie.

Boredom, not cold and rain, plagued the pickets in the southern California port. They whiled away their watches pitching horseshoes or playing baseball in vacant lots across from the docks in the Outer Harbor or relaxing in the shade behind a lumber pile. An entertainment committee sponsored dances, movies, ball games, boxing matches, and a soccer game between the crew of a British ship and a Maritime Federation team. In baseball the East beat the West, and the men beat the women in a softball game. Men's and women's basketball teams also competed. In a school auditorium the committee gave a puppet show for strikers' children, followed by vaudeville acts for their parents.

With arrests below normal during the strike, the strikers objected strenuously to the proposed appropriation of $44,500 for the 400 extra police on duty in the harbor, and they obtained signatures of 100,000 citizens on petitions opposing the appropriation. The strikers did not fully trust the shipowners' declaration that they would not operate their vessels. The Central Employment Bureau for Veterans advertised for guards for strike duty at $6.00 a day. The bureau sent applicants to the World Wide Detective Agency, which put them on a waiting list. The employers thus recruited over 200 by mid-November. The bureau claimed to be "taking no sides" in the strike, and the Community Chest, which gave $11,000 to the bureau, dodged the issue. The president of the Los Angeles Central Labor Council stated that "orders have already been placed with one private detective agency for 2,000 strikebreakers and an auxiliary police force is being organized as the beginning of a vigilante movement in Pedro."[9]

The shipowners reportedly tried to recruit scab engineers for standby on their vessels. The *New Orleans* managed to slip out of San Pedro with a scab crew, only to be disabled with cracked engine heads because the scabs forgot to turn on the cooling systems. The strikers speculated that the shipowners originally planned to open Los Angeles harbor after two weeks, but they changed their plans because of Roosevelt's decisive election victory, the strength of the Atlantic strike, the failure of the banana libel, and other setbacks. Whatever the reasons, the employers chose to leave their vessels idle at San Pedro and other Pacific Coast ports. At San Diego, 120 miles south of Los Angeles, 170 pickets patrolled the docks, where, among other vessels, the *Lake Francis* lay with eighty tons of dynamite aboard. The soup kitchen in the San Diego ILA hall fed 60 to 100 men each meal.

Campaign Against the Voice *Editor*

In the midst of the strike a major confrontation erupted over the editor of the *Voice of the Federation*. The paper testified strongly to the maritime workers' conviction that the imperative need for solidarity must override factional differences. The paper would present all sides fairly, thus enabling the membership to make intelligent decisions. Responsibility for allocating space and prominence to competing factions gave the editor tremendous potential power to use the *Voice* as a political tool. When the federation hired Barney Mayes as temporary editor in June 1936, the Communist Party took notice. The Communist *Western Worker* carried a front-page box exposing Mayes as really Barney Moss, a convicted felon who had served time in prison in Detroit for robbery. The editor of the *Voice* replied that Mayes was his pen name and he, indeed, served the time for a framed conspiracy charge connected with labor activities, not armed robbery. The Communist Party launched the campaign against him because he had been expelled from the Party as a Trotskyist.

On July 30, 1936, the newly elected editorial board sent four applications, including that of Barney Mayes, to the district councils to select a permanent editor. The Portland and San Pedro councils voted to confirm Mayes. San Francisco, reflecting Communist bloc strategy, endorsed William Grattan. In spite of the "campaign of innuendo, insinuation and falsification" launched against the paper, the editor, and the editorial board, by mid-November the *Voice* had increased from six pages and circulation of 9,000 copies to ten pages and 17,000 copies under Mayes's editorship.

The strike did not mute the campaign against Mayes and the paper. By then Seattle had endorsed Mayes, but Portland remained undecided. In a letter to the district councils November 28 the editorial board pleaded in vain for a daily paper to keep the membership informed during the strike. It charged that "there is and has been . . . a small minority group who have worked overtime in an attempt to destroy those responsible for the paper, even to the extent of trying to prevent the continuance of the Voice."[10]

The strategy appeared to be to strangle the paper. Communist bloc organizations, such as the Radio Telegraphists and Union Recreation Center, would decline to submit news, then claim the *Voice* discriminated against them and cut their bundles. The San Francisco Port Strike Committee refused to seat Mayes to work with the publicity committee, and a member of the Marine Fireman threatened to demand the recall of the editorial board if he were seated. Roy Pyle of the Telegraphists stated in the Policy Committee that strike information should be prohibited from the *Voice*.

Barney Mayes condemned the attack as political. "I was expelled from the Communist Party because I stuck up for democracy . . . and if you disagree with the Communist Party it means your character is going to be assassinated." He defended his refusal to publish an article submitted by the International Labor Defense because the ILD was "not an organization that represents the victims of the labor movement but on the contrary is a political instrument of the Communist Party and only engages in activity in behalf of that party and not in behalf of the working class."[11] He asserted that "I have turned down articles from the Communist Party and its auxiliary organizations, and I will continue to turn down those articles as long as I am editor of the Voice. . . . they have no place in our paper."[12]

While the editorial board pleaded for support, Harry Bridges, in his official capacity as Pacific Coast District ILA president, wrote to people Barney Mayes gave as references, implying "discrepancies" and requesting further information. Armed with one ambiguous answer to his queries and the knowledge that the Sailors' Union somehow received 500 free papers, Bridges took his charges against Mayes and the editorial board to the unions. He specifically exempted C.D. Bentley, who cooperated with the Communist bloc, from the charges. After hearing the ILA president, on December 3 the Northwest Joint Strike Committee voted 60-1/2 to 45-1/2 to condemn the editorial staff of the *Voice* and demand the removal of Mayes. The sixteen illegal votes of the Communist bloc Inland Boatmen and Cannery Workers tipped the results against Mayes. Those unions were seated in the Washington District Council but not affiliated with the Maritime Federation as coastwide organizations and paid no per capita to support the federation or the *Voice*; therefore, they had no right to vote on the editor. The Seattle Sailors Strike Committee tried without result to get the federation to rule on locally affiliated unions voting on coastwide issues.[13] Meetings of the San Francisco Marine Firemen and Local 38-79 also voted to remove the editor after Bridges spoke.

In a four-hour session December 9, attended by observers from the Marine Firemen, Radio Telegraphists, Boston Hunt of the Marine Cooks, Harry Lundeberg, and the entire Voice staff, the resident editorial board discussed the 500 free copies to the Sailors. Lundeberg objected that this was not "the time to start an internal squabble there is always time to do this when the strike is over." He warned that the *Voice* "does not belong to a few officials on this coast. If there is any immediate change on this paper I am in favor of a referendum vote of the rank and file and if such a thing is not done we are going to have a break up of the Voice of the Federation. . . . The rank and file on this coast built this paper. It is their property and as long as I am the secretary of the Sailors' Union I am going to see that the Voice is not used as a political foot-ball."[14] The editorial board decided to investigate Bridges's charges as soon as the rest of the members could be summoned to San Francisco.

The next day Bridges told the San Francisco Marine Cooks and Stewards that Mayes presented forged references, that the Sailors' Union "controlled the 'Voice'" and received 500 free copies each week, and that the women in the office were "told to 'keep their mouths shut'" about the irregularity. He said "Ryan's stooges and finks" backed Mayes, naming John Kucin and Elmer Bruce of San Pedro, and charged that the *Voice* "gave almost no space to the publicity campaign of the unions, even when uptown papers blazoned it on their front pages." In spite of Trotskyist rank-and-filer Boston Hunt's defense of the *Voice*, the meeting voted to "instruct the Editorial Board" to remove Barney Mayes.[15]

A public stenographer recorded verbatim the editorial board sessions December 11-13. Harry Bridges charged:

> 1. That the editor presented forged references with his application for the job as editor;
>
> 2. That with the knowledge of the editor, members of the editorial board and officials of the Sailors Union, the Sailors Union received 500 copies of the Voice free every week; and
>
> 3. The editorial policy regarding the Copeland Bill, that is injurious to the Federation.[16]

The board considered first the forgery charge. When pressed by Bridges, journalist Idwal Jones reneged on his initial reference for Mayes. Otherwise Bridges turned up nothing damaging. B.J. Widick, research director and associate editor for the United Rubber Workers, considered Bridges's letter hinting at "discrepancies" so surprising that he sent it and his reply to the editorial board. Widick wrote:

> I am at a complete loss to account for the insinuations and "investigations" of your editor. Inasmuch as I have already expressed myself regarding the qualifications of Brother Mayes and your board is in possession of that letter, it seemed to me that if the brilliant record of the VOICE under the direction of your editor needed any "investigating" that it should emanate from the body responsible to the membership for the policy and conduct of its official paper. . . .
>
> I can only hope that the slanderous campaign against your editor, which on occasions I have noted in the press of the so-called Communist Party, can be allayed before it results in serious injury to the strong front needed in your struggle against the shipowners.[17]

The board found the forgery charge unsubstantiated.

Examining the second charge of 500 free papers to the Sailors' Union and the innuendo that someone profited by their sale, the board found that the union had inadvertently not been billed for the extra papers and that three other people besides Mayes knew of the mistake. It reprimanded the staff for not correcting the mistake sooner and dismissed Bridges's charge of personal gain as "utterly ridiculous."

To substantiate his charge that the paper's editorial policy on the Copeland Act damaged the federation, Bridges quoted an article in the *Voice* November 26: "Outright repudiation of this Copeland fink book act and the anti-labor provisions of the subsidy acts alone will safeguard the rights and liberties of waterfront unionism." Bridges warned that the members opposed "striking against the Act of Congress," that to repudiate laws was "a good way of destroying unions."[18] In view of the fact that the unlicensed seamen on the Pacific Coast had pledged "never to accept the book as a condition of employment," the board stated that "the militant editorial policy carried on, especially in opposition to the Copeland Bill was 100% correct"[19] and dismissed the charge.

At the conclusion of the hearings Barney Mayes stated that he fought "not because I want to be editor, but because I am opposed to this unscrupulous machine, whose only weapons are not arguments in the open, but the frame-up, the attack on one's character; in other words, to discredit anybody and anything that stands in their way, to establish a strangle-hold over the trade unions in this country, . . ."[20]

The *Maritime Worker* answered Mayes: "The Communists do not want to dominate any union, or dictate its policies. We fight only for unity, for rank and file control, and a correct policy for the rank and file."[21]

The findings clearing Barney Mayes came after the board received the transcript of the hearings. Meanwhile, on December 16 the entire board—Fischer, Kelley, Dombroff, Schrimpf, and Bentley voted unanimously to remove him and appoint a temporary editor until the board reached a decision. Then the board would initiate the process for hiring a permanent editor. Mayes protested the hasty action: "I am being placed in the very unenviable position of being offered up as a sacrifice in order to please and serve the interests of the members of the Board." Bob Dombroff stated: "I believe that on the basis of all evidence presented, that the charges against Mayes have been proven absolutely unfounded. I consider the charges at this time union-smashing tactics. The only reason I am in favor of the temporary removal of Mayes, pending final settlement of the case, is to put a stop to the wrangling and dissension and to fight the shipowners."[22]

With Bentley dissenting, and over the protests of the Communist bloc, the board published the entire transcript of the hearing in the *Voice*. The board warned federation members: "We are, at present, engaged in a strike against the Shipowners, who have adopted a policy of passive resistance with the thought in mind of causing just such a split as we are now threatened with. These cries, charges and rumors pro and con have caused so much dissension that the solidarity of the Maritime Federation is gravely threatened."[23]

In his final issue as editor December 24, Barney Mayes defended the policies of the *Voice* and blasted his critics:

> The real explanation for the unusually vicious fight against me lies in the effort of the Communist Party to crucify me because I have resisted their attempts to dictate the policies of the VOICE. . . .
>
> I am opposed to the Communist Party, not because of its "radicalism," but because I consider it a reactionary force and an enemy of militant industrial unionism . . . I am sure that when an analysis of the present strike is made the representatives of the Communist Party within the Federation will be found among those who advocated steps which aimed at arresting the real effectiveness of the strike as well as sabotaging the formation of the National Maritime Federation.[24]

Bridges vs. Ryan

As the 1936-37 strike neared, Pacific Coast longshoremen sent Harry Bridges and Matt Meehan to New York to solicit support from the ILA nationally. They met with Joe Ryan and Atlantic and Gulf District officers. San Francisco Local 38-79 Publicity Committee reported October 1 that President Ryan "has assured the Pacific Coast that there will be complete co-operation between all Districts in support of the Pacific Coast should a lockout be forced by shipowners. The time has finally arrived when the Longshoremen of the United States are in complete agreement for their mutual benefit."[25]

After the tie-up began the strikers soon learned what International President Joe Ryan meant by support. He recognized as unfair only those companies that had rejected ILA demands, excluding the twenty-six intercoastal and foreign lines that had met the longshoremen's demands just before the strike. He also sided with ISU officials in breaking the East Coast seamen's strike. At first Bridges would not believe that East Coast longshoremen worked hot ships and upbraided the *Voice* editor for printing the story. When the reports proved true, in an open letter to Joe Ryan the Pacific Coast District Executive Board protested his ordering ILA men to work ships struck by the West Coast maritime unions and East Coast seamen. The board accused Ryan of strikebreaking and employing "gangsters and thugs" to attack seamen's picket lines.[26] Failing to gain Ryan's support, the district executive board sent Harry Bridges to the East Coast to appeal directly to longshoremen to stop working intercoastal vessels and strike all ships in sympathy. Bridges reported that in Philadelphia "gangsters" beat up rank-and-file longshoremen and stuffed the ballot box to defeat a strike vote. He found Boston longshoremen "sullen and bitter, but afraid to move."[27]

Joe Ryan's account of the trip is different. According to him, the Communist Party arranged mass meetings for Bridges in Philadelphia, Boston, Baltimore, and Madison Square Garden, where he shared the podium with Joe Curran and others. Sponsors did not invite local ILA or central labor council officials, and few longshoremen attended. In an acrimonious session in New York the Atlantic Coast District Executive Board criticized Bridges for butting in on East Coast affairs over the heads of the officers, and Ryan stopped his salary as Pacific Coast District international organizer for trying to disrupt the Atlantic Coast. The Pacific Coast District condemned and denounced Ryan for strikebreaking and demanded "that the arbitrary, unprincipled, disruptive order to remove Bridges be immediately withdrawn."[28] Harry Lundeberg called Ryan a "sell-out artist" and declared that he stands condemned in the eyes of the seamen for his scab herding and removing Bridges from office. Elmer Bruce declared that the Pacific Coast District should pay its own officers' salaries and not be beholden to the international.[29]

Negotiations

The unions resumed negotiations with the steam schooner operators November 28. The Marine Cooks and Stewards reached a tentative agreement, but talks with the Masters, Mates and Pilots ended December 9 when the licensed deck officers rejected an offer 578 to 18 because it did not grant union preference. The method of settling disputes emerged as a key issue. The *Log* of the Joint Policy Committee, a condensation of the minutes, noted December 4: "At this period all motions in minutes, judging from the makers thereof, indicate that Schmidt, Halling, Charlot, O'Grady, etc., (CP) were trying to put over the [San Francisco] NEWS PLAN for a PORT COMMITTEE, etc."[30] The plan, proposed at the instigation of Assistant Secretary of Labor McGrady, provided for a committee of employer and union representatives with a permanent neutral person named by the Labor Department to decide deadlocked issues.

Full-page newspaper ads by the Coast Committee for the Shipowners punctuated the negotiations. The ad December 10 urged "our employees": "COME ON, BOYS, let's settle this thing. Let's Negotiate—and Arbitrate. That's the good, clean, American way . . ."[31] At the request of the Department of Labor, Harry Lundeberg, Eugene Burke of the Marine Cooks, and John E. Ferguson of the Marine Firemen began negotiations with Tom Plant and Thomas B. Wilson of Alaska Steamship Company. The *San Francisco Chronicle* headlined December 15, "Three Sea Unions Near Pact With Owners on Pay Raise, Hiring Plan," and the *San Francisco News* echoed the next day, "SAILORS' WAGE PACT NEARS." The *Voice of the Federation* headline December 17 announced: "STRIKE END LOOMS." The Sailors' Union intended to submit tentative agreements to the regular meeting December 21.

Back from his unsuccessful East Coast trip, Harry Bridges requested a Policy Committee meeting for that day to "counteract publicity in press that strike is almost ended." With the Sailors' Union absent, the committee reaffirmed its previous position, "that report be made to JPC [Joint Policy Committee] before any tentative agreements are submitted to a referendum vote."[32] The committee sent a delegation to the Sailors to urge the union not to vote until all unions received acceptable offers. Disregarding Bridges, the meeting approved the offshore agreement and part of the Alaska agreement and rejected half the steam schooner offer. Members understood that the union would not vote formally until all unions reached agreement. The reconvened Policy Committee meeting December 21 again went on record that "*before* completed negotiations are submitted to rank and file for vote, that a report of negotiations committee be made to POLICY COMMITTEE." The committee condemned the *Voice* headline, "Strike End Looms" as "false, misleading, disruptive and inimical to best interests of rank and file of Maritime Federation,"[33] and called on the district councils to remove Barney Mayes immediately and install William Grattan as editor. Mayes put out his last issue of the paper December 24.

The next day, according to Austen Hansen in the *West Coast Sailors*, the ILA 38-79 *Strike Bulletin* contained "a mass of hints and innuendoes which must be answered." The "disruptive faction," he declared, hinted that Harry Lundeberg met secretly with the shipowners and that their conferences contained something "crooked." He charged the "disruptive faction [Communist bloc] . . . with seizing control of all publicity sources in San Francisco emanating from maritime unions" and not permitting any Sailors' Union representatives to speak on the radio time they helped pay for. Hansen warned them: "YOU WILL NOT SUCCEED IN SACRIFICING THE INTERESTS OF THE SAILORS TO THE INTERESTS OF A NARROW POLITICAL FACTION," continuing: "And if Brother Bridges is sore because he had nothing to do with negotiating an agreement for the sailors—it's just too bad! . . . he has been warned publicly today to keep his hands and his nose out of the sailors' business."[34]

Both the Joint Policy Committee and Harry Bridges condemned the recent strike settlement stories as misleading; they caused a serious drop in relief contributions needed to sustain the San Francisco strikers. Tom Plant jumped in with a blast at Bridges, charging him with seeking to prolong the strike until the East Coast seamen reached a settlement. The ILA 38-79 *Strike Bulletin* called the negotiations with heads of the unlicensed seamen's unions a "serious mistake." "Unfortunately, the Sailors, and Cooks and Firemen innocently walked into this trap." It charged that the shipowners tried to split the solidarity of the unions by settling with one union and warned that they were "quietly arranging to follow up the attacks of the presses upon the longshoremen BY RUNNING IN STRIKEBREAKERS."[35]

Harry Lundeberg branded the charge of "secret negotiations" a lie: the members knew of the meetings, and that the rule and practice in the federation was "that all organizations have complete autonomy in the negotiating of agreements . . . and the only agreement governing same is the agreement NOT TO RENEW OR SIGN until all are satisfied."[36] No one objected when the Masters, Mates and Pilots submitted an offer to a coastwide vote. Lundeberg contended that Sailors' Union members, not the Policy Committee, should be the proper body to pass on the terms of their agreement. He branded as "false to the core" the argument that the tentative agreement put other unions "on the spot." On the contrary, the agreement "certainly puts the shipowners in an untenable and ridiculous position in refusing to grant similar concessions to other unions." Denouncing as "vilest slanders" the implication that the union would sign an agreement before "other unions on strike have concluded satisfactory agreements," Lundeberg stated:

> We denounce these factionalists and disrupters of the workers struggle. We accuse them of attempting to utilize a militant strike struggle for better economic conditions as

a publicity campaign for the building of "leaders" and "heroes" . . . We do not believe in the practice of building "heroes" for the workers to bow to. We are fighting for and are determined to get better conditions for ourselves and all maritime workers, and nobody is going to utilize our struggles for another purpose.[37]

A federation mass meeting of 7,000 members December 23 adopted a resolution introduced by Al Quittenton, Sailors' Union assistant secretary and Communist bloc activist, expressing confidence in Harry Bridges and his policies. In the auditorium sailors distributed copies of the *West Coast Sailors* with Hansen's ultimatum to Bridges. The meeting approved a resolution from the ILA providing:

1. That no union submit to its membership for ratification any tentative agreement with employers "until all unions have arrived at tentative agreements" so ratification can be simultaneous.
2. That there be no more one-man negotiating committees, but that "a full Coast negotiating committee" be assembled in San Francisco to continue bargaining with ship operators.[38]

The next day the *Chronicle* aired at length the *West Coast Sailors* article and Local 38-79's reply, with the headline, "Lundeberg Followers Join Shipowners in Attack on Bridges." Lundeberg wired from Klamath Falls on his way to Seattle, "I repudiate all personal attacks on any other leader while the strike situation exists. Unity is absolutely necessary."[39] A special meeting of the Sailors' Union called December 24 by Communist bloc adherents repudiated the December 22 *West Coast Sailors* and apologized to "fellow unionists in other organizations for any attack made on leaders of other organizations." It voted for a joint strike bulletin for all unions. The *Chronicle* reported the meeting the next day, "Sailors Vote Full Accord with Strikers." The Communist bloc takeover attempt soon ended. The regular meeting December 28 nonconcurred in the business of the special meeting by a vote of 569 to 67. In the annual election of officers Harry Lundeberg defeated Al Quittenton for secretary-treasurer by a vote of 2,878 to 732, 75 percent.

The Policy Committee *Log* of January 25 recorded the attack of Marine Firemen delegate Walter Stack on Harry Lundeberg:

Reports that there is no *proof* that either Ferguson or Lundeberg took money, so he is not making any accusations, but there are rumors that Ferguson was paid off with Lundeberg. Says Secty. showed up shortly before meeting opened and started a very vicious attack against Curran and East Coast and assured membership the main danger was not from Scharrenberg and such, but those people who are being led by Union Square [Communists].[40]

The Sailors' Union condemned Walter Stack "as a provocateur for his lying, malicious, and slanderous statements"[41] and asked him to appear before a meeting to explain them. Stack replied that he had not accused Lundeberg of "selling out" or being a "shipowners' agent." Thus Stack evaded a libel suit.

Unions Negotiate Agreements

By late December, 234 vessels lay strikebound in Pacific ports, 141 deep-water vessels, 61 steam schooners, and 32 foreign ships. Seventy-six lay idle at San Pedro, seventy-three in San Francisco Bay, twenty-four at Portland, forty-two at Seattle, seven at Vancouver, B.C., and twelve at other Pacific Coast and Hawaiian ports. An Associated Press reporter dubbed the tie-up "the streamlined strike," marveling that the strikers had "been molded into a social and economic unit without parallel in the history of industrial labor." He related:

> Forty thousand men on strike but none of them idle.
>
> Nearly 250 ships tied up . . . business losses estimated at $7,000,000 a day . . . foreign trade badly affected . . . thousands of families tightening their belts as they await Christmas.
>
> But nobody killed . . . no disorder . . . no arrests for picketing . . . no extra police needed . . . union police who maintain perfect order.

The reporter compared the strikers to an army "with one notable exception—its 'generals' do nothing conclusive without first consulting the all-important rank and file."[42]

The shipowners pursued their campaign to split the unions with a full-page ad, "WHO Is Blocking Maritime Peace?"[43] Citing the tentative agreements with the Sailors and Marine Firemen, the ad accused Harry Bridges and a "small and selfish group" of delaying settlement until employers met demands of East Coast seamen and striking Bay Area machinists. Antilabor groups began to demand that the government deport the alien Bridges to his native Australia. Whatever influence thay had on public opinion, these attacks convinced many strikers that Bridges was indeed their fearless leader.

Negotiations between the offshore owners and licensed officers broke off over union preference the end of December. Tom Plant declared that "under no circumstances can [the shipowners] agree to union interference in the free selection of licensed officers for their ships. . . . They are responsible for the safety of the ships, passengers, crews and cargoes. Employers can never agree that these officers shall be forced into the unions and subjected to the dictates of union agents."[44] The unions replied that 95 percent of the officers already belonged to their unions. Meanwhile, shipowners on the East and Gulf coasts, in collusion with federal officials, sent vessels to sea with inexperienced scab crews and incompetent radio operators, causing accidents and shipwrecks.

The government estimated the end of December that the loss to Pacific Coast business thus far reached $450 million, as against $200 million in the 1934 strike. Foreign steamship lines, particularly Japanese, profited by the strike. With negotiations deadlocked, the press speculated that Congress might consider legislation to settle industrial disputes, and in a nationwide radio broadcast January 5 San Francisco Mayor Angelo Rossi called on President Roosevelt to intervene to settle the strike.

The longshoremen finally met with their employers. Just before the 1936-37 strike began the Waterfront Employers had offered to renew the 1934 award, and Harry

Shipowners ignored safety at sea. (SUP striker Robert L. Scanlon in N.W. Joint Strike Committee Bulletin*)*

Bridges had stated on the eve of the strike that "the fundamental demands of the ILA had been granted" and the longshoremen would "be striking in support of the other unions."[45] But in November the East Coast ILA had negotiated a raise for North Atlantic ports to $1.00 an hour and $1.50 overtime. When negotiations resumed on January 5, the Pacific Coast District demanded the North Atlantic scale in addition to the provisions of the 1934 award, which the twenty-six companies had offered on October 23. The Waterfront Employers refused to separate Atlantic wages and hours; if the longshoremen wanted the Atlantic scale they would have to accept an eight-hour day. They repeated their offer to renew the 1934 award with "enforcement and compliance provisions" similar to those negotiated with the Sailors and Marine Firemen.

The ILA rejected the offer indignantly. Plant's reference to the Sailors' terms brought another blast from the ILA. The San Francisco Local 38-79 *Strike Bulletin* January 7 objected strongly to accepting the port committee language in the Sailors' agreement. Gangs would be forced to work "under unsafe gear and practices." The provisions would be the "first steps to wreck our union," signaling a "return to the speed-up system, big loads, star gangs, Blue-Book Bosses, Blue-Book working rules, and the placing in the hands of the Labor Relations Committee, the power to expel any man from the waterfront." They would force union members to work with scabs. "It is certainly not the business of the Longshoremen—if the Sailors wish to work under

STRIKE BULLETIN

ISSUED BY N.W. JOINT STRIKE COMMITTEE

January 25, 1937 SEATTLE, WASHINGTON NO. 71

*******A SINISTER PRECEDENT*******

From the New York Post, published January 18th, comes the following comment on the Copeland Fink Book:

"We wonder whether any of the old Liberty League crowd, who were so strong against regimentation, will join Congressman Sirovich and the Joint Maritime Strike Council in their fight against the "continuous discharge book", as provided by the Copeland Bill?

If legislation provide for similar "continuous discharge books" in the rest of American business and industry, every worker would carry a card with his name, number, picture and the notations made on it by previous employers.

No worker could obtain a job without showing a card. The card could be revoked by a government board for "misbehavior." And there would not be any provision in the law - as there is none in the Copeland Act - for review by an independent tribunal of an act taking away a man's livelihood.

The "continuous discharge book" is not necessary to safety-at-sea regulations. Neither Copelandnor the shipping interests he represents, nor the Department of Commerce has shown itself particularly concerned about safety at sea. On the contrary, while the Department of Commerce has broken a promise to suspend the "continuous discharge book" while revision was debated in congress, it has not hesitated to suspend the provision of the law requiring competency certificates for employment as a seaman.

This provision was suspended so that the shipping lines could hire in-experienced men to break the maritime strike, at no matter what the cost to the traveling public. But no similar action has been taken on the "continuous discharge book" despite the promises of Secretary Perkins and Secretary Roper.

(OVER)

Shipowners resisted unions of licensed officers. (SUP striker Robert L. Scanlon in N.W. Joint Strike Committee Bulletin*)*

such terms—but the membership must resist to the very end this latest maneuver of the shipowners, to shackle such an agreement onto the I.L.A." "This is by no means a criticism of the Sailors' agreement," the bulletin concluded, but the ILA viewed "with extreme suspicion and distrust any provisions in an agreement *which the employers insist on.*"[46]

Assistant Secretary of Labor Edward McGrady had called the licensed officers' demand for union preference "the toughest nut to crack."[47] When they resumed negotiations January 7 the Masters, Mates and Pilots appeared ready to compromise the issue if it became "the sole remaining obstacle to peace."[48] Talks with both offshore and coastwide operators moved toward agreements for all crafts.

In the Northwest, January brought cold and snow as pickets huddled around their oil drums. The snow reached San Francisco Bay, where the temperature fell to 30 degrees on January 21—the coldest California winter on record. Pickets ignored the warning of Dr. J.C. Geiger, health director, that pneumonia threatened if they did not abandon their shacks along the Embarcadero. The employers added their pressure to the weather. In another full-page ad January 20 the offshore operators declared: "After nearly three months of industrial strife, the time has come to publicly record the lengths to which the Pacific Coast maritime industry has gone in a sincere effort to settle the strike."[49] The ad stated the employers' final offers and proposed to submit remaining issues in dispute to President Roosevelt.

Combined strikebreaking of longshoremen's and seamen's international officers forced East Coast seamen to return to work without gaining their demands. They ended the strike January 24 after a promise that the National Labor Relations Board would hold elections on the steamship lines. Intercoastal ships remained hot until the West Coast strike ended. Negotiations continued at San Francisco. The ILA accepted the existing wage scale with a guaranteed six-hour day January 28, settling the last major issue. The Policy Committee recommended January 30 that all unions vote immediately on ratifying their agreements and that the strike would be ended upon a majority vote of federation members to ratify.

Strikers Return to Work

Not all the unions approved completely the terms they submitted to their members coastwide. The Cooks and Stewards settled for nine hours on passenger vessels, and the Marine Firemen did not like their work rules. The ILA Checkers had union preference and the hiring halls, but wages and hours remained to be negotiated or arbitrated. Licensed officers did not have union preference. But the strikers prepared to make the best of their bargains and return to work. A consensus developed that they had achieved the greatest possible gains, that prolonging the strike would add nothing. Steamship lines began accepting conditional bookings of passengers and freight January 29, and newspapers speculated on whether the Dollar liner *President Hoover* or Matson's *Monterey* would clear the Golden Gate first. Strikers tacked a sign to a picket shack on the Embarcadero, "For sale on Tuesday," and the *Chronicle* reported February 3:

Picket shack at Oceanic Terminal, Portland, February 4, 1937. (Courtesy Oregon Historical Society, OrHi neg. 81693)

> Rank and filers did not wait for the ponderous machinery of the voting process to grind out what they considered to be a foregone conclusion.
>
> They demonstrated yesterday that no doubt exists in their minds. Grinning groups of them ranged the Embarcadero, burning the picket shacks that have provided them some protection from the weather during the more than three months they have been on strike.[50]

Hawaiian longshoremen had no cause to rejoice. On instructions from the Joint Policy Committee they returned to work without recognition or an agreement. The settlement also left out British Columbia in spite of the ILA district's promise that any agreement would include all BC locals.

As the strike wound down seamen faced the choice of taking the fink book or defying the government. The unions' massive outcry against the Copeland Act forced Congress to reconsider the law. On January 22, 1937, Congressman William I. Sirovich of New York introduced a bill to make the continuous discharge book and certificate of efficiency optional. Ignoring union demands that the Maritime Commission postpone enforcement of the book while Congress considered legislation to amend the act, the Bureau of Marine Inspection and Navigation began to issue continuous discharge books and certificates of efficiency on January 26. At San Francisco the first day some 300 nonunion seamen, principally from tankers, received the books.

The 20,000 union seamen on the Pacific Coast had pledged to refuse to accept the fink book. January 27 at San Francisco 4,000 union seamen reaffirmed their refusal to take the book, but a mass meeting of all strikers the next day heeded Harry Bridges's warning against "job action" against the government and declined to endorse the seamen's stand. That same night Secretary of Labor Perkins notified the unions that enforcement of the requirement for discharge books and certificates of efficiency would be suspended until March 26. Striking seamen could return to their ships without taking the fink book. As the strike ended the Sailors' Union reminded its members that "THERE IS NO PENALTY WHATSOEVER" for not taking the fink books, and shipowners whose crews did not have books suffered no penalty. "If you take the Copeland Fink Book," the union warned, "you can rest assured that in six months you will have no union."[51]

In spite of repeated assurances from the Department of Labor that the act would not be enforced, the seamen realized by February 10 that the shipping commissioner in San Francisco "was going to insist on men accepting the Discharge Book before he would sign articles."[52] Likewise, at San Pedro the *Iowan* and *Point Brava* lay idle because the shipping commissioner refused to allow their crews to sign on without books. The seamen sought legal relief. Federal Judge Michael D. Roche granted an injunction requested by the Sailors' Union, Marine Firemen, and Marine Cooks and Stewards restraining the San Francisco commissioner from requiring the books. The Sailors' Union obtained similar restraining orders for the ports of Seattle, Portland, San Pedro, and New York.

The Pacific Coast referendum to accept the agreements carried overwhelmingly. After ninety-seven days on the picket lines seamen and longshoremen returned to the ships and docks. The *Voice of the Federation* summarized their gains:

> Longshoremen, numbering approximately 18,000 the length of the Pacific Coast, returned to work at their old wage rate of 95 cents an hour straight time and $1.40 overtime, but got a guarantee of overtime after their basic six-hour day; factual control of employment [with the union dispatcher].
>
> Sailors, 7,000 in number, obtained hiring hall control, an eight-hour day, cash for overtime, and a $10 per month wage increase.
>
> Cooks and Stewards, 4,000, got hiring control, an eight-hour day on freighters, a nine-hour day on passenger ships, and a $10 wage boost.
>
> Marine Firemen, Oilers, Watertenders, and Wipers, 3,000, hiring control, eight-hour day, cash for overtime, $10 pay increase.
>
> Marine Engineers, 3,000, recognition, eight-hour day, cash for overtime, $15 pay raise.
>
> Masters, Mates and Pilots, 3,000, recognition, cash for overtime, $15 pay raise.
>
> Telegraphists, 2,000, hiring control, eight-hour radio day without clerical duties, $10 wage increase.
>
> Owners, observance of agreements without regard to job action and penalties for violations, selectivity of licensed personnel, practical and definite methods of enforcing agreement terms, and a better working morale.[53]

The Joint Policy Committee acclaimed the victory: "A publicity campaign which brought home to every union member and the general public the real facts of the strike, and placed blame where it belonged—on the shipowners, the Industrial Association and other employers' organizations—was a compelling factor in these victories."[54] The Trotskyists disagreed: "The main lesson of the Maritime strike is short and absolutely unmistakable: a militant picket line speaks the only language a boss can understand."[55]

Publicly the shipowners lauded the agreement as laying the foundation "for an enduring industrial peace in the maritime industry,"[56] but privately they licked their wounds. In a meeting of the Seattle Waterfront Employers February 4, someone suggested that employers should have a business agent similar to unions to protect their interests. They approved a letter by Keith Middleton to O.K. Cushing and Tom Plant proposing to make the Coast Committee permanent and enlarge it to include representatives of other major ports. It would establish a coastwide authority to interpret the agreements and provide for their enforcement.

In a letter to strikers at the end of November Frank Spector, San Francisco Communist Party organizer, informed them "with deep pride and satisfaction that over 100 of your fellow-strikers have joined our party since the strike began" because "they saw in actual life what a powerful aid the Communist Party is to the Maritime strikers."[57] William Schneiderman, California Communist Party organizer, credited Harry Bridges and his followers with the victory and charged Harry Lundeberg, the "super-militants," and the Trotskyists with weakening and prolonging the strike. He concluded:

> Summing up the role of the Party in the strike, its main task was the STRUGGLE FOR UNITY, which was the key to the victory finally won. . . . The strike was won because the fight for unity was successful, because the membership of the Maritime Federation . . . was mobilized against every splitting maneuver and red-baiting, and never allowed itself to be stampeded into a position where that unity was broken, even by leaders such as Lundeberg who often influenced some sections of the seamen with his syndicalist practices.[58]

Many members would disagree with Schneiderman. As they saw it, they won the strike and preserved the federation in spite of, not because of, the Communist Party's ceaseless drive for control of the unions. During the struggle with the shipowners the great concept of solidarity withstood threats to its supremacy. Victory confirmed union power and removed employer pressure. More than ever, competing programs and ideologies would endanger maritime solidarity.

15

The CIO Invasion

The surge of unionism among Pacific Coast maritime workers during the mid-1930s reflected the gigantic surge that swept across the nation. Within the union movement the debate soon focused on what form of union could best serve the hundreds of thousands of potential members in the mass production industries. Initially, the American Federation of Labor granted federal charters to workers in automobile, rubber, radio, and other industries. Craft unionists wanted to divide these new members among existing unions. Industrial unionists wanted to combine the federal locals in each industry in new international unions without regard for craft jurisdiction. A compromise at the 1934 convention provided that the AFL would charter new unions in auto, rubber, radio, cement, and aluminum while protecting the rights of craft unions.

After a year of organizational inaction, during which discouraged new members abandoned their federal locals, the controversy over industrial unions escalated at the 1935 convention. John L. Lewis, president of the United Mine Workers, emerged as the leader of the industrial union faction. Although support increased, the convention voted down the industrial resolution 18,024 to 10,933.

Soon after the convention Lewis and officers of other industrial unions formed the Committee for Industrial Organization (CIO) "to encourage and promote organization of workers in the mass production and unorganized industries of the nation and affiliation with the American Federation of Labor."[1] The AFL denounced the committee as illegal and suspended the ten affiliated unions in September 1936. Ignoring the AFL's continued protests and threats, the CIO helped workers in steel, automobile, rubber, and other industries to organize and bargain. The AFL Executive Council responded to the victories in March 1937 by ordering state federations and city central councils to expel all CIO unions. Some obeyed. The CIO executive officers countered with a resolution authorizing the committee "to issue certificates of affiliation to national, international, state, regional, city central bodies and local groups whenever it is deemed such action is advisable."[2] Thus the union officials squared off for labor's approaching civil war.

Communist Position on the CIO

The CIO debate reached Pacific Coast waterfronts after the 1936-37 strike. With members and followers active in both AFL and CIO unions, the Communist Party supported the CIO industrial union program but advocated remaining within the AFL. Writing at the end of March 1937, Party leader William Z. Foster declared:

CIO organizing pamphlet, 1936. (Author's Collection)

"The Communist Party has played a very active part in mobilizing the trade unionists against the suspension of the C.I.O. unions by the A. F. of L. Executive Council . . . It called upon the workers to refuse to suspend the C.I.O. locals from the city and state central labor councils, and thus keep the movement intact at the bottom in spite of the split among the officialdom."[3] Perhaps foreshadowing the party's maturing decision to throw its entire resources into the CIO, he predicted that the great bulk of marine transport workers would "eventually join it."[4]

But not yet. Maritime Federation District Council No. 1 sponsored a conference in Seattle April 11 to promote labor unity. The delegates pledged themselves "To support and further the aims of the C.I.O. within the A.F. of L., discouraging any attempts of unions to split away from the A.F. of L."[5] *Hook and Anchor*, the Communist Party paper on the Seattle waterfront, on May 1 called for "A STRONG AMERICAN FEDERATION OF LABOR" and condemned "so-called super militants, acting as stooges for Trotsky disrupters [who were] advocating that Pacific Coast workers sever all connections with workers in other sections of the U.S."[6] The Pacific Coast District ILA convention in mid-May rejected a resolution to withdraw from the AFL and voted to support the CIO program and work for AFL-CIO unity.

Jurisdictional Disputes

While the rival labor centers moved toward an irrevocable split, jurisdictional disputes erupted after the 1936-37 strike. The first one, initiated by the employers, concerned the ancient question of sailors working cargo on steam schooners. During the 1936 Maritime Federation convention a committee of sailors, longshoremen, and mates worked out an agreement accepted by the three unions. Resolution 59–A provided that all front or sling men (on the dock) must be ILA men and that steam schooners having eight or more hold men must use gang operation, with two or more men on deck. An ILA hatch required an ILA hatch tender, but a sailor gang need not have an ILA hatch tender or winch driver. The resolution reserved one hatch for sailors, and they might move to another hatch not previously worked. Mates would not be required to tend hatch. The unions observed the arrangement until the strike.

At the end of the strike, for the first time the Pacific Coast District ILA signed an agreement with the Shipowners' Association of the Pacific Coast, the steam schooner operators. The employers refused to include reference to established union jurisdiction for cargo work. Instead, they insisted on a statement that neither they nor the ILA "shall be committed with reference to the scope or nature of the duties of longshoremen or members of the crews of steam schooners."[7]

Armed with this ambiguous clause, the employers initiated a series of arbitrations. In the first one at San Pedro on March 13, Paul Dodd limited sailors to one hatch and ruled that longshoremen could replace those who quit. In a decision two weeks later for the Columbia River District, F.D. Tull ruled that sailors could drive winches and tend hatch for longshore gangs. In the third case in Seattle the arbitrator decided that a longshore hatch tender must be used in mixed gangs with a majority of longshoremen. Accusing the Sailors' Union of forming a united front with the shipowners because it intervened in the arbitrations, the ILA called upon the Sailors to abide by Resolution 59–A.

The Sailors replied that before the strike the operators had used eight sailors in a hatch and carried two winch drivers, but now they cut the hold men to the ILA number of six and shipped only one winch driver. They explained that the convention passed Resolution 59–A to prevent employers from knocking off longshoremen in the afternoon and replacing them with sailors to avoid paying overtime. Steam schooner sailors had always driven their own winches, for longshore hatches as well as their own, but an ILA hatch tender always worked above ILA members. The Sailors contended that the San Pedro ruling that longshoremen would replace sailors who quit violated customary practice and the intent of Resolution 59–A, that each craft furnish its own replacements. The employers tried to force the sailors to increase their loads from 1,800 pounds to the new proposed ILA maximum of 2,100.

The Pacific Coast District ILA convention condemned the Sailors' Union for "aiding the employers in their efforts to have seamen and licensed officers perform the work on steam schooners at a cheaper rate of pay."[8] More arbitrations upheld ILA claims. E.D. Hodge ruled in Tacoma that ILA and mixed gangs must have ILA hatch tenders and winch drivers. Arbitrator O'Connell decided that at Port Gamble mixed gangs must have longshore hatch tenders, and the San Francisco arbitrator limited sailors to one hatch and allowed one mixed gang that included sailors. A decision at Everett limited sailors to one hatch. Elmer Bruce of San Pedro warned that the steam schooner arbitrations helped to build a "wall of MISUNDERSTANDING" against the Sailors: "nothing can be gained except dissension, and the employers will be the winner if we do not stop this Union-splitting wrangling."[9]

More disputes arose between the Scalers and the Sailors' Union over maintenance work in port for Matson and other steamship companies and between the Inland Boatmen and the Sailors over crews of ocean-going tugs and Canadian steamers running between British Columbia and U.S. Pacific Coast ports.

Jurisdiction on Intercoastal Vessels

When it became apparent late in the strike that West Coast seamen would gain wage increases, cash overtime, and better working conditions, the ISU officials negotiated comparable improvements under the Atlantic agreement, bringing able seamen's wages to $72.50 and 70 cents overtime. The agreement ran until December 31, 1937. On the Pacific Coast February 4 the Joint Policy Committee adopted a motion by Harry Bridges relating to jurisdiction on intercoastal vessels. He explained, "Intent of this motion is to LET THE MEN AFFECTED DECIDE as to who represents and who will negotiate for them; he does not see it as a jurisdictional dispute."[10] Luckenbach and Luckenbach Gulf Steamship companies had signed the Sailors' Union offshore agreement, as well as the ISU Atlantic agreement. On March 1 the Eastern and Gulf District Rank and File Committee asked all Pacific Coast unions and the Maritime Federation "for the purpose of strengthening our national unity . . . to officially reaffirm their previous recognition" of the district's jurisdiction over intercoastal companies "that have been in the past and are now under East Coast Agreement."[11] The letter referred to the Bridges motion of February 4.

Although the East coast rebel seamen initially vowed to refuse to take fink books, the Rank and File Atlantic District ISU voted at a mass meeting in New York February 15 that "When, as a condition for getting a job and holding it, the men were forced to accept the fink book, then they should take it."[12] Refusing the books, they claimed, would allow ISU officials to ship scab crews. In March Congress passed the Sirovich amendments making the book optional and eliminating the most objectionable features of the certificates.

Over Communist bloc protests, the Sailors' Union opened a hall in New York. According to Harry Lundeberg, the East Coast Rank and File Committee compelled seamen to take Luckenbach North Atlantic ships to the West Coast with fink books, forcing those who refused off the vessels. At Philadelphia the crew of the *Susan Luckenbach* held up the ship for ten days refusing the books, until the Rank and File Committee pulled them off and shipped another crew with books. Meanwhile, two more Luckenbach vessels sailed to the West Coast in March, the *Florence* with a crew of ISU finks from New Orleans, and the *F.J.* with an East Coast rank-and-file crew with fink books. On March 9 District Council No. 2 refused to support an attempt to remove the crew of the *F.J.* in San Francisco; the *Voice* reported, "The I.L.A. District Executive Board voted to abide by the decision of the Joint Policy Committee that Luckenbach intercoastal ships remain under East Coast agreements."[13]

When the *Susan Luckenbach* arrived in San Pedro March 10 the Marine Firemen picketed, and the Sailors' Union tried to pull the crew off. The next day, according to a letter from the crew in the *ISU Pilot*, a federation mass meeting "voted the East Coast Brothers and especially Brothers sailing on Luckenbach ships a clean bill of health."[14] During a West Coast tour Joseph Curran appealed to District Council No. 2 on March 16 to stop West Coast officials from pulling strike-clear East Coast seamen off vessels because they carried fink books, He charged that "present conditions are building a wall between East Coast and West Coast men" and objected to the SUP hiring hall in New York. The *Voice of the Federation* editorialized:

> Certain elements among unions in the Maritime Federation . . . are running wild . . . . these misguided members are "dumping" or trying to "dump" East Coast crews arriving in Pacific waters because some of the East Coast seamen have taken the Copeland Fink Book . . . .
>
> . . . Could it be that some of the men advocating "dumping" East Coast crews could be taking money from the shipowners to see to it that East and West and Gulf never join hands? . . . They are certainly playing the game exactly as the shipowners would have it played.[15]

Harry Lundeberg replied that many East Coast seamen also refused the book, that the New York meeting with only 150 present which voted to take it did not represent rank-and-file sentiment. In Baltimore to avoid the book, West Coast seamen elected an SUP member to do their dispatching. New York SUP agent Thomas Hookey received threats that if he didn't close the hall it would be closed for him. The SUP hall shipped for about fifty West Coast vessels, as against thirty that the Rank and File Committee controlled. Lundeberg suggested that the East Coast leaders "spend a little more time and energy" in closing the twenty to thirty fink halls around New York instead of trying to close the SUP hall. He pointed out that the West Coast unions had improved wages and conditions on Luckenbach ships and were "in a position to give real protection to the men sailing on those ships," and continued:

> If the existence of the East Coast rank and file movement hinges on the "control" of intercoastal ships, we don't think much of it. For the benefit of both East and West Coast SEAMEN it would be best to have those ships under WEST COAST AGREEMENTS. The East Coast "leaders" haven't been successful in doing a damn thing for the seamen on the Intercoastal run—and neither are they recognized by the owners.[16]

The communist bloc in the ILA strongly supported the East Coast rank and file against the Sailors' Union. In his report to the Pacific Coast District convention Harry Bridges condemned the Sailors and Marine Firemen for plotting "to steal the East Coast ships and to dump the East Coast seamen and Curran." He charged that "the deal is to have the SUP take over all East Coast ships with Lundeberg working in conjunction with the ISU."[17]

East Coast seamen had returned to work with the promise of representation elections, but the National Labor Relations Board decided that it could not intervene in an internal union dispute, Accordingly, in May the Rank and File Seamen's Committee hastily transformed itself into the National Maritime Union (NMU) so it could petition the NLRB for elections. District Council No. 2 immediately endorsed the new organization. E.M. Evans, former NMU sailor's agent in Mobile, told the Maritime Federation convention: "We had nothing to do with the forming of the NMU in New York. They sent down NMU books on board ships and sold clearance cards. We did go on board ships and sold clearance cards to every man who scabbed during the strike for 25¢. If he did not have ten dollars to take an NMU book, we put a note in the book saying 'Ten dollars owing on this book.'"[18] Of the 60,000 seamen on the Atlantic and Gulf coasts, Evans estimated in June 1937 that probably 25,000 carried ISU books and an equal number NMU books, including the 25-cent books. About 10,000 belonged to the IWW Marine Transport Workers 510, including many who also had NMU books. He thought that 510 could best represent the seamen.

After the strike Pacific Coast employers responded to picket lines with lockouts. When sailors and firemen at San Pedro picketed the freighter *Lancaster* to force Weyerhaeuser to recognize her West Coast status, and longshoremen refused to cross the lines, the Waterfront Employers locked them out March 23. The next day the San Francisco Waterfront Employers locked out that port because longshoremen refused to cross the picket line of the *Knoxville City*, established to remove four ISU members who had scabbed during the East Coast strike. Following the lockouts Harry Bridges signed a statement March 25:

> The I.L.A. Pacific Coast District recognizes the fact that jurisdictional disputes between the various maritime unions and other disputes that are now occurring, involves unnecessary hardship on the employers through strikes, stoppages of work, etc.
>
> The I.L.A. Pacific Coast District hereby assures the employers parties to the 1936 agreement as amended, that such disputes as herein described will not be recognized or supported by the membership of the I.L.A. by indulging in illegal strikes or stoppages of work.[19]

Sailors' Union Affiliation Vote

Pacific Coast seamen began to consider CIO affiliation. When a proposed merger with the AFL Commercial Telegraphers Union failed, the independent American Radio Telegraphists' Association received a CIO charter April 14, 1937, becoming the first CIO union in the Maritime Federation. The Pacific Coast Marine Firemen voted in March to ballot on CIO affiliation, then postponed a decision until after a projected ISU rank-and-file convention.

The Sailors' Union voted April 19 to ballot on whether to affiliate with the CIO or continue to fight for an ISU charter. Five days later the ISU Executive Board moved to restore the SUP charter. Representatives of the Sailors' Union, Marine Firemen, and Marine Cooks and Stewards met with ISU Secretary-Treasurer Ivan Hunter May 3 and 4 in Los Angeles. With the Sailors' Union membership, agreements, and hiring hall intact, and defections to the CIO an immediate threat, the international had no leverage to demand concessions. Hunter agreed to recommend to the ISU Executive Board to:

1. Suspend all amendments to the ISU constitution adopted at the 1936 convention, thus reinstating the old constitution.
2. Waive all per capita tax due from the Pacific Coast unlicensed seamen to May 1937 without reducing their voting power.
3. Remove Selim Silver as West Coast ISU representative and close the San Francisco office.
4. Take steps to remove Clyde Deal as an ISU vice-president.
5. Remove Paul Scharrenberg as legislative representative.
6. Hold a national ISU convention in Los Angeles beginning July 19, with guarantees that delegates from both the Rank and File Committee and the recognized ISU would be fairly elected and seated.

The ISU Executive Board would meet May 13 to act on the proposed agreement with West Coast representatives attending. Harry Lundeberg commented on the offer: "From the foregoing, it will be evident to all that we are now in a position to carry through the program for which we have been fighting!"[20] The international accepted the terms at the Chicago meeting May 13, and the Pacific Coast representatives agreed afterward to recommend that the three unions go back into the ISU. But the Communist bloc had a different agenda. Headquarters meetings May 20 of the Marine Firemen and Marine Cooks and Stewards voted down motions to resume paying per capita to the ISU and instead voted to endorse the NMU and postpone a vote on ISU affiliation.

Before returning to the coast, Lundeberg met with John L. Lewis in Washington, D.C. He described the meeting in a letter to selected Sailors' Union activists May 22:

> I told him definitely the whole score. In turn he stated to me that he was not giving the new NMU a CIO charter – that they had been approached to do so, but had referred them to the SUP. In other words, he was stalling them off, until such time as he knew what the score was . . . I in turn told Lewis it would be impossible for us to recognize or work with this outfit calling themselves the NMU, with their present political connections, control and dictation of Union Square. Lewis told me definitely that if the SUP wants to affiliate with the CIO, he would give us the CHARTER. This is NOT FOR PUBLICATION as yet, due to the fact that I want first to find out what the guys think about it. The SUP will be granted the charter, and we will be the nucleus to re-establish the American seamen's movement, and would have full support from Lewis, and the CIO, and the SUP would retain its autonomy, run its own affairs, etc., and organize the rest of the industry with the CIO help on the Lakes and the East Coast.

Lundeberg discounted the National Maritime Union's professed interest in CIO affiliation, declaring that "this is the last thing they really want to do – their main objective is to GET A VOTE BACK THERE WHICH WILL ENABLE THEM TO REPRESENT THE SEAMEN, and then FORCE THE A.F. OF L. TO

RECOGNIZE THEM." As for the ISU, it was "nothing but a shell. They have nothing to offer us in the way of protection – but on the contrary are expecting to use the prestige of the SUP to pull the old fakers out of the hole they have gotten themselves into."[21]

Two days later the Sailors' Union headquarters meeting voted to ballot by referendum on affiliating with the CIO or reaffiliating with the ISU. The two-week referendum began May 25. Lundeberg predicted that the vote for CIO affiliation would be practically unanimous. The *West Coast Sailors* promised members: "By affiliating with the CIO, the SUP will retain its *OWN CONSTITUTION;* its own FUNDS AND PROPERTY and its own autonomy in conducting its own affairs."[22]

Progressive Union Committee

Ever since 1933 the Communist Party had organized caucuses on Pacific Coast waterfronts, the Albion Hall group in San Francisco and caucuses in other ports. The anti-Communists proposed a coastwide caucus without the Party's conspiratorial secrecy. Frank Lovell, an SUP member and a Trotskyist, contacted independent activists, who agreed that they needed an organization that would "function openly, and campaign for a militant policy within the Federation."[23] A group met in San Francisco April 3 and formed the Progressive Union Committee, with Harry Lundeberg chair and Boston Hunt of the Marine Cooks and Stewards, a reputed Trotskyist, secretary. Other sponsors included Harry Christoffersen, San Pedro Sailors' agent; Ed Coester, Portland Sailors' agent; Bob Dombroff from the Seattle Sailors; William Fischer, Portland longshoreman and president of the Maritime Federation; and Charles F. May of San Francisco, president of Masters, Mates and Pilots Local 90.

Three days later the committee put out "A Call to Action—To All Progressive Union Men." Here the anti-Communists appropriated the term "progressive," long used by the Party to signify political correctness. They warned that "if the mud-slinging and phoney policies employed by the Communist Party stooges is allowed to go unchallenged, the Federation will find itself in a very bad position." They charged that Harry Bridges followed a policy "either to control the Federation, or to wreck it, and consequently the entire maritime labor movement." The committee noted that the Bridges statement to the employers March 25 "will prevent the longshoremen from giving any effective support to the other unions in the Federation."[24]

The group proposed that progressive elements in each port meet weekly to formulate policies, and the San Francisco center would issue a weekly bulletin to be distributed on the coast. Donations would finance the project. The *Voice of the Federation* treated the call as a conspiracy: "Longshoremen Bare 'Call To Action' Plan in Federation Ranks, "and Bridges compared it to the "identical arguments of Joe Ryan and the reactionary A.F. of L. machine."[25] Although the Progressive Union Committee disappeared, its members continued to seek other means to work together against the Communist bloc in the Federation.

The Bridges administration controlled the Pacific Coast District ILA when the 1937 convention met in May. Opposition delegates remained silent on many subjects. However, a resolution introduced by Harry Bridges that condemned the Maritime Federation officers for favoring the Sailors' Union and called President William Fischer "incompetent, prejudiced, and therefore unfit" for the office evoked a spirited debate. Elmer Bruce, Cliff Thurston, Con Negstad, and eight more delegates protested in a signed statement against accusing and judging people not present to defend themselves. "The same people," they declared, "who loudly proclaim to the high heavens that we have a democratic Rank and File organization, stand here and deny, by their actions, the accused his inherent right to a fair trial conducted before all the representatives of all the component Unions in a decent, orderly way before an unprejudiced jury."[26]

San Francisco delegate Henry Schmidt produced the Progressive Union Committee's April 6 statement to prove the charges against Fischer and the Sailors' Union. John Schomaker, also Local 38-79, compared the statement to the discredited *Maritime Mirror*. Speaking of anonymous bulletins, Thurston wanted to know "why the famous scandal sheet, 'The Frisco Waterfront Worker' was not put out of business when it condemned everybody on no sound basis whatsoever." Bridges replied that it reflected "the minds of the workers."[27] Disregarding Fischer's defense, the delegates passed the resolution condemning him.

Charles Peabody of Portland voiced the distaste of his own local members and many delegates for "political factions": "Any ideas or policy that develop should emanate from within the organization and not from without. I don't care who the person is, when he transacts union business and union business only, no one should try to put ideas in his head, concocted by men or groups on the outside."[28] But the delegates rejected a resolution to expel members found guilty of working in concert to advance an outside political program, declaring it a violation of freedom of speech and expression.

Scanning the roster of delegates, Julius White of the Proletarian Party catalogued them according to ideological affinity. Among the Seattle longshoremen he placed George Clark, Burt Nelson, Louis Taggart, Bruce Hannon, and Thomas Richardson in the Communist bloc; William Craft and J.J. Whitney were politicians/opportunists. Art Krumholz of Aberdeen was a "C.P. sympathizer – individualist – claims he's anarchist – an ex-Wob." From the Portland local he labeled Matt Meehan, John Brost, and Jack Mowrey Communist bloc adherents and Charles Peabody and Cliff Thurston "O.K. – shrewd, able." From San Francisco Local 38-79 he tagged Harry Bridges as a CP member, "party name 'Gorgas,'" and Henry Schmidt as a CP member or worker, "'Bridges attorney!' – shrewd, able, slick article." John Schomaker, John Larsen, Joe White, Otto Klieman, and Germain Bulcke were with the Communist bloc; Eugene Deitrich was a politician/opportunist – "a two-faced fence-riding S." William Marlowe was "O.K.," also Henry Schrimpf, "ex CPM – Trotskyite in Socialist Party." Of the San Pedro delegation he put Tom Brown and Roy Donnelly in the Communist bloc and labeled the rest "O.K.," citing Elmer Bruce's "great ability."[29]

Besides condemning Joe Ryan for his failure to support striking East Coast seamen, the convention protested "the inactivity" of the Pacific Coast members of the

International Executive Council, M. D. Rodgers, Robert Hardin, and Bill Lewis, for their failure to censure Ryan for his strikebreaking activities. Although Richard Francis of the CIO welcomed affiliation of West Coast longshoremen, he warned the delegates that it "would be splitting the movement of the ILA, . . . While it may be alright for you on the Pacific Coast, you may weaken your brothers on the Atlantic and Gulf Coasts and make them a greater prey to Ryan and the others."[30]

During 1935, port committees had negotiated uniform working rules which included penalty cargo rates for three districts, San Francisco Bay, Portland and the Columbia River, and Washington state. Employers blocked similar agreements on load limits, fearing they would be leveled downward. The delegates considered the proposed coast-wide agreements on penalty cargo rates and load limits. A poll of longshore locals on whether the maximum load of 2,100 pounds would benefit their ports resulted in eighteen answering yes and sixteen no. Besides Northwest lumber ports, San Francisco, San Pedro, Tacoma, and Cliff Thurston of Portland said no. To overcome strong opposition in San Francisco, where longshoremen hoisted 1,800 pounds, Henry Schmidt asked Seattle Local 38-12 to send members to Local 38-79 "to speak in favor of the Uniform Load on a coast wise policy."[31] Twenty voted yes and nine no on penalty cargo rates, with six, including San Francisco, not voting. Members approved both agreements by a coastwide referendum vote.

1937 Maritime Federation Convention

For the third consecutive year representatives of the Pacific Coast maritime unions assembled to deliberate and legislate for the future of their federation. Ten delegates presented credentials from a new coastwide organization, the Inland Boatmen's Union. Longshoremen from British Columbia and Hawaii came to plead support for their beleaguered locals. Three representatives from the National Maritime Union arrived at the invitation of District Council No. 2. The same old insoluble problems confronted the delegates gathering in the Portland Labor Temple. They must balance power between the large and small unions, preserving the autonomy of each organization while maximizing federation strength by united action, and present a solid front to their employers whether on a single vessel or dock or the whole coast.

But this year the delegates faced a new challenge that overshadowed their perennial problems: whether or not to affiliate their unions and/or the federation with the CIO. For many the new labor center seemed a realization of their hope for industrial unionism. For others it was an unknown and elusive factor still to be defined. Apparently the Communist Party had finally made the decision to throw all its influence into the CIO with the aim, many believed, of capturing the organization. The Woodworkers' Federation had just voted to ballot on CIO affiliation. The Inland Boatmen prepared to vote on the CIO. The Communist bloc supported the CIO in both these unions. The Bridges group in the ILA advocated joining the CIO.

From the outset the Communist bloc appeared determined to control the convention. Unions instructed their delegates on issues and candidates, and a stream of wires and letters poured in from locals and ships' crews urging support for

Communist bloc positions. The bloc insisted on voting strength for the Inland Boatmen's Union based on a year's membership, although the union had been affiliated for only two months, deadlocking the convention. Finally, on the fifth day the Inland Boatmen agreed to accept votes based on two months' per capita.

Not all Communist bloc adherents considered themselves Marxists or Leninists. Most probably accepted no more than the Communist Party's immediate trade union program. The Party's aggressive defense of their rights attracted African Americans. Many union people began to believe the image of Harry Bridges, the great leader, carefully fostered by the Party and the mass media, and others simply drifted toward the winning camp, obviously the Bridges administration. Occasionally, voluntarily or on instructions, an articulate activist migrated to another port to strengthen the Communist presence. Thus, longshoreman Harry Pilcher moved from Everett to Portland, and marine fireman Walter Stack moved from Seattle to San Francisco.

CIO organizer John Brophy addressed the convention at length on the merits of CIO affiliation and the need to make an immediate decision. Then delegates questioned him for hours. He admitted that the CIO had no written constitution and that no date had been set for a convention. Members' voluntary contributions instead of a per capita tax financed the organization, and the presidents of affiliated unions comprised the executive committee, which made all decisions and appointed all staff. Harry Lundeberg wanted to know if the Sailors' Union could get a charter, as he had understood John L. Lewis to promise in May. Brophy defended Lewis as a man "who does not lightly make commitments," but, he hedged, "I don't know anything as to what John L. Lewis may have promised and I don't know of his changing his mind as to any commitments he may have made to you." Bob Dombroff pursued the subject: If the West Coast longshoremen voted to affiliate with the CIO, would they be granted a charter? Yes, Brophy replied, but he refused to say whether or not the Sailors' Union would likewise be granted a charter.

> Dombroff, Q: If the body of unlicensed seamen on the Pacific Coast also voted they still would not be granted a charter.
> Brophy, A: I wouldn't say that. I repeat what I have already said, that I am interested in encouraging the greatest measure of unity among the progressive forces. In the event that fails we will have to deal with it on the basis of conditions that exist.[32]

Harry Bridges asked Brophy which he would recommend, a vote by individual unions or by the federation, explaining, "We all know if we take a vote of the whole Federation and a couple of unions vote against the C.I.O. and don't affiliate the general rule of the C.I.O. is that they should go along anyway." Brophy recommended "that you act speedily and that you act through this body if there is the authority within it."[33] Thus the delegates defined the issue: Should the federation be involved in or committed to the question of CIO affiliation, or should each affiliated union proceed independently? The Communist bloc wanted the convention "to go on record as immediately *instructing* (emphasis added) all maritime unions affiliated with the Federation to take an immediate referendum" on CIO affiliation.[34] After hours of debate the convention voted "to go on record as *recommending* (emphasis added) that each organization . . . take a referendum . . . as soon as possible according to the rules of each organization."[35] The delegates endorsed a National Maritime Federation after deleting reference to CIO affiliation.

The Communist bloc longshoremen did not even wait for the delegates to return home and report on Brophy's talk and the ensuing discussion. An ILA caucus June 10 voted 27 to 9 to ballot on CIO affiliation, and the district sent out 26,000 ballots to the locals on June 15. Three days later the district executive board met in Seattle. The board members did not know that by then Harry Bridges had been appointed West Coast CIO director, although his union just began to vote on affiliation. The *Pacific Coast Longshoreman* attributed the district's abrupt about-face on the CIO to the new Communist Party line. Bridges said at a Seattle conference April 11 "that to leave and go to the C.I.O. without the whole I.L.A. going was only a way to divide unions here." A month later at the ILA district convention he reiterated the need to stay in the AFL. "A few days later, however, he flew to a conference with [John L.] Lewis. What was said or promised there is still a mystery, but we do know that the party at that time came out in the open for the C.I.O. without reservation."[36]

The NMU Debate

A resolution by the Inland Boatmen to support the National Maritime Union and call a national unity convention triggered a major battle. Contradicting assertions by NMU activists Jack Lawrenson and Ferdinand Smith that the NMU operated democratically, E.M. Evans, former Mobile sailors' agent, described how the union's national committee had imposed policies on the membership. In a roll call vote of 99.189 to 78.924, the convention voted to support East Coast seamen in their right to establish a democratic union, to "go on record to endorse the organization chosen by referendum ballot of the bona fide seamen of the East Coast and Gulf,"[37] and then to call a national seamen's convention.

In another controversial resolution from the ILA convention, Harry Bridges accused the West Coast unions of "taking the position against the East Coast rank and file seamen and in line with the reactionaries of the ISU" and "obstructing the struggle for rank and file control of the East Coast seamen by such methods as attempting to steal East Coast ships and bring them under West Coast jurisdiction, maintaining hiring halls in the East and Gulf seaports, as well as . . . on occasion of actually picketing East Coast ships, with full rank and file crews on them, because they were forced to accept the Copeland Fink Book." The resolution protested "these anti-union tactics" and refused "to support any West Coast union attempting to raid the East Coast jurisdiction and maintaining West Coast hiring halls in East Coast ports."[38]

Harry Lundeberg condemned the resolution as an "attempt to discredit the Sailors' Union . . . a disruptive move which rather than solidifying the Federation will split it wide open." He reminded the delegates that the Sailors' Union had consistently supported the East Coast rank-and-file movement from its inception. As for stealing

East Coast ships, "we would like to know what the I.L.A. has got to say about whose jurisdiction the ships should come under. They would get along a lot better on this Coast if they would mind their own business and not start jurisdiction squabbles."[39] He defended West Coast claims to represent seamen on Luckenbach, Shepard, and Union Sulphur intercoastal vessels because those unions had organized the ships and improved their wages and conditions after the 1934 strike. He asserted that the Sailors' Union hall in New York and the fight against the fink book benefited all seamen.

Henry Schmidt of Local 38-79 moved an amendment to delete most of the resolution. Elmer Bruce described the debate: "The attitude of the most vociferous supporters in the ILA convention was in this one to beg forgetfulness. They were almost vicious in the ILA convention and were abject beggars in the Maritime Federation convention. The seamen retorted that they were anxious for Unity, but it could not be bought that way. It must come if at all, by mutual respect."[40] The delegates voted down the resolution.

The Inland Boatmen made another jurisdictional claim against the Sailors' Union. When the sailors introduced a resolution recognizing the SUP "as the sole collective bargaining agency for the unlicensed personnel of the deck department on the Pacific Coast," the Inland Boatmen moved an amendment to limit the Sailors' jurisdiction to "offshore vessels." Rather than involve the federation in a jurisdictional dispute, the SUP delegates asked to withdraw the resolution. After more discussion and limiting amendments, the convention tabled the resolution.[41]

Henry Schmidt's statement at a federation mass meeting in San Francisco June 20 that "sailors were represented at the Maritime Convention by disrupters and had better get rid of them"[42] prompted a resolution from the Sailors' Union condemning "such back-biting tactics . . . as attacking fellow delegates when they are not present to defend themselves."[43] By mistake the Sailors attributed the statement to Harry Bridges. Acknowledging the error, Harry Lundeberg added, "However, we, the sailors delegation, know Bridges has condemned the Sailors officials and delegates in other meetings all up and down the coast."[44] John Kucin stated that the Masters, Mates and Pilots "resent the attitude and question the right of Delegate Bridges, President of the ILA, visiting ships in order to create dissension among the mates by telling them that their delegates are phoney and that Delegate O'Grady is the only Delegate truly representing the M M & P, when it is clearly evident that such is not the case, because Delegate O'Grady has sided in with the Longshoremen on almost every rising vote that affects the M M & P, . . ."[45]

Predictably, another partisan storm swirled around the *Voice of the Federation.* James O'Neil, who had succeeded Barney Mayes as editor, submitted a report to the convention in which he represented the paper as "solvent and progressing rapidly" and called reports of mismanagement and increasing debt "malicious lies."[46] He blamed Mayes and the editorial board for the paper's problems. Elmer Bruce of San Pedro termed the statement "a real gem for insinuation, braggadocio and self-laudation."[47] Rejecting a Communist bloc motion to table O'Neil's report, the delegates voted 91.7

to 81.543 to "condemn the editor for his report due to the many lies in his report and that this convention requests his immediate removal from the editorship of the VOICE."[48]

The locked-out British Columbia longshoremen remained a standing reproach to the Maritime Federation, and the open-shop ports constituted a dangerous gap in union defenses. After ordering them to strike with the U.S. ports and promising that they would be included in the settlement, the Pacific Coast District abandoned the Canadian ILA locals after the strike. West Coast crews of U. S. vessels refused to allow scab longshoremen on board their ships at Victoria and Vancouver, with the result that those vessels stopped calling at British Columbia ports. But Pacific Coast longshoremen worked foreign vessels loaded by scabs in those ports. Henry Schmidt declared in the convention that ILA members would be locked out coastwide if they refused to work the ships. Confronted with this prospect, the delegates acknowledged their impotence and overwhelmingly voted down sympathetic action.

Factional Battle Lines

Sharp factional lines emerged on most issues. The ILA had 61 votes, which represented 34 percent of the total in the 1937 Maritime Federation Convention. Of those 61 votes, the Communist bloc controlled 37.6 or 62 percent, and the anti-Communists 17.3 or 28 percent; 6.1 votes, 10 percent seemed uncommitted. The California delegates supported the Communist bloc, except for Elmer Bruce of San Pedro, Henry Schrimpf and William Marlowe in the San Francisco longshoremen, and David Harrington in the San Francisco warehousemen. The Portland longshore delegation split three to two for the anti-Communists, and Astoria and North Bend, Oregon sided with the anti-Communists. In Washington, Seattle split between Communist bloc and uncommitted delegates; Tacoma, Grays Harbor, and Olympia voted anti-Communist; and Everett, Bellingham, and Raymond identified with the Communist bloc.

Among the other crafts the Radio Telegraphists and Inland Boatmen voted solid Communist bloc; the Alaska Fishermen split between Seattle anti and San Francisco pro; and the Marine Cooks and Stewards split, with Seattle and Portland against and San Pedro and San Francisco for the Communist bloc after a headquarters meeting recalled Trotskyist delegate Boston Hunt. The Seattle Marine Firemen supported the Communist bloc, with the rest of the ports vociferously anti-Communist. Four attempts in headquarters meetings during the convention to recall the San Francisco delegates failed, and after the last attempt the meeting gave the delegates a standing vote of confidence. In the Masters, Mates and Pilots only E.B. O'Grady, the AFL staffer who had organized Local 90 in 1933, supported the Communist bloc. All delegates from the Sailors' Union and Marine Engineers voted anti-Communist. In the shipyard trades the Boilermakers voted anti-Communist, the Machinists leaned toward the Communist bloc, and the Shipwrights split. In the convention the anti-Communists had 102.54 votes, 55.6 percent; the Communist bloc 75.72 votes, 41.1 percent; and 6.15 votes, 3.3 percent seemed uncommitted.

The delegates frequently crossed factional lines when considering the federation structure. A constitutional amendment to limit votes on policy to those organizations "directly involved in the signing of agreements, strikes, lock-outs or major disputes"[49] failed to gain the necessary two-thirds majority. This proposal reflected dissatisfaction with representatives of unions such as the Cannery Workers and Inland Boatmen, who sometimes voted on strike policies in district councils. The convention sent to referendum a proposed amendment to raise per capita tax from 5 to 10 cents, 6 cents for the federation, 3 cents for district councils, and 1 cent for the *Voice of the Federation*; an amendment to reduce the federation executive board to one member from each coastwide organization, the board to be responsible for hiring an editor and publishing the paper; and an amendment to require only a simple majority to send a proposed amendment to referendum.

With officers already limited to two consecutive terms, the convention debated a proposal that an officer "shall have been actively engaged as a wage earner under the jurisdiction of his respective organization . . . for at least six months within the preceding three years prior to nomination,"[50] and providing that a former officer must work for another six months before again being eligible for office. Elmer Bruce, the ex-Wobbly from San Pedro, commented:

> The effect would have been to effectively stop anyone from building up an official family in the Union. Of course the Superman theory was trotted out and we heard about how we must rely on our Saviors to lead us . . . Personally I think it is a good thing for a worker to become acquainted with the job after having been an officer. . . . it gives another the chance to make good, and it KEEPS OUT THE OFFICEHOLDING OPPORTUNIST. . . . The Roll Call vote is interesting as to who believes in saviors."[51]

The Communist bloc and two paid officials from the Marine Engineers opposed the amendment.

No matter how bitterly the delegates and factions argued, most maritime workers still believed deeply and unquestioningly that the solidarity of the Maritime Federation must be preserved regardless of other differences. The delegates' unanimous support for resolutions affirming that solidarity testified to this conviction. They recommended that crews refer disputes on board ships over discipline, food, or supplies to their respective organizations, and that component unions educate their members on the need for respect, cooperation, and harmony between licensed and unlicensed crew members. The day after the convention voted down the Bridges resolution attacking the Sailors' Union, the delegates unanimously endorsed a resolution condemning character vilification and personal attack on federation members and pledging a fair trial and "just punishment" for unsubstantiated charges.[52]

CIO Maritime Unity Conference

Once again the delegates debated the CIO when Elmer Bruce and Henry Schrimpf introduced a resolution July 1 to accept John L. Lewis's invitation to participate in the Maritime Unity Conference July 7 in Washington, D.C. The resolution recommended democratic procedures for conducting the conference and proposed to send a representative from the federation. Over Communist bloc opposition the delegates adopted the resolution 93.4 to 80 and elected Marine Engineers delegate P.J. Fitzpatrick to attend. The one-day conference agreed on a program to form a national industrial maritime federation affiliated with the CIO: For longshoremen, if possible, the ILA would be affiliated as a national unit. For unlicensed seamen, a national conference would, if possible, establish one national CIO union. For licensed officers, the present unions would be affiliated as national units. For the fishing industry, the CIO would charter the Federated Fishermen's Council of the Pacific Coast, covering fishermen and cannery workers.

The next day the federation convention delegates received two wires, one from Lewis and Brophy asking endorsement of the CIO program, and the other from Fitzpatrick that "conference set up to my opinion is rather dubious."[53] When Mervyn Rathborne of the Telegraphists and Joe Curran of the NMU learned that the Maritime Federation refused to endorse their plans, they tried unsuccessfully to have Fitzpatrick unseated. A committee that included Vincent J. Malone of the Pacific Coast Marine Firemen and Harry Bridges remained in session in Washington after the CIO Maritime Conference. SUP activist Robert Stowell, also attending the conference, wired Harry Lundeberg July 9: "Rathborne announced with Brophy present that if West Coast unions refused to go along charter would be issued to NMU and CIO would send organizers into the field to organize West Coast."

In answer to this threat the Marine Firemen introduced a motion in the Maritime Federation Convention to recognize "only the S.U.P. as the sole collective bargaining agency for the unlicensed personnel of the deck department on the Pacific Coast."[54] The Communist bloc moved to qualify the support "according to past practices" and limit it to offshore vessels, recognizing the Inland Boatmen on inland waters. After a furious debate, the convention affirmed the jurisdiction of the Sailors' Union, Marine Firemen, and Marine Cooks and Stewards over West Coast unlicensed seamen. In a final word on job action the last day of the convention, over the protests of the Sailors' Union, the delegates voted not to recognize any picket line on a ship or dock until the area district council concurred in the dispute.

The weary delegates elected Maritime Federation officers Friday night, July 9. Relying on the tradition that delegates will support their fellow union member, the Communist bloc captured the nineteen Marine Firemen's votes to elect James Engstrom, Seattle port agent, president of the federation. The anti-Communists took the rest of the offices: Robert Benson of the Grays Harbor longshoremen, vice-president; John Kucin of the San Pedro Masters, Mates and Pilots, secretary; and N.P. Robertson of the Portland Marine Cooks and Stewards, Bob Dombroff of the Seattle Sailors, and David Harrington of the San Francisco Warehousemen, trustees. Engstrom proved to be an expensive president. After his election he moved to San Francisco. In addition to his salary of $2,118.48, he collected $1,477.45 expenses under the provision for $4.00 per diem while away from his home port.

The Maritime Federation had survived another acrimonious convention. The combination of conservatives and militants had prevented the Communists from capturing the organization. But now the pending CIO votes threatened to shatter the federation and destroy the remaining fragile pretentions of solidarity. Perhaps the convention reports exemplify the attitudes of the various groups at midsummer 1937.

Eugene Dennett, Puget Sound delegate from the Inland Boatmen and an active Communist Party worker, expressed optimism about future maritime unity. Acknowledging that the decision rested with each union, he noted that referendum votes so far favored the CIO overwhelmingly. He glossed over the endless hours of angry debate, the ugly disagreements that delegates never patched up, concluding that the convention brushed "aside the temporary differences to present a united front before the enemy."[55]

By contrast, Elmer Bruce gave the San Pedro longshoremen a gloomy picture of the "distinct alignment of groups" that characterized the convention and the disputes that lengthened it beyond expectations. "I say therefore," he declared, "that today we the Maritime Workers stand at the crossroads and that THERE NEVER WAS A TIME IN THE HISTORY OF THE LABOR MOVEMENT WHEN WE NEEDED TO THINK INDEPENDENTLY AND FEARLESSLY AS WE DO NOW."[56]

The *West Coast Sailors* exulted over the defeat of the "Union Square prophets" and their resolutions condemning the Sailors as "splitters and disrupters." "Delegates Strengthen Maritime Federation," the paper headlined.[57] But in his report to ILA Local 38-79 John Schomaker dismissed the federation convention without comment and praised the CIO program during this "reorganization period" for maritime workers to achieve national unity.[58] They both missed the mark. Nothing could strengthen the federation with the overriding issue of national affiliation tearing it to pieces, and rather than promoting national unity, CIO affiliation would sever the last restraints and inaugurate the fratricidal wars that destroyed maritime solidarity.

16

The AFL and CIO Checkerboard

More than in any other area, the AFL dominated the union upsurge on the Pacific Coast, and especially in the Northwest. The 1934 maritime strike, the seminal event, and the lumber victory a year later, fostered the growth of a militant union movement before the CIO era. The CIO threat had been a remote abstraction until the Communist Party decided at the end of May 1937 to attempt to capture the new CIO movement. Suddenly, lumber and maritime unions faced bitter internal struggles over national affiliation. The Woodworkers Federation, with almost 100,000 members, balloted on CIO affiliation, and debate over the issue convulsed the Maritime Federation.

Washington and Oregon AFL unions denounced the threatened raids by the dual federation. Ben T. Osborne, executive secretary of the Oregon State Federation of Labor, charged that Harry Bridges dominated the ILA "by shouting rank-and-file while following the pattern of dictators which have arisen in other countries." Bridges controlled the International Longshoremen's Association "by bringing in workers who are outside the industry": warehouse, bag factory, and cannery workers. Osborne predicted that the AFL would "remain in a commanding position" in the Northwest and would be "in a position to provide the greatest measure of support in times of stress."[1]

In a joint statement the Tacoma Central Labor Council and Building Trades Council condemned the "destructive group calling itself the C.I.O." Departing from their original legitimate object of organizing the unorganized, these "self-appointed saviors of the working class" soon began raiding other unions. "This dual movement," the joint statement continued, "shortly developed a policy of piracy within the organized union movement and is now dominated and completely controlled by undesirables and Communists bent on destroying the legitimate trade union movement of this country." The councils vowed to "rigorously oppose all forms of dual unionism" and "do everything in our power to eradicate all organizations that would destroy our movement." They would pursue this policy "against the enemy, whether or not it be the C.I.O. or the open-shop employers."[2] Thus the CIO invasion polarized union members.

Seamen Repudiate CIO

Sailors' Union delegates to the 1937 Maritime Federation convention listened with growing alarm to CIO representative John Brophy evade their questions about the promised charter. The daylong session June 9 left them wondering whether John L. Lewis double-crossed them. The SUP referendum ballot had probably carried overwhelmingly for CIO affiliation on the strength of Harry Lundeberg's understanding that the Sailors would retain their own constitution, funds, and property, and have full autonomy in conducting their own affairs. But it appeared that if the CIO granted one national seamen's charter, an East Coast majority would dominate the national union. The San Francisco *Call-Bulletin* reported June 10 that the Sailors' Union and the National Maritime Union were racing for the first CIO seamen's charter.

Headquarters meeting June 14 voted to hold up the results of the referendum ballot. According to the *Voice of the Federation*, Lundeberg "said the membership must be 'assured of protection' before CIO affiliation is considered. He said certain promises made by Lewis have not yet been fulfilled."[3] Subsequent developments proved that the Sailors' Union would not receive a CIO charter under the conditions described in the referendum. By overwhelming majorities, headquarters and branch meetings August 2 voted to burn the ballots. Impelled by the same misgivings, the Marine Firemen's Union voted July 29 to destroy similar referendum ballots, reported to be 816 to 40 at the Marine Firemen's headquarters for the CIO. CIO supporters denounced as arbitrary and dictatorial the votes to throw out the ballots. By then the debate had shifted from the merits of industrial unionism to the desirability of joining a Communist-dominated national maritime organization.

Faced with the prospect of new and unpredictable alignments, the anti-Communists in the seafaring unions drew together. Following adjournment of the Maritime Federation convention, delegates from the Sailors' Union, Marine Firemen, Marine Cooks and Stewards, Masters, Mates and Pilots, and Marine Engineers met in Portland July 10. The Radio Telegraphists stayed away. The conferees agreed "that in the event of any changes in the set up of the Maritime Federation of the Pacific, or any of the component SEAFARING UNIONS, that we agree that a coastwise conference be called immediately of all seafaring groups to protect the interests of all seafaring unions involved."[4]

Across the continent, the National Maritime Union held the first convention in New York City July 19-30, with delegates representing 35,000 seamen. The NMU *Pilot* hailed the sessions as "democratic to the core" with "no cliques, no factionalism." Eugene Burke, fraternal delegate from the Pacific Coast Marine Cooks and Stewards, called the convention "the greatest step toward National Unity he had witnessed in his 36 years in the maritime labor movement."[5] Others reported less favorably. An SUP member observing the proceedings from the gallery noted that the convention was "pretty well under the control of Curran & Co." A "pretty healthy opposition . . . raised its voice occasionally, but was smashed because they lacked leadership and program." He compared the constitution, drafted by Tommy Ray, a leading Communist, and the NMU attorney, to the old ISU constitution, with power concentrated in the district committee, which could "make or break any action—or member!"[6]

Vincent J. Malone, fraternal delegate from the Marine Firemen, reported that the proposed constitution "was a tremendous disappointment, not only to ourselves out here on the Pacific Coast, but to practically every delegate from the ships and the membership off the ships in the port of New York." It gave "almost unlimited power" to the executive council. West Coast unions could not afford to send representatives to quarterly meetings of the national council in New York, especially with the national office requiring 12-1/2 percent of local affiliates' income. He deplored the Firemen's hasty referendum ballot and recommended against NMU or CIO affiliation without much more careful analysis of just what we stand to lose when we go into the CIO."[7]

While the NMU convention met in New York, delegates from branches and headquarters of the Sailors' Union and Marine Firemen convened in San Francisco July 22 to formulate a joint policy for the agreements expiring September 30. Repeated urging failed to bring delegates from the Marine Cooks and Stewards to the conference because headquarters opposed the gathering. The Masters, Mates and Pilots and Marine Engineers sent fraternal delegates to coordinate September 30 plans. The conference recommended against strike action to gain improved working rules in the agreements.

Vincent Malone returned from New York, bringing his critical report of the NMU convention to the meeting. The group recommended against sending representatives to the CIO Maritime Unity Conference in Chicago August 16 because delegates had to go with the power to act and no opportunity to refer policies back to members for final decision, "creating a dictatorship of the worst order."[8] Echoing Malone's reservations, the delegates condemned the autocratic structure of the NMU and CIO, in which their members would sacrifice democratic rights and privileges. To promote closer cooperation among West Coast seafaring unions, the conference resolved that disputes between crafts aboard vessels should be settled in the main coast ports, rather than jeopardizing the welfare of the unions by tying up vessels in foreign or outports.

The rest of the seafaring unions chose up sides. The Marine Engineers' Beneficial Association, independent since 1923, voted in 1937 to join the CIO. Contrary to the usual pattern in maritime organizations, Communist pressure had very little influence: the union simply gave up attempting to resolve the jurisdictional dispute with the AFL Machinists Union over repairs on vessels in port, which blocked AFL affiliation. Local 90 of the Masters, Mates and Pilots sent Charles F. May to observe the CIO Maritime Conference in Washington, D.C. July 7. He criticized the CIO for lack of a constitution and appointing instead of electing officers. The MMP nationally voted to remain AFL. Clyde W. Deal reached an understanding with Harry Bridges, moving the Inland Boatmen's Union into the CIO with a charter October 8, 1937. The Marine Cooks and Stewards split along ideological lines: Seattle and San Pedro branches demanded their CIO ballots back uncounted, but headquarters upheld the 87 percent vote for the CIO.

Longshoremen Go CIO

The district ILA extended CIO balloting for two weeks until the middle of July because Grays Harbor refused at first to vote. The result announced July 16 favored CIO affiliation 11,441 to 3,349. All the major ports except Tacoma voted CIO: Seattle 850 to 235, Portland 734 to 169, San Francisco longshoremen 2,220 to 703, San Francisco warehousemen 2,445 to 411, and San Pedro 1,500 to 444. Twenty-eight locals rejected the CIO on the first ballot, but most of them voted the second time to go along with the rest of the coast. Anti-Communists charged the district applied pressure on these reluctant locals. Late returns brought coastwide totals to 12,079 yes and 3,479 no. When AFL central labor councils unseated the CIO longshore locals, the Communist bloc sponsored a unity council in each port of what they termed progressive organizations "to try to work out a program to Unite Labor."[9]

The CIO chartered the International Longshoremen's and Warehousemen's Union (ILWU) on August 11, 1937. Without holding a convention, adopting a constitution, or electing officers, the Pacific Coast District ILA Executive Board simply declared itself the ILWU on September 10. To protect their treasuries the ILA locals that would soon be ILWU locals divided their funds among members, who then deposited them in benevolent associations. Thus, San Francisco Local 38-79 members each received $13.15, which became the initiation fee for the Bay Area Longshoremen's Benevolent Association. The association then received an ILWU charter on September 27 as Local 1-10.

Five days after receiving the CIO charter, on August 16, the ILWU declared war on the ILA. "CIO LAUNCHES BIG LONGSHORE DRIVE," the NMU *Pilot* headlined. The CIO Maritime Committee "decided to take the offensive in the battle for East Coast longshore jurisdiction,"[10] placing fifty organizers in the field. The *I.L.W.U. Bulletin* published glowing accounts of progress at Providence, Boston, New York, and other Atlantic ports. Mervyn Rathborne, chair of the CIO Maritime Committee, exulted: "Nine out of ten longshoremen along the Atlantic and Gulf are determined to end once and for all the machine rule of Ryan, and set up in the industry a rank and file democratic union affiliated to the C.I.O."[11] Rathborne's prediction did not come true, leaving East Coast and West Coast longshoremen permanently divided.

ILA supporters on the Pacific Coast fought back against the CIO blitz. Dissidents from the CIO ports of Portland, Astoria, San Francisco, and San Pedro joined delegates from the ILA ports of Tacoma and Olympia in an emergency convention at San Francisco September 20, 1937. The ILA international paid expenses of $10.00 a day for one delegate from each port. They included many old timers who had been active in reorganizing the Pacific Coast in 1933: Bill Lewis, Albin Kullberg, Roger McKenna, and Harry Curtis from San Francisco; Paddy Morris and Tiny Thronson from Tacoma; Charles Peabody and Con Negstad from Portland; and Elmer Bruce and C.H. Lindegren from San Pedro. Eugene Dietrich remained international organizer.

The convention reconstituted as Pacific Coast District ILA Local 38 with Bill Lewis president. Besides Tacoma, the district comprised several small Washington locals, checkers, walking bosses, and handfuls of ILA dissidents in the CIO ports of Portland, San Francisco, and San Pedro. They were termed the "lost battalion" and "dirty dozen" by the CIO majority. The international financed these minority ILA ports. The San Francisco dissidents moved back into the old ILA hall at 113 Steuart. In San Pedro the ILA minority sued Local 38-82, the only incorporated union, to retain possession of the properties, rights, and corporate and contract privileges of the union;

the action involved $60,000 in property and funds. Many maritime workers who opposed the CIO disapproved of this attempt to grab the union by legal means against the wishes of the members. After almost a year in court the ILWU local won possession of its property and rights.

Not all anti-CIO longshoremen agreed with the strategy pursued by a handful of dissidents in forming an ILA local in a CIO port. In San Francisco at first, James F. Kennedy, Ralph Mallen, and Henry Schrimpf tried to work within the CIO local. Kennedy and Mallen soon joined the ILA minority, but Schrimpf continued to oppose the Communist bloc in the ILWU local. Tiny Thronson called the dirty dozens "a tactical mistake." Not only did they fail to split the CIO ports, but they removed from the locals and isolated articulate and effective opponents of the Communist bloc in those ports.

The ILWU charter coincided with a major confrontation with the Teamsters Union over warehousemen. In 1936 the AFL ruled that the Teamsters had jurisdiction over uptown warehouses and the ILA over marine warehouses. Defying the ruling, the Bridges administration undertook an aggressive organizing campaign in uptown warehouses, with the result that by May 1937 ILA membership among warehouse workers had increased from 1,800 to 9,000.

Early in 1937 California Packing Corporation in San Francisco fired seventy-five warehousemen for joining ILA Local 38-44 and closed the North Beach warehouse. The first of September Cal-Pack signed an agreement with the Teamsters and hired their members to empty the warehouse. Faced with 500 pickets from the locked-out warehousemen the second day, the teamsters refused to cross the line. Teamsters Local 85 picketed the waterfront, demanding that the warehousemen join the Teamsters. Cargo that truckers refused to haul clogged the piers. After the Teamsters Union declined to submit the question of affiliation to a vote of the 11,000 warehousemen it claimed, the National Labor Relations Board ruled that the ILWU represented them.

Four hundred teamster pickets appeared on the San Francisco waterfront on Thursday, September 23, and pickets patrolled the East Bay docks. The shipowners notified the Sailors' Union "that they would prefer charges of mutiny against sailors who refused to pass through picket lines of the Teamsters, and refusal of the Union to supply crews would be considered a violation of the agreement and agreement would be considered cancelled." In a special meeting that afternoon Sailors' Union officials warned members that if they went through the Teamsters' picket line "the safety clauses in any agreement would not be worth the paper they were written on in the future to respect other picket lines."[12] The members voted to ask the Teamsters to withdraw their pickets. Meetings of Marine Engineers and Marine Firemen backed the Warehousemen.

An ILWU leaflet the next day pictured a teamster thug ordering rank and filers to picket with the "gangster-like command" to "Keep your shirts on and your mouths shut!" The flyer urged maritime workers not to respect this "picket line of the Teamsters officials working hand in hand with the employers to wreck the Maritime Federation and the Pacific Coast labor movement."[13] An ILWU sound truck cruised

"KEEP YOUR SHIRTS ON AND YOUR MOUTHS SHUT!"

With this gangster-like command hurled at them by their officials, 400 rank and file teamsters are ordered to extend Dave Beck's picket lines from East Bay docks to the full length of the Embarcadero.

In the New York dailies of September 18, the ghost of Judas Joe Ryan foretold what is taking place today in the Bay Area. On that day, Ryan said: "Before next week is out we will have completed a strong working arrangement with the Teamsters, the ILA and the Sailors Union of the Pacific."

The "strong working arrangement" is now completed. The "strong working arrangement" to wreck the Maritime Federation is now in action.

While Joe Ryan smirks with joy in New York, 400 teamsters in San Francisco are ordered to "keep your shirts on and your mouths shut" -- and go out on picket, they don't know what for.

While Dave Beck roars with glee in Seattle, officers of the Sailors Union in San Francisco state: "We will respect the teamsters' picket line." <u>But the rank and file of the S.U.P. said NO!</u>

What is this picket line, that Ryan has blessed, that Beck has ordered, that Sailors officials refuse to pass ---
<u>and which 400 rank and file teamsters have no stomach for?</u>

Is it a picket line for better wages and working conditions?
Is it a picket line of labor united in one cause against employers?
<u>Or is it a picket line of the Teamsters officials working hand in hand with the employers to wreck the Maritime Federation and the Pacific Coast labor movement?</u>

A few days ago, E. J. Vizzard, secretary of the Draymen's Association, said: "The teamsters are fighting our battle."

How happy those 400 teamsters must feel to know that they are fighting a battle for Mr. Vizzard! How happy their wives and children must feel to know that their bread-winners are unemployed and on the picket line in the interests of Mr. Vizzard and the Draymen's Association.

And the rank and file sailors -- we can just picture them bowing in "respect" to a picket line that has the sanction and blessing of an employers' association. Thursday they voted not to respect bosses' picket lines.
It is easy to see what the rank and file workers of the maritime unions are destined for if they let themselves be duped into becoming tools for this Ryan-Beck-Draymen's Association conspiracy. . . .Back to the loving arms of Scharrenberg,and the days of the phony ISU leadership.

Back to the days when the rank and file of the maritime unions were also forced to obey commands and edicts like "Keep your shirts on and your mouths shut." Back to the days when there was no Maritime Federation of the Pacific! Back to the blue book and the fink hall!

GOOD UNION MEN DON'T RESPECT THE BOSSES' PICKET LINES

<u>September 24, 1937</u>
<u>UOPWA 34</u>

Membership and officials of the
Longshoremen and Warehousemen's Union
27 Clay Street --- San Francisco

ILWU leaflet during the confrontation with the Teamsters Union, San Francisco, September 1937. (Author's Collection)

Henry Schmidt urging longshoremen to cross teamster picket lines, San Francisco, September 25, 1937. (Courtesy San Francisco Public Library)

the waterfront, while hundreds of longshoremen and warehousemen marched up the Embarcadero to meet the teamster pickets. Longshoremen and seamen crossed the Teamsters' picket lines. *The West Coast Sailors* commented sadly: "The shipowners have spent millions the last three years in an effort to accomplish what was done within twenty-four hours in the Port of San Francisco today. . . . Picket lines were ignored, and the shipowners ordered the sailors to do likewise or they'd cancel their agreement and revoke their licenses!"[14]

The confrontation reached a noisy climax on Monday, the 27th, in the "battle of the sound trucks," an exchange in front of Pier 15 between President Henry Schmidt of ILWU Local 1-10 and Michael Casey of the Teamsters, while thousands of maritime workers and teamsters in opposing camps listened and demonstrated. Acceding to farmers' pleas that the embargo on moving their perishable crops meant ruin, the Teamsters withdrew their pickets that night without relinquishing their claims to warehousemen. The ILWU asserted that rank-and-file opposition and rebellion caused the Teamsters to lift the boycott. Thus ended the jurisdictional picket line that pitted union people against each other rather than against the boss. More would soon follow.

The West Coast Firemen

A scandal over a meeting packed with nonmembers renewed the struggle for control of the Marine Firemen. At the September 16 meeting, during the Teamster-Longshoremen confrontation, five Communist bloc adherents charged that someone packed the meeting in anticipation of a vote to shut off steam on all vessels to support the Teamsters. Bloc activist Robert Fitzgerald related: "The proof was positive and beyond any doubt whatsoever and upon the exposure some 70 to 80 men . . . left the hall leaving full Union books behind them. These books were formerly the property of members who had taken withdrawal cards or were books that had been lost and they had been passed out at a secret meeting previous to the regular meeting by Ferguson and others."[15]

The Marine Firemen expelled Secretary John E. Ferguson and several others. Headquarters replaced the dismissed officials with Communist bloc followers. Vincent Malone, who resigned as port committeeman, roundly condemned the "political clique" for spreading rumors implicating him in the fraud. Harry Bridges injected himself into the scandal, charging at a meeting of Marine Engineers No. 97 that P. J. Fitzpatrick, one of their members, had participated in the plot to pack the meeting. After an investigating committee established that Fitzpatrick was at sea on the date in question, the union voted to bar Bridges from the hall until he could furnish proofs.

A group of firemen challenged the Communist-dominated administration of their union. The *West Coast Firemen* appeared on October 19, a weekly four-page tabloid, with the announced mission "to give the rank and file sea-going firemen a strong, clear voice in their own affairs." It deplored headquarters meetings "packed with longshore and warehouse permit men" who did not go to sea. The "illegally elected headquarters officers" had "embarked on a deliberate campaign to wipe out the branches, gag the rank and file, and sell the Marine Firemen's Union down the river." The paper declared:

> Our four pages will have to buck a powerful propaganda machine—a lie-machine well oiled by years of experience in the business of slandering and steam-rollering genuine trade union militants, of splitting and wrecking fighting unions, of "using" the labor movement for the interests of the Communist Party.
>
> We intend to fight the policy of the Communist Party not because it is "RED" BUT BECAUSE IT ISN'T. BECAUSE THIS OUTFIT BETRAYS EVERY REAL PRINCIPLE OF CLASS-CONSCIOUS, MILITANT TRADE UNIONISM.

The entire back page resembled a display ad: "The Undersigned Members of the PACIFIC COAST MARINE FIREMEN, OILERS, WIPERS, AND WATER-TENDERS Almost Every Man of Them Veterans of the 1934 and 1936 Strike, Endorse Our Publication of the Progressive Views of the SEAGOING FIREMEN ON THE PACIFIC COAST."[16] Then followed the names and book numbers of forty-eight members.

The *West Coast Firemen* advocated a concrete internal program. It condemned the recent issuance of a second CIO ballot over the opposition of three branches,

Seattle, Portland, and San Pedro, and cried "foul" when ballots turned up at NMU halls in New York, Baltimore, and New Orleans. It opposed joining the CIO both because the branches wanted more information and because affiliation would cost the union about $250 a month per capita when it was already $16,000 in debt. Instead, the paper supported amalgamation of the Pacific Coast unlicensed seamen's unions. Many supporters of the paper believed the Trotskyists were involved in the paper.

The headquarters meeting October 21 condemned the paper as a reactionary rag, published "to prevent the firemen from voting in a democratic referendum."[17] To counter Walter Stack's charge that the AFL was subsidizing the paper with about $250 a week, the second issue carried a financial statement showing expenses of $60.95 for 5,000 copies and income from listed donors of $67.00. Each issue thereafter included a financial statement. The Communist *Maritime Worker* called the tabloid the "most hated paper" and its endorsers "Ferguson stooges." The *West Coast Firemen* replied: "We know the Commissars believe that any fireman who doesn't bow three times a day before Stalin's icon would stab his grandmother. That's a major reason why the rank and file is fed up with their stupid and dogmatic dictation."[18]

Headquarters approved a resolution from the crew of the *Monterey* proposing that endorsers of the *West Coast Firemen* be denied shipping privileges. If, as the paper charged, the Communist bloc originally planned to expel the endorsers, their numbers soon made punishment impossible. The second issue contained 109 more names, the third 76 more, the fourth 184 more, until by the middle of January 1938 the back page was covered with 1,157 names in fine print, and the paper stopped listing them.

Seattle, Portland, and San Pedro endorsed the paper. On every policy the branches and their paper battled headquarters. They sent an emergency committee to San Francisco to investigate the election, which they considered illegal, of Robert Fitzgerald as secretary and Allan Yates as port committeeman. They supported economy measures proposed by Vincent Malone. He blamed former secretary Ferguson for mismanaging funds so that the union went into the 1936-37 strike with a treasury of $6,000 and emerged owing $35,000. When the Communist bloc took over, the union still owed over $13,000, and the debt began to increase.

Branch observers sent to headquarters to monitor the referendum vote charged that ballots had been improperly distributed and membership records not accurately kept. Over branch protests, headquarters announced a vote of 1,189 to 306 to affiliate with the CIO and 1,284 to 197 to send delegates to the San Francisco CIO Unity Conference. The anti-Communist slate won every office but one in the coastwide election of officers for 1938. Vincent Malone defeated Robert Fitzgerald for secretary 1,427 to 1,052, and Jimmy Quinn of San Pedro, one of the founders of the *West Coast Firemen*, defeated Allan Yates for assistant secretary 1,412 to 1,052. Communist bloc leader Walter Stack won election as San Francisco first patrolman with 39 percent of the votes in a field of seven candidates. Unquestionably, the *West Coast Firemen* accounted for the Communist bloc defeat.

While unions debated affiliation, a group of sailors and firemen, probably independent militants and Trotskyists, put forth a program for unlicensed seamen. Dismissing the old ISU as completely bankrupt, they also condemned the CIO for making "a deal with the Communist Party to turn the leadership of the maritime movement over to the fly-by-night outfit of Curran and Co., which as far as its leading bureaucracy is concerned, is nothing but an appendage of the Communist Party." The group proposed:

1. To safeguard full union autonomy "in any relationship with the general labor movement."

2. To amalgamate the three West Coast unlicensed seamen's unions in a single industrial union.

3. To encourage East Coast seamen in the NMU "to oust the Communist bureaucrats."

4. To preserve the solidarity of the Maritime Federation and maintain friendly relations with the AFL movement on the Pacific Coast.

5. To support the *West Coast Sailors* and the *Voice of the Federation* and prevent the *Voice* from again falling "into the hands of factional disrupters."[19]

The Communist bloc charged the plan to amalgamate the Sailors' Union, Marine Firemen, and Marine Cooks and Stewards amounted to an attack on the NMU and seamen's unity. One rank-and-file letter predicted the main purpose of amalgamation would be "to fight the West Coast longshoremen and the East Coast seaman," and another letter asserted the group backing it "only seeks to sabotage any harmony with the East Coast."[20] Supporters contended that Pacific coast amalgamation would provide needed industrial solidarity. It would "serve to strengthen and solidify the Maritime Federation of the Pacific and start the march toward a genuine, rank and file controlled, national industrial union of seamen on all coasts."[21] Although Portland, Seattle, and San Pedro branches of the Marine Firemen demanded a referendum on calling a convention to amalgamate, headquarters refused to put the issue to a vote. The Seattle and Portland Marine Cooks and Stewards also supported amalgamation. The Sailors' Union voted to put out a referendum ballot on amalgamation.

Jurisdictional Disputes

Ideological differences and the need to provide jobs for members sharpened the jurisdictional disputes that divided the unions. The new inland division of the Sailors' Union collided with the Inland Boatmen over crews of ocean-going tugs and inland craft at San Pedro and on San Francisco Bay. In view of his past record the Sailors thoroughly distrusted IBU Secretary Clyde Deal, a CIO organizer appointed by Harry Bridges. They believed that given the opportunity he would cooperate with the NMU to take over West Coast deck crews. The Scalers and Sailors accused each other of scabbing (working below scale) in the maintenance yards of major steamship lines. The Communist bloc charged that the Sailors' Union created a clique to control headquarters meetings by putting key members to work in the Matson shore gangs.

The dispute over cargo work on steam schooners festered. The Sailors' Union negotiated the steam schooner agreement with the Coastwise Line, which began operating on the West Coast in March 1937. The vessels worked schooner style (sailors worked cargo, as on steam schooners) with no objection from the longshoremen prior to the agreement. Then the district recommended that Seattle not furnish men unless the local could dispatch gangs for the whole ship. On August 22, after the Seattle Longshoremen refused to furnish sling men for the sailors' hatch on the *Coast Merchant*, the ILA worked the entire ship. When the *Coast Merchant* returned August 28 and the *Coast Banker* arrived September 2, the Longshoremen again refused sling men for the sailors' hatch. The Sailors offered to furnish the men, but instead the company ordered full longshore gangs. Thereupon the Sailors picketed and firemen refused steam to the longshore gangs, tying up the vessels. The Sailors' Union dismissed as "ridiculous" a recommendation of the ILWU Executive Board September 10 that the locals "take the winch drivers on these steam schooners into the [ILWU]" and then "take over the steam schooners for the [ILWU] and do away with the Sailors Hatch."[22]

A Maritime Federation mass meeting in Seattle September 16 voted "to uphold the SUP in its claim to certain work on the coastwise vessels, and further that we abide by Resolution 59-A as passed at the 1936 Maritime Federation Convention, which gives the Sailors the right to one hatch."[23] That night a delegation from the Sailors' Union addressed the Longshoremen's meeting. The *Voice* correspondent reported: "After the S.U.P. members had assured the membership that under no circumstances were the Alaska ships to be worked schooner style on Puget Sound, a motion releasing the coast liners and requesting both Lundeberg and Bridges to meet and reach an agreement as to when a vessel is or is not a schooner was put and passed."[24] But next day the longshore officers refused to release the vessels. That night the Maritime Federation District Council voted 64 to 20 on a roll call to support the Sailors, with Inland Boatmen and Seattle Longshoremen opposed. After ILWU members began to circulate a petition for a special meeting to recall specific officials, the local agreed to dispatch the disputed sling men for the *Coast Merchant* and *Coast Banker.*

Harry Lundeberg charged that the "CIO-longshore leaders, failing to get anything in the last two years . . . excepting miserable concessions to the bosses must make some sort of showing to their own rank and file if they are to keep absolute control of the longshoremen. They can't get it from the bosses so they'll take it from the sailors: they have consistently tried to move the steamschooner sailors off the steamschooners."[25] The ILWU denied that it wanted the steam schooner work, "especially under the wages and conditions that the S.U.P. officials and the owners think are good enough for this work." It charged that on the Coastwise Line "The S.U.P. got together with the shipowners and insisted the crew work cargo with the result that those crews now make another $8.00 or $10.00 per month and work like hell. It was further understood that if the crews did not produce plenty on the jobs" they would be fired.[26] The Sailors' Union replied that all steam schooner personnel enjoyed better wages and conditions because the crew worked cargo. Moreover, sailors worked under better conditions than longshoremen: eight instead of six men in the hold and a load limit of 1,800 instead of 2,100 pounds.

Besides fighting jurisdictional wars, the seamen battled a hostile government. The Sailors' Union defended the right of noncitizen members to continue to sail on steam schooners in spite of efforts to enforce new regulations requiring citizenship. The unions objected strenuously to a proposed federal mediation board that would curtail their right to strike. The Sailors' Union condemned a decision that the master of a vessel could break watches of seamen in outside ports on the Pacific Coast. The practice, the union contended, disregarded safety. "Some of these old tubs," the *West Coast Sailors* growled, "are so rotten that it would pay the operators to see them on the bottom, and lately altogether too many of these death traps have endangered the lives of our members."[27]

The Sailors' Union dissented vigorously from a request by Harry Bridges and the ILWU for the La Follette Civil Liberties Committee to investigate industrial spies and provocateurs in the maritime unions. The union notified the committee "that the maritime unions of the Pacific Coast are capable of settling their own problems and determined to resist any interference from unauthorized political agents or interests which are outside of, foreign to, and repeatedly hostile to those of the membership."[28] The *West Coast Firemen* called the request "mistaken, insulting and dangerous," providing a "field day" for enemies of the maritime unions. If Bridges had such evidence, he should present it to the Maritime Federation, not the government, which had "over and over again acted with the shipowners."[29]

The unions muted their quarrels to organize the tankers. With the substantial gains of the 1936-37 strike as evidence of strength, the Sailors' Union and Marine Firemen launched an organizing drive among tanker seamen the spring of 1937. Some crew members already carried union books. The oil companies raised wages $10.00 following the strike. The Marine Cooks and Stewards and Radio Telegraphists joined the drive. The unions filed petitions for NLRB elections on twenty-six tankers operated by five oil companies. No union challenged Standard Oil.

While the unions waited for hearings, the oil companies cleaned up their vessels, improving food and quarters and raising pay. They fired union militants and brought replacements from the East Coast. In the elections finally held in May 1938, the Sailors' Union won on four Richfield tankers, two Hillcone, four General Petroleum, and six Associated Oil. The Marine Cooks and Stewards won on Richfield, Hillcone, and General Petroleum; the Marine Firemen on Richfield and Hillcone; and the Radio Telegraphists on Hillcone. A company union won the engine department on Associated, and all unions lost on Union Oil. The Marine Engineers won bargaining rights on Richfield tankers with a majority of signed union authorization cards.

Oregon Lumber War

The bitterest jurisdictional battle of all tore apart the Oregon labor movement and spilled over into the divided maritime unions. When the Woodworkers Federation voted CIO in July 1937, the Brotherhood of Carpenters vowed to boycott CIO lumber. Building Trades Council pickets appeared at seven major Portland mills when their Lumber and Sawmill Workers locals joined the International Woodworkers of America, CIO, on August 14. Thereupon the mills closed, blaming the jurisdictional dispute. The CIO unions accused the mills of locking our their members to force them back into the AFL, but others held that the depressed lumber market was responsible for the shutdowns. Violence erupted when the mills tried to open in early September, with both AFL and CIO goon squads beating up pickets and workers. Ed Coester of the Sailors reported death threats "beginning to mark the mill war here, when three workers were fired upon from across the river."

When the *W.R. Chamberlin, Jr.* docked at the CIO West Oregon mill in September, sailors and firemen threatened to quit rather than work under the unsafe conditions of a picket line and police protection. But after listening to a delegation of CIO Woodworkers, the Portland branch of the Sailors' Union voted September 13 not to recognize jurisdictional picket lines "as long as the men working are bona fide union men."[30] The next morning the *W.R. Chamberlin* reappeared at the West Oregon mill with sixteen police officers on hand. Three sailors quit rather than work under police protection, and the firemen quit at 5:00 p.m. The cooks and stewards came off the next day, and the rest of the sailors on Thursday. The unions dispatched another crew to the vessel. The San Pedro Sailors correspondent noted:

> As docks become glutted with cargo and more ships lie idle, it is increasingly apparent that the mistakes and blunders of the CIO "leaders" providing excuses for the AF of L officialdom to "crack down" can result only in a widening of the rift that now exists. Nowhere else in America had the CIO been maneuvered into such a helpless position, and nowhere else is there such an open and devastating split in the labor movement.[31]

The Aberdeen Sailors complained of the idle men stranded there: "This condition did not exist before the CIO came out to this coast to organize the unorganized but instead started raiding the strongest organized unions in the world today and caused a split in what was the strongest weapon any group of organized labor has ever possessed to win a strike, namely, the MARITIME FEDERATION OF THE PACIFIC COAST."[32]

The Portland Central Labor Council pursued the CIO lumber boycott vigorously, disregarding NLRB certification of the CIO in October for the seven mills. By November the Portland lumber war had thrown an estimated 4,000 out of work. When the *W.R. Chamberlin, Jr.* arrived at San Pedro in early November with her second load of CIO lumber, ILWU longshoremen went through AFL picket lines to work the vessel. The ILA predicted that the lumber would remain rough piled on the dock untouched by teamsters and boycotted by carpenters.

CIO longshoremen could not keep their promise to support CIO lumber workers. Threatened with a port lockout, Harry Bridges and others persuaded the Forest Grove CIO Woodworkers local to withdraw pickets from eleven cars of lumber, which Portland longshoremen then loaded on the *Hegira* on November 11. The next month

ILWU men loaded AFL lumber on the *West Ira*. When Newport CIO Woodworkers picketed AFL lumber being loaded on the *Anna Shafer*, ILWU Secretary Matt Meehan wired the longshoremen, "If not a strong picket line go through it and work cargo."[33] They did. Thus, the longshoremen abandoned their CIO brothers rather that violate their agreement by refusing to handle hot cargo. The war hurt longshoremen as well as lumber workers. Bellingham longshoremen's wages dropped from $150 to $70 a month, and in Portland normally 60 percent of cargo was lumber. In Everett shipping declined 60 percent, and Grays Harbor had 12,000 unemployed lumber workers and longshoremen.

Portland ILWU Local 1-8 explained to the Woodworkers in February 1938 that "the best way in which the longshoremen could support the lumber workers was by remaining on the job, giving financial support, and doing everything in their power to use the strength of their organization to assist the I.W.A." If the employers had been able "to provoke the longshoremen into stoppages of work," a lockout would have resulted "by which they could smash both organizations at the same time, particularly as the shipowners would not have lost much by suspending operations."[34] By then mills in the Columbia River district had reopened, fourteen AFL, seven CIO, and five with undetermined affiliation. Some had no union contracts.

In early March 1938, Bay Area District Council No. 2 concurred in a resolution from ILWU Local 1-10 to "take immediate steps leading to a refusal to load, unload, or transport any lumber whatsoever"[35] unless the Carpenters lifted the boycott on CIO lumber. The Sailors' Union replied that it would not support a steam schooner tie-up involving some 500 members over a jurisdictional squabble and reiterated the resolution at the beginning of the lumber war to "go on record as not supporting either faction by an official walk off or declaration of support."[36] In a stormy two-day session the Columbia River District Council tabled the resolution, and Washington District Council refused to endorse the boycott threat. In a joint ILWU-IWA meeting in Portland April 18 Harry Bridges reportedly told the Woodworkers to "get their men back on the job 'under any kind of agreement you can get.'"[37]

The Communist bloc objected strongly to crews tying up vessels. On a trip from Tacoma to San Pedro in November 1937, in several ports the steam schooner *James Griffiths* failed to provide meals for the crew, and with no steam up the fo'c'sle was too cold to sleep in. When the ship docked at San Pedro November 28 the sailors walked off demanding meal and room money. The captain fired them, and the firemen quit in sympathy. With the cooks still aboard, a tug with an Inland Boatmen's crew towed the *James Griffiths* to Long Beach to load. Reinforced by District Council No. 2's refusal to back the sailors, the steam schooner operators would not consider the crew's demands and threatened to suspend relations with the Sailors' Union. With the threat of a coastwide tie-up and uncertain support from the San Francisco Marine Firemen, the crew brought the vessel to San Francisco to settle the beef.

Harry Bridges charged in the *San Francisco Chronicle* December 7: "This whole thing is a provocative plot worked up by the Sailors' officials in collaboration with the

Shipowners' Association." When Harry Lundeberg demanded an explanation, Bridges replied: "At no time did I make any official statement charging collaboration between the Sailors' Union and the shipowners."[38] The *Chronicle* chimed in with an editorial: "Seafaring Unions Require Better Union Discipline." The paper condemned the crew for initially tying up the *James Griffiths* in San Pedro instead of continuing to work while the port committee settled the grievance:

> The question still remains what sort of control the union officers have over their men that permits such a stupid outbreak to occur in the first place. If the officers do not maintain sufficient discipline to be able to prevent their men from violating their agreements in a case so clear cut as this one then it is high time for the good of the men and their union, that their official structure be reorganized.
>
> The seafaring unions have not liked the Maritime Commission's pointed criticism of sea discipline. They do not leave themselves much room to complain when they exhibit, as they did at San Pedro, such a lack of discipline as union men."[39]

Walter Stack declared: "No hot meal is worth precipitating a coastwise lockout, throwing hundreds of men out of work and strengthening the case of Copeland who has bills before the House to place us under Coast Guard management . . . . Can there be any connection between the Sailors' and Firemen's officials, the A.F. of L. and the Maritime Commission? Your guess is as good as mine."[40] The Sailors won the beef. The shipowners port committee agreed December 11 that the *James Griffiths* should pay the crew for five hot meals and furnish comfortable heated quarters at night and on Sundays and holidays.

On Puget Sound, ILA Tacoma longshoremen supported their ILWU brothers in Seattle when the Waterfront Employers tried to impose new methods of work that would have eliminated half of their jobs. In late December the Canadian coastwise steamer *Border Prince* collected cargo from small Puget Sound ports. Arriving in Seattle, she prepared to transfer the cargo on lift boards directly to an American-Hawaiian vessel moored at the same pier. When Seattle longshore gangs refused to touch the cargo unless it was first landed on the dock, the Waterfront Employers locked out the port January 4, 1938, and diverted other cargo to Tacoma. A delegation from the neighboring ILA local pledged support to Seattle. ILWU Local 1-19 recommended "that all locals work any and all ships and cargo coming to your respective ports" so as to "confine the present dispute to Seattle alone."[41] Seattle dispatched over 300 men to Tacoma to work the diverted ships. The ILWU notified the employers January 12: "We will co-operate with you strictly in maintaining the provisions of the agreement to provide continuous work on the Seattle waterfront."[42] The next day the employers opened the port and the longshoremen returned to work. The lockout did not change port practices.

"Is the Federation to Survive?"

After the 1937 Maritime Federation convention fired James O'Neil, the editorial board hired Ralph Chaplin as temporary editor in August. The new editor, a former member of the Industrial Workers of the World, had served five years in prison for

IWW activity during World War I. He soon demonstrated his objection to Communist bloc domination. When the confrontation between the Longshoremen and Teamsters erupted on the San Francisco waterfront in September, Chaplin warned of the danger to the federation:

> The Teamsters . . . look upon the Federation as "Harry Bridges' Baby." Other A.F. of L. unions claim that Bridges is out to destroy the Federation because he cannot control it and make it an adjunct of the communist party. In spite of the fact that no solidarity is possible on the waterfront without the cooperation of the teamsters, the "Voice" finds itself in the embarrassing position of filling its columns with one-sided C.I.O. anti-teamster propaganda . . . .
>
> The official publication of the Federation, therefore, has become a battle ground in which the very efficient machine-made propaganda of the C.I.O. is opposed half-heartedly by a group of indignant unions rightly or wrongly convinced that they are "not defeated but outnumbered."[43]

More rousing editorials urged members to defend the federation because, Chaplin declared, "solidarity is all that has ever stood between the rank and file and the economic serfdom from which they have been attempting to free themselves."[44] A few rank and filers responded to his pleas. SUP member John Pugh warned that the Communist Party planned to liquidate the federation. "The M.F.P.C. is our first line of defense," he declared:

> Should the shipowners succeed in wrecking it, they would break us one by one as they have always done before . . . . We who do the work, must consider the situation in the light of past experiences and hold together the Maritime Federation of the Pacific Coast, at least until such time as we can have something better. The half-baked hodge-podge now being offered on a silver platter offers no temptation to change.[45]

Other letters condemned Chaplin as a reactionary and employers' tool. Both factions continued to fill the *Voice* with violent partisan attacks. The Sailors' Union had been publishing its own four-page weekly tabloid, the *West Coast Sailors*, since May 1937. Another four-page weekly tabloid appeared on September 20, the *I.L.W.U. Bulletin*, published by the Bay Area locals of the International Longshoremen's and Warehousemen's Union and edited by James O'Neil.

Trustee Dave Harrington's resignation brought John Schomaker of San Francisco Local 38-79, an articulate Communist, to the *Voice* editorial board. Although the amendment had been adopted providing for a combined executive and editorial board of one member from each affiliated union, the old editorial board continued to function until the organizations could select their members. Federation President James Engstrom called a meeting of the board for October 30, attended on such short notice by only Secretary John Kucin, Chaplin, and Schomaker. The new trustee asked who wrote the editorials and whether they were "supposed to reflect the membership's views." Schomaker condemned the paper as "all wrong." He and "Chaplin engage in a personal crossfire and President calls meeting to order," the minutes stated.[46] The Communist Party and the CIO absolutely had to silence Chaplin's forthright criticisms in the paper. Chaplin put out the November 4 issue of the *Voice* and submitted his resignation. He left with a front-page blast: "The blow has fallen at last!" he declared:

> Following a process of slow and deliberate strangulation, the stooges of the Communist Party have the "Voice" right where they want it—on the rocks.
>
> "Comrade" Shoemaker, newly elected member of the Editorial Board, gloated over the fact at last Monday's board meeting.
>
> Comrade Shoemaker cooly announced that the "Voice" must be dumped. He claims that it is the "rank and file" that is doing the dumping. The reason given is that the policy of the "Voice" is not approved by the "rank and file." Responsibility for the disaster is placed on the shoulders of the present editor. . . .
>
> The principles of genuine industrial unionism upon which the Maritime Federation . . . was founded are too important to be discarded for the cheap substitute proposed by the Communist C.I.O. "Maritime Council."[47]

The *Voice* was truly in danger of perishing on the rocks. From a peak circulation of 17,000, the paper declined to a run of 14,000 by July 15, 1937, and debts mounted. The board cut back from ten to eight pages. Unions expressed their opinion of the paper by the size of their bundles. When James O'Neil edited the paper the San Francisco Sailors cut the bundle to 50 copies, then raised it to 250 when Chaplin took over. At that time the San Francisco longshoremen, then ILWU Local 1-10, cut their bundle from 2,000 to 250 copies. Other comparable fluctuations brought circulation to 11,000 in November. Moreover, according to the advertising manager, "groups went along the waterfront telling our advertisers to go into the [CIO] Labor Herald."[48] Many did this, and others ceased advertising because of finances. Bad debts, unpaid bundle orders that John Kucin could not collect, increased the burden.

Following Chaplin's resignation the full board met to consider the financial crisis. John Schomaker doubted "if confidence in the paper can be restored."[49] The board hired R. Dunavon temporary editor and recommended a referendum ballot on retaining the federation and the *Voice*. The board ordered a list of delinquent accounts published, totaling $2,445.47, of which the National Maritime Union owed $1,364.43. "Is the Federation to Survive?" the board asked in a front-page editorial November 11. It charged:

> In the wrangling between the A.F. of L. and C.I.O., the Federation has been pushed far in the background. [Vital issues have] been overlooked while these self-styled "leaders" wage their battle over who's going to collect dues from the workers.
>
> Many of these "leaders" have even gone so far as to say, "We no longer need the Federation." . . . Many times in recent weeks, the Federation has been on the verge of collapse and the only thing that has held it together has been, not the "leaders," but the solidarity of the members on the job. . . . because of the fight for power, it is necessary for the membership to take things in their own hands and notify all factions that we intend to keep the Federation and we shall not sit back and allow anyone to destroy it. We feel the best way to serve this notice is by a referendum ballot of the entire membership.

The board described the crisis with the *Voice*: lack of support from affiliates and threats of a boycott against advertisers, warning that "the Voice is what the name stands for, the Voice of the Federation. Once those who are attempting to wreck the Federation have gagged that voice it will be so much easier to strangle the Maritime Federation of the Pacific Coast."[50]

The Communist bloc scuttled the board's recommendation for the referendum on supporting the Maritime Federation and the *Voice.* District Council No. 2 condemned and nonconcurred, branding the proposal "disruptive," and referred to the affiliates without comment a federation request to try to get more advertising for the *Voice.* The Columbia River and Southern California councils filed the recommendation. On a roll call, Washington District Council No. 1 voted in favor of the referendum 80-2/3 to 38-1/3 and sent the federation letter to all affiliates. Thus ended the referendum proposal to reaffirm support for the federation and the *Voice.*

The *Voice* sank deeper into debt. A lawsuit filed by attorney Aaron Sapiro for $2,200 in legal fees owed by the Modesto Defense Committee and writs of attachment served on the Masters, Mates and Pilots, Marine Engineers, Sailors' Union, and Marine Cooks and Stewards prevented their paying the required per capita to the federation. The new executive and editorial board met in January 1938. Since July the *Voice* debt to the Golden Gate Press had increased from $6,000 to $8,200. The press wanted $2,000 immediately. Debtors still owed money, including $2,000 from the NMU. Advertisements dropped by half from August through December, and circulation declined to about 8,300 creating a deficit of $150 each issue. The board voted "to do everything in their power" to get the affiliated unions to subscribe to the *Voice* for 25 percent of the membership of seagoing unions and 45 percent for shoreside groups.[51] The Sailors' Union immediately loaned the *Voice* $750, to be applied later against per capita taxes, and after hearing John Kucin, Washington District Council No. 1 loaned $500. Portland Longshoremen responded to Federation Vice-President Robert Benson's appeal with another $500. The *Voice* continued publication.

Sailors' Union Ballot

The Sailors' Union voted again on national affiliation. During December 1937 the union put out a three-way ballot: AFL, CIO, or Independent. The AFL offered:

> To abolish the I.S.U. and reorganize it under a charter satisfactory to us and under a name to be chosen by us; complete autonomy; complete control of funds and property; right to negociate and sign our own agreements; call strikes on or off; guarantees no political assessments; election of officers by referendum; no check-off; right to select organizers as needed.

The CIO offered:

> An invitation to attend a National Seamen's Conference in January called by the N.M.U., the I.B.U., and the Marine Cooks and Stewards of the Pacific Coast, at which conference a national seamen's unity structure covering autonomy, property, jurisdiction, etc., under the C.I.O. will be determined.

Independent offered:

> Complete recognition by shipowners as collective bargaining agent for West Coast sailors; control of our own hiring halls; complete autonomy; absolute control of funds and property; to keep our jurisdiction over the steamschooner work, our jurisdiction over Sailors maintenance work, without danger of these jurisdictions being traded off; no dictation by top committees or executive boards; control by the membership; and government by our own constitution only.[52]

Controversy raged both within and without the Sailors' Union. In a pamphlet, *Steady As She Goes*, ordered published by a headquarters meeting, the Sailors argued that the vote did not concern industrial unionism because so far the CIO had failed to build industrial unionism. CIO affiliation meant "actually becoming part of the NMU, completely controlled by the already-established National Executive Committee of the NMU." While AFL members had supported the Sailors "to the limit, both morally and financially," AFL officials had never helped them. Therefore, considering the progress during the twenty-two months since it was expelled from the

Sailor's Union votes to remain independent, December 1937. (Author's Collection)

ISU, the Sailors' Union should remain independent. "NEEDLESS TO SAY," the pamphlet pointed out, "THE IDENTICAL MEN AND FORCES WHICH TODAY ARE ATTEMPTING TO DRIVE US INTO AFFILIATION WITH THE CIO WERE THE ONES WHO WERE LOUDEST IN THEIR DENUNCIATION OF SUP POLICY AT THAT TIME TO FIGHT THESE LABOR FAKERS TO A STANDSTILL, AND UTTERED DIRE THREATS AGAINST US IF WE DID NOT RETURN TO THE AFL-ISU FOLD." The pamphlet called upon the union to "lay greater stress and devote more energy towards building" the Maritime Federation and to work for amalgamation of West Coast unlicensed seamen.[53]

A group of Sailors' Union members put out a pamphlet for CIO affiliation. They quoted John L. Lewis's letter to the union "that joining the C.I.O., the seamen will be assured of organization on an industrial basis, . . . as well as the right to have a national organization, democratically controlled by rank and file majorities." For "full protection of its autonomy, property and democratic rights" he referred the union to "the enactment of adequate constitutional safeguards at the national convention." They advocated CIO affiliation to assure national unity. "On the other hand," they warned, "if we remain divided as we are now on a national scale, then the day will eventually come when our unions will be wiped out, because we will be divided nationally and the shipowners will be united nationally." To avoid destruction the union must unite with other Pacific Coast unions in the CIO. "And remaining independent," they charged, "is just another road that takes you to support of the A.F. of L."[54]

The Longshoremen jumped into the Sailors' referendum with a front-page article in the *I.L.W.U. Bulletin* December 2, headlined, "I.L.W.U. ASKS UNITY PROGRAM – Coast Longshoremen Vitally Concerned in SUP Ballot." They condemned the ballot as "a tricky word maneuver to throw dust in the eyes of the seamen": independence would open "the back door for Sailors to enter the A.F.L." They warned that "without waterfront unity—complete unity," the job of facing and fighting employer attacks would be impossible.[55] Another editorial the next week repeated: "We don't want independent unionism, meaning that we can rely on our selves—that we don't need support from other unions. Along this course lies disaster."[56]

Replying for the Sailors that longshore officials "have been dictating to us long enough, with the aid of stooges in our outfit," activist Charles Cates advised them:

> Attend to your own business, and act like union men and not like snipers. . . . We can make our own decisions without your advice. . . .
>
> Stop all the S.U.P. baiting. Be real honest-to-God union men and take care of your own troubles; we can take care of ours, and when the time comes that either one of us, or both of us, have to unite to fight the bosses, the sailors will be ready and willing to cooperate with any bonafide union and expect the same treatment from any union organization.[57]

District Council No. 2 held a mass meeting December 3, reportedly attended by 1,200 to 1,500 men, to discuss the question of AFL, CIO, or independent. Of the three invited speakers, Harry Bridges, Edward Vandeleur of the San Francisco Labor Council, and Harry Lundeberg, only Bridges showed up. He made a long speech attacking the independent position as a vote for the AFL, charging falsely that the Sailors' Union East Coast representative, John Lempe, was on Joe Ryan's payroll. A barrage of rank-and-file letters repeated all the arguments attacking SUP "super- militants."

The Communist bloc also campaigned for its "progressive slate" in the Sailors' annual election of officers. The *West Coast Sailors* denounced editorially "one of the most vicious campaigns of slander, libel and slimy lies in the history of West Coast labor . . . directed against the Sailors' Union and its officials in a last stand effort to deliver the Union into the hands of the commissars." Other unions and their members bought radio time and circulated anonymous slates for "progressive candidates." In all its history, the paper protested, "the Union has never been so grossly insulted as they have been lately—by the members of other unions openly supporting and electioneering for office in the Sailors' Union. . . . For what reason or purpose do they pay for the use of the radio so that propaganda can be broadcast in favor of the candidates who are pledged to go down the line for political action, the Party and the CIO?" The writer asserted that the bloc needed "to gain control of the Sailors' Union" because "in no other way can Bridges deliver the maritime industry to the CIO as he boasted to Lewis that he could."[58]

The Communist *Western Worker* contributed to the campaign with an item December 13, "Lundeberg's a Stool," based on a *Newsweek* story that "Lundeberg had instigated the present deportation charges against Bridges." Lundeberg demanded a retraction from *Newsweek* and threatened to sue the *Western Worker*; the paper retracted the story December 30.

The Sailors' Union voted 2,204 to remain independent to 641 for AFL or CIO, and 2,382 to 565 for amalgamation of West Coast unlicensed seamen. Harry Lundeberg defeated the Communist bloc candidate, Harry Mayer, for secretary 2,496 to 453, and anti-Communists won over the entire progressive slate. Likewise, in Masters, Mates and Pilots Local 90 Charles F. May defeated J. Greenbeck, the Communist bloc candidate, 771 to 226.

Rival Seamen's Organizations

While CIO advocates bombarded the Sailors' Union with advice, CIO seamen prepared for their constitutional convention in San Francisco. The National Maritime Union had voted CIO 19,072 to 1,084. Convention sponsors proclaimed the goal of "one union! one book! one constitution!" but the *West Coast Firemen* charged it was "designed to crush the Sailors' Union of the Pacific."[59] Delegates from the NMU, Marine Cooks and Stewards, Inland Boatmen, and Marine Firemen participated in the convention, which opened January 17, 1938. Refusal of the Sailors' Union to participate turned the proposed national union into the United Seamen's Council of North America, composed of the existing separate CIO seamen's unions. The delegates pledged to "abolish jurisdictional questions by Industrial Unionism, Universal transfer rights, and Uniform agreements." *The National Seaman* praised the convention for "the harmonious manner by which the delegates worked together to . . . bring forth a program by which all seamen will unite 'to bargain more effectively with the shipowners and to secure better working-living conditions and wages for all'!"[60]

Vincent Malone, delegate from the Marine Firemen, disagreed. In an open letter to his membership he blasted the "well oiled propaganda machine" that tried to twist his signature on recommendations for procedure to endorsement of the convention's draft program. He withdrew his signature entirely, stating "that I believe parts of the program and setup offered by the Convention to be completely undesirable and calculated to disrupt and disunite West Coast Seamen, . . . rather than to unite it on a sound, practical, and progressive basis as proposed in the Amalgamation plan already endorsed by all the branches on the Coast."[61] The *West Coast Firemen* called the draft agreement a "program of disunity and destruction" because it specified CIO affiliation, when the Sailors' Union had just rejected the CIO by 78 percent and the Marine Firemen had defeated candidates favoring the CIO.[62] The Portland branch "rejected this spurious unity program and branded it for what it was—a declaration of war against our brothers who have fought with us on the picket lines . . ."[63] The United Seamen's Council remained a paper organization.

As antagonisms deepened in the Maritime Federation, the anti-Communists condemned Bay Area District Council No. 2 as a propaganda tool. During a federation executive board meeting in January 1938, SUP representative Carl Tillman charged that "a certain group" used monthly mass meetings "in their interest rather than in the interest of the Federation," and some meetings caused "more friction amongst the ranks of the workers than ever before in the name of unity." Federation Secretary John Kucin related that he decided to go to a meeting unannounced. After he had informed the secretary that he would not be there, "Brother Brown had my name called out and a fellow got up and said I didn't have guts enough to attend the meeting and otherwise blasted the M.F. officials. I was convinced by what was going on that the meeting was only a mud slinging session."

Randolph Meriwether of the Marine Engineers agreed that the meetings "cause too much discontent," and Oscar Rolstad of the Masters, Mates and Pilots declared that "it has been a disgrace the way the meetings have been carried on." They have "always been a character destroying proposition, and just because another person doesn't believe as someone else believes he is called a faker and a phoney."[64] Both organizations objected to being billed for pro rata expenses of such meetings. Subsequently the Marine Engineers, Masters, Mates and Pilots, and Sailors withdrew their delegates from the council.

District Council No. 2 provoked another controversy by endorsing the National Maritime Union January 25. Federation Vice-President Robert Benson related in a letter to John Kucin that Washington District Council No. 1 tabled the resolution "until we have further information." Then "Matt Meehan sent wires to all I.L.W.U. Locals in the Northwest requesting them to have delegates in Friday night's District

Council meeting. Evidently with the purpose in mind of putting across the N.M.U. . . . The seafaring groups on the Pacific Coast have a 'beef' with the N.M.U. and . . . 'Shore' groups [dominated by the Communist bloc] have no business trying to cram the N.M.U. down the throats of West Coast seamen."[65]

When the council meeting February 25 voted to seek further information on the NMU, delegates from the Marine Firemen; Sailors; Marine Cooks; and Masters, Mates and Pilots Local 90 caucused and then stated "that if this Council insists on going through with the idea of recognizing the NMU that their delegates will have to leave as it is a dual organization. . . . Discussion for about 3 hours on the unity of the past and the disunity of the present. What can be done to regain the unity of the past."[66] At the meeting the next week the council voted 69 to 34 "to take no action in regards to recognition or endorsement of the NMU until . . . the NMU is not considered hostile or dual by any of the seafaring groups affiliated with this council."[67]

The activities of women's auxiliaries of the longshoremen and Maritime Federation varied according to the ideology of the majority group. Women relatives of longshoremen organized auxiliaries during the 1934 strike, and women relatives of other maritime workers came together as the 1936 strike approached. In auxiliaries not dominated by Communists, the women helped with strike relief, raised money with bazaars and other events, and gave Christmas parties for children of union members. District Council No. 1 Maritime Federation Auxiliary in Seattle produced a pocket size booklet, *Union Labels for Union Men*, to guide maritime workers in buying union products. The Longshoremen refused to purchase any because the booklet included a rhyme by Ralph Chaplin about union labels.

By contrast, in addition to conventional women's support work, two Communist-dominated auxiliaries participated in District Council No. 2. The Masters, Mates and Pilots objected to "the Ladies Auxiliaries discussing our problems and also criticizing us at any time they see fit. . . . They have injected themselves into many arguments, with which they have no concern, . . . and we resent it. We have our own auxiliary and we subsidize it; they assist us in many ways, yet never enter into our business. We enjoy the association."[68]

District Council No. 2 endorsed a letter from the ILWU Ladies Auxiliary condemning the *West Coast Firemen*. When the headquarters meeting of the Marine Firemen concurred in the letter, the paper commented, "Ah, but it breaks our hearts to have the frails turn up their piquant snub noses at us. . . . but what, we ask, does the Ladies Auxiliary know about firing a ship, oiling an engine, or running the firemen's union?"[69]

Anti-Communist seamen continued to seek some way to cooperate regardless of affiliation. The Seafarers' Federation originated in a mass meeting of 650 seamen and fishermen in Seattle February 17, 1938. Deploring attempts to drive them apart, the meeting declared: "Now more than ever before it is necessary for the Seafaring men to be once again united that we may be able to maintain the conditions that we have won and be able to secure more improvements and also be united in order to defeat the proposed legislation in Congress, which will put us back in slavery." The meeting resolved to organize a Seafarers' Federation composed of unions of Sailors, Firemen, Cooks and Stewards, Fishermen, Masters, Mates and Pilots, Marine Engineers, and Radio Telegraphists. It would be "strictly an Economic Organization" and would "at all times work in harmony with the Maritime Federation and its affiliated unions with the ultimate aim of unification of all seafaring unions on a nationwide basis."[70]

Factional alignments dictated reception of the new organization coastwide. In Seattle the Sailors, Firemen, Cooks and Stewards, Mates, and two unions of fishermen organized a port council. Sailors and Firemen in Portland endorsed the federation. In San Francisco the Sailors, Firemen, Mates, and Marine Engineers formed a council, and in San Pedro the same unions favored the organization. No Radio Telegraphists participated. The San Francisco meeting of the Seafarers' Federation March 1 adopted a uniform policy to request $10,000 war risk insurance for crews of vessels sailing into belligerent areas where those vessels carried war risk insurance. The meeting also voted "that all questions and problems directly involving the seafaring unions be taken up and decided by the seafaring unions alone . . . as their uniform policy and such policies be presented to the MFPC as our policy."[71]

The Communist bloc condemned the Seafarers as a move to destroy the Maritime Federation. A District Council No. 2 mass meeting March 8 resolved "that we stand unalterably opposed to any move that would split the unity of the Federation or divide the seamen from the longshoremen" and condemned "the efforts of the shipowners or any other group to split the Maritime Federation or to establish any form of dual Federation."[72]

The *West Coast Sailors* replied that seagoing unions had organized to restore the balance of power in the federation, which had been tipped toward shoreside unions by recent affiliations. "Far from being an attempt to split the MFPC," the paper declared, "this is a move to save the Maritime Federation by strengthening one of its most important aims. . . . Today the Maritime Federation is a Federation on paper, and every informed trade unionist knows it." But the Sailors' Union would "do our damndest to make the Maritime Federation again a reality in actual practice for the benefit of its members."[73] Tragic events would soon confirm the federation's impotence.

Thus the maritime workers struggled with their newly created enemies. Besides the employers, ever present and waiting, they now had the national labor federations, personified in their own unions, that they must either defend or condemn. But most union members still believed that the principle of solidarity prevailed over all differences—that neither partisan alliances nor fear of employers could induce them to betray each other. They would soon learn how irrelevant their solidarity had become.

17

The Shepard Line Beef

From enthusiastic financial and moral support for the insurgent East Coast seamen early in 1936, the Sailors' Union of the Pacific shifted two years later to hostility toward the Communist leadership of the National Maritime Union and sympathy for its membership controlled by those officials. The Sailors criticized the NMU for accepting the fink book and for ignoring working and living conditions in its eagerness to sign agreements. A report from San Pedro illustrates the union's contempt for the NMU officials.

Weyerhaeuser chartered the *Pacific* of the Argonaut Line, under East Coast agreement, to carry cargoes on the West Coast. When she arrived at San Pedro from Portland, Oregon, with the crew complaining of bedbugs, she took two replacements in the engine room and one on deck. The *West Coast Sailors* correspondent commented: "East Coast replacements were shipped. We informed them that all vessels under West Coast agreement are forced to fumigate. We do not make a practice of shipping fresh meat to the running-stock of any scow. But Sailors' and Firemen's Unions here had to depart from the established practice to safe-guard Mr. Curran's sacred contracts."[1]

The Sailors' Union resented the National Maritime Union's increasing interference with intercoastal vessels under West Coast agreements. In the Shepard Line beef mutual bad feeling would escalate into a bitter confrontation in which CIO longshoremen would crash SUP picket lines to support their ideological brothers in the NMU.

The Shepard Agreement

The Sailors Union signed agreements in April 1937 with two small intercoastal companies claimed by East Coast rank and filers, the Shepard Line and Union Sulphur, which had carried West Coast crews since 1935. When the 1936 strike began, West Coast crews tied up three Shepard vessels in Atlantic ports. After two weeks the East Coast Strike Strategy Committee "made an agreement with the Shepard Line to let their ships run coastwise on the Atlantic Coast during the strike."[2] After the strike the vessels sailed intercoastal with East Coast crews and no agreements. When the Shepard liner *Harpoon* arrived in San Francisco with complaints of poor conditions and disputed overtime, a leaflet appeared on the waterfront April 15 signed by most of the crew. It challenged District Organizer Joe Curran's credentials as a democratically elected official and urged East Coast rank-and-file seamen to join the

Sailors' Union. Two days later the crews of the *Harpoon* and *Wind Rush,* also a Shepard vessel, struck for a West Coast agreement.

In a letter to the rank-and-file East Coast District Committee, Adamo D'Ambrosio and John Cahill of the *Harpoon* urged the East Coast Committee to repudiate "any political group that may be dominating you" and merge with the West Coast unions. They argued that the rank and file on both coasts wanted "one union, one agreement, one constitution, one book," and contended that "our outlaw power [to fight the autocratic ISU] lies in our Pacific District unions and that merging of both these powers into one would immediately put us in a position to put out the old line officials forever more."[3] The *ISU Pilot* replied with a furious blast, charging D'Ambrosio was planted on the *Harpoon* as a disrupter, that he had scabbed in previous strikes, and that he had tried to wreck the rank-and-file movement.

With two of his ships tied up, T.H. Shepard flew out to San Francisco. District Council No. 2 refused to support the striking crews, and, according to Harry Lundeberg, Harry Bridges threatened the owner with "trouble" if he signed an agreement. Nevertheless, the Sailors' Union signed an agreement with Shepard on April 28, to run until September 30, 1937. The Marine Firemen and Marine Cooks and Stewards signed similar agreements with the company. With no notice of termination, the agreements automatically extended to September 30, 1938. According to the NMU *Pilot,* Shepard intended to disregard the West Coast agreements: "During the time the ships were tied up the Shepard Line was in constant communication with the NMU asking it to reach an understanding with the SUP so that the ships could be released. After the ships were released, the company affirmed its original contract with the NMU." Joe Curran argued that Shepard signed the agreement to move the ships. "However, there was no indication on the part of Shepard or anyone else that this contract took the form of a legal contract over a period of time."[4]

While the AFL and ILA President Joe Ryan tried to organize a viable seamen's union on the East Coast to block the CIO drive, the National Maritime Union gained bargaining rights in NLRB elections. During the last half of 1937 seamen voted 85 percent for the NMU over the AFL. The NMU won elections on twenty-seven lines, the AFL on three, and no union on two. In one of these elections on the Shepard vessels during October, unlicensed seamen voted 112 for the NMU, 5 for the AFL, and 13 for neither. The Sailors' Union did not appear on the ballot. A crew member notified the Sailors' Union of the NLRB election on Shepard. Harry Lundeberg wired NLRB Chairman Warren G. Madden October 13:

> In your general notice of elections among seamen you name Shepard Steamship Company, Pennsylvania Shipping Company and United Fruit stop. Previously you conducted elections in Luckenbach over our protest stop. For your information Sailors Union of the Pacific has agreement with Shepard Steamship Company covering all its ships and is recognized by that company as bargaining agent for sailors stop. SUP also has agreement and is recognized by Penn Shipping and United Fruit for all ships of those companies operating on West Coast stop. SUP has agreement and is recognized by Luckenbach for all

> ships in Gulf to West Coast run stop. Apparently bonafide union agreements are being disregarded by your board and your representative at New York has repeatedly failed to maintain an impartial attitude in these matters stop.... West Coast sailors have concluded that they cannot rely on your board for fair treatment under the present set up, and that their only recourse in the matter of agreements mentioned above will be economic action whenever necessary and leave it to you to pacify the affected operators.[5]

Upon receiving Lundeberg's wire the NLRB asked the company about West Coast agreements. Otis Shepard replied November 4: "We do not know that we have any binding agreement with any of the unions representing unlicensed personnel at the present time. We have had agreements with both the Union on the Pacific Coast and the Union on the Atlantic Coast. All of these agreements, however, have expired and we are now operating on verbal understandings with both of the unions."

Taking Shepard's word, the NLRB replied to the Sailors' Union on November 9, ruling the Shepard election in order because the vessels operated out of Atlantic and Gulf ports. The board advised Lundeberg to communicate with the regional office in New York "if you think that in any specific case the Board has posted and voted a ship whose home port is on the Pacific Coast."[6] On January 10, 1938, the NLRB certified the NMU as bargaining agent for Shepard. On the Pacific Coast the Marine Firemen defended the validity of the West Coast Shepard agreements, but the Marine Cooks and Stewards, reflecting the Communist line, recognized NMU jurisdiction.

SUP vs. NMU

Besides an unresponsive government board, the Sailors' Union faced hostile CIO unions on the West Coast openly supporting the NMU. Moreover, the union believed that the Communist Party deliberately placed NMU members on West Coast ships to cause trouble. The SUP saw in the *Willmoto* beef an attempt to sabotage the union and lose the ship. The deck crew included, as it did on many intercoastal vessels, NMU men sailing with SUP permits. In Baltimore during September the company fired two cooks at the crew's insistence and sent them back first class to the West Coast. Then the firemen demanded East Coast articles and refused to sign on. John Lempe, SUP representative, insisted that the deck gang would sign West Coast articles "or else." The SUP correspondent charged that "Practically all the beefs caused on our ships on this coast is instigated by Permit men. The Willmoto is entirely dominated by commissars.... Upon looking at the crew list on that ship we find that only two or three men are members of the SUP; the balance are NMU men issued permits to sail on West Coast ships by our union."[7]

As a result of the *Willmoto* incident, the Sailors' Union instructed "all ships crews and ships delegates not to tie up or delay the sailing of any ship in any port whatsoever unless so authorized by members of the SUP and to bring their troubles back to the mainland of the Pacific Coast to be settled."[8] To spread jobs during slack shipping, the SUP closed the books to new members and voted to issue no more permits until March 1, 1938. The union would give preference to SUP members, rotate jobs for permit men, and tighten up on rules for probationary members.

In the *Canadian* beef the end of December, the Sailors' Union accused the NMU of stealing a West Coast ship. On her return to New York after a trip to South America, the American-Hawaiian vessel took six replacements from the SUP hall. A squad of NMU men boarded the ship, beat the 112-pound deck delegate severely, and forced the West Coast men off the vessel. Joe Curran told Joe Voltaro of the SUP: "The West Coast men who were dumped can go back on the Canadian only if they ship through the NMU hall."[9] In March the *Canadian* shipped a full West Coast crew from the New York SUP hall. The Baltimore SUP hall, supported by donations from crews, shipped replacements for all unlicensed seamen.

Tension between the two unions increased. Roland E. Perry, West Coast NMU representative, complained of NMU deck and engine men being pulled off West Coast ships in Pacific ports. "Not a day passes but one or more men are pulled off. A week ago 12 men were forced off in one day."[10] In a registered letter to the SUP February 2 the NMU asked "whether this policy of discrimination is to continue" and if the union would "continue to pull all men who are not members of the SUP off West Coast ships." If the SUP policy continued, the NMU declared that SUP members "sailing on East Coast ships shall be obliged to transfer into the NMU or to be removed from the ships."[11]

The Sailors' Union replied to the ultimatum with an open letter to East Coast seamen, charging that the Communist Party controlled the NMU leadership and was "responsible for weakening and selling out the bonafide seamen's movement back East, and also have attempted to disrupt and smash the SUP." The union dismissed the NMU demand as an empty threat because "you don't control shipping on the East Coast." Many vessels shipped through "crimps [employment agencies] and off the docks. . . . The A.F. of L. seamen have control of quite a few ships, and also the shipowners control the shipping in lots of ships regardless of the color of a seaman's book!"[12]

Trouble increased on Shepard vessels. The NMU charged that in November the San Pedro SUP branch pulled five members off the *Harpoon*. In January two SUP replacements shipped on the *Sea Thrush* at San Francisco demanded West Coast shipping articles. Harry Bridges, acting on authority from Joe Curran, advised the NMU sailors and sympathetic firemen to sit down and force the SUP replacements off. The SUP told its members to stay put. After two days "the skipper told the sit-downers that they had better start standing up or they would be paid off immediately." A second warning ended the sit-down, and the *Sea Thrush* sailed with the West Coast men aboard, "plus round trip articles for the SUP members and first class transportation if they were forced off on the East Coast."[13] In Seattle, the Sailors branch voted January 10 to pull NMU men off "all ships where Sailors' Union of the Pacific men have been discriminated against by NMU crews." They expected a Shepard vessel to arrive that night "with a clear-cut case of discrimination against SUP members."[14]

Another Shepard vessel, the *Wind Rush*, arrived in New York January 20 with a full SUP crew. The NMU sent a party of about thirty-five to chase the West Coast men off the ship, but the SUP countered with a protective squad of ten or twelve, mostly Wobs from the Marine Transport Workers 510 hall. The SUP crew stayed on the vessel, but instead of sailing, steamboat inspectors ordered the *Wind Rush* to drydock for repairs. The company promised the crew their jobs when she came out of drydock.

Not all NMU members approved of the war on the Sailors' Union. After a lengthy discussion, a turbulent NMU meeting in New York January 24 voted 420 to 221 to give SUP men until the end of February to join the NMU or get off the ships; thereupon, about 300 men walked out. An Anti-Communist opposition movement emerged with the appearance in March of the *Rank and File NMU Pilot*, and by the end of the month the New York dailies headlined the NMU internal struggle and expulsion of the rank-and-file editor.

When the *Wind Rush* went back into commission on Monday, April 11, she shipped a crew from the NMU hall, although SUP men were available. Shepard said he had been notified to deal with the NMU. The New York SUP branch immediately declared the *Wind Rush* hot "until the Shepard Line lived up to their agreement with the SUP and shipped SUP men thru the SUP hall." That same night the SUP headquarters meeting in San Francisco voted to "tie up all Shepard Line ships on the Pacific Coast until they lived up to their agreement with the SUP."[15] The economic action that Harry Lundeberg promised the NLRB would begin.

Sailors' Union Picket Lines

With the *Sea Thrush* due in Portland the next day, the Sailors' Union agent Ed Coester called a special meeting of the executive board of Columbia River District Council No. 3 on Tuesday, April 12. The meeting voted to endorse the SUP embargo. When the *Sea Thrush* docked at the Oceanic terminal on Wednesday morning, ILWU longshoremen refused to cross the picket line and fraternized with SUP pickets. Six Sailors' Union members left the ship, but licensed officers and several West Coast cooks stayed aboard, as well as the NMU engine room crew. The Marine Cooks agent called another district council meeting at noon to reconsider the embargo, and all crafts but the Sailors, Marine Firemen, and Boilermakers voted not to support the picket line.

The convention of the International Longshoremen's and Warehousemen's Union in session in Aberdeen instructed the local to return to work immediately. Harry Bridges explained "that these ships were under East Coast agreement and jurisdiction."[16] The delegates labeled the tie-up, a "phoney beef, . . . no more than a jurisdictional raid upon a legitimate union,"[17] and Bridges charged that it was a "deliberate action to cause a lockout of longshoremen."[18] He proclaimed, according to the Associated Press, that if the Sailors "get away with this on these ships in Portland and Seattle, I'll instruct our east coast men to tie them up there and they'll do it too."[19]

Citing violations of the union contract, the Waterfront Employers requested a Labor Relations Committee meeting. The Portland ILWU Local 1-8 meeting Wednesday night voted to ask the Sailors' Union to withdraw the pickets and refer the matter to the

Maritime Federation. On Thursday morning, April 14, three longshore gangs went through the picket line of 100 sailors and firemen to work the *Sea Thrush*. Police, armed with machine guns and sawed-off shotguns, "snarled at the sailors they had better abandon their picket line, or get worse than they got in 1934."[20] About twenty longshoremen would not go through the line, and an NMU member sent from San Francisco as a replacement refused to board the vessel and turned in his shipping card at the SUP hall. At noon police turned back twenty carloads of longshoremen who came to the dock to replace the police and "handle the situation ourselves." Deck officers refused to obey the order of Masters, Mates and Pilots Local 90 to leave the ship, and she sailed for San Francisco Friday morning.

A Sailors' Union picket line greeted the second Shepard vessel, the *Timber Rush*, when she docked at Pier 6 in Seattle on Wednesday afternoon, April 13. Six NMU members quit the ship rather than work behind the SUP picket line; subsequently the SUP saw to their needs. The vessel lay idle Thursday as longshoremen ignored the ILWU convention order to go to work. Harry Bridges pledged to the Waterfront Employers that longshoremen would work the ship.

Longshoremen crash Sailors' Union picket line on the Shepard Line Timber Rush, *Seattle, April 15, 1938. (Courtesy Museum of History and Industry,* Seattle Post-Intelligencer *Collection, photograph #24097)*

In a special meeting Friday morning members of ILWU Local 1-19 heard delegations from the Sailors' Union and the NMU crew. Then, according to *Voice* correspondent Burt Nelson, Harry Bridges "thoroughly explained the set up," charging that the SUP cooperated with Joe Ryan to defeat the NMU on the East Coast. This "picket line was every bit as phoney as that of the teamsters in Frisco. The teamsters hoped to break the ILWU and so does Lundeberg." The Longshoremen voted to ask the Sailors to remove their pickets and refer the dispute to the Maritime Federation. Regardless of pickets, the longshoremen would go back to work at noon.

When the men assembled at noon "President Richardson instructed the members to put their hands in their pockets and walk through the line." Nelson noted that "a large number of cops were at Pier six apparently at the insistence of the SUP as the ILWU had not asked them to be there." He continued: "The men then moved in a body to Pier six and after a brief delay the cops moved off down the street. A wedge was then formed of the five gangs going to work and supported by approximately three hundred other members they moved through the picket line led by President Richardson of the Seattle Local and Brother Bridges."[21]

The longshoremen passed out leaflets requesting "the rank and file of the S.U.P." to "disperse this line" and "demand a meeting of the executive board of the M.F.P.C. to get on this matter at once." Seattle branch agent Pete Gill replied that the sailors would keep on picketing. "We wouldn't have a chance against the longshoremen in the federation if it came to a vote."[22] A reporter quoted Bridges, "I tried to be the first through the picket line but some beat me to it."[23] The Seattle longshoremen finished the ship without incident, and she moved to Tacoma during the night.

With no pickets in sight, Tacoma longshoremen worked the *Timber Rush* on April 16. According to Tiny Thronson, the sailors stayed away by arrangement, and the ILA deliberately staged the spectacle of longshoremen working the vessel to bolster their case that only an intimidating picket line could keep them away. On Monday morning, April 18, 150 "sailor" pickets surrounded the *Timber Rush* lying at Milwaukee Dock No. 2 waiting to load 600 tons of pulp. The longshore gangs returned to the hall, refusing to work under unsafe conditions. Most of the pickets belonged to the Lumber and Sawmill Workers Union, along with a few actual SUP members. AFL longshoremen and lumber workers supported the sailors against their common ideological opponent.

The ILWU convention approved a letter to the Sailors' Union contending that at the end of the 1936-37 strike the unions, including the SUP, unanimously "agreed that jurisdiction of the Shepard line would remain with the East Coast union, namely the NMU, and an agreement to that effect would be entered into between the Shepard line, the NMU and the Policy Committee represented by Harry Bridges."[24] Although the Joint Policy Committee may have passed such a motion, there is no evidence that the Sailors' Union ever agreed to it or surrendered jurisdiction over Shepard vessels.

The ILWU charged that the picket lines "were supported by the Portland and Seattle police and Teamster goons." The longshoremen tried to explain away the embarrassing police presence:

> The police on both the Portland and Seattle picket lines must have been there to protect the SUP pickets because when have the police ever been used to protect a bona fide picket line? . . . because much of the SUP picket lines was of the same nature as those thrown out against the ILWU by the Teamster officials. We are firmly of the opinion that the police and machine guns as described in the West Coast Sailor were there to protect the sailors and not the longshoremen.[25]

San Francisco: the Sea Thrush *Battle*

With several hundred Sailors' Union pickets gathered at Pier 41 in San Francisco, the *Sea Thrush* tied up at one o'clock Monday afternoon, April 18. Some distance away hundreds of longshoremen surrounded an auto equipped with a loud speaker, over which ILWU Local 1-10 Vice-President Germain Bulcke urged the SUP to disperse the pickets and refer the dispute to the Maritime Federation: "You sailors will only force us to violate our agreement and enable the employers to close down the port. It is not necessary to have picket lines against member unions."[26]

President James Engstrom of the Maritime Federation and Secretary Z.R. Brown of District Council No. 2 also spoke, defending the longshoremen's decision to work Shepard vessels. But a leaflet from the Old Timers Committee of ILWU Local 1-10 urged longshoremen not to crash the picket lines: "If we work the *Sea Thrush* we

Harry Lundeberg exhorting the longshoremen not to crash the Sailors' Union picket line on the Shepard Line Sea Thrush, *San Francisco, April 18, 1938. (Courtesy Sailors' Union of the Pacific)*

are definitely through as a union organization. . . . The Maritime Federation is completely destroyed should we refuse to respect this picket line."[27]

Mounting a cornerstone of the pier, Harry Lundeberg told the crowd around the entrance, "This is a fight against the Shepard Line . . . against an open shop drive . . . for protection of seamen's hiring halls."[28] Continuing over the loud speaker, he declared, "If these shipowners, who hold a contract with the Sailors' Union of the Pacific, are able to get away with this, it means the opening wedge of an open shop drive on the West Coast."[29]

That morning the dispatcher chose carefully the three gangs to work the *Sea Thrush*. Many regular longshoremen would not crash the sailors' picket line. The ILWU pulled the permits of five SUP members, winch drivers who had worked out of the longshore hall for three years, after they refused the assignment. But permit men from other unions—warehousemen, scalers, and cannery workers—made up the gangs. Teamsters standing by at Pier 41 pledged support to the Sailors.

As the time neared for the longshoremen to begin work, police moved all but twenty pickets to the other side of the Embarcadero. At 1:30 a voice over the loud speaker told the longshoremen to go to work, and the fifty-four men moved slowly toward the pier entrance, "then dug in their toes and with heads and shoulders down, dived into the line."[30] "Give it to 'em!" shouted Lundeberg, clipping "the first fink that attempted to pass that picket line—right on the button!"[31] The rest of the sailors surged across the street to join the pickets, as twenty police officers "swung their clubs freely" to break up the picket line.

"Fists were swung, men shouted and cursed," the *Chronicle* reported. "Blood dripped from bruised noses and the smack of fists on flesh sounded above the din."[32] The voice from the loud speaker urged the officers to do their duty and reminded the longshoremen that they would be replaced if they did not move up and "Get aboard the ship and go to work."[33] The fight lasted over fifteen minutes before the gangs got through to the ship and went to work with bruised faces and skinned knuckles. Reinforced by more officers, police forced the sailors back fifty yards from the pier entrance. "The cops broke up our picket line," Lundeberg told 250 sailors. "Not a rank and file longshoreman went through that picket line. They were outsiders."[34]

Twenty-five or thirty men fell with bleeding faces and bruised eyes. Three went to the hospital: John Dibble, a Seattle warehousemen whom Charles Brenner hit on the head with a baseball bat; Brenner, an SUP militant; and SUP Assistant Secretary Rangvald Johansen, suffering a fractured cheek bone and concussion from a police club. After Brenner hit Dibble, a group of longshoremen dragged the sailor aside, beat him severely, and gave him the boots. The Sailors' Union charged that assassins made two deliberate attempts to kill Lundeberg during the fight. Sailors deflected a blow with a heavy iron bolt wrapped in newspaper that was aimed at the back of his head, and later they stopped a knife hidden in a handkerchief directed toward his back.

ILWU members informed police of a box containing thirty new baseball bats in the back of Lundeberg's car, identical with the one Charles Brenner used. Questioned by police, Lundeberg charged that Communists planted the bats in his car after it was parked. After several hours police permitted the Sailors to restore the picket line of twenty. Lundeberg stated the *Sea Thrush* sailed short handed, with only two ABs, two ordinary seamen, and a carpenter on deck, and that she carried three passengers against steamboat inspection rules. Mates on the vessel refused Local 90's order to respect the picket line, labeling it a jurisdictional dispute. The *Sea Thrush* moved to Alameda Tuesday morning, followed by fifteen Sailors' Union pickets and supporting teamsters, who turned back truckloads of provisions. She finished loading there and sailed for San Pedro. Federation Secretary John Kucin commented sadly on the spectacle of "brother slugging brother":

> Men who were the best of friends before, became bitter enemies later. Men who had suffered side by side and stood shoulder to shoulder on other picket lines now were battering each other down. . . . Had the police not interfered (and I cannot be convinced that they had no intention of interfering, because it would have been to the advantage of the Industrial Association), had they permitted the incident to assume greater proportions than it did, there is no telling how much damage would have been done that day in front of Pier 41.[35]

The union papers reflected the bitter confrontation: "LUNDEBERG SLUG-FEST DANGERS FEDERATION: SHIPPERS HAPPY," the *I.L.W.U. Bulletin* headlined, "SUP Head in Open Alliance With Teamster Goon Captains, Vandeleur AFL Machine, Leads Bloody Attack on Longshoremen; Defies All Pleas for Unity." In an open letter to Sailors' Union members, the ILWU charged that the Shepard picket lines had "one object in view," explaining: "That was to force us out on the bricks and cause the shipowners to declare a lockout of the entire Pacific Coast. Then the Beck-Vandeleur machine would be in a position to start a 'back to work' movement, using the Joe Ryan stooges who are camped at 113 Steuart street and who were down at Pier 41 to see how well your leader has done their dirty work."[36]

In an anonymous open letter to Lundeberg, signed only by "ILWU 1-10 Rank and File," perhaps to avoid a libel action, the writer insinuated that someone paid Lundeberg to wreck the federation: "How much is Joe Ryan paying for this stuff, Harry? How much are the shipowners paying you? . . . Somebody, somewhere wants this Federation smashed. Somebody, somewhere, benefits tremendously by it. And you're not doing it for love. Scharrenberg didn't do it for love and you're no charity heel, Harry."

Referring to the San Francisco patrolman's recent embezzlement of $2,000, the writer taunted, "He had sticky fingers, Harry, and there is more than a suspicion that yours aren't too clean either." He charged that Lundeberg transferred money from the bank to a safe deposit box because "It's a whole lot easier to grab in a box for the dough," and wanted to know if the money was all there. "Every cent of it? You wouldn't kid the rank and file by any chance would you?"[37]

The *West Coast Sailors* headlined, "POLICE AID NMU-ILWU OFFICIALS IN OPEN SHOP DRIVE BY SHEPARD LINE ON SAILORS UNION." Another caption proclaimed, "Sailors' Heads Are Bloody But Unbowed! Real Longshoremen Stay Away From Pier As Commissar Stooges Write Black Page In Maritime Labor

Record." In an open letter to all longshoremen, the Sailors repeated that Shepard was not a jurisdictional beef, but "a fight against the shipowners." They warned that open shop and fink halls would result "if longshore workers are bamboozled by discredited spellbinders into . . . fighting shoulder to shoulder with shotgun carrying cops." They suggested that "Shepard has 'paid off' to someone to get this agreement out of their hair!"[38]

Back in New York a Sailors' Union picket line, honored by longshoremen, checkers, and teamsters, kept the *Wind Rush* tied up. Four hundred NMU members and Communist sympathizers tried to storm the line on April 19. "In face of our resistance," SUP representative Frank Berry wired, "they sheered off and established picket lines now facing each other separated by New York police."[39] One day NMU members on the *Bunoventura*, lying at the next pier, invited SUP pickets aboard for dinner, "and as a result of this East-West Coast solidarity, several more seamen will join the 99-Year Club, and be kicked out of the NMU by the commissars."[40] Seamen expelled from the NMU for ninety-nine years for opposing Joe Curran and the Communist bloc belonged to the club.

Maritime Federation Condemns Sailors

The Maritime Federation Executive Board, composed of one member from each coastwide organization met on April 20 to consider the Shepard Line beef. The Sailors' Union did not attend. In a long resolution the ILWU Executive Board condemned the SUP for threatening "the very existence" of the federation with a jurisdictional picket line "backed by teamster goons and AFL cannery finks and company stooges," that "attacked ILWU members, slugging a longshoreman over the head with a baseball bat." It accused the Sailors of "disregarding the interests of component members of the Federation" and pursuing an "individual policy" that "has castigated and nullified time and again the powerful influence of the Federation." The ILWU condemned the SUP for "picketing against a decision of the NLRB" and proposed that the union withdraw the pickets and refer the dispute to the upcoming Maritime Federation convention.[41]

Vincent Malone, secretary-treasurer of the Marine Firemen, disagreed and defended the validity of the Shepard agreements, declaring:

> Regardless of what the National Labor Relations Board decides, the agreements of members of the Federation should be held inviolate. They should not be discarded or thrown overboard when the East Coast moves in. If you go on record to say the Firemen's agreement is worthless, you can do the same thing if the East Coast moves in on the American-Hawaiian ships or intercoastal trade ships.[42]

Malone proposed that representatives of the Sailors' Union and the NMU meet immediately, with a fifth impartial man, to agree on a decision that both unions would honor. He blamed the Sailors for picketing and the ILWU for crashing the picket lines. Pending a settlement he called upon the Sailors to withdraw their pickets. Harry

Norman of the Marine Engineers and Federation Secretary John Kucin supported Malone's proposal. Federation President James Engstrom presented a plan for a series of referendum votes to determine federation policy. No one supported his plan. In a letter to the board the Sailors' Union presumed "that the Executive Board . . . is not trying to assume the power to negotiate nor settle a strictly SUP dispute, when the SUP has not referred the matter to the MFPC."[43]

John Schomaker of the ILWU condemned the SUP for choosing to "battle us through goon squads" rather than settle the dispute in the NLRB or the federation. The Longshoremen were "the backbone of the Federation. If it becomes necessary to expel any union, let us do it and make a solid front of the organizations that are left." He charged that Lundeberg was "planning with the teamsters to lock out the entire coast." The ILWU wanted to know whether the Sailors were "in the Federation or out. We know we can get along without them because we feel that the organizations that are left can maintain a close unity and beat the shipowners by themselves." Henry Schmidt, president of San Francisco ILWU Local 1-10, declared:

> The SUP has no intention of going along with the Federation program. . . . If they don't want to go along with the program of the majority, let them get out. Morally and otherwise they are absolutely no good to the Federation. . . .
> If there is going to be war on the waterfront, I think the Longshoremen are in a position to handle it. We will recognize no jurisdictional picket lines. . . . If these picket lines are established again we will go to town on them and remove them like we did before.[44]

John Kucin defended the Sailors' Union. The NLRB, he charged, erred in ignoring the SUP protest and holding the Shepard election "while the West Coast unions had working agreements in existence for that company." As to charges that the Sailors wrecked the federation, he reminded the board that only the SUP loaned money immediately when the federation faced a financial crisis. He asserted that working agreements, not port of registry, determined East or West coast ships, pointing out that Alaska Steamship Company vessels, although registered in New York, never left the Pacific Coast. He maintained "that the organization who has the agreement in this case should be given some consideration." The ILWU "would expect the same consideration, the same faithfulness from other members of the Federation that they expect from you." Kucin reminded the board that seamen did not always obey the NLRB and the government without question, citing the NMU's current picketing of government fink halls and the Maritime Commission. All seamen opposed the recently opened government hiring halls on the East Coast. Kucin took issue with speeches that, in fact, "put an organization on trial," stating:

> Brothers made statements that if organizations don't go along with the majority we will kick them out. Have any of you stopped to think what that means? Now you have a complete Federation. Every unit in the Federation needed—I don't care who they are . . . You kick out one organization and you have no Federation. . . . Do the Executive Board members that spoke before me perhaps mean that we will kick them out and agree with

the claims made by the Sailors Union that we are going to move in on them with another union—to set up a union dual to them?[45]

At the end of the two-day meeting representatives of the Alaska Fishermen, Radio Telegraphists, Inland Boatmen, Machinists, Longshoremen, and Marine Cooks and Stewards voted for the ILWU resolution, and the Marine Engineers and Marine Firemen against. The Sailors' Union and Masters, Mates and Pilots stayed away. District Council No. 1 voted 53 to 37 to concur, District Council No. 2 unanimously, and District Council No. 3, 31 to 30. The federation officers notified the affiliates that the SUP picket line "is to be removed and the matter referred to the Maritime Federation Convention." They urged the unions to take action at the convention "to stop this procedure of one organization placing picket lines against other component organizations in the Federation, which is to the disadvantage of the entire Maritime Federation."[46] Predictably, the Sailors did not withdraw their pickets, and the dispute proceeded without regard for the federation directive.

The Shepard Line beef followed the *Sea Thrush* to San Pedro, where a picket line of 500 sailors and firemen greeted the vessel on Saturday morning, April 23. After longshoremen went through their line, firemen shut off steam on nine other vessels unloading lumber, and sailors and firemen voted to strike all vessels and picket all docks in the harbor. The sailors and firemen resumed work the next day. Sailors and firemen picketed the next Shepard vessel, the *Sage Brush*, when she arrived at San Pedro April 27 from the East Coast. Harry Bridges led the longshoremen through the line to work the vessel. The Marine Engineers national office threatened to revoke the San Pedro association's charter for supporting the sailors and firemen. The *West Coast Firemen* charged that Bridges pressured the MEBA to make the threat.

Joseph Curran proposed that the NMU and the SUP meet with the NLRB to resolve the dispute, the meeting to be "contingent upon maintaining status quo on Shepard Line ships."[47] Harry Lundeberg replied that the SUP would meet provided the NMU recognized the West Coast agreements. Joe Curran complained that the "SUP does not want these hearings but instead wants to continue to harass and embarrass the National Maritime Union, and not legally establish the fact that they have an outstanding agreement with the Shepard Line."[48]

The NLRB held a hearing April 25, attended by representatives of the NMU and the company. The SUP did not appear. The board ruled the Shepard agreement with the SUP invalid because: First, the company recognized the Sailors' Union as a bargaining agent for all unlicensed personnel, whereas it represented only the deck crews. Second, SUP membership "was practically confined" to the *Wind Rush* and *Harpoon*, and the company "continued to operate as an East Coast operator." Therefore, the ruling concluded, "the contract was invalid at its inception."[49] Third, the contract was extended without proof that the Sailors' Union had a majority of employees and with an NLRB election already scheduled. For these reasons the board reaffirmed NMU jurisdiction of Shepard vessels. The decision did not surprise the Sailors—nor did it deter them from continuing their economic action.

Timber Rush *at Tacoma*

With longshoremen refusing to cross the Sailors' Union picket line, the *Timber Rush* remained tied up at Tacoma. The Sailors' Union removed twenty-one crew members and put them up in a Seattle hotel—shanghaied them, the NMU charged. When the Labor Relations Committee met April 19, Tacoma ILA Local 38-97 representatives contended that the picket line constituted an unsafe condition, not subject to arbitration under the agreement. Business Agent George Smith declared, "We haven't got any 'fighting men' in this town. We'll respect anybody's picket line." The *Tacoma Times* commented that the employers favored the CIO: "Although they have not said so bluntly, they were elated when CIO men refused to honor the sailor pickets and chagrined when AFL men in Tacoma took the opposite stand."[50]

At the Waterfront Employers' request, the Secretary of Labor appointed Rev. M.E. Bollen of Seattle to arbitrate the dispute. The vessel had been tied up a week when the arbitrator heard the case on April 25. Twice a day ILA gangs dispatched to work the ship returned to the hall when faced by pickets. The longshoremen denied "the right of either party to request an arbitration" and the "authority of the Secretary of Labor in this instance to appoint the arbitrator."[51] Therefore, they refused to participate in the proceedings. The arbitrator ruled April 26 that a disagreement existed between the Tacoma ILA and the Waterfront Employers, that the longshoremen had failed to prove the picket line constituted an unsafe working condition, and that they had violated the agreement by refusing to attend the hearing.

The longshoremen ignored the decision and continued to honor the Sailors' Union picket line. The crew members returned to the *Timber Rush* in groups with police escort. With the concurrence of the Pacific Coast Waterfront Employers, the Seattle Waterfront Employers threatened to close the port of Tacoma. Every available longshoreman worked, as shippers rushed to clear vessels before the closure deadline, set for Saturday morning, April 30. Four gangs dispatched to the *Timber Rush* the morning of the 29th found themselves outnumbered three to one by pickets and left. A dozen ships cleared the port the last day, some leaving cargo behind on the docks. On Saturday morning longshoremen again refused to cross the picket line, and the employers declared the port closed at 8:00 a.m. Only the *Timber Rush* remained in the harbor.

Meanwhile, the *Sage Brush* made her way up the coast from San Pedro. At San Francisco May 2 several hundred longshoremen beat up and chased away six sailors picketing the vessel at Pier 54. The Old Timers Committee bulletin charged the "longshoremen" were paid $2.00 apiece for the job. The *San Francisco Chronicle* praised the longshoremen editorially for "their great ingenuity and resourcefulness" in circumventing the rule "that no picket line must ever be passed." When the longshoremen went down to work the *Sage Brush:*

> Two hundred of them first "removed" the Sailors picket line. The longshoremen then were able to work the ship without breaking their own cardinal rule.
>
> The example is a useful one. Some time San Francisco may awaken to the fact that the longshoremen themselves have suggested a sound method of dealing with super-annoying picket lines.[52]

At 8:00 a.m. on May 4 four gangs of longshoremen went through the *Sage Brush* picket line of thirty-five sailors with handkerchiefs around their necks for identification. When Local 1-10 President Henry Schmidt arrived half an hour later he pulled the men off the vessel and directed them to disperse the pickets. Fist fights broke out as the longshoremen routed the sailors. With no pickets in evidence, union teamsters hauled cargo from the dock. The Sailors' Union warned "that if there were any more dumping of S.U.P. pickets they would pull all ships on the Pacific Coast."[53] A picket line of 200 sailors and firemen faced the *Sage Brush* when she tied up at the Oceanic terminal in Portland the morning of May 11. After three gangs of longshoremen went to work at 1:00 p.m., 150 more sailors and firemen from six ships in the harbor "all hit the picket line as a protest against the longshoremen going through the Sailors' picket line."[54] They picketed until the *Sage Brush* left for Puget Sound that night.

Tacoma citizens objected strongly to the closure of their port. Representatives of the locked-out longshoremen and waterfront employers reiterated their previous positions in a city council hearing May 2. Dr. Bollen, the Labor Department arbitrator, asserted that "The C.I.O. is very close to the waterfront employers."[55] Mayor George Smitley wired Almon W. Roth of the Pacific Coast Waterfront Employers and Secretary of Labor Perkins to end the port closure immediately. Roth referred him to the Seattle employers, and Perkins said nothing. In a front-page editorial the *Tacoma Times* complained: "Tacoma Made 'Goat' In Tieup Of Her Shipping." The paper demanded: "Let Madame Perkins, the NLRB and Mr. Roth of the waterfront employers' association settle this thing at San Francisco or Boston—not at Tacoma, at Tacoma's costly expense."[56] The Sailors' Union donated $1,000 to the locked-out longshoremen. ILA Local 38-97 declared all cargo diverted from Tacoma or destined for that port hot.

The action shifted to Seattle as sailors and firemen honored the ban on Tacoma cargo. By May 7 they had five vessels with hot cargo tied up in Seattle, the *Makiki, Matthew Luckenbach, Point San Pablo, Lurline Burns,* and *Lake Francis*. The Seattle Marine Cooks and Stewards labeled the dispute jurisdictional and instructed members to stay aboard their vessels and respect NMU books. Masters refused to pay off the men who quit, charging the sympathetic strike violated the agreement. But in the steamboat inspection board inquiry, crew members from the *Makiki* denied a concerted walkout. They quit individually because "mother in poor health – lumbago – didn't like sleeping next to steam pipes – just wanted to get off," and so on. Captain James E. Dollard declared that "there certainly should be a law to keep men from walking off whenever they feel like it."[57]

A delegation from the Tacoma ILA appealed without success for support to Seattle ILWU Local 1-19. The Seattle longshoremen voted to "continue working as usual and that we give the Tacoma longshoremen preference in working cargo diverted to Seattle from Tacoma." The meeting also endorsed the ILWU statement on the lockout:

> This beef was hashed up by Ryan, Paddy Morris and Lundeberg to break up the Maritime Federation, to smash the longshoremen and thus weaken our organizing drive on the East Coast, and also to drive the longshoremen and sailors back into the AFL, which has been overwhelmingly repudiated by the membership.
>
> The shipowners working with this group are seizing the opportunity to use this tie-up as a hot cargo beef in order to carry out their union-smashing drive and extend it to the whole coast.[58]

Tacoma longshoremen disagreed. They accused the waterfront employers of converting the ILWU into an "instrument for use against bona fide unionists. They made it a company union." They charged that the "rich, chiseling, tricky" Shepard Line, "aided and abetted by the communist controlled company union known as the N.M.U. . . . and by the N.L.R.B. . . . treated its contract with the S.U.P. like a scrap of paper." The ILA explained:

> At other ports the I.L.W.U. completing the transformation of militant trade unionists into stooges of the Waterfront Employers Association continued to crash S.U.P. picket lines, . . .
>
> Orders have been issued by the party that any longshoreman refusing to obey the orders to crash the picket line must be disciplined by withdrawal of work according to statements made by them. Even at that many have carefully refrained from ratting to please the W.E.A. and the party goonmen.[59]

The Sailors' Union delivered an ultimatum on Wednesday, May 11, that unless the Waterfront Employers opened the port of Tacoma by 5:00 p.m. the next day, "We call all our union members out of all vessels trading in and out of Seattle and in the meantime our members are not permitted to leave any vessel."[60] The threat worked. Dr. John R. Steelman, director of the U.S. Conciliation Service, arranged a truce with Otis Shepard and the Pacific Coast Waterfront Employers to open the port. Eight hundred members of the Sailors' Union, Marine Firemen, and Tacoma ILA accepted the terms at a special meeting in Seattle at 1:00 a.m. Friday morning, May 13. The sailors and firemen agreed to call off the strike provided:

> A. Waterfront employers open up the port of Tacoma for all ships excepting Shepard Line ships.
>
> B. Shepard to move the Timberrush out of Tacoma as is and no other Shepard Line Ship to move into port of Tacoma except Shepard Ships with full West Coast crews.
>
> 2. The Sailors Union, in compliance with request of Department of Labor, agrees to ten-day truce on the Pacific Coast and to send the Secretary of the SUP to Washington, D.C., to meet in conference with Department of Labor and Shepard Line officials.[61]

The Waterfront Employers accepted the truce, and the *Timber Rush* steamed out of Tacoma, headed for Lake Union. The Seattle Sailors correspondent called the truce terms "a face-saving device for the shipowners as a graceful settlement of a situation that had become very distasteful to them."[62] Sailors and Firemen would resume economic action if Shepard did not recognize their agreement. During the lockout members of the Inland Boatmen in Seattle and Tacoma refused to touch hot cargo. The Sailors' Union spent $12,000 from the strike fund on the Shepard Line beef.

Shepard Line Capitulates

As instructed, Harry Lundeberg met with an NLRB representative, Otis Shepard, and his attorney in Washington, D.C. He reported:

> I . . . stated that the Sailors' Union of the Pacific membership did not intend to let the National Labor Relations Board . . . come in and arbitrarily certify another union through phoney manipulations, and stated that we demanded that the Shepard Steamship Company live up to our agreement with them, . . .
>
> From the beginning it was apparent that both the Shepard Line and the NLRB were hostile to the SUP and favoring the NMU, but this was no surprise. Why shouldn't the Shepard Line favor a union whose leadership had only a few days prior, recommended to their membership to accept an open shop agreement and conditions far below the West Coast agreements and who has also openly recommended to their membership to ship through the Maritime Commission's hiring halls.[63]

Special meetings of the Sailors' Union rejected two Shepard Line proposals approved by the NLRB and Joe Curran:

> 1. Give the SUP control of all Shepard Line ships until September 30, then turn them over, lock stock and barrel to the NMU, or
> 2. Give the SUP control of two ships, the NMU control of two ships, and tie up the fifth ship.[64]

During this time the *Harpoon* carried a West Coast crew. The *Wind Rush* shipped a crew of sailors and firemen from the New York SUP hall April 24. They charged that the departing NMU crew deliberately wrecked equipment and messed up the crew's quarters before leaving the vessel. When she reached Philadelphia a gang of men, presumably from the NMU, dumped five crew members when they went ashore. They beat severely Joseph Martin, an oiler, and robbed him of money and personal belongings. The NMU denied the dumpings. When the *Wind Rush* arrived at San Francisco an investigating committee of the Marine Firemen cleared the engine room gang, including two Wobblies shipped in New York when no members of the Firemen would take the job.

The *Sea Thrush* docked at Brooklyn May 21. With Sailors' Union pickets out, ILA tugboat crews refused to move the ship. Shepard fired the NMU men and shipped a crew from the SUP hall, to turn to May 23. But the NMU men refused to get off. Shepard notified Frank Berry May 27 that the company recognized the validity of the

SUP agreement, and federal marshals evicted the NMU crew. The New York Maritime Council accused ILA President Joe Ryan of collusion with Shepard against the NMU and staged a one-day protest strike June 2 in New York.

Pickets met the *Sage Brush* at San Pedro May 30, the last Shepard vessel with an NMU crew, and again all but a few veteran longshoremen went through the line. With Shepard resigned to dealing with the Sailors' Union, the company fired the NMU crew when the ship reached Philadelphia the end of June. Although the Bureau of Navigation and Steamboat Inspection had outlawed sitdown strikes in American ports, the NMU ordered the crew to refuse to leave. Federal marshals hauled them off to jail with bail set at $250. While 300 protestors picketed the ship, West Coast sailors and firemen shipped a crew from the AFL seamen's hall. An NMU beef squad surrounded the hall threatening to dump the West Coast and AFL men, but a heavy police presence prevented a serious fight. By agreement, in New York members of the Marine Firemen replaced three AFL seamen who shipped to complete the engine room gang, and the *Sage Brush* sailed with a full West Coast crew. The *Timber Rush* came out of Lake Union the end of July with an SUP crew.

Against the combined pressure of the company, the federal government, the waterfront employers, and Communist bloc seamen and longshoremen, the Sailors' Union compelled Shepard to recognize its agreement. The economic action that Harry Lundeberg promised the NLRB worked. On the East Coast, AFL longshoremen respected SUP picket lines, immobilizing Shepard vessels. On the West Coast, the Waterfront Employers deserted Shepard and opened the port of Tacoma when the Sailors' Union threatened to strike the port of Seattle. By coincidence or because of economic pressure, Shepard attorneys decided the Sailors' Union agreement was legal and binding, and the NLRB ceased to declare that the NMU represented Shepard seamen.

The threats and predictions of Harry Bridges did not materialize. East Coast longshoremen supported the Sailors' Union of the Pacific, not the National Maritime Union, because Bridges was unable to persuade them to abandon the International Longshoremen's Association and join the Congress of Industrial Organizations. The Pacific Coast Waterfront Employers did not use SUP picket lines as an excuse to lock out longshoremen. What did the International Longshoremen's and Warehousemen's Union accomplish by forcing members to fight their way through SUP picket lines? Was the ugly confrontation an inevitable result of the national AFL-CIO struggle, or an inevitable result of the Communist Party's drive to control the maritime unions? Without the influence of these outside forces, would sailors and longshoremen have faced each other as enemies on picket lines? In an open letter to ILWU members the *Pacific Coast Longshoreman* charged that their "party line leaders" had isolated them by their CIO affiliation:

> You got disunity where you had solidarity. You have secession where an injury to one was the concern of all. You have disruption. You have had your treasuries rifled and

> looted. You fought friends and lined up with foes. You allowed yourselves to be herded as scabs to aid in breaking the signed contract with the S.U.P. You went back on every principle of unionism in which you once took pride. Your fellow workers regard you as outlaws ready to go thru picket lines to aid employers break contracts.[65]

The Sailors officially branded longshoremen who crossed their picket line "finks," the vilest epithet in labor. The CIO longshoremen accused Harry Lundeberg of "criminal disruption," of working with the shipowners to destroy their union and the Maritime Federation. Yet in spite of the deadly hostility and bitter invective, a few people still believed in the imperative need for solidarity. They would try to fashion a truce to save the Maritime Federation.

18

Dissolution of the Maritime Federation

While the *Sea Thrush* steamed toward San Francisco and the tragic confrontation between sailors and longshoremen at Pier 41, maritime workers celebrated the third anniversary of their federation. Secretary Fred Kelley had promised them in the first issue of the *Voice of the Federation* in June 1935: "The slogan, 'An Injury to One is an Injury to All,' means exactly what it says. Each affiliated organization, large and small, is assured that it has the support of the rest of the Federation in getting its just demands. It is only by unity of action that these demands are brought to the front and eventually won."[1]

During these troubled years the members yearned for that lost assurance. In the anniversary edition of the *Voice*, the federation pleaded for the return of former strength:

> Yesterday was 1934—a bitter, hard, cold day, when maritime workers fought for release from virtual peonage. The battle once it was won gave birth to a monument to Labor's perseverance and courage and unity—the Maritime Federation of the Pacific Coast. Today that Maritime Federation is beset by reactionaries within and without. Today we must again exhibit the courage, fortitude, and unity of yesterday, "1934." We must each of us be a committee of one—self–appointed to safeguard that Federation, or tomorrow what will we have?[2]

The Shepard Line beef drove the Sailors' Union into the AFL. Accusing the CIO of a "boss-collaboration, labor smashing crusade" in the maritime industry, "as evidenced by their approval of government hiring halls, their violent picket line smashing tactics, and their attempts to establish the NMU on the West Coast," the union resolved on May 16 to vote by coastwide referendum on "accepting a national charter from the AF of L on our own terms."[3] Marine Firemen remained split, with a vociferous Communist bloc minority concentrated in San Francisco. Over Communist opposition the Firemen voted 976 to remain independent, as against 170 for CIO and 40 for AFL affiliation, and voted 1,015 to 171 to amalgamate with the Sailors' Union and Marine Cooks in an independent industrial union. But the Marine Cooks and Stewards, dominated by the Communist bloc, remained firmly anchored in the CIO. Marine Engineers No. 97 had withdrawn from the Bay Area Federation District Council, and Masters, Mates and Pilots Local 90 balloted coastwide on leaving the federation. In an NLRB hearing AFL and CIO longshoremen contested for possession of the bargaining agreement with the Pacific Coast Waterfront Employers. In these grim circumstances delegates gathered in San Francisco in 1938 for the fourth annual convention of the Maritime Federation.

Secretary John Kucin prepared for the convention as if the federation might survive—as if well-intentioned delegates would come together in good faith to reaffirm the mutual solidarity of their unions. Others were not as sanguine. At the request of the branches, the Sailors' Union sent five members from headquarters to the convention, perhaps to avoid unnecessary transportation expense. The Marine Firemen's branches elected Secretary Vincent Malone and San Francisco patrolman J. Nance O'Neill, and headquarters elected Walter Stack, the only Communist bloc adherent in the delegation, and Assistant Secretary Jimmy Quinn. In spite of John Kucin's urging, most of the Marine Engineers voted not to participate; only Seattle No. 38 sent C.R. French to the convention. The *West Coast Firemen* predicted that "the party strategy will be to introduce resolutions of such a nature that will make it impossible for some of the founding organizations to remain. . . . As the thing stands now the convention will be a party rump convention in which they will capture themselves."[4]

Battle Over Seating Tacoma Longshoremen

In his welcome to the convention June 6, Henry Schmidt, president of District Council No. 2, pointed out that the "good ship 'FEDERATION' is very much in need of repairs. . . . she has sprung a leak,"[5] and he appealed for solidarity to repair the damage. The next day the delegates took up the issue that would drive three major founding organizations out of the convention: the question of seating the Tacoma longshoremen. The credentials committee voted seven to five not to seat ILA Local 38-97 because the AFL longshoremen no longer had a coastwide organization. A minority report recommended seating them:

> Can we as workers penalize and censure a group of workers who have been under union conditions 20 years, who are a vital link in our Federation as workers in a solid and United Front against the employer because they have failed to go CIO?
>
> . . . for no reason other than their choice of affiliation, a loyal member local—one whom we fought shoulder to shoulder with in the 1934 Marine strike—the 1935 Timber Workers strike—the strike in 1936 and 1937, a group of workers who have respected every picket line established by a member of the Maritime Federation of the Pacific, willing at all times to strike in support of a distressed member local as was shown in the Seattle lockout of this year is to be unseated because of their affiliation and not their principles.[6]

Jimmy Quinn of the Firemen warned that "if you refuse to seat these delegates that you are deliberately breaking up the convention."[7] Walter stack replied: "If you recognize Tacoma as a coastwise organization it means you recognize Ryan, Morris and his strike-breakers outright . . . you will recognize such as the 'Dirty Dozen' and the 'Lost Battalion.' Joseph P. Ryan and that gang are out publicly on record to break the Maritime Federation because eighty per cent of the Maritime Federation is CIO."[8]

C.R. French of the Marine Engineers defended the Tacoma longshoremen: "Now if you want a Maritime Federation you had better seat them. If you don't want it now is the time to say so, for that is what we came down here for—to find out whether you really, and honestly and sincerely want a Maritime Federation or not. . . . these men are Union longshoremen and I don't give a damn whether they are CIO or AFL."[9]

John Brost of the Portland longshoremen accused the Sailors' Union of "attempting to use this as an issue to do something that has been tried for a long, long time, to find some excuse to break up the Maritime Federation,"[10] and Joe Simons, San Pedro longshoreman, charged that during the open-shop years the Tacoma local "was only kept there for that one purpose, to see that Industrial Unionism is never established on this Pacific Coast. (Applause)"[11] John Kucin pleaded for cooperative effort:

> I don't care what you think of each other personally, that should not enter into it here—you are all Union men. Your union membership directs you to take certain action and I think the quicker you sit down and use your minds instead of your animosity and get together the sooner we are going to have something out of this Federation, because the good ship "FEDERATION" has not only sprung a leak, it has lost its rudder and its stem is badly bent and the ribs are busting and we should all get together here and patch it up.[12]

Ignoring Kucin's plea, Harry Bridges made a long speech accusing the Sailors' Union and Tacoma longshoremen of betraying the rest of the coast. He charged that in 1926 the San Francisco longshoremen "were kept in the Blue Book by Ryan and by the SUP and with the help of Tacoma. . . . We organized on the Pacific Coast and dumped the Blue Book, not because of Tacoma, but in spite of Tacoma and everything that they could do to stop us." He charged Paddy Morris and Tacoma with attempting to sell out the 1934 strike and advocating that the longshoremen settle separately. "Every time—every move that has been made for solidarity on this Pacific Coast, it has been fought and blocked by Tacoma." Bridges asserted that Bill Lewis and others drew $75.00 a week from the ILA, continuing: "Paddy Morris never worked for a principal in his life; they will work for anybody for seventy-five bucks a week, and will stoop to anything to do it too. . . . Tacoma has been kept in the picture to keep the coast divided. . . . We know that there is one big local and one big port that the whole wheel turns around and that is the port of San Francisco."[13]

F.G. Fetzer, San Pedro longshoreman, insinuated that Tacoma had been a company union: "It seems strange to me that when every port on the coast was struggling with bum conditions, low wages and the black ball system that there was a local on this coast who maintained a charter from Ryan."[14] Revels Cayton, Marine Cooks and Stewards, charged that the Tacoma longshoremen "have been a whip in the hands of the shipowners to break the unions and block them whenever necessary."[15]

Charles May, Masters, Mates and Pilots, reminded the delegates of talk in the 1937 convention that "We are going to be CIO all of us pretty soon" and the statement of Bridges at the Washingon CIO Maritime Unity Conference that "the Federation has served its purpose." Now the same group "was hollering today for unity and solidarity."[16]

Eugene Dennett, Inland Boatmen, contended that the Tacoma delegation, Andy Larsen, George Soule, and Tiny Thronson, did not really represent the rank-and-file

Tacoma longshoremen: "that when we turn down a minority report that in no way can be construed as cutting the Tacoma longshoremen adrift. . . . The distinction is that those persons who have devoted their whole time and energy to wrecking the Maritime Federation are being cut adrift making it possible for the rank and file to actually express themselves and work themselves in conjunction with solidarity— . . ."[17]

Henry Schmidt declared that the delegates were "making a mountain out of a mole hill. I am sure that the Federation will continue to function if the delegates are not seated."[18] But John Kucin urged them to "remember that organizations are on the verge of withdrawing from the Federation. One foolish action will mean the breaking up of the Federation."[19] Probably Schmidt and every other delegate knew that meetings of Sailors and Firemen up and down the coast the night before instructed their delegates to withdraw from the convention if the body voted not to seat the Tacoma longshoremen. Without giving the Tacoma delegates a chance to speak, the convention voted down the minority report and adopted the majority report 55 to 17. Tacoma was out.

Then the Marine Firemen read telegrams instructing them to withdraw, and Carl Tillman read a statement from the Sailors' Union, concluding that "we will not be a party to the attempted use of the Federation as a whole to club other organizations into accepting either the one or the other of the national affiliations today offered Labor." Charles May declared for the Masters, Mates and Pilots, "We are bound to support the Tacoma men because they have always supported us, we cannot remain here now that you have denied them a seat."[20] At 3:10 p.m. on June 9, delegates from the Sailors' Union, Masters, Mates and Pilots, and all except Walter Stack of the Marine Firemen walked out of the convention with the Tacoma delegation. Stack condemned the Firemen's walkout as illegal.

John Kucin pleaded with Harry Bridges, "You are the leader of these men here from the ILWU and one word from you would do much to heal this breach."[21] Schmidt replied that after a two-hour discussion without Bridges in attendance, the ILWU caucus voted unanimously to exclude the Tacoma ILA. Bridges declared that the "SUP has been out of this Federation for the last two years . . . They have never been willing to accept majority rule and as long as they won't, we are better off without them."[22] Federation President James Engstrom stated, "I have been attending Federation conventions and meetings for four years, and I know that this move was planned approximately four years ago. . . . Ryan and Morris and a number of others were always planning and Morris even made a statement to the effect that he was going to bust the Federation."[23]

The convention sent delegations to meetings of the unions that had walked out to try to persuade them to return. Robert Benson, federation vice-president from the Grays Harbor longshoremen, Roy Donnelly, Joe Simons, and F.W. McCormick spoke to the Masters, Mates and Pilots meeting that night. Instead of making the expected speech, Benson told them the real cause of the walkout was "because we have packed those [district] councils with organizations who do not belong in the Maritime Federation." He named the Cannery Workers, which belonged "in the food stuffs working industry." He believed that if the federation "got back to the original seven unions . . . the MM&P would be only too willing and too glad to come back."[24] For this speech the convention delegates called him a traitor and threatened to prefer charges.

The delegates who walked out of the convention issued a statement declaring that "it was with amazement that we witnessed this deliberate attempt on the part of CIO adherents to . . . use the Maritime Federation of the Pacific to club unions into the CIO."[25] In a federation mass meeting June 9, convention delegates explained their refusal to seat the Tacoma longshoremen to some 2,000 members. That night a five-hour meeting of 700 Marine Firemen heard a delegation from the convention urge them to send delegates back to the convention; Tacoma longshoremen, Robert Benson, Rangvald Johansen, and members of Local 90 showed up to defend the delegates who withdrew. The membership repudiated the walkout and elected new delegates.

The Sailors' Union meeting June 13 refused to admit James Engstrom and Revels Cayton from the convention because they had opposed the union in the Shepard Line beef. The rest of the delegation, Karl Isaksen of the Everett longshoremen and C.R. French of the Marine Engineers, could not persuade the sailors to return to the convention. Vincent Malone and others from the Marine Firemen and Tiny Thronson of the Tacoma longshoremen also spoke. The SUP members concurred in their delegates' recommendation "that we stay out of the Federation until such time as it is back to where it originally started, and is back in the hands of the maritime workers and out of the clutches of the CIO politicians." The meeting also accepted the delegates' recommendation:

> [To seek] a friendly alliance with the Masters, Mates and Pilots, the Marine Firemen, the Marine Engineers, the Teamsters and the Tacoma longshoremen; this alliance to be made for the specific purpose of self-protection against the employers if they attempt to move in on us and take over our hiring halls, or any of our hard-won gains, and that we will back one another up in lockouts or strikes, and each and every organization . . . to mind their own business and not attempt to interfere with the internal affairs of any other union.[26]

The next day the unions that had left the convention acted on the Sailors' Union recommendation. Representatives of the Sailors; Marine Firemen; Masters, Mates and Pilots Local 90; and Tacoma longshoremen endorsed a program for "solidifying our economic power" for the September 30 negotiations. They proposed:

> 1. No compromise on union control of hiring through our own hiring halls.
> 2. No wage cuts—no increase in regular working hours—no chiseling on working conditions.
> 3. United front for possible wage increases and better working conditions.
> 4. Uncompromising fight against any form of government control.
> 5. Against the arbitration of any of these fundamental union principles.[27]

The federation convention condemned "these moves by Lundeberg, Malone and Ryan's representatives" as "deliberate attempts to break the Federation" and branded them "as helping the shipowners and against the best interests of every working man and woman on the Pacific Coast."[28]

The convention report of the Masters, Mates and Pilots reflected their disappointment with the federation. They had welcomed the founding, believing that "we could get closer together, settle any differences among ourselves and meet the employers united, provide work for our members under the best possible working conditions and wages." Now the unions were farther apart than in 1933. "The will of one is constantly being forced on another and if the other refuses to accept that will it becomes the further butt of other attacks. . . . The Federation has been used for many purposes which our members feel were not our concern. Internal strife has torn it apart and it is failing in its purpose." During the past year the "CIO issue appeared to be more important than any effort to set a policy for closer relationship, harmony between organizations and a legislative program."[29]

Secretary John Kucin's Report

John Kucin defended the concept of the Maritime Federation in his report:

> When it was formed it was on the principle of uniting all groups in one industry, to coordinate the policies advanced by each and bring forth some ONE plan of action that would be acceptable to all. It is a voluntary organization in that no group loses its identity nor autonomy. Each organization's internal affairs are its own and of no concern to anyone else. It was formed without regard to each group's parent affiliation. . . .
>
> It was formed for the preservation of each component group; one to assist the other against encroachment upon its rights, privileges and jurisdiction. And each to receive the respect of the other. The ideas of one group to receive the same consideration and respect another would expect to receive for its ideas.[30]

Kucin deplored the interference with another union's internal affairs that caused "the harsh feelings between the ILWU and the SUP."[31] He criticized Harry Bridges for injecting himself into a dispute between the Sailors' Union and Inland Boatmen and again into the *James Griffiths* dispute with the steam schooner operators. Members ignored the federation instead of referring disputes to that body. In the Shepard Line beef Harry Lundeberg "adopted the attitude that the SUP had taken the position not to refer the dispute after District Council No. 3 reversed itself. He felt the cards were stacked against the SUP and that the Federation would rule in favor of the NMU. He gave the impression that an effort was being made to move the SUP out of existence and replace it with the NMU."[32]

Instead of the spectacle of longshoremen crashing sailors' picket lines, Kucin had hoped that the Portland longshoremen would respect the line on the *Sea Thrush* and refer the dispute to the federation. He stated:

> If the ports had been tied up a day or two over this dispute, all groups would have been

> affected and the pressure on the SUP would have been too intense to ignore. There would have been no rioting and the sanctity of the picket line still upheld. Now the press and the employers were given that which they have been hoping for and the picket line is something to be sneered at.

The last paragraph of the *Chronicle* editorial of May 4 "invited the public to incite riot whenever it encounters a picket line."[33]

By condemning the Sailors' Union, the federation executive board, in effect, "admitted to the SUP that their contentions were correct. That we were going to drive them out of existence and replace them with some other group." Kucin called the Shepard Line beef "the most serious dispute the Federation has ever had on its hands; greater in my mind than our strikes of the past." The resultant bitterness "will be a long time in healing." He warned that continued jurisdictional disputes "can only lead to one end—the loss of confidence of our members in our organizations and the destruction of the Maritime Federation, in the increased hostile attitude of the public and regulation of our organizations by the government through unfavorable legislation and compulsory arbitration."[34]

Kucin warned that the federation structure threatened to break down. Only the Northwest District Council functioned properly, with regular weekly meetings in which all the component organizations participated. Three major unions had dropped out of the Bay Area council, complaining that delegates from the women's auxiliaries "inject themselves into matters that do not concern them and express themselves too freely on matters pertaining to the internal affairs of other unions." They also objected to local affiliates interfering "with Federation matters of a coastwise nature" and to the amount of time and money spent "on matters not pertaining to the Federation." The Columbia River council met irregularly with poor attendance, and the San Pedro council had "broken down entirely."[35]

Kucin declared that the *Voice* "has been the cause of much controversy since the day of its first issue. . . . Each faction has tried to control it and use it for its own purpose." With nothing censored, the rank-and-file columns "contained some of the most slanderous and vitriolic comments I have ever read." He criticized "News and Notes" of organizations:

> These items . . . would carry vituperative remarks about other Federation groups. Delighting in informing the world of some other group's activities at its meetings and tearing a sister organization to pieces—this being called "constructive criticism.". . .
>
> On the front page would be an article describing the solidarity and militancy of the Federation, and then the inside pages would belie those articles through the bickering and hatred described therein.[36]

Kucin reminded the delegates that the federation was organized as a voluntary association in which each union retained autonomy "in the conduct of its internal affairs." Majority rule became possible "only if each group consents to actions sponsored by a majority. If one group decides that it cannot accept the decision of the rest for any reason, there is no rule that will compel them to." Although the unions agreed unanimously in their purpose, to secure "better wages, hours, working conditions and increased employment," they differed in methods. "We have permitted too many interests other than wages and conditions to capture our attention. We have permitted grudges and personal differences to sway us from our original purpose, and we have permitted outside influences to inject themselves into our scheme of things."[37]

Predictably, the delegates did not like Kucin's report. His "many misconceptions and misstatements" detracted "somewhat from the value of his conclusions." His proposed solution in the Shepard Line dispute "would not only have put the SUP out of business, but the MFPC and all its component organizations as well." The federation executive board "was correct in condemning the sailors' picket line."[38] Kucin replied:

> None of the delegates here know how often President Engstrom and myself have been told to mind our own business when we attempted to inject ourselves into any dispute, even when we attempted to bring about a settlement of the dispute between the firemen and engineers on the fruit ships. . . . You had better stop talking about cooperation and pledging support to the Federation and start acting cooperation and giving support. . . . So far as the vote of thanks is concerned, I didn't expect any, didn't ask for any, and don't want any and you can keep it.[39]

After the rising vote of thanks C.R. French stated for the record: "I won't insult a brother licensed officer by standing up here and giving him a vote of confidence after the most dirty, lying, libelous, and scandalous remarks that I have ever heard on the floor of any convention. The idea is to elect a licensed officer for a front, and then make a doormat and a donkey out of him."[40]

The End of the Federation

Rejecting the possibility of compromise, the convention delegates formalized in resolutions the monolithic organization that had emerged from their actions. They resolved to "put teeth" in the constitution, "even to the extent of empowering the Executive Board to expel any organization which takes action which will injure the unions affiliated and eventually destroy them and the Federation," provided a membership referendum ratified the penalty.[41] They created a joint negotiating committee for September 30, which would conduct "all negotiations of all coastwise agreements with the shipowners." All "coastwise agreements entered into by a component organization" were to be "countersigned by the joint negotiating committee and the officers of the Maritime Federation" after approval by the union.[42]

With the opposition driven out, the convention elected all officers by acclamation: James Engstrom of the Seattle Marine Firemen, president; H.F. McGrath of the San Francisco Machinists, vice-president; Bruce Hannon of the Seattle Longshoremen, secretary-treasurer; and Revels Cayton, Randolph Meriwether, and John Schomaker, trustees. Revels Cayton made the final unity speech:

> The task the delegates and officers have is to build a fighting organization so that the maritime unions will continue to live and prosper and grow strong. . . . The Federation

> must revive in the spirit of 1934. . . . and be really aggressive and strong against those who want to destroy our union. . . . we must carry on the fight and be on the offensive instead of on the defensive.[43]

The delegates applauded.

The 1938 convention destroyed the federation, although the name and newspaper lingered for several years. For the young militants who fought so hard for and believed so intensely in the Maritime Federation, the future suddenly disappeared. The long road of solidarity no longer stretched away toward the dawn of social justice. No road existed, and probably no dawn—ever. The solidarity of the Maritime Federation became empty rhetoric.

But beneath the ruined structure, regardless of quarrels over national affiliation, maritime workers drew together in defense against shipowners' aggression. The Marine Firemen rejected a Shepard Line attempt to use them against the Sailors' Union, and both unions supported the Marine Cooks and Stewards in gaining an agreement with the company. The Sailors' Union assured the Longshoremen and Warehousemen that "if attempts are made by employers to crush any section of the maritime workers, and these workers decide they are forced to strike to protect their status, the Sailors' Union of the Pacific stands now, as always—to back them up at all times!"[44]

Although the federation perished, the individual organizations remained strong. Members held fast to their unions and hiring halls. Neither employers nor government could break them. Among these union bastions, shorn of rhetoric, fragments of solidarity endured.

Glossary

Able-bodied seaman (able seaman, AB) — An experienced sailor on deck, equivalent to journeyman rating ashore.

Agreement, union — A contract between a union or group of unions and an employer or group of employers. Customarily it includes minimum wage rates, hours, and conditions of work, provisions for benefits, method for settling grievances, union security clause, and other matters.

American Plan — Campaign of antiunion employers during the 1920s equating the open shop with patriotism and the closed or union shop with subversive aims and disloyalty.

Arbitration — A method of settling disputes by calling in a third party (arbitrator), whose decision is final and binding.

Assessment — A fixed sum of money levied on all union members for a specific purpose, such as a strike assessment to create a strike fund.

Bargaining unit — A group of employees who negotiate collectively with their employer or employers.

Beef — A dispute between different unions or a union and management.

Blacklist — A list circulated among employers of undesirable workers whom they will not hire because of union membership or activity.

Blue Book union — A company union instituted on the San Francisco waterfront in 1919, named for the cover of the membership book.

Boatswain (bo'sun) — In a large crew, the able seaman who transmits orders from mate to sailors, equivalent to working foreman ashore.

Boom — A spar attached to the mast of a ship that is rigged with tackle. The boom is swung out when working cargo.

Boycott — Concerted refusal by union members and supporters to handle or buy a product or service.

Business agent (or representative) — Union member, usually paid, authorized to represent the union in negotiations with employers and other matters.

Casual — Extra worker.

Central labor council — A voluntary association of local unions in a geographical area for mutual protection and advancement.

Certification — Official designation of a union as the exclusive bargaining representative for employees in a particular bargaining unit.

Charter — Large engraved certificate of affiliation issued by a national union to a local union or council.

Checker — In Northwest ports the person who tallies cargo being stowed aboard or unloaded from a ship.

Closed shop — A contract provision that requires employers to hire only union members, outlawed by Taft-Hartley Act except in construction and maritime industries.

Coastwide — Embracing the entire coast in contrast to one locality.

Coastwise — In the shipping trade, coastwise refers to voyages along the coast, in contrast to offshore voyages.

Collective bargaining — The process of negotiating agreements or settling disputes between management and employees, in which a union represents all workers in the bargaining unit.

Company union — Sometimes called an employee representation plan. A union fostered and dominated by the employer to discourage organization of a bona fide union.

Conciliation — Efforts by a third party to persuade a union and management to reach agreement in a dispute. The conciliator or mediator tries to find a basis for settlement without having the authority to impose a settlement on either side. In contrast to arbitration, the recommendations are not binding.

Cost-of-living index — An index measuring the change in the cost of typical worker purchases of goods and services as expressed as a percentage of the cost of those same goods and services in some base period. Also called consumer price index.

Craft union — A union confined to one craft, but may include unskilled helpers as well as skilled journeymen.

Death benefit — A cash payment by the union to the family upon the death of a member, or payment of funeral expenses.

Deep water — A 19th century term for voyages across oceans in contrast to coastwise shipping routes.

Delegate — The union representative in a ship's crew.

Direct action — Action taken by workers at the point of production, either individually or collectively, to make immediate change in their work situation.

Discharge — A certificate of release from a vessel issued to a seaman at the end of a voyage.

Discrimination — Unequal treatment of workers because of race, nationality, religion, sex, sexual preference, age, or union activity.

Dispatcher — Official in a hiring hall who sends people out on jobs.

Dual union — A rival union covering the same jurisdiction as that claimed by an already established union.

Dues — Fees, usually monthly, that the union votes for and collects from all members to pay the expenses of the union.

Dumping — Beating up a person with fists, brass knuckles, or saps.

Extras — Laborers hired for longshore work at peak times.

Faker, fakir — Derogatory term for a union official implying a lazy, self-serving, and/or corrupt official.

Fink — Scab, strikebreaker.

Fink book — Continuous discharge book that employers required seamen to carry to sail on the Pacific Coast, 1921–1934.

Fink hall — Employers' hiring hall for seamen and longshoremen.

Fo'c'sle (forecastle) — The unlicensed seamen's quarters, usually in the forward part of a vessel.

Forepeak — The extreme forward lower compartment of a vessel.

Free riders, free loaders — Employees who secure whatever benefits derive from the union's activities without paying dues.

Galley — The kitchen of a vessel.

Gang — A longshore work team.

Gang boss — The leader of the longshore work team, often the hatch tender.

General strike — Sympathetic strike of all workers in a geographic area or industry for a common demand in support of a group of workers already on strike.

Grievance — A dispute between union and management over a workplace situation or the interpretation of an agreement.

Hang the hook — To stop work suddenly, generally because of a grievance or an accident. Also a strike.

Hatch — An opening in the deck of a ship giving access to the hold where cargo is stowed.

Hatch tender — A longshoreman positioned so that he can see the gang in the ship's hold and at the same time signal the winch driver where and when to position the load. Usually the gang boss.

Hot cargo — Unfair material that has been produced or handled by scabs.

Industrial union — Union of all workers in an industry regardless of the kind of work they perform, in contrast to separate unions for workers of each craft in the industry.

Initiation fee — The entrance fee to join a union.

Intercoastal — The shipping route between the Atlantic, Gulf, and Pacific coasts by way of the Panama Canal.

International representative — A representative of the international union, usually paid, who assists local unions in a certain area or industry.

International union — A body composed of affiliated local unions, usually including some locals outside the United Sates.

Job action — Same as direct action.

Jurisdictional dispute — A controversy between two or more unions over the right to the same work.

Local union — A voluntary association of working people organized for their mutual protection and advancement, the basic unit of labor organization.

Lockout — The withdrawing of employment by an employer and the whole or partial closing of the establishment to gain concessions from or resist demands of employees.

Longshoremen — During the 19th century the term referred to workers handling cargo on docks, in contrast to stevedores and riggers who worked aboard vessels. During the 20th century the term came to mean workers discharging and loading cargo and trucking cargo on the docks.

Marine cook, steward, waiter, salonman, messman — Experience ratings of unlicensed seamen in the stewards' department of a vessel.

Marine fireman, oiler, watertender, wiper — Experience ratings of unlicensed seamen in the engine room of a vessel.

Marine unions — The seagoing crafts.

Maritime unions — Includes all seagoing and shoreside crafts.

Mate — A licensed deck officer ranking below the captain.

Mediation — Same as conciliation.

National Labor Relations Act (Wagner Act, 1935) — Federal law guaranteeing workers in industries engaged in interstate commerce the right to organize and bargain collectively.

National Labor Relations Board (NLRB) — National board and regional boards established by the Wagner Act to conduct secret ballot elections to determine employees' choice of bargaining agent. Also to hear and determine unfair labor practices under the law.

NRA (National Recovery Administration) — The federal agency created to administer the National Industrial Recovery Act passed June 16, 1933. Principal labor provisions of the act stated that employees had the right to organize and bargain collectively through representatives of their own choosing and set maximum hours and minimum wages in industry codes.

Offshore — The modern term for deep water. Refers to voyages across the ocean in contrast to coastwise routes.

Open shop — A workplace where no union is recognized by the employer and frequently union membership is discouraged or prohibited.

Ordinary seaman — A sailor on deck without sufficient experience to qualify as an able seaman, equivalent to an apprentice ashore.

Overtime — Time worked beyond the established working hours. Overtime pay is the premium rate in effect during those hours worked.

Patrolman — Paid representative of a seagoing union who visits ships in port to collect dues, sign up new members, and settle disputes.

Per capita tax — That portion of local union dues which is remitted to the parent body or to councils with which the local union is affiliated.

Permit, work — An authorization given by a union to work temporarily on a union job without joining the union. Usually the permit holder pays a monthly fee equal to union dues.

Pick — The process of dispatching longshoremen to jobs. At selected times the members line up in the hiring hall and are "picked" according to classification and earnings.

Picket — To patrol alongside the premises of an employer to prevent people, goods, or equipment from entering the establishment during a strike or lockout.

Picket line — One or more persons with signs patrolling an unfair or struck establishment or unfair product to isolate it.

Pie card — A derogatory term applied to a paid union official.

Piecework pay — Wages paid on the basis of number of units produced, rather than the time spent in production.

Quickie strike — Work stoppage called without advance notice and often not authorized by the union.

Raiding — A union's attempt to enroll workers belonging to or represented by another union.

Rank and file — Union members in contrast to union officers.

Rat — Scab, strikebreaker.

Real wages — The amount of goods and services that money wages will buy.

Sabotage — Destruction of an employer's property or the hindering of production by discontented workers.

Scab — A person who takes a striker's job or works behind a picket line in an unfair establishment.

Scab hall — Employers' hiring hall.

Secondary boycott — Refusal of union people to handle or work on a product that has been previously handled or worked on by scabs, or is diverted from a workplace where workers are on strike or locked out.

Seniority — Workers' length of service with an employer, often used to determine the order of layoffs, recalls, promotions, and other matters.

Shape-up — A method of selecting longshoremen whereby the workers assemble at the pier and a gang boss selects the crew.

Ship clerk — Term for checker in California ports.

Shop committee — Designated union representatives in the work place.

Shop steward — Union representative on the job, usually authorized to collect dues, solicit new members, and receive, investigate, and attempt to settle grievances.

Speedup — Increased productivity achieved by either increasing the speed of the machine or driving the worker harder to get maximum output.

Steam schooner — Popular name for lumber and general cargo vessels on the Pacific Coast.

Stevedore: Employer — A person or firm loading and unloading vessels under a contract with a shipping company. *Worker* — A longshoreman stowing or breaking out cargo aboard ship or building loads at the ship's side, in contrast to a trucker.

Strike — To stop work or withhold services collectively.

Strikebreakers — Workers hired during a strike to break a strike. Polite name for scabs.

Sympathetic strike — A strike by workers in support of other workers already on strike.

Tackle — Ship's gear used to load and unload cargo.

Tackle to tackle — The movement of cargo from the time it leaves the ship to the first place of rest on the dock.

Traveling card — A card issued by a local union enabling a member in good standing to transfer to another local of the same international union without joining as a new member.

Trim a ship — Stow cargo so that the ship will not list or capsize.

Trip card — Work permit for one voyage in seagoing unions.

Trucker — A dock worker who moves cargo from dock to warehouse by hand truck, jitney, or forklift.

Unfair — A term applied to employers involved in a labor dispute or their goods and services made or handled by scabs.

Unfair list — List of names circulated by unions of employers and products boycotted by labor.

Union busting — Planned course of action to destroy or eliminate a union.

Union recognition — Employer acceptance of a union as the exclusive bargaining agent for all employees in a bargaining unit.

Union security — Contract provision defining conditions under which employees may or may not be required to become and remain members of a union.

Union shop — A union security provision requiring all present employees to become and remain members of the union and all new employees to become and remain members of the union after a certain time. Also a workplace in which all employees are union members.

Unlicensed seamen — Members of crews in the deck department, engine department, and stewards' department of vessels below the rank of licensed officers.

Wagner Act — See National Labor Relations Act.

Walking boss — The foreman of longshore gangs and hatch tenders on a dock.

Warehouseman — Worker whose primary responsibility is in cargo storage area.

Winch driver — Operator of equipment that hoists cargo to and from the dock and the ship's hold.

Notes

Chapter 1. Fink Hall Years: Seamen

1 *Seamen's Journal*, Feb. 15, 1922.
2 Ibid.
3 *Cornelius Andersen vs. Shipowners' Association of the Pacific Coast and Pacific American Steamship Association*: Transcript of Record, United States Circuit Court of Appeals for the Ninth Circuit (1927) p. 6.
4 Ibid., pp. 6-7.
5 *Seamen's Journal*, Feb. 15, 1922.
6 Ibid.
7 Ibid.
8 *Memorial to the Honorable United States Senate and Members of the House of Representatives, Relating to the Shipowners' Monopoly, and the Case of Street vs. Shipowners' Association of the Pacific Coast and Pacific American Shipowners Association.* International Seamen's Union of America (n.d.) p. 7.
9 Walter J. Petersen, *Marine Labor Union Leadership* (San Francisco, 1925) pp. 45-52.
10 Byron Times in *Seamen's Journal*, Feb. 22, 1922.
11 *New York Times*, Aug. 28, 1925.
12 *Andersen vs. Shipowners*, p. 6.
13 Ibid., p. 397.
14 Ibid., p. 341.
15 Ibid., p. 138.
16 Ibid., pp. 153-54.
17 Ibid., p. 362.
18 Ibid., p. 98.
19 Ibid., p. 191.
20 *Seamen's Journal*, May 1928.
21 U.S. Shipping Board report Jan. 26, 1928, quoted in petition of Andrew Furuseth to the House of Representatives Nov. 15, 1929.
22 *Industrial Solidarity*, Apr. 1, 1925.
23 *Andersen vs. Shipowners*, p. 368.
24 *Industrial Solidarity*, Jan. 15, 1927.
25 The facts in this section are taken from *The Colored Marine Employees Benevolent Association of the Pacific 1931-1934 or Implications of Vertical Mobility for Negro Stewards in Seattle* by Joseph Sylvester Jackson. M.A. thesis, University of Washington, 1939. Interpretation and conclusions are mine.
26 Jackson, *Colored Marine Employees*, p. 52.
27 Industrial Workers of the World, *The Story of the Sea: Marine Transport Workers' Hand Book* (Chicago, n.d.) p. 39.
28 *Seamen's Journal*, Mar. 1925.
29 *Andersen vs. Shipowners*, p. 401.
30 *Seamen's Journal*, Oct. 1926.

Chapter 2. Fink Hall Years: Longshoremen

1 International Lonshoremen's Association Convention Proceedings (1927) p. 151.
2 Pacific Coast District ILA Convention Proceedings (1924) p. 6.
3 George Michael Jones, *Longshore Unionism on Puget Sound: A Seattle-Tacoma Comparison.* M.A. thesis, University of Washington (1957) p. 52.

4 Waterfront Employers of Seattle Minutes, May 26, 1920.
5 International Longshoremen's Association Convention Proceedings (1921) p. 396, Madsen to Executive Council.
6 Frank P. Foisie, *Decasualizing Longshore Labor and the Seattle Experience* (Seattle, 1934) p.10.
7 Ibid., p. 20.
8 Joint Organization Through Employee Representation of Longshoreman and Truckers, and Waterfront Employers of Seattle, Joint Employment Committee Minutes, Mar. 29, 1921.
9 W.C. Dawson, "Brief History of the Waterfront Employers of Seattle, 1908-1936," p. 4.
10 Keith J. Middleton in Northwest Waterfront Employers Minutes, Jul. 20, 1921.
11 Pacific Coast District ILA Convention Proceedings (1922) p. 35.
12 Ibid., p. 39.
13 Ibid., p. 40.
14 Seattle Joint Executive Committee Minutes, Aug. 9, 1923.
15 Ibid., Oct. 12, 1923.
16 Seattle *Longshore Log*, Apr. 1924.
17 Northwest Waterfront Employers Association Minutes, Apr. 18, 1925.
18 *Tacoma Labor Advocate*, Jun. 8, 1934.
19 Northwest Waterfront Employers Association Minutes, Jul. 20, 1921.
20 Pacific Coast District ILA Convention Proceedings (1924) p. 6.
21 Ibid. (1923) p. 24.
22 Ibid. (1924) p. 5.
23 Ibid. (1926).
24 International Longshoremen's Association Convention Proceedings (1923) pp. 36-37.
25 Pacific Coast District ILA Convention Proceedings (1927) p. 2.
26 *Labor Advocate*, Jul. 19, 1929.
27 See Pacific Coast District ILA Convention Proceedings (1917) p. 54; (1918) p. 63; and (1920) p. 54. See also Ronald E. Magden, *The Working Longshoreman* (Tacoma, 1991) p.87 and Ronald E. Magden, *A History of Seattle Waterfront Workers, 1884-1934* (Seattle, 1991) p. 109.
28 National Longshoremen's Board Arbitration Proceedings, Vol. 21, p. 1758.
29 Ibid., p. 1759.
30 Pacific Coast District ILA Convention Proceedings (1929) p. 2.
31 Ibid. (1930) p. 8.
32 Sailors' Union of the Pacific archives, San Francisco.
33 Pacific Coast District ILA Convention Proceedings (1930) p. 8.
34 Ibid., p. 9.

Chapter 3. The Vise of the Depression

1 *Labor Advocate*, Nov. 29, 1929.
2 Ibid., Aug. 28, 1931.
3 *Industrial Worker*, Feb. 21, 1931.
4 Report to Secretary of Commerce Roper, "Report on the Satus of Working Conditions of Seamen in the American Merchant Marine," 1936, introduced in testimony on H.R. 2662, Exhibit 5. Quoted in *Nailing the Shipowners' Lies*, International Longshoremen's and Warehousemen's Union (San Francisco, 1948).
5 *Industrial Worker*, Jun. 13, 1931.
6 Ibid., Jul. 26, 1932.
7 N. Sparks, *Struggle of the Marine Workers*, International Pamphlets No. 5 (New York, 1930) p. 46.
8 Ibid., p. 49.
9 International Longshoremen's Association Convention Proceedings (1931) pp. 68-69, report of J.C. Bjorklund.

10 ILA Local 38-12 Minutes, May 7, 1931.
11 Joint Employment Committee Minutes, Apr. 10, 1931.
12 *Labor Advocate*, Dec. 2, 1932.
13 Pacific Coast District ILA Convention Proceedings (1932).
14 National Longshoremen's Board Arbitration Proceedings, Vol. 19, p. 1517. Quoted in Dwight Livingstone Palmer, *Pacific Coast Maritime Labor*, Ph. D. dissertation (Stanford University, 1935) p. 284.
15 Ibid., Vol. 14, p. 1037, quoted in Palmer, p. 284.
16 Joint Executive Committee Minutes, Oct. 23, 1931.
17 Ibid.
18 Pacific Coast District ILA Convention Proceedings (1932) p. 5.
19 Ibid., p. 6.
20 Joint Executive Committee Minutes, Jan. 20, 1932.
21 Pacific Coast District ILA Convention Proceedings (1932) p. 6.
22 Joint Executive Committee Minutes, Jun. 3, 1932.
23 *Wage Scale, Rules and Working Conditions on the Tacoma Waterfront* (1932) p.3.
24 Pacific Coast District ILA Convention Proceedings (1932) p. 4.
25 Ibid.
26 Ibid., p. 5.
27 Pacific Coast District ILA Convention Proceedings (1931) p. 8.
28 Ibid., p. 19.
29 *Labor Advocate*, Jun. 8, 1934.
30 Joint Executive Committee Minutes, Dec. 15, 1932.
31 Ibid., Dec. 22, 1932.
32 *Labor Advocate*, Dec. 2, 1932.

Chapter 4. The New Deal on the Waterfront

1 *Labor Advocate*, Jun. 9, 1933.
2 Robert Coleman Francis, *A History of Labor on the San Francisco Waterfront.* Ph. D. dissertation, University of California (1934) p. 188.
3 International Longshoremen's Association Convention Proceedings (1935) pp. 252-53.
4 *Waterfront Worker*, Jul. 1933.
5 Seattle Waterfront Employers archives.
6 Seattle Waterfront Employers Minutes, Aug. 28, 1933.
7 Leaflet in *San Francisco Waterfront Strikes, 1934: A Collection of Pamphlets, Broadsides, etc.*, 2 Vols. International Longshore and Warehouse Union Library, San Francisco (hereafter cited as *Waterfront Strikes Collection*).
8 Jack Bjorklund to Lee Holman, Aug. 21, 1933, as quoted in Robert W. Cherny, unpublished manuscript on the life of Harry Bridges.
9 Seattle Waterfront Employers Minutes, Sep. 18, 1933.
10 ILA Local 38-79 Executive Committee Minutes, Oct. 2, 9, 1933.
11 *San Francisco Chronicle*, Oct. 18, 1933.
12 This account is based on the *San Francisco Chronicle, San Francisco Examiner, San Francisco News*, and an interview with William J. Lewis.
13 *Labor Advocate*, Sep. 8, 1933.
14 *Voice of Action*, Oct. 2, 1933.
15 Ibid.
16 Joint Executive Committee Minutes, Nov. 15, 1933.
17 Seattle Waterfront Employers Minutes dated Nov. 27, 1933, but probably Nov. 21, 1933.
18 *Industrial Worker*, Sep. 5, 1933.

19 *Labor Advocate*, Nov. 24, 1933.
20 Ibid., Dec. 1, 1933.
21 Ibid., Jan. 5, 1934.
22 Seattle Waterfront Employers Minutes, Jan. 3, 15, 1934.
23 Documents of National Longshoremen's Board. Quoted in Palmer, *Pacific Coast Maritime Labor*, p. 307.
24 *Labor Advocate*, Feb. 16, 1934.
25 *Voice of Action*, Feb. 5, 1934.
26 Ibid., Dec. 11, 1933.
27 Pacific Coast District ILA Convention Proceedings (1934) p. 6.
28 Ibid., pp. 86-87.
29 *Waterfront Worker*, n.d., author's collection.
30 Pacific Coast District ILA Convention Proceedings (1934) p. 118.
31 Ibid., p. 119.
32 Ibid., pp. 119-20, 133.
33 Ibid., p. 132.
34 Ibid., p. 135.
35 Ibid., p. 140.
36 Ibid., p. 135.
37 Ibid., p. 138.
38 Ibid., p. 141.
39 Ibid., p. 142.
40 Ibid., p. 143.
41 Ibid.
42 Ibid., p. 144.
43 Ibid., p. 106.
44 Ibid., p. 154.
45 Ibid., p. 149.
46 *Program of the Communist International* (New York, 1936). Quoted in James C. Oneal and G.A. Warner, *American Communism* (New York, 1947) p. 389.
47 "Instructions for Communist Factions in Non-Party Institutions and Organizations," adopted by the Executive Committee of the Communist International, Moscow, Feb. 27, 1934. In Oneal and Warner, *American Communism*, pp. 384-85.
48 Eugene V. Dennett, *Agitprop: The Life of an American Working-Class Radical* (New York, 1990) p. 213.
49 *Voice of Action*, Mar. 13, 1934.
50 Stephen Schwartz, *Brotherhood of the Sea: A History of the Sailors' Union of the Pacific 1885-1985* (San Francisco, 1986) p. 87.
51 Paul Eliel, *The Waterfront and General Strikes, San Francisco, 1934* (San Francisco, 1934) p. 188.
52 Charles P. Larrowe, *Harry Bridges: The Rise and Fall of Radical Labor in the United States* (New York, 1972) p. 28.
53 *Pacific Shipper* (San Francisco) Mar. 26, 1934.
54 *Labor Advocate*, Mar. 23, 1934.
55 Mike Quin, *The Big Strike* (New York, 1979) p. 43.
56 Eliel, *Waterfront and General Strikes*, p. 7.
57 *Labor Advocate*, Apr. 13, 1934.
58 Eliel, *Waterfront and General Strikes*, p. 195.
59 *San Francisco News*, May 8, 1934, quoted in Eliel, p. 13.

Chapter 5. Strike!

1 *Labor Advocate*, May 11, 1934.
2 Pacific Coast District ILA Convention Proceedings (1935) May 10.
3 *Labor Clarion* (San Francisco) May 11, 1934.
4 *Portland News-Telegram*, May 10, 1934.
5 Ibid., May 11, 1934.
6 *Oregon Labor Press*, May 18, 1934.
7 Albert Farmer, "The Diary of a Longshore Dispatcher, 1928-1934," May 12, 1934. Albert Farmer papers, University of Washington, Seattle.
8 *Industrial Worker*, May 24, 1934.
9 *Seattle Post-Intelligencer*, May 12, 1934.
10 *Labor Advocate*, May 18, 1934.
11 *Post-Intelligencer*, May 13, 1934.
12 Ibid.
13 Memorandum of San Francisco Waterfront Employers' Union, *Waterfront Strikes Collection.*
14 Ibid.
15 Tacoma Central Labor Council Minutes, May 16, 1934.
16 *Post-Intelligencer*, May 18, 1934.
17 Farmer, "Diary," May 18, 1934.
18 *Post-Intelligencer*, May 19, 1934.
19 San Francisco Waterfront Employers' Union, *Waterfront Strikes Collection.*
20 *Labor Clarion*, Jun. 8, 1934.
21 *Spokesman* (San Francisco), May 17, 1934.
22 Ibid., Jul. 12, 1934.
23 ILA Local 38-79 leaflet, "To All Negro People," May 16, 1934, quoted in Cherny, Harry Bridges manuscript.
24 *San Pedro News-Pilot*, May 15, 1934.
25 *Citizen*, (Los Angeles), May 25, 1934.
26 SUP Minutes in Schwartz, *Brotherhood of the Sea*, p. 90.
27 MWIU Bulletin in *Waterfront Strikes Collection.*
28 Schwartz, *Brotherhood of the Sea*, p. 92.
29 Marine Engineers' Beneficial Association Convention Proceedings (1935), report of District Deputy Morrison, p. 121.
30 *Post-Intelligencer*, May 22, 1934.
31 *Labor Advocate*, Jun. 1, 1934.
32 *Pacific Shipper*, May 21, 1934.
33 Ibid.
34 *News-Telegram*, May 11, 1934.
35 Carl Lynch in *Joint Marine Journal*, Atlantic and Gulf, No. 5, Aug. 14, 1934, *Waterfront Strikes Collection.*
36 *Citizen*, May 18, 1934.
37 *San Francisco News*, May 19, 1934, in Eliel, *Waterfront and General Strikes*, p. 25.
38 *Chronicle*, May 21, 1934, in Eliel, pp. 26-27.
39 *Oakland Tribune*, May 21, 1934, in Eliel, p. 27.
40 *News-Telegram*, May 24, 1934.
41 *Labor Advocate*, May 25, 1934.
42 Joint Northwest Strike Committee Minutes, May 24, 1934, p. 4.
43 Ibid, May 25-26, 1934, p. 6.

Chapter 6, Negotiations

1 Pacific Coast District ILA Convention Proceedings (1935) May 10.
2 *San Francisco News*, May 26, 1934, quoted in Eliel, *Waterfront and General Strikes*, p. 31.
3 *Post-Intelligencer*, May 27, 1934.
4 *San Francisco Examiner*, May 27, 1934, quoted in Eliel, p. 32.
5 Joint Northwest Strike Committee Minutes, May 26-27, 1934, p. 6.
6 *Pacific Shipper*, May 28, 1934.
7 *Chronicle*, May 25, 1934.
8 Eliel, *Waterfront and General Strikes*, p. 206.
9 *Chronicle*, May 29, 1934.
10 Eliel, *Waterfront and General Strikes*, pp. 206-7.
11 *Call-Bulletin* (San Francisco), May 29, 1934, quoted in Eliel, p. 34.
12 Joint Northwest Strike Committee Minutes, May 29, 1934, p. 1.
13 Joseph P. Ryan to Luckenbach Steamship Co., May 31, 1934, quoted in Cherney, Harry Bridges manuscript.
14 *Tacoma News Tribune*, May 31, 1934.
15 Ibid., Jun. 2, 1934.
16 Waterfront Employers' Union bulletin, *Waterfront Strikes Collection..*
17 *Labor Clarion*, Jun. 15, 1934.
18 *News Tribune*, Jun. 9, 1934.
19 *Los Angeles Times*, Jun. 13, 1934.
20 Ibid., May 18, 1934.
21 *News-Pilot*, Jun. 7, 1934.
22 Letter from A.H. Petersen in *Labor Advocate*, Jun. 15, 1934.
23 Joint Northwest Strike Committee Minutes, Jun. 13, 1934, pp. 1-2.
24 *Labor Advocate*, Jun. 15, 1934.
25 *News Tribune*, Jun. 8, 1934.
26 Carl Carter to George Larsen, May 26, 1934, quoted in Schwartz, *Brotherhood of the Sea*, p. 94.
27 *News-Telegram*, Jun. 7, 1934.
28 Joint Northwest Strike Committee Minutes, Jun. 8, 1934, p. 1.
29 Ibid., Jun. 7, 1934, p. 1.
30 MWIU leaflet in *Waterfront Strikes Collection.*
31 Ibid.
32 Ibid.
33 Joint Northwest Strike Committee Minutes, Jun. 9, 1934, pp. 1-2.
34 Ibid., p. 3.
35 Ibid., Jun. 13, 1934, p. 2.
36 *Voice of Action*, Jun. 8, 1934.
37 Leaflet, *Waterfront Strikes Collection.*
38 *News Tribune*, Jun. 8, 1934.
39 Eliel, *Waterfront and General Strikes*, p. 23.
40 *Post-Intelligencer*, Jun. 13, 1934.
41 *Labor Advocate*, Jun. 15, 1934.
42 Joint Northwest Strike Committee Minutes, Jun. 12, 1934, pp. 3-4.
43 International Longshoremen's Association Convention Proceedings (1935) p. 104.
44 Joint Northwest Strike Committee Minutes, Jun. 12, 1934, p. 1.
45 *Post-Intelligencer*, Jun. 16, 1934.
46 *News Tribune*, Jun. 15, 1934.
47 Ibid.

48 *Labor Advocate*, Jun. 15, 1934.
49 Eliel, *Waterfront and General Strikes*, pp. 209-10.
50 Ibid., p. 213.
51 International Longshoremen's Association Convention Proceedings (1935) p. 108.
52 Eliel, *Waterfront and General Strikes*, pp. 217-18.
53 International Longshoremen's Association Convention Proceedings (1935) pp. 108-9.
54 Ibid., p. 105.
55 Eliel, *Waterfront and General Strikes*, pp. 62-63.
56 International Longshoremen's Association Convention Proceedings (1935) p. 109.
57 Pacific Coast District ILA Convention Proceedings (1935) May 10.
58 *Examiner*, Jun. 19, 1934, in Eliel, p. 73.
59 Ibid., in Eliel, p. 74.
60 *Chronicle*, Jun. 17, 1934.
61 *Post-Intelligencer*, Jun. 18, 1934.
62 *Chronicle*, Jun. 17, 1934.
63 *Post-Intelligencer*, Jun. 18, 1934.
64 *Chronicle*, Jun. 17, 1934.
65 *Post-Intelligencer*, Jun. 18, 1934.
66 Eliel, *Waterfront and General Strikes*, p. 75.
67 *Chronicle*, Jun. 18, 1934.
68 *Examiner*, Jun. 18, 1934, in Eliel, p. 76.
69 Ibid.

Chapter 7. Open the Ports!

1 Pacific Coast District ILA Convention Proceedings (1935) May 10.
2 Eliel, *Waterfront and General Strikes*, p. 221.
3 *Labor Clarion*, Jun. 22, 1934.
4 *San Francisco News*, Jun. 19, 1934, in Eliel, p. 81.
5 Leaflet, *Waterfront Strikes Collection.*
6 *Chronicle*, Jun. 20, 1934.
7 Joint Marine Strike Committee Minutes, Jun. 19, 1934.
8 *Pacific Shipper*, Jun. 25, 1934.
9 *Examiner*, Jun. 22, 1934.
10 Eliel, *Waterfront and General Strikes*, p. 221.
11 Ibid., p. 88.
12 Schwartz, *Brotherhood of the Sea*, p. 98.
13 Ibid.
14 Ibid., p. 99.
15 *Waterfront Strikes Collection.*
16 *Labor Clarion*, Jun. 29, 1934.
17 *Waterfront Strikes Collection.*
18 Ibid.
19 Joint Northwest Strike Committee Minutes, Jun. 29, 1934. Letter from W.R. Patterson, Jun. 22, 1934.
20 Ibid., Jun. 18, 1934, p. 3.
21 *Examiner*, Jun. 21, 1934, in Eliel, p. 84.
22 Joint Northwest Strike Committee Minutes, Jun. 20, 1934, p. 4.
23 *News Tribune*, Jun. 20, 1934.
24 Joint Northwest Strike Committee Minutes, Jun. 20, 1934, p. 2.
25 Seattle Central Labor Council Minutes, Jun. 20, 1934.

26 *Post-Intelligencer*, Jun. 22, 1934.
27 Joint Northwest Strike Committee Minutes, Jun. 21, 1934, p. 3.
28 *News Tribune*, Jun. 23, 1934.
29 Ibid., Jun. 18, 1934.
30 Ibid., Jun. 20, 1934.
31 Tacoma Central Labor Council Minutes, Jun. 20, 1934.
32 Mimeographed letter in author's collection.
33 *Labor Advocate*, Jun. 22, 1934.
34 Jackson, *Colored Marine Employees*, p. 56.
35 Seattle Central Labor Council Minutes, Jun. 27, 1934.
36 *Voice of Action*, Jul. 6, 1934.
37 Joint Northwest Strike Committee Minutes, Jun. 29, 1934, p. 1.
38 *Labor Advocate*, Jul. 6, 1934.
39 Joint Northwest Strike Committee Minutes, Jul. 5, 1934, p. 3.
40 Ibid., p. 4.
41 *News Tribune*, Jul. 5, 1934.
42 Joint Northwest Strike Committee Minutes, Jul. 9, 1934, p. 2.
43 *News-Telegram*, Jun. 18, 1934.
44 Ibid.
45 Ibid., Jun. 19, 1934.
46 Ibid., Jun. 20, 1934.
47 Ibid., Jun. 22, 1934.
48 Joint Northwest Strike Committee Minutes, Jun. 30, 1934, p. 2.
49 Charles Peabody papers, Portland.
50 *News-Telegram*, Jul. 7, 1934.
51 Ibid.
52 *Oregon Labor Press*, Jul. 13, 1934.
53 Ibid.
54 *News-Telegram*, Jul. 11, 1934.
55 Ibid.
56 Ibid., Jul. 12, 1934.
57 *Oregon Labor Press*, Jul. 20, 1934.
58 Ibid.
59 *Waterfront Worker*, Jun. 25, 1934.
60 *Examiner*, Jun. 24, 1934.
61 Ibid., Jun. 27, 1934.
62 Seattle Waterfront Employers Minutes, Jul. 16, 1934.
63 *Examiner*, Jun. 28, 1934.
64 Ibid., Jun. 29, 1934.
65 Ibid.
66 *Waterfront Strikes Collection.*
67 Ibid.
68 Ibid.
69 ISU Strike Bulletin, Jun. 29, 1934, *Waterfront Strikes Collection.*
70 Ibid.
71 *Waterfront Strikes Collection.*
72 Eliel, *Waterfront and General Strikes*, pp. 226-27.
73 *Joint Marine Journal*, Jul. 3, 1934, *Waterfront Strikes Collection.*
74 ILA Strike Bulletin, Jul. 2, 1934, *Waterfront Strikes Collection.*
75 *Chronicle*, Jul. 3, 1934.

Chapter 8. Bloody Thursday

1 *Chronicle*, Jul. 4, 1934.
2 Eliel, *Waterfront and General Strikes*, p. 229.
3 ILA Strike Bulletin No. 10, Jul. 3, 1934, *Waterfront Strikes Collection.*
4 *Joint Marine Journal*, Jul. 4, 1934.
5 *Post-Intelligencer*, Jul. 6, 1934.
6 *San Francisco News*, Jul. 5, 1934.
7 Ibid.
8 Joint Marine Strike Committee Minutes, Jul. 5, 1934.
9 Donald Mackenzie Brown, "Dividends and Stevedores," *Scribners*, Jan. 1935, p. 54.
10 *Tacoma Daily Ledger*, Jul. 6, 1934.
11 Brown, "Dividends and Stevedores," p. 54.
12 Larrowe, *Harry Bridges*, p. 68.
13 *Chronicle*, Jul. 6, 1934.
14 ILA leaflet Jul. 6, 1934, and Joint Marine Strike Committee leaflet, c. Jul. 14, 1934, *Waterfront Strikes Collection.*
15 *Daily Ledger*, Jul. 6, 1934.
16 Brown, "Dividends and Stevedores," p. 54.
17 George P. Hedley, *The San Francisco Strike As I Have Seen It* (San Francisco, 1934) p. 8.
18 Quin, *The Big Strike*, p. 115.
19 Brown, "Dividends and Stevedores," p. 55.
20 Marine Firemen's Union Minutes, Jul. 5, 1934, *Waterfront Strikes Collection.*
21 *Labor Clarion*, Jul. 13, 1934.
22 *San Francisco News*, Jul. 6, 1934.
23 Ibid.
24 *Joint Marine Journal*, Jul. 7, 1934.
25 *Post-Intelligencer*, Jul. 7, 1934.
26 *Joint Marine Journal*, Jul. 7, 1934.
27 *Waterfront Strikes Collection.*
28 *Labor Clarion*, Jul. 13, 1934.
29 *Post-Intelligencer*, Jul. 7, 1934.
30 *Labor Clarion*, Jul. 13, 1934.
31 *Waterfront Strikes Collection.*
32 ILA Strike Bulletin, Jul. 7, 1934.
33 *Joint Marine Journal*, Jul. 8, 1934.
34 *Waterfront Strikes Collection.*
35 *Chronicle*, Jul. 10, 1934.
36 *Joint Marine Journal*, Jul. 7, 1934.
37 ILA Strike Bulletin, Jul. 6, 1934.
38 *Joint Marine Journal*, Jul. 7, 1934.
39 Ibid.
40 Ibid., Jul. 10, 1934.
41 National Longshoremen's Board Mediation Proceedings, Vol. 1, pp. 6-7, quoted in Palmer, *Pacific Coast Maritime Labor.*
42 Joint Northwest Strike Committee Minutes, Jul. 5, 1934, p. 3.
43 National Longshoremen's Board Mediation Proceedings, Vol. 2, pp. 86-88, quoted in Palmer, *Pacific Coast Maritime Labor.*
44 *San Francisco News*, Jul. 11, 1934, in Eliel, *Waterfront and General Strikes*, p. 130.
45 Seattle Waterfront Employers Minutes, Jul. 11, 1934.

46 ILA leaflet, Jul. 14, 1934, *Waterfront Strikes Collection.*
47 Ibid., Jul. 16, 1934.
48 *Joint Marine Journal*, Jul. 12, 1934.
49 Ibid., Jul. 17, 1934.
50 ILA Strike Bulletin, Jul. 18, 1934.
51 *Waterfront Strikes Collection.*
52 *Call-Bulletin*, Jul. 6, 1934, in Eliel, *Waterfront and General Strikes*, p. 119.
53 ILA leaflet, Jul. 6, 1934, *Waterfront Strikes Collection.*
54 *Labor Clarion*, Jul. 13, 1934.
55 ILA Strike Bulletin, Jul. 7, 1934.
56 *Post-Intelligencer*, Jul. 7, 1934.
57 *Labor Clarion*, Jul. 13, 1934.
58 *Examiner*, Jul. 9, 1934, in Eliel, *Waterfront and General Strikes*, p. 124.
59 *Chronicle*, Jul. 9, 1934.
60 *Labor Clarion*, Jul. 13, 1934.
61 General Strike Committee Minutes, San Francisco Labor Council archives.
62 Pacific Coast District ILA Convention Proceedings (1935) May 10.
63 William F. Dunne, *The Great San Francisco General Strike* (New York, 1934) p. 68, "Lessons of Recent Strike Struggles." Resolution adopted by the meeting of the Central Committee of the Communist Party, Sep. 5-6, 1934.
64 *Labor Clarion*, Jul. 20, 1934.
65 Ibid.
66 *Joint Marine Journal*, Jul. 17, 1934.
67 *Chronicle*, Jul. 16, 1934.
68 *Post-Intelligencer*, Jul. 16, 1934.
69 *Los Angeles Times*, Jul. 15, 1934.
70 *Call-Bulletin*, Jul. 17, 1934.
71 *Post-Intelligencer*, Jul. 18, 1934.
72 *Labor Advocate*, Aug. 10, 1934.
73 *Chronicle*, Jul. 18, 1934.
74 *Western Worker*, Jul. 18, 1934.
75 *Labor Clarion*, Jul. 20, 1934.
76 *Chronicle*, Jul. 20, 1934.

Chapter 9. Strike Settlement

1 *San Francisco News*, Jul. 20, 1934, in Eliel, *Waterfront and General Strikes*, p. 170.
2 *Joint Marine Journal*, Jul. 19, 1934.
3 *Examiner*, Jul. 21, 1934, in Eliel, pp. 170-71.
4 *New York Daily News*, Jul. 20, 1934, in *Labor Clarion*, Jul. 27, 1934.
5 *Tacoma Times*, Jul. 25, 1934.
6 *Post-Intelligencer*, Jul. 17, 1934.
7 *New York Times*, Jul. 18,1934.
8 *New York Post*, Jul. 19, 1934, in *Labor Clarion*, Aug. 10, 1934.
9 *Labor Clarion*, Jul. 27, 1934.
10 Ibid.
11 *Citizen*, Jul. 20, 1934.
12 *Labor Advocate*, Jul. 20, 1934.
13 Seattle Central Labor Council Minutes, Jul. 18, 1934.
14 *Post-Intelligencer*, Jul. 20, 1934.
15 *Joint Marine Journal*, Jul. 26, 1934.

16 *News-Telegram*, Jul. 20, 1934.
17 *Post-Intelligencer*, Jul. 20, 1934.
18 *News-Telegram*, Jul. 20, 1934.
19 Ibid., Jul. 21, 1934.
20 Joint Northwest Strike Committee Minutes, Jul. 21, 1934, p. 3.
21 Copy of letter in San Francisco Labor Council archives.
22 *Joint Marine Journal*, Jul. 20, 1934.
23 *San Francisco News*, Jul. 21, 1934, in Eliel, p. 172.
24 *News Tribune*, Jul. 24, 1934.
25 *Chronicle*, Jul. 24, 1934.
26 *Labor Advocate*, Jul. 27, 1934.
27 Ibid.
28 *Joint Marine Journal*, Jul. 23, 1934.
29 Ibid.
30 ILA Strike Bulletin, Jul. 23, 1934.
31 Ibid.
32 Ibid., Jul. 24, 1934.
33 *Joint Marine Journal*, Jul. 27, 1934.
34 *Examiner*, Jul. 27, 1934, in Eliel, p. 180.
35 Ibid., Jul. 28, 1934, in Eliel, p. 179.
36 Ibid., in Eliel, p. 180.
37 ILA Strike Bulletin, Jul. 28, 1934.
38 *Examiner*, Jul. 27, 1934, in Eliel, p. 176.
39 Letter in *Waterfront Strikes Collection*.
40 *Joint Marine Journal*, Jul. 28, 1934.
41 Ibid., Jul. 27, 1934.
42 ILA Strike Bulletin, Jul. 28, 1934.
43 Schwartz, *Brotherhood of the Sea*, p. 109.
44 Ibid., p. 110.
45 Ibid.
46 ILA Strike Bulletin, Jul. 30, 1934.
47 *Chronicle*, Jul. 31, 1934.
48 *Voice of Action*, Aug. 3, 1934.
49 Sam Darcy, "The San Francisco Bay Area General Strike." *The Communist* (Oct. 1934). Quoted in Cherny, Harry Bridges manuscript.
50 Dunne, *Great San Francisco General Strike*, pp. 9-10.
51 Ibid., p. 46.
52 *Voice of the Federation* (San Francisco) Jun. 14, 1935.

Chapter 10. Confirming the Victory

1 National Longshoremen's Board Arbitration Proceedings, Aug. 16, 1934, pp. 11-12.
2 *Spokesman* (San Francisco) Aug. 16, 1934.
3 Portland ILA Bulletin, *Waterfront Strikes Collection*.
4 *Labor Advocate*, Dec. 14, 1934.
5 Longshoremen's Board Proceedings, Vol. 28, p. 38. Statement of Herman Phleger, Sep. 25, 1934.
6 Ibid., pp. 42, 50.
7 Seattle Waterfront Employers Minutes, Oct. 1, 1934.
8 Arbitration Award Handed Down by National Longshoremen's Board, Sec. 11, in Quin, *Big Strike*, p. 258.
9 *Waterfront Worker*, Oct. 15, 1934.

10 *Voice of Action*, Oct. 19, 1934.
11 Waterfront Employers' press release, *Waterfront Strikes Collection.*
12 *Waterfront Worker*, Oct. 22, 1934.
13 *Labor Advocate*, Apr. 19, 1935.
14 Waterfront Employers' Union, *Waterfront Strikes Collection.*
15 *Waterfront Worker*, Nov. 19, 1934.
16 Ibid., Dec. 10, 1934.
17 Sloss Award, p. 3. Quoted in Richard Alan Liebes. *Longshore Labor Relations on the Pacific Coast, 1934-1942*. Ph. D. dissertation (University of California, Berkeley, 1942).
18 *Waterfront Worker*, Nov. 19, 1934.
19 Ibid., Nov. 26, 1934.
20 Ibid., Dec. 14, 1934.
21 *New Waterfront Worker*, May 9, 1935. Author's collection.
22 *Voice of Action,* Aug. 16, 1934.
23 Seattle Waterfront Employers Minutes, Jan. 22, 1935.
24 Wire Jan. 31, 1935, Waterfront Employers' Union, *Waterfront Strikes Collection.*
25 Report of Examiner (discrimination) to the National Longshoremen's Board, Oct. 31, 1934. Quoted in Palmer, *Pacific Coast Maritime Labor*, pp. 442-44.
26 *Pacific Seaman*, Sep. 22, 1934.
27 National Longshoremen's Board Documents, in Palmer, *Pacific Coast Maritime Labor*, p. 456.
28 Ibid., p. 450.
29 *ISU of A Journal*, Aug. 1934.
30 *Waterfront Worker*, Oct. 22, 1934.
31 Ibid., Nov. 26, 1934.
32 *Pacific Seaman*, Sep. 22, 1934.
33 Ibid., Oct. 20, 1934.
34 *Seamen's Journal*, Feb. 1935.
35 *Pacific Seaman*, Oct. 6, 1934.
36 *Seamen's Journal*, May 1935.
37 *Voice of the Federation*, Jul. 19, 1935.
38 *Pacific Seaman*, Oct. 27, 1934.
39 *Voice of the Federation*, Jul. 12, 1935.
40 Vincent J. Malone, "The Story of the Marine Firemen's Union." San Francisco, 1945.
41 *Post-Intelligencer*, Mar. 27, 1935.
42 *Voice of Action*, Jan. 11, 1935.
43 *Waterfront Worker*, Jan. 21, 1935.
44 *Post-Intelligencer*, Mar. 20, 1935.
45 Ibid., Mar. 22, 1935.
46 *Waterfront Worker*, Apr. 1, 1935.
47 *Seamen's Voice* (April 1935?) *Waterfront Strikes Collection.*
48 *West Coast Sailors*, Oct. 15, 1937.
49 *Post-Intelligencer*, Mar. 17, 1935.
50 *Seattle Star*, Apr. 16, 1935.
51 Report to Maritime Federation Emergency Convention, Nov. 12, 1935, p. 1. Author's collection.
52 *Seamen's Journal*, Jul. 1935.
53 *Voice of the Federation*, Jul. 19, 1935.

Chapter 11. Hot Cargo

1 ILA Local 38-12 Minutes, Dec. 6, 1934.
2 Maritime Federation of the Pacific Coast Convention Proceedings (1938) p. 38.

3 Letter from Pacific Coast District ILA, Jan. 17, 1935. Author's collection.
4 *Waterfront Worker*, Jan. 14, 1935.
5 Ibid., Jan. 21, 1935.
6 Ibid., Feb. 4, 1935.
7 *Voice of Action*, Mar. 8, Mar. 22, 1935.
8 Maritime Federation Convention Proceedings (1935) Apr. 18.
9 Maritime Federation Constitution (1935) p. 2.
10 Ibid., p. 11.
11 Ibid., p. 5.
12 *Voice of Action*, Apr. 26, 1935.
13 Ibid., May 3, 1935.
14 *Waterfront Worker*, May 13, 1935.
15 International Longshoremen's Association Convention Proceedings (1935) p. 153.
16 Ibid., p. 251.
17 *A.F. of L. Rank and File Federationist*, Sep. 1935, p. 10.
18 *Labor Advocate*, Aug. 5, 1935.
19 Letter Feb. 2, 1935. U.S. Congress, Report of the Committee on Education and Labor, *Violations of Free Speech and the Rights of Labor*, 78th Congress, 1st Session, Senate Report No. 398 (1943) p. 1058. (Hereafter cited as LoFollette Committee Report.)
20 Seattle Waterfront Employers Minutes, Mar. 15, 1935.
21 San Francisco Waterfront Employers' Assn. Minutes Apr. 17, 1935. LaFollette Committee Report, p. 1049.
22 Letter to Seattle agent, American-Hawaiian S.S. Co. Jan. 8, 1935. Ibid., p. 1050.
23 LaFollette Committee Report, p. 1054.
24 *Pacific Coast Longshoreman,* Mar. 23, 1938.
25 Lundeberg report to Maritime Federation Emergency Convention, Nov. 12, 1935, p. 3.
26 LaFollette Committee Report, p. 1055.
27 Waterfront Employers' Assn., *Waterfront Strikes Collection.*
28 Waterfront Employers' Assn. Minutes, Jul. 8, 1935. LaFollette Committee Report, p. 1055.
29 Ibid., Jul. 15, 1935, p. 1056.
30 Pacific Coast District ILA Executive Board Minutes, Aug. 1, 1935. Author's collection.
31 *Voice of the Federation*, Aug. 10, 1935.
32 Seattle Waterfront Employers Minutes, Aug. 8, 1935.
33 *Voice of the Federation*, Aug. 10, 1935.
34 District 38 letter to all affiliated locals, Aug. 21, 1935. Author's collection.
35 *Voice of the Federation*, Sep. 13, 1935.
36 *Pacific Coast Longshoreman,* Sep. 23, 1935.
37 *Chronicle*, Sep. 22, 1935.
38 Ibid.
39 *Pacific Coast Longshoreman*, Apr. 6, 1936.
40 Ibid.
41 Pacific American Shipowners and Waterfront Employers of San Francisco, Seattle, Portland and San Pedro. *Hot Cargo: The Longshoremen's Alibi for Arbitration Award Violations* (San Francisco, 1935) pp. 7-8.
42 *Waterfront Worker*, Sep. 30, 1935.
43 Pacific Coast District ILA Convention Proceedings (1936) p. 207.
44 *Voice of the Federation*, Oct. 6, 1935.
45 *Pacific Coast Longshoreman*, Oct. 7, 1935.
46 *Voice of the Federation*, Oct. 10, 1935.
47 Ibid.
48 Seattle Waterfront Employers Minutes, Dec. 9, 1935.

Chapter 12. Testing the Federation

1 *Voice of the Federation*, Oct. 17, 1935.
2 Ibid., Oct. 24, 1935.
3 Ibid.
4 Ibid., Oct. 31, 1935.
5 *Waterfront Worker*, Nov. 4, 1935.
6 *Pacific Coast Longshoreman*, Oct. 7, 1935.
7 *Daily Commercial News*, Nov. 27, 1935. Quoted in Liebes, *Longshore Labor Relations*.
8 Author's collection.
9 Maritime Federation Emergency Convention (1935) Resolution No. 18 and Digest of Convention Proceedings, p. 8.
10 Ibid., Proceedings, Nov. 20, pp. 14-15.
11 Ibid., Nov. 21, p. 10.
12 *Voice of the Federation*, Nov. 21, 1935.
13 *Pacific Coast Longshoreman*, Dec. 2, 1935.
14 *Waterfront Worker*, Dec. 16, 1935.
15 *Pacific Coast Longshoreman*, Feb. 10, 1936.
16 *Voice of the Federation*, Feb. 20, 1936.
17 *Pacific Coast Longshoreman*, Mar. 9, 1936.
18 Ibid., Mar. 23, 1936.
19 *Labor Advocate*, Dec. 6, 1935.
20 Waterfront Employers' Assn. Minutes, Dec. 9, 1935. LaFollette Committee Report, p. 1061.
21 Ibid., p. 1062.
22 *Voice of the Federation*, Jan. 30, 1936.
23 Meeting Jan. 7, 1936. LaFollette Committee Report, pp. 1064-65.
24 Ibid., p. 1066.
25 Pacific Coast District ILA Convention Proceedings (1936) p. 209.
26 Ibid., p. 163.
27 LaFollette Committee Report, p. 1057.
28 *Voice of the Federation*, Dec. 27, 1935.
29 Author's collection.
30 International Seamen's Union Convention Proceedings (1936). *Seamen's Journal*, Apr. 1936, p. 129.
31 Ibid., p. 136.
32 Sailors' Union of the Pacific Emergency Committee (SUPEC) Report to Maritime Federation Convention (May 1936) p. 2. Author's collection.
33 *Voice of the Federation*, Jan. 30, 1936.
34 *Waterfront Worker*, Feb. 3, 1936.
35 SUPEC Report, p. 3.
36 Ibid.
37 *Pacific Coast Longshoreman*, Feb. 24, 1936.
38 SUPEC Report, p. 2.
39 Gill related this incident to the author.
40 *Voice of the Federation*, Feb. 27, 1936.
41 LaFollette Committee Report, p. 1067.
42 *Pacific Coast Longshoreman*, Mar. 2, 1936.
43 *Voice of the Federation*, Mar. 5, 1936.
44 Ibid., Feb. 27, 1936.
45 Author's collection.
46 *Voice of the Federation*, Apr. 16, 1936.

47 Ibid., May 14, 1936.
48 Ibid., Jan. 10, 1936.
49 Pacific Coast District ILA Convention Proceedings (1936) p. 209.
50 Ibid., p. 210.
51 *Pacific Coast Longshoreman*, Apr. 27, 1936.
52 Ibid.
53 Letter to Bob Dombroff, Apr. 23, 1936. Author's collection.
54 *Pacific Coast Longshoreman*, Apr. 27, 1936.
55 *Voice of the Federation*, Apr. 16, 1936.
56 *Pacific Coast Longshoreman*, Apr. 27, 1936.
57 *Voice of the Federation*, Apr. 16, 1936.
58 LaFollette Committee Report, p. 1069.
59 *Pacific Coast Longshoreman*, Apr. 27, 1936.
60 Ibid.
61 Pacific Coast District ILA Convention Proceedings (1936) p. 160.
62 *April 21 Agreement Between Waterfront Employers Association of San Francisco and International Longshoremen's Association Dist. No. 38 – Local 38-79* (San Francisco, 1936) pp. 1-2.
63 *Pacific Coast Longshoreman*, Apr. 27, 1936.
64 *April 21 Agreement*, p. 9.
65 Pacific Coast District ILA Convention Proceedings (1936) p. 162.
66 Ibid.
67 *Voice of the Federation*, Apr. 21, 1936.
68 Pacific Coast District ILA Convention Proceedings (1936) p. 162.
69 Letter to Bob Dombroff, Apr. 23, 1936.
70 *Pacific Coast Longshoreman*, Apr. 27, 1936.
71 Ibid., May 4, 1936.
72 Pacific Coast District ILA Convention Proceedings (1936) p. 19.
73 Ibid., pp. 122-23.
74 Ibid., p. 124.
75 Ibid., p. 146.
76 Ibid., pp. 151-53.
77 Ibid., p. 159.
78 Ibid., p. 163.
79 Ibid., p. 178.
80 Ibid., p. 221.
81 Ibid., p. 218.
82 Ibid., p. 179.
83 Ibid., p. 184.
84 Ibid., p. 187.
85 Ibid., p. 191.
86 Ibid., p. 196.
87 Ibid., p. 199.
88 Ibid., pp. 200-1.
89 Resolution, ibid., p. 37.
90 Resolution, ibid., p. 16.
91 Maritime Federation Constitution (1936) p. 2.
92 Ibid., p. 13.
93 Maritime Federation Convention Proceedings (1936) Minutes Jun. 5, pp. 3-4.
94 Ibid., Minutes Jun. 10, p. 7.
95 Ibid., p. 10.

96 *Maritime Worker*, Jun. 15, 1936.
97 *Voice of the Federation*, Jun. 11, 1936.

Chapter 13. The 1936-1937 Strike

1 "Views of the Sailors' Union of the Pacific Toward the Seamen's Act H.R. 8597," Jan. 15, 1937 (Brief presented to Marine Committee by Harry Lundeberg). Author's collection.
2 Ibid.
3 *Voice of the Federation,* Jun. 25, 1936.
4 Ibid., Jul. 2, 1936.
5 "Views of the Sailors' Union . . ."
6 Ibid.
7 *Voice of the Federation*, Jun. 18, 1936.
8 "Memorandum of Terms of Settlement of Differences Between International Seamen's Union and Sailors' Union of the Pacific," Jul. 1936. Author's collection.
9 *Voice of the Federation*, Jul. 23, 1936.
10 Ibid., Jul. 30, 1936.
11 Ibid., Aug. 13, 1936.
12 Ibid., Aug. 20, 1936.
13 LaFollette Committee Report, p. 1080.
14 Ibid., p. 1081.
15 *Pacific Coast Longshoreman*, Sep. 7, 1936.
16 Ibid., Sep. 14, 1936.
17 LaFollette Committee Report, p. 1084.
18 Ibid., p. 1085. Minutes of San Francisco Waterfront Employers' Assn., Oct. 1, 1936.
19 *Voice of the Federation,* Sep. 3, 1936.
20 Ibid., Sep. 10, 1936.
21 Ibid., Sep. 24, 1936.
22 Ibid., Sep. 17, 1936.
23 Ibid., Oct. 1, 1936.
24 Ibid.
25 Ibid., Oct. 8, 1936.
26 Ibid., Nov. 5, 1936, "SUP Notes."
27 Ibid., Oct. 15, 1936.
28 Ibid., Oct. 22, 1936.
29 Ibid., Oct. 29, 1936.
30 Report of the Negotiating Committee, Oct. 25, 1936. Author's collection.
31 *Log of the Joint Negotiating Committee*, p. 14. (Hereafter cited as *Log*.)
32 *Black Gang News*, Nov. 6, 1936. Author's collection.
33 *Seattle Star*, Nov. 2, 1936.
34 *Chronicle,* Oct. 31, 1936.
35 *Star*, Oct. 30, 1936.
36 Ibid., Nov. 2, 1936.
37 *Log*, p. 15.
38 Minutes of Maritime Federation District Council No. 1, Nov. 6, 1936. Author's collection.
39 *Chronicle*, Nov. 9, 1936.
40 *Log*, p. 21.
41 San Pedro *Maritime Strike News*, Nov. 14, 1936. Author's collection.
42 *West Coast Sailors*, Nov. 9, 1936. Author's collection.
43 *Voice of the Federation*, Nov. 19, 1936.
44 Ibid., Jan. 14, 1937.

45 *Chronicle*, Oct. 31, 1936.
46 Ibid., Nov. 1, 1936.
47 *West Coast Sailors*, Nov. 17, 1936.
48 *Log*, p. 19.
49 Lundeberg to Dombroff, Nov. 6, 1936. Author's collection.
50 Minutes of Seattle Branch SUP, Nov. 9, 1936. Author's collection.
51 *Log*, p. 20.
52 Ibid., p. 21.
53 *N.W. Joint Strike Committee Bulletin*, Jan. 21, 1937. Author's collection.
54 Ibid., Jan. 22, 1937.
55 *Log*, p. 17.
56 *Chronicle*, Nov. 6, 1936.
57 *Voice of the Federation*, Nov. 12, 1936.
58 *West Coast Sailors*, Nov. 28, 1936.
59 *Chronicle*, Nov. 3, 1936.

Chapter 14. On the Picket Lines

1 *N.W. Joint Strike Committee Bulletin*, Nov. 6, 1936.
2 ILA Local 38-126 *Strike Bulletin*, Nov. 24, 1936. Author's collection.
3 *N.W. Joint Strike Committee Bulletin*, Jan. 12, 1937.
4 *Log*, p. 20.
5 Ibid.
6 *Chronicle*, Oct. 31, 1936.
7 *West Coast Sailors*, Nov. 9, 1936.
8 *Maritime Strike News*, Nov. 19, 1936.
9 *West Coast Sailors*, Nov. 9, 1936.
10 *Voice of the Federation* correspondence, Nov. 28, 1936. Author's collection.
11 Minutes, *Voice of the Federation* Editorial Board, Nov. 17, 1936, pp. 5, 8. Author's collection. (Hereafter cited as Minutes Editorial Board.)
12 "Report of Meeting of the Editorial Board, Voice of the Federation," p. 360. Author's collection. (Hereafter cited as Editorial Board Meeting.)
13 Minutes of Northwest Joint Strike Committee, Dec. 1, 3, 1936; wire from Seattle Sailors Strike Committee to Harry Lundeberg, Dec. 12, 1936.
14 Minutes Editorial Board, Dec. 9, 1936.
15 Editorial Board Meeting, pp. 303-5.
16 "Findings of the Editorial Board of the Voice of the Federation in Regard to the Mayes Investigation," p. 1. Author's collection. (Hereafter cited as Editorial Board Findings.)
17 Editorial Board Meeting, p. 319.
18 Ibid., pp. 217-18.
19 Editorial Board Findings, p. 4.
20 Editorial Board Meeting, p. 361.
21 *Maritime Worker*, Dec. 14, 1936.
22 Minutes Editorial Board, Dec. 16, 1936.
23 Letter "To All Members," Dec. 16, 1936. Author's collection.
24 *Voice of the Federation*, Dec. 24, 1936.
25 Ibid., Oct. 1, 1936.
26 *Maritime Strike News*, Dec. 3, 1936.
27 Ibid., Dec. 30, 1936.
28 Resolution, Pacific Coast District ILA Executive Board Minutes, Dec. 18, 1936. Author's collection.
29 *Voice of the Federation*, Dec. 17, 1936.

30 *Log*, p. 22.
31 *Chronicle*, Dec. 10, 1936.
32 *Log*, p. 23.
33 Ibid., p. 25.
34 *West Coast Sailors*, Dec. 22, 1936.
35 *Voice of the Federation*, Dec. 24, 1936.
36 Ibid.
37 Ibid.
38 *Chronicle*, Dec. 24, 1936.
39 Ibid.
40 *Log*, p. 28, Minutes Jan. 25, 1937.
41 *West Coast Sailors*, Feb. 2, 1937.
42 *Chronicle*, Dec. 20, 1936.
43 Ibid., Dec. 26, 1936.
44 Ibid., Dec. 29, 1936.
45 *Log*, p. 14.
46 ILA Local 38-79 *Strike Bulletin*, Jan. 7, 1937.
47 *Chronicle*, Dec. 21, 1936.
48 Ibid., Jan. 8, 1937.
49 Ibid., Jan. 20, 1937.
50 Ibid., Feb. 3, 1937.
51 *N.W. Joint Strike Committee Bulletin*, Feb. 2, 1937.
52 *West Coast Sailors*, Feb. 12, 1937.
53 *Voice of the Federation*, Feb. 11, 1937.
54 Ibid., Feb. 4, 1937.
55 Mimeographed pamphlet, no title, no date, p. 3. Author's collection.
56 C.E. Wheeler, *Chronicle*, Feb. 6, 1937.
57 *Maritime Worker*, Nov. 30, 1936.
58 William Schneiderman. *The Pacific Coast Maritime Strike* (San Francisco, 1937) pp. 21-22.

Chapter 15. The CIO Invasion

1 Committee for Industrial Organization. *The C.I.O.: What It Is and How It Came to Be* (Washington, D.C., 1937) p. 10.
2 Ibid., p. 22.
3 William Z. Foster. *American Trade Unionism: Principles and Organization, Strategy and Tactics* (New York, 1947) pp. 213–14.
4 Ibid., p. 216.
5 Leaflet, Maritime Federation District Council No. 1.
6 Author's collection.
7 Agreement Between Pacific Coast District, Local 38 of the International Longshoremen's Association and Shipowners' Association of the Pacific Coast, Feb. 4, 1937, p. 13.
8 Pacific Coast District ILA Convention Proceedings (1937) p. 214.
9 Elmer Bruce, Report to ILA Local 38-82 of 1937 Maritime Federation Convention, p. 2. Author's collection.
10 *Log*, p. 29.
11 *ISU Pilot*, Mar. 30, 1937.
12 Ibid., Feb. 23, 1937.
13 *Voice of the Federation*, Mar. 11, 1937.
14 *Pilot*, Mar. 23, 1937.
15 *Voice of the Federation*, Mar. 18, 1937.

16 Ibid., Mar. 25, 1937.
17 Pacific Coast District ILA Convention Proceedings (1937) p. 123.
18 Maritime Federation Convention Proceedings (1937) afternoon session, Jun. 28, p. 2.
19 "A Call to Action," Apr. 6, 1937, p. 2. Author's collection.
20 *West Coast Sailors*, "Report on Los Angeles Conference, May 3-4, 1937," p. 3.
21 Author's collection.
22 *West Coast Sailors*, May 25, 1937.
23 Copy of letter to Norma Perrie, Feb. 15, 1937. Author's collection.
24 "Call to Action," pp. 1-3.
25 *Voice of the Federation*, May 27, 1937.
26 Pacific Coast District ILA Convention Proceedings (1937) p. 183.
27 Ibid., p. 190.
28 Ibid., p. 72.
29 Author's collection.
30 Pacific Coast District ILA Convention Proceedings (1937) p. 135.
31 Minutes ILA Local 38-12, Jun. 17, 1937.
32 Maritime Federation Convention Proceedings (1937) afternoon session, Jun. 9, p. 34.
33 Ibid., pp. 41-42.
34 Ibid., Resolutions, p. 56, No. 73.
35 Ibid., afternoon session, Jun. 14, p. 6.
36 *Pacific Coast Longshoreman,* Oct. 20, 1937.
37 Maritime Federation Convention Proceedings (1937) morning session, Jun. 28, p. 8.
38 Ibid., Resolutions, pp. 30-31, No. 39.
39 Ibid., evening session, Jun. 29, p. 3.
40 Bruce Report to Local 38-82, p. 6.
41 Maritime Federation Convention Proceedings (1937) Resolutions, p. 51, No. 67; morning session, Jun. 28, pp. 9-12.
42 Ibid., morning session, Jun. 22, p. 7.
43 Ibid., morning session, Jun. 24, p. 5.
44 Ibid., p. 7.
45 Ibid., p. 6.
46 "Official Report of the Editor of the Voice of the Federation Submitted to Maritime Federation of the Pacific Coast Convention at Portland, Oregon, June 7, 1937," p. 1. Author's collection.
47 Bruce Report to Local 38-82, p. 7.
48 Maritime Federation Convention Proceedings (1937) night session, Jul. 8, p. 6.
49 Ibid., afternoon session, Jun. 26, p. 3.
50 Ibid., afternoon session, Jun. 30, p. 3.
51 Bruce Report to Local 38-82, p. 6.
52 Maritime Federation Convention Proceedings (1937) Resolutions, p. 47, No. 61.
53 Ibid., morning session, Jul. 8, p. 7.
54 Ibid., morning session, Jul. 9, p. 11.
55 Eugene Dennett, "Inland Boatmen Report on Maritime Convention," n.d. Author's collection.
56 Bruce Report to Local 38-82, p. 1.
57 *West Coast Sailors*, Jul. 9, 1937.
58 *Voice of the Federation*, Jul. 15, 1937.

Chapter 16. The AFL and CIO Checkerboard

1 *Sunday Oregonian*, Jul. 4, 1937, Magazine Section, p. 8.
2 "Statement," Jul. 22, 1937. Author's collection.
3 *Voice of the Federation*, Jun. 17, 1937.

4 Ibid., Jul. 15, 1937.
5 *Pilot*, Jul. 30, 1937.
6 *West Coast Sailors*, Aug. 6, 1937.
7 Ibid., Jul. 30, 1937.
8 *Voice of the Federation*, Aug. 5, 1937.
9 Minutes ILA Local 38-12, Aug. 15, 1937.
10 *Pilot*, Aug. 20, 1937.
11 *I.L.W.U. Bulletin*, Oct. 4, 1937.
12 *West Coast Sailors*, Sep. 24, 1937.
13 Author's collection.
14 *West Coast Sailors*, Sep. 24, 1937.
15 *Voice of the Federation*, Oct. 14, 1937.
16 *West Coast Firemen*, Oct. 19, 1937.
17 *Voice of the Federation*, Oct. 28, 1937.
18 *West Coast Firemen*, Nov. 18, 1937.
19 *Voice of the Federation*, Sep. 9, 1937.
20 Ibid., Nov. 11, 1937.
21 *West Coast Firemen*, Nov. 2, 1937.
22 *West Coast Sailors*, Sep. 17, 1937.
23 Ibid., Sep. 24, 1937.
24 *Voice of the Federation*, Sep. 23, 1937.
25 *West Coast Sailors*, Oct. 29, 1937.
26 *Voice of the Federation*, Dec. 23, 1937.
27 *West Coast Sailors*, Dec. 17, 1937.
28 *Voice of the Federation*, Dec. 23, 1937.
29 *West Coast Firemen*, Dec. 21, 1937.
30 *West Coast Sailors*, Sep. 17, 1937.
31 Ibid.
32 Ibid., Sep. 24, 1937.
33 *Pacific Coast Longshoreman*, Jan. 19, 1938.
34 Mimeographed letter, Feb. 24, 1938. Author's collection.
35 *I.L.W.U. Bulletin*, Mar. 5, 1938.
36 *West Coast Sailors*, Mar. 4, 1938.
37 *ILA 38-78 Bulletin*, Apr. 20, 1938. Author's collection.
38 *West Coast Sailors*, Dec. 10, 1937.
39 Ibid.
40 *Voice of the Federation*, Dec. 9, 1937.
41 Letter Jan. 6, 1938. Copy in author's collection.
42 *Pacific Coast Longshoreman*, Jan. 19, 1938.
43 *Voice of the Federation*, Sep. 9, 1937.
44 Ibid., Sep. 30, 1937.
45 Ibid., Sep. 23, 1937.
46 Minutes Editorial Board, Oct. 30, 1937.
47 *Voice of the Federation*, Nov. 4, 1937.
48 Minutes Maritime Federation Executive Board, Jan. 15, 1938.
49 Minutes Editorial Board, Nov. 6, 1937.
50 *Voice of the Federation*, Nov. 11, 1937.
51 Minutes Federation Executive Board, Jan. 15, 1938.
52 *West Coast Sailors*, Nov. 26, 1937.
53 Sailors' Union of the Pacific, *Steady As She Goes* (San Francisco, 1937).

54 [Sailors' Union Members], *C.I.O., A.F. of L., or Independent* (San Francisco, 1937.)
55 *I.L.W.U. Bulletin*, Dec. 2, 1937.
56 Ibid., Dec. 9, 1937.
57 *Voice of the Federation*, Dec. 9, 1937.
58 *West Coast Sailors*, Dec. 24, 1937.
59 *West Coast Firemen*, Dec. 21, 1937.
60 *National Seaman*, Jan. 24, 1938.
61 *West Coast Firemen,* Jan. 25, 1938.
62 Ibid.
63 Ibid., Feb. 1, 1938.
64 Minutes Federation Executive Board, Jan. 14, 1938.
65 Letter Feb. 28, 1938. Copy in author's collection.
66 Minutes Maritime Federation District Council No. 1, Feb. 25, 1938.
67 Ibid., Mar. 4, 1938.
68 Maritime Federation Convention Proceedings (1938) p. 184.
69 *West Coast Firemen*, Nov. 30, 1937.
70 Resolution Feb. 16, 1938. Author's collection.
71 Minutes Seafarers' Federation, Mar. 1, 1938. Author's collection.
72 *Voice of the Federation*, Mar. 17, 1938.
73 *West Coast Sailors*, Mar. 4, 1938.

Chapter 17. The Shepard Line Beef

1 *West Coast Sailors*, Feb. 18, 1938.
2 Ibid., Apr. 15, 1938.
3 *Voice of the Federation*, Apr. 22, 1937.
4 *Pilot*, Apr. 22, 1938.
5 *West Coast Sailors*, Oct. 15, 1937.
6 Decisions and Orders of the National Labor Relations Board, Vol. 7, p. 82.
7 *West Coast Sailors*, Oct. 8, 1937.
8 Ibid., Oct. 15, 1937.
9 Ibid., Jan. 7, 1938.
10 Ibid., Jan. 14, 1938.
11 *Pilot*, Feb. 18, 1938.
12 *West Coast Sailors*, Feb. 11, 1938.
13 *Voice of the Federation*, Jan. 13, 1938.
14 *West Coast Sailors*, Jan. 14, 1938.
15 Ibid., Apr. 15, 1938.
16 International Longshoremen's and Warehousemen's Union Convention Proceedings (1938) p. 48.
17 Ibid., p. 53.
18 *Morning Oregonian*, Apr. 15, 1938.
19 Ibid., Apr. 14, 1938.
20 *West Coast Sailors*, Apr. 15, 1938.
21 *Voice of the Federation*, Apr 21, 1938.
22 *Post-Intelligencer*, Apr. 16, 1938.
23 *Pacific Coast Longshoreman*, Apr. 20, 1938.
24 ILWU Convention Proceedings (1938) p. 87.
25 Ibid., pp. 87-88.
26 *Chronicle*, Apr. 19, 1938.
27 *West Coast Firemen*, Apr. 19, 1938.
28 *West Coast Sailors,* Apr. 19, 1938.

29 *Chronicle*, Apr. 19, 1938.
30 Ibid.
31 *West Coast Sailors*, Apr. 19, 1938.
32 *Chronicle*, Apr. 19, 1938.
33 *West Coast Sailors*, Apr. 19, 1938.
34 *Chronicle*, Apr. 19, 1938.
35 Maritime Federation Convention Proceedings (1938) p. 112.
36 *I.L.W.U. Bulletin*, Apr. 21, 1938.
37 Ibid.
38 *West Coast Sailors*, Apr. 19, 1938.
39 Ibid.
40 Ibid., Apr. 22, 1938.
41 *Voice of the Federation*, May 19, 1938.
42 Ibid., Apr. 28, 1938.
43 Ibid.
44 Ibid., May 5, 1938.
45 Ibid.
46 Ibid., May 19, 1938.
47 *West Coast Sailors*, May 20, 1938.
48 *Pilot*, Apr. 22, 1938.
49 NLRB Decisions, Vol. 7, p. 83.
50 *Tacoma Times*, Apr. 22, 1938.
51 *Statement and Award* in re Refusal of Longshoremen to Work Cargo on S.S. Timber Rush (Shepard Steamship Co.) Port of Tacoma, Washington, by M.E. Bollen, Arbitrator, Apr. 26, 1938, p. 2. Author's collection.
52 *Chronicle*, May 4, 1938. Quoted in Maritime Federation Convention Proceedings (1938) p. 113.
53 *Pacific Coast Longshoreman*, May 11, 1938.
54 *West Coast Sailors*, May 13, 1938.
55 *Pacific Coast Longshoreman*, May 11, 1938.
56 *Tacoma Times*, May 4, 1938.
57 *Post-Intelligencer*, May 10, 1938.
58 *I.L.W.U. Bulletin*, May 12, 1938.
59 *Pacific Coast Longshoreman*, May 11, 1938.
60 *Tacoma News Tribune*, May 12, 1938.
61 *West Coast Sailors*, May 13, 1938.
62 Ibid., May 20, 1938.
63 Ibid., May 27, 1938.
64 Ibid.
65 *Pacific Coast Longshoreman*, May 4, 1938.

Chapter 18. Dissolution of the Maritime Federation

1 *Voice of the Federation*, Jun. 14, 1935.
2 Ibid., Apr. 14, 1938.
3 *West Coast Sailors*, May 20, 1938.
4 *West Coast Firemen*, May 17, 1938.
5 Maritime Federation Convention Proceedings (1938) p. 2.
6 Ibid., p. 9.
7 Ibid., p. 10.
8 Ibid.
9 Ibid., p. 11.

10 Ibid., p. 12.
11 Ibid., P. 18.
12 Ibid., p. 11.
13 Ibid., pp. 22-25.
14 Ibid., pp. 25-26.
15 Ibid., p. 27.
16 Ibid., p. 28.
17 Ibid., p. 30.
18 Ibid.
19 Ibid., p. 34.
20 Ibid., p. 37.
21 Ibid., p. 38.
22 Ibid., p. 39.
23 Ibid.
24 Ibid., pp. 70-71.
25 Statement Jun. 7, 1938, signed by delegates from MM&P Local 90, MFOW&W, and SUP. Copy in author's collection.
26 *West Coast Sailors*, Jun. 17, 1938.
27 Ibid.
28 Maritime Federation Convention Proceedings (1938) p. 267.
29 Ibid., pp. 184-85.
30 Ibid., p. 105.
31 Ibid., p. 107.
32 Ibid., p. 112.
33 Ibid., pp. 113-14,
34 Ibid., p. 114.
35 Ibid., pp. 119-20.
36 Ibid., pp. 127-28.
37 Ibid., pp. 140-41.
38 Ibid., p. 276.
39 Ibid., p. 279.
40 Ibid., pp. 279-80.
41 Ibid., p. 336.
42 Ibid., p. 343.
43 Ibid., p. 309.
44 *West Coast Sailors*, Sep. 9, 1938.

Illustrations

Abbreviations

AFL	American Federation of Labor
ARTA	American Radio Telegraphists' Association
CIO	Committee for Industrial Organization
CIO	Congress of Industrial Organizations
IBU	Inland Boatmen's Union
ILA	International Longshoremen's Association
ILWU	International Longshoremen's and Warehousemen's Union (now International Longshore and Warehouse Union)
ISU	International Seamen's Union
IWW	Industrial Workers of the World
MCS	Marine Cooks and Stewards' Association of the Pacific Coast
MEBA	Marine Engineers' Beneficial Association
MFOW	Pacific Coast Marine Firemen, Oilers, Watertenders and Wipers' Association
MFPC	Maritime Federation of the Pacific Coast
MMP	National Organization of Masters, Mates and Pilots
MTW	Marine Transport Workers Industrial Union 510, IWW
MWIU	Marine Workers Industrial Union
NLRB	National Labor Relations Board
NRA	National Recovery Administration
SUP	Sailors' Union of the Pacific

Pacific Coast Maritime History Committee

Clyde H. Hupp, Chair – Former Secretary-Treasurer, Pierce County Central Labor Council

Philip Lelli, Vice-Chair – Past President, International Longshore and Warehouse Union Local 23, Tacoma

T.A. Thronson – Retired Longshoreman and 1934 Strike Veteran

John W. Thompson – Secretary-Treasurer, Pierce County Central Labor Council

James Ruble – Educator, Puyallup, Washington

Archie Green – Author and Labor Folklorist, San Francisco

Robert W. Cherny – San Francisco State University

Bob Markholt – American Federation of Teachers Local 1789, Seattle

Nellie Fox-Edwards – Former Legislative and Political Education Director, Oregon AFL-CIO

Greg Mowat – American Federation of State, County and Municipal Employees Local 443, Olympia

Lou Stewart – Former Education Director, Washington State Labor Council

Ross Rieder – Pacific Northwest Labor History Association

Gunnar Lundeberg – Sailors' Union of the Pacific, San Francisco

Allen Seager – Simon Fraser University, British Columbia

Marcus Widenor – Labor Education and Research Center, University of Oregon

Shaun Maloney – Past President, International Longshore and Warehouse Union Local 19, Seattle

Dallas DeLay – International Longshore and Warehouse Union Local 19, Seattle

Arthur Alméida – Past President, International Longshore and Warehouse Union Local 13, Wilmington

Blaine Johnson – Author, Tacoma

John Ehly – Retired, International Longshore and Warehouse Union Local 23, Tacoma

Vance Lelli – International Longshore and Warehouse Union Local 23, Tacoma

Ottilie Markholt, Author – Office and Professional Employees International Union Local 23, Tacoma

T.A. "Tiny" Thronson

1905-1999

On April 1, 1999, while Maritime Solidarity was being printed, Tiny Thronson passed away. During our many years of research and writing, Tiny contributed his first-hand knowledge and understanding of events to make the book a faithful record of the struggles of maritime workers during the 1930s. When we formed a committee to publish Maritime Solidarity, Tiny was our first and faithful member. We wish that we could have placed a book in his hands. We will miss him.

Bibliography

Primary Sources

Oral History

Peter B. Gill, Sailors' Union of the Pacific, Seattle. Discussions in depth 1939-1942.

T.A. Thronson, International Longshoremen's Association, Tacoma. Discussions in depth 1961-62 and intermittently 1985 to present.

Edward Coester, Sailor's Union, Portland and Seattle. Conversations 1937-39 and interview December 1963.

Emil Miljus, Sailors' Union, Seattle. Conversations 1936-37.

William T. Morris, Pacific Coast District ILA, Tacoma. Interview c. 1941.

Art Will, ILA, Seattle. Interview c. 1941.

M.J. Cannalonga, Marine Firemen's Union, Seattle. Interview c. 1940.

Members of Sailors' Union, Seattle. Interviews arranged by Pete Gill, c. 1941: Meyers, Morse, Mike Chismar, Charles Cates, Poole.

Martin Frederickson, ILA Local 38-97, Tacoma. Interview c. 1960.

William J. Lewis, ILA, San Francisco. Interview October 1963.

Charles G. Peabody, ILA Local 38-78, Portland. Interview November 21, 1963.

Jack Connors, Marine Cooks and Stewards, Seattle. Interview December 1963.

Dudley Robinson, Sailors' Union, Seattle. Interview December 1963.

Minutes of Union Locals, Councils, and Committees

International Longshoremen's Association Local 38-12, Seattle, 1918-1938.

Joint Marine Strike Committee, San Francisco, 1934.

Joint Northwest Strike Committee, Tacoma, 1934.

Log of Joint Negotiation/Policy Committee, San Francisco, 1936-37.

Maritime Federation District Council No. 1, Seattle, 1936-38.

Maritime Federation District Council No. 2, San Francisco, 1936-38.

Maritime Federation District Council No. 3, Portland, 1935-38.

Maritime Federation District Council No. 4, San Pedro, 1937-38.

Riggers' and Stevedores' Union, San Francisco (Independent and ILA Local 38-33) 1906-1919.

San Francisco General Strike Committee, 1934.

Seattle Central Labor Council, 1915-1934.

Tacoma Central Labor Council, 1907-1937.

Voice of the Federation Editorial Board, San Francisco, 1936-37.

Proceedings of Union Conventions

International Longshoremen's Association. Proceedings of Conventions, 1899-1935.

International Longshoremen's and Warehousemen's Union. Convention Proceedings, 1938.

Marine Council of the Pacific Coast. Convention Proceedings, July 1933.

Marine Engineers' Beneficial Association. Proceedings of Conventions, 1917-1935.

Maritime Federation of the Pacific Coast. Convention Proceedings, 1935-38.

Pacific Coast District, International Longshoremen's Association. Proceedings of Annual Conventions, 1910-1920 and 1922-1938.

Washington State Federation of Labor. Proceedings of 33rd Annual Convention, 1934, and Minutes of Executive Board Meeting, July 7-12, 1934.

Union Constitutions

International Longshoremen's Association, 1935.

ILA, Pacific Coast District 38, 1935.

ILA Local 38-30, Tacoma, 1924.

International Longshoremen's and Warehousemen's Union, 1941.

ILWU Local 1-8, Seattle, 1937.

International Seamen's Union, 1936.

Maritime Federation of the Pacific Coast, 1935-37.

Maritime Federation, Columbia River District Council No. 3.

Sailors' Union of the Pacific, 1935-37.

Union Agreements

American Radio Telegraphists' Association. Agreement, 1937.

ILA District 38. Alaska Agreement, 1934.

ILA Portland and Columbia River District. *Working Rules, Wages and Conditions,* Jun. 7, 1935.

ILA, San Francisco Bay District. *Wage Scale and Working Rules,* Jan. 12, 1935.

ILA Washington State. *Wages, Hours and Working Rules,* May 2, 1935.

ILA District 38. Agreement Between Waterfront Employers of Seattle, Portland, San Francisco, Southern California, and Shipowners' Association of the Pacific Coast, 1937.

ILA District 38. *Maximum Loads for Standard Commodities,* 1937.

ILA District 38. *Penalty Cargo Rates,* 1937.

Marine Firemen, Oilers, Watertenders and Wipers, Seattle Branch. Wages and Working Rules on Alaska Cargo Ships, Cannery Ships, and Whalers, 1935.

Masters, Mates and Pilots. Agreement for Intercoastal and Offshore Trades and Alaska Lines, 1937.

Sailors' Union. Agreement for Intercoastal and Offshore Trades and Alaska Lines, 1937.

Sailors' Union. Agreement with Shepard Steamship Co., 1937.

Maritime Labor Bulletins

Harbor Unity, Seattle, 1938.

ILA Local 38-78 Bulletin, Portland, 1937-38.

ILA Local 38-79 Strike Bulletin, San Francisco, 1934.

ILA Local 38-79 Bulletin, San Francisco, 1937-38.

ILWU 1-19 Bulletin, Seattle, 1937-38.

International Seamen's Union Strike Bulletin, San Francisco, 1934.

I.W.W. Seaman, New York, 1937-39.

Joint Marine Journal, San Francisco, 1934.

Marine Workers Industrial Union Strike Bulletin, San Francisco, 1934.

Maritime Strike News, San Pedro, 1936-37.

N.W. Joint Strike Committee Bulletin, Seattle, 1936-37.

Pacific Coast District 38 ILA Bulletin, Seattle, 1938.

West Coast Sailors, San Francisco (bulletin Nov. 1936-May 1937).

Labor Newspapers

Black Gang News, San Francisco, 1936-37.

The Citizen, Los Angeles.

I.L.W.U. Bulletin, San Francisco.

Industrial Solidarity, Chicago.

Industrial Worker, Seattle and Chicago.

I.S.U. Pilot, then *Pilot* (NMU), New York.

Labor Clarion, San Francisco.

Oregon Labor Press, Portland.

Pacific Coast Longshoreman, Seattle (1935-36), Tacoma (1937-38).

Pacific Seaman/American Seaman, San Francisco 1934-36.

Seamen's Journal, San Francisco and Washington, D.C. (*Coast Seamen's Journal* before 1918).

Seattle Union Record.

Tacoma Labor Advocate.

Voice of Action, Seattle.

Voice of the Federation, San Francisco.

Waterfront Worker, San Francisco.

West Coast Firemen, San Francisco.

West Coast Sailors, San Francisco.

Labor Pamphlets

A.F. of L. News Service. *President Green Declares That American Federation of Labor's Relentless Opposition to Minority Rule Is Real Issue in C.I.O. Controversy.* Washington, D.C.: 1937.

A.F. of L. News Service. *President Green Declares That Democratic Rule in the A.F. of L. is Real Issue in Controversy with Industrial Organization.* Washington, D.C.: 1936.

A.F. of L. News Service. *President Green Extols Labor Movement as Shield of Democracy and Relentless Foe of Dictatorships.* Washington, D.C.: 1936.

A.F. of L. News Service. *President Green Sounds Warning Against Continued Existence of Committee for Industrial Organization.* Washington, D.C.: 1936.

A.F. of L. News Service. *Ten international unions affiliated with the A.F. of L. stand automatically suspended for failure to withdraw from Committee on Industrial Organization.* Washington, D.C.: 1936.

April 21 Agreement Between Waterfront Employers Association of San Francisco and International Longshoremen's Association District No. 38 – Local 38-79. San Francisco: 1936.

Committee for Industrial Organization. *The Case for Industrial Organization.* Washington, D.C.: 1936.

Committee for Industrial Organization. *The C.I.O.: What It Is and How It Came to Be.* Washington, D.C.: 1937.

Committee for Industrial Organization. *Questions and Answers on the C.I.O.* c. 1936.

Committee for United Seamen of America. *Proposed Constitution for One Industrial Union of All American Seamen.* San Francisco: 1937.

Curran, Joseph. *Maritime Unity.* New York: National Maritime Union, 1937.

Dunne, William F. *The Great San Francisco General Strike: The Story of the West Coast Strike—the Bay Counties' General Strike and the Maritime Workers' Strike.* New York: Workers Library, 1934.

Foster, William Z. *Industrial Unionism.* New York: Workers Library, 1936.

Furuseth, Andrew. *Petition to the Honorable, the Speaker, and the Members of the House of Representatives.* Washington, D.C.: International Seamen's Union of America, Nov. 15, 1929.

Haas, Eric. *John L. Lewis Exposed.* New York: Socialist Labor Party, 1938.

Hedley, George P. *The San Francisco Strike As I Have Seen It.* An Address Before the Church Council for Social Education, Berkeley, July 19, 1934. Fourth Edition. San Francisco: Conference for Labor's Civil Rights, 1934.

Industrial Workers of the World. *The Story of the Sea: Marine Transport Worker's Hand Book.* Chicago: c. 1925.

International Juridical Association. *Report on the Status and Working Conditions of Seamen in the American Merchant Marine.* New York: 1936.

International Longshoremen's Association Local 38-79. *The Maritime Crisis: What It Is and What It Isn't.* San Francisco: 1936.

________________. *The Truth About the Waterfront: The I.L.A. States Its Case to the Public.* San Francisco: 1935.

International Longshoremen's Association Local 38-83, Local 38-86, Local 38-97. *Brief of Petitioners Before the National Labor Relations Board.* Tacoma: 1941.

International Longshoremen's and Warehousemen's Union. *Nailing the Shipowners' Lies.* San Francisco: 1948.

International Seamen's Union of America. *Memorial to the Honorable United States Senators and Members of the House of Representatives, Relating to the Shipowners' Monopoly and the case of Street v. Shipowners' Association of the Pacific Coast and Pacific American Steamship Association.* c. 1925.

______________. *Seamen's Discharge Books: The "Character Mark."* Excerpts from Proceedings of Twenty-ninth Convention, International Seamen's Union of America, January 11-19, 1926. Washington, D.C.

______________, Legislative Committee. *The Seamen's View of the "Proposed Codification of the Navigation Laws" and the "Suggested Amendments": An Open Letter the U.S. Shipping Board.* San Francisco: Sep. 8, 1927.

International Seamen's Union, Pacific District. *The Shipowners Promise "A Square Deal."* San Francisco: c. 1922.

Joint Marine Modesto Defense Committee. *The Modesto Frame-Up.* San Francisco: 1935.

King-Ramsay-Conner Defense Committee. *The Ship Murder: The Story of a Frameup.* San Francisco: 1937.

Morris, George. *A Tale of Two Waterfronts.* New York: Daily Worker, 1953.

[Sailors' Union Members]. *C.I.O., A.F. of L., or Independent.* San Francisco: 1937.

Sailors' Union of the Pacific. *Steady As She Goes.* San Francisco: 1937.

Schneiderman, William. *The Pacific Coast Maritime Strike.* San Francisco: 1937.

Sparks, N. *The Struggle of the Marine Workers.* New York: International Publishers, 1930.

Miscellaneous Labor Records

Deal, Clyde W. "The Tide Turns." Clyde W. Deal papers, University of Washington, Seattle.

Farmer, Albert. "The Diary of a Longshore Dispatcher, 1928-1934." Albert Farmer papers, University of Washington, Seattle.

ILA Local 38-30, Tacoma. Earnings record, 1930. Courtesy Morris Thorsen.

ILA Local 38-78, Portland. *Day Book,* 1931-1933.

Malone, Vincent J. "The Story of the Marine Firemen's Union," 1945. Marine Firemen, Oilers, Watertenders and Wipers Association, San Francisco.

Noonan, George. Collection includes early history of Seattle and Tacoma longshore unions and union documents, 1900-1941. Tacoma Public Library.

Pacific Coast District ILA. "Draft of Proposed Code for Longshoremen, Checkers and Grain Handlers." July 31, 1933.

Pacific Coast District ILA office Tacoma, 1941. Miscellaneous papers.

Peabody, Charles G. Papers relating to ILA Local 38-78, Portland.

San Francisco Waterfront Strikes, 1934: A Collection of Pamphlets, Broadsides, etc., 2 Vols. ILWU Library, San Francisco.

Strike file, 1934. San Francisco Labor Council.

Author's collection of correspondence, minutes, and other documents.

Minutes and Publications of Maritime Employers

Dawson, W.C. "Brief History of the Waterfront Employers of Seattle, 1908-1936." Pacific Maritime Assn. (PMA) Files, Seattle.

Foisie, Frank P. *Decasualizing Longshore Labor and the Seattle Experience.* Seattle: Waterfront Employers of Seattle, 1934.

Joint Organization Through Employee Representation of Longshoremen and Truckers and Waterfront Employers of Seattle. Minutes of Joint Executive Committee and Joint Employment Committee. PMA Files.

Northwest Waterfront Employers' Union. Minutes. PMA Files.

Pacific American Shipowners and Waterfront Employers of San Francisco, Seattle, Portland and San Pedro. *Hot Cargo: The Longshoremen's Alibi for Arbitration Award Violations.* San Francisco: 1935.

Pacific Coast Marine Safety Code Committee. *Pacific Coast Marine Safety Code: Stevedoring Operations on Board Ship.* 1931.

Pacific Shipper, San Francisco.

Petersen, Walter J. *Marine Labor Union Leadership.* San Francisco: Waterfront Employers' Union, 1925.

San Francisco Chamber of Commerce. *Law and Order in San Francisco: A Beginning.* San Francisco: 1916.

Seattle Longshore Log.

Waterfront Employers of Seattle. Minutes. PMA Files.

Waterfront Employers' Union of San Francisco. *Full and By, A Message from the Waterfront Employers' Union.* San Francisco: 1921.

____________. *The Pacific Coast Longshoremen's Strike of 1934: Statement of Thomas G. Plant, President, . . . to the National Longshoremen's Board.* San Francisco: 1934.

____________ (Waterfront Employers' Association after Feb. 1935). Miscellaneous papers in Graduate Social Science Library, University of California, Berkeley.

Waterfront Employers' Union of Tacoma. Minutes. PMA Files.

Waterfront Wage Scales and Working Rules

Standard Practice Handbook for Longshoremen and Employers. Portland, 1934.

Standard Practice Handbook, Joint Organization Through Employee Representation of Longshoremen and Truckers and Waterfront Employers of Seattle. January 1932.

Wage Scale and Working Rules of the Longshoremen's Association of the Port of San Francisco and Bay District. December 10, 1927-December 9, 1929.

Wage Scale and Working Rules of the Longshoremen's Association of the Port of San Francisco and Bay District. December 10, 1933-December 9, 1934.

Wage Scale, Rules and Working Conditions on the Tacoma Waterfront. 1924.

Wage Scale, Rules and Working Conditions on the Tacoma Waterfront. January 1932.

Government Documents and Publications

Albrecht, Arthur Emil. *International Seamen's Union of America: A Study of Its History and Problems.* Bulletin of the United States Bureau of Labor Statics, Miscellaneous Series, No. 342. Washington, D.C.: Government Printing Office, 1923.

Bass, Robert P. *Marine and Dock Labor: Work, Wages and Industrial Relations During the Period of the War.* Washington, D.C.: Government Printing Office, 1919.

Bureau of Labor of the State of Oregon. *Tenth Biennial Report, 1921-1922.* Salem, Oregon: 1922.

Macarthur, Walter, Compiler. *American Seamen's Law: Appendix, Court Decisions, Department Circulars, Statutes and Acts, Table of Wages.* San Francisco: 1931.

Stern, Boris. *A Report on Longshore Labor Conditions in the United States and Port Decasualization.* Washington, D.C.: November 10, 1933.

U.S. Circuit Court of Appeals for the Ninth Circuit. *Cornelius Andersen vs. Shipowners' Association of the Pacific Coast and Pacific American Steamship Association.* San Francisco: 1928.

U.S. Congress. Senate. Subcommittee of the Committee on Education and Labor. *Violations of Free Speech and the Rights of Labor.* Hearings, Part 60, 76th Cong., 3rd sess. Washington, D.C.: 1940.

______________. Subcommittee of the Committee on Education and Labor. *Violations of Free Speech and the Rights of Labor.* 77th Cong., 2d sess., S. Rept. 1150, Part 2. Washington, D.C.: 1942.

______________. Subcommittee of the Committee on Education and Labor. *Violations of Free Speech and the Rights of Labor,* 78th Cong., 1st sess., S. Rept. 398, Part 3. Washington, D.C.: 1943.

U.S. National Labor Relations Board. *Decisions and Orders . . .,* Vols. 1-7. Washington, D.C.: 1936-38.

U.S. National Longshoremen's Board. *Proceedings before the National Longshoremen's Board . . . to Arbitrate Controversies between the Waterfront Employers and the International Longshoremen's Association, Local 38, Pacific Coast District,* Vols. 21, 27, and 28. San Francisco: 1934.

U.S. Shipping Board. *Third National Conference on the Merchant Marine.* Washington, D.C.: 1930.

Secondary Sources

Newspapers

Los Angeles Times.

Morning Oregonian, Portland.

Portland News-Telegram.

San Francisco Chronicle.

San Francisco Examiner.

San Francisco News.

San Pedro Daily Pilot.

San Pedro News-Pilot.

Seattle Post-Intelligencer.

Seattle Star.

The Spokesman, San Francisco.

Tacoma Daily Ledger.

Tacoma News Tribune.

Tacoma Times.

Western American, Oakland.

Articles

Adams, William. "The Shipping Conspiracy." *Nation,* Sep. 5 and 12, 1934.

Booth, Caesar. "Bridges Leads Scabs on Sailors' Union." *Industrial Unionist,* May 1938.

Brown, Donald Mackenzie. "Dividends and Stevedores." *Scribner's,* Jan. 1935, pp. 52-56.

Cantwell, Robert. "War on the West Coast: I. The Gentlemen of San Francisco." *New Republic,* Aug. 1, 1934, pp. 308-10.

"Dailies Helped Break General Strike." Editorial, *Nation.* Aug. 8, 1934.

DeFord, Miriam Allen. "Riot Guns in San Francisco." *Nation,* Jul. 7, 1934.

_______________. "San Francisco: An Autopsy on the General Strike." *Nation,* Aug. 1, 1934.

Green, William. "Does the U.S. Want a Labor Dictator?" *Reader's Digest,* Dec. 1937.

IWW Card No. X13068. "West Coast Chaos—The CIO-AFL Inter-union War." *One Big Union Monthly,* Oct. 1937.

Lerner, Tillie. "The Strike." *Partisan Review,* Sep.-Oct. 1934. Reprinted in Jack Salzman, Editor. *Years of Protest.* New York: Pegasus, 1970.

"Longshore Labor Conditions in the United States – Part I." *Monthly Labor Review,* Oct. 1930, pp. 1-20.

"Longshore Labor Conditions in the United States – Part II." *Monthly Labor Review,* Nov. 1930, pp. 11-25.

"The Maritime Unions." *Fortune,* Sep. 1937.

McFadden, Bernard. "Our Merchant Marine Smells to High Heaven." *Liberty,* Mar. 5, 1938.

McFee, William. "Seagoing Soviets." *Saturday Evening Post,* Sep. 21, 1940.

Mills, Herb, and David Wellman. "Contractually Sanctioned Job Action and Workers' Control: The Case of San Francisco Longshoremen." *Labor History,* Spring 1987.

P.C. "The Longshoremen's Convention—and After." *A.F. ofL. Rank and File Federationist,* Sep. 1935.

Seely, Evelyn. "San Francisco's Labor War." *Nation,* Jun. 13, 1934.

________________. "War on the West Coast: II. Journalistic Strikebreakers." *New Republic,* Aug. 1, 1934, pp. 310-12.

Wayne, Elvar. "Sloss's 'Impartial' Arbitration." *Pacific Weekly,* Oct. 14, 1935.

West, George P. "Andrew Furuseth and the Radicals." *Survey,* Nov. 5, 1921, pp. 207-9.

________________. "Andrew Furuseth Stands Pat." *Survey,* Oct. 15, 1923, pp. 86-90.

Books

*Indicates background source.

*Barnes, Charles B. *The Longshoremen.* New York: Survey Associates, 1915.

Bernstein, Irving. *The Lean Years: A History of the American Worker, 1920-1933.* Boston: Houghton Mifflin, 1960.

________________. *Turbulent Years: A History of the American Worker, 1933-1941.* Boston: Houghton Mifflin, 1970.

*Borkinau, Franz. *World Communism: A History of the Communist International.* 1939. Reprint. Ann Arbor, Michigan: University of Michigan Press, 1962.

*Brecher, Jeremy. *Strike!* San Francisco: Straight Arrow Books, 1972.

*Brody, David. *Workers in Industrial America: Essays on the 20th Century Struggle.* New York: Oxford University Press, 1980.

Buchanan, Roger B. *Dock Strike: History of the 1934 Waterfront Strike in Portland, Oregon.* Everett, Washington: The Working Press, 1975.

Chaplin, Ralph. *Wobbly: The Rough-and-Tumble Story of an American Radical.* Chicago: University of Chicago Press, 1948.

Cochran, Bert. *Labor and Communism: The Conflict that Shaped American Unions.* Princeton: Princeton University Press, 1977.

Cross, Ira B. *A History of the Labor Movement in California.* Berkeley: University of California Press, 1935.

Dennett, Eugene V. *Agitprop: The Life of an American Working-Class Radical: The Autobiography of Eugene V. Dennett.* Albany: State University of New York Press, 1990.

*Draper, Theodore. *The Roots of American Communism.* New York: Viking Press, 1937.

*Dubofsky, Melvyn. *We Shall Be All: A History of the Industrial Workers of the World.* New York: Quadrangle/New York Times Book Co., 1969.

Eliel, Paul. *The Waterfront and General Strike, San Francisco, 1934: A Brief History.* San Francisco: Hooper Printing Co., 1934.

Foster, William Z. *American Trade Unionism: Principles and Organization, Strategy and Tactics.* New York: International Publishers, 1947.

*Gambs, John S. *The Decline of the I.W.W.* New York: Columbia University Press, 1932.

Gorter, Wytze, and George H. Hildebrand. *The Pacific Coast Maritime Industry, 1930-1948.* Vo. 1: *An Economic Profile,* Vol. 2: *An Analysis of Performance.* Berkeley: University of California Press, 1952 and 1954.

Hall, Burton, Editor. *Autocracy and Insurgency in Organized Labor.* New Brunswick, N.J.: Transaction Books, 1972.

International Longshoremen's and Warehousemen's Union. *The ILWU Story: Three Decades of Militant Unionism.* San Francisco: ILWU, 1963.

Jensen, Vernon H. *Lumber and Labor.* 1945. Reprint. New York: Arno Press, 1971.

Kimeldorf, Howard. *Reds or Rackets? The Making of Radical and Conservative Unions on the Waterfront.* Berkeley: University of California Press, 1988.

*Klehr, Harvey, and John Earl Haynes. *The American Communist Movement: Storming Heaven Itself.* New York: Twayne Publishers, 1992.

*Krebs, Richard [Jan Valtine]. *Out of the Night.* New York: Alliance Book Corp., 1941.

Lang, Frederick J. *Maritime: A Historical Sketch and a Worker's Program.* 2nd ed. New York: Pioneer Publishers, 1945.

Larrowe, Charles P. *Harry Bridges: The Rise and Fall of Radical Labor in the United States.* 2nd ed. Westport: Lawrence Hill, 1977.

______________. *Shape-up and Hiring Hall: A Comparison of Hiring Methods and Labor Relations on the New York and Seattle Waterfronts.* Berkeley: University of California Press, 1955.

Madison, Charles A. *American Labor Leaders.* New York: Harper & Brothers Publishers, 1950.

Magden, Ronald E. *A History of Seattle Waterfront Workers, 1884-1934.* Seattle: International Longshoremen's and Warehousemen's Union, Local 19 and Washington Commission for the Humanities, 1991.

____________. *The Working Longshoreman.* Tacoma, Washington: International Longshoremen's and Warehousemen's Union, Local 23, 1991.

Magden, Ronald E., and A.D. Martinson. *The Working Waterfront: The Story of Tacoma's Ships and Men.* Tacoma, Washington: International Longshoremen's and Warehousemen's Union, Local 23, and Washington Commission for the Humanities, 1982.

Mears, E.G. *Maritime Trade of Western United States.* Palo Alto: Stanford University Press, 1935.

Mers, Gilbert. *Working the Waterfront: The Ups and Downs of a Rebel Longshoreman.* Austin, Texas: University of Texas Press, 1988.

Minton, Bruce, and John Stuart. *Men Who Lead Labor.* New York: Modern Age Books, 1937.

Nelson, Bruce. *Workers on the Waterfront: Seamen, Longshoremen, and Unionism in the 1930s.* Urbana: University of Illinois Press, 1988.

*O'Connor, Harvey. *Revolution in Seattle.* 1964. Reprint. Seattle: Left Bank Books, 1981.

Oneal, James C., and G.A. Warner. *American Communism: A Critical Analysis of its Origins, Development and Programs.* Revised ed. New York: E.P. Dutton & Co., Inc., 1947.

Pacific Coast Marine Firemen, Oilers, Watertenders and Wipers Association. *From Hell Hole to High Tech: Historical Highlights.* San Francisco: 1983.

________________. *The Story of the Marine Firemen's Union.* San Francisco: 1945.

*Perlman, Selig. *A Theory of the Labor Movement.* 1928. Reprint. Philadelphia: Porcupine Press, Inc., 1979.

*Perlman, Selig, and Philip Taft. *History of Labor in the United States, 1896-1932. Vo. 4: Labor Movements.* New York: Macmillan, 1935.

Pilcher, William W. *The Portland Longshoremen: A Dispersed Urban Community.* New York: Holt, Rinehart and Winston, 1972.

Quin, Mike [Paul William Ryan]. *The Big Strike.* 1949. Reprint. New York: International Publishers, 1979.

*Rosenberg, Daniel. *New Orleans Dockworkers: Race, Labor, and Unionism, 1892-1923.* Albany: State University of New York, 1988.

Russell, Maud. *Men Along the Shore: The I.L.A. and its History.* New York: Brussel & Brussel, Inc., 1966.

San Francisco Bay Area District Council No. 2, Maritime Federation of the Pacific Coast. *Men and Ships: A Pictorial of the Maritime Industry.* San Francisco: 1937.

Schneider, Betty V.H. *Industrial Relations in the West Coast Maritime Industry.* Berkeley: University of California, Institute of Industrial Relations, 1958.

Schneider, Betty V.H., and Abraham Siegel. *Industrial Relations in the Pacific Coast Longshore Industry.* Berkeley: University of California, Institute of Industrial Relations, 1956.

Schwartz, Stephen. *Brotherhood of the Sea: A History of the Sailors' Union of the Pacific.* 1885-1985. New Brunswick, N.J.: Transaction Books, 1986.

Selvin, David. *Sky Full of Storm: A Brief History of California Labor.* Berkeley: University of California, Institute of Industrial Relations, 1966.

*Spero, Sterling D., and Abram L. Harris. *The Black Worker: The Negro and the Labor Movement.* 1931. Reprint. New York: Athaneum, 1968.

Taylor, Paul S. *The Sailors Union of the Pacific.* New York: Ronald Press, 1923.

*Thompson, Fred. W. *The I.W.W.: Its First Fifty Years, 1905-1955.* Chicago: Industrial Workers of the World, 1955.

*Vorse, Mary Heaton. *Labor's New Millions.* New York: Modern Age Books, 1938.

Weintraub, Hyman. *Andrew Furuseth: Emancipator of the Seamen.* Berkeley: University of California Press, 1959.

Unpublished Manuscripts, Dissertations, and Theses

Brown, Giles T. *The Admiral Line and Its Competitors: The Zenith and Decline of Shipping Along the Pacific Coast, 1916-1936.* Ph. D. dissertation, Claremont College, 1948.

Cherny, Robert W. Manuscript on the life of Harry Bridges.

__________. *"Deport Harry Bridges!" Anti-Communism and the Department of Labor, 1934-1940.*

__________. *"Transforming a Company Union"? The Strange Case of the San Francisco Blue Book, 1919-1934.* Prepared for the annual meeting of the Southwest Labor Studies Association, at California State University, Dominguez Hills, April 20-21, 1990.

Dorfman, Joe. *The Longshoremen Strikes of 1922 and After.* B.A. thesis, Reed College, Portland, 1924.

Fast, Lisette Emery. *The Efficiency of Cargo Handling in Relation to the Decasualization of Longshore Labor on the Seattle Waterfront.* M.B.A. thesis, University of Washington, 1921.

Francis, Robert Coleman. *A History of Labor on the San Francisco Waterfront.* Ph. D. dissertation, University of California, Berkleley, 1934.

Gramm, Warren Stanley. *Employer Association Development in Seattle and Vicinity.* M.A. thesis, University of Washington, 1948.

Jackson, Joseph Sylvester. *The Colored Marine Employees Benevolent Association of the Pacific, 1931-1934, or Implications of Vertical Mobility for Negro Stewards in Seattle.* M.A. thesis, University of Washington, 1939.

Jones, George Michael. *Longshore Unionism on Puget Sound: A Seattle-Tacoma Comparison.* M.A. thesis, University of Washington, 1947.

Lampman, Robert James. *Collective Bargaining of West Coast Sailors, 1885-1947: A Case Study in Unionism.* Ph. D. dissertation, University of Wisconsin, 1950.

Liebes, Richard Alan. *Longhsore Labor Relations on the Pacific Coast, 1934-1942.* Ph. D. dissertation, University of California, Berkeley, 1942.

Lucy, George Edward. *Group Employer-Employee Industrial Relations in the San Francisco Maritime Industry, 1888-1947.* Ph. D. dissertation, St. Louis University, 1948.

Palmer, Dwight Livingstone. *Pacific Coast Maritime Labor.* Ph. D. dissertation, Stanford University, 1935.

Pitts, Robert Bedford. *Organized Labor and the Negro in Seattle.* M.A. thesis, University of Washington, 1941.

Thompson, Margaret Jane. *Development and Comparison of Industrial Relationships in Seattle.* M.B.A. thesis, University of Washington, 1929.

Thor, Howard Andrew. *A History of the Marine Engineers Beneficial Association.* M.A. thesis, University of California, 1954.

Tobie, Harvey Elmer. *Oregon Labor Disputes 1919-1923: A Study of Representative Controversies and Current Thought.* Ph.D. dissertation, University of Oregon, 1936.

Index